A BLACK CIVILIZATION

harper torchbooks

A reference-list of Harper Torchbooks, classified by subjects, is printed at the end of this volume.

Two Dancers Crying Out to the Python.
(See Section D, Gunabibi Ceremony, page 288.)

A BLACK CIVILIZATION

A Social Study of an Australian Tribe

Revised Edition

BY

W. Lloyd Warner

HARPER TORCHBOOKS  *The University Library*

HARPER & ROW, PUBLISHERS
NEW YORK, EVANSTON AND LONDON

To

A. R. RADCLIFFE-BROWN

A BLACK CIVILIZATION: A Study
of an Australian Tribe

Revised Edition

Printed in the United States of America

This book was originally published in 1937 by Harper & Brothers, with a revised edition in 1958. The Torchbook edition omits pages 41-51 and 472-565 of the revised edition.

First HARPER TORCHBOOK edition published 1964 by
Harper & Row, Publishers, Incorporated
49 East 33rd Street
New York, N.Y. 10016

Library of Congress catalog number: 58-7939

CONTENTS

PREFACE ix

INTRODUCTION by Robert H. Lowie xiii

PART I

A GENERAL STATEMENT

I. THE MURNGIN 3

PART II

SOCIAL STRUCTURE

II. THE LOCAL ORGANIZATION 15

Detailed exposition of the various local institutions—clan, moiety, phratry, and tribe; their relations to the fundamental social pattern—the kinship structure.

III. THE FAMILY AND KINSHIP STRUCTURE 41

The immediate and extended systems of kin; the Murngin sub-section system; further interpretations of the customs of the Mirriri and Wakinu and the relationship systems generally.

IV. AGE GRADING 114

The several groupings of the individuals of Murngin society on the basis of age, sex, marital status, ritual position, etc.; the functions of certain *rites de passage*.

V. PRIMARY ADAPTATIONS AND TECHNOLOGY 127

The Murngin economic group, the horde, and its relation to tribal ritual; division of labor; man a species in a biological configuration.

VI. WARFARE 144

Clan feuds, causes of war, kinds of battles, effects of war on social institutions and ritual; detailed history of a particular blood feud.

PART III

ABSOLUTE LOGICS

VII. MURNGIN MAGIC AND MEDICINE 183

Detailed exposition of the kinds and types of Murngin magics and medicines.

VIII. A SOCIOLOGICAL INTERPRETATION OF MAGIC 213

IX. MURNGIN TOTEMISM I 234

Statement of the problem and method of analysis; the fundamental oral rite or myth and the associated rituals: the Wawilak constellation.

X. MURNGIN TOTEMISM II 325

The Djunkgao constellation.

XI. AN INTERPRETATION OF MURNGIN TOTEMISM AND OF ITS RITUAL LOGICS 361

XII. MORTUARY RITES 402

Customs, rites, and general social behavior surrounding death; place of totemism in the observances.

XIII. INTERPRETATION OF MURNGIN DEATH RITUALS —AN INTEGRATION OF MURNGIN SOCIETY 433

PART IV

SOCIAL CHANGE

XIV. SOCIAL CHANGE IN NORTH AUSTRALIA 443

Reconstruction of Murngin History by use of early documents, archaeology and ethnological methods.

PART V

PERSONAL HISTORY

XV. MAHKAROLLA AND MURNGIN SOCIETY 467

The life and opinions of a Murngin man told by him; the present author's friendship with him.

GLOSSARY OF KIN, NATIVE, AND TECHNICAL TERMS 491

INDEX 496

PLATES

(Plates appear between pages 464–465.)

Frontispiece. Two Dancers Crying Out to the Python

IA. Stone Artifacts

IB. Articles Worn

IIA. Spear Throwers

IIB. Spear-Heads

IIIA. Baskets

IIIB. Totemic Emblems

IVA. War Party

IVB. Warrior

VA. Blowing the Python Trumpet over the Iguana

VB. Iguana Dancers in the Djungguan Ceremony

VIA. Yermerlindi, the Python's Emblems in the Gunabibi

VIB. Preparing a Dancer for the Gunabibi Ceremony

VIIA. Chorus and Dancers in the Ulmark Ceremony

VIIB. Grub Dancers in the Ulmark Ceremony

VIIIA. Dancing Flood Water in the Narra Ceremony

VIIIB. Boys Receiving Instruction in the Narra Ceremony

CHARTS

I. Murngin Society as a General Configuration 11

II. Murngin Kinship System 48

III. Ego's Kinship Personality 93

IV. Daughter and Gift Reciprocation by the Son-in-law and Father-in-law 97

V. Structural Analysis of the Gift and Daughter Exchange 97

VI. Structural Analysis of the Murngin Kinship System 103

VII. The Murngin Sub-section System 108

VIII. Matrilineal Cycles of the Sub-section System 109

IX. The Relation of Ego and His Families to His Spatial Position in the Camp, and His Age Grade Status 124

X. Constellation of the Wawilak Myth and Its Rituals 238

XI. Rain Chart for Port Darwin (46-Year Record) 370

XII. Wawilak Totemic Logic 395

XIII. Djunkgao Totemic Logic 397

XIV. Social Logic of Murngin Totemism 398

XV. Nature and Social Organization in Their Relation to Totemism 401

XVI. The Place of Death in the Murngin Social Structure 439

FIGURES

1. The Maringo Type of Battle Formation 161

2. Symbolic Totem Well for Curing Ritual 217

3. The Triangular Dance Ground of the Snake's Body 255

MAP

Tribes and Clans of the Murngin Area 40

PREFACE

THIS book is the result of three years (1926-1929) spent in Australia in two field trips to northeastern Arnhem Land in the country bounded on the eastern and northern limits by the Sea of Arafura and the western shores of the Gulf of Carpentaria. The field research was done under the auspices of the Rockefeller Foundation for the first year and the Australian National Research Council for the last two; without their generous financial assistance it could not have been attempted. I am indeed grateful. Part of the data has been published in certain of the scientific journals, to whom I offer my thanks for allowing me to republish that part of my material in its present form.

The present Torchbook edition of BLACK CIVILIZATION, with a few changes herein noted, is exactly the same as the previous one. To improve readability and reduce unnecessary length, a long list of tribal terms for the clans previously in Chapter II has been eliminated and several ethnographic appendices intended for specialists have been excluded. Two former appendices of broader interests, one on social change and the other a "personal history" of Mahkarolla were retained and converted into chapters. This preface to the Torchbook edition combines the texts of the previous two; most of the first (1937) and all of the second one (1957) are present.

That this book is essentially a communal creation rather than the work of an individual is clearly demonstrated to the author when he finally has completed his task. If the essential elements of genius could be analyzed I believe that a large proportion of the fundamental factors involved would be shorn from the so-called creator and given to his contemporary society. If this is partly true of genius it is almost wholly true of the ordinary fellow who does research in the social sciences and publishes his results as I have done in the pages that follow. In a sense, when I express my deep gratitude and my many obligations to those whose names are to be found in the next few paragraphs either for practical assistance which made the field work easier or because of their molding of the fundamentals of my thinking in the field of social anthropology, I am only partially recognizing their communal labor in creating this study of the North Australian aborigines.

My deepest obligation is to the Murngin people themselves, who gave me a fine, whole-hearted hospitality. I am particularly indebted to one of them, Mahkarolla, one of the finest men I have had the good luck to count among my friends. I sometimes wonder at the futility of so-called progress when I think of him.

I wish to thank my friend and first teacher, Robert H. Lowie, one of the few great American social anthropologists, for first taking in hand my rather difficult human material and molding out of it, if not an anthropologist, then at least the semblance of one. He did this not only by his great learning and keen intelligence, but also by his generous friendship.

To A. R. Radcliffe-Brown I feel a similar gratitude; as his friend and pupil I was fortunate indeed in receiving his wise and ever helpful direction of my research in North Australia. For these reasons as well as many others I have taken the liberty of dedicating this volume to him.

Since the publication of the first edition (1937) of this volume and the earlier papers on Murngin kinship,[1] a rather extensive literature on what has been called "the Murngin controversy" has been published.[2] The "controversy" is not one but many. Since this book is an ethnographic monograph and since most of the important issues are broadly theoretical and methodological and have to do with many or all peoples and not only the Murngin, I will do no more here than review and draw attention to some of the more important publications and leave the discussion of such problems for a more appropriate time. Moreover, since the later research of the Berndts on the Murngin has validated my own findings on the kinship system and subsections (classes), I shall not here argue the case again.[3] I hope presently to complete a book on the family and kinship structure which will deal with the larger tech-

[1] W. Lloyd Warner, "Morphology and Functions of the Australian Murngin Type of Kinship, Part I," *American Anthropologist,* vol. 32, no. 2, pp. 207-256; "Part II," vol. 33, no. 2, pp. 172-198; "Kinship Morphology of Forty-One North Australian Tribes," *ibid.,* vol. 35, no. 1, pp. 63-86.

[2] A. R. Radcliffe-Brown, "The Social Organization of Australian Tribes," *Oceania Monograph,* No. 1; L. Sharp, "The Social Organization of the Yir-Yoront Tribe, Cape York Peninsula," *Oceania,* vol. 4, pp. 404-31.

[3] Ronald M. Berndt, "'Murngin' (Wulamba) Social Organization," *American Anthropologist,* vol. 57, no. 1, pp. 84-196; *Kunapipi,* International Universities Press and Cheshires, 1951.

nical, methodological, and theoretical problems of which the Murngin system is but one among many.

The several issues argued in the many publications have to do with: (1) the substantive nature of Murngin asymmetrical marriage;[4] (2) the subsection system and its significance for regulating marriage and descent; (3) the way the kinship system and the subsection system are interrelated;[5] (4) more implicitly, the way the nuclear families of orientation and procreation relate to the kinship system and the social structure system;[6] (5) the nature of the unilineal local organization; and (6) the relation of the clans and other territorial groupings to the kinship system line of descent and the subsection systems.[7]

All these are also dealt with at a more theoretical level. Some publications are primarily concerned with the comparative study of Australian social organizations;[8] others more broadly view the entire range of human kinship systems.[9] The systems of Lévi-Strauss and Lawrence suffer from an inadequate methodology. They have two fatal defects: they do not use genealogical evidence to found their systems and they start from the most general and abstract of the kinship groupings, namely the subsection system, instead of examining the nuclear families first and then with genealogical evidence found their theories about the structure, functions, and meaning of the section systems. Lévi-Strauss' theoretical system consequently twists the structure of Murngin life to fit his theory about sections and subsections.

[4] T. T. Webb, "Tribal Organization in Eastern Arnhem Land," *Oceania,* vol. 3, 1933, pp. 406-411.

[5] A. P. Elkin, "Marriage and Descent in Arnhem Land," *Oceania 3*:412-416; *The Australian Aborigines,* Sydney, 1938; "Murngin Kinship Re-examined and Remarks on Some Generalizations," *American Anthropologist 55*:412-419; A. R. Radcliffe-Brown, "Murngin Social Organization," *American Anthropologist, 53*:37-55; W. E. Lawrence and G. P. Murdock, "Murngin Social Organization," *American Anthropologist, 51*:58-65; G. P. Murdock, *Social Structure,* Macmillan, 1949.

[6] W. Lloyd Warner, "The Family and Principles of Kinship Structure in Australia," *American Sociological Review,* vol. 2, no. 1, pp. 43-54.

[7] Ronald M. Berndt, " 'Murngin' (Wulamba) Social Organization," *American Anthropologist,* vol. 57, no. 1; "In Reply to Radcliffe-Brown on Australian Local Organization," *American Anthropologist,* vol. 59, no. 2, pp. 346-351; A. R. Radcliffe-Brown, "On Australian Local Organization," *American Anthropologist,* vol. 58, no. 2, pp. 363-367.

[8] A. R. Radcliffe-Brown, "Murngin Social Organization," *American Anthropologist,* vol. 53, no. 1, pp. 37-55; William E. Lawrence, "Alternating Generations in Australia," George P. Murdock (ed.), *Studies in the Science of Society,* pp. 319-354, New Haven: Yale University Press and London: H. Milford and Oxford University Press, 1937.

[9] C. Lévi-Strauss, *Les Structures élémentaires de la parenté,* Presses Universitaires de France, 1949; "Social Structure," in *Anthropology Today,* by A. Kroeber *et al.,* Univer-

Once again I wish to pay my deep respect and extend my thanks to my anthropological teachers and friends, A. R. Radcliffe-Brown and Robert R. Lowie, and to Mahkarolla, my Murngin teacher and friend. All these have died since the first edition was published. I hope that this volume as fact and symbol states some of the significances that made life meaningful and exciting to all of us as friends and as men who wanted to learn more about the nature of human life. I love and cherish each of them.

W. LLOYD WARNER

(1937, 1957, 1964)

---

sity of Chicago Press, 1953; E. R. Leach, "The Structural Implications of Matrilateral Cross-Cousin Marriage," *Journal of the Royal Anthropological Institute, 81*:23-55; George C. Homans and David M. Schneider, *Marriage, Authority, and Final Causes: A Study of Unilateral Cross-Cousin Marriage,* The Free Press, 1955; Kingsley Davis and W. Lloyd Warner, "Structural Analysis of Kinship," *American Anthropologist,* vol. 39, no. 2, pp. 291-313.

INTRODUCTION

From the time of their discovery, Australian aborigines have naturally attracted the attention of anthropologists. Their very appearance suggested a departure from known types of man: while their dark skin and long skulls would bring them under the popular category of Negroes, these "blackfellows" lacked woolly hair, were heavily bearded, and had unusually strong brow-ridges, which seemed to stamp them with a morphologically inferior character. Their mode of life in its obvious external features—the lack of bow and arrow, pottery, weaving, and farming—was unequivocally rude, corresponding to that of "lower hunters." Thus there developed the picture of a singularly low surviving sample of Stone Age humanity, which some definitely identified with the Mousterian culture stage and with the Neanderthal race of that period.

As more information accumulated, this conception underwent material changes. Whatever anatomical peculiarities might be ascribed to the Australian, he was recognized as an unexceptionable member of *Homo sapiens*, in others words, as incomparably closer to the Caucasian race than to any known extinct species. Some enthusiasts were even led to proclaim a differential affinity with the White as against other living races, a conclusion for which there is no warrant, though saner spirits affirm a connection with the darker types of southern India. What particularly stirred the imagination of scholars, however, was the seeming paradox of an extremely intricate social and ceremonial system that went hand in hand with technological deficiency. One could hardly wish for a better illustration of our present axiom that advancement is far from uniform, lagging behind in one direction while it forges ahead in another. To accept the complex scheme of Australian society as that of primeval mankind would be preposterous, for it bore upon its face evidence of a varied and checkered history. But to forego the hope of finding in Australia the earliest patterns of human ceremonial, supernaturalism, and family life is not tantamount to renouncing interest in the natives, who claim our attention irrespective of any light they may shed on ultimate "origins." Accordingly, there have been within the last forty years a series of distinguished studies illuminating all phases of aboriginal activity.

In trying to assign to Professor Warner's book its rightful place among these publications, an Americanist cannot presume to speak with authority; he can merely voice impressions based on what he happens to know about the relevant literature and about the currents of thought which find expression in the present volume.

So far as I am aware, then, Professor Warner is the first to deal with amplitude of the structure and supernaturalism of a *tropical* Australian people. I am not forgetting the admirable *Bulletins of North Queensland Ethnography* issued by the late Dr. Walter E. Roth. But to Dr. Roth, as his subsequent and equally valuable South American researches indicate, technology was the most congenial aspect of culture and the one in which he especially excelled. As for Professor Spencer's work, his trips to the north country were relatively brief and their results accordingly do not rival in authoritativeness his important work on the central tribes. It seems to me, then, that this new book for the first time sets forth at length how a people regulated their society and ritual in the northern third of the island continent. It extends the perspective hitherto afforded, thereby enabling us to form a clearer notion of the range of ideas that find expression among the "blackfellows," to set off what is local from what is continental.

In his theoretical approach Professor Warner represents a novel fusion of ideas. He received his early anthropological training at the University of California and thus imbibed the brand of theory dispensed by Professor A. L. Kroeber and myself, respectively. I am not fond of catchwords, so I will not label it as "American." My conviction grows that there are nearly as many "American" points of view as there are American anthropologists; and that individual temperament and aptitude count for far more than does adherence to a scientific profession of faith. Classification into such a group seems in most instances a barren procedure. I, for example, am reckoned a conservative right-wing ethnographer in America, but have been described abroad both as a functionalist and as virtually a member of the *Kulturkreis* school. Yet I am not conscious of being a split personality. However this may be, in Berkeley Mr. Warner was exposed to the tenet that tribal contacts and chronological relations are matters of scientific concern; and this position was not foreign to his purposes when he reached the Murngin. Accordingly, there is here a summary of archaeological work, meager as its findings turned out to be. Far more significant is the discussion of Malay contacts. These had already been indicated in Ratzel's "Völkerkunde"; but it is the present author's merit to have discriminatingly reduced these alien influences to their proper proportion.

During the summer of 1926, Professor Bronislaw Malinowski lectured in Berkeley, and Mr. Warner was thus brought face to face with a consistently functionalist philosophy of culture. Soon Professor A. R. Radcliffe-Brown was able to afford him an opportunity to study in Australia some people still approximately living a life undebauched by white civilization, and the several years of field-work under his supervision gave Mr. Warner still another outlook on the subject. Specifically, it intensified a nascent devotion to kinship nomenclatures and introduced Mr. Warner to the French sociologists led by the late Professor Durkheim and nowadays most authoritatively represented by Professor Mauss.

These several influences explain the deviations of this treatise from the norm of monographs printed in this country. Much unquestionably coincides in aim with what trained ethnographers of whatever school would endeavor to secure. It also seems to me that the fruitful attempt to correlate specific aspects of Murngin culture with one another—as in the chapter on Warfare—is closely paralleled in general aim by Dr. A. H. Gayton's study of the interweaving of Yokuts shamanism and chieftaincy and by Dr. Cora Du Bois' recent demonstration of how the wealth concept integrates culture in southwestern Oregon. On the other hand, there is also in Professor Warner's approach a good deal that differs in organization and the statement of problems, in fact, in the very nature of the problems themselves. To these portions the reader's response will inevitably vary with his attitude toward the sociological philosophy from which the author has drawn his inspiration. It may, however, not be superfluous to add that, as the discussion of magic proves, he cannot be considered a servile follower of Durkheim. Altogether, American anthropology has in the past been preponderantly molded by British and German influences, and except on one or two writers sociology as a distinct discipline has been without discernible effect. The advent of a French—and, at that a sociological—flavor is thus not without piquancy.

Personally, I prefer to judge anthropological productions without reference to their author's "political" affiliations. Consequently, I will content myself with mentioning several features of this book that have appealed to me. I have already referred to the section on Malay-Murngin intercourse, which I am convinced is no mere sop to the historical-minded, but a recognition of the part played by contacts in the shaping of culture. From the sections on family and kinship I get a sharp picture of the workings of the Murngin system and from my more limited reading accept Professor Radcliffe-Brown's verdict that it embodies the clearest report available on Australian conditions. The description of supernaturalism brings out forcibly the patterns that shape it; and the definite way in which myth and ritual are related is striking and, indeed, surprising.

There seems to be here a solid mass of factual material that bears testimony to Professor Warner's zeal and skill as an observer, not to omit his obvious sympathy with his subjects. And anthropologists will eagerly watch the synthesis toward which the manifold trends that have molded his professional development are tending.

Robert H. Lowie

University of California
Berkeley (1936)

PART I

A GENERAL STATEMENT

CHAPTER I

THE MURNGIN

THE northern shores of Australia are separated in the east from New Guinea by the Torres Strait and the Gulf of Carpentaria, and in the west by the shallow Sea of Arafura. The Indian Ocean lies between Australia and the East Indian island of Timor. Below the Arafura is Arnhem Land, that almost blank space on the map which extends from the Gulf of Carpentaria to the Indian Ocean. In the furthermost northern and eastern parts of this latter region are several tribes which may be referred to collectively as the Murngin. Their ancestors lived here many hundreds and probably thousands of years before them.[1]

Eastern and northern Arnhem Land are unpopulated by whites except for a half dozen or more missionaries who are stationed at three comparatively recent Christian outposts. Traders infrequently sail their two-masted luggers into the shallow harbors and mouths of the tidal rivers to exchange their goods with the natives; all other economic efforts have been unprofitable. On the southern borders of this huge territory white civilization is making a melancholy and profitless effort to implant its own markings in the form of cattle ranches on the bleak country that lies along the southern banks of the Roper River. A telegraph system which unites white Australia with the rest of the British Empire stretches from the populous cities of southern Australia across the barren central desert into the western border of Arnhem Land and terminates at the tiny, isolated town of Port Darwin.

The Murngin live some ten to fifteen degrees south of the equator in a land which has little elevation. The climate is tropical and marked by the sharp, seasonal cycles of the rainy and dry periods, with corresponding changes in the prevailing winds or monsoons. The long flat coastal regions have a savanna type of vegetation, with the ubiquitous mangrove here and there forming dense jungle groves along the flat sandy islands, bays, and tidal rivers. The groves of ti trees in this region are green oases which the native sees as he journeys in from the barren

[1] See Chapter XIV, Social Change in North Australia.

alkaline plains and approaches the marshy lakes that are abundantly present in the rainy season and frequently absent in the dry period. The acacia and the eucalyptus are familiar and frequent in both the low and the high lands, and spear grass covers the land in dense growths during the months of rain.

The animals, with certain minor variations, are the usual marsupials and monotremes found in Australia, with the bat and wild domestic dog the only mammalia living in the region. Nature is bountiful with many varieties of birds, fish, and other animals; but vegetable foods, although plentiful, are limited in variety.

The Murngin people belong to the aboriginal Australoid race found throughout Australia—not Mongoloid, Negroid, or Caucasian, but a variant group which seems to be a blend of many of the features of the white and black races.[2] Their language is one of the Australo-Dravidian linguistic group. They belong to a Stone Age culture; were they placed in our own chronology, their technological development would fall somewhere between the Old and the New Stone Ages.

The Murngin civilization is a simple Australian culture with a small hunting and gathering population which lives off the sea and the land. The natural environment which surrounds it and drastically affects native behavior consists of *two changes which make up the yearly cycle*; one of these is extremely rainy, producing a period of scarcity, and the other a dry period when there is an abundance of food. The technology can be described briefly as the adaptive mechanisms of the general society to these two parts of the cycle of nature.

The social organization must be given in a more detailed description. The fundamental basis of the society is an elaborate kinship[3] system in which everyone is related to everyone else. This kinship system is organized into more general units which are patrilineal,[3] exogamic[3] clans[3] which have local territories that were "given to them by the totems."[3] All parts of the clan land have totemic references. Each clan has multiple totems; all clans have at least one, possibly more, sacred water holes where live the high totems, the totemic ancestors, the ancestral dead, and the totemic spirits of the unborn. The names of all clansmen have totemic significance, and the whole general totemic pattern is related to the clan.

[2] The term "Black" in the title of this book, *A Black Civilization,* is not to be interpreted as describing these people as purely Negroid. The term refers, rather, to their popular name, "Australian Blacks," and to the name they accept for themselves from the Australian whites, "Blackfellows."

[3] See Glossary of Technical Terms.

The clans are of basic importance. They are the largest units of solidarity, and open conflict never occurs within them, as it would not between a man's clan and his wife's and mother's clan. It is through his clan that a man establishes his totemic relations and identifies himself with the sacred world by virtue of a mystical experience of his father. The mother is supposed to be spiritually fertilized by the entrance into her uterus of the infant's soul when it has come from the child's father's totemic well. Many ethnologists have insisted that the Australian aborigines have no knowledge of physiological conception. Although I held this opinion during the first part of my field work, I later came to the conclusion that knowledge of procreation is general to the Murngin but is considered of little importance.[4]

The blood feud is forever present and tends to kill a sufficient number of young men to allow the system of polygyny[5] to function. The Murngin have developed a number of well-constructed types of warfare which form dramatic episodes in the several chains of feuds linking the dead generations of the past to those of the living.

The moiety[5] is a still larger unit than the clan, dividing the sixty-odd clans into two groups which intermarry. By the device of the moiety, the whole of the life of the Murngin, as well as nature, is placed in two opposing groups called Yiritja and Dua.

A final important structure in Murngin society is the age-grading[5] institution. It divides, first, the men from the women (see page 120, Age Grading) on the basis of those who are initiated into the mysteries and those who are not, and then redivides the men on an age-graded scale based primarily on the place a man achieves within the rest of his social organization through *rites de passage*.

Within this social configuration the life of each Murngin male goes through an exact cycle. The first life crisis occurs when the Murngin soul, through the father's mystic experience, leaves the totemic well and enters the womb of the mother. By circumcision around the age of six to eight years the individual passes from the social status of a woman to that of a man. When at about the age of eighteen he achieves parenthood and is shown his totems for the first time, he goes to another, higher status; and to a still higher when, at about thirty-five, he sees the high totems. At death he passes through a very elaborate mortuary rite, returns to his totemic well, and the circle is complete. The personality before birth is purely spiritual; it becomes almost completely profane or unspiritual in the earlier period of its

[4] See pages 23-25.

[5] See Glossary of Technical Terms.

life when it is classed socially with the females, gradually becomes more and more ritualized and sacred as the individual grows older and approaches death, and at death once more becomes completely spiritual and sacred. This is the life of all Murngin men. A woman, on the other hand, passes out of the sacred existence of the unborn to the profane existence of the born and living, and back again to the sacred existence of the dead; but little sacred progress is made during her lifetime.

Obviously the principle of the social bifurcation of the sexes has been used to create the lowest status, that of women and children. The women's group remains comparatively undifferentiated, while the men's group becomes highly segmented and graded through participation in the totemic mysteries. The age-grading structure largely controls the degree of participation a man has in his society. The older men exercise their control largely through their power to say whether or not a man can go from one age grade to another. It is only they who possess the knowledge which makes up the totemic ideology.

The participation of a Murngin in the age-grading structure revolves around, first, his position in the immediate family structure, and, secondly, his place in the ceremonial mysteries. The life of man is divided into a number of stages marked by the *rites de passage*. The life crises of an individual, including birth, maturity, and death, are set off by elaborate rituals. These rituals correspond roughly to a man's position in the family structure. When he is circumcised he moves out of his family of orientation[6] into a men's camp; and at the time he creates his own family, that of procreation,[6] he moves into higher age grades by seeing his totems in a series of rituals. Chart I, page 11, expresses in summary fashion the relation of man's place in the social organization to his place in the age-graded ceremonial life.

The first principle of age grading, the sexual bifurcation by which women are excluded from participation in the totemic mysteries, immediately limits female behavior in the society and tends to simplify their personalities. The man's social personality, on the contrary, expands and becomes more complex by his participation in the various elaborate age-graded rituals. There seems to be considerable evidence for a relationship between this and a man's comparatively complex technological behavior and a woman's more simple type. The Murngin man handles more complicated tools and weapons, and uses more complex techniques in making and using them than does his female kinswoman;

[6] See Glossary of Technical Terms.

it is one of the theses of this book that a man's social value is correspondingly more important, and his place in the rituals is partly due to and partly expresses this fact.

A man's or woman's place in Murngin society is fixed by his or her position in the kinship structure. The totality of his behavior toward all the people in his community and of their behavior in relation to him, with all the concomitant obligations, duties, and privileges, is determined by his being placed exactly in this social structure through the operation of certain mechanisms. Social space in the sense of social stratification has no vertical extension in Murngin society; but the kinship space[7] has the usual kind of vertical structure found in all kinship systems, namely, the extension which is created by the generations above and below a man (ego). Generation recognition does not extend beyond the usual five of the normal vertical kinship structure, but the lateral structure has been extended to three lines on both sides (paternal and maternal) of the line of a man's own lineage, making a total of seven.

The whole of the social organization is built on the pattern of kinship. The kinship system is the fundamental form into which the rest of the social organization has been integrated. The greater part of the behavior of the Murngin can be understood only in terms of his behavior as a kinsman. The very complex kinship structure with its seven lines of descent and five generations in each line is but an elaboration of the immediate families of orientation[8] and of procreation,[8] that is, of the family into which an individual is born and that which he creates at marriage. The underlying mechanism controlling the relations of these two families is that of asymmetrical cross-cousin marriage, which here means that a man marries his maternal uncle's daughter but not his father's sister's daughter. As will be demonstrated in other parts of this chapter, the result of this asymmetry has been to give a tremendous lateral spread to the kinship structure instead of keeping it narrowed to the two lines of descent where symmetrical cross-cousin marriage takes place.

The Murngin have doubled the count of thirty-five relatives created by five generations and seven lines of descent, through the division of each of these on the basis of brother and sister relation. In addition, by the use of the principle of age in generation, separating older

[7] See Warner, W. L., et al., *Social Class in America,* Harper Torchbooks, New York, 1960.

[8] See Glossary of Technical Terms.

from younger brother in the terminology, there is one extra relative, making a total of seventy-one for each member of the society.

Every individual in Murngin society, looked at from the point of view of the totality of his behavior in the society, expresses all of the kinship relations. At one moment he is behaving as a son to his father, and in the next as a father to his son, or as a son-in-law to his father-in-law, and then reversing this latter relationship with some other person. Because of the classificatory or tribal type of kinship reckoning, each Murngin has every type of relationship expressed by the system.

One of the most general statements that can be made about Murngin kinship structure is that the perpendicular or vertical lines in the structure are very strong; they consist primarily of fathers and children. The lateral or horizontal lines are comparatively weak, since they consist primarily of the extension of the kinship structure through marriage. This comparative weakness and strength are an important determinant in the behavior of the Murngin. Various devices are used and customs formed around the feeling of weakness expressed in all the individual's behavior within the laterally extended kinship structure. The most dramatic examples are found in the mirrirri and wakinū customs which surround the relation of tabooed brother to sister, and of the maternal grandmother's brother to sister's daughter's son.

Although from the simple relations found within the immediate family the Murngin have worked out this very elaborate, extended kinship structure in great detail, they also, in common with many other Australian tribes, have reversed the process and reclassified the relatives into more general kin groupings, termed subsections by the later anthropologists and mistakenly called marriage classes by the earlier. The subsection terminology groups all seventy-one relatives into but eight exogamic units. This simplification aids greatly in determining a man's relationship to people from more distant areas and functions openly during the gatherings of the people for their great rituals when such identifications become necessary.

Geographical space is injected formally into the Murngin social system by the territorial extension given the clan. The various areas with their natural phenomena such as pools, rivers, lakes, trees, larger stones, hills, and plains have totemic references associated with the clan. The clans, as has been stated, are regrouped into two exogamic divisions or moieties which by virtue of their classification of the clans also have spatial expression. Vaguer local groups, bands, or phratries group together certain clans within one moiety.

The tribe is almost a non-existent unit among these people. Its most explicit element is a dialectic unity, but even here the linguistic variation within small local groups is very highly developed. The organized tribe with the use of chiefs does not exist. The tribe is not the war-making group nor does it enforce law.

It has long been the theory of a great number of anthropological authorities that magic is an individual phenomenon, whereas religion is a social phenomenon. The Durkheim or French school of sociology has been in agreement with this general point of view, although its members differed radically from the American, English, and German schools in their interpretation of religion. Although I am in general agreement with the social interpretation of religion by Durkheim, I cannot follow him or his school in his separation of magic from religion. It is another thesis of this book that magic is also as much a "church" in the Durkheim sense as religion. A test situation is available in this region because, although the peoples of the northern area believe in magic, they have no magicians such as are found in the south. Their substitution of ordinary religious rituals reveals much about the nature of magic.

The social mechanisms which are placed in operation within the group by the spread of the knowledge that a black magician has stolen a man's soul, that is, successfully operated on a man, are presented and analyzed in the chapter on magic. When magic is believed to be functioning, all the members of the society act in a manner exactly opposite to the ordinary in their relations with the unfortunate victim. This means that instead of helping to sustain the individual and allowing him to function as a normal person, these protective devices are withdrawn and the attitude is taken that the man is "half dead" and will shortly die. The effect upon the suggestive individual, it is contended in this book, is sufficient to set up certain psycho-physiological reactions which tend to destroy him. When this individual becomes very ill, the movement of social withdrawal from him ceases, and pressure is then applied through mortuary rites which perform the function of attempting to remove him from the society of the living to that of the dead, further destroying his desire to live and frequently bringing about his ultimate death.

The sacred world of the Murngin is totemically conceived; each individual by virtue of his clan membership possesses and belongs to a number of totems which are grouped into hierarchies of sacred values. Several fundamental myths organize the conceptual scheme of the social life and of the outside world which surrounds it. Elaborate community rituals allow the individual by means of symbolic dances, songs, and ritual speech to participate physically in the expression of the group's conceptions of the absolute.

The primary purpose of the several chapters on myth and ritual in this book is to attempt to solve the problem of the social meanings of the symbols used in these oral and dramatic rites. The major mythologies are creation stories which tell of the lives of two sisters who lived in the days when the world was different and man and beast had an existence usually the exact opposite of their manner of life today. The dramatic episodes in the journey of these creator women from the unknown interior to the coastal plains are saturated with social meaning and social value. Within them are the ultimate clues to the problem of Murngin social logic.

Generally speaking, it will be the purpose of this book, not only to present the civilization of the Murngin in the description of the various parts of tribal life, but to attempt to discover some of the general principles which govern their social life. To do this we shall examine, particularly in the chapter on technology, their primary adaptation to their natural environment. We shall see what complete technological systems have been organized by them to make and manipulate their tools and implements and adjust themselves as men to the ordered cycle of nature with its rainy season of scarcity and its dry season of plenty. We shall then, in the chapters on local organization, kinship, age grading, and warfare, look at their social order and determine how they regulate the human relations, not only of individual to individual, but of smaller groups to larger groups, of family to clan, and clan to tribe. Finally, we shall present the Murngin religious life and see what it means and how it regulates, organizes, and integrates their behavior into that of a complete and well-organized society.

To be more technical, when we have completed our study we shall have seen the primary articulation of Murngin society with its natural environment by the agency of its technology; secondly, we shall have examined the secondary adaptation of the several tribes by which their social organization disciplines and organizes the human behavior of the individuals of the culture and their relations with one another as members of the several internal institutions of the tribe; and, finally, we shall have viewed the tertiary adaptation of the people, namely, their totemic rituals, myths, and absolute logics which integrate the group and relate each of the separate parts of the society and of nature into a larger and general unity.

The following chart presents the various parts of the society and their various relationships in a working whole.

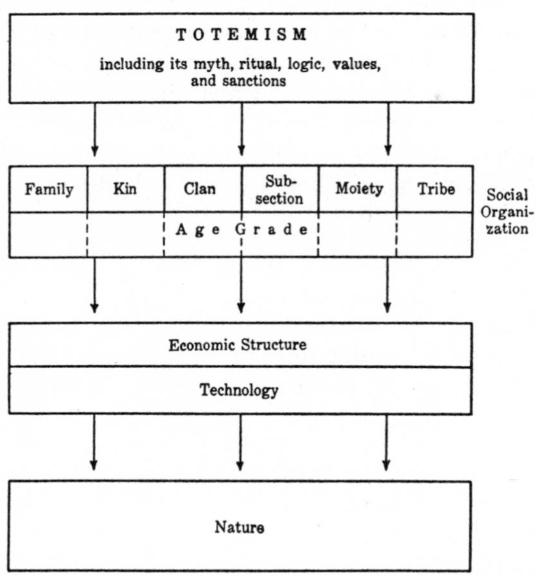

CHART I.—MURNGIN SOCIETY AS A GENERAL CONFIGURATION

Beginning at the foot of the chart, we see the arrows pointing downward from Technology to Nature to indicate the subordination of nature to man's technological adaptation. The Economic Structure is placed in the general rectangle with Technology, for it organizes and disciplines this material culture of the Murngin. In turn, the economic and technological structure is subordinate to the general social structure which is divided into its various inner segments, the chart indicating that age grading cuts across all other Murngin institutions. At the top of the chart the totemic religious structure disciplines and gives final sanctions to the social organization as related to nature through the rest of the society. A series of upward-pointing arrows might be included to symbolize the influence directly or indirectly of the lower on the upper divisions.

It seems to the author that the important chapters of this book are those which endeavor to contribute to our theoretical understanding of social behavior. These chapters are VIII, A Sociological Interpretation of Magic; XI, An Interpretation of Murngin Totemism and of its Ritual Logics; XIII, Interpretation of Murngin Death Rituals—An Integration of Murngin Society; and the latter parts of Chapter III, where certain kinship customs are interpreted, and of Chapter IV, where the functions of the *rites de passage* in Murngin society are treated. However, it is necessary to read the descriptive parts of the book if the reader is properly to understand the interpretation. I also consider Chapter XIV, Social Change in North Australia, of importance, since it helps the ethnologist to untangle the relations between Australia and Southeastern Asia.

PART II

SOCIAL STRUCTURE

CHAPTER II

THE LOCAL ORGANIZATION

THE eight tribes[1] considered in this book, of which the Murngin[2] (fire sparks) is the principal one, have the same kinship system, the same form of local organization, largely the same myths and ceremonies, and, in general, the same culture, with only those minor variations found in any homogeneous civilization. This similarity is particularly true of the basic structure of the local organization.

The Murngin and surrounding peoples have the following institutions which organize them into local groupings:[3] (1) patrilineal clans, (2) moieties, (3) phratries, (4) tribes, and (5) economic groups called hordes. Within these institutions and helping to integrate them functionally into a more complex society are a limited family, a classificatory kinship system, and a modified subsection system described in Chapter III.

The clan and moiety are the two most important units in the local organization.[4] The clan will be examined first, then the moiety with the clan grouping, and after this the phratry and tribe—the clan and moiety first, because they are the fundamental structures found

[1] See map, page 40, for the following tribes: Yaernungo, Burera, Murngin, Barlamomo, Djinba, Ritarngo, Yandjinung, and Dai.

[2] As stated earlier the tribe can hardly be said to exist in this area, and of all the tribes studied, the Murngin is the weakest in form. The word Murngin was found as a designation only after much effort. The people do not think of themselves under this name or classification. The word has been used by me as a general term for all of the eight tribes in the area and for the groups of people located in the central part of the territory of the eight tribes. I have seized upon this name as a convenient and concise way of talking about this whole group of people; had any of the other tribes who possess the particular type of social organization found in this area been located in the center of the group, I should have used the name of that tribe rather than Murngin.

[3] See Glossary for all native and technical terms.

[4] On pages 39 ff. of the revised edition of 1958 will be found a list of clans, with the English equivalents of the native clan names. The common or ordinary name is given in most cases, as well as the sacred or totemic name. This list has been omitted from the Torchbook edition.

throughout the eight tribes. The horde, dealt with in the chapter on technology, and the phratry may or may not be present in a given area. The tribe is of minor importance in native life.

The Clan

The Murngin clan is an exogamic patrilineal group averaging forty or fifty individuals who possess a common territory which averages 360 square miles.[5] This group possesses one or more sacred totemic water holes, formed by a creator totem, in which the whole of the tribal life is focussed; all members of the clan are born from this water hole, and all go back to it at death; in it the totem's spirits live with the mythological ancestor, the souls of the dead, and the unborn children. The male members of the clan who can be the permanent occupants of the group's land possess totemic emblems in common.

A clan frequently has an exclusive name for its people and another preferred one that defines the language spoken by this people as different from that of all other clans. The clan is exogamous by virtue of belonging to a moiety, which prevents marriage within its half of the tribe. Theoretically an individual can marry into any one of the clans in the opposite moiety. The tribal and intertribal myths of the moiety which are saturated with themes expressing the local organization of these people always devote small parts of their stories to the special circumstances of the creation of a clan. They also give its association with the totems and other elements of tribal life considered important by these people. The more localized myths which concern only two or three clans usually symbolize intra-clan solidarity and inter-clan antagonism. The ceremonies possessed by a clan, like the totems, are ordinarily owned by other similar groups belonging to the same moiety, although local variations in totem and ceremony occur.

The following relatives are always found in a clan: marikmo[6] (father's father and father's father's sister), bapa (father), mokul bapa (father's sister), wawa (older brother), yukiyuko (younger brother), yeppa (sister), gatu (son and daughter), and maraitcha (son's son and son's daughter). In other words, these relatives are in ego's brother's

[5] For additional elements in the clan configuration see Part III.

[6] See Chart II, page 48, for the place of kinship terms in the kinship system. Native terms have been used more frequently than the author would have liked, but it was impossible always to give an exact translation in a few words. It seems better to define a word carefully at least once, and thereafter use the term. (See Glossary of Native Terms.)

lineage, either as consanguine or classificatory kin. Other lines of relatives are sometimes found, but no relative from the opposite moiety ever belongs to ego's clan. The mari and kutara lines are sometimes members of ego's clan (mari, mother's mother, mother's mother's brother; kutara, sister's daughter's daughter, sister's daughter's son).

An important activity of the clan is war, the clan being the war-making group.[7] Within this group no violent conflict ever takes place, no matter how much cause is given. Members may quarrel, but for clansmen to fight one another would be considered an unnatural act in Murngin society and it never occurs. When the clan is at war the ceremonial leader almost always acts as the war leader. A clan seldom goes to battle as a group against another one, but usually has an eternal feud with certain others which results in occasional ambushes in which a man or two is killed.

The demographic aspects of Murngin society are extremely difficult to ascertain, owing to the roving life and impossibility of a head census. Genealogies showed the Kolpa (northern Wessel Island)[8] to be a group of about twenty-five relatives. The clan itself, as well as those who did not belong to it or their (the Yaernungo) tribe, considered this below the normal population level. The Liaalaomir (Glyde River) clan genealogies include around fifty people; the clansmen seem satisfied with their numbers, possessing a sense of well-being as a group not evident among the Kolpa. This was also true of clans like the Liagaomir (the mainland south of Howard Island) and the Daiuror (interior south of Howard Island). The Wangurri have some sixty or seventy members in their clan. The Warumeri, to their north, now have about forty people, since the last generation suffered a severe loss through a disastrous fight with the Wangurri over the right to certain women.

The Yalukal and Barlmawi at the present time have only one male member each. It is highly likely that such clans will disappear, continuance being dependent upon the male line. The land will continue to belong to the dead clan until in several generations the memory of it is lost and new traditions have filled the thought of the natives. The land and water holes will then belong to another group which will have been occupying it since the demise of its former owners. The

[7] The statement that the clan is a war-making group needs further elaboration and amendments which are given in Chapter VI.

[8] See map, page 40.

writer recorded statements from some younger men that certain territory belonged to the people now living upon it, while a few old men said this land really belonged to an older group that had died out. Once these old men are dead, it is likely that all memory of the ownership by a former clan will be gone.

Clan territory always has as a central core the land surrounding the water hole. Near the water hole the camps are usually made. Unless a river, lake, or other body of water defines it, no exact boundary exists between two clans. Usually a river or lake is occupied by one clan and the barren plains between form the outer limits for it and its neighbors. When one traverses a dry, unproductive part of the country, those parts of it near billibong (Australian white term: small lake or pool), lily places, and water locations are known to all peoples to belong to a definite clan; but as one moves across the dry plains toward the water hole of another group, there is considerable doubt as to which clan owns the plains area. No native would bother himself about it; it is looked upon as without significance in the lives of the people.

The land along the sea, the bays, inlets and tidal rivers, however, has very definite boundaries, well known to all peoples. Usually myths or folk tales record the facts of territorial ownership in the tribal tradition. The land of the clan is not always contiguous but may be separated by a distance of twenty or thirty miles. The home of a clan, however, is usually one continuous tract. The Gwiyamil, situated in the interior on Buckingham River, possess a small island in Caddell Straits between Elcho and Howard Islands. The island, piled high with boulders and with one wind-blown tree, cannot be more than 200 feet in diameter. Its natural geographic affinities are with Elcho Island, but it is "owned" by this inland clan. The Murngin say that Garrawark, a creator totemic fish, dived underground from the Gwiyamil well in the interior and came up at this island, made it, and called it Gwiyamil country. Garrawark also made other clan countries, but he did not call them Gwiyamil, which exposes the rationalization in this answer. A guess, based on similar types of association among the Murngin, is that some peculiarity in the country and the island associated the two places in their minds. The Milyingi, Djirin, Warumeri, Marungun and other clans all have additional territory away from their clan home and water holes.

No land can be taken from a clan by an act of war. A clan does not possess its land by strength of arms but by immemorial tradition and as an integral part of the culture. Murngin myth dies hard, and ownership of land is in Murngin myth even after the final destruction of a particular clan. It would never occur to a victorious group to annex another's territory, even though the entire male population were destroyed and the dead men's women and children taken by the victors. In the passage of time the clan using it would absorb it into their own territory and the myth would unconsciously change to express this. In the thought of the Murngin, land and water, people and clan are an act of the creator totem and the mythological ancestors, who always announce in myth and ceremony that this is the country of such and such a clan; to expropriate this land as a conscious act would be impossible. Just as the totem, the creator, and the members are a permanent and inextricable part of the culture, so is the clan's ownership of the land. This will become clearer when the concepts of birth, death, and totem are associated, and the sacred wells of the clans considered.

The forty or fifty-odd people who belong to a clan do not all live in the land of the clan. All sisters and daughters, since the rule of marriage is patrilocal after the first year or two, go to their husband's clan to live and rear their families. This means that fully half of the members of the clan live after the age of puberty with a group belonging to the opposite moiety. On the other hand, the wives of the clansmen have come from clans of the opposite moiety and make up the difference in population caused by the loss of the group's own females.

Friendly clans always live together during the seasons when food is plentiful in certain area. When the turtles of Buckingham Bay are laying hundreds of eggs nightly along the Djirin coast, the Birkili and Wangurri may be found there. When the cycad palm nuts are ready for picking on Millingimbi Island, the surrounding clans gather for the period of plenty. This is done as a right, no invitation being necessary and no one questioning this right as long as peace reigns. Let there be trouble and cause for a possible killing, and the visitors return to their own land, even though their visit has taken on the nature of a permanent residence.

The most important unifying concept in the whole of clan ideology is that of the sacred water hole in which reposes the spiritual unity of clan life. It is the fundamental symbol of clan solidarity. From it come all the eternal qualities, and to it those qualities return when they have been lived or used by members of the clan. Water, in Murngin thought, is one of the most important symbols of spiritual life.

In the rainy season great torrents of tropical rain fall daily, making large portions of the mainland south of the Arafura Sea, for weeks and sometimes months at a time, a series of islands in a shallow sea of mud and water. Then, with rare interruptions, there is continuous drought for six or seven months. During the wet season tropical vegetation has sprung up everywhere; giant spear grass sometimes grows to twelve and fourteen feet in height, covering all the country and paths, making communication a difficult matter at best, and in many places impossible. The water recedes, the water holes become drier and drier, and a large number disappear entirely; birds and fish are gone, and the many varieties of lilies and yams disappear. It is then that the native appreciates the value of water, just as before he realized the harm it could do him. It is doubtful if anyone ever died of thirst in this country, but it is certain that many have felt its pangs. Deaths have occurred from the great floods. It is small wonder that with the food and drink of life dependent on the water holes, and possible death resulting from the great floods, the native has made water his chief symbol of the clan's spiritual life.

The water hole may be an ordinary small lake or billibong, a river or creek flooding through the domain of the clan, a spring of water, or a native well or water hole; and in a few cases it may be the ocean itself, but this last form is usually associated with a tidal spring.[9] All the water holes found in the territory of a clan are divided into two classes: they are either garma wells or narra (ranga) wells. The first are totemic but not sacred; they were made by the lower order of totems, whose emblems may be displayed in camp and seen by the women. The narra wells are always sacred; they were made by the higher wongar totems, whose emblems are ranga (higher emblems) and can be seen only by the initiated young men after the age of puberty. A clan always has at least one and sometimes three or four of the latter.

The narra water hole is usually not taboo to women. They may obtain water there, bathe in the pool, and possibly fish or gather yams and lily bulbs. Occasionally a well becomes so taboo that no woman is allowed near it. Such is the great well, Mir-rir-min-a, of the

[9] The following native terms are used: a water hole or well, mang-o-tji (literally, eye); a spring, mil-min-jerk; river, man-i (literally, throat); creek, par-ka; a small rill running from a spring or artesian well, ri-el-la; billibong, lum-mi (upper thigh); rock-basin water, gar-ra (rain) nar-ku-la (water); fresh-water bog, mar-a-ka; saline but drinkable bog water, gal-la-min-dir; the ocean, or salt spring, or any salt water which is undrinkable, ka-pu mon-ok (water salt).

Liaalaomir clan on the Glyde River. Here was enacted the great drama of the Rock Python swallowing the two Creator Sisters which has tremendous import in ceremonial and mythological activity.[10] Even the men will not stay on or near this spot at night. The Gunabibi ceremony, although an enactment of this great event, is not conducted here for fear of disturbing the peace of the great father snake, thus causing him once again to come out of his subterranean depths and swallow those who have angered him.

All clan totems are thought to lie below the clan water hole in the subterranean waters. Here too will be found the old mythological ancestors who lived in the time of the activities of the totems on earth in the great mythological days when the world was made and named. When a ranga (higher totemic emblem) has been made by the men of the clan for a ceremony and has been used during the night time, it is put back into the mud of the water hole so that the wongar (spirit of the totem) which is felt to be in the emblem may return to the well.

When a child is born it comes from this well as a spirit. In the well it has the appearance of a very small fish. The spirit comes to the father who is to be, and asks for its mother so that it may be born. The father points out the mother and the spirit child enters her vagina. This happens while the father is dreaming; or when he is out hunting he may notice something peculiar about the actions of an animal or bird which will lead him to the conclusion that his wife is going to have a child.

My informant arrived one morning obviously anxious to talk:

I had a nice dream the other night. I dreamed that a boy child walked past all the other humpies [Australian white term for native huts] in the camp and kept coming until he got to my house. He beat on the bark wall. He called out, "Father! Father! Where are you?"

"Here I am."

"Where is mother?"

I told him and wakened up. I thought to myself, "True." Yesterday I went fishing with my wife at the creek. I went up one side of the creek and she went up the other. By and by a bream fish came up and took her hook. He came up to it easily and quietly. My wife did not have to pull on the line, for he came in to her like he wanted to. My mielk [woman] was standing in the water only up to her ankles. He came up to her even though she was in the shallow water. Then he stopped quickly, shook

[10] See Chapter IX for a detailed description of the myth and ceremonies centered around this totemic well.

himself against her leg, broke the line, and went back into the deep water. We did not see him again. I came across to her; I said, "What was that?" She said, "A bream fish." I said, "What did he do?" She told me. She said, "My father went fishing like this when my little brother was born; I think this fish shook against my leg for that.' I said, "Oh you know that." "Yes." "You remember my dream I told you about?" She said, "Yes, that's what I think. I won't menstruate any longer now because that baby fish is inside me."

A man from another clan told me this story:

My brothers and I took a dugout canoe and went fishing. We went a long way that day. It was dark when we came back. When we passed the long sand beach on Rabuma Island a turtle came out of the sea and looked at me. I heard him splash the water. It was dark and I was afraid. I said, "What's that?" I heard nothing then. We went on. We paddled slowly, for it was very late, and we were very tired. I heard something go "Wah!" I said, "What is that one?"—That turtle looked at me. All the men heard me call out.—We went on. The tide came in. The moon was still up. The Big Star came out. No light yet. We paddled slowly. Pretty soon that fellow came out again. He looked at me. It was light now, the birds had started to sing.—We were home. I left my canoe and went to my camp. This one followed me [the informant pointed to his third and last child, a small girl]. She had been in the canoe all the time, but I didn't know her.

I went to sleep. I dreamed she came to me. I went to the mainland next day. Willidjungo's mother saw my younger wife. A child had been sucking her breast. It had left a wet spot on the nipple. The old woman said, "That one will have a child soon."

I came home and quarreled with this wife. My other wife said, "Don't fight with her. She is going to have a baby." I stopped scolding. She was too young to know that a baby was inside her when I came from where the turtle had followed me and this baby had come home with me from that narra well.

If the child should die as a baby it would go back to the well, stay awhile and then return to the same mother. Narnarngo's wife's baby died. The baby went back to its waterhole to become a fish again for a little while and stay beside its wongar.

Narnarngo walked by his water hole. He had just killed a dugong. When he slept that night he dreamed that the child's marikmo (father's father) came to him and said, "I'm bringing my maraitcha [son's son] back to you." Soon the child was born. Everyone knew that it was the same baby because of the child's resemblance to the one that had died, which proved that the father's dream was true.

In 1898 Spencer and Gillen published their book, *Native Tribes of Central Australia,* in which they declare, "We have amongst the Arunta, Luritcha and Ilparra tribes, and probably also among others, such as the Warramunga, the idea firmly held that the child is not the direct result of intercourse, that it may come without this, which merely, as it were, prepares the mother for the reception and birth also of an already formed spirit child who inhabits one of the local totem centers. Time after time we have questioned them on this point and always received the reply that the child was not the direct result of intercourse." This is in reference to the opinion that among the natives of central and northern Australia there is no knowledge of physiological conception and that they believe impregnation of a woman to be entirely due to spiritual causes. Spencer and Gillen rather insisted on this fact because many of the whites of Australia believe that the natives practice the rite of subincision in the attempt to prevent conception. This operation is found throughout a large part of Australia; Spencer and Gillen rightly point out that it has nothing to do with birth control practices.

I was in very intimate contact with the Murngin natives. During my first eight or nine months among them I was firmly convinced that the people had no understanding of physiological conception and believed in the spiritual impregnation of a woman by a totemic child spirit. All the fathers told me their children had come to them in dreams as totemic souls, or in some extra-mundane experience, and asked that their mothers be pointed out to them. The men had complied with the request of the children, who had entered the vaginas of the mothers. During all this time, although I was in constant relationship with a large number of the men and there was practically no taboo on our conversations, which were of the most intimate nature, I could find no indication of any knowledge whatsoever of physiological conception; yet in the study I was making of the people, while looking at the problem from the point of view of the "total situation," that is, considering the whole of the culture, there were strong indications that the natives understood the true nature of the father's physical function.

The second time I entered the area I determined to go into this matter further, since the people I studied were but an extension of the central tribes on which Spencer and Gillen had reported. An occasion arose in which I could inquire directly of certain old men just what the semen did when it entered the uterus of a woman. They all looked at me with much contempt for my ignorance and informed me that "that was what made babies." I had not been able to obtain this information earlier because the ordinary savage is far more interested in the child's spiritual conception, which determines its place in the social life of the people, than he is in the physiological mechanism of conception. He would far rather talk about ritual and myth than about ordinary mundane affairs. The relationship between the primitive men of northeastern Arnhem Land and me as a field worker would be the same as that between the colonial Puritans of Massachusetts and the traditional visitor from Mars. Had the latter asked Cotton Mather or any other member of the community "where babies came from," he would have discovered that they came from heaven, that God sent them, and that it was the special duty of the church to look out for them. He might have been told that the stork brought them, and discovered totemic "spiritual conception." He would have been told this for approximately the same reason that the ordinary anthropological field investigator is informed by the natives that the totemic spirit is what causes impregnation.

I know it is dangerous to assume that, because the tribes I studied knew about physiological conception, the people Spencer and Gillen investigated had similar knowledge. I do feel, though, the necessity of throwing doubt upon the validity of the conclusions reached by Spencer and Gillen and others who claim there is no knowledge of physiological conception among certain savage tribes. I think that possibly this knowledge does exist but is not considered important, the spiritual conception of the child looming so large in native thinking that the field worker obtains nothing but facts concerning the latter.[11]

When a man dies he goes straight to his narra well. He is taken there by his marikmo (paternal grandfather). He never comes back but always remains a spirit. Usually a Murngin who is about to die, particularly if severely wounded in a spear fight, dances his death dance, which is symbolical of the ceremonial actions of his totem. This is to send his spirit back to his ranga well.

"We can drink that narra water; we can see the bottom of the well.

[11] This point perhaps has been labored by me, but a large number of sociological and anthropological theories have been built out of the idea that there are many savage peoples who are ignorant of the facts of procreation. It is time some check be placed upon such speculation until further proof is accumulated by field workers.

That is nothing. That man is far down below in the deep water with his ranga, with his wongar and his old marikmo."

The soul of the dead (bir-im-bir) then returns to its totem and the totem lives in the sacred narra well. This is true for both men and women.

A Warumeri clansman was unconscious and near death. The relatives sang the garma sea-way (a cycle of songs about the sea and those totems which are connected with it). While they sang, it was thought, the spirit of marikmo was listening to the song. They then sang crayfish, which is a Warumeri totem. The hand of the dying one moved convulsively like a crayfish. They sang whale, also the clan's totem, and the person dying kicked in imitation of a whale. This meant he was going to die, and he was telling his people. He wanted them to sing his song, it was believed, so that his marikmo and old gatu (father's father's father) would know and come to him.

The dying one stiffened and was quiet. He was dead according to tribal thought, although his heart beat. "I see that go," one relative said about the heart of the dying man, "and I knew he was dead, but that his marikmo was looking out for him. I could see that because that old man marikmo moved inside his heart. He was taking that spirit back to the Warumeri well."

After death and before the burial ceremony, the symbol of the narra well of the deceased is painted on his chest and abdomen—in this instance, the wild duck well. This is done in order that all the dead of the well can see the one who has just died and take him immediately away to his water hole.

When, during the Djungguan ceremony for the great snake, Yurlunggur, and during the Narra ceremony for the other totemic emblems, a ranga is made, not only does the totem or the totem's essence enter into it through the singing of the men, but also the birimbir spirits of the dead ancestors—illustrating the close association of the clan members with their totems and dead ancestors.

The mythological ancestors who are in the well and who had some part in its formation are called old marikmo or old gatu. Their names express clearly the affiliation of the mythical men to the narra well and to the totem.

The names of the wells show the same totemic affiliation either directly or indirectly. Like the names of the mythological ancestors, they are of two types, the sacred and the camp variety. The sacred ones are used only during the great ceremonies, usually the Narra for the great majority of totems. It is then that all the wells of a moiety and the names of its dead ancestors are called out by the leader. The camp name is the one known by both men and women. No woman knows the sacred name of a well, or, for that matter, anything else that has to do with the sacred tribal life.

The chief totem of the Liaalaomir clan is a carpet snake. The names of the well are carpet snake's nose and menstruation blood, the latter referring indirectly to the actions of the snake.

The Djirin clan has the shark for a totem and the following names for its well: shark's head, ripples from a shark's swimming, hill from a tidal wave made by the shark when he created this country.

Although the well names refer to a totem which belongs to the other clans in the moiety, they also refer in particular to geographical aspects of one clan's territory, so that they have local significance. The same is true of the names of the mythological ancestors.

A man's name is taken from his male mari (mother's mother's brother) and his male marikmo (father's father). All sacred names are his marikmo's and not his mari's, but a man's camp names come chiefly from his mari; these latter also usually reflect totemic affiliation.

The symbol of the well is also painted on a man after his initiation and when he receives his totemic name in the Narra corroboree, and on a small boy when he is to be circumcised.

In addition to the relatives listed on page 16 as always included in the clan, there may be included within the clan: mari, male and female (mother's mother and mother's mother's brother); mokul rumeru (mother's mother's brother's daughter); marelker (mother's mother's brother's son); kutara, male and female (sister's daughter's son and sister's daughter's daughter); gurrong, male and female (father's sister's daughter's son and father's sister's daughter's daughter).

These relatives, too, may be blood or tribal in their relationship to ego. Men, for example, may be called brothers by ego and be clan members only remotely related to ego. The usual Murngin method of reckoning kin does not always operate within the clan, for, when there have been wrong marriages,[12] the practice of tracing descent through the mother and ignoring the father does not function. This

[12] See pages 94-95.

keeps the kinship position of offspring of such a marriage adjusted to the organization of his group. The son of a woman and man who have married wrong and who are not dué (father's sister's son) and galle (mother's brother's daughter) to each other is called gatu by the man and waku by the woman, just as is a son by correct marriage. The sons by another wife of the man would call this child of an improper marriage brother, and the other members of the patrilineal line of the clan would call him by the kinship term they would use if he were the offspring of a proper marriage.[13]

The practice of tracing the descent of relatives within the clan through the father, and outside through the mother, although largely designed to strengthen the clan solidarity and create a sharp line of demarcation between it and other such groups, at times has had the opposite effect.

The Warumeri and Wangurri clans have until recently been bitter rivals for the possession of women of clans in the other moiety. Certain members of the Warumeri clan in the last generation married women who should have become the wives of Wangurri clansmen, since their fathers stood in the relationship of mother's brother to ego.

[13] The relatives from other clans would ignore the relationship of the son to the father in the case of a wrong marriage and call the child the proper term applied to him when tracing his place in the kinship system through the mother. Thus if ego's father married a woman ego called momo (father's mother), ego would call their child brother, for he would trace the relationship through his father, because of the influence of the clan and family; but ego's nati (mother's father), for example, would call the child waku (sister's son), instead of kaminyer (daughter's son, daughter's daughter) as he calls ego.

Nati, being outside the clan, would trace his relationship to the child of the wrong marriage through the mother. The mother in the above example would be nati's sister, so that the child would be sister's son to him. Ego's gawel (mother's brother) would call this child of ego's father by a wrong marriage to ego's momo, dué, instead of the usual waku, since he is father's sister's son if the relationship is traced through the mother.

It can be seen that this process of reckoning relationship through the mother by all outside clans is continually changing the kinship composition of the various clans. New lines of descent are constantly springing out of different clans for those of the kin who are outside its limits. A clan that would for a period have only a mari and marelker and a mari and mokul for the male and female relatives in one's clan other than one's own patrilineal line, could, by a wrong marriage of the male mari—let us say, to a waku—create a gurrong-kutara line of descent for ego on the old mari-marelker clan.

When a clan develops a subclan within it, and this smaller unit is rather strongly organized, there is a possibility of the same process being applied within the clan that ordinarily takes place outside it. When this happens the mari-marelker and gurrong-kutara lines may be found within the clan. This occurs very rarely because these subgroups are unusual within the clan.

The Wangurri organized a raid, killed many of the Warumeri men and took the women for themselves. The children who were born from the Warumeri fathers before the capture of their mothers by the other clan were called gatu by the men who had captured their mothers, and wawa or yukiyuko by these men's sons, who were their progeny through proper marriage. The sons of these women by Wangurri fathers were also called wawa or yukiyuko by the Wangurri sons, not only because the fathers reckoned their relationship through the clan but because the mother too was in the right relationship.

In addition to reckoning kin as above, the Wangurri sons, by tracing the relationship of the Warumeri sons of these women through the mother, would call them brothers, just as the new husbands of these women would apply the term gatu to these children. The same procedure would be true of the Warumeri for the Wangurri offspring. Thus, instead of strengthening the differences between two clans, the tracing of descent through the mother for outside clans has broken down the ordinary clan walls and has done much to hasten the process of consolidation that can be seen taking place at the present time between two clans which possess contiguous territories and hold most of their totems in common. A Wangurri man is now head of both clans.

Below are listed the clans which usually intermarry. This does not mean that these clans do not also marry into other groups. It is felt, however, according to my informants, that the clans listed in the right-hand column are the ones into which those listed in the left-hand column prefer to marry.

Barlmawi	⟷	Liaalaomir
Birkili	⟷	Perango, Djirin, Gwiyula
Bringel	⟷	Mandelpui, Liaalaomir, Wawilak
Daiuror	⟷	Liagaomir, Naladaer, Djirin, Liaalaomir
Djawark	⟷	Darlwongo
Djirin	⟷	Warumeri, Birkili, Daiuror, Wangurri
Gunalbingu	⟷	Kurkamarnapia
Gwiyamil	⟷	Liagaomir, Liaalaomir
Gwiyula	⟷	Birkili
Karmalanga	⟷	Burera (tribe), Wulkara
Kiki	⟷	Maradunggimi
Kolpa	⟷	Perango, Murru
Komaits	⟷	Riraidjingo
Liagaomir	⟷	Wulkara, Gwiyamil, Daiuror
Lummami	⟷	Riraidjingo

Marderpa	⟷	Marungun
Marungun	⟷	Yalukal, Yandjinung (tribe)
Merango	⟷	Darlwongo
Naladaer	⟷	Daiuror
Perango	⟷	Kolpa, Birkili
Wangurri	⟷	Kalpu, Maradunggimi, Djirin, Kapin
Warumeri	⟷	Kalpu
Yalukal	⟷	Marungun

Examining this list of intermarrying clans in connection with the map (page 40), we see that they usually adjoin or are but a short distance apart. When Murngin warfare is discussed later in this chapter, it will be seen that the clans which are in competition for women from another particular clan are usually antagonistic groups and belong to opposing sides in the clan feuds.

A man always calls his own totems bapa (father), marikmo (paternal grandfather), or occasionally old gatu (paternal grandfather's father), according to the relationship term that his father applies to the emblem. If his father calls a totem bapa, ego applies the term marikmo to it; when the father addresses it as older brother, ego calls it bapa. In other words, a man applies the rule of kinship to his relationship with his totem by tracing his relationship to it as though it were an actual relative of his father. Often this nicety is not completely observed, and all the ranga are called by the single term bapa. Ego traces his relationship to totems of another clan through his nearest and most important relative in that clan. He would apply the term mari to a totem if it came from a clan having the mari and marelker line of descent as ego's nearest relatives in it, or he would use the term gawel (mother's brother) or arndi (mother) if the totem came from his mother's group. The members of a clan may all call the same outside clan's totems by different terms, since they may all be in different relationships to the men within these outside groups. The use of this kinship device further articulates ego with the local organization outside his own group, which gives him a greater sense of solidarity.

Sharing of totems occurs largely with clans belonging to the same moiety and will be discussed under the sections on moiety and phratries.

Murngin Moieties

Yiritja and Dua are the intertribal names for the moieties of this North Australian culture. All of the eight tribes considered in this paper, except the Burera, refer to their moieties by these names. The native word for moiety is ba-per-u, meaning the four subsections that belong to each moiety. It probably has reference to bapa (father), although the natives are unconscious of any such association.

The members of each moiety are supposed to speak different languages. The clans around Buckingham Bay, Arnhem Bay, Elcho Island and down the east coast of the Gulf of Carpentaria say they speak the Ko-par-ping-u language if they belong to the Yiritja moiety, and Djam-bar-ping-u if they are Dua. Actually, vocabularies gathered by the author show no difference between the two so-called languages. Language, however, is a native criterion—the final test—used to differentiate local groups. Even each clan is said to have a "language"; and some have a different dialect, but most within a given area speak the same one. The clans claim "languages" of their own by giving themselves linguistic names in addition to group names.

The people surrounding the Koparpingu and Djambarpingu area say their moieties have linguistic differences that are like Koparpingu and Djambarpingu, but do not consider themselves as being Koparpingu and Djambarpingu. There is considerable regional dialectic variation among the Murngin clans; the division, however, is not on the basis of moiety, but on that of groups of contiguous clan hordes belonging to the same tribe or to different tribes.

Everything in Murngin civilization is divided on this dual basis. There is nothing in the whole universe—plant, animal, mineral, star, man, or culture—that has not a place in one of the two categories. This division is as clear cut to a Murngin as heaven and hell to a mediaeval theologian, although of course never on the basis of good or bad. The allocation is made by an association that sometimes seems irrational to a European but is perfectly reasonable to the native mind. When one inquires into the underlying concept back of such seeming syncretisms, the reasoning is as justifiable, granted the premise, as for our own classifications.

To illustrate the principle: a red parrot is Dua because of his early association with the Dua creator women; red parrot feathers, one of the chief articles of decoration, are Dua because of this; baskets covered with red parrot feathers are Dua. The spear thrower is Dua, the sting-ray spear belongs to the same moiety, but the wooden spear is Yiritja. The shark belongs to the Dua moiety; the barrimundi is Yiritja, as is black duck.

The above association of objects may seem arbitrary and haphazard to the reader, but every article fits into an elaborate ideological system which finds its expression in myth and folklore. The white man is Yiritja, therefore all of his culture is Yiritja; so that if a tin can is thrown away at a mission station the native who captures this valued prize knows that it is Yiritja and has a convenient and workable category in which to place it. The white man is Yiritja because the Malay trader before him was Yiritja, and Malay and white man, to the native, are obviously alike.

The moiety division is a most fundamental category in the native mind. It divides the mother's people from the father's. Ego's mother's brother, his mother, and his wife are in the opposite moiety to him, for the descent is patrilineal, while his own father and father's sister are in his own moiety. Below will be found a list of the relatives who belong to each moiety.[14] We shall place ego in the Dua moiety in order to orientate the relatives to him.

DUA

marikmo (father's father and father's father's sister)
bapa (father)
mokul bapa (father's sister)
wawa (older brother) (ego)
yukiyuko (younger brother)
yeppa (sister)
gatu (son and daughter)
maraitcha (son's son and son's daughter)
mari (mother's mother's brother and mother's mother)
marelker (mother's mother's brother's son)
mokul rumeru (mother's mother's brother's daughter) (mother-in-law)
gurrong (father's sister's daughter's son and daughter)
kutara (sister's daughter's son and daughter)

YIRITJA

nati (mother's father)
momo (father's mother)
gawel (mother's brother)
arndi (mother)
galle (mother's brother's daughter [ego's wife] and mother's brother's son)
waku (sister's son and daughter, and father's father's sister's son and daughter)
dué (father's sister's son and daughter)
natjiwalker (mother's mother's mother's brother's son)
momelker (mother's mother's mother's brother's daughter)
dumungur (father's sister's daughter's daughter's son and daughter)
nati (mother's father)
kaminyer (daughter's son and daughter)

Incest rules are very rigid, sexual intercourse not being allowed between members of the same moiety. The rigidity of the taboo is illus-

[14] The kinship terms which are here divided into the two moieties are fully described in the next chapter.

trated in an autobiography collected by the writer: The narrator said laughingly that as very small children (three or four years old) the boys and girls "played house" together, and although they did not know what galle and dué (husband and wife) meant, the two sexes called each other by these terms when they were playing as though they were in the right relationship; but he added, "No Yiritja boy ever played house with a Yiritja girl and no Dua boy ever did this with a Dua girl. We always did this properly." On being asked how they, as children, knew this was the right way, he said, "That is something I always knew." Other similar occurrences related of the author's informant's and others' childhood indicate the emotional depth of the dual division in the mental make-up of these people, for it goes back of memory in the experience of the individual. Since a native's memory for the events of his early life is even better than our own, it will be seen how early the discipline of the dual division makes itself felt.

The great ceremonies also help to keep the things of the universe in their correct categories and to establish their correct relationships to each other, since at least once each year they dramatize the mythologies. Most of the great ceremonies belong to the Dua moiety—the Ul-mark, Djung-guan, Gun-a-bi-bi, and Marn-di-el-la—while the Nar-ra totemic ceremony is divided into two parts, one for each moiety; the first three ceremonies of the garma corroborees, which celebrate the spiritual life of the lesser totems, are Dua, because they are associated with Yur-lung-gur and Mu-it, the great snakes, which are Dua, and because they are connected with the two creator sisters who belong to this moiety. Even though the larger ceremonies are supposedly Dua in ownership, actually both groups participate, and in their structure both are given an equal rôle. The only practical difference in these dramatic rituals is that all ceremonies owned by the Dua are led by headmen of clans belonging to this moiety.

There are no headmen for moieties, although, as will be seen in the discussion of myth and ceremony, the headman of the Liaalaomir holds a place almost equaling in position that which the leader of a moiety would possess.

Intra-moiety fights are common; in fact, more common than warfare with clans of the opposing moiety. No clans would join together to fight another people simply because they belong to the same moiety; nor, were this reason advanced, would it prevent fighting within the moiety. The struggle for women among members of the same moiety is too keen to be overcome by an appeal to moiety solidarity.

Various parts of the ceremonies are used to give expression to the dual division. In the Djungguan ceremony, subsections, when calling up their dead ancestors, are placed in the moiety order; that is, first the four Dua subsections and then the four Yiritja take turns in calling the names and the illustrious deeds of their dead ancestors. At the end of this ceremony, when food is eaten ritualistically, the members of the two groups exchange food. During the Gunabibi only Dua men paint themselves, since it is taboo for Yiritja men so to decorate themselves for this particular ceremony. Dua men, however, cannot construct the great Yer-mer-lin-di totemic emblem, and this duty and privilege devolves upon Yiritja men, in exchange for which service the Dua men present the Yiritja men with food and other presents. The Dua use a round grave post to mark their burial spots or when they wish to erect a monument to the spirit of a newly dead person belonging to their moiety, whereas the coastal Yiritja raise a ceremonial mast for their dead. The Dua use red feather decorations for their Narra ceremonies; the Yiritja use opossum fur.

The totems themselves are largely divided on the basis of the moiety. Most clans of one moiety possess their totems in common. There is a considerable regional variation, but the differences are not due to clan divisions. Very occasionally a clan will possess a totem that no other owns, but this is only a temporary condition, for the myth of the two creator women usually is sufficient proof of ownership to other clans, so that in a short time they accept this new totem as their own, provided they belong to the same moiety as the original clan. For example, on the eastern side of Arnhem Land, along the coast of the Gulf of Carpentaria, all of the Dua clan have totems such as a yam stick, old woman, and young woman, while the Dua clans in the west, which center around the Goyder River, are more concerned with a snake and a complex of totems which surround it, and less with the women and their totemic objects. There seems to be an historical basis for this division which will be discussed later.

The Phratry

There is a weak attempt on the part of the Murngin to form groups of clans within the moiety, based on the mythological idea of a common association with a common creator totem or an alleged similarity of language differentiating one group from surrounding groups of clans. This grouping on a phratry basis, by no means general, is very weak and of no great importance.

The Warumeri, Wangurri, Wulkara, and Gwiyamil all call themselves Man-dji-kai (sand fly), supposedly the general name for their several languages. Although there is a considerable dialectic variation among the clans within this group, each claiming a distinct language for itself, they all insist that these languages are similar, and distinct and separate from those of all other clans. Even a cursory examination of the vocabularies shows that this is a rationalization, and once again a use of the linguistic criterion which the native feels he must have to separate peoples as his own or as different. The Kolpa of the Yaernungo tribe on Wessel Island and the Wallamungo of the Burera tribe on Millingimbi in the Crocodile group are sometimes added to the Mandjikai group. The Wallamungo speak a very different language so that one who knew only the Murngin tongue could not understand their language; thus it is impossible for the native to apply his linguistic criterion here as a definition for the phratry solidarity. Here, then, they fall back on their mythological association: in the days of Wongar (when totems walked the earth as men), Barrimundi came from the Wangurri country and tried to go on through to the other clans, but the whale and crayfish totems prevented him; in his efforts to force his way through, he smashed himself into many pieces which flew for many miles and landed in the territories of the other totemic clans in his phratry group and made their totemic water holes.

A Murngin says, "When I am in trouble I remember my ranga (high totem) and I go ask his people for help." What he means is not that he would go to the whole of his moiety, but that he would appeal to members of his phratry, connected with him by a myth which is confined to the clans in the smaller group. This manifestation of phratry solidarity is weak, however, and frequently the people within it are the very ones who are in the most intense disputes. Instead of going to members of his own phratry in a time of crisis, a clansman would be far more likely to appeal to his mother's clan. In other words, his kinship organization is more powerful in directing his actions than is his local organization, since it is the demands the kinship organization makes upon the members of the clan which force the whole group to act, rather than the demands made by the clan organized as a local unit.

Other phratries are the Garl-ba-nuk (catfish) of the Mandelpui and

Liaalaomir clans, and the Durili and Ding Ding phratries. The last two named are too nebulous in their composition to give their clan membership. Some informants name all the Dua clans as belonging to both, while others place only part of the eastern local units in these groups.

The phratry in Murngin society represents a weak attempt within the culture to create new and larger groups than the clan to control the intra-moiety antagonisms. It is an expression of the moiety weakness in controlling the antagonisms of the clans within it. The rivalry for women, as well as the other competitions, excites emotions too strong to be suppressed by phratry solidarity. It is only in the clan that one finds sufficient pressure placed on the antagonisms to prevent open war.

There is an interesting association between the Warumeri on one side and the Wawilak of the Ritarngo tribe on the other. The two are seventy-five miles apart, a long distance in this culture; yet according to native accounts the black duck totem is supposed to have lived with and performed certain significant acts for each clan in a mythological period, so they are most friendly. Actually, the two do not compete for women, although belonging to the same moiety; but the clans that lie between these two and belong to their moiety do compete, so that the Wawilak and Warumeri have common enemies and like grievances, and possess a convenient myth as a rallying point to express solidarity when associated in warfare against mutual enemies. This association of the two clans, although of considerable importance in their activities, is unnamed and does not class them as a phratry.

The Tribe

The tribes of northeastern Arnhem Land, of which Murngin is one, are very weak social units, and when measured by the ordinary definitions of what constitutes a tribe fail almost completely. The tribe is not the war-making group. On the contrary, it is usually within it that the most intensive feuds are found. Tribal membership of the clans on the borders of two tribes is uncertain and changing, or the people may sometimes insist that they belong to both tribes. Even clans well toward the center of a tribe's territory will, under certain circumstances, range themselves with another group, as will be seen as we examine in the following paragraphs the Murngin tribe.

The name Murngin, as stated, is little used, the principle of dual organization being so strong that the moiety names of a particular area are used much more commonly than the tribal to describe a particular people.

Arnhem Land, north of the Roper River and the upper waters of the Katherine River, has four large cultural groups. The differences are mostly in immaterial culture, and although of considerable importance from a local point of view, the cultures are but subtypes of a larger culture. The four divisions, the first the Murngin, are found among the eight tribes that inhabit the country from Cape Wessel in the northeast, the islands and the coast of the eastern side of the Gulf of Carpentaria to Blue Mud Bay, and eastward over to the upper waters of the Goyder and Glyde Rivers. This culture continues westward to Cape Stewart along the coast line of the Arafura Sea. West of them, including the tribe on each side of Caddell and Liverpool Rivers to the seacoast of Van Diemen's Gulf, the Kariera type of social organization is found. South of Blue Mud Bay, along the seacoast, the Mara-Anula form of social organization appears, and the Arunta type is found in the islands of this region.[15]

The Murngin type of culture is possessed by eight tribes: the Murngin, Yaernungo, Burera, Yandjinung, Djinba, Ritarngo, Barlamomo, and Dai. The Yaernungo, Burera, Yandjinung, Djinba and Ritarngo are definitely recognized divisions in the culture, although their exact boundaries are not known, for a border-line clan may be in one group for some purposes and in another for others. The Dai, Barlamomo, and Murngin are not clearly defined in the minds of the natives and the designations are of little consequence in their thinking and seldom used. The Ritarngo and Djinba tribesmen to the south and west call these people to the north of them Murngin, and distinguish them as different from themselves. The Yaernungo, north of the Murngin, do the same, but to a lesser degree. The Yandjinung also call the clans in different areas, including the Karmalanga of Banyan Island and the Wulkara of Howard Island, by the name of Murngin; the Murngin, however, look upon them as members of the Yandjinung tribe. The people of these islands usually consider themselves as belonging to the Yandjinung but occasionally place themselves in the Yaernungo tribe.

The Dai are very frequently classed as Murngin. The dialect of this tribe is that of the clans north of it, which are classed as Murngin.

[15] The names Arunta, Kariera, Mara-Anula, and Murngin are used here not as tribal distinctions, but as types of kinship organizations which form the basic foundation for general variations in the social organization.

The Barlamomo occupy a similar position in relation to the Murngin. The Dai and Barlamomo can hardly be ranked as tribes, except that the terms are loosely used by the natives for groups of clans belonging to either moiety; and since they cannot be phratries and belong to both groups of the dual division, and since there is a vague recognition of their distinctiveness in their having names and being considered by the people to the north as each one people, they have been ranked as tribes by the writer, with full recognition that such a designation is too ample and solid a term to describe them.

The Djawark and Darlwongo clans sometimes are included among the Dai; the Marderpa group may be classed as Dai, Murngin, or Ritarngo, according to the feeling of the people within the clan or those without who distinguish them.

Within the region east of the Yandjinung, Burera, Djinba, and Ritarngo tribes, and including the peoples known as Yaernungo, Dai, Barlamomo, and Murngin, there is considerable linguistic homogeneity. All the peoples included in the latter four tribes can understand the various dialectic variations found throughout the area. The greatest divergence in dialect is among the Yaernungo, but the Liaalaomir of the Goyder River on the one hand, and the Wanguri and Warumeri of Árnhem Bay on the other, also present considerable variation in speech. The peoples belonging to the tribes in the area mentioned above cannot understand the languages of the other tribes along their borders unless they have learned them as separate tongues. Linguistic ability is very marked among all these people. It would be difficult to find a Murngin adult who could not speak three or four languages, and frequently men speak seven and eight.

There is greater difference between these northern languages of Australia than there is between French and English. The Burera have the most divergent tongue and are definitely affiliated linguistically with the more western peoples such as the Gun-wing-u and Maung.

As will be seen from the map, the Murngin have many more clans than the other tribes. It cannot be stated as a definite hypothesis, but very likely that the group of the Murngin associated together under the moiety "linguistic" terms as Djambarpingu and Koparpingu are one people and differentiated from the rest of the Murngin. When asked to what people they belong, they always reply Djambarpingu or Koparpingu, according to the moiety. The clans usually classed as belonging to the two groups are:

Djambarpingu (Dua)	Koparpingu (Yiritja)
Liagaomir	Daiuror
Naladaer	Gwiyamil
Djirin	Birkili
Gwiyula	Burilung (sometimes classed with Barlamomo tribe)
Djapu	
Maradunggimi (sometimes classed with Barlamomo tribe)	
Djawark	

If the above hypothesis is true, this group in an earlier period was confined to the area around Buckingham Bay, Arnhem Bay, Elcho Island, and the English Company Islands. I was unable to find a general name covering both divisions to substantiate this historical contention. The Malay trader undoubtedly widened the horizon of the society by his movements along the coast, and with the introduction of the dugout canoe made possible longer, more rapid journeys and wider contacts among the peoples of the various clans comprising this and the present Murngin group; before this time the only means of travel had been by foot or by the frail bark canoe and rafts. It seems likely to me that the Malay's advent, which occurred at least several hundred years ago, provides sufficient explanation for the breakdown of the earlier tribal grouping—which, if similar to that of present-day tribes was a very weak manifestation at best—and for the formation of a larger Murngin group.

Pronunciation varies greatly locally. This linguistic differentiation does not coincide with tribal areas, although there is a tendency for the tribes to be linguistically distinguished. As has been stated, all the clans consider themselves linguistically distinct, and members of the two moieties believe they speak different dialects. This insistence on linguistic difference is so extreme that members of the same clan pronounce their words with a suitable amount of variation. Any attempt to state that this dialect or that method of pronunciation is a standard and exact one is likely to be a projection of our own ethnocentric linguistic values. The western Europeans and the Americans, particularly since the advent of the public school, have made an extreme fetish of standard English and correct pronunciation. There has been, with the general urge, a general standardization of speech. We frequently assume that the primitives always do as we do in their speech habits. This may or may not be true. The Murngin have an extreme degree of variation; and as far as I could determine, the chief criteria which tended toward uniformity in the language are a use and a pronunciation of the various words sufficiently varied to identify a person with his own linguistic area, and yet with enough speech uniformity to be understood by the people as a whole.

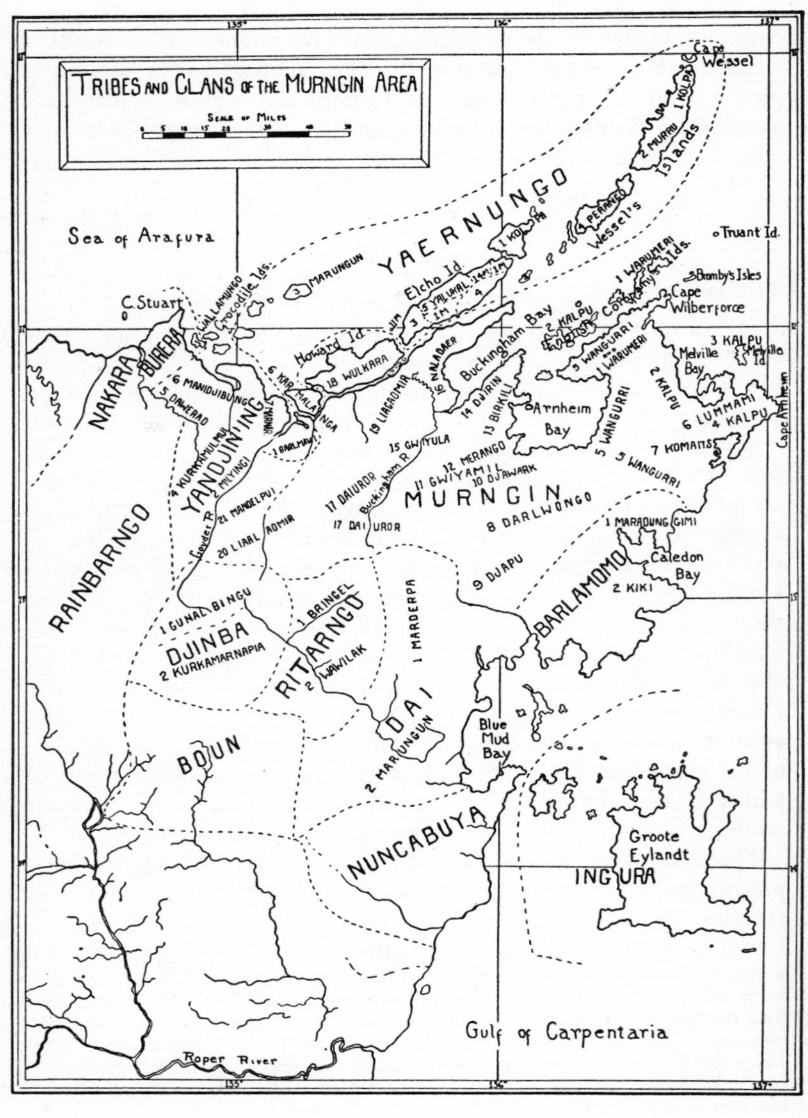
TRIBES AND CLANS OF THE MURNGIN AREA
SCALE OF MILES
0 5 10 15 20 30 40 50
135°
136°
137°
Sea of Arafura
Cape Wessel
1 KOLPA
2 MURRU
Islands
YAERNUNGO
3 PERANGO
Wessel's
1 KOLPA
Truant Id.
Crocodile Ids.
3 MARUNGUN
WALLAMUNGO
Elcho Id.
3 YALUKAL
4
C. Stuart
Bromby's Isles
1 WARUMERI
Cape Wilberforce
Buckingham Bay
2 KALPU
English Co.'s
Howard Id.
3 WANGURRI
1 WARUMERI
3 KALPU
Melville Id.
Melville Bay
NAKARA
BURERA
6 MANIDJIBUNG
5 DAWERAD
6 KAR
MALA
NGA
18 WULKARA
19 LIAGAOMIR
16 NALADAER
Buckingham
14 DJIRIN
13 BIRKILI
Arnheim Bay
5 WANGURRI
2 KALPU
6 LUMMAMI
4 KALPU
Cape Arnheim
YANDJINUNG
4 KURKAMULMUI
MILYINGI
1 BARLMAU
15 GWIYULA
12 MERANGO
11 GWIYAMIL
10 DJAWARK
7 KOMAITS
5 WANGURRI
17 DAIURDR
Buckingham R.
MURNGIN
21 MANDELPUI
RAINBARNGO
20 LIAALAOMIR
Goyder R.
17 DAIURDR
8 DARLWONGO
1 MARADUNG GIMI
Caledon Bay
9 DJAPU
BARLAMOMO
2 KIKI
1 GUNALBINGU
DJINBA
2 KURKAMARNAPIA
1 BRINGEL
RITARNGO
2 WAWILAK
1 MARDERPA
DAI
2 MARUNGUN
Blue Mud Bay
BOUN
NUNCABUYA
Groote Eylandt
INGURA
Gulf of Carpentaria
Roper River

CHAPTER III

THE FAMILY AND KINSHIP STRUCTURE

The Immediate Families of Orientation and Procreation

It seems unnecessary to say that the elementary family is found among the Murngin.[1] However, some of the earlier writers on aboriginal life stated that the general family system as known in other continental areas did not occur among the Australians, leaving an erroneous impression which still holds among many modern thinkers on primitive Australia. The elementary families of orientation and procreation are present and form the nuclear elements around which the larger kinship organization is built. The families of orientation and procreation are fundamental integrating factors in the social personality of the kinship ego. He is born into the first and orientated by it to the kinship organization of his own tribe and to the neighboring tribes. His filial relations to his father place him in his patrilineal clan and moiety and in a marrying relation with his mother's clan and moiety. The simple reciprocal[2] of the son and father ties him by a set of organized attitudes and behaviors to one-half the tribe and, more immediately, to his clan. The direct mother-son reciprocal is the foundation on which is built his entire set of relations by affinity, since it is the mother's brother's daughter who becomes the son's wife.

The underlying basis of the Murngin families of orientation and procreation is the incest taboo; no one within the two elementary families can have sexual relations with any other member of the two

[1] The family of orientation is the immediate family into which ego (a man or woman) is born; in its upper generation it includes the father and mother and in its lower ego's brothers and sisters. The primary function of the family of orientation from the point of view of ego is to socialize his organism and orientate it to the general community. When ego marries and has children, he establishes his family of procreation where his functions are reversed, since he is now in the position of helping in the creation of new organisms and in their socialization. All normal men and women in Murngin society, as well as other societies, live in these two families. Too frequently when kinship systems are examined these two families are considered not as separate but as one; and since all kinship structures are based on the position of ego, this has served to confuse many expositions of kinship structure.

[2] See Glossary of Technical Terms.

groups (except, of course, ego's father with ego's mother and ego with his wife). The membership of each family is the same as in Euro-American families and includes the same members as found here, the only difference being that a man can have a number of wives, which means in Murngin society that the children have a number of mothers. The sister is not only sexually taboo to her brothers, but any direct contact with her is also taboo. The incest idea is enlarged upon to include these additional restrictions in the general behavior of the opposite sexes of one generation within the family. This extreme form of the incest taboo in the total behavior of brothers and sisters, expressed overtly in concrete negative acts (avoidance), contributes to the organization of the family of orientation. The avoidance rules become concrete symbols of the underlying rule of incest which forces marriage outside the family of orientation and thereby creates the family of procreation out of extra-familial personalities.

The father-son reciprocal is the solid bond around which ego's spiritual affiliations are organized, since by a mystical experience of his father he leaves the totem well as a tiny fish and is directed by his male parent into his mother's womb. The father's mystical experience is the expression of the creation of the family of procreation. It is in fact the first element in the filio-parental relationship, since it is the first moment when either parent is supposed to know the beginning of this new generation within his own family. The annunciation of the child to the father by a dream symbolizes the parents' sexual intercourse, and in Murngin thought both dream and intercourse are necessary for conception and birth.

This first spiritual bond built on the father-son reciprocal determines the child's place in the totemic ceremonies which are of major import in his adult life: his whole spiritual identity, including his totem and power names; his sacred well where his soul will return after death; and the dogma and ritual which surround all these spiritual entities. So much for the orientating relations of ego's generation and that of his parents. Within his own generation and his family of orientation his brothers and sisters are to be found. His brothers and he occupy an identical place within the social structure. They are in the same patrilineal line as he and enjoy the same solidarity with the father as he, the primary differentiating factor being the distinction between older and younger brothers, as expressed in the kinship terminology. The brothers are spiritually almost identical, since they have the same totem and clan well, and their names, although somewhat different, are items from the same totemic configuration. They marry under the same rules and regulations and obtain for wives the same social personality (their mother's brother's daughters) and, by the action of the levirate and sororate, sometimes the identical women. In every respect the brothers are equivalent, primarily because of this occupation of the same sociological place in the family of procreation. The equivalence of brothers is one of the basic principles underlying the fundamental structure of the kinship organization.

The brother-sister reciprocal is fundamentally powerful and primarily the same as in Euro-American society. There is also a considerable degree of equivalence between brothers and sisters. They occupy the same generation and same line of descent. From a structural point of view, the horizontal generation line cross-sects the perpendicular patrilineal line at the same point for both the sisters and the brothers. They are therefore from the same totem well, they have the same totems, et cetera, but because of their sexual difference they are not completely equivalent. Further, they marry people who occupy different points within the social kinship structure, which tends to differentiate them.

The marriage of a male ego to his wife is something more than the modern marriage contract to any woman out of a general group. He marries into his wife's family of orientation, a group of four personalities who are his mother's brother, his mother's brother's wife (who is also part of another family), his wife's brother, and his wife's sister, who is also mother's brother's daughter. Ego, then, is constantly looking to his mother's people for his wives while he is a member of his own family of orientation and while forming his family of procreation, and when he has a son he still seeks the father of his mother's group to obtain wives for his male offspring. On the other hand, he has nothing to obtain during childhood and early manhood from his father's side of the family. When he has a daughter old enough for marriage, he wants a son-in-law; but he is then not a seeker but the one sought after by his sister's son, which puts him in a very strong position. To summarize: in his family of orientation he is weak in his relations with his mother's people and strong with his father's; in his family of procreation this still holds true. It is to be noted that on his father's side there are no tabooed collateral relatives with the exception of his sister, who is a part of his own family; but on his mother's side two are taboo: mokul rumeru and momelker. The elementary family tends to be much more stable in Murngin society than it does in our own because of the operation of the sororate and levirate, since if a man obtains two or more sisters for wives and they are looked upon as mothers, the death of any one of them does not disrupt the equilibrium of the family structure; if the husband dies, his brothers inherit the wives and children and there is still no break within the general structure, since the children have, as the classificatory terminology attests, regarded their father's brothers as fathers.

An examination of the relationship of the two elementary families to the entire kinship system shows that all the perpendicular patrilineal lines of descent except the two extremes to the right and left of ego (the natchiwalker-gawel and the dumungur-waku line)[3] are all in direct familial structural articulation with ego's elementary families of orientation and procreation. This is of extreme importance in the formation of the kinship pattern and partially explains it. To understand this properly, the kinship terms as separate entities must be forgotten and the total kinship system looked upon as a group of interlocking elementary familial units, in each of which there are certain social elements which have an intercellular unity and system of relations of their own.

Five of the patrilineal lines and all of the horizontal lines of generation interlock directly with ego's elementary families of procreation and orientation. The emotional content of the organized system of attitudes and behavior in ego's family is directly connected with the organized emotional content of the other families, and from these latter groups the larger structure and the total kinship system is constructed. The termination of the perpendicular patrilineal lines two generations above and below ego is partially accounted for by the fact that the direct contact with ego's elementary families stops exactly there, with marikmo on one end and maraitcha at the other. The only important personalities left out of this interlocking group of elementary families' structures are dumungur (lower left-hand corner of the kinship chart), mari (male), marelker and momelker. The mari-male and momelker personalities cluster about the mokul rumeru entity. These people all belong to her family of orientation, since one is her father, one her mother (see also mari-kutara reciprocal, page 88 f.), and one her brother. She is in a critical relation to ego because she is the wife of gawel, who controls ego's chances of obtaining a wife. She is at the same time

[3] See Chart II, page 48, for these lines. The reader should use this chart throughout the present chapter.

the daughter of mari. Mari and his wife momelker, who, as her parents, control her behavior, also stand in a powerful relation with gawel's mother (mari's sister): by virtue of the considerable control exercised by brothers over sisters and reflected through gawel's mother upon gawel, ego is given further power over gawel. It seems likely, in the light of what has just been said, that mokul rumeru's extreme importance has allowed her whole family of orientation to be given kinship personalities. The brother-brother, sister-sister, and for some purposes brother-sister equivalence has brought natchiwalker into the larger kinship group within which he is not a strong personality.

The Murngin familial structure is the fundamental basis of their social organization. In its simplest form it consists of restricted elementary families; in its more elaborate expression it includes the complicated extended kinship system which is built out of a formalization of a large number of elementary families. It also includes a further generalization of the kinship personalities into a grouping of lineage and descent called the subsection system, and finally a dual organization which divides the many totemic clans between the two moieties. We shall now examine the familial system of elementary families and the extended kin group and the latter structure's more general form, the subsection system.

The Kinship System

The Murngin system of reckoning kin, in common with those of other tribes of Australia where kinship structures have been studied, groups relatives by the Dakota classificatory method. That is, there is first a bifurcation of all the members of the group by a separation of the mother's kin from the father's, and, second, collateral relatives are merged with lineal ones through the operations of the principle of the equivalence of brothers. Everyone in the tribe and in all other tribes known to the Murngin is related to a given man and woman by this system of social recognition. A man's paternal uncles are addressed by the same term as his father because they are equivalent to the father in Murngin thinking. The same principle operates in the next ascending generation: the paternal grandfather and his brothers are given one term by the father's children. This logic holds in the classification of all seventy-one relatives found in the Murngin system; for example, the paternal grandfather's sons are called by the same term as the father because they are the male offspring of men given the same term as a man's own paternal grandfather. In other words, a large group of men are called father who are classificatory, not actual, male parents; and the sons of these classificatory fathers are called brother by each other although they are not blood brothers. Each brother calls the offspring of every other brother as well as his own, sons and daughters, and the latter reciprocate with father. On the mother's side the mother's sisters are called mother and all the brothers of one's mother's father are given the same term as the maternal grandfather, which means, by the logic of equivalences, that the daughters of these maternal grandfathers must be called mother and these women's brothers are classed as maternal uncles. It can be seen that such a system of classifying collateral kin with a man's own lineage, given the passage of a few generations, associates under one term actual blood relatives and a whole group of men who may not be related.

The kinship system, as stated, recognizes the total of seventy-one kinds of relatives. There are seven lines of descent and five generations in each lineage. The seven lines of descent include a man's or woman's own patrilineal line, three lines of descent related to him through his father and three through his mother. Since each of the seven lines has five generations, it means that thirty-five relatives are created by the lineage and generation principles alone. This number is doubled by a sexual division of the relatives recognized. The males and females of each line and generation either are given separate terms, or their separation is effected by adding a male or female adjective to the general term. For example, son and daughter are called gatu, but the former is called gatu diramo (man) and the latter gatu mielk (woman).

The division of the brother relation on the basis of age accounts for the final kinship term. A brother who was born before his own brothers calls them by a term which means younger brother and they call him by a word which designates him as older brother.

The system as thus far described has concerned only descent and its relationships. The whole structure rests upon a law of marriage by which a man's wife is his maternal uncle's daughter and a woman's husband is her paternal aunt's son. The woman sought by a man is his consanguine mother's brother's child; but if no one of that near relationship is available, the one as near by blood as can be obtained is preferred. The same principle holds true for a woman's spouse. This marriage is not symmetrical, in the sense that a man's mother's brother does not marry his father's sister and thereby have offspring who are related to him through both his father's side and his mother's line, as under the marriage rules of many primitive tribes. The Murngin cross-cousin marriage is asymmetrical because father's sister's daughter is not mother's brother's daughter and the former marries outside ego's mother's or father's line; the maternal uncle's son is not at the same time father's sister's son, and he too marries someone outside the two lines rather than ego's sister, as he would if this cross-cousin marriage were symmetrical. The outside marriage of the two, because of this asymmetry of the basic preferential marriage mechanism, is fundamentally responsible for the enlargement of the kinship system into the seven lines of descent. The wife and husband of these two members, father's sister's daughter and father's sister's son, are recognized in each of the generations, and the brothers and sisters of their spouses are also recognized because of the feeling for including a whole family in the terminology if any one of its members is recognized. This general problem of the elaborating of the kinship system will be discussed later. Chart II depicts the whole Murngin kinship system. Ego's line is the one in the center of the chart and ego is placed in the position of brother, since he and brother occupy the same space in the scheme. The whole system is related or articulated in the chart to ego because the system itself is formed on this basis. This means that the kinship terminology is always from the point of view of a man speaking or being spoken to. For example, a man or woman calls his father's father marikmo and the latter calls his son's son maraitcha. The chart shows this by putting marikmo two generations above ego and in the same line. Ego's son's son calls ego marikmo, is termed maraitcha by him, and is articulated into the general chart by placing him two generations below in ego's line. The = signs designate marriage. It is important to notice that they tie two lines directly together. The sign ┌──┐ symbolizes a brother and sister relationship. For example, yeppa (sister) and wawa (older brother) have their direct relationship symbolized by this device, as do arndi (mother) and gawel (mother's brother). The = sign shows that ego and his brothers marry galle and that ego's sisters marry dué. The abbreviated English descriptive terms found above each of these relatives will enable the reader to trace their "blood" relationship to ego.

A perusal of the chart shows that a number of the terms are repeated; for example, mother and mother's brother are called arndi and gawel, respectively, and so are the daughter and son of one's wife's brother.

The whole kinship system of the Murngin people is made up of fundamental kinship reciprocals, such as brother and sister, father

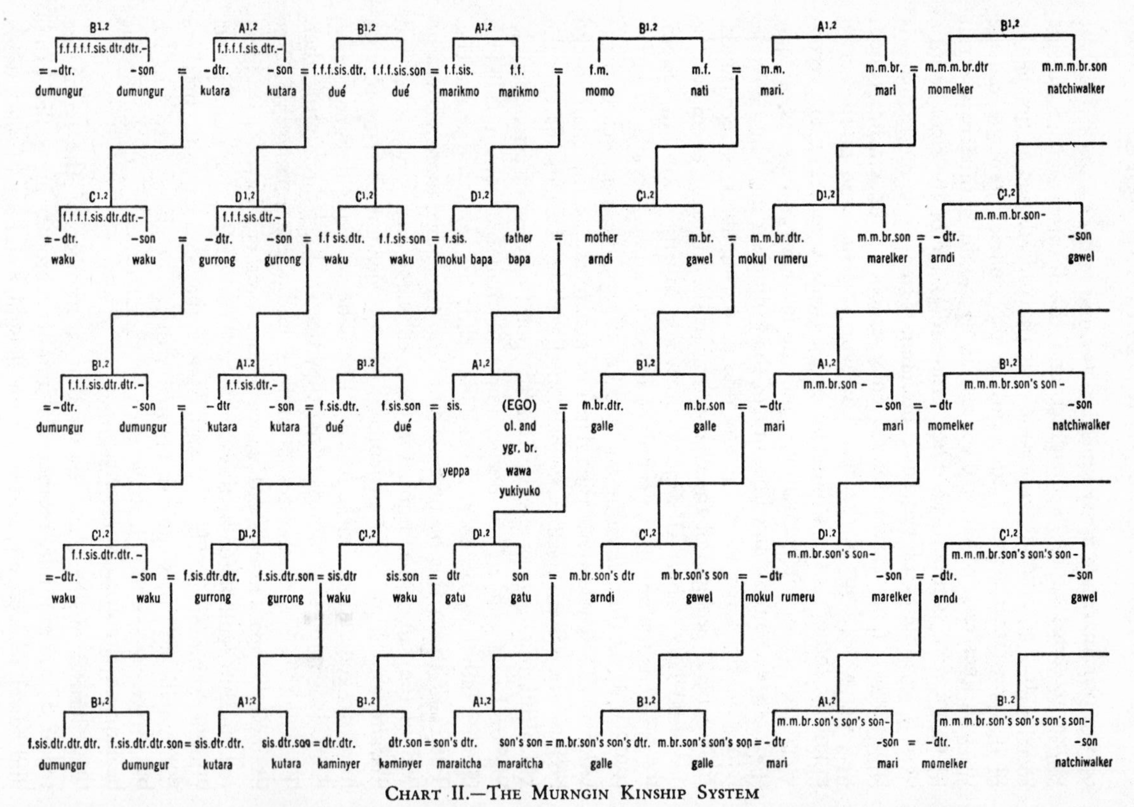

Chart II.—The Murngin Kinship System

and son, maternal uncle and sister's son. Every individual term represents a complex nexus of social behavior which creates a well-defined social personality. Each of these social personalities is but one element of the larger personality of each individual within the whole society, since each male has all the male terms in the kinship system applied to him, and every woman all the female terms.

Each of the reciprocals is considered below in structural order according to patrilineal line. The first relationships considered are those in a man's own line, beginning with those of his own generation—older and younger brother, brother and sister, and sister and sister. We next consider the collateral relatives in the patrilineal lines outside ego's own, beginning with the husband and wife relationship.

Wawa ⟷ *Yukiyuko* (older brother ⟷ younger brother)

The general type of this relationship has several varieties of which the natives are conscious when they use the two general terms. They comprise: (1) Two brothers from the same father and same mother; (2) two brothers from the same father and two mothers who are sisters; (3) from the same mother and two fathers who are brothers; (4) from two fathers who are brothers, and two mothers who are sisters; (5) brothers belonging to the same clan but only tribal in relationship; (6) brothers from nearby clans; (7) brothers from more remote clans and tribes. The intensity of behavior decreases from the first to the last mentioned; indeed, the last two varieties may have little in common with the other five; yet given normal conditions, the Murngin and other tribes with their type of kinship would consider it wrong if certain, though not all, of the rules regulating this relationship were broken. Hence it will be necessary to differentiate among the various kinds of brothers.[4]

The junior levirate is a prominent mechanism. When an older brother dies the brother next in age and consanguinity receives his wives and becomes father to the children. This is not only a privilege, but a duty. Frequently wives thus acquired, being past the age of bearing children or gathering food, are really an economic liability to the heir; yet he must take and look after them.

The junior levirate functions even before the death of the older brother. A gawel (father-in-law) is supposed to give his waku (son-in-law) all the female offspring from his own wives, but there is a

[4] An aborigine, speaking fair English, described the first two varieties as "my proper wawa," the third and fourth as "my proper wawa, but little bit different," the fifth as "close-up wawa," the sixth and seventh as "far-off wawas."

strong feeling that a man who has acquired two wives or all the issue of his gawel's first wife should allow his younger brother to have his share of the women from the gawel and mokul. The older brother, however, has the first right to them, and his gawel will ask his permission before giving the third daughter to the younger man. He will say: "It is better that your yukiyuko have this woman, for you have two already, and he has none. It is better that I have more waku to help me." Unless the older brother is an extraordinarily selfish person, he immediately replies, "Yes, you tell him to feed her" (give her to him for a wife); and he helps his younger brother procure the presents he must give gawel and mokul for this wife.

Mutual help prevails between wawa and yukiyuko in giving frequent presents to gawel and mokul. When wawa is making presents for his first wives, yukiyuko gives him spears, game from the hunt, and whatever wawa might like to present to his parents-in-law. When yukiyuko's turn comes, wawa is equally helpful. There is no obligation on yukiyuko to make presents to wawa for the latter's right to the galle that are to come to the former. Rather, wawa frequently asks gawel to give his other daughters to yukiyuko and makes presents to gawel for this purpose. Several motives guide him in this procedure. The first is brotherly affection and family pride. Own brothers through one father and one mother or father's brothers and mother's sisters are one's best friends, and most like one socially. Then there is frequently the fear that yukiyuko will fornicate with wawa's wives. This is no uncommon thing; the jungle and Australian bush offer ample opportunities for secret meetings. An old man usually suffers this indignity in silence, since he knows that his senility forces his wives to go to other men for sexual satisfaction and that his younger brothers who will inherit them are the proper ones for them. If the older brother has this situation too forcibly thrust upon him by camp gossip, he must attempt to discipline the younger man by scolding him—but "he doesn't talk very hard." Among younger men this would cause considerable trouble and would not happen very often except among tribal brothers, the whole pressure of society being against the younger man: all the relatives in his male line and those of the clan would defend the rights of the older man and condemn the younger. Finally, an older brother always helps a younger brother to acquire a wife because it settles the younger man and tends to prevent his getting into trouble with more remote wawas, yukiyukos, and other kin, by copulating with their wives, thereby forcing the wawa to defend his brother from their vengeance.

Because all of the members of a group of brothers are all dué to the same galle and the women thereby are the potential wives of all yukiyukos of this group, there is a strong tribal rule that no yukiyuko can talk to or be near wawa's wives, but wawa can talk to and be near yukiyuko's. (This would not be true of a woman beyond the age when she would be sexually interested in yukiyuko, nor of boys below the age of puberty.) The rule holds against all yukiyukos, near or distant, except where blood brothers are involved who have a tremendous love and trust in each other. Breaking of the rule by blood brothers was observed, but not by tribal brothers.

There is still another method by which the junior levirate operates. A wawa often gives one or two of his younger wives to yukiyuko. These wives may merely be those promised by a gawel and for whom wawa has made presents (wawa would be forced to obtain permission from gawel in this case); or wawa may give yukiyuko wives he has already lived with, in which circumstances permission need not be asked.

If wawa has four or five wives, he may say to a single yukiyuko, "You see that one—you take her and feed her." Yukiyuko usually says, if wawa is an old man, "No, you are an old man. I'll wait until you die, then I'll have them all." Wawa replies, "No, you take her now, yukiyuko. I have many wives and you have none." Yukiyuko then takes her, and she belongs to him permanently. Wawa loses all right to her sexually and economically, and she cannot be returned to him. If yukiyuko died, his new wife would go to his younger brother, even though he were not consanguine but only tribal.

Ordinarily a man would present his younger brother with a wife if particularly pleased with some exploit of yukiyuko's, such as the successful termination of a punitive expedition against common enemies.

One of Warlumbopo's older brothers (actual) had been ambushed and mortally wounded by a tribal yukiyuko.

Shortly after this Warlumbopo walked into the camp of the dying man.

Warlumbopo wailed for his dead brother. He refused to allow the wives of the dead man to bury him until he had killed the slayer of his wawa, when he returned to his dead brother and buried him.

When Daurlung, an older brother to Warlumbopo and younger to the dead man, heard the news he said, "We'll get all our Ritarngo people and go fight them." "No," said Warlumbopo. He had not told Daurlung of his killing their brother's slayer since the latter had been a good friend of Daurlung's. Daurlung said, "Yes, we must go kill our brother's slayer." "You can't kill him now." "Why?" "He's dead." "Who killed him?" "I did." "My own brother! Good! I'll give you two of my wives."[5]

This episode not only illustrates the operation of the junior levirate during the life of an older brother, but shows clearly the solidarity among a group of consanguine brothers and its lack between "far-off" brothers.

Wawa always is at the head of a family of brothers and has the strongest voice in their affairs if the father is very old or dead. However, if wawa is not of an assertive type, whereas one of the younger brothers is, the latter could hold equal authority with him and frequently would have the final decision on any problem that confronted them.

The oldest brother, who has the rights of ceremonial leadership for certain of the clan and moiety ceremonies, usually has the next oldest help him, and they confer over ceremonial matters on an almost equal basis; but, given two personalities of equal strength, the older would be by virtue of his age the more powerful in family affairs.

Usually two brothers cooperate in making a canoe, since of all economic labors this is the most difficult and extends over the greatest period of time. A canoe, too, has the highest economic value of all the Murngin's technological articles. Wawa has the most control over the canoe, although yukiyuko, if a man of will, may have an equal say in its management. If it were traded to another group, all the brothers would feel they had an ownership in it, even if they had not helped make it.

The brothers usually have an equal right to the property of each, although it is definitely known that a spear, a club, a basket, or any other such article belongs to one man and not to the group. A dog is known to belong to one man; yet the other brothers have a feeling of secondary ownership, and the dog recognizes them as secondary masters, much as with us a boy may own a dog and receive primary obedience and loyalty from his pet, while his brothers are secondary masters. These latter would look upon the dog as their brother's, but as "ours" in relation to outsiders.

If a son of one brother dies, the others always join in the ceremonial

[5] There is a full account of this incident in Warlumbopo's life as a warrior in the chapter on warfare, pages 166-179.

dances in the mourning for him. All varieties of brothers within the clan are included, the activity being really more a clan than a fraternal function.

Among brothers within the clan fighting is not allowed, but among brothers who belong to adjoining clans warfare is quite common.

Although the Murngin and the other seven tribes who share their type of kinship have a very strong feeling against the younger brother's copulating with an older brother's wife under ordinary circumstances, there is a period among the peoples practicing the Gunabibi ceremony when sexual "license" is recognized and even demanded between brothers and their wives. This is, however, strictly regulated; only brothers from more distant clans would be invited and allowed to exchange wives for ceremonial copulation. The tribal ideal of this custom is that a few nights before the end of the ceremony older brothers call their consanguine younger brothers and ask the latter to go to the nearby camp of the distant brothers in attendance at this ceremony, taking the older men's wives with them. The older brothers in the visitors' camp do likewise. The men and women paint themselves and go into the bush in the nearby jungle for copulation. The last night one woman may stay with several men, for a larger proportion of men than women always attend, since wifeless brothers usually enter into this ceremony. After a man has had intercourse with a tribal brother's wife, the husband puts his sweat on both of his guest's legs "so that he won't be sick from it." The men meanwhile have been giving presents to the women for some time before the ceremony and the women turn the gifts over to their husbands, although they frequently keep part for themselves. In reality, there is an exchange of presents, as well as of wives, among these more distant brothers.

The above is a tribal ideal. Actually, copulation purely for pleasure starts early in the ceremony, while the last night's indulgence is a purification rite supposed to cleanse a man and woman of impurities and to avoid illness during the period between the present ceremony and the next. The men and women have clandestine meetings, but it is generally known which people are having these assignations in the surrounding bush or jungle, and many broadly humorous remarks are passed by both sexes about their various lovers. However, some men and women would not enter into this earlier secret copulation, but would wait until the last night.[6]

[6] The ritual place of wife exchange and its significance are treated in the chapter on Murngin totemism, particularly pages 296-298.

Yeppa ⟷ *Wawa* and *Yukiyuko* (sister ⟷ older and younger brother)

There are the same varieties of yeppa as of wawa and yukiyuko. There is little difference in the behavior of a yukiyuko-yeppa and a wawa-yeppa relationship, except that if yukiyuko is an adolescent or child, he will not have an older brother's control over his sisters; but if he is an adult he has as much influence in directing their affairs as has his older brother. Yeppa calls any brother born before her "wawa" and any brother born after her "yukiyuko," exactly as a man would. With the above reservation, we can treat the yukiyuko-yeppa and the wawa-yeppa relationships as one, remembering of course the varying degree of closeness in the relationship between wawa and yukiyuko, and realizing its effect on the relationship we are now considering.

The sister and brother relationship is surrounded with taboos. If a brother speaks in the hearing of his sister, tribal or blood, he utters his words in a low voice, since she is not supposed to hear him. She speaks in the same manner before him. He never talks to her directly, nor she to him. He does not use obscenities in front of her as he would before most women (including his mother, daughter's daughter, and father's sister), nor will he allow anyone else to indulge in such language before her in his presence. They never sleep in the same hut or camp except as infants. At a very early age they are separated. Yeppa always helps her brothers if they are involved in a fight. She would not only ask assistance of her relatives but also give aid herself unless she felt a divided loyalty, in which case she would, with the help of other women, try to prevent a fight.

A brother is like a second father to a sister. If she is caught in adultery he gives her a beating and, if not stopped, tries to kill her. When Daoper's wife ran off with Bengaliwe her near brothers gave her an unmerciful beating and might have killed her had not other relatives interfered. Even if a brother saw her own husband copulating with his sister, he would become angry and try to beat her. However, he is careful not to see them.

A yukiyuko always accompanies yeppa when she first goes to her husband's clan to live after their marriage. The brother is usually preadolescent, but sometimes he may be older. He is supposed to look out for his sister, seeing that she does not commit adultery, preventing other men from seducing her, and by his presence protecting her from ill treatment by her husband.

Brothers look to their sisters to supply them with wakus for their daughters to marry. A waku's importance to a man is no less than that of a son. A brother always makes presents to his sister for her son, as well as to her husband.

A brother, but no sister, may eat a youth's kill of kangaroo, emu, et cetera, until the youth's wife has had a child. A sister is supposed to help carry the ruddled bones of the first kangaroo or emu killed by her brother, just as she helps carry her dead brother's bones.

A brother and father always know and keep the tabooed names of a girl. No woman knows her ceremonial name.

There are two sets of behavior in the relationship of a brother and sister that must be treated together (see pages 99-101 for an interpretation of the Wakinu and Mirriri customs). First, she is called wakinu by all her brothers. In its primary sense, wakinu means a person without kin, and secondarily "worthless" or, more expressively, "rubbish." Bamapama, the trickster hero, a much-loved scoundrel who lived in the olden days and broke all laws, is always wakinu after some particularly fantastic escapade of his has been retold. Wakinu is used during a fight as an appropriate term against one's enemies. Secondly, no brother can hear his sister sworn at or hear obscene speech in her presence, such as is very common otherwise. Ordinarily, when a man's anger rises, he immediately bursts into an almost pyrotechnical display of abuse, most of it centering around sex, breaking of incest taboos, peculiarities of the genitalia, irregularities in the sexual act between men and women, et cetera. The aversion to hearing or using such profanity in front of a sister is called "mirriri" (ear-thing). It really means, "My ear can't hear obscenity in front of my sister." An older man said, "It is just the same as if I had been hit on the head with a club when I hear that." Another said, "My heart jumps and stops, jumps and stops, when I hear that mirriri."

Malambunu had come home and found his food unprepared by his wife, Dangra. A quarrel resulted in which he called her matamakmi (incestuous). She did not swear at him. A near-clan brother of Dangra, Badunga, heard the swearing and became very angry. He gathered a bundle of spears, hooked them one by one to his spear-thrower, and threw them at a large number of the women in the native camp, including Dangra. An investigation showed that every one of the women at whom he threw was called yeppa by him.

Balli, an adolescent girl, called her own mother dalardumaru (big vagina).

Natjurili, a near-clan brother of the mother, heard the girl use this term. He, too, threw spears at all his sisters, tribal and blood.

A general camp fight was on; Dimala, who wanted the combatants to stop, cried, "Stop swearing at each other. If you don't stop calling each other names, I'll have to go throw spears at all my sisters."

If Malambunu had sworn at Badunga's near brother as he had at Badunga's sister, there would have been a quarrel and possible fight; such swearing between men, however, only happens when there is already a fight on. If Balli had sworn at Natjurili's mother or daughter, he would have done nothing.[7]

The person who swears most frequently at a man's sister is her husband, especially in a connubial quarrel. The husband is ego's dué, with whom he has one of the strongest relationships.

Yeppa ⟷ *Yeppa* (sister ⟷ sister)

There are the following varieties of this relationship: (1) sisters from the same father and mother and having the same husband; (2) sisters from the same father and mother but having different husbands; (3) sisters having the same husband but different fathers and mothers; (4) wives of brothers of one clan; (5) near-clan sisters; and (6) distant-clan sisters.

There are no taboos between sisters. Younger sisters are disciplined and protected by the older ones. The older ones also teach the younger ones how to make baskets, earn their living, and do the things they should as members of Murngin culture.

Bapa ⟷ *Gatu* (father ⟷ child)

There are five varieties of this relationship, in the following order of importance: (1) the blood father; (2) his brothers; (3) fathers more remote than the first two, but in the same clan; (4) fathers from nearby clans; and (5) fathers from remote clans.

A definite distinction is made between actual father and father's brothers, blood sons and brothers' sons; between father's own brothers and clan brothers of the father. Clan solidarity sharply divides fathers within and outside of the clan. There may or may not be a difference in the emotional attitude of a father and son from a nearby clan and a father and son from a more distant clan. The usual behavior between father and son generally does not hold between a distant son and

[7] There is some evidence that the father is also supposed to participate in the mirriri, but this feeling must be very weak since no concrete evidence was collected and it was spoken of but once by a Murngin man, and then only in passing.

father; frequently, because of the opportunities of competition for women among distant groups, there are actual animosity and warfare.

Since older and younger brothers are clearly differentiated by separate terms, wawa and yukiyuko, and have a definitely regulated behavior toward each other, the relationship of bapa and his sons must be considered from this point of view. Does a father distinguish between older and younger sons, even though there is no term to express these functional differences and all sons are gatu? The answer is decidedly in the affirmative, as will be seen below from the chronologically ordered account of the normal relationship from the period before birth of the son until the death of both father and son.

When a "married" man has no children, he must observe a number of food taboos until a wife announces pregnancy. He cannot eat, whether he or another kills or gathers them, porcupine, emu eggs, snake eggs, iguana eggs, turkey eggs, crayfish, large barrimundi, or crabs, until he acquires the right by old age. A child's birth removes all these taboos, but the child must be his, not a brother's.

The ideas surrounding birth give the father a prominent part in the procedure. The various spirits of the unborn and the dead live with the clan totems in the clan wells. As stated, a father dreams that the child comes to him, asking where it can find its mother, and enters the mother's vagina. The next day the man informs the wife that she is going to have a child, or, if it is his first child, to test the value of his dream he may keep it a secret. The natives believe these dreams are always true since a wife usually tells her husband a few days later that she has felt the movements of a child within her. The husband knows then that his dream is true. He sharpens his spears, rewraps his spear-thrower, and prepares to go hunting, for he knows that he will be successful because his child has come from the totemic spirits within the water, bringing good luck with it. He kills an abundance of game and brings it home. A slight ceremony takes place, after which he may eat all food, for, according to Murngin thought his wife having conceived, he is now a father. This removal of taboos on his diet furnishes one of the reasons for a man's eagerness to have children.

A child comes from its father's well on the father's clan territory, for clan descent is patrilineal. Sometimes the father may be in another part of the country and may dream that the child came from the well of the local clan. Then it would inherit not only its own clan's totems, but also those of the other, yet it would be a member only of his father's clan. The second water hole must belong to the same moiety as his father's; for a father to be Yiritja and the son Dua would be impossible. No man has ever dreamed such an unorthodox concept—either because the moiety idea is such a complete part of Murngin thought that their dreams conform to it, or the men who have such dreams place no importance upon them and forget or suppress them. At all events, a child, male or female, ordinarily inherits only its father's clan and totems, and occasionally inherits in addition totems of another clan. Further, the dream clearly demonstrates a sociological connection between father and child even before birth. The author has recorded no birth without the dream.

Sometimes a man steals another's wife while she is pregnant. The child when born is considered a member of the new man's clan; when he becomes older he usually returns to his own father's clan and identifies himself with it, although he may have strong attachments to his second father's group.

All this indicates that patrilineal inheritance is from the actual father and his group, and not from a different clan, though of the same moiety; it also shows the importance of the actual father in Murngin thought.

Several informants volunteered that a man must abstain from the tabooed foods until he has had a child, because the release from the taboo made him quiet and settled so he would stop running after other women and would stay in one place to take care of his wives, children, and parents-in-law. The social implications of this are very important. By becoming a father he has finally become a husband; he has extended his patrilineal line descendingly and thereby strengthened his own family; and, third, he has, also through this child, strengthened his relationship to his wife's brother, to gawel (father-in-law), mokul (mother-in-law), and marelker (mother-in-law's brother). For, instead of only one direct reciprocal relation, he now has an additional indirect reciprocation with each. His son (or daughter) calls his wife's brothers "gawel" and has a strong bond of mutual aid and obligation with them. His son calls ego's mother-in-law "mari" and has a strong untabooed attachment to her; and to marelker the son also has a strong emotional relationship because ego's marelker is mari to the son. The creation of these social personalities shows the enormous addition to one's kinship personality through the birth of a son, who strengthens ego's position, adding to his security within the clan, the tribe, and with other tribes.

On the other hand, the birth of a daughter is of equal importance.

It gives the father added bonds with waku (his sister's son) because the latter becomes husband to the daughter; it strengthens his position with daughter's son, who is waku to ego's son. A man prefers a son, however, because of his value in the constant tribal feuds, not only through his own assistance and the aid he brings to his relations (as, of course, the daughter does through her marriage), but also because almost the entire ceremonial life of the father's clan and tribe is centered around the males. A son inherits the right to perform certain dances through his father and never through his mother. By a son's initiation into the various ceremonies the father's social participation is further increased as it would not be if the child were a daughter.[8]

Each clan has ceremonial leaders for one or all of the ceremonies it owns. The leadership is inherited by the oldest son if he is old enough. If not, the deceased father's next oldest brother inherits the right until the son is old enough; or at the death or senility of the second brother the son becomes leader. The course taken depends largely upon the personalities of the two men, but in all events the son is looked upon as the heir to these rights. Such ceremonial leadership makes of a person a kind of clan headman.

When a boy is to be circumcised (at from six to nine years of age), it is the father who decides the type of initiation ceremony. The other old men of the tribe confer with him as to time, place, and other arrangements. The father and the mother make presents to the man who paints the child's body in preparation for the initiation. The father is one of those who teach his son how to hunt, fight, and conduct himself in the best possible way in the practical affairs of life. If the father is a ceremonial leader he instructs his son in the routine of songs, dances, and words that make up the great ceremonies.

Before the actual circumcision the neophyte is sent on a journey through the country of the various clans to inform the people of the coming ceremony and to collect presents. The father may refuse to send his son if he wishes; or, if he wants the boy to go, he may order him to leave and to take a certain route. No one else could do this.

A father never corrects his children. This is left to other kin (see mari, nati, et cetera).

Fathers and sons often cooperate in making a canoe. A son must always acquiesce in a father's request for the use of a canoe, or of any of the son's property. A father occupies a place much like an older

[8] For a full account of the individual's change of status, see Chapter IV, Age Grading.

brother's, and, with the father's senility recognized, the oldest son assumes his place as head of the family; at least he is looked to for guidance by the brothers and sisters.

Before circumcision, when a small boy finds a wild bees' nest, the honey of which is a greatly prized delicacy, he goes to tell his father (mari, gawel, and others, too), who will open the hollow tree for the boy and allow him with the aid of his small brothers to eat all of it, but will not eat it himself nor allow any but the brothers to touch it. This rule is very important, for it rests upon a magical idea that the boy will have good luck in the hunt and in later finding large nests. Should a man eat any of the boy's first wild bees' honey, a father would consider this more than sufficient cause to fight him. It is the father who takes the initiative in protecting the small boy's interest.

When a child, particularly a son, becomes ill, the father either treats him magically or uses native remedies. Should a mother neglect her child, or through misadventure allow it to be harmed, most fathers would become angry and beat her, and in some cases try to kill her.

When a son dies, the actual father and his brothers lead in the mourning ceremonies; when a father dies, all the varieties of sons within the limits of the clan cooperate in leading these ceremonies. When the bones of a man are exhumed after burial, it is the father who opens the grave and, with the help of the son's dué (the father's waku), cleans the putrid flesh off the bones.

The death of a son is a great social loss to the father, since there is no one to take his place; but the death of a father is felt less severely by the children. If the children are small, they and their mother pass through the levirate to the father's younger brother. If the children are grown, the father usually has become very old and his death causes them little social loss. The death of a father in our own society creates a greater social maladjustment than in the native society. The Murngin children have been calling the father's brother father, and, further, their behavior toward this younger brother of their father has differed but slightly from that toward their own father. The mother does not go back to her own but continues in the same social group. There is no change in the social adjustment of the children or other members of the kinship system. The personal loss of a father to the family and to society is usually keenly felt, as is the death of sons by a father. When a son dies a father beats his own head and attempts to wound himself to show his sorrow.

Thus far, the whole relationship is one of solidarity, and little potentiality for conflict appears.

Murngin polygyny usually implies that a man will acquire wives throughout his lifetime. Through the operation of tribal laws a very old man frequently gets young girls for wives. All these women are arndi to the sons, but often young men cohabit clandestinely with their father's younger wives. These must be only tribal relatives of the sons' actual mothers. Even so, the practice is considered wrong, but the feeling is not strong enough to prevent a sexually active son from cohabiting with a father's wife. Should the old man discover it, he would be very angry and reprove his son by calling him a dog, et cetera, but it is generally agreed that an old man beyond the age where sexual life interests him would not "growl very hard."

Sometimes when a son is too young to marry, a father may take his boy's galle as a wife (she is "small" arndi to the father) to keep someone else from getting her, because of the son's immaturity. The son would call this woman arndi until the father's death; then he inherits her and calls her galle. Any children born to her by the father would be called yukiyuko or yeppa and not gatu by the son. Frequently a son considers it his right to copulate with her (not openly), which causes the father much pain. The younger man would have abuse heaped on his head, but there would never be a fight over such a problem, or any other, between a father and son so long as they belonged to the same clan; however, a dispute between "sons" and "fathers" of different clans often leads to fights and occasional killings.

If a daughter runs away from her husband (the father's waku), the father with the aid of his sons brings the runaway back to his waku. She receives a beating from him and is advised to remain faithful to her husband. Quarreling daughters who are the wives of one man are instructed by their father to live in peace, for he considers the welfare of his waku of the greatest importance. He and her brothers also keep his daughter's totemic name for her since she is not allowed to know it.

Marikmo ⟷ *Maraitcha* (diramo and mielk)[9] (father's father; father's father's sister ⟷ son's son; son's daughter; brother's son's son; brother's son's daughter)

This relationship conforms to the father-children type, having the same five varieties as found in the bapa-gatu relationship.

[9] *Diramo,* man, male; *mielk,* woman, female.

The marikmo-maraitcha reciprocation is far less powerful than the wawa-yukiyuko or bapa-gatu relationship. The female marikmo is seldom considered at all. A marikmo diramo is of more importance to a maraitcha diramo after death than before. It is largely because of this post-mortem relationship that the living tie is of importance.

A spirit child comes from the water hole of the clan where the spirit of the dead marikmo is. This marikmo takes a special interest in the unborn child. A maraitcha receives some of his names, including all his totemic names, from his marikmo diramo. A maraitcha mielk receives her names from her female marikmo and mari.

When a man dies, the spirit of his marikmo comes out of the well for him, and takes the dead man's good soul[10] back to the well whence it had come as a spirit child. When a man lies dying, the spirit of marikmo (also mari) comes to his maraitcha and calls for the spirit to come out and join him. The natives believe that sometimes just as the man dies, while the heart is still beating, the marikmo's spirit enters the heart, and that is why the heart continues to beat. He then takes the soul of the dead man out of the heart and leaves for the other world through the dead man's mouth. Frequently, the spirit of a dead marikmo fights with the mokoi (the evil ghosts who live in jungles) for the spirit of the dead man, for they claim it as theirs. The father and others paint the body of the dead man or woman with the design of the totemic water hole and sing a totemic song so that marikmo can hear and lead his maraitcha to the totemic well and save it from the attacks of the mokoi.

When the bones are exhumed the women carry them for a time. A marikmo mielk helps in this, but her participation is small and of little importance.

A marikmo diramo has a claim on a man's canoe. Both male and female marikmo seem to acquire what powers they have because they are in the patrilineal line and are pale reflections of the father.

Mokul Bapa ⟷ *Gatu* (diramo and mielk) (father's sister ⟷ brother's child)

The varieties of mokul bapa correspond to those of bapa. The mokul bapa, say the natives, is a kind of female father. No taboos surround her relations with gatu except the ordinary restrictions between men and women of the same moiety. Gatu diramo looks upon her not only as a sister to his father, but also as a mother of his dué, a most impor-

[10] Birimbir, warro; see Glossary of Native Terms.

tant person. Gatu mielk sees her as a possible mother of her husband and, with marriage matters definitely settled, would make presents to her as such. Husband's mother and son's wife are usually together after the second year of marriage. Gatu diramo would always go to his mokul bapa among others for food if he were hungry.

When a man dies and his father is exhuming his bones, all the other women relatives are kept back of a windbreak and forbidden to have a full view of the proceedings; but mokul bapa is allowed to stand by the men and watch, occupying in a lesser degree the position her brother holds in this respect. Further, she, among others, is given the bones of her dead gatu to carry before they are finally put into a hollow log coffin.

She occupies as an individual the same position as the father's brothers, who also call their brother's children sons and daughters. She belongs to the same generation and patrilineal line as father's brothers and except for sex she is in every respect the same as they; her brother's children treat her with the respect due their fathers. A better understanding of her position can be gained by examining the relations of brother and sister.

So far we have discussed only the social personalities in ego's own patrilineal line. We now turn to two new lines of descent—the alternating dué-waku line which terminates in the term kaminyer; and the momo-nati and arndi-gawel line found, with galle added, in ego's own generation and the second descending generation.

Dué ⟷ *Galle* (diramo and mielk) (father's sister's child ⟷ mother's brother's child)

This reciprocal has four varieties: (1) dué (man) and galle (woman); (2) dué (man) and galle (man); (3) dué (woman) and galle (woman); and (4) dué (woman) and galle (man).

There are five varieties of the first relationship: (1) cohabiting galle and dué who are actually father's sister's sons and mother's brother's daughters; (2) cohabiting galle and dué who are from more distant clans; (3) actual father's sister's sons and mother's brother's daughters who are married to other dué and galle; (4) galle and dué from the same clan as the father's sister's husband and mother's brother; and (5) galle and dué from more remote clans.

The dué diramo and galle mielk relationship regulates the greater part of sexual behavior. The basic idea that a man may have an indefinite number of wives but a woman only one husband at a time underlies this most fundamental lateral relationship. Given the correlated basic complex of the junior levirate, by which the next eldest brother inherits a dead man's wife, it would be impossible not to have polygyny; and it is rather difficult to see how the entire system of kinship could exist without the levirate in some form.

A man always tries to obtain his actual mother's brother's daughter; if he cannot get her, he tries to marry someone as near to her in consanguinity as possible.

Usually an older male dué and male galle have an understanding that their sons and daughters shall marry. Such a betrothal could occur before the birth of either child. Sometimes a gawel will promise his wife's next daughter to his waku. Thus, even before birth there is a recognized relationship between dué and galle.

There are several degrees of marriage. As soon as a boy is circumcised and old enough to understand and remember what is told him, his galle is pointed out. At a similar age a galle mielk has her dué diramo shown to her. This is done by the male parents of both children.

The young men and women older than the two usually tease the young couple with somewhat obscene jokes about their relationship and its meaning in their physical behavior. The youngsters are usually shy and ashamed when confronted with such humor; however, as small children, when away from the elders, they play house together. They are fully aware of the sexual act and of sex differences.

About the time facial hair appears upon a boy and the breasts of a girl swell, that is, when sexual intercourse is in their power and of interest to both, they start making love trysts in the bush. They may not copulate at first, but they simulate the act in close contact.

When a girl has her first menses the mother and older women put her inside a house (no special one) and leave her. She is supposed to remain in one place and move with digging sticks as crutches. This represents the myth of the two old women who made the present world, walking with the aid of digging sticks; the older of the two was menstruating. It is believed that menstruation is due to the sexual act, and that the blood is not dangerous to a woman since it comes from the abdomen and not the heart.

When a girl's first menses are over, her father (gawel to her dué) says to her mother (mokul to her dué), "You go make a house for them and fix a camp for them. She is big enough now" (see page 118).

After this, a young couple start living together and are recognized as husband and wife. They have been copulating before, frequently with the knowledge of the father and mother, but the latter pretend ignorance.

Usually an older man with a wife or two acquires a young woman in her adolescent period. A young girl often starts living in her husband's household before menstruation. The dué usually takes her for fear of having her stolen from her parents by some other dué. He has no intercourse with her during this period. When the girl is old enough he may without ceremony start actual intercourse. Or he may take her out into the bush on the ruse that they are going fishing. He asks her to get some drinking water or some wood. While she is gone he ties a small piece of opossum fur string around his index finger, and when she comes back he asks her to lie down. He places the finger inside her vagina; then they return to camp, and sexual intercourse starts. This minor ceremony is not frequently practiced.

When an older man takes a pre-adolescent girl he helps the mother perform the ceremony at her first menstruation. After this is over the husband paints her with red ochre (this is always done for mourners after the death of a relative to avoid ceremonial uncleanliness, and is used in ceremonies).

Ordinarily there is but little taboo on a menstruating woman. She sleeps in the same house or camp with her husband, though the couple do not copulate. The only restriction in daily life is that no man would allow a wife or any other woman to go out in a canoe with him during this period, for otherwise the great mythical snake, Bapa Indi (the Great Father), would swallow them all. The story is told that not so long ago a man took his two wives in a canoe for a trip from one island to another. One of them was menstruating. When they had gone for a short time Yurlunggur (Bapa Indi) smelt the unclean odor, came out of the subterranean depths, and swallowed them all. This modern folk tale, which is believed by all Murngin, fits into the tribe's most fundamental myth of the two old creator sisters.

The above describes how a man ordinarily obtains a wife and what usually happens; but often a woman is not taken from her parents for some time because her future husband may be away in the country of a more distant clan. Various men may also dispute the right to her, owing to a gawel's exceeding his rights by promising her to several men, or because of a wrong marriage of the mokul or gawel, with the true gurrong of mokul demanding the daughter and the true waku of gawel claiming her. If the marriage had been according to tribal law, the waku of gawel and the gurrong of mokul would have been the same person; with the wrong marriage a discord is created in the first ascending generation, and sometimes considerable time elapses before a woman is taken in marriage.

After marriage a young man usually lives for a short period of varying length with his parents-in-law. After this he may go to his own people and take his wife with him. There is often much protest by the wife when she leaves her parents, but they aid her husband. When a child is born, its parents, if not already with the wife's parents, return there so the grandparents can see the baby. This is only for the first child, although the parents of both the husband and wife are always pleased and anxious to see all the grandchildren.

When a girl leaves her parents for the first time, a younger brother accompanies her (see page 54), a custom called "olokork." (The sister's husband is also dué to her young brother, just as this younger brother is galle to his sister's dué.) The husband looks out for the younger man and assumes the place of a father to him during his residence there.

When a child is born the new union is greatly solidified; it now has become a fully developed family, and except for the wife's being stolen by another man there would be little chance of permanent rupture even if she ran away. Tribal sentiment would be against her and her paramour or anyone who might have stolen her. The children would seldom go with her in such a case, and the strong attachment a Murngin mother has for her offspring would force her to come back to them. The writer has recorded several instances of a woman's going through the most difficult privations and risking probable death to return to her children after she had been stolen by a man from another tribe.

If a camp has been ambushed and the men all killed in a general tribal war, the women and children are taken by the conquerors and given as wives to the men who are in the right relationship to them.

A man wants as many wives as he can get and still keep his peace with the other males of his clan. The average is about three and a half for middle-aged men; but there is a recorded case of one native with seventeen wives, the majority having been obtained by stealing them or killing their husbands. He also married "wrong." There is a close correlation of having many wives with fighting strength, or with being the son of a man powerful in war who had thereby acquired a large number of women whose brothers would be gawels to the son. A dué likes many wives because he tires of cohabiting with one and because such multiplicity creates more sons and daughters, so that he will have more waku, dué, and galle, with stronger bonds between him and them.

When in camp a woman sleeps with her back to her husband. If intercourse takes place it is in this position so that no one can be aware of what they are doing.

A dué and galle never copulate during a woman's pregnancy, lest the child be born dead or die early in infancy, the mother's milk being soured by her husband's semen. If a child is born dead the parents are blamed. If a baby dies, the brother and father of the mother criticize their actions throughout the camp in loud voices for her and other members of the tribe to hear. Since sexual intercourse has usually occurred between dué and galle after what they feel should have been the regulated time, they say nothing and do not resent the criticism.

After a child is born the woman and man wait several days before resuming sexual relations. The wife goes through a short ceremony that is both therapeutic and ritualistic. She enters the bush with a female relative such as momo, mari, or mokul bapa, and places some stones on a fire. When these are hot she squats over the fire and the other woman throws water over the stones. The steam is supposed to heal, cleanse and close her uterus and make it small again.

A woman during this period sleeps facing her husband, who does not try to touch her but waits until she turns from him and starts making casual conversation. He realizes then that she wants him. After his first intercourse with his wife following the birth of a child, the husband always rises early and bathes himself. If he did not, he would look like an animal to the other men and feel ashamed before them.[11]

A woman gathers the small game, nuts, bulbs, yams, and other vegetable food, as well as all shell food for the family. A man always has first right to the food brought by her. She and her daughters have eaten all they wish while gathering it. A wife usually cooks the food she has brought for her husband. A large part of a family's larder is contributed by the wife. Big game is supplied by the men, who also bring in fish and large sea animals such as turtle, porpoise, dugong and shark.

[11] There is considerable evidence that there is a comparatively strong taboo on sexual relations between man and wife after the man has seen a totem the first time. It is said that the ceremonial leader for the totem would be so angry that he would attempt to spear the culprit.

Mutual fidelity is demanded by husband and wife. She is supposed to stay away from all other men, and according to tribal law he is not allowed to cohabit with any women except his wives. Nevertheless, adultery is very common. A woman, if she has not been married before, is supposed to come to her husband sexually untouched. The idea back of this is that she has always been his wife and could therefore not have had physical relations with another man. Frequently women have had intercourse with other dué before starting to live openly with their own husbands. This causes much indignation and usually results in a beating for the girl and a heated quarrel between the husband and the lover, who usually allows the outraged husband to use more vituperation, since the lover and the tribe recognize that he is in the wrong, and it pleases the husband to believe that he has had the better of the argument.

The attitude of the male part of the tribe toward the infidelity of a galle may be seen in the following story believed by the natives. It concerns the father of Danitcha, Danitcha's father's young galle, and her lover. Danitcha is an old man who is still living and belongs to the people along the Murngin borders. It happened when Danitcha was still a fish (unborn), he says, and when his father was a young man. We shall let Danitcha tell the tale.

Back in the bush my father came; he called to his young galle mielk, "Come on, we'll go look for wild honey." The woman went with him. Before this she had had no sexual relations with him. He saw the tracks of a bandicoot going inside a large hollow log. He crawled up to the tree. He said, "Come on, you come on up and look, too. I think we'll catch a bandicoot." She came up. He said, "You squat down with your hands on your knees ready to catch him if he comes out."

The man was lying down pretending to look into the hollow tree's hole, but he was casting his eye up at the girl's vagina. "Oh," he thought, "someone has opened her before, and she's my galle, and I haven't." He knew this because the opening was large. He got up. "I couldn't find anything in there," he said, "I think we'd better go." "Let's go drink some good water," he said. "Where?" "This way at a rock pool that I know about." They went to the rock. It rose straight into the air and was high like the clouds. The rock had a forked stick ladder. It was very long. He climbed up the pole. In the center of the rock was a deep hole that ran through it far down into the earth. It had water in it far below, and it stank with the dead bodies of women who had been untrue to their husbands. He pretended to drink, then came down. "Has it good water?" she asked. "Yes, it's full up. You go up and have a drink. I'll wait for you." She climbed higher and higher until she reached the top. She looked down and the man looked small. Then she found the rotting bones of the hundreds of women left there to die by their husbands since the time of Wongar because of their adulteries. She tried to hurry away. She looked down, the ladder was gone. She cried out. "Dué! Dué! Dué! I'm a young woman and I am yours, you've never had me. Look at me! This vagina is yours! These breasts are yours! Look!" He looked at her and in sign language he told her that she'd had another man. He walked away.

She cried and cried and looked down from all sides of the rock, but there was no way to escape. She cried and cried, but it was no use. She could see the forked stick ladder far below, where her dué had thrown it.

The dué went to camp. The girl's mother sent word (she was mokul rumeru to him and therefore could not talk to him) to ask where her daughter had gone. "I don't know," he lied, "I've been out by myself. She didn't come with me. All of you go look for her." They looked for five days, but no one found her. The man went away quietly. He went to the rock and stood off some distance to see if he could see her. "Ah, she's alive yet." He made a camp and stayed. At the large camp people still looked for her. He came back to the main camp. After six days he went again to the rock. The woman was very near death and in a state of coma. She was very weak and her eyes were closed. He went back to camp and stayed five or six days more and then came again to the rock. He couldn't see her. He raised the forked stick and crawled to the top of the rock. On top it was flat all over. In the middle was the deep hole. His galle, while kicking in her death struggle, had fallen into it. He took a spear, hooked it to his spear-thrower, and threw it straight into the air. The spear came down and went into the rock hole and fell into the body of the dead woman. When the spear hit her he could hear the drone of giant blow-flies in the depths of the rock cavern. He went back to camp. Everyone was still looking for the girl. The dué joined in the hunt. "I think," he said, "that maybe someone has stolen her, or it may be someone has killed her magically."

He sent word to all her people to help him find her. They looked for days and days but she was never found. This happened in the country of the Nullikan and Rainbarngo tribes.

Sometimes the husbands only keep their wives there a few days to teach them a lesson, and then let them return to camp. At other times the husband takes the lover and wife to this rock and leaves them. When they arrive at the rock the husband says, "You two can go get some water." They both go up at the same time. When the woman and her lover arrive on the flat stone, he takes the ladder down. One lover cried out, "What about this woman of yours? Don't you want her?" "Oh, you can have her now, I'll make her a present to you."

The story is told to the women and believed by them. It was recorded at a time when there was much serious talk among the men that two women caught by their husbands in adultery should be sent there.

If a wife continues to be unfaithful she might be killed by her dué and members of her own family. Usually the dué would depend upon a magician to accomplish this (see Magic, pages 184-196).

A beating is the usual punishment for a wife's adultery. Garawerpa, an old man of the Daiuror clan, put fire on his wives' vaginas, as did Binindaio when their galles copulated with Willidjungo, the medicine man. With the beating goes a severe tongue lashing. An outraged wife who has caught her husband in a sexual relation with another woman resorts to public abuse of her mate for his infidelities. Her obscenity and abuse are usually more proficiently and much more adequately expressed than a husband's.

At noon one day Bruk Bruk, the young and attractive wife of Lika, who had inherited her from an older brother, accused Djolli, a man from a more distant clan, of trying to seduce her in the bush. A tremendous noise was made in the camp. All the relatives of the parties concerned talked at once, and the two men armed themselves with spears, spear-throwers, and clubs and charged at each other, exchanging curses.

Djolli was angry because he claimed to be falsely accused; and so was Lika because he knew something was wrong, for either his wife had defended her virtue against Djolli, or she had succumbed and then accused him. In either case his self-esteem had been injured. Djolli's wife, an older woman, no longer attractive, stood by, and instead of helping her husband, the usual thing for a wife, screamed at him: "You belong to me. I am your sexual partner. You are like a dog. You are incestuous and sleep with your own mothers and sisters. Why don't you keep your penis where it belongs—in me, not other women?"

The galle has another recourse. She can attack and abuse her husband's mistress. A wife usually feels that it is the other woman's fault anyway.

Balliman, a young man noted for his fighting and dancing abilities, was Mumulaiki's lover, so camp gossip had it. Balliman's wife (he had inherited her), who was much older than he, took her digging stick and, with the aid of much cursing, gave Mumulaiki a thorough thrashing. Both women were in a fainting condition when the fight was stopped by others. Their heads were cut open and they were covered with bruises and cuts.

A further variation in the standards a husband and wife apply to each other may be seen in the following account. Here, too, it will be noticed, when dué is not very assertive, galle is on more or less equal terms with him.

Dimala's wife was known about the various tribes as a woman who usually had an affair with some other woman's husband and was not always particular whether these lovers stood in the right relationship of dué to her. Dimala, too, always had a number of affairs. One day his wife abused him for having such relationships. "Yes," he replied, "I've got one woman, and you can do nothing. You've got your lovers—I've got my sweethearts. My head can think two ways. When you stay quietly by me and have no lovers, I'll sit quietly by you and have no sweethearts."

Such an understanding between spouses is most unusual and considered somewhat asocial. Ordinarily a husband would feel it his duty to beat his wife when she conducted herself in an unlawful way with another man.

Dimala, too, would have felt it necessary to beat his wife and condemn her for the act if she had been caught openly fornicating with someone. Tribal feeling would have driven him to it if his pride had not.

Five varieties of extra-legal sexual relations between men and women are recognized as possible, i.e., the tribe would not condemn them as unpardonable offenses against customary law: (1) relations when the legal spouse of either or when both spouses are carrying on an affair without the mate's full knowledge; (2) runaway matches when the man and woman go to a distant clan to live—usually a true love match, but not always; (3) a union when a man steals a woman from her husband and takes her to his own clan; (4) a union when warring clansmen kill off the husbands of the women and keep them for themselves; and (5) the union of a daughter whose father has given her to a relative without a legal claim to her in another tribe.

Each of the above is considered illegal and condemned by all people, yet each is practiced to a considerable degree among all the tribes in this region, and each frequently leads to a permanent union that has full tribal recognition.

In the first type of liaison the man and woman usually meet in the bush for a lovers' assignation, which always means sexual intercourse. A man ordinarily would choose a galle for such affairs, and a woman a dué; but they occur between momo and kaminyer, little arndi and waku, gawel and waku, and one case has been reported of momelker and dumungur. This last is very rare and has a strong taboo against it. All relationships except the above are completely taboo, and no one would any more think of such an extra-legal union than a normal man in our society would consider a liaison with his own mother. All the above affairs would be with distant relatives and not the actual ones.

Much indignation usually is caused by a gawel-waku liaison if discovered, though several were observed. This sentiment would not be that of the injured wife or husband alone, but of the tribe generally. Men having such a relationship with waku or momelker would be called dogs and considered evil-doers even by their own people, who might be defending them at the time from the attacks of the girl's husbands and relatives. The woman would most certainly receive a severe beating and occasionally be killed.

The regulation that a younger brother is not allowed near an older brother's wife whereas an older brother may be near a younger brother's of course applies here, since, except through a wrong marriage, all men who call each other brothers would call the same women galle, and they in turn would call these men dué. Even with such limitations the dué-galle affair is a most common form of adultery because, with the exception of this one taboo, there is no restriction to deter the pair or to make the most orthodox Murngin feel he is doing anything wrong. The momo-kaminyer relationship is the next least provocative of social condemnation. Of course, this would not be actual father's mother and brother's son's son, but a younger woman and a man in this relationship.

The men's attitude toward sexual union is one of extreme interest. While some speak but little of it, others make sex, food, and war the three subjects of their conversation. The women, however, seem even more interested than the men. They, too, vary considerably in their attitude; some are continually in trouble because of attempting to satisfy their desires by seducing young men, while others remain quiet and faithful to one man. All the men testified that there were no cold women; or rather, as they put it, all women were interested in the sexual relation. The evidence seems to verify their contentions; but caution must be exercised here since no man would admit that women were not interested in him. However, many of the men complained that their wives and other female relatives had too great an interest.

The woman's attitude will be illustrated under the head of runaway unions.

If a man had a sweetheart in his early youth and the affair terminated after he had acquired his proper mates, he must always feed her if she comes to his camp, and she must always feed him if he goes to hers. Wives, however, always complain and cause trouble for the man who tries to follow this custom because of their jealous fear that he may return to the affair. They are anything but hospitable to a husband's former sweetheart who visits their camps. An understanding husband will allow hospitality, particularly if he and his wife's former lover are good friends and if there has been no early trouble between the two. Otherwise, the husband, too, would forbid a wife to feed her former paramour.

Lovers' unions often develop into permanent ones. If there is a dispute about a girl between two young men, one of whom has been living with her, it is likely that, all else being equal, the lover would get the girl, for, say the old men, "They were sweethearts." If the woman should be given to the other man, the lovers frequently run away, and the tribe later recognizes the union.

A number of customs are connected with sweethearting. At night the husbands generally make their wives sit in their own camps. A favorite time for the assignation of lovers, therefore, is during the day when the women are accessible out in the bush and mangrove jungle, where they gather bulbs and shellfish—in groups for companionship and for fear of being stolen. The young man sneaks up near her and taps a stone on the ground. The woman is on the alert and knows what this means. She tells her companions that she is thirsty, or with some other excuse slips away to join her lover.

Sometimes a man has a woman's friend—always a woman—drop a certain type of string in the loved one's basket. If the woman belongs to the Yiritja moiety and the man to the Dua he puts an opossum fur string into it; if he is Yiritja and she Dua, he uses a red parrot feather string. This, of course, occurs only after he feels fairly confident that his advances will have a favorable reception. She replies through her woman friend, and arrangements are made for a time and place.

The following is an account of the operation of this custom, its failure, the feelings of the relatives involved, and the general camp scene during trouble over adultery. Such camp brawls are not infrequent and play a prominent part in Murngin life. The following genealogy is necessary to understand the happenings:

Nar-narng'o = Ku-tjer-in'-o   Ben-ai-tji-ma-loi
ego   wife   galle

Djowa = Gur'-ain-gur'-ain
son-in-law   daughter
(waku)

Djowa had been away from home looking for kangaroo. He came home and while looking for tobacco discovered an opossum string in his wife's basket. Since his wife was Dua and the string had no red parrot feathers on it, his suspicions were not aroused. He was living, however, with his father-in-law, an older man by the name of Narnarngo. The latter's wife Kutjerino was Yiritja and her basket was hung beside that of the other woman. Narnarngo immediately jumped to the conclusion that it was Kutjerino the lover's string was meant for, and that her paramour had made a mistake and put the opossum string into the wrong basket. He was particularly sensitive to any such attempt, not only because of a volatile temperament that always had him in trouble, but also because recently one of his wives had been stolen. He accused Kutjerino. "To whom does this belong?" She replied, "I don't know." After questioning her for some time with no results, he approached Kutjerino's galle, Benaitjimaloi's wife, who was notorious for the number and frequency of her affairs, and accused her of placing the string in the basket. She informed him it was Bengaliwe's string, but denied placing it there.

Narnarngo began cursing Bengaliwe and accusing him of an affair with his wife, but not in his presence. A near relative of Bengaliwe heard Narnarngo's comments and rushed up to the men's camp, where he told Bengaliwe what the old man had been saying. The accused did not take the charges seriously, and went unarmed to Narnarngo's camp. When he was shown the opossum string he admitted it was his, but said that he had made it to wear around his head (opossum strings are usual ornaments). Narnarngo said that Bengaliwe was lying and had tried to fornicate with his wife.

Meanwhile another quarrel had developed in the camp because a father thought one of the black magicians was trying to kill his daughter. This second dispute developed into a general camp brawl in which Balliman, a near relative of Bengaliwe's, took part. He loved a fight for the sheer joy of exercising proficiency in battle. When his own fight had more or less quieted down, although all the participants were still excited, Balliman heard Narnarngo once again call Bengaliwe various profane terms, but not within the hearing of the latter. He went to the accused and told him.

"Let us go back and fight him," he said. The two took their spears and went. "Why do you keep on saying I try to lie with your wife? I didn't." Narnarngo called Bengaliwe "deindumeiu" (big testicles). Bengaliwe replied by calling Narnarngo "golitchirtommeru" (big kidneyed). Both terms designate a man who would break all laws of sexual behavior.

When Benaitjimaloi heard the quarrel he came over with his four brothers and stood back of Narnarngo to help him. He is true galle to Narnarngo. Other near male relatives joined each side and a new camp brawl was in progress. No one was killed or very much hurt in the fight that followed. It was later ascertained that a small boy, unaware of the string's significance, had taken it out of Bengaliwe's and placed it in Djowa's wife's basket.

Sometimes a woman attempts to seduce a young man into joining her for a lovers' assignation. She usually starts by sending him food. After these presents have been given for a while and he is sure of their meaning, he usually tells the woman who brings them for her friend to tell the other woman where he will meet her. If they have an assignation, he usually makes presents to her. Sometimes young men are so bashful that it takes much persuasion to force them into such a union.

A runaway marriage differs from a union caused by a man's stealing a woman in that the woman gives her consent; such an arrangement has the consent of neither her people nor his; whereas in the case of theft, a man's own people frequently support him, particularly if there has been hard feeling between the two clans and a conscious rivalry for the women of certain groups. The runaway union usually ends in his and her people attempting to send her back to her true dué, because it would lead to armed trouble between the man's people and the members of the right dué's clan, and also for the woman's people if they did not condemn the act by helping the true dué regain his wife. However, no man's clan would desert him in such a situation to the point of allowing him to be killed or attacked by the injured man's group. Ordinarily, such a situation ends in a "growling" match, in which the two sides stand armed behind the two opponents, the lover allowing the injured husband to have the better of the cursing. Sometimes such a runaway marriage leads to permanent union.

After a couple have been lovers for some time they may be so fond of each other as to risk everything and leave their own kin and go to a distant clan. Her people, the husband's gawel and galle, immediately help the injured spouse to regain his wife. The people of their groups generally frown upon the lovers' attempt. Further, her people consider it an affront to them by the people of her lover's clan, and it is necessary for them to protest that they had nothing to do with the matter and show good faith by helping get her back. A woman or a man can take the initiative in a runaway marriage, but most of the cases recorded were due to the influence of the woman.

Monalli had been the lover of another's wife. He had had trouble and had decided to return to his own clan. When he left, the wife went with him. He protested, when apprehended, that he did not want her and had asked her to remain with her own husband. The woman herself, although it meant a merciless beating, admitted she was the guilty one and still asked to be allowed to follow him.

Inyinyerri, a fine looking young man, ran away with Raiola's mokul rumeru (sister to the actual one) because they had been having an affair and because her dué's people had stolen Inyinyerri's own father's wives and he wished to even the mark. Inyinyerri's people protested that it would cause too much trouble, and he sent her back. A neutral man was given an opossum string with a loop at one end which was put over her head; and she was led to her gurrong, who brought her to her husband. When he accepted the string it was realized that he wanted her; had he cut the string it would have meant that he did not want her.

It occurs, but unusually, that a man who is stealing, or running away with, a woman uses the head circlet to take her.

If a galle mielk ran away and her father failed in forcing her back, it would be mandatory upon him to provide the dué (his waku) with a new galle. If he could not, he would try to help him obtain another and make presents to him for the loss. The same proceedings are gone through if a man's wife is childless.

If a husband runs away from his wife she goes to his people, usually to her mokul bapa (mother-in-law), for protection, and remains with the man's parents until his people bring him back, or she is given to a younger brother who is nearest of kin.

The author has recorded instances of a man's freely giving up his wife after she had run away.

Daoper, a youngster sixteen or eighteen years old, had a wife of about thirty-five who ran away with another. Her people brought her back to him. Her brother gave her a thorough beating, as did the husband, but the latter said, "He can have her, she causes me too much trouble. She's too old for me."

A custom halfway between a lovers' arrangement and a runaway union is illustrated by the action of two former lovers when the man, to obtain tribal recognition of his taking the woman to wife, walks into the husband's camp and takes her away. The husband always shows fight, but his people on this occasion stop him. There is a considerable interval before the next step, the new couple meanwhile going away to another country. When the three meet again the former husband comes over to their camp, eats with them, and accepts presents of food or the man's totemic emblem, signifying that they are friends, that he recognizes the rights of the new dué and has given up his own. This very seldom happens, for a man's importance in society rests largely on the large number of galle who bear him many children and gather quantities of food during the great tribal ceremonies. It would only occur when he and the old men of his clan had become bored with the actions of the woman and did not wish to kill her.

Although many customs, such as the use of a string to bring back or take a runaway woman, apply also to the stealing of women, the latter method of acquiring a woman nevertheless occupies a rather different place in the tribal life and local organization. If a woman is found to be really to blame, there frequently is no further trouble; but if it is believed she has been definitely stolen, difficulties are to be expected. The theft of a man's galle by a member of a rival clan is a recognized method of insulting all the members of the legal husband's clan. The clan into which she is taken consider it wrong but justifiable and it pleases them that their enemies have lost the woman.

Still another method of securing women—by ambush—differs from woman-stealing only in that the husband is first killed; capture is not the object of the fight except as retaliation for an earlier theft of women. The writer has recorded instances of a group of clans acquiring five or six women by this means.

The gift of a daughter to a far-off dué has two forms, according to the recognition given it by the tribe. If a gawel has no near waku, he is forced to find a man considerably removed from him in this relationship, and all the people feel that he has done right; but if a gawel has a near waku and gives his daughter to a distant one, the near waku's people feel that they have been treated unfairly. If they are a strong clan they force her return. In any case, there is a feeling of uncertainty about the marriage, and her husband is apprehensive of her being taken away by her near dué. Sometimes a man gains permission from his waku to give his daughter to a distant one, because of a complex of circumstances, such as: (1) the weakness of the near waku and his clan; (2) the strength of the far-off waku's clan; (3) the near waku's having a number of wives and no younger brothers; and (4) the possibility that the waku may want to go without wives. There are two cases of this last on record. The old men usually try to get a man to marry and marry properly. Not only is their personal pressure felt by a man who does not wish to marry, but the whole impact of society is placed against him in hundreds of direct and indirect ways. It would be a strong man with an intense dislike of women who could retain his bachelorhood against such odds.[12]

The reader may assume from this account of illegal unions that marriage is a very unstable institution. Such is not the case. Although love affairs are common, a lifelong marriage either of a galle mielk to one dué, or to him and his younger brothers through the levirate, is the normal thing. Murngin society could not exist were this not true.

From the cases of unfaithfulness and the mechanical manner of acquiring spouses through the relationship of the parents, conjugal love might appear impossible. Although rare, it does exist. The ideal wife and husband are those who remain faithful to their spouses; on the other hand, a promiscuous woman or man is disapproved of even though not openly condemned.

To illustrate a man's affection for his wife: Mun-yir-yir had had a magically powerful totemic string given him to keep preparatory to its being placed upon another's totemic emblem. No woman may see or even hear of such a thing. His galle was burning bush for bandicoots. The fire burned and destroyed the string. All his clansmen and those of the man to whom the string belonged were extremely angry. Women had been killed before for such an offense. An old man said

[12] Occasionally one hears accounts of a number of unmarried men collecting in a group of five or six, going out into the jungle with one woman and having group sexual relation with her. One woman I knew of had done this several times; the people severely disapproved of her. She seemed a woman of insatiable sexual appetite and was continually in trouble because of it. She also seemed to stimulate all the men sexually and had a greater interest for them than some of the other women who might have been obtained. Sometimes a youth who is having an affair with an older woman will tell his friends and have them accompany him to his assignation. The other men remain back when they arrive. According to one of the accounts given me, the woman says, "Who is with you?" He replies, "My friends." She says, "Do not bring your friends, I only like you, I only want to have you." The boy says, "No, they are my friends. I'll have you first, then they can." She objects, and he says, "But I feel very sorry for them. Maybe if you don't play with them they will come use black magic on you." He keeps on talking like that and the woman listens and agrees to his proposal. There seems to be considerable evidence that what is called nymphomania among modern women also exists among these aboriginal peoples.

at the time that it was to his clan as though she had killed a strong man. Her husband said nothing, but hurried her to a mission on a nearby island to shield her against possible attacks of his own people. He risked being injured himself for this, but he was more concerned for her. This was not merely because of her economic or child-bearing value. He had an older wife, who had borne him a daughter, whom he loved even more than his younger wife; and the older woman was still a sexual mate and a very able food-gatherer. Yet he told me he would have let them kill the old woman, for she was "rubbish," but that he liked the young galle "too much" and he could not let them kill her.

One further instance may be cited. One of Benaitjimaloi's three wives, the oldest, was notorious for her promiscuity. She had not only been beaten by him, but at one time all the people of a camp had thrashed her for her misconduct. Benaitjimaloi had acquired her by a runaway union. She had been caught in a sexual relation with Bindjerpuma. The husband fought the lover and then said to everybody that he was tired of her continual affairs, was through with her, and that she could go where she pleased. Then he gave her a thorough beating. One of the older men in the tribe, and one of the most intelligent, said, "He won't give her away. I see inside his head. He beat her after he said he'd thrown her away; that shows that he likes that woman too much." Benaitjimaloi kept his wife.

A man and all his wives live in the same camp. If he is going on a long journey he usually leaves some of them with their parents, taking only one with him. When a house is to be built the women usually construct the ordinary windbreak type, but sometimes a man helps them. The husband brings in the heavy stringy bark for the small, dome-shaped house used by most of the people during the rainy season. The women keep the house clean. It is felt that the house belongs to the man and the women.

The wives live in a fair degree of amiability, but there is sometimes jealousy over their husband.

Dorng, a man past middle age, but still very active, had three wives, of whom Opossum was the youngest. He complained one day:

"My wives growl at each other all the time. The two old ones are good friends, but they are jealous of Opossum. They say to her, 'Why don't you get another man? This man is our husband. He made our children come. He belongs to us. He doesn't belong to you.' Opossum says, 'Where am I to go? My other dué are too old; I'd be the same as dead if I lived with one of them.' The two old ones say, 'Your first man is dead already.' " [Dorng's brother died and he got Opossum through the levirate.] His old wives were very pleasant and kind to him, but Opossum was a scold. "When I want to sleep with one of the old sisters at night," he said, "Opossum won't go to sleep as she should. I wait and wait; sometimes morning comes, and that woman watches and won't go to sleep. All right, I wait no longer. I play with her. When I do, Opossum growls at me. The old sisters go to sleep, but sometimes they laugh at me when I play with Opossum."

When Mahkarolla's gawel and mokul gave him their second daughter, the first daughter, who was his wife, immediately quarreled with her younger sister and asked her what right she had to be sleeping with Mahkarolla, who belonged only to her. The first wife said nothing to the husband about her opposition to her sister. When her parents heard of it they said to their older daughter, "She is just the same as you. You are our daughter and she is our daughter. You have him for a husband, and we have given her to him, and now she has him for a husband. She is your young sister; you'll now have someone to look out for the wood for you, and she can help you gather food." This stopped all criticism, and the two sisters lived together as wives to Mahkarolla with the utmost amiability and friendship.

This is the usual situation in Murngin marriage when two sisters from one family marry a man. The older sister has more power than the younger one. Trouble between wives is only likely when he marries into two clans distant from each other.

A wife has considerable independence. She is not the badly treated woman of the older Australian ethnologists' theories. She usually asserts her rights. Women are more vocal than men in Murngin society. Frequently they discipline their husbands by refusing to give them food when the men have been away too long and the wives fear they have had a secret affair.

Husbands and wives are strongly united through their children, for both are very fond of their offspring and extremely demonstrative in their affection. To a European, the children are almost intolerable in their demands on their parents and those around them.

As an indication of connubial solidarity, the following is presented. A small child had died and been buried. A day or two after this a camp fight developed only a short distance from the child's grave. The voices of the mother and father could be heard above the din, first pleading with the combatants to stop, and then angrily cursing the people engaged in the trouble because it is believed a spirit of the dead should not be disturbed by fights until after the last mourning ceremony. It was as father and mother that the two protested, but evidently through the child there was a greater bond of solidarity between them.

When a young dué is circumcised, his near galle cut their thighs "to show their sorrow." A galle always carries her dué's bones after they have been exhumed.

Dué Diramo ⟷ *Galle Diramo* (father's sister's son ⟷ mother's brother's son)

There are as many variations in the dué-diramo and galle-diramo relationship as in the dué-diramo and galle-mielk type.

This is one of the strongest relationships between men. The actual brothers of ego's wife (who is the daughter of mother's brother) and the consanguine father's sister's son (who is the husband of ego's sister) have the strongest bond of any of the male dué and galle. Each always comes to the other for assistance when he gets into trouble. When a man is giving presents to gawel for gawel's daughter, he also offers them to galle diramo because he is brother to the wife.

When Narnarngo got himself into trouble with Bengaliwe his dué immediately came to his assistance (see page 75). This is only one instance of scores recorded by the writer.

Dué and galle engage in many enterprises together, such as canoe building. The bond between them finds a full expression in all the everyday activities of life. When a man is in trouble and needs a good supply of weapons it is always his brothers, and his dué and galle, who lend him extra spears and clubs, and who come to his assistance.

Male dué and galle have added strength given to their relationship through indirect ties; dué's son and galle's daughter will later be husband and wife; and galle will later be, or is, gawel to dué's son, just as dué is waku to galle's father. This last relationship is one of the most binding in Murngun society, and by indirect relationship it occurs twice in the reciprocity that exists between galle and dué: dué's son is waku to galle, and dué is waku to galle's father.

The full position of dué diramo and galle diramo cannot be realized until one studies the behavior of yeppa and her brother and her position as the wife of dué. The dué's position therefore includes the following relationships: (1) to his wife; (2) to galle's father; and (3) his son's relationship of waku to dué's galle. Every one of these elements contributes appreciably to the solidarity of the two men. Many elements make for conflict if the marriage is normal, but this is overcome by the Murngin with great brilliance in social engineering.

Galle diramo and dué mielk have little direct relationship. Their entire conduct is a pale reflection of the other galle-diramo and dué-diramo reciprocity. Galle diramo marries mari mielk and his wife's relatives belong to a different line from that of dué mielk; dué mielk's husband is kutara in still another line.

Gawel ⟷ *Waku* (diramo and mielk) (mother's brother ⟷ sister's child)

There are two types of the waku-gawel relationship since there are both a male and a female waku, the relationship with the latter being of little importance. There are six varieties of the gawel and waku-diramo type. They are, in descending order of significance: (1) the consanguine mother's brother (gawel) and sister's son, the latter having the former's daughter as a wife; (2) mother's brother whose daughters have been given to waku's brothers; (3) consanguine mother's brothers, but with no daughters given to the sister's son; (4) near mother's brothers and sister's sons; (5) distant mother's brothers and sister's sons, who have a trading reciprocation; and (6) distant mother's brothers and sister's sons.

The first three and the fifth are the important varieties in the eyes of the natives. The fifth will be treated by itself (see page 134), since it includes other elements of the Murngin culture either latent or non-existent in the relationships so far studied. The fundamental facts are that mother's brother is the man to whom sister's son looks for a wife, and that accordingly waku is the man from whom gawel receives many presents and favors.

As soon as a boy is old enough to comprehend, his parents point gawel out to him, or a gawel may tell the boy that he is his potential father-in-law and as such must receive special attention. This means that throughout waku's life he is always giving presents to gawel. The latter at times returns them. All the articles of the daily diet and material culture are included in this gift-making. When a waku has been initiated into the tribal secrets to the point where he knows and has seen his ranga, he often gives the string from it to his gawel. This is the finest gift one man could make to another, unless it were the ranga itself or a hair belt made from a dead clansman's hair. In a way, any of these presents would give an important part of the social personality of the waku to his gawel. The gifts are always more numerous from the younger man to the older; but when a gawel receives ranga string, a ranga, or the hair belt, he must reciprocate by giving a return present to show his appreciation, or he would offend his waku.

When a gawel gives his daughter to his sister's son, this is not merely a gift, for the waku by tribal law has a right to her and would fight for her if the gawel tried to give her to someone else. He would also feel that he had the right to gawel's wife's second daughter and the privilege of declining the offer of a third. There would be an obligation, too, on gawel to give his waku another wife if the first were barren or died before giving birth to a child. If a waku's wife runs away from him, his gawel would under almost all circumstances do everything possible to get her back for the husband. If he did not, he would feel obligated to give the waku another daughter in her place.

A gawel decides when the waku shall receive his daughter, or, in other words, he really determines when the tribe shall give its complete recognition to the marriage.

A group of brothers who were gawel would be divided up according to seniority among a group of waku who were brothers. The oldest gawel would have the oldest waku, and the next oldest gawel would have the next oldest waku. This is the ideal, naturally not always realized. Ideally, also, the first wife gives her first two daughters to the oldest waku and the next daughter to the next oldest waku.

When a gawel decides to give recognition to a marriage of his daughter to a waku, he instructs his wife (mokul rumeru to the waku) to build a camp for the two, and for a time residence is matrilocal (see page 66).

When it is decided that a waku is to get a gawel's daughter, the gawel shows his pleasure by giving presents to his dué, who is the boy's father, and also to yeppa, his sister, who is the boy's mother. The boy's mother would receive more than the father. A gawel is pleased, because a waku is like a second son to him, and he has strengthened his position in the tribe by this marriage tie to another clan, whereas a daughter is of little use in time of war. A waku would be of great help, both because of himself and his brothers, and also because of waku's other relatives.

Such a relationship would also prevent trouble. "If my bapa and my gawel tried to fight, I'd stop them," is a favorite remark among the Murngin men. "I wouldn't know which one to help. I'd stop both of them." This demonstrates clearly the strong bond between these relatives. Sometimes a waku's gawel is not galle to the waku's father except distantly. Obviously, given the above feelings, the gawel-waku relationship adds much to the strength of a clan and at the same time helps prevent trouble between the two groups.

If a fight developed, gawel would help waku with the loan of his spears, and, if necessary, by fighting for him. His own sons would also aid his waku, their dué. A waku is taught much of what he knows about fighting and hunting by gawel. If the older man is a magician he also teaches this art to his waku.

Gawel uses waku's property, or vice versa, with the freedom of a brother or father. If gawel's wife is misbehaving, waku tries by indirect threats of death to make her conform to the tribal ideal of conduct.

Sometimes a gawel promises a waku his daughter, the boy makes presents to him for a long period of time, and the gawel then refuses to give him the girl. This means trouble. Strong pressure would usually be put upon the older man to force him to give her to the boy. This might end in an interclan fight, or the waku would probably run away with her.

Another disappointing situation for waku that occasionally occurs is when a gawel says, "I'll give you the daughters from this wife." The waku makes presents over a period of time, meanwhile watching the woman to see if she is going to bear children. If she is barren or produces only sons he stops making his father-in-law presents and turns his attention to some other gawel.

The Australian aborigine is a most industrious trader. Articles of trade are passed over well-known trade routes for hundreds of miles and through many tribes. The Murngin and their neighbors are no exceptions to this rule. The Ritarngo and the Djinba trade stone spear heads to the seacoast tribes for red ocher and pipe clay, or for wooden spears. Ranga string is exchanged between them, as well as many other articles. The waku-gawel reciprocal is utilized for the trading. All men try to have as many distant waku as they can. Presents are constantly being exchanged between the two, not to acquire material wealth so much as to extend a man's sphere of influence beyond the nearby clans. It pleases a Murngin to have a present sent from a distant people and adds greatly to his social prestige. It also gives him a greater feeling of safety when traveling, to know that he has a waku or gawel with whom he has this trading relationship. Waku and gawel often visit each other and their behavior demonstrates real friendship when they meet.

The gawel and waku-mielk relationship is not very strong. The man would not ordinarily copulate with her in a clandestine affair. If he were caught he would be called a dog or other animal because of intimacy with too near a kinswoman.

Arndi ⟷ *Waku* (diramo and mielk) (mother ⟷ child)

There are two types of kinship in this reciprocal—mother and son, and mother and daughter. Each has a number of varieties according to the closeness of relation and the consequently stronger bonds. They are: (1) actual mother, and her sons and daughters; (2) mother's sisters who are wives of the actual father and his brothers; (3) mothers, and children from nearby clans. There is another type of arndi who is ego's son's mate. She is near or distant according to the blood or tribal connection.

The essential element in the relationship is that arndi is the mother of waku. Her sisters are considered near mothers; they may be one's father's wives or near father's wives.

There are no taboos between a mother and her children except sexual ones. Even here a waku often has an affair with a distant arndi. This is considered wrong, but it occurs. One's father's arndi would come from nati and mari, while one's son's arndi would have to come from galle and mari. Except under rare circumstances there would be no possible chance of a son's marrying a possible mate for a father, just as the opposite union would not be allowed.

A mother suckles her own children but her sisters often help if she happens to have two babies whose ages are close together. Sometimes a mother kills her newborn babe because it has followed too closely on her others and she has not enough milk to feed it. This would be done without the knowledge of the father, who would be most angry if he knew it. If a baby dies when born, the father is suspicious of his wife, believing that she might have smothered it in the bush.

Abortion, practiced for the same reason as infanticide, is not infrequent. The pregnant woman's sisters exert pressure on her abdomen with knees and hands.

When twins are born one is always killed, sometimes the second. But usually, if they are boy and girl, the latter is put to death. Waltjimi's wife killed the boy and allowed the girl to live. There was much indignation in the camp, for it was said that a boy made a people strong, while a girl only caused trouble. A woman kills a twin because it makes her feel like a dog to have a litter instead of one baby.

For a few days a mother carries her newborn child under her arm in a strip of paper bark. At this time she covers it with charcoal to make it turn black, for it is very light when born and it is thought that it will stay that color unless so painted. In a short time she holds her infant on her shoulder, its legs straddling her neck and its arms clinging to her head. She carries her children out into the bush with her while she gathers the plants, or shell food, for the family larder. When the little boy is about four years old he stays in camp with the other little ones. But the young girls continue going with their mothers, who during this early period start teaching them the countless things they must know about the fauna and flora, the land and the sea, in order to become good food-gatherers. When a boy is to be circumcised the mother always makes presents to the man who paints his body for the ceremony. When the son kills his first kangaroo or emu, the bones are painted and she carries them as she does those of a dead relative. This is to bring the son good luck in the hunt.

If the son's fathers are dead, the mother is sometimes consulted as to the proper time to circumcise him. When the boy returns from his journey to all the local clans, inviting them to come to his circumcision ceremony, it is she who brags about the number of presents given him. She always exaggerates because it is felt that this will also be helpful for the son in acquiring the good things in later life. While he is being circumcised she cries and beats herself. The actions are customary, but they are more than that to the mother, who is deeply affected when she hears her son's cries. The sisters to the mother act in the same way during this ceremony. A mother seldom corrects her child, this being left for mari and nati to do.

When a child is hurt or dead a mother always cuts and beats her head to show her grief. After the child is buried she paints herself with red ocher to cleanse herself of ceremonial impurity so that she can go out for wood and food with the other women. She waits until after burial to paint herself because the body would not decompose if she did it before. After the bones have been prepared for dispersal among the women she is one of the carriers and is usually the first to get them.

The child sees the mother's sisters as arndi not only because they are her sisters but because the father may die and the mother will be transferred to a younger brother of the father, or an older brother may die and his wives will be given to the child's father. In both cases the women would be arndi as wives to the child's father.

When a mother goes away with the father for a trip to distant kinspeople, the older children are left with the mother's sisters, the mother's mother, or the mother's brother. The children turn to the near mothers for food and care with the same feeling as to their own mother.

A mother is deeply fond of her children. Maritcha saved the life of a young man about fifteen years old when some of the former's clansmen plotted the boy's death. The mother heard of this. Maritcha's clan and her own had had a feud for many years, yet from gratitude she attempted to help Maritcha and stop her own people from fighting him at a later time.

When a girl has her first menses the mother helps paint her and take care of her.

There is constant tribal pressure on a mother to be good to her children. No Murngin mother would dare correct her children in the manner of a European woman, for she would be considered cruel and inhuman. Camp gossip and opinion would uniformly condemn her and liken her to an animal. On the other hand, there is less restraint on a son and daughter concerning their mother than in our own society. They frequently curse her, and there is no taboo on the conversation used before her.

Little arndi (son's wife) occupies a different place in the kinship system, although the general behavior toward her would be the same as toward the true mother (see page 61). Waku in this case would also be a different person. He would be father's sister's husband or husband's father to small arndi.

If a small arndi's husband runs away she goes back to her mokul bapa (husband's mother) until he returns or until she has been given to a younger brother of the husband.

Nati ⟷ *Kaminyer* (diramo and mielk) (mother's father ⟷ daughter's child)

There are two types of this relationship since there are a female and a male kaminyer and only a male nati. There are five varieties of nati: (1) gawel's and arndi's true father; (2) brothers of this nati; (3) brothers of momo married to marikmo; (4) near nati; and (5) distant nati.

Nati always feeds his male kaminyer, but not the female because he and she would be afraid people might think he was trying to seduce her. He would also be afraid that she might think so herself. The reason for this suspicion is that nati and kaminyer mielk are frequently lovers just as momo and kaminyer diramo are. It must be emphasized that they are not near relatives.

Nati takes a special interest in kaminyer diramo as a child; he and mari correct his manners and regulate his conduct more than any other relative does.

Nati is important not so much in direct relationship as indirectly. His marriage to mari mielk makes the relationship between nati and kaminyer much more important because mari mielk assumes a prominent place in a man's or woman's life. The fact that nati is the father of gawel and arndi also increases his importance.

Momo ⟷ *Kaminyer* (diramo and mielk) (father's mother ⟷ daughter's child)

Momo is of little direct influence in the life of kaminyer. She is frequently a sweetheart of his. This is of course not his father's mother, or any of her sisters or clan members, but a woman who stands in this tribal relation to him.

She carries the bones of a dead man, but it does not matter to his relatives or herself whether she does so, for the emotional and social bond is of too little consequence. She sometimes helps build kaminyer's first house when gawel gives him his daughter.

Mari ⟷ *Kutara* (diramo and mielk) (mother's mother, mother's mother's brother ⟷ woman's daughter's child, sister's daughter's child)

There are four types of reciprocals in this group of mari and kutara, both terms being used for both sexes. We shall first consider mari diramo and kutara diramo.

Mari is ego's mother's mother's brother, and kutara is sister's daughter's son. There are other mari and kutara, but they have been built out of this fundamental relationship. The mari-kutara behavior is one of the most interesting reciprocals in the whole of this kinship system. The relationship is very close and has a considerable emotional quality to it.

Personal names are greatly treasured by the Murngin, and both men and women receive them from their mari, such names being more important in daily life than those obtained from a marikmo. Besides the ordinary personal names given by a mari, one also obtains any nickname that might have been given to mari through some peculiar circumstance in the latter's life. The boy's father decides what names shall be given, which means that the father chooses the names from his marelker.

Kutara and mari always come to each other's assistance in times of danger. When a camp quarrel is being aired kutara invariably stands at mari's side. If one of them is killed the other will aid the avenging party. A black magician's tales of his killings speak of a mari who had lost his kutara in a spear fight and had come to the magician for aid to buy back his kutara's life. The sorcerer slew the kutara's killer by magic, and the mari paid for it with many handsome gifts.

Presents are always being exchanged between kutara and mari. When ranga string is being given away after some of the big ceremonies, mari and kutara are always prominent in the exchanges.

When kutara dies mari's spirit always comes for him, along with marikmo's. If the deceased was a young man, the dead mari's spirit condemns his relatives for not giving the child better treatment and for not preventing his death. They always explain to his mari's spirit that they have done all they could to keep him alive. Mari helps marikmo's spirit take the dead soul back to its totemic water hole and helps protect it against the evil ghosts who try to steal kutara's soul. So, in death as in life, mari is kutara's protector and guide. In the Djungguan circumcision ceremony mari's totemic name is always called out by his kutara, as is marikmo's, and it is believed that the spirit of mari appears at that time, although it is not seen.

Mari is usually the person who really teaches kutara his manners.

Mari is powerful not only because of his direct relationship with kutara, but also indirectly, for he is father of mokul (mother-in-law) and marelker (mokul's brother); he is marelker to kutara's bapa, and wawa or yukiyuko to mari mielk, who is mother to kutara's gawel.

The fact that mari is father to kutara's mokul, the woman with the strongest taboos around her and one who is very important to kutara, gives kutara a strength he would not otherwise possess. He can force mokul to give her daughter to him if the mokul is unfair about it, since mari can put pressure not only on her but on her husband, who is gawel to kutara. Mari occupies, because of this relationship with kutara's gawel and mokul, one of the most powerful positions. A man's whole position, security and well-being demand that he have a number of wives and children; he must look to gawel and mokul for the fruition of his wishes; if his mari and he are on good terms, which nearly always holds true, his mari will force these two to help him. In other words, the relatives with whom ego is weakest are those with whom his mari is strongest, and the latter's position in both power and relationship is exactly the opposite of his kutara's.

Mari mielk also occupies a position of considerable importance. She looks out for kutara when he is small. Instances of a man's having a greater affection for his mari mielk than for his own arndi were recorded several times. Mari mielk corrects the children when they are mischievous or bad-mannered. Chastisement is hardly ever practiced, but ridicule is effectively used. Her name is also called out in the sacred Djungguan ceremony when a boy is being initiated. She sometimes helps build the house for a man to live in after gawel has given him a wife. She can always be depended on for food. Kutara would also remember her, as he would her brother, if he had killed any game. When kutara kills his first emu or kangaroo, she helps carry the bones when they have been painted with red ocher, just as she carries kutara's bones after his death. She is important by indirect relationship, because she is mother of ego's mother and gawel, mokul bapa to ego's mokul rumeru, and mokul rumeru to his bapa.

To sum up, the relationships of mari diramo to kutara diramo and of mari mielk to both the female and male kutaras are the most important in the second ascending and descending generation, whereas the relationship of mari diramo and kutara mielk is of little importance.

Mokul ⟷ *Gurrong* (diramo and mielk) (mother's mother's brother's daughter ⟷ father's sister's daughter's children)

There are two types of this relationship, built on the fact that there are a male and a female gurrong. The relationship between mokul and gurrong diramo is very important, but that of the two women is of no significance. We will consider only the former. The fundamental fact is that mokul is the mother of gurrong's wife, and to her he is the man to whom she gives her daughter in marriage.

There are five varieties of mokul: (1) the actual daughter of ego's mother's mother's brother and mother of ego's wife; (2) the mothers of ego's wives who come from distant clans; (3) the daughters of actual mari, but not the mothers of ego's wives; (4) the daughters of near mari; and (5) the daughters of mari from distant clans. The two most important are the first and second, the third having a very strong emotional content; but as regards taboos the behavior toward all of them is more or less the same.

The whole relationship of mokul and gurrong is one of complete mutual avoidance. He cannot speak to her; she cannot speak to him. He does not look at her; she does not look at him. They do not hand any article to each other or use each other's names. Should they meet on a path they each turn aside and walk past with their eyes averted. There is no direct contact between the two, except in very unusual cases or in times of great emotion, such as during a fight, when a man or a woman is not aware of what he is doing. Their whole relationship is an indirect one.

A child before circumcision is exempt from the avoidance rules because he is considered too young to understand them. After this he is told to observe all of them in his relationship with all his mokul. A young mokul is also told at an early age that she must observe all the taboos surrounding gurrong. If a mokul has become very old it is possible to talk to her, receive food, and be near her, but the relationship is always most formal and reserved.

Should a mokul or gurrong disobey any of the taboos unwittingly (it would happen in no other way), a sore or large swelling would appear in the groin of the offender. Several persons were so afflicted, and all their tribesmen believed them to have broken this taboo and to be suffering the penalty.

Mokul and gurrong may be near each other around the same fire. An observer would not notice their avoidance unless aware of the custom and the relationship of the individuals; it then becomes quite marked.

This taboo does not imply any animosity between the two, their indirect relationship usually being most pleasant. A man is proud of his mokul and boasts of her kindness to him. She always sends him food and her most prized possessions through her daughter, and he sends presents to her through his wife. She, too, is equally proud of her gurrong, and tells of his many kindnesses to her.

If a man's galle misbehaves, mokul would always help him discipline her. Only in cases of extreme cruelty would the wife's mother take her part against the husband. If a gurrong is neglectful of his duty in giving presents to his parents-in-law, there is always a chance that, during the early part of a marriage before there are any children, the daughter will be taken away from him. The mokul takes a prominent part in this action, for she feels that he must look out for her.

A mokul who misbehaved herself as a wife to gawel would find her gurrong against her and he would help gawel punish her.

For a full appreciation of her relationship to gurrong, it is necessary to read the account of the gawel-waku reciprocal, keeping in mind that this waku is her gurrong when she is wife of the gawel.

Mokul and gurrong mielk are not taboo to each other. This relationship has no restrictions upon it.

Marelker ⟷ *Gurrong* (diramo and mielk) (mother's mother's brother's son ⟷ father's sister's daughter's children)

The same varieties of the marelker-gurrong relationship are found among the Murngin as the mokul-gurrong, since marelker is the brother of mokul; but the marelker-gurrong relationship, as well as that of marelker and gurrong diramo, is quite different. Avoidance and restraint are lacking between marelker and gurrong diramo; the two men are frequently together, particularly if ego has a son, because marelker is mari to the boy. Marelker is as fond of the child as its father and shows it as much attention. Gurrong makes presents to marelker whenever he gives anything to mokul, for as marelker is mokul's brother he has considerable control over her. The only taboo between the two men is that neither uses the other's personal names.

Marelker diramo and gurrong mielk are partly taboo to each other. They do not speak each other's names, and because of the moiety are sexually taboo. One of the most amusing stories in Murngin folk lore is an account of marelker seducing his female gurrong, the whole point of the story being that marelker is made to do the very things he is supposed to avoid in his daily behavior with gurrong.

Natchiwalker ⟷ *Dumungur* (diramo and mielk) (mother's mother's mother's brother's son ⟷ father's sister's daughter's daughter's child)

This relationship is built on the pattern of the nati-kaminyer reciprocity. Natchiwalker is important largely as a brother of momelker. His name is taboo to dumungur, and dumungur's is taboo to him.

Momelker ⟷ *Dumungur* (diramo and mielk) (mother's mother's mother's brother's daughter ⟷ father's sister's daughter's daughter's child)

Momelker is taboo to dumungur diramo just as fully as mokul is to gurrong diramo. She is the mother of mokul and she is also mokul to ego's gawel. Ego therefore uses the same behavior to her as does his gawel. There are no taboos between momelker and dumungur mielk. This relationship is unimportant.

There are the following varieties of momelker: (1) blood mother of mokul; (2) sisters of the first; (3) those from nearby clans; and (4) those from distant clans. There are the same varieties of natchiwalker, except that in the case of the first, he is the brother of the actual mother.

Kinship Personality of Ego

Ego's kinship personality is best summarized in Chart III. Here all the relations which are described in this chapter are found as a total

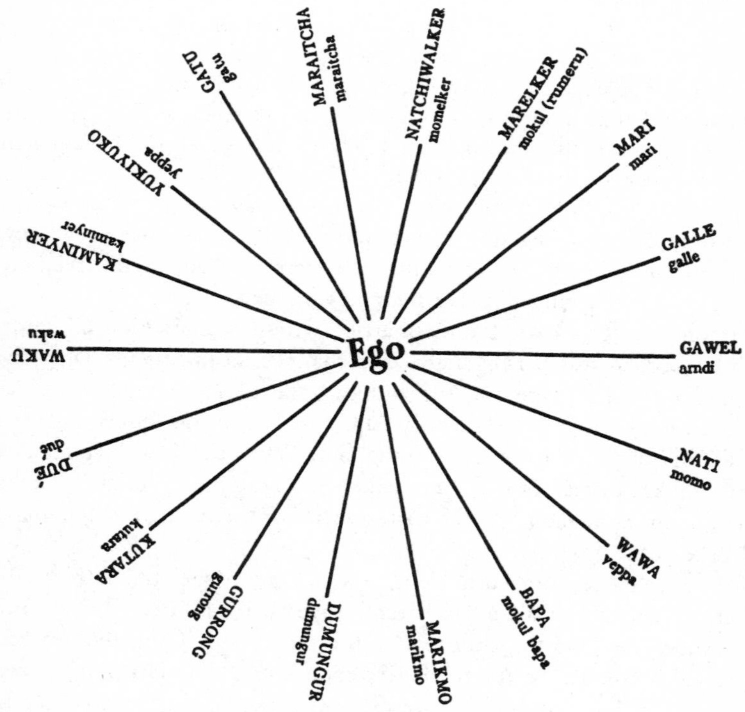

CHART III.—EGO'S KINSHIP PERSONALITY

of ego's kinship personality (except those between two women, if ego is a man, and vice versa); not only is ego wawa to yukiyuko, but he is yukiyuko to an older man he calls wawa; not only is he dumungur to natchiwalker, but he is natchiwalker to another man who is dumungur to him.

The small letters are for women; the larger type designates men. The figure shows that: (1) ego is all the male terms; (2) he is in direct relation to every female term; and (3) he is only indirectly concerned with the reciprocal relations of women. The reverse of these statements is true if ego is a woman.

Ego, as an expression of only one part—the kinship organization—of Murngin culture, is an extremely complex social personality. We must remember that he is a member of a tribe, a clan, and moiety; of a totemic system; of an economic group; of a system of mythology, ceremony and belief; and of many other mechanisms.

Each individual feels it is his right rather than his duty to keep his part of the system working; hence the proper functioning of the whole. A proper marriage is preferred because a Murngin man and woman usually feel that they have a right to each other, since their relationship has destined them to marriage. This is true of all the behavior of all the personalities in the system.

Nevertheless, wrong marriages occur (see also pages 26, 27). The Murngin have arranged a rather simple scheme to make the new marriage fit into the general kinship system and adjust the relationships of the offspring to other members of the society.

If one of ego's own family marries wrong the relationship term of the woman this person married is changed so that it fits what she would be called were she the proper galle of ego's relative. Thus, when ego's own galle is taken by bapa, the former no longer calls her galle, but arndi. This is true throughout. When natchiwalker marries ego's mokul instead of ego's momelker, ego no longer calls the woman mokul, but momelker; yet the correct term for the woman is known, as will be seen presently.

When children are born from a wrong marriage, the father calls them by the terms all other parents give their children (gatu). But everyone else calls the children by the term used if the mother had married normally. To use the native expression, "The father is thrown away."[13] There is only one exception: if a father marries ego's galle, ego would not call the children gatu, but wawa and yeppa. In all other cases the rule would hold; if ego's father married ego's momelker, ego would call the offspring marelker and mokul, and not brother and sister. There are recorded cases of this. When natchiwalker marries

[13] Radcliffe-Brown, A. R., "Three Tribes of Western Australia," Royal Anthropological Institute of Great Britain and Ireland. *Journal,* London, 1913, Vol. XLIII, pages 143-194.

mokul and the mokul is ego's mother's mother's blood-brother's daughter, he looks to this mokul to give him a daughter for his wife. Any offspring from the union would be called galle by ego.

This simple arrangement always keeps the kinship system functioning smoothly. The odd arrangement of the relatives created within the local clan has already been discussed in Chapter II.

A child inherits its totem from its father. When the totemic emblem is shown to the boy for the first time the father or clan leader says, "This is your father," or "your grandfather." The boy will always call it by one of these terms. Most men call their totem "father." Their mother's totem is called arndi or gawel, and the totems of other clans are traced by the nearest relative in these clans. If this relative is marelker, for instance, and he calls the totem father, ego would use the term mari for it. Since most of the mythology is connected with the totems and ceremonies, kinship permeates the whole of Murngin culture. Its relationship to the mythological system will be considered later.

Principles of Murngin Kinship Structure

The two main elements in Murngin kinship are the patrilineal lines and their lateral connections through the intermarriage of the five generations of the seven lines of descent.

Perpendicular Relationships

All perpendicular relationships are *strong* and *unbreakable* since they are patrilineal lines of fathers, sons, daughters, brothers, and sisters, belonging to the same totemic clans and interlocking families. Distant *tribal* relatives called father, son, et cetera, are not under consideration. Clan solidarity and family cohesion prevent strife among the relatives who fit into the perpendicular relationship. If ego, for our purposes, is shifted one line to the right, he takes galle's place, and gawel becomes his father; or if he is shifted to the left to dumungur, this again is a father and son line of descent. Each of the seven lines of descent is built out of the restricted family, which preserves its continuity by the patrilineal laws that regulate descent from fathers to sons. The mother, although still considered a member of her father's clan, is through her children firmly bound to *their* clan. To be fully understood, her position must also be considered from the point of view of sister—she must be seen as a sister to her brother no less than as ego's mother.

Lateral Relationships

Malinowski, in his *Argonauts of the Western Pacific*,[14] has given a splendid description and explanation of the economic ritual called the kula. Reciprocation is the fundamental basis of this ceremonial exchange which produces a stability and balance in the social relations of the groups and individuals involved. It organizes the structure of the economic group by the exchange of ceremonial objects.

The fundamentals of Murngin kinship also rest on reciprocation, the underlying basis of which, however, is a mutual antagonism between the kinship personalities who form the lateral relationships. This organized[15] antagonism is correlated with a sense of personal integrity or solidarity by each of the social personalities involved. An equilibrium between the organized antagonisms created by the ritual and economic reciprocity forms the smaller segments of kinship, as well as the completed structure when articulated to the perpendicular patrilineal lines of fathers and sons.

All lateral relationships are potentially much weaker than the perpendicular because they involve the partial destruction of an old family by taking a daughter and sister from it to become the wife and mother of a new family to be created. Social change of any kind in a society of this type involves weakness in that part of its structure where the movement takes place, and arouses antagonisms between the families and clans involved. Yet the change of a woman's status must continue if the society is to survive. Women must be given if they are to be acquired for wives and mothers to continue one's own clan's patrilineal line of descent as well as the family system.

It has just been said that the perpendicular structures are strong and the lateral relationships potentially weaker. The perpendicular relations are lines of fathers, brothers and sons, and the direct lateral relations are those of marriage by which the vertical relations are tied to each other. To repeat a statement made earlier, in each generation the men marry the line to the right of them in lateral articulation with their own patrilineal column, and the women of ego's patrilineal line unite by marriage with the line to the left (see Chart II).

Since all the relatives, all the generations, and all the seven lines do exactly the same thing, let us examine the immediate situation created

[14] Malinowski, Bronislaw, *Argonauts of the Western Pacific*, G. Routledge & Sons, Ltd., London, 1922.

[15] "Organized"; the term is used in its newer, sociological sense, meaning "socially controlled."

by the dué-galle (husband and wife) relationship, for there lies the basis of the social system's lateral structure. In brief, ego obtains from his mother's brother a woman with whom he copulates and creates a

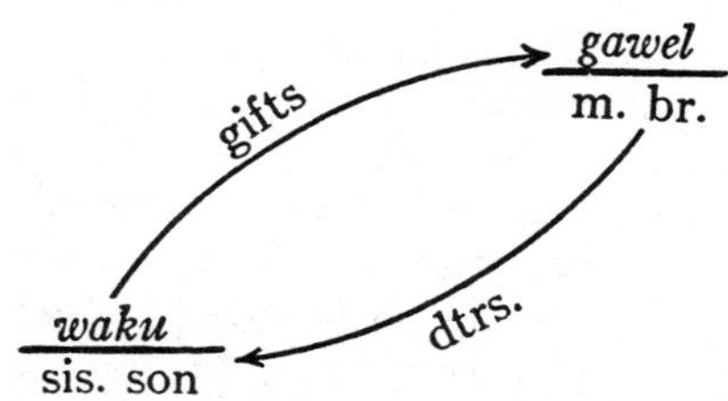

CHART IV.—THE DAUGHTER AND GIFT RECIPROCATION BY THE SON-IN-LAW AND FATHER-IN-LAW

new family; ego reciprocates by giving presents to his mother's brother. More generally, a group of brothers are always giving presents to another group of brothers for their daughters, while the first group of brothers are receiving presents for *their* daughters from still another group of brothers.

This can be symbolized with the pattern shown in Chart IV.

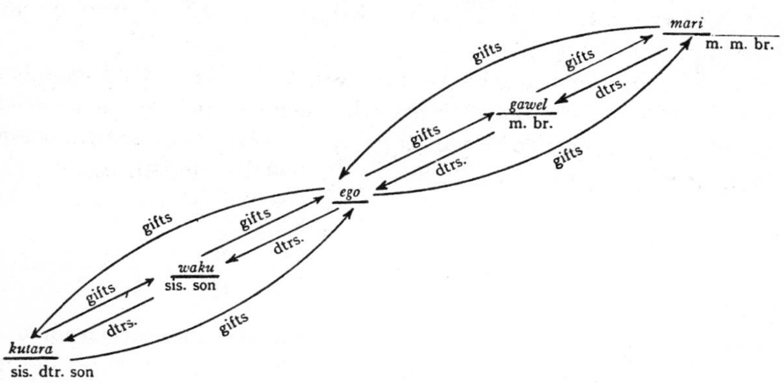

CHART V.—STRUCTURAL ANALYSIS OF THE GIFT AND DAUGHTER EXCHANGE

This diagonal reciprocation creates a line of five relatives running diagonally up from the second descending generation (kutara) to the second ascending generation (mari), who are forever exchanging women and presents.

In Chart V this reciprocation has been presented so as to show the core of the whole structure functioning at one time. Starting from the lower left-hand corner, kutara is seen making gifts to ego's waku for his daughters; waku is sending gifts to ego (waku's gawel) for his daughters; ego is performing the same exchange with gawel, while the latter is in a similar position with ego's mari. Thus we see running diagonally throughout the entire kinship system the reciprocation based on the exchange of daughters and compensated for it by gifts, while at the same time new families are being created by the change of the daughter and sister of the older family into the wife and mother of the newly created family (see Chart II).

This same small pattern of behavior (mother's brother ⟷ sister's son) creates other diagonal lines, the two most important of which are the line dumungur ⟷ gurrong ⟷ dué ⟷ bapa ⟷ nati; and the line, kaminyer ⟷ gatu ⟷ galle ⟷ marelker ⟷ natji walker. These lines are also exchanging women for presents, as ego's own line does. To see this clearly, let the reader consider bapa (father) in Chart II as ego, and it will be seen that from dumungur to nati there are people in the same relationship as kutara to mari.

There is always the danger that this reciprocity will be broken; that gawel will allow his daughter to go to another relative than waku; that a series of runaway marriages, wrong marriages, or wife-stealing will break these lateral and diagonal bonds, thereby breaking the relationship system.

Further, the organized antagonism felt by the family whose unity is injured by the removal of a marrying member may result in open conflict that would involve the larger interclan unities, destroying the social structure since its whole basis is the kinship organization.

Custom of the Mir-ri-ri

To discover additional methods for saving the structure from destruction because of asocial actions and to get at the real meaning of some customs that heretofore have appeared inexplicable, let us re-examine the Murngin kinship behavior centered around sisters and daughters.

Fathers and brothers treat a daughter and sister alike in that (1) they decide to which of her dués she will belong; (2) they stand responsible for her loss by runaway marriage, et cetera; (3) they beat her for misconduct; (4) they supply another daughter and sister to her dué if she dies or is sterile; and (5) they come to her assistance if she is excessively mistreated by dué.

The above largely summarizes a father's behavior toward a daughter, but gives only a part of a brother's relationship with his sister.

Except for the fifth case, the father and brother, so far as they obey tribal law, do all they can to force the daughter and sister into a permanent marriage and to censor the dué-galle relationship. The necessity of keeping a woman with her husband to protect the kinship structure of Murngin society is thus clearly felt by all people, including the members of her own family and clan, whose structures have been damaged by her going to a new family and clan.

The fifth element of behavior indicates a possibility of strife. No brother or father would interfere with a husband chastising his wife; indeed, they would help him. But if the wife were being brutally treated, or were killed for no just cause, they would interfere, which would usually mean a fight. Such an assumption of responsibility for the sister's and daughter's rights shows that she is still considered a part of her kinsmen's clan and family. It is only under the most extreme provocation that members of a woman's clan would act; no instance was recorded by the author. In case of a husband's brutality, his own clansmen apply pressure to prevent trouble with her clan, and also because of a feeling that such conduct is wrong.

If a brother killed his sister, no direct action would be taken by the clan, clan solidarity preventing it. This contrasts with the feeling of her own clan if her husband should kill her. It demonstrates that fundamentally she is considered as belonging to her own group, not to her husband's, even after she has been taken by the latter's clan.

Yet a brother calls his sister "wakinu," i.e., without relatives; and if her husband or anyone else swears at her in her brother's presence the latter throws spears at her and at all his other sisters, even though they are not involved in the quarrel. This behavior seemingly contradicts the above statement. There are several possible explanations. It might be said that he throws spears at her because he believes the swearing to be due to some fault of hers. A brief investigation proves this to be untrue. Balli called her mother by an obscene term because the latter was attempting to stop her from having an illegal relationship with a man who stood in the wrong kinship position to her. Natjurili knew this when he threw spears at her mother (his sister); still he felt impelled to throw them.

Possibly the structure of the kinship system will explain this seemingly anomalous behavior of a brother to his sister; or, to put it another way, structure can explain the function.

Yeppa does belong to her clan and family, but for most practical purposes her family and clan lose her to the husband's. If she is called "rubbish" and without relatives it means: "We put no real value on this woman, we have thrown her out of our clan, really she was never in it. Our family and clan have not been damaged by her loss as our sister and daughter since she is wakinu and does not belong to them, but we do value her as a wife and mother among your people; hence the various guarantees we make of keeping her with you. We don't want her back, we want to keep the relationship permanent; that is why we say, 'She is without relatives.' "

When dué swears at yeppa, and wawa or yukiyuko throws spears at her and her sisters, it is of course absurd that she, the offended, should suffer rather than the person responsible. The Murngin know this; they say, "It is silly, but when I hear those words at my sister I must do something. I throw spears at her."

In view of the feeling against hearing filthy speeches before one's sisters, the following structural interpretation seems to throw the most light on this behavior.

Yeppa is a member of one's own immediate family and patrilineal line. The emotional ties to her are very strong. She is from babyhood to childhood loved and petted by one's father. She is her brother's companion before he reaches the age of circumcision; thereafter, being felt to be such a near relative and with such a strong emotional reciprocation, she is of necessity taboo. This is the woman that a brother throws spears at for an act of which she is the victim. The interpretation is simple. Her patrilineal and family bond are very strong; everyone knows that in a final test a brother would fight his own dué if he went too far when mistreating her. Given the fact that a man cannot hear his sister sworn at, he must choose either to defend his sister and fight her husband,[16] or to do nothing. If he chose the first, it

[16] The situation in the relationship ego ⟷ sister's husband exists in all ego's other clan relationships: to attack any clan relative would cause trouble.

would immediately endanger and possibly destroy for a time the whole lateral structure of his clan's kinship with the rest of the tribe. A fight with a dué of another clan would immediately call clan solidarity into action; all the brother's brothers, sons, fathers, et cetera, would necessarily come to his aid, just as these same relatives of dué would help dué, so that a general fight would result. A general re-exchange of women by forceful means would be a very likely possibility. Obviously only the most extreme circumstances would force such action.

Doing nothing is conceivable, but extremely difficult if the emotions are highly aroused by the mirriri. It is out of keeping with general Murngin behavior not to express an emotion socially. Therefore an entirely different possibility has been seized upon and socialized. The sister is treated as though she were her husband, and spears are thrown at her as though she and not he were the culprit. This saves any trouble between the clans.

The custom of throwing spears gives ritualistic expression to the wakinu concept, and to its opposite. The woman has been called a person without relatives, something actually impossible in the social life. She is rubbish to her family when the question arises whether she is to stay in her new capacity as mother or go back to her own clan. When brothers throw spears at their sisters, they demonstrate that she is not a part of her own family, even though dué calls her by terms slandering her as well as her family and clan; they will not act against the husband or his clan. On the other hand, the custom expresses extreme displeasure at hearing one's sister abused. "This woman is called sister by me, I cannot hear obscenity used against her. I throw spears at her to show my dislike, because if I throw them at you, it would cause trouble out of proportion to the cause of it."

A man throws spears at his sister not only when her dué swears at her but when anyone else does. Because of clan solidarity, he could not throw them at any member of his own clan except yeppa, which is allowed by the wakinu concept.

The remaining problem is: Why does a man throw spears at *all* his sisters instead of confining his act to the one sworn at? All women who stand in the relation of sister to ego, no matter how distant the clan, are treated in exactly the same manner (not spoken to, touched, et cetera); the mirriri falls under this class of behavior, both as belonging to a general pattern and as an extension of the behavior that comes from the feeling surrounding a blood sister. Also, throwing spears at all sisters accentuates the ritualistic nature of the spear-throwing. Emotionally, throwing at several women instead of one is more satisfactory since the feelings linked with the mirriri are intense and need much activity to vent them.

Mari ⟷ Kutara Solidarity

As has been said, the lateral structure of the Murngin kinship system is potentially weak. The gawel-waku reciprocal is no exception, because of the change of daughter to wife and because gawel may not give his daughter to his proper waku. This relationship is most decidedly strengthened by the addition of the mari-marelker and gurrong-kutara lines of descent. The reason is simple. Ego's mari is gawel to ego's own gawel. This places ego's gawel in the same weak position toward ego's most generous and helpful friend (mari) as that in which ego finds himself toward his own gawel. Many natives have been recorded as saying the following: "Mari is the boss of my mokul rumeru and gawel and helps me get my galle." Through the mari-kutara tie there is strength between gawel and waku, so that a solid bond is established from mari in the second ascending generation and second lateral line to the right of ego, and kutara in the second descending generation and second lateral line to the left of ego.

Kutara inherits mari's personal names, hence an identity of personality in names. Since names are of the utmost importance in Murngin thought and there is a feeling of sameness about things bearing the same name, the great solidarity between mari and kutara can be understood. Even after mari's death he still comes to kutara's aid. He is an eternal source of health and comfort to kutara. The latter, usually a younger man, is also a great help to mari, for he can give physical aid in time of war, is an active huntsman, and, all in all, usually participates in the social life as a mature male still in his prime. Moreover, they belong to the same moiety, and frequently to the same clan, which adds to the strength of the positive relationship.

An examination of the kinship structure demonstrates the reasons for this solidarity. Mari's kutara uses the term gawel for the man who is in the relationship of waku to mari. In other words, the person to whom kutara stands in the weakest relationship, his gawel, is a social personality with whom kutara's mari is in exactly the opposite relationship—mari is strong with kutara's gawel where kutara is weak. Mari's relationship in this case is positive while kutara's is negative.

Mari balances this weakness in the gawel-kutara relationship by his complete solidarity with kutara.

The whole system can be given algebraic expression if we allow a negative or weak relationship to be symbolized by a minus sign and a positive or strong relationship by a plus. Chart VI illustrates and demonstrates clearly the dynamic equilibrium established in the kinship structure by reciprocation. It has in it, as will be shown later, explanations of the extent and limitation of the Murngin kinship structure.

Beginning with ego and examining the ascending relationships, we see that the short arrow, symbolizing the exchange of daughters and

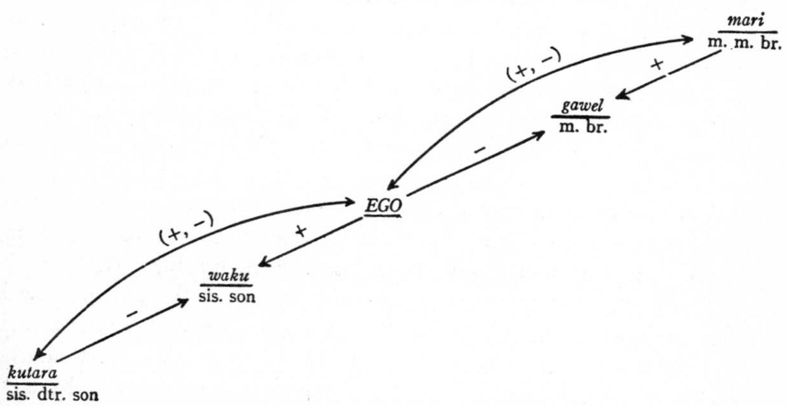

CHART VI.—STRUCTURAL ANALYSIS OF THE MURNGIN KINSHIP SYSTEM

gifts between ego and gawel, shows that ego is in a negative or weak position. The same situation obtains between ego's gawel and mari, for gawel is in the position of waku to ego's mari just as ego is in that position to gawel; and in the descending generations the situation is reversed, for ego is powerful in his relations with waku, whereas the latter is weak; the waku-kutara reciprocation is the same (for waku is gawel to ego's kutara). All the charts and all relatives in this chapter are presented from the point of view of ego. In Chart VI (to recapitulate before continuing), the arrow pointing from ego to gawel shows ego to be in a weak or minus relationship with gawel; from ego's point of view the arrow pointing from mari to gawel symbolizes that ego's mari is in a strong or plus relationship with gawel. The position is exactly reversed in the descending generations. The arrow running from ego to waku shows ego to be in a plus relationship with his sister's son, while the arrow pointing from kutara to waku shows that from ego's point of view kutara is in a minus relationship with his son-in-law (waku). These four relationships show two pluses and two minuses equally distributed on each side of ego.

The longer arrows (starting from ego) show that ego (who is kutara to mari) and mari both stand in a relationship which is completely balanced, as does ego with kutara in the descending relationship. The plus-minus relationship, both ascendingly and descendingly, in the mari-kutara relationship expresses the symmetrical balance that exists in the negative and positive relationships that obtain because of the intermediate relative—an equilibrium has been established in the kinship structure. The two plus signs are balanced by the two minus signs to both the right and the left of ego. Mari's antagonism for his son-in-law (ego's gawel) can be expressed by his help and sense of solidarity with ego (his kutara), and ego's sense of weakness with his gawel is compensated for by his feeling of strength when in association with mari.

The social personality of gawel is balanced by the two. He feels strong with his waku and weak with his own gawel, but the very solidarity of mari and kutara strengthens him, for his gawel (ego's mari) will do nothing to harm his interests when the person gawel stands strongest with, ego (his waku), is also strong with gawel's own gawel. Obviously the whole Murngin kinship structure, particularly in its lateral expressions, is a system of checks and balances and establishes a dynamic equilibrium in the kinship structure.

At first sight, the enormous extent of a Murngin kinship system seems unexplainable and almost fantastic. There seems no reason for the spread of the lateral lines. With the asymmetrical cross-cousin marriage system three lines of descent are automatically created: ego's line, the mother's line (which is ego's marrying line), and the sister's husband's line. They must be recognized by the culture because all people are counted as relatives.

Shall there be a recognition of a new line of relatives and the creation of a new set of social personalities? Or shall this additional line of kin be "thrown back" into one's own patrilineal line and called by the same terms as those found in each generation of ego's line? The latter expedient is used to set the final limits on the Murngin kinship structure. When the line beginning with natchiwalker in the upper right-hand corner of the kinship chart marries into the line at its right, this new line is again called the mari, mokul, marelker line to terminate the system.

The new line of kin, however, is necessary if the asymmetrical type of marriage is to remain stable, since, as has already been explained, the mari-kutara reciprocal creates an equilibrium in the kinship structure by balancing the inequalities of the gawel-waku reciprocal. Momelker and natjiwalker are important because the former is the mother of ego's mother-in-law and the latter is the brother of this woman. Dumungur, reciprocal of these terms, is emotionally important because, from the point of view of momelker and natchiwalker, he is the person who has a feeling of taboo for them since the woman is his mother-in-law's mother.

Marelker is mari's son. He follows his father's behavior toward ego. He later will be ego's son's mari. He treats ego's children with all the affection of a mother and father. He is gawel to ego's galle (wife's brother) to whom ego stands in the potentially weak relationship of dué. The whole mari-marelker line and gurrong-kutara line add a check to the gawel-galle line and balance the kinship system.

The momelker relationship is built out of the mokul rumeru behavior. Ego acts to her as his gawel does (she is gawel's mokul). She is the mother of mokul rumeru, the natives say; and just as one avoids a mother of one's wife, so one avoids her mother. The natchiwalker line also acts as a check on the mari line and further balances the kinship system as it stands in the relation of gawel and galle to mari-marelker line of descent.

Murngin Subsections

The Murngin, like the Kariera and Arunta relatives, are regrouped into larger reciprocal divisions. Professor Radcliffe-Brown has called these divisions "sections" when they number four, as among the Kariera; and "subsections" when they number eight, as among the Arunta. His brilliant paper also for the first time recognized the true importance of these divisions and gave them the formulary expression used in this book.[17]

The Murngin system shares many elements with the two major types of section and subsection found in Australia, but in certain respects it does not conform to either.

[17] Radcliffe-Brown, A. R., "The Social Organization of Australian Tribes," *Oceania,* Vol. I, 1930.

The Murngin subsections are based on a system of marriage and descent and they are essentially a kinship structure. They generalize on the larger kinship structure with its great number of relatives by placing a group of these relatives together and calling them by one term. By this regrouping process, all the kinship terms are reduced to eight, since the subsection system has eight divisions. The people who are to be placed in any one group are determined first by an alternation of generations in the kinship system. For example, a man's paternal grandfather is in the same subsection as himself, and his son's children are also in his subsection. This rule of alternation of generation, which is followed in all seven lines of descent, would create only two new groupings out of the kinship system. A second rule creating two additional groupings places all relatives in ego's own moiety in the same set of subsections as his own line and those relatives who are in the opposite moiety in opposing sections. (This does not necessarily mean that the moiety operates here to accomplish this, but that the same principles which underlie dual organization also operate in helping create the subsections.) The total of eight subsections is achieved by dividing each kinship personality (see, for example, marikmo, nati and mari, Chart II) into two. The existing marriage laws govern the behavior of each of the various subsections, and the kinship laws of descent regulate the descent of the offspring inasmuch as each of the patrilineal lines found in any one subsection determines the children's general place in this grouping. The only addition to the general rules of kinship behavior made by the subsection structure is the division of the patrilineal lines into new groupings on the basis of alternation of generation. The placement of collateral lines, such as mari with marikmo, in one group is already fundamental to this classificatory system of kinship by which collateral relatives are classed as lineal kin. The moiety and the clan, to a lesser extent, also class separate lines of descent and larger groupings by the same general principle. Even the principle of alternation of generation is already expressed in a number of the lines of descent where, as for example in a man's mother's mother's lineage, the alternate generations have the same kinship terms.

The eight subsections in the Murngin system, four in each moiety, are:[18]

[18] Each of the subsection names has been lettered to simplify presentation of the material.

Dua		Yiritja	
A^1	m. Buralung	B^1	m. Narit
	f. Kalint		f. Naritjin
A^2	m. Ballung (Belin)	B^2	m. Burlain
	f. Billindjint		f. Burlaindjint
D^1	m. Wamut	C^1	m. Kaidjawk
	f. Wamutjin		f. Koitjin
D^2	m. Kamerdung	C^2	m. Bangardi
	f. Kamindjint		f. Bangarditjin

Each subsection has a male and female term, the latter usually formed by suffixing "-djint" or "-tjint" to the root.

Murngin marriage rules differ from those of the other two major forms of section systems found in Australia. An A^1 male can marry women out of B^1 or B^2 subsections, and an A^2 male can marry the same women. The B^1 and B^2 subsections reciprocate with the A^1 and A^2 groups. The same is true of C^1 and C^2 and D^1 and D^2. In the Arunta system the four subsections of one moiety marry into the four subsections of the opposite moiety, but with the rule that only one subsection out of the first half can marry a single subsection out of the opposite four; with the Murngin, a man of one subsection can marry into either one or both of two subsections in the opposite moiety, but he cannot marry into the other two of the other moiety or into any of his own moiety. This reduces the subsections from the point of view of marriage to the four sections of the Kariera type:

$$A^{1,2} = B^{1,2}$$
$$C^{1,2} = D^{1,2}$$

The descent rules, however, follow the usual Arunta method. An A^1 or A^2 man marries a B^1 woman; her children are D^2. If an A^1 or A^2 man marries a B^2 woman, the children are D^1; if a B^1 or B^2 man marries an A^2 woman, the children are C^1; or if a B^1 or B^2 man marries an A^2 woman, the children are C^2.

When a C^1 or C^2 man marries a D^1 woman, the offspring of this union are B^1. If either of these men marries D^2, the children are B^2; if a D^1 or D^2 man has a C^1 wife, the children are A^2; or if they marry C^2, the children are A^1.

This can be expressed in the following chart (VII):[19]

A comparison of this with the Arunta and Kariera formulae shows the concrete differences in the three mechanisms and, further, how

[19] The = signs indicate marriage, and the arrows descent.

the Murngin subsection system combines elements of the other two forms.[20]

Although the Murngin have eight named subsections, the Arunta and Kariera charts compared with the Murngin ones show that these eight divisions are grouped into pairs, so that actually the A^1 and A^2 subsections, for example, are but an A section, and B^1 and B^2 a B section. In other words, there are two intermarrying groups in both Murngin and Kariera, although in Kariera each one of these groups has only one name for the male members, whereas in Murngin there are two names for each marrying section because it has been divided into subsections.

Further examination shows only two lines of descent in each moiety of the Kariera form, whereas in the Murngin there are four lines of descent in each moiety. If we turn to the Arunta formula, we see

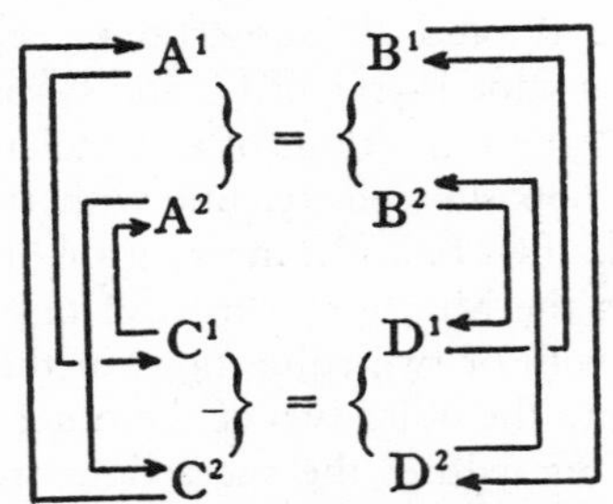

CHART VII.—THE MURNGIN SUBSECTION SYSTEM

eight lines of descent also, but four marriages instead of two as in the two other systems. To put this concretely, in Kariera the male lines of descent are A to D, D to A in moiety 1, and C to B, and B to C in moiety 2; for Arunta, A^1 to D^2, and from D^2 to A^1; from A^2 to D^1 and from D^1 to A^2 in moiety 1; and in moiety 2, from B^1 to C^1, C^1 to B^1, B^2 to C^2, and C^2 to B^2. In Murngin the son of an A^1 man may be either D^1 or D^2, depending upon which subsection the man married into; an A^2 man's children will also be D^1 or D^2. This is true of the male descent of all the subsections. In the Kariera, Arunta, and Murngin systems, in the event of a wrong marriage, "the father is thrown away." In the Kariera and Arunta this rule operates only for wrong marriages, since a member of a section or subsection in these systems can marry properly into only one other section or subsection. In Murn-

[20] See Warner, W. Lloyd, "Kinship Morphology of Forty-one North Australian Tribes," *American Anthropologist,* 1933, Vol. XXXV, No. 1, pages 63-86.

gin society this is also a device used for wrong marriages in the kinship system, but in the subsection system it has been formalized so that A^1 or A^2, for example, is made into a regular spouse of B^1 or B^2, and neither of the males of B^1 or B^2 has any control over the descent of their children from the wives of A^1 and A^2. The child's subsection is always determined by the mother's position in the eight subsections, never by the father's.

To restate the situation, the kinship system of the Murngin is patrilineal and matrilineal; but the subsection system in descent, which is only an extension of the kinship system, is purely matrilineal. For as far as the descent of the child is concerned, it makes no difference if

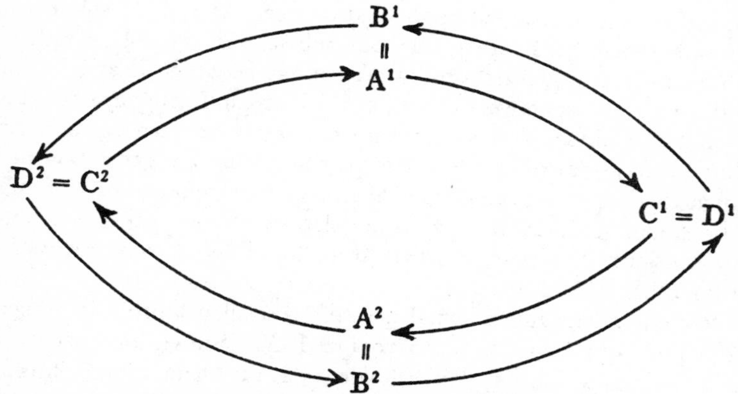

CHART VIII.—MATRILINEAL CYCLES OF THE SUBSECTION SYSTEM

the father belongs to the two regular subsections into which the mother's subsection ordinarily marries, or to an irregular one. The mother's subsection is final in determining the child's subsection.

Within the Murngin subsection system there are two unnamed matrilineal cycles or, to express it in another way, four lines of female descent (Chart VIII). The first is B^1—D^2—B^2—D^1—and B^1; the second, A^1—C^1—A^2—C^2—and A^1. These two unnamed cycles of descent through the female line show that, in addition to the named patrilineal moieties, the Murngin also have unnamed matrilineal moieties because of the descent through the mothers of a subsection. The child's subsection, however, is always in his father's moiety, even though his position in the subsection of his father's moiety is wholly dependent upon that of his mother's in her moiety.

These two cycles may be expressed by the following formula:

The descent cycles of the Murngin and the Arunta through the female lines are exactly the same, except that in Arunta the optional marriage is not permitted.

The articulation of the subsection to the kinship system is given in Chart II. It will be seen that each patrilineal line of the kinship system has four subsections in it, consisting of two alternating pairs. For example, the first line at the left of ego (Chart II) shows B^1 and B^2 alternating by generation with C^1 and C^2; in ego's own line A^1 and A^2 alternate by generation with D^1 and D^2.

This means that each group of relatives will be divided between A^1 and A^2 in a generation and line. In other words, all father's fathers and father's father's sisters are divided between A^1 and A^2 (there will of course be father's fathers in both subsections as well as father's father's sisters); all fathers and father's sisters between D^1 and D^2; all brothers and sisters between A^1 and A^2; all sons and daughters between D^1 and D^2; all son's sons and son's daughters between A^1 and A^2. Thus we have described ego's own patrilineal line by generation and shown that a pair of subsections alternates with another pair of subsections and separates the group of relatives of each generation into two divisions. The same is true, except for different subsections, for all the other lines of descent.

Here one of the fundamental laws of Australian kinship is broken, for sibling equivalence is well recognized in all subsection systems of the other tribes. This makes a slight maladjustment in the kinship system. The natives themselves feel this. They always say that a pair of subsections are "all the same as brothers, but different."

A glance at the articulation of the subsection system and the kinship system from the point of view of the subsection also throws further light on the subsection system. The relatives have been placed in the above grouping of four instead of eight because each relative will be found in two subsections, as has been said before; that is, some of ego's brothers and sisters will be in A^1 and others will be in A^2, just as some of ego's mother's brother's daughters will be in B^1 and others in B^2. The grouping of the relatives into four sections is exactly the same as the system used by the Kariera, and the contents of the above four pairs of subsections are the same as those of the four Kariera sections, except that Murngin has additional terms in each of the four groups.

The principle of alternation of generation is clearly demonstrated in the Murngin configuration. In the subsection arrangement, in the second ascending generation in ego's line, the marikmos are grouped as A, and the first ascending is D (the father's); and in ego's generation the brothers and sisters are grouped as A again. Ego's son is D and his son's son is A. To the right of ego the line from top to bottom runs B, C, B, C, and B, and to the left of ego the same alternation of generation is found. Ego's grandfather and ego's own generations are grouped together, and ego's son's son is also grouped with him. Ego's father and his son are placed together in a different subsection. In other words, alternating generations within patrilineal lines are grouped together, so that grandfathers and grandsons are considered to be members of one group.

The Murngin use their subsection system much as they do their kinship system; a man or a woman is called by his subsection term almost as often as by his kin designation. Even the children use a subsection title, usually employing it more frequently than the kinship term.

At large intertribal gatherings when the kinship term is difficult to obtain because of the remoteness of the various relatives, the subsection terminology is used; this with slight variations is the same throughout northeast Arnhem Land. Some of the people come from hundreds of miles for these great ceremonies in the lower Goyder and Glyde River districts, and their *kinship* terminology is utterly different. Since the section terms are practically the same and only eight in number, it is comparatively easy to discover one's subsection relationship to an utter stranger. The subsections also play a prominent rôle in three of the main ceremonies. In the Djungguan ceremony they regulate the order of certain dances and also the time for calling out the sacred names of the men's dead ancestors. The subsection as well as the clan and moiety system of the Murngin has a totemic significance, since each subsection has a group of totems attached to it, viz., A^1 Buralung: stone kangaroo, night heron, sultry albatross, and wallaby; A^2 Ballung: iguana; D^1 Wamut: wedge-tailed eagle; D^2 Kamerdung: sea eagle and the sun; B^1 Narit: gray kangaroo and a small fresh water fish; B^2 Burlain: emu and thin-legged kangaroo; C^1 Kaidjawk: ibis; C^2 Bangardi: brown-tailed hawk.

These totems and the subsections, as well as the position of the subsection in ceremonies, will be more fully discussed in the chapters dealing with totemism, local organization and ceremony.

The above description proves clearly that, contrary to the opinion of the older writers, the subsection and section system does not regulate marriage but serves rather as an extension of the kinship system. The earlier writers' own evidence shows that it does not regulate marriage, because the relationship of a woman and man finally determines what persons they marry. In Murngin as well as Kariera, ego always marries his mother's brother's daughter, and it is of no concern which subsection she is in—in Murngin he can marry a woman of B^1 or B^2 if he is an A^1 or A^2. It is her kinship relationship to him that really counts; further, in the group from which he takes his wife there are several women that he cannot marry—for example, father's mother.

Reciprocals

"Man speaking" and "woman speaking." These terms do not apply to the reciprocals of the Murngin people as they do among certain other Australian peoples. They follow a very simple rule: ego and his sister call all relatives by the same term. If ego calls a man or woman "kutara," she addresses them by the same term. This means that ego's son and daughter, whom he calls gatu, are also called gatu by his sister, while her children are called waku by him and by her. Ego's sister's husband calls her children gatu, and ego's sister's husband's sister would also call them gatu. Ego's mother calls him waku.

The above method, like most exotic systems of nomenclature, seems strange and "unnatural" to a European, yet they have only extended a method we partially use. To all ascending relatives, a sister and brother in our society apply the same terms (mother, father, aunt, uncle, grandfather, and grandmother). They also apply the same terms to certain lateral relatives, such as first and second cousin. The Murngin do the same except that they also include the descending relatives.

There is thus extended to sisters an equivalence with brothers almost as complete as is usual in primitive society.

The Murngin reciprocals are:

Wa-wa ⟷ Yu-ki-yu-ko
Wa-wa ⟷ Yep-pa
Yu-ki-yu-ko ⟷ Yep-pa
Yep-pa ⟷ Yep-pa
Du-mun-gur ⟷ Na-tji-wal-ker
Du-mun-gur ⟷ Mo-mel-ker
Wa-ku ⟷ Ga-wel

Wa-ku ⟷ Arn-di
Ku-tar-a ⟷ Mar-i
Gur-rong ⟷ Ma-rel-ker
Gur-rong ⟷ Mo-kul (ru-mer-u)
Dué ⟷ Gal-le
Ka-min-yer ⟷ Nat-i
Ka-min-yer ⟷ Mo-mo
Ma-rik-mo ⟷ Ma-rai-tcha
Ba-pa ⟷ Ga-tu
Mokul Bapa ⟷ Ga-tu

Kinship Terminology, Subsections, and Moieties

(Relations of a Man of A^1 or A^2)

Moiety 1	*Moiety 2*
$A^{1,2}$	$B^{1,2}$
Marikmo	Nati
Maraitcha	Kaminyer
Wawa (ego)	Momo
Yukiyuko	Galle
Yeppa	Dué
Mari	Natjiwalker

Moiety 1	*Moiety 2*
$D^{1,2}$	$C^{1,2}$
Kutara	Dumungur
Bapa	Momelker
Gatu	Gawel
Marelker	Waku
Mokul rumeru	Arndi
Gurrong	Waku

CHAPTER IV

AGE GRADING

THE male's life cycle is divided on the basis of definite social groupings ordinarily spoken of as age grades. Although these social changes which take place in a man's life are at more or less definite physical age levels for all of the men, purely social factors have an equal importance in determining a man's status within the age grades.

Age grading is a generalizing process that cuts across the whole group, and is generically connected with the immediate families of procreation and orientation. Status in the age grades is closely correlated with a man's family position.

The peoples of the different areas apply various terms to each of the age grades. The ones used here are those which seem to be in more general use by all the Murngin. Children up until the age of six or eight are called dji-mer-ku-li regardless of sex; but as soon as he is circumcised a boy may be called by a term that denotes the ceremony which was used for his circumcision. The boy who is circumcised by the Djungguan is called par-tung-o, the name of the ground where the bushes are put in the outside camp and where his blood falls. Sometimes the names mo-lu-lu and mor-da are used for the Djungguan initiates.—This circumcision name is used from the time a boy is cut until he is dead, but is looked upon as an age-grading term to separate a male from the uncircumcised group below him. Sometimes an uncut boy is called da-pi gar-da-ko or yo-to gar-da-ko (foreskin) from his birth until he is painted for his initiation.

Wangurri married men who belong to the age grade above the younger single men are called mir-ri ma-mi, "camp." The Djambarpingu people call an as yet childless married man wonga mirri, "camp-man," which distinguishes him as a man who still has an attenuated relation with his family of orientation and has not yet established his family of procreation, who has been initiated into the various ceremonials that represent the attainment of a mature age-grade status, and who is in the main married people's camp and not in the boys'.—During his entire life a man has age-segregating terms applied to him.

A small girl is called mielk yoto (woman child, or small child). A girl with breasts and without a child is referred to as wirkul mielk (breasts woman). From first pregnancy until death a woman is called gung-mun, literally, giver.

Very old men are more or less informally given an age-grade status and grouped under the term or-ung-o, and old women are called kar-kar-ang (white hair).

The tests of a man's ordinary status are (1) his responsibility in blood feuds and (2) the possession of children. The tests of a man's ritual status are (1) the areas of the sacred grounds into which he can penetrate and (2) the parts of the graded rituals in which he can participate. Although these two categories of status do not always coincide, they usually do, for it is felt that they should. Further, the effect of the ritual taboos of the different grades decidedly alters a man's ordinary participation in the community's daily round of events.

Small children, boys and girls, accompany their mothers to the lily swamps or oyster beds. They are carried astride their mothers' necks and put their hands around the mother's forehead. (This method is used in the initiation rituals when the little boys are carried by the men, to indicate the age status of the neophytes.)

Little girls continue to accompany their mothers and help them at first as a part of their play. Gradually they learn their part in the woman's division of labor. The division between men and women is concretely expressed by the manner in which they carry their personal baskets. The women place the string handle of the basket over their foreheads and allow the basket to hang down their backs. The men place the string handle over their arms and wear the basket hanging from their shoulders.

In due time the small boys form little groups and play by themselves such games as throwing mud balls at one another, throwing slender sticks in the manner of their fathers, and they indulge in many kinds of improvised and not very formalized play.

Young boys, before and after circumcision, carry small fish spears with them, but do not use spear-throwers. They play along the water's edge with the spears, and occasionally strike a small fish, developing their throwing technique to considerable accuracy. At this period they make quite a point of carrying their personal baskets under their arms in the manner of mature men.

When large animals such as kangaroos, sea turtles, or emus are harpooned or speared and are being prepared for the stone fires by the older men, the little boys stand about and watch, edging as close as they can and being constantly warned to get back. Meanwhile they quarrel among themselves over the tidbits given them, e.g., the shells of the turtles from which they pick bits of meat.

A boy remains with his family of orientation until he is six or eight years of age, when he is circumcised, leaves his family, and goes to live with the boys of his own age and those who are older in a male group presided over by an older man (or men) who does not possess a wife. This does not mean that he is not in constant contact with the members of his own family. It is felt to be wrong, however, for the young man to live in his parents' camp after he reaches this age because he will be aware of their sexual relations and will learn ways of behavior not proper for a boy who has not taken a wife. Sexual relations between married people are carried on in the bush in the daytime and in camp at night. In camp they lie in such a position that they will not be noticed by their camp mates. "It is all right for children to watch, for they don't know what's happening, but when a boy gets older he sees, and then he says, 'That's good for me, too.' He goes and gets a young girl, maybe a galle to him, and they go into the bush." "When he stays in the big camp he sees too many women. If sometimes you see a small boy from the men's camp sit down in the camp with the women, he hasn't learned which way to behave proper."

The sister taboos are put into force at this same period and are active deterrents in keeping the boy away from his own camp, since the young girls remain with their parents until they are taken by their spouses.

The youths are supposed to eat in their (boys', unmarried men's) camp and sleep there, not going around with women. The boys' camp is the place for them to learn the proper etiquette in their conduct with men and women. A boy is not supposed to look "hard" at a woman. Whenever a man stares at a woman he is thought to have designs upon her. "If a boy looks hard at that girl she says to herself, 'What does he look at me for that way? I think he wants to play with me.' She goes and talks then and makes trouble."

When the younger circumcised boys are put in the unmarried men's camp there is a definite recognition of age. They are seen no longer as babies but as growing boys; but if the young men stay in the men's camp after they grow a beard it is then not so much a matter of age grading as such as it is a single status that is being recognized, since they are now at the proper age for marriage. It is marriage which takes males out of the men's camp and puts them in the general camp. The young men's camp recognizes sex, marriage status, and age. A large number of men who are past the adolescence ceremonies, that is, the totem-seeing rituals, continue in the young men's camp because they have yet to obtain a wife. Further proof that marriage is a final criterion of status is found in the fact that men who travel without their women stay in the men's camp, since at that moment they are single men and not to be classed as married. The only deviation from this of which the writer knows is that occasionally a man will stay in a brother's camp if visiting outside his own clan's territory.

In the young men's camp the oldest man takes charge and reprimands all wrongdoers with the assistance of the near relatives of the offending youths. He also gives them instructions and advice about the totemic emblems when they have seen them, and informs them on the tribal mores, tradition, and mythology. At times there may be more than one old man in the men's camp. The division of authority and power is then based on the personalities of the old men, the more dominant achieving a greater control over the boys. Such authority is more explicit here than one finds it in almost any other part of the Murngin behavior, with the possible exception of the ceremonial ritual when the leader decides when and where it shall be held.

His near female relatives carry the bones of the animal when a boy makes his first kill. It is supposed to be done for all the animals a male kills until he has a baby. The bones of the animal or bird are painted with red ocher. If a boy kills a turkey or other large bird, he does not pick it up but leaves it, returns to the camp and tells some old man. He does not say the name of the turkey but calls out "Ka-ok," the sound the turkey makes, to tell his listener what has happened so that he can pick it up. If a young man finds a porcupine (echidna), he will not kill it but goes to tell an old man of his find. If it is killed, he cannot eat it. After they have been carried by the women, the bones of the larger animals are put in a basket made by the mother for this purpose. The basket is placed near the camp and no one touches it, for it would anger the relatives of the boy and a fight would follow.

For the purposes of the blood feud all children, including boys until the time they have a beard, are classed as women; it is felt wrong to kill very young men, who are usually not allowed to accompany the older men on fighting expeditions.

When a man sees the python totem for the first time he must have a moustache and beard. The young men who have not been initiated into the Djungguan by seeing the python totemic emblem are allowed to sit back of the brush hut where the totem is kept. If they are able to look through the wall, they must keep their heads down so that they cannot see what is inside. They are allowed to call out at the end of each song in the chorus with the older men.

When the time comes for them to paint for the last Djungguan ceremony, these young men who have not seen the totem go off to a little depression in the ground or behind some bushes some distance from the old men's camp and put their decorations on by themselves.

Men obtain their wives at almost any age after they have reached maturity, the first usually when the beard begins, and the others at any time after that through the operation of the levirate or because promised by their mother's brothers. For example, several old men over sixty had several female children promised them as wives. The best time for a boy to marry is when his moustache appears, when he "looks like a proper man," and not until then. His father and mother, as well as father-in-law, exert pressure on him to see that he remains single, and they also observe his behavior to make sure that he does not have contact with a girl before that, although usually their efforts are unsuccessful. "Gawel is on the lookout and no business happens with that girl. He says to the father and mother, 'I'll listen for you people too.'" A young man said to me, "We do not sleep with girls before we are married because we are afraid of the old people. Sometimes a girl who belongs to another man says yes and we do. If it is found out the proper husband raises a row, and maybe her father. Sometimes a boy gets killed this way and sometimes they only cut him until the blood comes" (in a makarata).

The proper time for a girl to marry is when her breasts first start developing.

In the married people's camp the husband and wife "own" the hut because they both participate in the making of it and both live in it. The woman ordinarily keeps it clean and throws away the garbage which collects about the floor. Usually she makes the fire and it is her duty to bring in the wood. It is also her duty to cook the shell food, yams, and other vegetable food. This is generally done communally by the women in the bush where the food is gathered, but women also cook within the camp. Men cook the larger animals, prepare the stone ovens, place the large chunks of meat in the fire, and tend the food to see that it is being properly treated.—It is considered as within the bounds of propriety for the man to move about the camp at night in the way he pleases, but "all women must stay in the house when the men are at home."

Definite taboos are removed from a man's diet when he becomes a father (see pages 57 and 58), as from a woman's when she becomes a mother or too old to have children. After the birth of the child, the parents paint themselves. He takes the bones of his first kills from the basket which had been made by his mother and carries them some distance from the camp. Here a hollow log is cut in the same shape as that for the bones of a dead man, and the bones are put inside it. The "coffin" is put up in the camp in the same manner as a dead man's carved hollow-log coffin. The people who have had meat from the boy while he could not eat put presents of food in his clan's symbolic well, made while he was painting himself.—If a man had eaten of the tabooed foods while in the lower age grades, it is supposed he would become weak and unable to throw a spear in a spear fight; in a makarata it is likely that a spear will go into his leg, it will swell up and his flesh grow rotten while the spear is in his leg. This will also happen if the bones of the animals killed are not put in a hollow log and treated properly. If a young childless man ate porcupine, he would not grow up because "porcupine is a short one."

The reason given for the release from the taboos (see also page 58) is that the young man "becomes more quiet then and does not run about everywhere after other women. He stays in one place and looks out for his own galle and children." In reality, his social personality has grown so that his actual relatives include descending relatives as well as ascending. The birth of a child heightens his emotional ties with his relatives who have children who will marry his children and, in all, puts him in a different status, which is expressed by the release of the food taboos. All this underlying thought agrees with the Murngin idea that marriage does not become complete and permanent until a child is born.

Age grading in Murngin societies is highly ritualistic and controls a man's religious life far more than it does his ordinary daily existence. A man's religious knowledge and his understanding of the sacred totemic lore, with the associated myths and rituals, are dependent upon how far he has been initiated into the sacred mysteries. The initiations elevate him from a lower and more profane existence to a higher and more sacred plane and mark his transition from one age grade to a higher and older one. Age grading, then, controls the degree of sacred participation a man has within the community.

The older men are the final repositories of all the sacred knowledge which can be obtained only by their willingness to initiate the younger men of the lower ranks into their own group. The older men, therefore, by virtue of the age-grade system, control the younger men fairly effectively. It is partly through the exercise of the sanction of refusing to allow a man to be initiated into certain ceremonies, or threatening to do so, that they can maintain the effectiveness of Murngin gerontocracy. In addition, the old men, felt to be in closer touch with the clan ancestors and totems through their deeper participation in the sacred myths and rituals, effect discipline by invoking the religious sanctions: dire things will happen to men who commit acts the old men frown on and which offend the totemic spirits and ancient ancestors. For example, a man who starts a fight or who commits adultery during a ceremony may be told that his real ancestors and his totemic ancestors will not allow the totemic fish soul to enter his wife, she will be childless—a thing all Murngin men would make every effort to avoid. The offending young man may also be told that the totemic ancestors will not come to direct him to his totemic water hole if he is killed in a fight, or that they will refuse to answer him in a time of need, as when he is in a fight or drowning.

The first effective age grading in the lives of the Murngin occurs when the entire group is sexually bifurcated. The young boy is circumcised and immediately enters the portals of a sacred realm which is forever taboo to his sister, promised wives, and the entire female population of a tribe. The pidgin-English expression found generally among Australian aborigines, "make him a young man," describes what takes place in the minds of the natives: that is, the boy is taken out of the social status of female and put in the social category of male by the use of certain rites of passage. His later initiations take him spiritually further and further from his original profane innocence of the uncircumcised child, where sociologically he is treated as a woman, and they translate him grade by grade into the group's mysteries. The young girl grows into womanhood and continues in the ordinary world with only an outsider's knowledge of the mysteries which center in the men's ground and overflow during parts of the rituals into the general camp where her world is centered.

The principle of sex, then, has been used to organize a status group, with the women and small children of either sex in one group and the initiated men in another. The women's group remains ritually undifferentiated in a status sense except for a tendency to give women near or in the menopause preference over younger women in those ceremonies in which women participate. For example, in the Gunabibi the old women beat the ground to stop Muit, and in the Djungguan it is felt to be more appropriate and effective for older women to dance around the warngaitja than for men to do so. This corresponds with the lifting of part of the feeling of taboo around the mother-in-law after she loses many of her secondary sexual characteristics and "gets to be an old woman and looks all the same as a man."

Murngin age grading is largely a religious phenomenon consisting of a series of rites of passage from one age group to another in the life cycle of the individual. It seems, therefore, nearer the truth of Murngin thought to treat the life of the individual as the complete entity it appears to be in the thought of the culture. Each Murngin's beginning is in the sacred totemic well of his ancestors, and each Murngin's end is within the same subterranean depths. His first status is that of the unborn child in the form of a small fish which exists with others of his kind beside the totemic spirits of the clan, the totemic mythological ancestors, the ancient clan dead, and those who have recently died. He is under the control of his ancestors and the totem, and his passage from the world of the unborn to that of the living depends on the good behavior of his parents, particularly of his father. The Murngin think of this from the parents' point of view and conduct their lives more carefully because of the fear of childlessness.

The Murngin baby comes from the totem well through a religious experience of the father, since it is the father who is in touch with the totem world of which the mother is supposed to have no knowledge. The father's mystical dream experience is itself a kind of rite of passage of the unborn and begins the child's socialization. The father's announcement to the mother of the child's arrival (frequently, it must be admitted, after she has reported her pregnancy to the father, who has kept silent, he says, to test the validity of his experience) changes the father's age-grade status. It removes certain ritualistic food taboos and definitely establishes his place in the older men's group. This means, then, that the father-child reciprocal functions as a unit: the consummation of his family of procreation through his first child's "birth" effects the father's spiritual birth into a recognized higher status in the community age grouping, and simultaneously the new being is taken into the lowest age grade.

As an old man, the Murngin learns the final mysteries of life by seeing the most esoteric of the totems. Ultimately he dies and assumes a new social status, and by the mourning rite of passage enters his last social grouping, for he still retains a social personality of his own as long as he is in the memory of his group. His ultimate fate is loss of social personality when he is forgotten as an individual and remembered only as an undifferentiated part of a long line of clan ancestors and is absorbed in the general sacredness of the clan well. The sacred power of the clan well derives in part from the knowledge of the souls of the long and the recent dead dwelling within it. The dead soul, when it is ceremonially ushered into the totemic well, is a spiritual part of the man's or woman's participation in the land of the living. The woman's spiritual existence, although not primary and direct as thought of by the Murngin, is nevertheless real and identifiable, for she has a number of sacred totemic names known to her father and brothers, she comes from the totemic water hole as a fish, and vicariously, and to some extent directly, participates in all the sacred totemic rituals. Her partial participation in these rituals which are enacted outside the men's ground also gives her a certain amount of ritualization.

As a man becomes more deeply integrated into his daily community life, that is, when he becomes old enough to go on expeditions as a responsible member of the blood feud and to be held accountable by the enemies of the clan as a part of his group, and when he marries and has children and extends his kinship personality by primary contacts, he at the same time grows deeper and deeper into his esoteric existence and becomes more deeply learned in the rituals and the sacred language.

A review of the chapter on economics and technology quickly convinces one that men make and use the greater number of the more complex tools, weapons, and implements. If all the complexities of the technological apparatus as a part of the society's adaptation to its natural environment were charted, each process receiving a line symbolizing its part in the general technical behavior, it would become apparent that the greater the complexity of the technology, the greater the participation of the men in it, and the simpler the technological processes, the more women participate. There is a possible correlation between the women's restricted social participation in such parts of the culture as ritual and myth and their simple technological behavior. Technological behavior obviously is connected with the age-grading situation in Murngin society. It is impossible to say which causes which—both are part of the male-female social dichotomy. There can be no question, however, but that the general profane participation of the women in the technological and economic life of the people is just as restricted when it comes to participating in the more elaborate and highly skilled technical processes as it is in the ritual of the tribe; and that the men's highly developed participation in Murngin ritual finds its counterpart in their greater participation in economic and technological processes which demand a greater degree of manual dexterity and skill and are far more complex techniques. The most elaborate and only complex technique a woman uses is that of making baskets. All other processes which she uses are comparatively simple, with the possible exception of helping to construct some of the bark houses. The same is true of her economic behavior. The digging of yams, the gathering of shells, of roots, of fruit, are probably the simplest of all the economic processes found in Murngin society. It is with these things she is chiefly engaged. Among men the harpooning of turtles—which includes such elaborate technical background as the making of a canoe, its sailing and proper use, the construction of the harpoon and its use—is probably at the maximum end of Murngin technological complexity. As a boy grows up his participation in the use of these techniques grows, paralleled by his ritual growth.

In other words, as he generally extends his social personality further into the group in his daily life, he is, at definite intervals, admitted into a deeper understanding of the religious life. If in no other way, he becomes aware of this by being part of the group which forces the younger men through these same rites. He realizes that he enters many of the ceremonies as a part of his older age group, and that he is becoming part of the Python spirit, as when he gives his blood to the Python's Djungguan rite or when he dances with the sacred blood on him. This identification with the essential holiness or final sacred power necessitates, he realizes, careful conduct and a minute regulation of his daily behavior, for he risks profaning this spirit within himself and resultant sickness or death. The best medicine man among the Murngin told several of his patients that Muit was angry and had made them sick because they failed to see the Gunabibi through to its conclusion—an affront to the Python. The men's group separates farther and farther from that of the women and uninitiated children. It is within this mentality that the essential elements of Murngin age grading have their foundations.

The meanings of the age-grade structure are further elaborated in the section in Chapter XIII, pages 433-440.

The Age Grade Chart

The accompanying chart is designed to show the general relation between a man's position in his family and his corresponding place

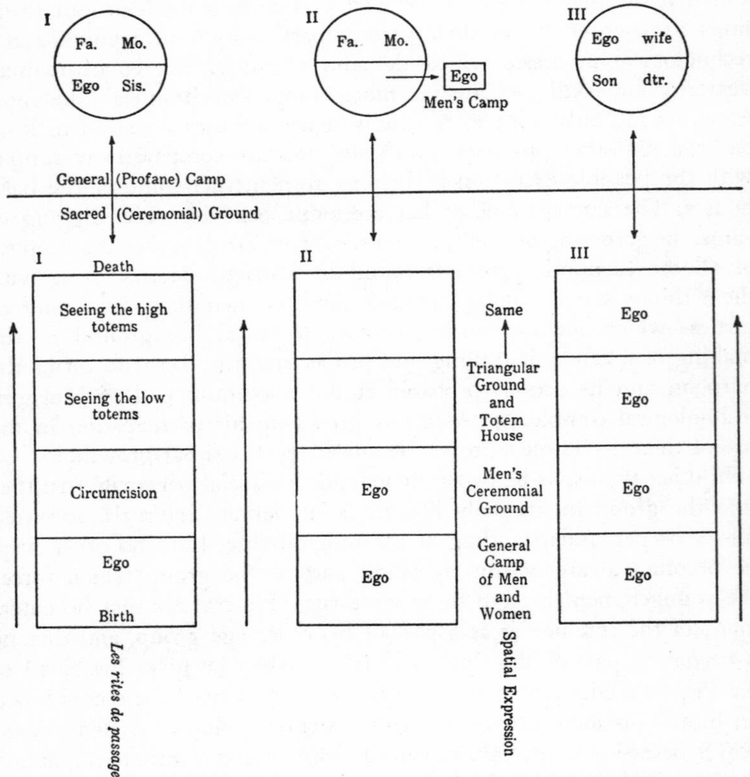

Chart IX.—The Relation of Ego and His Families to His Spatial Position in the Camp and His Age Grade Status

in the age grading during the various periods of his life. The family structure, represented by circles, is separated from the age-grade "ladders" by a horizontal line. The upper section of the chart represents the general or profane camp, and the lower section the sacred or ceremonial ground. The arrows pointing toward both the family circle and the age-grade ladder, and running through the line separating the sacred and profane areas, are devices to show the reciprocal relation existing between the two structures. For example, Family I is shown to be in relation to Age-grade Chart I, but one sees that at this period ego, the individual, is placed within the family in which he was born and in the lower generation. If one then turns to Age-grade Ladder I, one sees that ego is placed at the bottom, between birth and the line of circumcision. In the next family, II, one sees that ego has moved out of the lower generation of the family into the men's camp but has not yet established a family of his own, while in Age-grade Ladder II one sees that he participates not only in the group below the circumcision level but also in the group above and up to the line where he sees the lower totems. In the final family circle, III, ego is in the upper generation, his children in the lower, and the reciprocating arrow shows that in the age-grade ladder he has passed through the stage of seeing the lower totems, and, as an older man, has gone to the top of the ladder by seeing the high totems.

By the device of placing ego in the four spaces we can see that his participation is much fuller than it was in II, and we can visually determine the enormous growth of a man's ceremonial activities from the time when he was in but one segment in the first age-grade ladder.

Each of the rungs of the first ladder has been named, from the bottom to the top, respectively, birth, circumcision, seeing the low totems, and seeing the high totems. In the space between Ladders II and III each of the areas between the rungs of the age grade has been named from the point of view of its general spatial expression of the tribe's ceremonial grounds.

In general, we can say there is a correspondence between (1) the relation of ego's family of orientation and ego's spatial position in the general camp (see the position of ego in relation to the family on the upper part of the age-grade chart) and (2) his ritual status and degree of penetration into the men's ground. Although these two are separate to a considerable degree in the Murngin mind, nevertheless they closely parallel each other. When a boy is old enough to be circumcised, he is initiated by this means into the men's group (see the lower half of the age-grade chart where the "steps in the ladder" represent the different parts of the rites of passage) and enters the outer grounds but does not dance in the triangular ground (see the openings in the "ladder" generally classed as spatial expression); at the same time he moves to the boys' and unmarried men's camp. When a man is married he starts living openly in the main camp with his wife and becomes a wonga mirri. At approximately this time he sees Yurlunggur. At a later period, sometimes after only a year or two and other times much later, he gives his blood to Yurlunggur. In the Narra ceremonies a man tends to be much older before he sees the higher totems, which, ordinarily speaking, means he has had children or he is biologically in middle age. Although the initiation symbols vary for the older and less well-defined statuses, the fundamental division between men and women which usually identifies a man with the male group is in all initiations symbolized by the rite of circumcision, whether it be an element in the Djungguan, Marndiella, or other ritual. The circumcised penis has the mark of the snake upon it because the python has taken the foreskin and by the operation the blood has been let for the Great Father—it is a social mark on an individual.[1]

[1] See Chapter XV for an "autobiographical" account of a Murngin native which is also a statement of age grading as it is seen and felt by the individual experiencing it.

CHAPTER V

PRIMARY ADAPTATIONS AND TECHNOLOGY

THE GENERAL PROBLEM

THE economic life of a people is essentially concerned with relating the primary technological adaptation to nature and the community's secondary adaptation which is its social organization. Many peoples have developed a separate set of unified social mechanisms which are roughly called their economic systems, such as the organized market of modern capitalism or the simpler and less developed systems of agricultural barbarism. The tools and implements are formed into a general order of making and using to exact a supply of food and other creature necessities from nature, and they are then used by the population of a group in a systematized manner through a set of conventions and social usages which are dictated by the social organization. The social organization regulates the technology and helps discipline the distribution and consumption of its productivity.

The Murngin have not created a separate economic structure and are dependent on their other social institutions to regulate indirectly their technology and control the distribution and the consumption of goods and services.[1] The present chapter will be concerned with the purely economic aspects of the social structure, and with artifacts and their manufacture and use.

I. THE PLACE OF THE MURNGIN SOCIAL STRUCTURE IN ORGANIZING PRODUCTION OF CREATURE NECESSITIES

1. *The Horde*

The horde is an unstable economic group whose membership and size are regulated by the seasonal cycle. In the rainy months this group may be, and frequently is, only a kinship group composed of a few brothers and their wives and children or possibly "brothers-in-law" and their families. (These relatives are usually connected by blood.) When the dry season begins and the various food-producing areas are

[1] The economic horde organization is only partly an exception to this.

open to human occupation by the drying of the land, the burning of the spear grass, and the disappearance of the swarms of vicious insects, these smaller groups coalesce into larger units which may contain as many as thirty or forty people and will contain many more if a large ritual is being celebrated. Every member of this group is related closely to at least one or more other individuals in the group, but to the rest he is only tribally related. Where the sea-turtle eggs on the sand beaches are most plentiful, the oyster beds most prolific and accessible, sea-bird eggs most abundant, lily and yam swamps most productive, and the cycad palm nuts ripened and ready for picking, there will be found the horde groups.

All of the people in the horde will be of friendly clans which are usually closely intermarried; if there are antagonisms they are suppressed or given expression in a peace-making makarata, which allows those involved to remain in harmony. As soon as food is plentiful the better areas usually become locations for the great rituals which take place at this time; the ceremonial life definitely enlarges the size of the horde groups. The camp of the horde is organized spatially in the same way as the clan lands are spatially related to each other.

Ritual sanctions at this time help prevent open strife, which is always a possibility whenever the clans come together. The belief that the totem will be offended if clashes occur between opposing clansmen usually keeps the peace. Ritual sanction, then, is the most powerful force in regulating the peaceful behavior of these larger food-gathering hordes. If it were not for these extreme sanctions the larger hordes could not be formed. Peoples with a background of feud and warfare who might not otherwise risk meeting one another can be fairly certain of peace in a horde gathered for a ritual. Since the local clans which start the ceremony have it well under way and the totemic emblems have been made and are in the camp by the time the first guests arrive, hesitant visitors can feel comparatively safe in coming to the ceremony. The bitterly antagonistic clans, however, who have a continuous blood feud tradition and a record of killing back of them would never be present unless under extreme circumstances, for religious sanctions or peace-making duels would not prevent open strife and possible secret killings between them.

The horde, then, is governed by the seasonal fluctuation of plenty or scarcity, and its extreme in size is effected by the attractive stimuli of important ceremonies.

The usual division of labor obtains during the period of the larger horde gathering and is intensified by it. The women gather small animals and all vegetable food, and the men fish and kill larger animals, although a man might gather yams or lily bulbs for himself if he were hungry. The women of the various clans of allied groups often go on foraging expeditions together.

2. Gathering and Preparation of Food—Sexual Division of Labor

The women furnish the bulk of the daily food. The men's contribution of meat, although much more prized, is less certain. When kangaroos, wallabies, or emus are speared, turtles, dugong or porpoises harpooned, the whole group gorges itself after the meat has been divided properly and cooked in stone fires and ovens. The women are supposed to supply the food for the men while they perform the sacred rituals; although the men may hunt, fish, or go harpooning for sea animals at this time, they do it casually and not as part of their daily routine.

In the usual method of hunting kangaroos, a man or several men cover themselves with mud to prevent the kangaroo from seeing and smelling them and wait at a narrow part of the mangrove jungle. A group of young boys, sent to the other end of the jungle, spread out in a long line and start moving toward the men. They bark in a very high tone in imitation of the dingo. The boys progress fairly slowly in order not to frighten the kangaroos into too rapid motion. When the kangaroos get within throwing distance the men attempt to hit them with their stone spears. Kangaroos are also stalked; success here is possible because the animal usually sleeps in the daytime and can easily be approached to within accurate throwing distance.[2]

After an opossum has been treed and captured, it is hit on the head and the entrails are removed immediately. The intestinal fat is pulled off and cooked where the animal is captured. The intestines are carefully cleaned and opened and the gut is wrapped around the handle of a spear-thrower. When the opossum is to be cooked, all the openings of the carcass are closed, the hair is singed off, and the carcass put in the ashes and covered over with leaves and ashes. It is not cooked with a stone fire, as are larger animals, such as turtle, emu, kangaroo,

[2] The Murngin are expert in identifying footprints. A little girl eight or nine years old can immediately tell one who made a particular footprint even though there are a hundred or more people who have placed their imprints on the earth about it. This is true even though the member is not present and the print has been made sometime in the past. Small female children of this age would be the poorest of any of the Murngin at identifying footprints.

wallaby and dugong. The flying fox is prepared in the same way as the opossum.

Flying foxes are caught in the daytime. They sleep in the mangrove jungles. The most favorable time for hunting them is during the mating season when they make a noise during the daytime. The native sneaks up while it is light and climbs the tree where they are suspended. He either catches them with his hands or hits them with a club. The wing bones of the flying fox are pulled out, and sometimes the native closes the other apertures of the carcass, puts his lip to one of the wing-bone holes and blows up the fox with air. This is supposed to make the animal fatter. If a large number of these bats are caught, they are cooked in a stone fire instead of the ordinary ash fire.

A snake is either hit on the head when lying on the ground, or if hunted by an expert, pulled out of its hole. The people on the Goyder River kill the snake by hitting it on the back of the head. People farther east do not do this and are generally more afraid of snakes than those in the Goyder River district and the people west of them. The stunned snake is held by the head and whirled round and round. This tends to force the meat toward the tail. The snake is then stretched out and left until dead. Then it is coiled in a circle and tied in four places. It too is cooked in ashes, as are iguanas.

Birds, including the cockatoo, egret, duck, ibis, and other water birds, are stalked. A spearman with a fish spear and screen of branches stalks them until he gets within accurate throwing distance. All birds except the emu are cooked on a stone fire. Only the large ones are gutted. When an emu is seen, bushes are gathered and fashioned into a screen to be carried before the spearman, who maneuvers to a position in which the wind will be against him, no sound will carry, and the emu cannot smell his sweat. This method is also used for kangaroos and other game that is stalked. The spear is put in the spear-thrower and carried on the shoulder with the head pointing out over the bushes. Emus are sometimes hunted by waiting in a tree by the water hole where they come to drink. A long spear with double prongs is used here. Kangaroos are ordinarily not hunted in this manner but occasionally a man may wait at a well for rock kangaroos.

When an emu is speared the native rushes up and puts his foot on the abdomen. The bird is carefully watched to see if there is much excretion, for if so he is thought to be fat, otherwise he is considered thin and poor eating. The neck and legs are tied up for carrying, a fire is made, a paper-bark receptacle is fashioned, and water is brought and put beside the bird. The feathers are plucked and placed in the water, and the emu is put in the fire to remove the smaller feathers. The wet feathers are then made into a small brush which is rubbed against the body to remove the remaining feathers and burned quills.

The abdomen is opened down the center and a large enough aperture made to admit the hand and pull out the entrails. The heart may or may not be removed. When the intestines are pulled out they are cut up into eight-inch pieces, the crop being cut off by itself. A stick is used to turn the pieces, including the crop, inside out, and the inner lining is removed. All the pieces are washed and the two ends of the entrails tied with grass or string. A small hole is dug, heated stones from a large fire are placed in it, and, on top of them, large green leaves. The intestines are then put on the leaves and covered with another coating of leaves, stones, and a final covering of earth. The food is then left to steam until it is considered properly cooked. The intestines swell up and the intestinal fat melts. This is the purpose of turning them inside out and tying them, since the fat thus retained is considered a great delicacy. While the intestines are cooking other stones are pulled out of the large fire and a large hole is made in the ground in which the stones and a coating of leaves are placed. The emu is first filled with hot stones and then placed on the leaves and covered with more leaves and stones, and the hole is then filled up with earth and grass. While the emu cooks the intestines are eaten.

When a turtle has been harpooned and beached, the head and neck are cut off, hot stones which have been prepared are pushed inside, and the neck and anus are filled with leaves. This makes a kind of steam oven of the turtle's body. While steaming, the turtle is turned on its back. A sharp stone knife (now usually a steel one) is used to split the shell from neck to tail. A parallel split about one inch from the other is made and the strip of shell removed. Then the hunter, starting where the dorsal and ventral shells meet, pulls back on the shell or has a boy pull while he cuts, sometimes with the aid of a stone hitting against his knife.

After this, the leg bones are broken and chunks of meat cut from the animal. This opens the body so that the entrails are in view, now well steamed and, according to native taste, thoroughly cooked. They are eaten immediately. The liver is put in the fire and cooked with coals; it is eaten by the older men. The little boys are given the shells to pick. The blood is poured into a receptacle and drunk by the men.

Everything that can be digested is eaten, but nothing is done with bone or shell. When the Malays were trading with the natives the shell was exchanged for Malay products.

A man who goes turtle harpooning usually takes three or four men with him to paddle the canoe. He is considered the leader, but helps with the paddling while looking for turtle. The canoe goes beyond the breakwater out into the open sea. Along the sand beaches a goodly number of these animals can be found swimming in to shore to lay their eggs. When the head of the turtle is sighted all the oarsmen paddle as rapidly and silently as possible. They hold their heads and bodies down as low as possible so as not to be seen. When the canoe gets within range the harpooner articulates his harpoon to his spear-thrower and aims it just back of the turtle's head. If he strikes, the turtle dives, taking the head of the harpoon with the rope following to the sea bottom. The rope is held on to if it is possible; if not, it is picked up again when the animal rises sufficiently to bring the rope within reach. When the turtle comes up for air he is sometimes speared again, once more goes down, and the rope again held. When the rope becomes slack and it is felt that the turtle has tired itself, a man jumps overboard, puts his hands at the side of the turtle and attempts to turn it on its back. When he has it in this position the other men pull up on the rope. They catch hold of the turtle's legs and pull it on board. It is then hit on the head with a club. This has to be done carefully because a bite in a vulnerable spot would probably result in death.

Eggs of three species of turtle are eaten. Buckingham and Arnhem Bays are supposed to furnish the largest supply. Nests of crocodiles are sought out along the swampy river banks and their eggs gathered and eaten.

Sharks and crocodiles are harpooned, but usually speared. The backbone of a crocodile is chopped in back of the hind legs to sever the tail and to prevent its striking the hunter. When a sting ray is speared its tail is held in the mouth to prevent the fish's barbed prong from striking the spearsman while he is killing it.

The shallow rock bottoms along the seacoast or the white sand bottoms of the long low beaches where the water is knee to waist deep are the favorite fishing places. A spear-thrower is nearly always used with a fish spear.

Poison is sometimes used to stupefy fish, which then float in the water until gathered in. Dangi, an unidentified vegetable product, is macerated and placed in the pool. Some of the writer's informants claim that a poison grass is used similarly.

A fish is cut in halves the long way and cooked immediately because it is believed that if a bit old when eaten it causes leprosy (but see Magic, page 197).

Oysters, periwinkles, and the many varieties of bivalves gathered by the women are cooked on the shore at the spot where they are collected. A fire is made over stones and the shellfish put on the hot stones and embers. The shells open or crack and the flesh is removed and eaten by the women or placed in small receptacles to be carried home to the men.

Honey is gathered by both sexes, but usually by men. When a hive is discovered in a hollow tree that is not too large the tree is cut down and the trunk split open. The honey is usually eaten where found. Gathering honey is a painless task in Australia because the native bees are stingless. The honey is often put in a water-tight basket, mixed with water and drunk as a beverage. It is never allowed to ferment; the natives have no intoxicating drink. The wax is formed into a ball and put in the men's baskets to be used in the construction of various implements.

Pandanus fruit, ripening about August, is cut up into fine pieces and cooked. The small cabbage palm is gathered about the same time, the whole trunk of the plant being cooked and beaten on a log, and the glutinous product eaten. Spear grass is chewed by the children as well as the other people.

Cycad palm nuts are gathered from the center of the trees by the women with the aid of a forked stick placed against the trunk to make a rough ladder. The nuts are knocked off with a club if they are too high to reach. The outside skin is removed and the kernels are placed in a large basket which is submerged in a fresh-water pool and allowed to remain several days until the poisonous qualities of the green fruit are removed. Sometimes the women first heat the nuts, thus reducing the time for soaking them.

Several varieties of tree grubs are eaten. Both men and women gather them. They select trees which have the proper indications upon them, split open the trunk, and remove the grubs which are washed and eaten raw. They look much like the entrail of a fowl and taste much like a snail.

The nests of all the larger birds are robbed and the eggs eaten. During the proper season the various sea birds lay their eggs in great quantities regularly in certain spots along the coast. These eggs are greatly relished by the natives.[3]

3. *Kinship Customs*

The enlargement of a Murngin's economic behavior is dependent on two factors: (1) the horde; and (2) certain reciprocals in the kinship structure. All the relatives of a Murngin ordinarily exchange gifts with him, but certain kinship personalities do this much more than others. The mother's brother—sister's son relationship has been seized upon as the mechanism for enlarging the economic life of a Murngin man. "Far-off" wakus and gawels are sought by a man, distant not only socially but geographically; the greater distance a man has between him and a trading waku or gawel, the greater pride he exhibits when displaying articles sent or brought to him by his relative, and the greater satisfaction he feels when sending or returning gifts. (See chapter on kinship, page 84.)

The mari-kutara relationship is much the same, except that there is a tendency to indulge in ritual gifts much more than in those from the ordinary material culture. The feathered string which has been the decorative covering of the totemic poles is sent by mari or kutara to the other. This exchange of ritual goods plays a prominent part in the economic life of the people, since if a mari receives a gift from kutara he must, in a not too great period of time, return a present of like ritual value. The finely turned string, often used as ritual string, is usually made by women, at times hundreds of feet of it. It is generously covered with birds' feathers and used on one of the larger totem poles. Obviously a great amount of work on the part of the women and the killing of a large number of birds is required to meet the needs of ritual exchange. Only the red feathers from the breasts

[3] The people of the various areas, particularly those west and east of the Goyder, are always accusing each other of cannibalism. The author can vouch that no cannibals are present among the peoples east of the Goyder and roughly in the Murngin area. The Murngin tell a number of stories of the people south of Cape Stewart which to them prove the existence of cannibalism there. Some of them claim they have seen men's baskets filled with meat which was neither kangaroo nor dugong and which they were convinced was human flesh. In one account I collected, the narrator described watching a cannibal feast. The victim, a large man, was carved and prepared for cooking. There is much scornful joking among the Murngin about these people to the west of them. When they think they see human flesh in the basket of one of these people they say, "Ah, what is this one?" and another Murngin replies, "Oh, that's a kangaroo," with a sarcastic inflection in his voice. The other one says, "Yes, but it doesn't smell just like kangaroo," to which the reply is made, "Oh, well, maybe it's only a dead man."

of the red-breasted parrot can be used for certain totemic emblems. To collect a sufficient supply of red feathers to put on such totems as their fire, woman and other Dua moiety totemic emblems demands considerable industry not only on the part of the totem makers in their daily hunting and robbings of birds' nests but also in gift exchanges. This means that red ocher and other body paints, spear heads from the interior, carved wooden spears from the coastal belt, and other objects of economic value must be had to trade. Small white feathers from hawks' breasts and from the sulphur-crested cockatoo and the blue-eyed corella are also used for the string of many totems. The larger feathers of the cockatoos and the yellow crest of the sulphur-crested cockatoo are used for the great ritual headdresses made by the men with the aid of adhesive gathered from the ironwood tree and the honeybee's hive. Ironwood resin makes a very hard, durable cement and is used for many purposes for which the beeswax is too malleable. Ordinarily the beeswax is preferred for the molding of head pieces because the proper shapes can be more easily obtained.

Obviously the extension of the kinship personality of a man by the exchange of gifts between far-off relatives or the strengthening of the bonds between near kin such as mari and kutara definitely stimulates economic enterprise. More labor is necessary than if these mechanisms were not present. The goods themselves take on higher value from their use in the totemic ceremonies; the totemic strings absorb some of the clan ceremonial power and, once used, are taboo to the uninitiated. They are of course valuable in another ritual since they will be used by the receiver for his own totemic emblem and then be passed on to other reciprocating relatives.

4. *Property*

Relating Murngin technological articles to human beings by the concept of ownership is one of the methods of controlling and regulating this society's adaptation to the natural environment, since it incorporates the various articles of technology into the general social order. The Murngin concepts of property are developed into a variety of forms according to the type of thing owned. Land is divided among the clans; and definite areas and their natural objects such as trees, water holes, and the like are considered as belonging to these exogamic units. Derivatively the moieties are also supposed to have an "owning" relationship to the land areas of the country. This means that not only are spatial divisions organized by the separation of all things on the basis of their inherent nature of being Dua or Yiritja, but that the moiety grouping of things takes on spatial definitions and specific location. The importance of the intertwining of these two concepts can be seen in the larger myths such as Wawilak, Djunkgao, Barnumbir, which reflect their division of the things of nature and culture into two moiety categories and group the objects of nature accordingly because they are the property of the clans. The clans are thought of as owning their totems and the right to certain minute variations of the ritual. The ownership of the land includes the use of it, but there would be no thought of excluding the members of other clans from using it; rather, mutual use would be encouraged if the two groups were friendly.

The objects of the technology are personally owned, but a number of brothers and fathers and sons who have cooperated in an enterprise such as boat building have a feeling of collective ownership (see pages 52, 59.)

The concept of incorporeal property is not very highly developed. A man's name is his own, but other members of his clan could possess it if their parents or grandparents who named them had wished it so. There are no songs or painting designs, curing or killing magics, which are considered, as elsewhere, the property of any one individual or group. Certain totemic designs are associated with clans or moieties, and it would be impossible for members of the other clans or moiety to use these designs or emblems unless given permission under special circumstances; but these as well as totems and rituals are not so much properties in an economic sense as integral parts of the structure of the clan. To a great degree this is also true of the land. To remove these incorporeal elements from the clan and moiety structures would cause a complete reorganization of those structures, and only in a most secondary and derivative sense can they be thought of as in an economic category; yet the effect of their being part of the clan and moiety configuration has many of the attributes of our concept of property.

The Murngins' undeveloped sense of property seems to be associated with their lack of interest in developing their technological equipment, and both of these social elements seem to root in the desire to be free from the burdens and responsibilities of objects which would interfere with the society's itinerant existence. The equivalents of incorporeal property in other tribes are here felt to be part of the clan or moiety, i.e., not objects for the exclusive use of any one individual group to dispose of as it saw fit. The medicine man's magical ritual is a possible exception since he alone can exercise his magic; but here too the feeling is not so much of ownership as of having obtained his magical equipment by inherent ability combined with a mystic experience. In the west the magician's power can be passed from father to son, or to some extent from mother's brother to sister's son, and a man can acquire his magical rituals from others; but essentially the concept of magical power is much like our modern concept of talent and ability.

The governing principle in the evaluation of objects which will be kept permanently by their owner is the ease with which they can be transported by human carriage or dugout canoe. The amount of labor consumed in their manufacture contributes in some degree to their high value as individual property, and the relative scarcity of an object in nature or in trade also makes its contributions to Murngin economic values; but the final desideratum is the relative ease of transportation of the article, since this society has no domesticated beast of burden. Metal containers obtained in trade with white missionaries are extremely scarce and highly prized; yet if of very large size they will be given to someone remaining in camp or cut up and put to other uses.

The ultimate value is freedom of movement. Basically the largest factor contributing to this value is the shifting food supply which necessitates change of location; but the feeling for change of location permeates the whole society and has become the most positive motivating factor in the thinking of any Australian aborigine, including the Murngin. All the white ranchers and frontier settlers know and have to make allowance for the partially acculturated blacks' uncontrollable desire "to take a walk about," chiefly under the compulsion of movement from place to place but also because of love for homeland and native culture. The desire to go to other places is forever present in the mental constitution of a black's behavior. If he is in his own clan land where he was born and where he grew to maturity—the center of his cultural heritage—he still feels the urge to go to the next horde or food ground. A flexible material culture and a like technological equipment must, and do, form his adaptation to the natural environment.

(For further consideration of this economic problem, particularly from the point of view of the selection or rejection of exotic articles from other cultures, the reader should see Chapter XIV, Social Change in North Australia.)

It might be argued that the factor of transportation did not prevent a luxuriant growth of ceremonial paraphernalia, such as totemic emblems, grave posts, ceremonial objects of dress, etc. Although the native does consider his ritualistic objects necessary aids to hunting and gathering activities, they are not directly used; and while ceremonial string and the smaller objects are frequently kept after a ritual, the larger objects are ceremonially destroyed by burial or fire, for which, it is most likely, the burden of carrying them is largely responsible. The natives give a mythological reason, and the concept of destruction does fit into the ideas underlying the ceremony; but the destruction was undoubtedly influenced by the necessity of either carrying or destroying a heavy object to prevent women from seeing it.

Whether the Murngin's position as nomadic hunters and gatherers can be historically explained by their having been out of contact with the main centers of civilization and therefore not having risen to the horticultural stage and acquired permanent residence, seems to the writer open to argument. The Cape York Peninsula people had constant communication with the New Guinea horticulturalists, yet did not acquire horticulture as a mode of earning a living, even though they did borrow many other elements from the New Guinea culture. Although the Malays must have been in contact with North Australia for a long period of time, the Murngin again took over only a very small part of their rather extensive material culture.

II. Man, a Species in a Biological Configuration

1. *Man, the Animal, Relating Himself to Nature*

Murngin man is but one species in the general biological configuration of plants and animals which is in constant state of adjustment to the inorganic world. This human animal is from one point of view a purely environmental thing in the same way that a eucalyptus tree, a mangrove jungle, and a species of kangaroo, etc., form the natural environment in which a Murngin lives. It is only by a process of abstracting man from the rest of the organic and inorganic world that we see him as a separate creature and create the useful dichotomy of heredity and environment.

The Murngin native eats, drinks, sleeps, excretes, copulates and reproduces his kind, is born and dies, as do the dingo, the kangaroo, or the other animals who move over the land with him. He affects his environmental world, but it largely controls his behavior; and, generally speaking, his place in the natural economy is largely the same as, let us say, that of the kangaroo, which is an idea the Murngin take as axiomatic. The kangaroo has his peculiar set of articulations to the remainder of the environment, and nature is systematically related to him; but whereas the plant, other animals, and minerals could, with certain modifications, continue their existence without him, the kangaroo obviously cannot live without them, and he must make an organized effort within himself to keep his organism alive and to reproduce his kind during what should be the normal span of his life. Murngin man occupies exactly the same position. He too has a North Australian environment that is both favorable and unfavorable. With parts of his physical surroundings his articulation is made with ease and without effort, but with other elements of nature he must struggle to adapt himself to them or to change them to his needs. Unlike the kangaroo, the way man changes himself or nature is largely cultural, and it is usually that part of his societal life called technology or material culture which is primarily and directly concerned.

Technology, from the functional point of view, is a many-armed and many-handed mechanism. The major element in it is man's attempt to force the materials of nature, formed into artifacts, to do the things his hands, feet, mouth, and teeth are unable to do without their help. When his effort is needed to force nature to be more hospitable, technology multiplies his two hands and arms into many hands and arms. It organizes his animal scratching, pulling, clawing, digging, chewing, biting and other physical activities into culturally ruled ways of manipulating nature by the creation of tools and of techniques for their manufacture and use. The Murngin material culture is comparatively simple, and a study of their implements offers an opportunity to examine some of the physical activities of a people who have been disciplined by technological behavior.

The making of any one article of culture is associated with every technical process in the whole of the material culture of the tribe. Material culture, in its turn, articulates with every other branch of culture, so that starting with such a small element in technology as the making of a spear-thrower one must ultimately consider the whole of the civilization.

A spear-thrower (mangel) is made by (1) cutting down with a stone axe a branch or small tree, (2) splitting it with a stone axe and scraping it with a bivalve shell, (3) carving it into correct shape, and hafting with (4) fiber, (5) string, and (6) resin.

(1) The mere act of cutting the tree down with a stone axe connects the spear-thrower with an elaborate stone technique and system of

trade. (2) Scraping with the bivalve shell connects the mangel with the sexual division of labor, for women gather the shells, this not being considered man's work. (3) Hafting it with resin takes in the whole process of preparing the sap of a tree and forming it into a cement. (5) Hafting with fiber string brings in the process of using a digging stick to pull up the roots, breaking and cutting them up, soaking them in water and drying by a fire before a woman twists them into string. The spear-thrower presupposes a spear. If a stone spear is used once, then the spear-thrower connects with stone technique, with fiber string making, with the use of fire to straighten a shaft, etc.

All this could be carried much further, but it can be seen that not only are the various objects and processes of native material culture mutually dependent and intricately articulated, but also the materials with which these artifacts are made are connected into a unified system. The aborigine thus has, as one method (in addition to other methods) of classifying all objects of nature, the use to which those objects are put in the technology. Every native knows for what this tree or that stone is used. He usually thinks of them with such reference, or as elements in his ceremony and myth, or both.

2. *The Materials Selected from the Environment*

Murngin technology will be considered from three primary points of view: (1) the materials selected from the natural environment, such as kinds of wood, stone, vegetable, and animal products utilized in forming the various objects made by the culture; (2) the aims and methods of the makers of the various artifacts; and (3) the objects themselves and their functions in the society.

Vegetable, mineral, and animal materials, in the order of their quantitative importance (foods not being under consideration), are used in making the various artifacts of the northeast Arnhem Land culture.

The vegetable material consists of many varieties. The trees of the mangrove jungles with their long, slender, light trunks are utilized in the manufacture of spear shafts; their peculiarly curved roots, lying on the top of the oozing mud along the tidal rivers, are used in the manufacture of boomerangs and in the formation of pick-like clubs. The eucalyptus forests contribute bark, sap, and wood, and the Melaleuca (paper bark) tree gives its bark and wood. Every kind of tree found in the environment is used for some purpose. Wood, bark, resin, sap, leaves and grass—all of these are formed into tools by which the native adapts himself to his natural and cultural environment.

Wood is chosen for its degree of hardness and weight and also for its shape according to the purposes of the object to be made. The main forms used are (1) long, slender, light (or heavy) shafts; (2) hollow logs; (3) roots with a well-defined arc; (4) long, straight, slender trunks with thick roots running off at a right angle from the shaft; (5) forked sticks; (6) ends of branches with many twigs and leaves; (7) any variety of dry wood; and (8) very large light wood tree trunks.

Three types of bark are used: (1) a long, thick, wide type found on the trunk of the larger eucalyptus; (2) thin paper-like bark from the Melaleuca; and (3) long thin fibers of root bark easily macerated.

Many varieties of leaves are technological material. They are usually gathered in bundles by breaking off branches, but one large-leafed species is used singly as a plate on which to put fresh meat for cooking.

The long reeds of the water-lily ponds, spear grass particularly, and many other varieties of reeds are utilized.

The few animal materials used are, from land animals: kangaroo fat, kangaroo gut, kangaroo leg bones, bird feathers, bird bones (particularly leg), opossum fur, opossum gut and human hair; from sea animals: sting-ray prongs, fish and shark vertebrae, bivalve shells, and the melon shell.

Deposits of red ocher and pipe clay are mined along certain portions of the seacoast. Yellow ocher is found in outcroppings. Round river stones about the size of goose eggs are gathered. Diorite stones are also used. Quartzite is quarried from outcroppings. Ordinary earth and sand are used in making houses and ceremonial objects on the ground. Rock ledges forming caves are utilized as shelters during the rainy season. Rock basins which catch rain water are used as types of primitive cisterns to supply water in the absence of wells and fresh-water courses.

3. *General Description of Technical Methods Used in Making Raw Materials into Cultural Artifacts*

Only the general methods by which raw material is formed into artifacts will be discussed here. Each specific technique will be described in the section dealing with the articles manufactured.

The chief tools used with food are the ground stone axe,[4] a knife (formerly made of bone, but, since the Malay contacts, of iron), and a variety of bivalve shell.

Cylindrical wooden articles are made by cutting down a tree or

[4] The iron tomahawk is now used in its place.

limb of the right size, hacking and pulling off the outer and inner bark with the axe and fingers, and then scraping the wood to the proper size with the axe and unhafted bivalve shell.

Flat wooden artifacts are formed by first splitting the cylinder in half and then splitting off a segment from the flat inner surface. Axe and shell are then used to hew the wood into the proper shape.

Hollow cylindrical objects are made by cutting down a tree eaten out by white ants, stripping outer and inner bark from it, and then cutting and scraping it with axe and shell to the form desired.

Bark Technique.—To remove thick bark from the trunk of a tree, a cut is made around the bottom of the tree, and another just below the forks of the tree. A split is then made with the axe down the side of the tree from top to the bottom and the bark pulled from the trunk. The outer bark is then stripped off. Processes vary from here on according to the artifact to be manufactured. The bark may be soaked in water or heated to bend it to the shape desired; sometimes, as in house building, only pressure is applied to it.

Paper bark (Melaleuca), the thin white bark of the ti tree found in Arnhem Land in the swamps and where the ground is moist the year round, is used in a number of ways. It is usually removed from the tree by taking the handle end of the spear-thrower and inserting it until it hits the trunk of the tree, then pulling down upon it in the same way that a knife would be used. Along the seacoast this bark does not enter so much into the culture as in the more distant interior, since sea shells offer better material for containers, largely because they are more easily prepared for use than the vegetable material.

Paper bark is used for water and honey containers, as a ladle for dipping water from the well, for pubic covering, mats, "blankets," cigarette paper, exterior covering for houses, tinder material for starting fire, the core of many totemic emblems, the "dunce cap" of the Gunabibi ceremony, and for many other daily uses.

Stone Technique.—The Murngin go to the interior for their spear heads and stone knives, or obtain them in trade. The techniques used are the same as those described in Spencer and Gillen's *Arunta.*[5]

Cements.—The Murngin have four varieties of adhesives. Ironwood resin is the principal cement used. The roots of the ironwood tree are cut into strips a few feet in length and heated over a fire. The sap is scraped from the sticks and collected on a central wooden core where it cools and hardens. When wanted for use it is heated again in a

[5] Spencer and Gillen, *The Arunta,* Macmillan, London, 1927, pp. 540-548.

small fire. It is used to haft wooden spear heads to their shafts, to articulate the peg of the spear-thrower to the shaft, and also to haft the feathers of some of the larger headdresses to a wooden or bone shaft.

Beeswax is used to join the stone spear head to the shaft, it serves as the core for the various feather headdresses, it is used to make the mouth of the wooden trumpet small enough to fit the lips, and at times it is used as calking material for boats. It is also pushed into the hole always made in the septum to give the nose, for purely aesthetic reasons, a very concave form. (If beeswax is not used, small rings are made by wrapping two ends of cane together with fiber string and inserting them in the hole made in the septum.) When not in use, beeswax is molded into a flat mass and carried in a man's basket.

Human blood or the sap of an orchid bulb (djelkork) is used to glue feathers and paint to the dancers' bodies for the various ceremonies, and to stick these same materials on their totemic emblems. When the bulb is used, it is chewed and the macerated end rubbed on the object to be decorated.

Hafting.—Wooden objects to be hafted together are always carved to fit nicely. Ironwood resin or beeswax is heated and applied to the parts, which are then fitted together and wrapped with fiber string.

Murngin technology is forever subject to two fundamental changes: first, the constant movements from food ground to food ground, and, secondly and more radically, the exigencies of the alternate rainy and more favorable dry seasons. Both are essentially problems of environmental adaptation: the one involves the adjustment of man to his food supply rather than vice versa through an agricultural or pastoral economy; and the other is an adjustment to a semi-annual seasonal change which can best be stated in terms of fifty to sixty inches of rain during three or four months and none at all during the rest of the year. These adjustments have profoundly and fundamentally affected Murngin technology and, as we shall see later, their ritual and myth.

CHAPTER VI

WARFARE

WARFARE is one of the most important social activities of the Murngin and surrounding tribes. Without it, Murngin society as it is now constituted could not exist. Any social change consequent upon the loss of the trait would demand a decided alteration in the fundamental structures of the civilization. Warfare prevents modifications in the society that would possibly destroy it.

The tribe is not the war-making group in this society, nor is the moiety. Warfare is as likely to occur within these groups as outside them. The clan, the largest social unit without internal armed conflict, is usually the war-making group. The causes leading to warfare are the killing of a clansman by a member of another clan, and interclan rivalry for women. The latter is the usual cause of a killing. Blood vengeance forces further killings. Clans within a moiety are more likely to be fighting, since clans of the opposite exogamic moieties are not in competition for women. An analysis of battles and killings shows this to be true in most cases, but there are a number of instances in which groups belonging to opposite moieties have been in conflict.

Feuds between clans of opposite moieties are more likely to die out for lack of the stimulus provided by competition for women. Such clans are likely to allow a makarata to be held, where blood is ceremonially shed as repayment for the death of a clansman, in order that the feud may be definitely ended.

It seems a probable hypothesis that one of the fundamental reasons for the creation of a phratry is a drive within the civilization to create social structures intermediate in size between moiety and clan, where open conflict would be taboo, as it is now within clan limits. This feeling is not strong enough to counterbalance the open antagonisms resulting from the struggle for women. The clan structure is too solid and too powerful to yield any of its influence to a larger social institution.

As will be seen later, polygyny is possible under present conditions only because of warfare, and, conversely, is a decided factor in stimulating open conflict because of the resultant scarcity of women.

The kinship system of the Murngin, with its attendant set of obligations, duties, rights and privileges stated sufficiently often before, tends to enlarge the scope of a two-clan feud to four or possibly all of the clans of the several tribes. The waku-gawel relationship, and also the dué-galle, mari-kutara, and marelker-gurrong relationships express a very strong solidarity; and a man can depend upon any one of these relatives, distributed in eight or more clans besides his own, to come to his assistance. An isolated killing, owing to the strength of the kinship structure, usually results in the whole of northeastern Arnhem Land becoming a battle ground at fairly frequent intervals.

Kinship solidarity extends warfare but also has the opposite tendency: that of limiting its scope when it has reached very large proportions. All the clans are interrelated, and generally many will find their loyalties divided, for the kinship through marriage of certain members of a clan will dictate their helping one faction, while other members will be compelled by the laws of kinship to aid the other side. Since the solidarity of the clan prevents members fighting among themselves, those clans whose loyalties are divided usually try to pacify the warring ones. In a makarata, frequently arranged by them, they will usually be found doing all they can to have this peace-making ceremony end successfully.

Ceremony, Myth, and Warfare

People who gather to celebrate the great totemic ceremonies, such as the Gunabibi, Djungguan, or Narra rites, come from clan territories sometimes hundreds of miles apart. The leaders for the Gunabibi ceremony, for instance, frequently come up through the interior from the headwaters of the Roper River in the south to the mouth of the Goyder. Members from all the tribes in the northern Arnhem Land district attend yearly. A ceremony assumes greater importance the larger the number of people present and the greater the distance they have come. A man always brags about how far he traveled, how many clans he visited on his pilgrimage to invite the various peoples to his circumcision, and how many people attended.

Warfare is in direct opposition to ceremony. It tends to destroy the larger group solidarity and ultimately to reduce the people who are at peace with each other to the clan unit, since only here is there absolute assurance that fighting cannot take place.

If armed conflict breaks out in a camp where a ceremony is being celebrated, the ritual is usually stopped, either because the participants are afraid to stay, for they may be killed in their sleep, or because the leaders of the ceremony become angry at what they consider an insult to their totems.

It is believed that while a totemic emblem is in camp all fighting should cease, and any infraction of the tribal law is considered a direct insult to the totemic emblem and therefore to the clan. The leader of a Narra ceremony, at which the totemic emblems are used, almost always stops the ritual if there has been any serious infraction of tribal law, because he does not want to accept the consequences of an affront to his totem. It is believed that the totem itself would seek vengeance upon any leader who did not protect its interests at such a time. The writer saw two Narra, a Djungguan, and two Gunabibi ceremonies terminated because of the outbreak of fighting. The two Narra were stopped by the leaders because they said their totems were insulted, the Djungguan and Gunabibi because of the fighters' fear of death and also because of the anger of the leader of the ceremony. Another Narra ceremony was not stopped when a fight followed the catching of two women in adultery by their husbands. The women were thoroughly beaten—less because of the offense itself than because it took place while a great ceremony was being held—and might have been killed but for their escape in the black of night by swimming to a nearby island.

The deliberate stopping of a ceremony demonstrates that warfare and ceremony have clearly antithetical traits. The great ceremonies tend to enlarge the group solidarity both in numbers and in extent of territory and to create a smoothly functioning unit out of a large number of clans, but warfare destroys this unity and reduces the limits of solidarity to the clan.

Since both traits are necessary to the tribe's social organization, a nice periodical balance has been struck; at one period ceremonialism controls the people's activities, and later war is uppermost in the relations of the local groups.

Effects of Warfare on Population

A fairly accurate estimate places the population of this area around three thousand. The genealogical material gathered by the writer shows about an equal number of women and men, with possibly slightly more men than women. This means that there are about fifteen hundred men, more than half of whom have not reached the age of sixteen. This leaves approximately seven hundred men who are looking for mates among the same number of women. The statistical average of wives to one middle-aged man is three and one-half. Part of the discrepancy between the total numbers of married women and men is accounted for by the fact that women are taken in marriage just before they reach the age of puberty; although sexual intercourse is not indulged in until after puberty, the women otherwise are treated as wives. A second factor in establishing the unequal ratio is that men up to the age of twenty, and frequently to twenty-five, are without wives or have only one wife; they must wait either for the action of the levirate or for some of the younger females to mature. The two factors just named as expressions of the disproportionate sexual ratio in marriage do not account, however, for a sufficient number of women to make up the difference. The killing of young men below the age of twenty-five, because of the ever-present blood feuds, makes up the balance.

The one important effect of warfare on Murngin society is the seasonal slaying of a small proportion of young men who have passed adolescence and are potential or eligible mates.

In the summary of men killed in battle the writer recorded about one hundred deaths in the last twenty years caused by war. These figures obviously do not include all of the deaths from this cause. There are none recorded for the people south of Caledon Bay and only a few for those around Wessel Island and the English Company Islands, where heavy fighting has always taken place. It would be safe, on the basis of population, to add another hundred deaths to the figure above, making a total of two hundred men killed. Since each man averages three and one-half women, these men would have appropriated seven hundred women of the available supply, or, in terms of the present situation, the tribes needed seven hundred women less than they would have, had the men lived.

Warfare, then, is one of the mechanisms on which polygyny is based. If war were abolished, the percentage of men would increase, and the pressure on the social structure created by seeking mates would probably be too strong for the present form of polygyny, with its attendant mechanisms, the levirate and sororate, to survive. Since these latter mechanisms do much toward strengthening the society and preventing chaos attendant on the transfer of a woman from one clan to another, it will be seen that warfare, while destroying one type of solidarity (ceremonial), is partly responsible for the solid foundation of the kinship structure in Murngin society. Warfare also helps to prevent the breaking of tribal laws by the threat of retaliation from other social groups. Finally, it acts as the ultimate police power in the functioning of Murngin society. It is the threat of its force which ultimately prevents flagrant breaking of tribal taboos.

Causes of War

Of seventy-two recorded battles of the last twenty years in which members of Murngin factions were killed, fifty were for blood revenge —the desire to avenge the killing of a relative, usually a clansman, by members of another clan. Of these, fifteen were deliberate killings, against the tradition of what is fair cause for a war, and because it was felt that the enemies had killed the wrong people. Ten killings were due to stealing or obtaining by illegal means a woman who belonged to another clan. Five supposedly guilty magicians were killed by the clan members of victims of black magic. Five men were slain for looking at a totemic emblem under improper circumstances and thereby insulting the owning clan and endangering the clan's spiritual strength.

The idea underlying most Murngin warfare is that the same injury should be inflicted upon the enemy group that one's own group has suffered. This accomplished, a clan feels satisfied; otherwise, there is a constant compulsion toward vengeance, causing a continuous restlessness among those who are out to "buy back" the killing of one of their clansmen. The stealing of a woman provokes the same spirit, since the group feels itself injured; and only the return of the woman and a ceremonial fight, or the stealing of another woman, will satisfy the hurt to its self-esteem, unless the clan has retaliated by killing or wounding one of the enemy clansmen. The same feeling is instigated by the improper viewing of the totem—an insult and an injury to the entire clan.

Any of the above causes for war may be given deliberately or by accident, but in either case warfare is a certain consequence. If a young man chances upon an old man engaged in making a totemic emblem, the former is killed; or if a man is accidentally killed in a fight by a member of a friendly group, the dead man's people retaliate. There is, nevertheless, considerable feeling that an accident should not cause open hostilities, but it has small influence upon the public opinion of those who believe themselves injured.

There are a number of forms of ritualistic injury. If women look at a totemic emblem they are killed by their own group, with the help of any other group that has been offended by their actions. The clan to which they belong is not held responsible except in a minor way. Some years ago the Liagaomir clan was holding a totemic ceremony, using its carpet snake totemic emblems (painted wooden trumpets). Two women stole up to the ceremonial ground and watched the men blowing the trumpet, went back to the women's camp and told them what they had seen. When the men came back to camp and heard of their behavior, Yanindja, the leader, said, "When will we kill them?"

Everyone replied, "Immediately."

The two women were instantly put to death by members of their own clan with the help of the men from the other group.

Maritja, one of the most conventional men in the society, was making a shark totemic emblem. He had hidden it in a hollow tree near the border of the men's ceremonial grounds. Some women belonging to the visiting Burera tribe had walked near it. This had been established by the identification of their footprints by Maritja and his brothers. Maritja went down to the Burera camp and said to the assembled group, "You all know I never make trouble unless there is very good cause for it. You know I look for peace, but your women have done my people a great wrong. They have walked near the place where I had my totem hidden. I shall be sick and maybe I'll die."

The Burera men said, "You are right. If they have done this you may kill them if you wish." Nothing further was done since it was not considered a very great wrong; but had the women actually looked at his totemic emblem he could have killed them, and their clan would not have retaliated.

Munyiryir's wife was burning a patch of brush while hunting for bandicoot. The husband had hidden the string for his totemic emblem in the bushes. The fire destroyed it. The string belonged to the Daiuror clan. They tried to kill her and would have succeeded, but she escaped to the mission with the help of her husband. He was felt to have done wrong in helping her.

A young Warumeri clansman illicitly viewed a stone totemic emblem that is situated on Elcho Island. The men of the clan followed his footsteps and saw what he had done. When they caught him they immediately killed him.

A Mandelpui boy came upon two old Liaalaomir men making a totemic emblem. When they saw him they said, "Come look," and with smiles and gestures indicated their approval of his having a closer view of their totem. This was to put him off his guard; a few days later they ambushed and killed him.

If one of the members of a clan breaks a number of the ritualistic taboos he is seldom killed by members of his own clan. Usually the old men arrange for his death by members of another clan. If such offenses went unpunished the whole structure of Murngin society would fall to pieces, since in time the women and children would be aware of the secrets of the men's associations, and with the knowledge common, the ceremonial ideas would lose their significance.

Should a young man make a totemic emblem without the permission of the clan's ceremonial leader, the usual method of dealing with this insult to the clan would be to kill him.

The finding of the first wild bees' nest, because of its magical significance, is a very important matter to a young boy. Should an older man eat any of it or not allow the boy to consume the honey that was found, the father and father-in-law of the boy would start a camp fight with the man's group.

At the beginning of the dry season all the underbrush is burned off to secure better hunting, frequently destroying a log coffin. The dead man's clan is always offended, but killing seldom results, for the deed is felt to have been accidental, and no strong feeling surrounds the bones of a dead man.

The use of obscenity and profanity against a man always results in a camp fight. Profanity usually reflects not only on the man but on his clan and carries an incestuous connotation. Occasionally quarrels result from an unfair division of the game killed in the hunt, but not always open warfare, since those who feel they had a right to the game are near relatives whose solidarity is too strong to allow fighting.

Adulteries may cause a husband to give only his wife a thorough beating, but usually the lover is also held responsible and a fight is a consequence. The fights are ordinarily of the nirimaoi-yolno (a fight within the camp) type. If the lover attempts to steal her the more serious narrup (secret killing) and maringo (night attack on a camp) are used, because wife-stealing is a much more serious offense.

A number of customs attend these killings that serve as causes for war. When the body of a man killed in a fight or by magic is disinterred, the finger bones are given both to the near relatives of the victim's clan and to related groups as relics to remind them of their duty of blood vengeance. The relic is wrapped with fiber string and covered with beeswax and parrot feathers. It is placed at the bottom of the man's personal basket. A piece of a spear that has been broken off and left in the body of the victim is also used as a relic. When a man has been wounded he sometimes soaks pieces of paper bark in his blood and presents them to his relatives to be used as reminders of their duty to compensate him for his injury by helping him kill or wound a member of the offending man's clan. When a man obtains one of the relics, it is an almost absolute demand on him to kill a member of the slayer's group. This is particularly true if it is given to a young man. The older men usually give their relics to the younger males.

The spirit of the dead is supposed to go with the relic, and the relic has magic power. It can be thrown into an intended victim's fire and cause him to go to sleep, or the possessor can blow his breath against it and produce the same effect. It is often carried in the mouth during a battle to make an opponent tired and heavy-footed and to prevent him from dodging spears. Relics play a prominent part in all feuds.

Occasionally men are killed within the clan, but this is not a cause for war or retaliation by members of the clan or by near relatives from without the clan. A man may be such a notorious killer and cause so much trouble for his own clansmen that the entire group will kill him to stop further disturbances. At times men are slain by their own clan for breaking ceremonial taboos, such as divulging secrets of the old men to the women or the uninitiated, and for viewing ceremonial objects before their initiation.

If a fight is on and a near relative is accidentally hit by a club or spear, the person responsible hits himself on the head while saying he is sorry. Here, too, the underlying idea is to inflict an injury on the responsible person similar to the one the injured party suffered.

Military honor also contributes its share to the causes for war. A man will brave the spears of a whole clan to demonstrate his fearlessness. The writer has seen two brothers defy fifteen men in a spear fight. The Murngin people are a brave and courageous group. Fear of death while in a fight is seldom seen. A man who shows an unwillingness to fight is called a woman and held in extreme contempt.

The fundamental principle underlying all the causes of Murngin warfare is that of reciprocity: if a harm has been done to an individual or a group, it is felt by the injured people that they must repay the ones who have harmed them by an injury that at least equals the one they have suffered. When the total cultural situation of Murngin life is further examined, this negative reciprocation is found to fit into a larger reciprocation. In the chapters on Murngin kinship and local organization it was seen that the foundations of these structures are built entirely on reciprocity, and that the whole civilization might be described as in dynamic equilibrium.

Magic and War

Another belief centered around killing as a cause for war is that the spirit of the dead man enters the body of the killer and gives him double strength and actually increases his body size. When a man kills another during a tribal or interclan feud, he returns home and does not eat cooked food but subsists only on cold edibles until the soul of the dead man approaches him. He can hear the dead man's soul coming because the shaft of the spear which hangs from the stone head within the man drags on the ground and hits against the trees and bushes as he walks. When the spirit is very near, the killer can hear sounds coming from the dead man's wound (in a night fight the attacker usually strikes the sleeper's gullet).

The killer, ordinarily a young man and very frightened, in his fear runs to the camp of the old men. An old man tells him that he should not be afraid, but return and take the spear with which he has killed the man, remove the spear head, and put the spear end of the shaft between his own big toe and the toe next to it. The other end of the shaft is placed against his left shoulder. The left foot and side of the killer are used if he is right-handed, and the right side is used if he is left-handed. This is done so that the dead man's soul will not be afraid of the hand that killed its body.

The soul then enters the socket where the spear head was, and pushes its way upward into the leg of the killer, and finally into the body. It walks like an ant. It finally enters the stomach and shuts it up. The man feels sick and his abdomen becomes feverish. The killer rubs his stomach and calls out the proper name of the man he has killed (not his totem name, but his profane name). This cures him and he becomes normal again, for the spirit leaves the stomach and enters his heart. When the spirit enters the heart it has the same effect as if the blood of the dead man had been given to the killer. It is as though the man, before he died, had given his life's blood (powers, physical and spiritual) to the man who was to kill him.

The slayer, grown larger and exceedingly strong, acquires all the life strength the dead man once possessed. When the slayer dreams, the soul tells him that he has food for him and gives directions where to go to find it. He says, "Down there by the river you will find many kangaroo," or, "In that old tree there is a large honeybees' nest," or, "Near that large sand bank you will harpoon a very large turtle and find many eggs on the beach."

The killer listens, and after a little time sneaks away from camp by himself and goes out in the bush, where he meets the soul of the dead man. The soul comes very close and lies down. The slayer is frightened and cries, "Who is that? Somebody is near me." When he draws near where the spirit of the dead man was he finds a kangaroo, or, if he has gone to the sea beach, he discovers a turtle. It is unusually small. He looks at it and understands the meaning of its being there in the place where he had heard the movements of the dead man's soul. He takes sweat from under his arm and rubs it on his right arm, if he is right-handed, and on his left, if he is left-handed. He picks up his spear and calls out the name of the dead man and spears the animal. The animal is immediately killed but becomes much larger while dying. The man attempts to lift it. He finds it impossible because it has grown so large. He leaves the kill and returns to camp to tell his friends. He says when he arrives, "I have just killed the soul of the dead man. Do not let anyone hear of this because he might get angry again." His more intimate friends and relatives go out with him to help skin the animal and prepare it for eating. When they cut it up they find fat everywhere, which is considered one of the greatest delicacies in the native larder. When they cook it, only very small pieces are placed on the fire at first. They are tasted with much care, and the meat always tastes unpleasant.

Then the whole animal is cooked and a feast made with the parts more appreciated by the natives. The remainder is carried back to the main camp. The old men of the camp look and see that it is an animal of enormous size. They gather around it and someone asks, "Where did you kill him?"

"Up there by the river."

The old men know that this is no ordinary kill because there is fat everywhere. After some little time one of the old men asks, "Did you see somebody's soul out there in the bush?"

"No," lies the young man.

The old men then taste the flesh of the animal, but it does not taste the same as it ordinarily does. It has a slightly different flavor, it is not like a natural kangaroo or turtle.

The old men shake their heads affirmatively and click their tongues: "You have seen the dead man's soul all right."

"Yes, he came to me yesterday and went inside my body. Last night when I dreamed he told me to go out in the bush. Today I went out and he came to me. I knew it was the soul of the dead man. When I sneaked up closer to make sure, I saw a small kangaroo lying there. I put sweat from my armpit on my throwing arm and killed him. The kangaroo grew as big as you see it now."

One of the old men replies to this effect: "We knew straightaway that this had happened because it always happens like this. It happened to most of us when we were young men."

No woman is allowed to eat any of the flesh of such an animal; only the old men, the killer, and his immediate male relatives partake of it. When a member of the Yiritija moiety is killed the killer sees an animal of that same moiety; after a Dua man is slain an animal from that moiety is later seen and killed.

Often the spirit of a man who has been killed appears in the guise of a crow, cockatoo, or other bird, and circles around and around the head of the slayer, or at times a honeybee may appear. When such creatures take the place of the spirit they always belong to the moiety of the dead man, and their function is to lead the slayer to the larger animal just as the soul does when it appears. A man only acquires the soul of the dead in a night fight, never in the daytime, because the one who has been killed sees the killer and his anger prevents the soul from entering the body of his killer.

When Mahkarolla had grown to early maturity he went with an expedition to an enemy clan and there killed one of its members in a night attack. He had been home but a few days when he noticed a crow flying back and forth very near his head. It seemed to have selected him from all the other men of the camp for its attention. The crow is Dua; the dead man's clan was Dua.

"This crow flew a little way from my camp. I looked and I saw a Dua honeybee flying away. I followed, for I thought it might be that I would find the honeybee's hive. I went into the bush and watched that honeybee. I went and went and I saw that tree, and up in the top of the tree that same crow was sitting. I knew what this meant. I took sweat from under my arm and rubbed it on my right arm. I looked up now and I could not see that crow any more. I think that he has changed into a honeybee. The tree was a small one when I first looked. Now it had become very large. I took my axe and cut it down. Most bees' hives are only in a part of a hollow log, but the honey in this one went from the ground all the way up the tree. When I split it open the tree grew even bigger. I understood now, for this dead man I had killed had brought me here.

"When I went fighting that time I was a very young man. No one had told me that when one killed a man his spirit entered one's heart, but after I had killed him the old men asked me if I had seen a soul and I said no and asked them what they meant. They said, 'There is a very big meaning for that; it is something maraiin [spiritual, taboo, sacred].' I understood then what they meant. I began to look for it.

"When I took the honey from the tree there were about seven or eight baskets full. I did not take it home. I left it. I went back to the camp by myself. I said to the old men, 'I have found out there a very large honey-bees' nest. I have left the honey at the tree.'

"Some of the old men said, 'Let us walk just a little way from the camp and we will have a talk.' When we had walked a short distance and had sat down one old man said to me, 'What have you done? Have you dreamed anything?'

" 'Yes,' I said, 'I dreamed, but I did not understand then. I do not believe its meaning. I was going about then like a fool. This crow came, went round and round, and sat on a tree. Even then I thought that crow flew for nothing. I did not believe this one. Then I looked and saw the honeybee fly this way and that. I think then maybe I better follow him. The bee had something white on its nose and looked all the same as a bird.' I then told the old men how I found the honeybees' nest and what happened. The old people said, 'All the members of the dead man's clan are going to hear about this, and they are going to be very angry.' "

It can be seen that this belief would furnish ample cause, if there were no others, for young men anxious to become strong and adult to go out and kill enemies of the clan.

Types of Armed Conflict

There are six distinct varieties of warfare among the Murngin. Each has a separate pattern of behavior and an individual name. In addition to these there is another form in which only the women participate. The names are nirimaoi yolno, a fight within the camp; narrup or djawarlt, a secret method of killing; maringo (death adder), a night attack in which the entire camp is surrounded; milwerangel, a general open fight between at least two groups; gaingar (ghost spear), a pitched battle; and makarata, a ceremonial peace-making fight which is partly an ordeal. Each of the six forms will be described in detail.

In the seventy-two recorded engagements involving killings, twenty-nine men were slain by a gaingar fight, thirty-five by maringo, twenty-seven by narrup, three by milwerangel, and two by nirimaoi yolno. Although the last is the most frequent type of fight, it seldom results in killings; gaingar, on the other hand, has happened only twice in the last twenty years, yet it has accounted for the deaths of twenty-nine men.

The wooden or stone-headed spear, the spear-thrower and the club, as well as the stone knife, are used in these engagements. The spear is the chief weapon, although in camp fights clubs play a prominent part. The stone axe, which is primarily utilized as an implement, also serves as a weapon. No shield is found here. The Murngin depend on the spear thrower to ward off spears and on their well-developed agility to avoid thrusts. In all fights except the nirimaoi yolno and the narrup, the people coat themselves with war paint of white clay.

Nirimaoi Yolno

Nirimaoi fights are very frequent and are usually the result of quarrels caused by adultery or the husband's belief that someone has been attempting to make him a cuckold. The injured man goes to the camp of the lover and accuses him. He carries a bundle of spears and possibly a club with him. Words follow, swearing starts, and indignation is felt on both sides. Relatives of each contestant help him if the quarrel is felt to be very serious. The women usually attempt to hold the arms of the men to stop the fight from becoming too serious, meanwhile cursing the opponents of their brothers and husbands. At times, however, women pick up their digging sticks or a man's club and help their male relatives; very occasionally a woman is wounded and in certain very rare cases killed.

The nirimaoi yolno fight seldom results in anyone's being killed. Friends of both parties always stand back of the men and hit the spear-throwers or hold them when the fighters attempt to hurl their spears at each other. The contestants usually depend upon this and talk much "harder" (dal) to each other than they would if they knew that they were going to be allowed to have free play at each other. They increase their own sense of importance through the interest of others in their actions and possess a feeling that they are much braver warriors and are filled with a much more intense desire to kill than they would have if no one interfered. By remonstrating with their friends and struggling to get free from them, they are able to vent their outraged emotions and prove to the community that no one can infringe upon their rights without a valiant effort being made to prevent it. Obviously on some occasions there is a certain amount of bluff in the conduct of the contestants. The writer observed one nirimaoi yolno fight when, for some unaccountable reason, the contestants' friends did not attempt to hold them. They had counted on being restrained when they rushed at each other while hurling threats of death and covering each other with obscenity and profanity. When they reached each other no clubs were wielded or spears thrown; the men stood breast to breast and obviously felt a bit ridiculous. The usual results of the nirimaoi yolno are a few bruises, much obscenity, many threats, but few killings.

It must be borne in mind that members of a camp usually come from several clans, or fighting would never take place. Although the clan is undoubtedly involved in this variety of battle, the fight is almost always an individual affair, with a few of the combatants' relatives joining the fray. The nirimaoi yolno is also used as a kind of debate where angry men may air their fancied or actual grievances and state their position in controversial matters. This latter function is very important and is in most cases the primary basis of the nirimaoi yolno.

Narrup or Djawarlt

The narrup generally results in someone's being killed or badly injured. It is one of the most deadly forms of Murngin warfare for it occurs at night and by stealth. It is usually conducted by a few individuals who may be members of one clan, or by a party composed of members of one's own clan, the mother's clan, and the wife's group. Such relatives as gawel, waku, dué, galle, bapa, gatu, maraitcha, and marikmo are frequently members of this type of expedition.

The success of the narrup depends upon surprise. A man is usually attacked while sleeping. Warlumbopo's slaying of his brother's killer at Blue Mud Bay, Maiangula's killing of Kamata, and Natjimbui's killing of the Marderpa man in the feud described in this chapter are examples of the narrup night attack.

Although the narrup may be an individual affair, the entire clan is held responsible for the killing. The young men usually attempt to gain the sanction of their elders for a maringo expedition but do not feel they need to for the narrup, which is therefore a favorite fighting method. At times an old man may prefer to remain in the background and have a young man do his killing so that he will not be held as the one primarily responsible, and because of his desire for secrecy the other old men of the clan would not be consulted. The "pusher" (pidgin English word describing the instigator) is a social personality most prominent in the narrup warfare. When young men kill, everyone speculates on who did the "pushing," for it is always assumed that an old man is really responsible. Although not always true, it is a rule of pragmatic value for a clan to follow when meting out vengeance. Waltjimi, in the feud that is described in this chapter, is a good example of the "pusher" type of war personality, just as the old Darlwongo men are later the causes of the continuation of the feud when they "push" Natjimbui.

Maringo

The maringo (death adder) obtains its name both because of the snake-like formation of the attackers that surround the camp of the enemy and because of its deadliness. Killings or severe wounds always result.

When a maringo expedition to avenge the slaying of a clan's relative is decided upon, the following magical procedure is gone through before the warriors leave camp. Relics of the dead man are always carried by some of the relatives. The oldest man who holds one of these relics goes out into the bush some little distance from the camp and makes a fire and hut for himself. He draws the likeness of a man on the earth or molds it on the ground with his hands, giving it the name of the killer.

He then instructs a young man to go into the main camp and tell the old men, who organize themselves and go out in a body. They stop some little distance from where the old man and the image are camped. The leader sends two men ahead as spies. They pretend to look for the camp of the image, which represents their enemy's camp, and to discover if the "killer" is there.

Everyone in the group is as stealthily quiet as if he were on an actual expedition. The two young men sneak around the camp of the image. They return and announce that there is no one there and they could not find the "killer."

They sit down and say nothing. The others also remain quiet, unless they express regret that "he" has escaped and it is of no use to continue the expedition.

The two young men eat; when they have finished they pick up some pieces of white clay or other paint material and throw them into the ring of men. Everyone knows then that the image, the killer in this magical ritual, is there. The two leaders of the expedition divide their men into two groups; one side goes to the left of the camp of the image and the other to the right. They form a circle of spearmen about the camp. When the advancing leaders have met and the camp is completely surrounded, they ask if the "killer" is there, and use his name; and then, with shouts and cries, the expedition rushes in and throws its spears into the body of the image.

The above follows very closely the usual maringo fight of the blacks. If the expedition is successful the killer's body takes the place of the image, and possibly several of his relatives are also slain.

After the spears have been thrown into the image, the owner of the relic kneels on both knees beside it. He puts a piece of fire that has been taken from the camp fire into the image. He places his basket before his mouth; in the basket he has the relic, wrapped up in fiber string or paper bark, so that no profane eye can see it. He addresses the relic as follows: "Where is the killer?" There is no answer. He then starts naming the various possible places where the slayer could be found and asks the relic, which has the spirit of the dead man, where the enemy is. The naming of place is continued until a kind of click is heard. This is supposed to come from the bone and is in answer to the question.

The owner of the relic says, "Ah, that is the place." He once more addresses the relic: "You are not lying to me? You are telling me the truth?" The click is heard again. Next day the avenging expedition sets out and goes to the place designated to kill the slayer of their relative. It is thought that such an expedition must be successful after the ritual has been performed.

The best description of a maringo can be found in the following myth from the Durili people of Cape Grey, which tells of a night attack made by the snakes against a certain clan. It conforms to the accounts of the modern maringo fighting and in addition gives the idealized form according to the best native standards.

"The people were catching fish in the creek. They had caught a lot of fish with a line [for hooks the Murngin used nails from planks that were brought in on the tide]. While some of the men were catching fish others were busy making a fire. They burned the bones and scales in the fire. An eastern wind came up.

"A small blue-tongued lizard [Dua moiety] who was in the nearby bush smelt the fish bones cooking. 'Ah,' he said, 'they are cooking fish; I shall go.'

"He came close; he ate the bones and scales. The men got up. 'What is this?' they said. They had never seen a blue-tongued lizard before, for although he looked like a snake he was different. Someone picked up a stick and hit this lizard on the head and killed it.

"Far back in the jungle the lizard's father waited for him. He was poisonous and very vicious. He was a barananna and wongar.

"Presently the soul of the little blue-tongued lizard entered the heart of his father. The father trembled as it did this and realized what had happened. 'Someone has killed my son,' he said. He was very angry.

"The father sent word to all the snakes and lizards. They all came. He was far down in his well. They all went into his well. The father snake lifted the stone which was at the bottom of the well and made it much larger. They all came out of the well, the snakes first and the lizards after. They made three groups and formed three rings. The head man moved his body and the earth shook.

"The men who had killed the blue-tongued lizard said, 'What is the matter with this ground? It is moving.' The father snake came out of the well and sent two of his sons to look at the enemy. When they returned the father and his two sons led the three groups. The parent snake came behind the whole army.

"They walked until they were close to the camp. When but a short distance away the snakes sharpened their teeth to prepare for the battle.

"The two sons said, 'You stay here. We will go look to see how many men there are.' They looked. 'Good,' they said, 'all of them are here.'

"Then every snake painted himself with white paint while the sons were away. The two came back and went to their father.

" 'What did you find?'

" 'Nothing,' they said, 'no one was there, only tracks.'

"They lied.

"The father said, 'Why did we come here for nothing?' He was very angry. The two sons borrowed pieces of white clay and threw them into the center of the ring of warriors. The father said, 'Ah, that is good. There are plenty of them there. We will go now.' It is like we Murngin do now when we go to fight. We send men to look at the camp. When they come back they say, 'Nobody is there,' but then they throw white paint in the ring, which means that there are a number, that we can fight them. We do that today because Wongar did that and because everybody knows that means we will fight.

All the larger snakes as they advanced walked on their tails like men, and they stood very high. Meanwhile the clansmen had taken refuge on a small island in the creek because they were afraid of the earthquake and they did not know what was going to happen. The snakes arrived at the old camp and followed the men's footprints to the island.

"The Wongar snake said, 'We will sleep here on the bank until early morning, then we will surround the camp while they sleep and kill them all.'

"The morning star came out. The father saw it and he said, 'We will show these people now that they cannot kill our sons.'

"The clansmen heard the noise of the snakes swimming in the river. They thought it the sound of a tide. The men were in the center of the island. The snakes surrounded them in the following formation:[1]

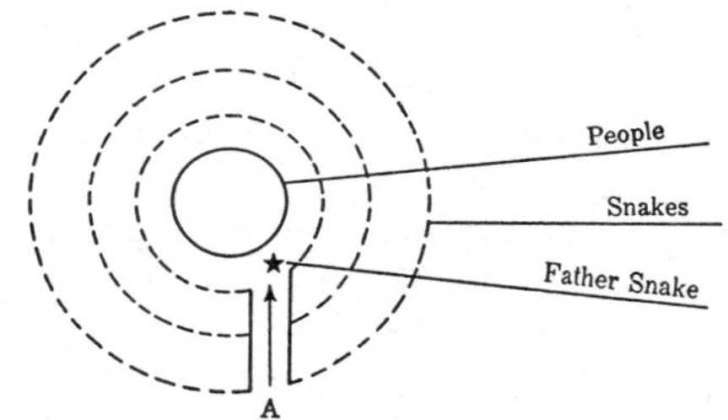

FIGURE 1.—THE MARINGO TYPE OF BATTLE FORMATION

"The father snake went in the aisle at A, just as the leader does now. They killed all the men and left them. One man escaped by climbing up a mangrove tree where the snakes did not see him.

"When the snakes went back to their own country that man came down. He went to his own clan and recruited a number of men to come fight the snakes. The Wongar snake hit them with several thunderbolts and defeated them."[2]

Milwerangel

The Milwerangel is a general fight between members of several clans. The element of surprise is not used. The participants know it will take place at a certain location, usually an open plain with jungle growths bordering it. After a few minutes of fighting, the combat resembles a brawl. Spears and clubs are used, but the latter play only a minor rôle. An excellent concrete example of a milwerangel will be found in the account of the feud described later in this chapter. Further generalization is unnecessary except to say that the milwerangel is a recognized type of battle and therefore has a specific name.

Gaingar

The gaingar is so deadly and results in so many casualties that it is rarely used and then only under the most extreme provocation. There

[1] This diagram is a copy of one made by a native informant.

[2] Certain elements of the myth which have nothing to do with a maringo fight have been omitted.

are only two recorded cases in the last twenty years, one between the peoples of the Caledon Bay area and those of Buckingham Bay; the other between the peoples west of the Goyder River and along the seacoast and those east of the Goyder and in the interior. The gaingar represents a regional fight involving a large number of clans rather than the usual type in which only a few clans participate.

The writer recorded fifteen deaths in the Caledon Bay fight, and fourteen killed and one severely wounded in the Goyder River combat. Such casualty lists show clearly that the sparse population of the Murngin and the surrounding tribes cannot afford such a military luxury except at very rare intervals.

The fight is held between the members of several clans and is the result of regional antagonisms. It may be within the tribe or intertribal. It always follows a long-protracted series of killings in which each side is stimulated to an almost hysterical pitch. When one group of clans finally decides to invite its enemies for a gaingar, the people always say that this is a spear fight to end spear fights, so that from that time on there will be peace for all the clans and tribes. It is sincerely believed at the time that this is an effort to stop clan feuds.[3]

The ideal gaingar takes place in the following way: The challengers make two small spears of a special type. They are wrapped with ceremonial feathered string; two pendants of the same material and tipped with feathers hang from each. One spear has short arms and the other much longer ones. The first symbolizes the Dua moiety, the second the Yiritja. The arms are also symbolic of the men killed by each side before the challenge is sent. Dua men are put in a Dua spear, and the Yiritja are supposed to be placed in the weapon of their moiety. Although the arms may sometimes symbolize only one man, more frequently it is a whole group.

After the spears are completed they are hidden until the following day. In the morning two young men take them and run up and down in front of the warriors while the latter throw their spears at the ceremonial ones. Should one of the spears be hit, it is believed that the war party will be defeated and some of their own men killed. If they are not struck no one of their side will be killed and the expedition will be a success.

In the afternoon the two spears are placed in the ground at a throw-

[3] Talk of this kind, however, has such a familiar ring to a European of this generation that one can only smile at the seeming incongruity of a Stone Age man mouthing the meaty phrases of our twentieth-century peacemakers.

ing distance, and once more spears are thrown at them, but this time there is an effort made actually to strike them, since now they represent the enemies, whereas in the morning they represented the challenging clan. The spears are then sent by messenger to the enemy. They are a ceremonial invitation for battle. The enemy goes through the same ceremony if it decides to accept. The two parties then meet halfway between their respective territories.

Short spears are used in the gaingar because they can be thrown from any position and are difficult to parry or avoid. The two lines of warriors stand about fifty feet apart. Leadership is almost completely absent after the fight starts. Trickery is used if possible. In the gaingar that was held in the Goyder River district, the sea people who challenged the men from the interior hid part of their forces on each side of the plain in a mangrove jungle. They placed a small party down at the forward end of the plain for the advancing people to see. As the enemy advanced this small group retreated to the jungle growth at the far end. They thus enticed their antagonists into the avenue of hidden warriors. The sea people then surrounded those from the interior and killed a large number.

Maḳarata

The makarata is a ceremonial peacemaking fight. It is a kind of general duel and partial ordeal which allows the aggrieved parties to vent their feelings by throwing spears at their enemies or by seeing the latter's blood run in expiation.

Frequently the makarata does not follow the ideal pattern; instead of providing a peacemaking mechanism, it produces only another battle in the interminable blood feud of the clans.

When sufficient time has elapsed after an injury or death of a member for the clan's emotions to calm, the men send a message to their enemies saying they are ready for a makarata. The other side usually agrees to enter into this peacemaking ceremony, although there is always suspicion of treachery. The injured group always sends the invitation, and the other must wait for them to decide when they wish to have it. Frequently makarata are held after some of the totemic ceremonies have taken place, since it is at this time that most of the clans will be present. When the warriors of the injured clan or clans arrive on the dueling ground they are covered with white clay. They dance in, singing a song which is descriptive of the water of their totemic well. The other side has also painted itself. The two sides stand a little more than spear-throwing distance apart, and each is so situated that it has a mangrove jungle back of it for protection in case the makarata becomes a real fight and it is necessary to take cover. The clan which considers itself injured performs the dance connected with its chief totem. It is of the garma or non-sacred variety. The Warumeri clan, for instance, would dance the garawark (mythological fish) totemic dance; the Djirin clan would perform its shark dance. The challenging group dances over to its antagonists, stops, and without further ceremony walks back to its own side. After the men have reformed their ranks, their opponents dance toward them, using the latter's totemic dance for this military ritual. They return to their own side and reform their line to make ready for the actual duel.

The men who are supposed to have "pushed" the killers then start running in a zigzag in the middle of the field, facing their opponents. They are accompanied by two close relatives who are also near kin of the other side. The function of the latter runners is to deter the aggrieved clan from throwing spears with too deadly an intent for fear of hitting their kin, and to help knock down spears which might hit the "pushers." The "pushers" are made a target for spears whose stone heads have been removed. Every member of the clan or clans which feels itself injured throws at least once at the runners. When an individual's turn to throw arrives he advances from the group and moves toward the runners. If he feels very strongly he continues throwing spears until he has chased the runners into the jungle. This action is repeated by the more indignant members of the offended clan three or four times. The injured clan curses the members of the other group; the offending group cannot reply, for this is supposed to add additional insult; they must run and say nothing. Finally, when their emotions have subsided to a considerable extent, one of the older men of the offended group says that they have had enough and the spear throwing stops.

After the "pushers," the actual killers run. The spear head is not removed from the shaft; the throwers continue hurling their spears, at first as a group and finally as individuals, until they have exhausted their emotions. While all this is taking place, the old men of both sides walk back and forth from one group to the other, telling the throwers to be careful and not kill or hurt anyone. The offending clan's old men ask the younger men to be quiet and not to become angry, and when they hear insults thrown at them not to reply or throw spears since they are in the wrong. When the old men of the injured clan feel that they have sated their anger as a group they call out to the young men to stop, and each man then throws singly at the killers. He may throw as long as he pleases.

When this part of the ceremony has been completed, the whole offending group dances up to the other, and one of the latter jabs a spear through the thighs of the killers. If this happens it means that no further retaliatory action will be taken. The killers can feel free to go into the country of their enemies without fear of injury. If only a slight wound is made the offenders know they are not forgiven and the truce is only temporary. Sometimes no wound is made at all. This acts as a direct statement of the offended clan's intention to wreak vengeance on the other side.

After the wound has been made the two sides dance together as one group to prove their feeling of solidarity and to express ritually that they are not openly warring groups, but one people. They also perform the usual water dance.

The above is the idealized form of the makarata. If all goes well, this procedure is followed through until the end, and the makarata's purpose is fulfilled. The following things can happen to turn the makarata into a real fight: (1) the old men may not have enough power to keep their young men in control; (2) the offending side may start swearing or throwing spears, which immediately turns the whole performance into a fight; (3) one of the runners may be badly wounded, which is likely to stimulate his clan members to attack the other side; (4) treachery may be resorted to; (5) the accidental wounding of an outsider may sometimes result; and (6) a member of either side may deliberately throw a spear into the other group because he is anxious to start a general fight.

Women's Fights

Brawls in which only women are engaged are fairly frequent. The fights usually take place between two women, almost always because a young woman has seduced another's husband. Occasionally more than two women are involved, sisters taking sides with their kin; or several wives of one man may attack his sweetheart, in which case the latter usually calls upon her own relatives for help. The women's ironwood digging sticks are the usual weapons, although if a man's club is within reach the women often use it. They strike each other on the head. The fights are of such intensity that bloodshed always results.

Wergild

The conception of wergild is present among the Murngin, but it is very poorly developed and seldom solves the problem of terminating a feud. Whenever a war is in actual progress there is always talk by the offending party of sending food, which usually consists of palm nut bread, to the injured group. The person who has inflicted the injury is the one who is supposed to send it to the nearest relative of the deceased or to the man who has been wounded. Tobacco is also a favorite article sent for the wergild. If the man who receives the bread eats it or if he smokes the tobacco, it is a sign that he has accepted the payment, that the blood feud is terminated, and there will be no further retaliation as far as he is concerned. Every member of the clan, as well as the near kin of other clans, must also eat of this food or smoke the tobacco to make the wergild effective. This is almost always an impossibility and as a consequence the wergild is hardly ever a success. The chief basis of its ineffectiveness is that the solidarity of the clan group is interfered with by the operation of the kinship system; if clan members alone were concerned, it is likely that all frequently could and would enter into the ritual of eating the bread or smoking the tobacco.

History of a Clan Feud

Some twenty years ago a Darlwongo clansman and a Warumeri clansman both desired a woman of the Djapu group. A fight resulted and the Warumeri man was killed. The triangular arrangement of these particular clans, two of the Yiritja moiety competing for women of the Dua Djapu clan whose territories lie between the two competing groups, has always been in existence and reflects itself even in the folklore. The death of the Warumeri clansman not only procured the woman for the Darlwongo but added one more mark to the score of the interminable blood feud that also has always been a part of the relationship of the two clans.

Two or three years later one of Warlumbopo's eldest brother's sons, of the Bringel clan and Ritarngo tribe, killed a Darlwongo man to "buy back" the dead Warumeri, because "he remembered his black duck totem." The story of the black duck ranga (totem) which relates the Warumeri and Bringel groups in mythological times is given the credit for this solidarity by the natives; but, although it does give a splendid rationalization in the tribal system of thought for such an alliance, it is not the real explanation; the Darlwongo are perhaps even more closely related by myth to their enemies than they are to their friends. Actually, the antagonism of the Warumeri and Bringel against the same clan, with the lack of rivalry for women, has made them very friendly, and there is a considerable solidarity in the activities of the two groups.

A few years following the last killing recounted here, Warlumbopo's brother and his son, Danginbir, went up to the Marderpa clan's highland country for a visit. They were taking the usual route to the Blue Mud Bay seacoast. When they arrived an old Marderpa man told his sons, "You go kill Danginbir's father." He wanted this done because the father-in-law of the Darlwongo who had been killed had sent him as a present a red parrot belt made from the hair of the dead man. It was maraiin, had as much power as a totemic emblem, and was therefore taboo and feared. The old Marderpa felt ashamed when he saw it, since no one had avenged the death of the owner of the hair; he made the Darlwongo quarrel his own. (It is highly likely that there was already a considerable background of antagonism between the Marderpa and the enemies of the Darlwongo.)[4]

He took Danginbir to a paper-bark tree jungle on an expedition for yams. The young Marderpa accompanied the father on another route.

The old Marderpa, Kamata by name, sharpened his axe. It, too, had been the property of the dead Darlwongo and had later been transferred to the father-in-law, now deceased, who in turn had sent it as further pressure on the Marderpa to help him avenge the taking of his son-in-law's life by killing the Ritarngo.

As Kamata sharpened his axe, Danginbir grew suspicious. He asked, "Why are you sharpening that tomahawk?"

"I am going to look for a wild bees' nest," said Kamata.

It was late morning and they had already gathered some yams and killed some small game. They made a fire and cooked and ate their food. They slept.

The Marderpa only pretended to sleep, and when everyone else was deep in slumber he stealthily arose and hit Danginbir on the back of the neck. He severed Danginbir's head from his body. The Marderpa threw the head and body into the river.

Meanwhile the boy's father and the other Marderpa had gathered a good quantity of yams. A Marderpa picked up his spear and said, "I am going to look for some kangaroo. You pick up the yams and take them back to camp." He hooked his spear to his spear-thrower, and while the man who was carrying the yams walked toward camp he sneaked up behind him and speared him in the back. He did not succeed in killing him, for the wounded man dropped his burden and ran toward camp. The Marderpa stopped and picked up the yams that were dropped and did not follow. When the old man arrived in camp he said, "Where is my son?"

Someone said, "He has been killed."

[4] There is less information recorded by the writer on this matter because the Marderpa group lay at the farther end of the Murngin country.

"Well," said he, "it can't be helped. I can do nothing, for my son started it first." He collected his wives and belongings and said, "We will go now. I think this wound will kill me before I get home."

After they had walked for several days he felt too ill to continue his journey.

"When I die," he said, "you wives put me in my grave and go straight to Warlumbopo [his younger brother] and tell him what has happened to his elder brother."

Shortly after he had spoken, Warlumbopo walked into the dying man's camp. He cried and cried. Then the old man raised himself to a sitting position. He danced the dance of the black duck totem flying home, for he remembered his totemic water hole and he wanted his soul to go straight to it when it left his body, and then he fell back dead.[5]

Warlumbopo said, "I won't show my sorrow now. I will go buy you back first, my brother." He did not bury his brother, and he told the wives of the deceased not to bury him. He picked up his spears and basket and went away. He went down to the Blue Mud Bay country where the Marderpa people had gone after his brother had left them. He went over to Woodah Island. It was daytime.

The Marderpa people saw him. They conferred together. "We must kill him too," they said. They got ready. Groote Eyelandt and Barlamomo people were also there. Warlumbopo walked straight into the camp as though nothing had happened. All the men of the camp hooked up their spears. "Why have you people got your spears hooked up? What is the matter?" He pretended he knew nothing.

"Haven't you heard anything?" someone said.

"No," he replied. "I have come down here to hunt for emu."

The old Marderpa man who had killed his brother sang the water of the Ritarngo well and the water of the Marderpa clan's well, then he said the dead man's name. "We killed him and his son," he said.

"Oh," said Warlumbopo, "and a good thing it was, too. He was a wakinu [without relatives and asocial]. I have a spear mark from him too." He showed a scar upon his leg (from an engagement with an enemy, not from his brother).

Warlumbopo painted himself for a makarata peacemaking ceremony, and so did the old men of the Marderpa group. They went out to the dueling ground. Two old men and two boys ran for Warlumbopo to throw his spears at them. He took the stone heads out of his spears and threw two shafts at them.

[5] All clansmen perform this death ceremony. A Wangurri would dance and call out his Garawark, the son of Barrimundi; and a Liaalaomir man would dance the great python and imitate the thunder of his totem.

"All right," he said, "I am satisfied. My brother was no good, and I cannot be angry."

The four men came up for him to spear the man who had done the killing. "No," said Warlumbopo, "I don't want to spear your leg. I am through." (He did not want to take this action which is symbolical of finishing a feud, so that he could kill the man at a later date.)

"No," said the man, "you spear my leg."

Warlumbopo took his spear head and just broke the skin of his enemy. He wanted the latter to think that it did not mean very much to him, but inwardly it signified that he intended to kill him later.

They all went back to camp. He slept there with them that night. The Marderpa men watched him, for they believed he might be pretending and they were too wise not to know that all the people in the north resort to trickery whenever it is possible. Warlumbopo remained quiet. He stayed there for over a week and did nothing. He carried only one spear to keep suspicion down. It was a big red stone spear. He put a longer shaft to it. The fact that he carried only one spear served partially to quiet the suspicions of his enemies, for ordinarily when there is trouble a man carries a large bundle of them.

One night when it was dark he slept nearer the main camp. The camp dogs came in from their places in the surrounding bush. They were nosing about the refuse while they hunted for turtle bones. Two dogs became engaged in a noisy fight over a bone. One of them was Warlumbopo's. While they were howling he picked up his spear and started calling the dog's name, "Latera!" (also the name of the stones around his clan well), and running toward the dogs, which brought him to the side of the old man who had killed his brother. The old Marderpa was awakened by the noise and raised up on his elbow. As he did this, Warlumbopo shoved his spear downward into the man's gullet. He started running again, calling for his dog as he went across to the mainland on the sand bank that connects the island with it during low tide. When he was out of the firelight's glow in the darkness of the surrounding bush he stopped and called back to the Marderpa, "You people do not know what is at the bottom of new spring water."[6]

Warlumbopo went back into the bush to the camp of his dead brother. The body had swollen. It was very large. The wives of the dead man were still there. He dug a hole and rolled the body into it, covered it, and went back to his Ritarngo country with the wives. When he arrived home he

[6] This cryptic, rather epigrammatic remark, with a touch of sardonic humor about it, very typical of Murngin thought, refers to the fact that every year, after the long wet season is past and the flood waters have gone, new fresh-water springs are found and it is always a matter of speculation from where they come. Warlumbopo had likened himself to a spring and the cause of his arrival in the Marderpa camp to the underground source of a spring's water supply.

sang the water song of their clan well to another older brother, Daurlung, and thereby told him of their elder brother's death, since the name of the dead is taboo. Daurlung cried. After he had finished he said, "We will get all our Ritarngo people and go fight the Marderpa."

"No," said Warlumbopo. He had not told his brother of what he had done to avenge their older brother's death, because he believed Daurlung was a good friend to the man he had killed, and he wanted first to tell the whole story. When Daurlung heard that his friend (a distant tribal younger brother) had not tried to save the lives of his own brother and son, he was very angry. He said, "We will go kill that one first."

Warlumbopo said quietly, "You cannot kill him now."

"Why?"

"He is dead."

"Who killed him?"

"I did."

"My own brother!" said Daurlung. "Good! I shall give you two of my wives." He then gave Warlumbopo two of his wives to show his appreciation.

This ends the episode of Blue Mud Bay.

Meanwhile rivalry for women among certain clans had caused another feud to continue between the Djirin and the Naladaer on one side and the Gwiyula on the other. The Daiuror clan, which is closely related to the former two by marriage, always sided with them in a dispute, but the Gwiyula usually had much the best of the fighting for their clan had two of the most feared and deadly fighters, known throughout the tribes of the eastern Arafura Sea. They are Parpar and Drona (the kangaroo-legged one), who has a deformed leg.

Parpar, about fifteen years ago, killed Djingaran, a Djirin clansman, the father of Maiangula, for revenge in a narrup fight. Maritja, a son of Djingaran's brother and a member of the Djirin clan, a few years later killed a Gwiyula in a maringo fight. Parpar and Drona then killed several Naladaer people, including Ginda, the brother of Berundais, who will be mentioned with Maiangula a little later in this story. They also wounded Waltjimi, a member of the Daiuror clan.

They put the corpse of Berundais' brother in a tree. Djowa and a number of his people some few months later cleaned the bones and took them away. Djowa found the spear head with the skeleton. He wrapped it with paper bark and fiber string, as is always done with such relics, and put it in his basket. All the members of the party that gathered the bones received one or more small bones as relics.

Djowa and Berundais kept the spear in their baskets. A short time after this they conferred and decided to transfer it to someone else. They gave it to Watia (Liagaomir clan). Watia kept the relic for a considerable period of time and finally, tired of having it in his possession, presented it to Bengaliwe (Djirin clan). He said, "This comes from Drona and Parpar. You can do something about this, for I am tired." Time passed and Bengaliwe also lost interest in the relic. The killing had occurred so long before the time of his possession that it did not have great emotional interest for him. He even considered throwing it away, but it still remained in his personal basket. One day Balliman (Djirin clan) looked into his relative's basket. He saw the relic wrapped in the fiber string and, since he was still a very young man, his curiosity was aroused to the point of his asking Bengaliwe what it meant. Bengaliwe said, "That belongs to you people. It comes from Parpar's brother." Since the Naladaer and Djirin clansmen are considered more or less one people, for the Naladaer has a very undifferentiated existence from the Djirin, the statement of Bengaliwe was true.

Balliman's interest was aroused. He was a natural fighter, and always keen on organizing an expedition to fight someone, no matter what the cause. He went to his near brother, a member of the Djirin clan, Maiangula, and said, "I have something here for you. It is an old gatu [son]. It belongs to us. The spear that killed him is in Bengaliwe's basket." Maiangula, a large man of a more or less even temperament, said, "What do you think we had better do? Do you think we ought to steal it away from Bengaliwe? He can't go fight them for that. His people are too near relatives to them for him to fight Parpar and Drona. They are like one people."

Maiangula then went to see Bengaliwe and was given the relic.

Maiangula had been a small boy when his father was killed, so he had done nothing at the time to avenge his father's death. About three years before he received the relic from Bengaliwe and about two years after the killing of Ginda, the Naladaer, Waltjimi, the war leader of the Daiuror group, who was Maiangula's father-in-law, said to the young man, "You have a spear head, Maiangula, that was found in the body of Ginda when we painted his body with red ocher and took it from the tree. He was my waku [son-in-law]. You go kill Parpar and Drona and I will give you one of my daughters for a present to become your wife."

After a conference, Maritja, the leader of the Djirin, agreed to head the party. He agreed to go on the expedition only after he had stipulated that Parpar and Drona be the only two men killed, since they were such notorious killers that there was a general feeling among the older men throughout north Arnhem Land that the clan to which the two belonged should not be held responsible for their behavior. This feeling, however, became uppermost in the minds of the old men only at those times when they were most philosophical and there had been no recent slaying, for during their more emotional states they felt that the whole clan should be destroyed. Maiangula and the younger men, although agreeing to this consideration of Maritja, were out to kill for blood vengeance and did not concern themselves with whether to kill Parpar and Drona or other members of their clan. In the war party which left in search of Parpar and Drona were Maritja (Djirin), Balliman (Djirin), Maiangula (Djirin), Djowa (Daiuror), Berundais (Naladaer), as well as many other members of the three clans. The first two were actual brothers, and the third a classificatory brother of the first two, since his father was a brother of their father. Djowa was a son of Waltjimi's older brother.

Narnarngo, a Liagaomir clansman who had reared Parpar when the latter's father's father died, heard of the expedition and dispatched Kamata[7] and Gurnboko, the first a Bringel and the second a Gwiyula, to warn Parpar of his danger. They joined the camp where the others were staying. The information spread among the war party that these new people were going to warn Parpar. The younger men immediately decided among themselves to give up the expedition and kill Kamata and Gurnboko. The leader, Maritja, a much older man than the others, attempted to prevent this but failed.

Maiangula, the leader of the younger men, said, "Narnarngo, who knows all the news, talks too much; he has found out we are going to kill Parpar and Drona. Parpar is a 'son' of Narnarngo. These two men here we can kill now. They are close enough relatives to those others for us to kill them even though they are a little bit 'far off' in their relationship. Because they are a little far, we will not tell Maritja. He is an old man and understands too much, and he will know that we are doing something a little bit wrong. I cannot think that way in my head; I think too much about my father. This young man is a brother that belongs to Parpar; he is close enough."

Maritja knew from the behavior of the younger men that they were plotting the death of the two young men. He said, "I have lived a long time. I saw the old men and the way they acted before you young men were born. I have seen them grow very quiet and their bodies look like they were dead when they were filled inside with a desire to fight. I have seen myself that way. It is better that we go back to our camp. If we stay here you will kill somebody who is not a close enough relative to Parpar and Drona, who killed our relatives."

He warned the prospective victims of their danger and asked them to leave immediately, but they were too young fully to believe him. When it was dusk, the three young men, Maiangula, Balliman and Berundais, formed a camp by themselves against the old men's protests. It was behind a large pandanus palm tree, about eight or ten feet away from the others. Maritja, to make sure that no harm would fall upon the young Gwiyula

[7] This younger Kamata must not be confused with the first one who was killed in the earlier part of the history here related.

and his companion, had them sleep beside him. After a time they all went to sleep. Maritja felt something in his hair. He raised up, sat down by the fire; he said to his young charges, "Don't you go to sleep now. Something was walking about in my hair. I think it was sent to warn me. Maybe it was a spirit to tell me that somebody would get speared tonight." He talked very loudly for everyone to hear, in the hope that it might frighten the younger men and prevent them from carrying out their plot. Everyone remained quiet.

A little bird (willy wagtail) lost its footing in a nearby tree and fluttered about in the branches. Maritja knew then that something was going to happen. "That bird," he said to the young men, "is telling us a story. He has always come and told us black men when trouble and spearmen were around. Then that one walked in my hair; that meant something. I think you boys had better go. I think something is going to happen."

Kamata, one of the young men, said, "No, we will stay here. I am going to lie down. I want to go to sleep."

The young men lay down and Maritja put his legs over the body of the smaller one. Presently Maritja and the two boys were in a deep sleep. By this time it was late. The moon was high in the sky. When the moon had gone down and it was very dark, Balliman and Maiangula awakened. Maiangula said, "You, Balliman, you go kill Gurlbaiili. You, Djowa, you go kill Kamata. I am going to kill Gurnboko." Balliman and Maiangula arose, but Djowa remained quiet. Balliman with Berundais sneaked up to Gurlbaiili's camp. Djowa, meanwhile, had placed his spear in the fire to make it hot so that he could straighten it, and because it would cut better when he tried to kill the sleeping man. While this was occurring, Maiangula removed the steel blade from his spear and sharpened it. He sneaked up on Kamata himself with the spear head in his hand and sank it into the latter's jugular vein. Maiangula then turned his attention to the second man, but he was nervous and attempted to dispatch him too quickly. Instead of hitting him in the gullet, he struck his side. The young man who was wounded started crying, "Mother, Mother, Mother." Balliman, meanwhile, in attempting to approach near enough to Gurlbaiili to sink his spear into him, had run into a pandanus patch, which was around the sleeping man's camp, and because of its thickness and the sharpness of the thorns, he was unable to get through it. He walked around the edge of the pandanus trying to find a path, but just before he was near enough to stab him he heard the thud of the spear entering the small boy's body; he was afraid, and he and Berundais ran away.

In the morning the news of the killing was carried to the nearby camps. Raiola, a brother of the slain man, arrived with some of his kinsmen. Raiola cursed Maiangula and started fighting with him, but when he saw Berundais he thought that this man was probably to blame for the killing, since he believed that it was Berundais who had given Maiangula the relic. He struck Berundais on the head with a club. Maritja, although a very near relative of Berundais, commanded his people not to fight Raiola because he had a right to attack them, since one of his relatives had been slain. Dimala was then attacked by Raiola because he was a brother-in-law of Maiangula's. They fought with knives, but because of the intervention of their mutual friends and relatives, neither of them was hurt. Maiangula and the killers meanwhile had hidden in the bush.

After things had quieted and the general camp brawl which had resulted from the slaying had ceased, the inevitable series of discussions commenced among the various old men who had gathered from the clans to determine just what was back of the killing and to attempt to find out if anyone had "pushed" the younger men. The opinions were very divergent upon the actual motivation, but it was felt by all that Maiangula had killed a man who was too far removed from his real enemies, Parpar and Drona. There was also a secondary sentiment that Maiangula's father had been too long dead for Maiangula to retaliate. It was also believed by most of the men that some older man, probably Waltjimi, had directed him to kill the boy, for Waltjimi was a bitter enemy of the Bringel clan. The wounding of the younger man was not so severely criticized, for he was near enough in relationship to Parpar. The chief fault found with his wounding was that he was too young, so that even this attempt to avenge his father's death was held against Maiangula.

After a week or more, when Raiola with his relatives had gone back into the interior to their clan's territory and the general excitement had died down considerably, it was decided to send a messenger from the camp of the Djirin and Naladaer peoples to the Gwiyula to discover what their feelings were about the matter and to attempt to arrange a makarata to settle matters. Birindjaoi was chosen to go because it was thought he would not be hurt by the other side, since he had near relatives among them.[8] Baerwit, the recognized leader of the Ritarngo clans, was the unofficial head of the group of clansmen who had gathered by a small lake in the interior country. Birindjaoi met Raiola, who was his friend. All of the men's bodies were painted with white clay to show that they were on the warpath. He and Raiola went over to the part of the camp where the Ritarngo were situated. They took tobacco and food to Baerwit. He invited them to sit down. Birindjaoi, who distrusted Baerwit, said that he preferred to stand. Three of the young Ritarngo were standing with their spears ready to throw them. They were all blood sons of Baerwit.

The older leader picked up a paper-bark water basin and invited the messenger to have a drink of fresh water. The latter realized it was

[8] He was identified also with the Crocodile Island mission.

trickery, and that he was attempting to get him to bend his face down so that his sons could spear him, so he said he was not thirsty and that he had decided to leave. Baerwit said, "Before you go I want to make my people one in a makarata. They are three groups now." Birindjaoi said, "Yes, you do that so that we won't have a lot of spear troubles." The Djinba and Ritarngo peoples who were under Baerwit's leadership stood up and looked meaningly at each other; but the other group, the Gunalbingi, stood up and looked at the ground, which indicated they were not at one with the others in their plot to kill Birindjaoi. While they stood there a white light seemed to play all over his body like the reflection of the sun's light in a pool. Raiola noticed that Birindjaoi's body seemed to change. The light came and went several times. The first time that it came it was a spirit to warn him and Raiola that trouble was there for them. The former did not see it, but Raiola did. Raiola saw it like the flash of lightning in a dark night, and it made him shut his eyes.

Birindjaoi said again to Baerwit, "Go ahead and make these people one."

Baerwit said, "My legs are tired. You go ahead and we will come behind you."

Birindjaoi said, "No, we will walk together."

Raiola and he walked together. Raiola talked to him in a distant language which the others could not understand. He said, "They don't understand me in this language. I saw three lights shine on you. I know now those men want to hurt you." The group of men meanwhile had been walking toward a wooded plain. When they were very near it Baerwit started walking rapidly toward the two. He cried out to his chief fighter, "Tjari, you run and catch Raiola. We cannot hurt him; he belongs to our own people, but he will fight if we try to spear Birindjaoi." The group of clansmen formed around them. An old man, who was a near relative to Birindjaoi, quietly stood up beside him and put his abdomen against his back so that no one could spear him when he was not looking. Raiola, before this had happened, had given him a spear, and Blumberi, also a relative by marriage to Birindjaoi, had presented him with a spear-thrower. Raiola then turned to Baerwit. He said, "You think you are going to kill him? You kill him and I will kill one of your men. No, I won't kill one; I shall kill two. Birindjaoi is a messenger man and you have no right to kill him. You are doing wrong. All right; I will do wrong and kill people who are near to me."

Tjari ran at Birindjaoi with his spear pointed at him. Raiola turned upon him with his spear, as did Birindjaoi. Tjari moved back into his group. One of the Djinba warriors threw a spear at Birindjaoi when he was not looking. The old man called out in time for him to grab the spear before it hit him. Raiola threw a spear at his attacker and caught the latter in the thigh. The man fell on his knee and from this position threw at Raiola and missed him. The two men, while the attack was being made against them, had hurried toward the river which flowed in the middle of the wooded plain. They ran; spears were thrown at them, but they were not hit. Their enemies in an attempt to stop their running and prevent their escape, held in their mouths bones of men, for it is believed that the spirits of the dead do all in their power to help those who are supposed to be avenging their deaths. The men ran faster. They jumped in the river and swam for the other side. It was dusk by this time and difficult to see them. They swam until they came to a mangrove jungle. They lay within it until morning.

After the two left, the Ritarngo, Djinba and Gunalbingu people heard that the Rainbarngo, Wulaki, and Yandjinung tribes were coming to fight them. This latter group of tribes live along the western border of the others.

The report was true, and when the westerners were within some distance of the eastern group the latter hid in the paper-bark swamp until their enemies were close to them. They arose and chased them but hit no one. One of the enemy was captured. They turned him loose, and as he ran away they threw spears at him. Two of them mortally wounded him. The emotions of all the people were deeply affected, and the general lust to kill was felt by all of them. Baerwit and his group turned upon their allies, the Djinba, who, being in the minority, ran away. Baerwit then turned upon the Gunalbingu to slake his desire for killing, but they too were afraid and retreated to their own country. It is unlikely that anyone would have been killed, since the three groups were too closely related.

A few weeks later, when interest in the blood feud had quieted and emotions were no longer at fever heat, a great makarata was held. Raiola and other Ritarngo, Djinba, Warumeri and one Wangurri were against Maiangula and his clan. Just before the rainy season had arrived and a few months after Maiangula had killed the young Kamata, his gawel [mother's brother], Minyipiriwi, came to the grave, opened it with the aid of several others, cleaned the bones, painted them, placed them in a paper-bark container, and took them back to the Bringel clan's country. He gave one of the smaller bones to Natjimbui, a Djirin, as he did to all the Ritarngo. Natjimbui was a clansman of Maiangula, which made it irregular for him to receive this relic, but the Djirin clan had always been friendly with the Bringel.

Natjimbui, because he belonged to the same clan, could not kill one of his own clansmen, and had no desire to inflict an injury on his own group, but he did feel compulsion to do something for the Bringel, since they were friends of his. He took the bone and started for the Marderpa country to kill the slayer of Kamata's brother. On his way he went through the

Darlwongo country and found the Marderpa man who, many years ago, had cut Danginbir's head off (see page 167).

Two Darlwongo men approached Natjimbui and told him that this Marderpa man chased them with spears while they were preparing to make their honeybee totem. This is a great crime among the Murngin and a deliberate insult to the totem of the clan. Because of this they were forced to take the string from off the emblem and put it back in their baskets, since the emblem would have lost its efficacy had they continued making it after this occurrence.

Natjimbui the next morning went to look for food. He was followed again by the two Darlwongo old men. When they had penetrated into a nearby jungle for some distance they came upon Natjimbui digging yams. Once more they said to him, "That Marderpa man chased us with spears while we were making our totem. Don't you feel sorry for your mother?" (Their totemic emblem was called mother by Natjimbui because his mother was the nearest relative through whom he could trace his relationship to it.)

"Yes, I will do it. I do not forget my mother. I will do it tonight."

When night came the married men of the camp gave food to the single men. Everyone sat down at dusk and sang and talked. The Marderpa man was suspicious and did not trust the Darlwongo clansmen. He said out loud, for all the camp to hear, "I am all the same as a kangaroo. I sit up all night and watch."

Natjimbui sat down in the main camp. He did not sleep; he too watched. Hours went by. He grew tired of waiting and reached in his basket and took out the bone of the dead man. He unwrapped the paper bark from the relic and cut the bone in half. He wrapped one half and placed it once more in his basket. He held the other in his hand. He was far enough away from the Marderpa and other members of the camp so that no one could see what he was doing.

Natjimbui arose and walked over and sat down at the fire beside the Marderpa man. He started talking to him. While they talked he threw small stones into the fire, then he pretended to pick up a stone to throw, but instead of the stone he threw the bone into the fire. He was sure then that the Marderpa would soon be sleeping, since this was done to make the spirit come out of the bone and act upon the Marderpa in such a way that he would be easy to kill. By and by the Marderpa boy said, "I am very sleepy. I think I will go to sleep." They both lay down. Natjimbui continued talking. He asked questions, after some little time, to see if anyone would answer him. No one did. They were all asleep. He stealthily rubbed his spear with the other part of the relic to make it go straight and kill quickly, for he knew that the spirit would guide his spear. He hooked up his spear and pointed at the Marderpa, but too many small boys were sleeping around the man. He took his leg and pushed the young boys to one side. He held his spear in his hand and shoved it into the other man's abdomen.

The wounded man groaned and cried, "What is wrong?"

"Danginbir! You remember him, don't you? He was the one whose head and body you threw in the water."

General confusion prevailed in the camp. Everyone cried, "Why did you do that?"

"This one [the man he had just killed], a long time ago, killed that little boy's [Kamata's] brother. He [Kamata] had no older brother to look out for him and he was killed. This bone I have in my hand brought him back. It was just as if that little brother [Kamata] had opened my mind when he died, for I forgot that big brother. I thought about him now."

After the excitement had died, everyone said, "That is too long ago for a young man like Natjimbui to think about it. It is much too long. He did not think for that far back."

Several of the older men turned to the two old Darlwongo and said, "We think that you told that young man something." They emphatically denied it, as old men always do when they have "pushed" young men into a killing. While everyone was talking and shouting and the relatives of the man who had been speared were wailing, the Marderpa men of the camp tried to make a ring of spearmen around Natjimbui. Natjimbui edged out of the group so that no one was at his back. "You people stand back there," he said. "If you come close I will kill another one of you." They stood back. "You people sleep over there," continued Natjimbui, "I will sleep over here away from you. Tomorrow morning I will come out for you." (This meant that he would run before them in a makarata.)

The two old men went with him so that he could sleep. In the morning he painted himself, as did the Marderpa; he ran before the Marderpa, with the two old men accompanying him. They chased him inside a mangrove jungle. This was done a number of times. Finally they grew tired and the old men of the Marderpa clan said that they had had enough.

Natjimbui danced the net dance, which symbolized his catching the soul of the man who had been killed. After that he put his leg out to have it stabbed, but the Marderpa refused.

They buried the body, left the Darlwongo country, and after one night's camp arrived in the Gwiyula territory. Natjimbui accompanied them. When they had buried the Marderpa man a Kalpu man had cut the armlets off the Marderpa. When Natjimbui arrived here he said that he was going to leave them and go to the Crocodile Islands. The father of Gurnboko (the young man wounded by Maiangula) said, "No. Let us wait and sleep here tonight. We will all go tomorrow."

That afternoon omens of ill luck appeared to Natjimbui. His spear fell down and the stone head broke. Probably a mokoi (evil ghost) tried to break this spear. If a man's feather headdress or parrot-feather arm streamers fall off during the war period, it is a mokoi's doing.

The Kalpu man knocked off little pieces from the edge of his stone spear head. He chipped it only on one side to make it very sharp. Night had come. Natjimbui's wives slept on each side of him. He lay on his side near a small fire. The Kalpu man, when everyone was deep in sleep, sneaked up to Natjimbui's side and shoved his spear into his body at the base of the ribs. Natjimbui rose on his elbow but did not cry out. Gurnboko's father began shouting. Everyone started crying, and once more general confusion reigned throughout the camp. They cried, "Maringo! maringo!" They thought that an enemy group had surrounded the camp. Someone called, "Djawarlt!" Natjimbui arose to his feet with the spear in his side and gathered up his own spear and spear-thrower. He walked back from the camp and its firelight until he was in the darkness. A Marango clansman called out his name, but he did not answer. He hooked up his spear and threw it at him. He missed. Another Marango came close to him and called his name. Natjimbui speared him in the abdomen. He then turned and walked away from the camp carrying his spear-thrower. His spears were depleted. He walked away and then came back to the fire. He pulled the handle of the spear out of his own body, but the stone head of the spear remained inside. He burned the handle of his spear-thrower until it was red hot, and put it against his wound. This was to make it smaller and so that it would close up properly. He walked slowly away from the fire until he came to the mangrove jungle. He retraced his steps, leaving his tracks in the mud pointing toward the river. He came back from the river walking on the low limbs of the mangrove trees, attempting to make it impossible for his enemies to trace him. He came to a dry place in the rocks and walked along the stones and grass to a mangrove creek. He went into the water and then back to a dry place and then crossed another small creek.

Blood was dripping from his wound. He put grass inside the hole. He dropped his spear-thrower for he was growing weak. The tracks went a little farther and were lost. He had not been found at the time the author left the Murngin country. The searching party which had followed the trail decided he must have crawled on his hands and knees so as not to make tracks, and that he had successfully stopped the flow of blood.

A makarata was held, in which Natjimbui's relatives chased the Kalpu.

This is the last episode in the Murngin feud that I followed while in the north. When I left, plots were being formed to continue its eternal flow through the lives of the clans participating in the blood feud. The history of this feud shows clearly that although clan solidarity is of considerable importance, and at times it is even possible that two or more clans may ally themselves for a short period, the kinship system tends to break down these solidarities and make a feud almost the activity of one individual.

PART III

ABSOLUTE LOGICS

CHAPTER VII

MURNGIN MAGIC AND MEDICINE

DESCRIPTION OF MURNGIN MAGIC, WITH DETAILED DATA

A. Introduction

Among all the clans of the eight tribes and all the members of the groups there is a profound belief in magic. The effects of its power are twofold: it can harm and destroy, or it can benefit and cure. Among the northern clans of the Murngin and Yaernungo tribes there is a belief in magic but there are no magicians of any kind, while among the southern and more western tribes magicians, both evil and good, are found everywhere. The "black" magician (sorcerer) can injure or kill his victim, and the "white" magician can cure him or restore his lost faculties. All deaths, sicknesses, certain types of bad luck, and, in general, all those occasions on which the individual is seriously out of adjustment with his community, physically, mentally, or socially, are looked upon as the effects of black magic; and in almost every case except that of soul-stealing the white magician is called in to remedy the situation.[1] There is here a kind of warfare between the forces which do good and those which do harm to man. The latter are related to an organized set of concrete techniques embodied in the person of the black magician, while an entirely different set gives practical expression, in the personality of the white magician, to those forces which control the effects of black magic. The struggle then becomes a warfare between these two types of magical personalities. This does not mean that they are necessarily enemies, though they usually are; furthermore, a black magician is not looked upon by all men as fearsome: to those of his own group he is a constant source of strength, since they seek his aid in repaying a wrong done to them by another group.

Occasionally when a very old person dies the diagnosis is, "It was nothing, just old age"; but this is very rare. Among some of the magical causes are: the machinations of an evil magician; possession by an

[1] Whenever a magician, black or white, is called upon, payment must be made to him.

evil ghost (mokoi); and ritual uncleanliness. Their effects can be cured by: ritual; white magic; and very occasionally, natural remedies. We shall first describe black magic and the sorcerer, then white magic and the healer, and finally analyze these concrete data in order to determine the nature of Murngin magic. To do this we shall first examine the internal evidence presented by the activities of the black and white magicians in the southern areas in the hope that we shall thus illuminate our understanding of the functions of magic. We shall next consider the northern area, which is without magicians, comparing it with the southern area to ascertain if this test situation throws any light upon the nature of magic and its possible relation to ritual and religion. After this we shall apply our findings to the theories held by Hubert, Mauss, and Durkheim,[2] particularly to their theory that magic is an individualistic technique without a church, therefore different from and antithetical to religion, the fundamental basis of which is its church organization. The last section of the chapter will present a sociological interpretation of black and white magic which will take account of all the Murngin magical data, demonstrating that magic is a part of religion and, like it, has its church.

B. Black Magic and the Sorcerer

The Murngin believe in a number of methods by which sorcerers can kill their victims. One of the more popular ideas is that the magician goes secretly into the bush and makes a long turtle rope, brings it near the camp, and hides it in preparation for the magical slaying of a tribesman. In the middle of the night or early morning he and an accomplice approach the camp where the one they intend to kill is asleep. They crawl up near him. One takes the rope, makes a loop in it, and slides it over the victim's head, lying down beside him so as not to be observed by anyone who might be awake; or, if the victim should waken, to make him believe the magician is one of the victim's wives. If all goes well, he pushes the rope around the sleeping man's neck. Meanwhile, the accomplice holds the opposite end of the rope some few paces away from the main camp. He has been told before that as soon as a pull is given on the rope, the cord will have been properly adjusted. The helper starts twisting the rope while the other sneaks to him. He continues to twist it until he starts

[2] Durkheim, Émile, *Elementary Forms of the Religious Life* (trans., J. W. Swain), The Macmillan Company, New York, 1926; Hubert and Mauss, "Théorie Générale de la Magie," *Année Sociologique*, Paris, Vol. VII.

choking the sleeper. The two then pull the struggling man toward them, pick him up and carry him to a safe place in the jungle. The one who had crawled into the camp returns and lies beside the man's wives, with whom he is supposed to copulate in the perfect killing.

The other magician, meanwhile, opens the left side of the man, who is now presumed to be in a dead faint, slits the skin between two ribs, somewhat below the heart, and pulls the two ribs back. He covers his arm and hand with orchid juice [3] and places a small sharpened hardwood stick in his palm with the sharpened end in his fingers. The victim is breathing heavily; when he inhales the magician pushes his hand upward between the ribs, when he exhales the magician holds his hand. When the sorcerer reaches the heart he thrusts the killing stick into it and withdraws his hand from the body.

The victim's body is now held so that the trunk is leaning down, and the blood is allowed to run into a paper-bark receptacle or a waterproof basket. When the heart stops beating the soul is let out; in native thinking the heart's blood is different from the body's blood, the home of the soul being in the heart. The basket of blood is hidden some distance away. The magician returns, puts the ribs in place, and smooths the flesh upon them. He builds a small fire, heats his spear-thrower in it, and rubs it against the wound. Previous to the killing he has gathered a nest of green ants and a small lizard, which are mashed together. The juice is taken from them and rubbed on the wound. The heating and rubbing continue until the opening is completely closed and all traces of the wound are gone.

The magician turns the body on its face. The large intestine protrudes several feet because of the magical death. A few green ants are shaken on the cut. They bite the flesh and the intestine retreats within the hole much like a snake.

The spear-thrower is then dipped in the heart's blood and whirled around the victim's head. The body quivers. The weapon is once more dipped into the heart's blood and waved again. He breathes heavily. The operation is repeated several times until the man who lost his soul sits up and looks very much as before the magical "killing."

The operator now hits him on the head and tells him he will not remember what has happened to him. He is ordered to open his mouth

[3] An orchid bulb, green ants, and sometimes a lizard are collected preparatory to a killing. The juice of the bulb is rubbed on the operating arm. The green ants and lizard are used to bite the intestine to make it withdraw or to bite a wound and cause it to close; sometimes ointments for the same purposes are made of the ants and of the lizard.

and the magician twists his tongue so that the top of it lies on the bottom of the mouth and the reverse side faces the palate. He is told that in three days—but there is no particular set time or magical number—he will die: "The first day you will be very happy, the next day you will be sick, and the third day you will die." After he leaves the spot where the operation has taken place, the magician runs ahead, hides, and waits for him, hits him with a club and cuts his body in two. One part of the body flies in the air in one direction and the other in the opposite. They become like leaves in the wind and disappear.[4] Several hundred feet away they reappear and the body becomes whole again. This process is repeated a number of times until the victim is near his camp, to which he returns. The magician sneaks away in the bush and returns to his own camp.

The man who has lost his soul feels very weak. His wives ask if he has had his soul stolen, and he says, "Oh, no, I have had dysentery, and I am very sick from it." The first day he feels very well, finds an abundance of food and seems very cheerful; the second day he sickens, and the third day he dies. A "white" magician is then called by the relatives to ascertain who has been responsible. He looks at the dead man to see what spirits are standing beside him, for the spirits of the killers are nearly always to be found by their victim's corpse, though only medicine men can see them. The doctor then announces the name of the killer and the relatives discuss the best way of avenging the death.

When a woman is killed the operation is considerably different. The rope is placed around her neck, she is dragged from the camp to a hiding place in the jungle, a fire is built, a paper-bark or basket receptacle is made ready, and green ants, a lizard and an orchid bulb are collected; but instead of making an incision below the heart the magician enters the body of the woman through her vagina. In operating on a man the magician faces his victim in a squatting position, but in opening a woman he works from the side with his legs pressed together for fear sexual desire will overcome his magic.

He has the killing stick in his palm. The skin around the Mount of Venus is pushed back until it reaches the navel. The magician inserts his hand in the vaginal orifice, goes forward when the woman inhales and keeps his hand quiet when she exhales. The woman is kept in a

[4] The word "warro" means leaf, also house, as well as the soul. The warro (soul) makes a malli or shade. A leaf does the same thing. This is possibly the association of ideas which gives the two the same name. Houses are shelters and are made of leaves.

squatting position with her buttocks on her heels. The basket or bark receptacle has been placed under her vagina and the blood is allowed to flow into the basket. Sometimes a large blue fly is put inside her and allowed to come out her mouth; it flies off with her soul, which becomes the creature and familiar of the magician. After the heart has been punctured and the soul released, the same process of alternating the hot spear-thrower and the green ant and lizard ointment is followed, and the hole in the uterus and the outer wound are closed.

The large intestine protrudes. She is turned over on her face to be given the same treatment as in the case of the man. When it has disappeared the spear-thrower once more is dipped in blood and whirled around the head, the same procedure being followed as with the man, until the female victim has recovered her senses and is told when she will die and that she will not be able to tell anyone what has happened to her. He cuts her in two a number of times on her way back to camp. She lives her allotted number of days and then, on the day set, she dies.

Other times the sorcerer sneaks up on a man while he is asleep and bites his nasal bone. This closes the nose and makes the man open his mouth. He takes a deep breath of air, which opens his heart, where everybody's life is. His soul comes out with the breath and goes down the doctor's mouth. He swallows it. The magician, with the aid of his helpers, then takes the man out into the bush and finishes the magical treatment ordinarily associated with soul-stealing.

Individuality and Social Personality of the Sorcerer

Individually the sorcerer is not different from the ordinary man in the community. He participates in the culture and in the daily round of affairs exactly like other men.

His difference from the average man lies in his having a special power. There were a large number of these soul-stealers in the southern and western parts of the Murngin country. Among them was Dulperro, who was credited with killing seven men and one woman; a number of expeditions had been sent out to spear him, but they had not killed him, although one succeeded in wounding him badly. Laindjura, from Marunga Island, was another outstanding killer; several of his case histories will be presented later. Goonga, of the Burera, was also a famous killer with sinister reputation. All of these men were taught by their fathers or maternal uncles how "to kill a man and make him alive to die." The black magician always gains his power originally from a near relative, usually his father, often his maternal uncle, but at times his paternal uncle. The father takes his son and says to him, "You do this way and that way, and by and by, after I die, you can do this too." Although there is a tendency for the son to obtain his magical power almost by right from his father, the novice must associate with the older sorcerer in a killing or two before he can secure sufficient mana in his group to be considered a sorcerer. First, the power is transmitted from a man who is a killer and master of the souls of several dead men; and, second, the beginner must have been associated with the killing of a man and therefore with the dead before he is given the social personality of a sorcerer by his community. In brief, his personality as a sorcerer is by double association with the power of the dead. He has the power to change the living into the dead before his sacred power comes from the sacred dead.

Case Histories of the Sorcerer Laindjura

One of the most noted killers in the southeastern Murngin country was Laindjura, who had destroyed many victims by black magic. As an individual he was not very different from the ordinary man in the tribe, although possibly a bit more alert. He was a good hunter as well as an excellent wood carver, and had several wives and a number of children. There was nothing sinister, peculiar, or psychopathic about him; he was perfectly normal in all of his behavior. Among his own people the attitudes were no different toward him than toward any other man in the clan. It was extremely difficult, however, to obtain Laindjura's confidence to the point where he would talk about his activities as a sorcerer. Although he and I were on very friendly terms, it was not until my second field trip into the area that he gave me long accounts of his various killings.

It is impossible definitely to evaluate how far Laindjura and other killers believed the case histories which they gave me. There was no doubt in my own thinking that Laindjura believed a great part of them. Since he was constantly credited and blamed by friends and enemies for certain deaths, he may at first have taken an attitude "as if" he had done these things and ultimately have come to believe that he had actually performed the operations he claimed he had. A black sorcerer who is credited with many killings has a rather difficult time among the people surrounding his own group, and under most circumstances it is more difficult and unpleasant to be so classed than as an ordinary man; hence a man would not practice such complete duplicity as these stories might indicate unless the setting were extraordinary from our point of view.

The Killing of Bom-li-tjir-i-li's wife.—"All of us were camping at Marunga Island. We were looking for oysters. This woman I was about to kill was hunting for lilies that day, for the other women had gone another way to search for oysters. I carried a hatchet with me and watched her. The woman gathered her lily bulbs, then left the swamp, went back on the sandy land and lay down in the shade. She covered herself with paper bark to keep warm because she had been in the lily pond and felt cold. Only her head came out from the bark. She could not see me.

"I sneaked up and hit her between the eyes with the head of a tomahawk. She kicked and tried to raise up but she couldn't. Her eyes turned up like she was dead. I picked her up under the arms and dragged her to a mangrove jungle and laid her down. She was a young girl.

"I split a mangrove stick from off a tree and sharpened it. I took some djel-kurk [orchid bulb] first and got it ready. I did not have my spear-thrower with me, so I took the handle off my tomahawk and jabbed about the skin on her Mount of Venus which was attached to her vagina and pushed it back. I pushed the skin up to her navel.

"Her large intestine protruded as though it were red calico. I covered my arm with orchid juice. I covered the killing stick with it, too. I put the stick in the palm of my hand so that I could push the point upward with my thumb. When she inhaled I pushed my arm in a little. When she exhaled I stopped. Little by little I got my hand inside her. Finally I touched her heart. I pushed the killing stick with my thumb up over the palm, which pressed the stick against my fingers, into her heart. She had a very large heart and I had to push harder than usual.

"I pulled the stick out. I stood back of her and held her up with her breasts in my hands. She was in a squatting position.

"Her heart's blood ran out into the paper-bark basket I had left to catch it in. It ran slower and slower and then stopped. I laid her down and took the blood away. I hid it. I came back and broke a nest of green ants off a tree. I laid it near her. I put the live ants on her skin. (See Wawilak myth, page 247.) I did not squeeze them, for I was in a hurry because I was afraid her relatives would come looking for her. The skin, when bitten by the ants, moved by itself downward from her navel and covered her bones over her Mount of Venus.

"I then took some dry mud from an old lily pond. I put my sweat on the mud and warmed it over the fire. I put it against her to heal the wound so that no trace would be left of what I had done. I was careful none of her pubic hair would be left inside her vagina so that it would be felt by her husband or seen by the women. I kept up the mud applications until the vagina looked as it did before. I put blood and sweat in the mud and warmed it and put it inside the uterus. I did this again, using the mud. sweat, and blood. I did this six or eight times. The inside now was like it was before.

"I turned her over. Her large intestine stuck out several feet. I shook some green ants on it. It went in some little way. I shook some more on, and a little receded. I shook some more, and all of it went in. Everything was all right now. There was no trace of the wound.

"I took the tomahawk handle which had her heart's blood on it. I whirled it around her head. Her head moved slowly. I whirled it again. She moved some more. The spirit that belonged to that dead woman went into my heart then. I felt it go in. I whirled the stick again and she gasped for breath. I jumped over her and straightened her toes and fingers. She blew some breath out of her mouth and was all right.

"It was noontime. I said to her, 'You go eat some lilies.' The woman got up and walked away. She went around another way. I said to that woman, 'You will live two days. One day you will be happy, the next day you will be sick.' The woman went to the place where I had found her. She went to sleep. I took her blood and went away. The other women came from where they had been gathering oysters. They were laughing and talking. They awakened the girl. She picked up her lily bulbs and went to the camp with the women.

"The next day she walked around and played, laughed, talked, and made fun and gathered a lot of oysters and lilies. She came back to camp that night. She brought the things she had gathered into camp. She lay down and died that night."

Mar-a-wa.—"I came to the Mission on the Crocodile Islands. They were making a Narra ceremony here. I killed Bonira's wife's brother (Marawa), a Burera man, while he was here.

"Marawa went out hunting palm nuts with his wife. She is the woman who is now Ilkara's wife. I followed them. They went to Balmal, on the other side of Millingimbi Island.

"Before this Marawa and I had fought on Marunga Island. He had hit me with a club that time. I was pretending to hunt for kangaroo. That is what I told the people in the camp. I went along through the bush until I heard Marawa breaking up palm fruit on a log with a small mallet. He was getting this food ready for the Narra ceremony. His wife had gone on for a long distance.

"When I saw this, I came out beside him and sat down. I asked him if anyone were there. 'Where are your women?' He said, 'They have gone to the boomerang well.' 'Are you going to camp with them?' 'No, I am going first and they are coming after me.'

"I started thinking, 'This fellow is a big man and I have no one to help me carry him.' The people had been cleaning palm-nut fruit there and left a lot of logs on which they had beaten the nuts. I got up and picked up a log. I said, 'Why don't you use this good one?' He said, 'No, this is all right.' He was sitting with his back to me. I hit him on the back of the neck [the base of the brain]. When I struck him he fell over and spewed. I thought, 'You are a big man all right, but you have fallen down now and you are not too big for me now.' I couldn't lift him, so I put my hands and arms under his body and dragged him. I put him in a cycad palm jungle.

"I laid him on his side and cut him open under his heart. I used a sharpened spear-thrower to open him, not a knife. I tore his flesh around to the center of his stomach, where his ribs ended. I bent back three ribs, one at a time. I rubbed my arm with orchid juice. I had an old gan-djur-ma [killing stick] with me. Sometimes I use the backbone of a kangaroo's lower leg or a sting-ray prong. As he inhaled I went in, and when he exhaled I stopped. I kept this up until I reached the heart. It is easy to do this on a man because I have to reach in only to the wrist, but on a woman one has to push the arm to the elbow. I pushed my right arm into him. I always use the right arm both on men and women [he made a point of this]. I pushed the stick with my thumb and fingers into his heart. I pulled it out, laid the body on its side, with the left side down so that the heart's blood would run into the hole I had made to receive it. When he breathed the blood ran faster than when he did not. I next filled a paper-bark basket with Marawa's blood. I covered up the hole which had the blood in it, but before doing this I took some of it and put it on a leaf. I took the paper-bark basket of blood and hid it. I came back and cleaned up the place. I warmed the spear-thrower until it was burning hot. I put it on the sore. The skin went in a little. I straightened the ribs. I warmed and straightened and warmed and straightened them. I next squeezed some ant juice on the hole. This stung him and he jumped. I kept this up until the hole was only a small thing. I burned it until it was closed and looked as it did before.

"I took some ants and shook them on his lower intestine. They bit him and it receded. I did this three times until it went back into his hole. It went like the sun in a rift of clouds. It went slow until it got to the edge, then dropped in quickly. I took some blood and put it on the spear-thrower and whirled the spear-thrower around his head several times. The body jerked. I whirled it again and he inhaled heavily. I pulled his eyelashes and fingers and toes. He awakened and looked around. He got up and sat down. He blew on his lips, making a noise like a drone pipe.

"I hit him on the head. I said, 'A Yandjinung man will hit you with a spear and kill you. There will be three of them that do this to you.' The man said nothing. I twisted his tongue upside down. I said to him then, 'You go down and get that food you were fixing and take it down to the camp.' He picked up his food and went to the main camp.

"The man slept two nights. The third day he got up and went to the Burera country near Cape Stewart. Ilkara was here at the Mission. The wife of Marawa had been a sweetheart of Ilkara's before she had become Marawa's wife. Ilkara wanted her now. I followed Marawa from the Mission. Ilkara took three of his maris and one of his wakus. They didn't know I had killed Marawa with magic.

"They followed him and came up on his left side. One of them threw a spear. He raised his arm to knock it off but the spear went to the place where I had opened him. He was kneeling down when they sneaked up on him. He stood up when he was hit. He stood still. He did not try to run, he did not try to raise his spear-thrower to protect himself, he did nothing. He did not try to throw his spear, for when a man is killed by magic he can do nothing.

"Ilkara's mari hooked up his spear to his spear-thrower and threw it. Marawa did not move, but stood like a tree. He fell over and died. After he died another mari speared him in the back. Ilkara took Marawa's woman."

Ka-per-ar-a, Sister of Bomlitjirli and Wife of Dorng.—"I killed her because she and Dorng had promised Waryi Waryi a tomahawk, but instead of giving it to him they gave it to Jerrimerrili. This made Waryi Waryi very angry. He told me and asked me to kill this woman. I was at the Mission. That woman went to look for palm nuts. I told everyone I was going to look for kangaroo. Before this Waryi Waryi and I had planned how it would be done. Waryi Waryi went to sleep at the well on the other side of Millingimbi Island, and I was to stay on this side and we were to meet halfway.

"I had only gone part way when I saw this woman. I followed her for a long distance. She was walking toward the other side of the island. There were a number of women with her. When they got well into the bush the party broke up and went in different directions. She went by herself.

"Waryi Waryi was coming the other way. He had a dog with him and was catching bandicoot. The dog was helping him. I followed the woman. I had a fish spear with me. I sneaked up to within a few feet of her and threw the fish spear through the calf of her leg.

"She screamed, 'Ya-kai! Ya-kai! Ya-kai!' I jumped and grabbed her from behind. She became very frightened but I held her. I put my foot against her Mount of Venus. She changed until she felt as if she were dead.

"Waryi Waryi came up closer. He looked at us. He thought that she and I were having sexual intercourse. When I saw him I was a very little frightened. I walked a little distance away and fell down on my knees and tried to crawl away, but Waryi Waryi called out, 'Don't be afraid, I'll come help you.'

"I told him to fix her up because it was his job, while I made a fire to cook the bandicoots he and his dog had killed, because I felt hungry. I cooked the bandicoots while he operated. I didn't tell him what to do, for he knew as much as I do about these things. Waryi Waryi opened up her vagina as I do. He put the blood some distance away. The last drops from the heart were put in a small basket. I put this blood away and came back and ate my bandicoot. Waryi Waryi worked. He burned the spear-thrower, he put sweat on it, then applied it to the wound, then put some ant juice on and kept doing this. The hole kept getting smaller and smaller. It closed. He put strong mud in the fire and pushed it into the uterus. The mud was withdrawn and more put in. He always put his sweat on first. The wound that had been made closed and the mud dropped out.

"He asked, 'Have you finished eating bandicoot?'

"I said, 'Yes.'

"He said, 'I'll eat now; you come work.'

"He went to the bandicoot and started eating. I took some green ants and a small lizard. I turned the woman on her stomach. The lizard was alive. I opened its mouth. I put it against the woman's large intestine. He bit. The intestine jumped back like it was afraid of the lizard. I shook green ants on it and it went back very quickly. After it went inside I turned her over. I rubbed the spear-thrower with her blood. She breathed deeply when I waved it over her. I pulled her eyelashes and fingers and toes. I whirled the spear-thrower around her again. She spat out her breath. She stretched and got up. She picked up her basket and yam stick and left.

"Waryi Waryi said to me, 'That bandicoot belongs to you that is left over. You can finish this woman. I am going the other way.'

"I ran ahead of her and waited for her. When she came past me I had a small stick with me. I hit her across the stomach. It cut her in two. The chest and head fell one way, the abdomen and legs the other, then I couldn't see her at all. I looked and looked. About fifty yards ahead she appeared again. I ran up ahead of her again and hid. When she came I hit her again and cut her in half. The head went one way, the body the other. I saw them fall on the ground. While I looked the body disappeared. I looked the way she was going for I knew she would appear in that way. She fell down to the ground like a leaf. When she hit the ground she was like a woman and carried her yam stick and basket. She carried her firewood and went home with her palm nuts. I went another way. She lived four days and died. I gave her that time."

Na-yil-li-wil-li.—"I killed him at night. My young brother, Gunnumbilli, helped me. My brother is dead now. Afterwards someone killed him with magic. Indjoka's brother [a Birkili clansman] had been killed. Somebody had killed him with magic and then a spear had got him. His pubic covering had blood on it. Dorng took it off the dead man and gave it to me. 'My kutara has been killed,' he said, 'you buy him back for me.'

"We two brothers left our Marunga camp and sneaked up on the Rarungalk camp where this man was. When we got to the Rarungalk camp we sat down. We had a turtle rope with us twenty feet long. Each of us took an end of the rope. I sneaked up while my brother held the rope. I made a loop in it before I got there. Nayilliwilli was asleep. I put one arm under him and lifted his head up and put the loop over it. I did not tighten it. I pulled on the rope to tell my brother to twist it. He twisted it by rolling it on his thigh with his hand. I stood by the sleeping man and kept the loops straight on the neck. It came tighter and tighter and then he couldn't call out. He did not jump about. His eyes protruded. He gurgled when the rope broke his Adam's apple.

"I pulled the rope and my brother slackened it. I pulled it again and my brother carried the rope and walked toward me. The rope was put on the dead man's chest. My brother picked him up by the legs and I carried him by the head. We sneaked out with him to the jungle down by the sea. Our tracks were covered up by the young people and women when they walked around in the morning, so they could not follow us. Nayilliwilli had a very old wife. She slept by herself. I did not, nor did my brother, sleep with her.

"When we had carried him to the jungle I opened him up and pulled back three ribs, and by the way I told you before I got into the heart and stuck it with a stick. The blood went 'drrrrr—rrr—r-r-r-r' at first and then 'dirt!—dirt!—dirt!' We had made a very large paper-bark basket that day at the same time we had made the rope to kill him. The stick was not pulled out until we had him lying on his side and elbow in the proper way. When the blood stopped running I picked him up again.

"I hid the spear-thrower and applied the green ants. I always put sweat on the spear-thrower first to make it strong. (I do not use mud or lizard at night because you can't find them. I use it in the daytime with both men and women.) I then painted the speart-thrower with blood and whirled it around his head. He gasped. I whirled it again, and he kicked. I left him this way. I took another nest of green ants and shook it on the large intestine. When it comes out it is all red and swells. It is alive and it is like the heart.

"The ants bit him and the large intestine went back. The next time I shook them it went back further. The fourth time I did it, it ran in.

"I painted the spear-thrower with blood and whirled it around his head. He moved and breathed as though he were properly alive. I turned his tongue upside down and then hit him on the head with the spear-thrower. He spat his breath out and trilled his lips as he did it.

"I said, 'You go there,' and pointed toward his camp fire. I watched him as he walked. He went to his camp and sat down. He coughed and cleared his throat as he did this. I took the blood and put it over by the trees which are near the Macassar well. I circled through the mangrove jungle and came out by the camp. Before I left I told him he had three days to live. 'You will sleep one night here on the island and the next night you will sleep on the mainland. The next day you will die.'

"He got over on the mainland that next day and died."

Li-a-nun-ga (*Burera young man*).—"I went over to Cape Stewart to eat some palm trunk food. Lianunga had come over another way to this country. He was there ahead of me. He had gone out to get palm trunk food and had gathered it and put it by the well where he was burning and pounding it to make it ready for eating. I asked, 'Are you here by yourself?' He said, 'Yes.'

"He got up and walked a little way. I threw a fish spear and hit him in the left side under the arm. I use a fish spear so that it will not make a large hole and draw too much blood as other spears do. He fell down when he was hit. I left him and walked over and gathered some djelkurk [orchid] and morlupana [a lizard found around fresh water]. I also got some green ants.

"I pulled the spear and the blood came with it. The blood was black. I knew it was from the heart. I turned him on his side and elbow. It ran out very quickly, and it was black and not red. Soon it ran slowly and stopped. I took sweat from my nose and warmed my fingers over the fire. I put sweat on the spear-thrower after that. I didn't use green ants because the hole was a little one and they were not needed. I painted the spear-thrower with blood and whirled it around his head. He moved. I turned him over then and worked on the large intestine. I threw green ants on it. It came back a little way and stopped. Finally it went inside. I put more blood on the spear-thrower and hit him on the head and turned his tongue. I painted the spear-thrower again and whirled it. He breathed deeply and blew on his lips. I straightened his fingers and toes and eyelashes.

"I said, 'You go along to the sun beach with your food.' He went to look for fish. I came out to the camp too. I saw him and sat down. I had told him he would die next day. The next day he was dead."

Mur-in-dit.—"Murindit was cooking fish on the mainland on this side of Cape Stewart. I followed his tracks down there. Milanginunga, an old man, asked me to kill Murindit because the young man was sweethearting with his wife. He did not want to fight that boy because Murindit was young and strong and Milanginunga was old. I gave him a sting-ray fish. I told him to go wash it while I went to spear some more. I went down to the sea and speared a shark. While I was doing this I thought, 'That old man has asked me to kill him.'

"I looked around. The men were a long way off. I was going to kill him by magic with the fish spear but he was in the jungle looking for fresh water. I went down to the well. He had started to clean the stingray. I sat down beside him and helped him. When the cleaning was finished he gave me some of the fish. I stood up. While I stood there I thought, 'I'll get him now.'

"I grabbed him. He fought and fought. He tried to get away. I held his arms. I put a hand down on his scrotum and pulled it. This broke the strings holding it. He fell down. I looked around for an orchid to cover my hands and arms but I found another tree, barlk barlk.

"I opened him at the shoulder bone because I was in a hurry. I took the spear-thrower and broke the flesh where the bone meets the shoulder on the left side and pushed my hands in until I felt his heart. [There is a belief among the Murngin that the throat and heart have direct connection and that the heart inhales and exhales breath through the throat.]

"I stuck the heart with my killing stick and pulled the stick out and held the body at the waist with the head and trunk down. The blood came very quickly, and then slowly until it stopped. I swallowed his soul. I closed up the wound I had made with ants and the spear-thrower as I told you before. I took my killing stick and stuck a necklace of marks all around his neck because he was Dua. This was to make him like a flying fox hanging from a tree. I mixed up grease from my nose and sweat from my arms and rubbed these holes and shut them up. I rubbed blood then on my spear-thrower and whirled it. He turned a little.

"I then turned him over and fixed his large intestine. I got a large nest of green ants and scattered them on the large intestine. I did this four times.

"I then carried the basket of blood and hid it away. I took a little out with the spear-thrower. I rubbed it on the spear-thrower and hit him on the head and twisted his tongue. I pulled his eyelashes, fingers and toes. I told him for two days he would be alive and the third day he would die.

" 'Come in,' he said, 'we'll cook this sting ray and eat it.'

"I said, 'You have been asleep and left me all the work to do.'

"He said, 'Yes, I have been in a very deep sleep.'

"He didn't eat and went home. I came the other way. He slept that night. Next day he went out fishing and got some oysters. He went another day. Next day he tied his chest and head up with a curing string. He was sick. He died without eating, in the middle of the night."

Other Varieties of Magic

In addition to the ordinary soul-stealing there are several other varieties of magic found among the Murngin. Among them are projection of foreign objects into the victim (see under white magic), image magic, singing magic, possession by an evil spirit, and dream magic.

Image magic (bidji).—This can be performed by anyone. The person (or persons) who is interested in destroying another mixes up a number of colors and paints the image of his intended victim on a large stone. The head represents that of the man, the nose and ears are kangaroo's, the arms, fingers and legs a human being's, the foot kangaroo's, the scrotum a man's, and the penis kangaroo's. During the period of painting, the man or men talk to the image, saying, "You will kill So and So." The name of the victim is pronounced. When the image is completed the magicians gather a large quantity of firewood and place it underneath the stone and around it, light it, and while the blaze burns they talk to it: "You must let us know by and by when you break, Stone, you must let us know when you make that popping noise when you break." The fire burns, and the stone becomes so heated that it finally breaks. Meanwhile the men who have painted the image watch and listen. When the stone finally breaks they know that the soul of their victim, who may be far away, will scream in pain "Ya-kai! Ya-kai!" because the soul and heart of the man have been affected in exactly the same way as the stone; the men who have painted the image can always hear the man cry out.

It is believed that in two or three days after the stone breaks the victim will wake up from his sleep and feel very weak and ill, that his body will swell up, his ears grow large and his nose run with blood, that his elbows and nails will split and his skin and testes crack. The man will walk around one year or more before he dies. The men who have done the killing tell of it after a time, saying, "We did this thing for him, we killed him." The news travels and soon everyone knows it. Gradually the living man's fingers slough off, and in time he dies.

From the above description of how image magic affects its victims it can be discerned that leprosy is felt to result from this variety of sorcery. The relatives of a man who has died of leprosy always feel that they must retaliate, for they believe that members of an enemy clan have caused the disease—despite the fact that the victim may have eaten stale fish (see page 133).

Singing Magic.—The Murngin believe that certain songs are the most deadly of all magic. Three men were spoken of as singing magicians, all of them being trusted informants of mine. Not one of them would admit that he had this ability. It was my belief that they were telling the truth. Possibly the tribes farther south use some sort of singing death magic, but I collected no evidence in proof of this. There is no question but that everyone is extremely afraid of it. All warned me not to attempt to have anyone sing it for me, since it was too dangerous and would be likely to kill me. This was said even by the men who were willing and anxious to demonstrate the sorcery which removed the soul by the opening of the heart.

If a man who has sung another suddenly changes his mind and wishes to save him, he can swim out into the water at daylight, wash himself, return to the shore, and paint himself with red ocher. But it is insisted that if the singer did not swim and paint himself his victim would surely die. According to the natives the far-off country to the south is where all the people sing this death magic against the men of the north. This region to the south is no definite place. It is here "that stones walk like men." "These stones walk around and sing these songs, and men follow and listen and learn them and sing them and make the men in the north sick."

One of the most deadly songs is the whitefish song. The breath of its victim comes rapidly and very hard, which means that the fish has eaten out the insides of the person. The tide regulates the time of the death. When it comes in, the victim becomes extremely ill, his heart beats very fast, and everyone says, "Who has done this and who has sung this song?" When the tide goes out again, the person becomes a little stronger, and when it has reached its lowest ebb he feels almost normal. As the tide comes in the victim becomes sicker and continues to grow weaker until at full tide he dies.

Balliman's sister was very ill with bronchial pneumonia. Everyone knew she had been "sung" by the whitefish song because she continued to expectorate and vomit. When she became sick the tide was well in; when it went out she got better. Ultimately, in spite of this extremely strong magic, she recovered. During the crisis there was talk about everyone's being forced to go in swimming in order that the old men could see who had done the singing by observing those who refused to go in: they would be guilty. Nothing came of the talk. Although the woman was supposed to die from this powerful magic and everyone was certain she had been sung, there seemed to be no criticism of the belief after it had failed to operate.

Possession by a Mokoi.—The Murngin believe that deafness, dumbness, and insanity are due to possession of the afflicted one by a mokoi. Other illnesses are also caused by the entrance of a mokoi into the head of the victim. There were two deaf and dumb men in the group, one of them a near inbecile, the other mentally normal. The first had to be watched and taken care of by all the others in order to remain alive, while the second provided for himself and was treated like any other man except that he talked and was spoken to by a sign language. The relatives of these two assume that mokois had entered their heads and that some day they would be led out into the bush, where someone would steal their souls, for "plenty of crazy men have been killed that way." It is thought that when these men were babies a dog had walked over the body of the more normal one a few times but had then been kicked out of the way; while the dog had walked over the other one several times, thus making him much more insane. "That one [the normal one]," said his brother, "when he was a baby a dog walked over him once and maybe twice. That made it so he couldn't hear or talk. I think that other one had a dog walk over him five or six times before his mother kicked that dog. I think that when the mother of that first boy kicked that dog he yelped and that is the reason he is not silly like that other crazy man. That other dog just went 'Unh' and didn't call out, and that is the reason his head is no good."

Image Whipping.—Another form of magic is to draw an image and then go over the whole of the body, naming each part and using the name of the intended victim. The image is then whipped with strings. This will cause a man's body to rot to pieces, and it is supposed to have killed several men among the various tribes in northeastern Arnhem Land.

Dreaming and Magic.—A bad dream can also cause sickness. Dreams of an open grave, of a recently dead man, or of the totemic emblem are among those which cause a man to rise from his sleep, build up his fire, put a branch of green leaves in the fire until it is smoking, brush himself off, and, if it seems to have been a particularly unpleasant dream, brush off the members of his immediate family.

Excretion and Magic.—There is a certain amount of fear among the Murngin that excreta or waste food products will be picked up by an enemy sorcerer and used to inflict sickness upon them. The belief, however, is not very strong, since no great care is exercised to hide this matter so that it cannot be used by the sorcerers. A man, however, before urinating or defecating, digs a hole and squats over it. He is seldom seen standing while urinating. Women squat too, but when in the bush put their hands on their knees and bend their knees slightly while remaining partially upright.

If there is a particular fear of magic, fish bones, kangaroo bones, anything that a man or woman has been eating are carefully picked up and hidden.

The magicians are believed to take the excrement at times and place it in a fire where there are hot stones which are supposed to make the victim very ill; at other times it is placed between the limbs of two trees, as are the pieces of refuse; the rubbing of the branches causes a sore in the victim's throat.

C. White Magic and the Healer

White magic is an effective force used to cure sickness, heal wounds, take away the malignant effect of a snake bite, and, in general, to remove from the individual a feeling of dysphoria and to give him a sense of well-being and adjustment to his community.

The white magician usually performs this function and applies this power. He can remove foreign objects which have been shot into the body of the sick man, and diagnose on the principle that the patient can live if the cause of illness is only a foreign object, but must die if his soul is stolen.

Individuality and Social Personality of the White Magician.—The individuality of the white magician is not different from that of the ordinary man. The only noticeable tendency in all the observed healers was their joviality and pleasantness in their ordinary social relations. There were no indications of the psychopathic personality, for psychologically and physically they were a very normal group.

The social personality of the healer is different from that of the ordinary man's only because of his additional magical powers; otherwise he participates in the culture much the same as anyone else. He marries, has children, hunts, fishes, fights, and enters the ceremonial life in a manner no different from that of other men. There is but one rigid taboo on his behavior: he canont submerge himself in salt water without losing his power. Evidence is conflicting as to the existence of food taboos. If there are such, they were not observed nor did the magicians admit any. The most successful healers were observed eating the foods which some of the evidence claimed were taboo to them. The reason for the belief in such restrictions seems to be that during their novitiate they undergo certain food privations.

The healer gains his power through extraordinary experiences with two or possibly three soul-children who afterwards become his helpers. Both the medicine man and his familiars are called marngit. He can, in some cases, foretell the future and read a man's mind.

The doctor diagnoses but does not announce the findings in his case. If the illness has been caused by intrusion, he uses a gentle massage to force the foreign object within the victim's body to a certain spot where it can be sucked out by the healer. If the sick man's soul has been stolen the magician can look through his body, see that his heart is empty and his body rotten, and he immediately predicts death. He may say that a man is possessed by a mokoi, since he is deaf, dumb, or insane. Other variations in the diagnostic process will be described later.

A good doctor can always find out who has stolen the soul of a man murdered by magic. One means of diagnosis is to take the armlet or hair of a dead man, place it on a stick which is put in the ground, stand off at some distance, stare continuously at the stick, and concentrate upon it. The doctor then sneaks up to the stick and hits it with his spirit bag. The spirits of the magicians who have killed the man jump out and the doctor recognizes them. He then informs the victim's clansmen. Sometimes he catches the spirits of the magicians when they jump. Everyone watches him, for the performance is public. When the medicine man tells the relatives of the dead man the names of the black magicians, the kinsmen ask him to try to kill the spirits of the sorcerers. Sometimes the diagnostician takes the hairs of the magician and crushes their spirits in his hands, which is supposed to kill the sorcerers.

One of the wives of a prominent man in the camp had recently died. Amburro, one of the older white magicians, came up to the hut. He saw some of the woman's hair. He said, "Amburro has come too late. If I had come before, she would not have died. She did not die for nothing. Somebody has stolen her soul and has killed her." Amburro said to the husband, "Have you got anything that I can have that belongs to that woman?" The husband said, "Yes, I have her hair here." The husband took some of the hair and enclosed it in the palms of his hands as directed by the doctor, whom he approached, opening his hands very slowly. Amburro grabbed the hair and held it in his fist. He opened it very slowly. He looked inside. He said immediately, "Those two magicians from inside the bush did that," and he gave their names.

The Ma-tji-tji or Spirit Bag of the White Magician.—White magicians usually have a small woven bag stuffed with bush cotton and attached to a head circlet, which is placed around the head so that the bag hangs by the ear of the wearer. The familiars of the magician are supposed to inhabit the matjitji; and when a magician parts with an old one he first rubs it under his arms and then against the new bag to allow his spirits to enter this other bag.

The natives in the western part of the territory of the eight tribes use these bags generally for good luck in hunting or to hold in their mouths when they are fighting. Its use is not confined to the magician.

Willidjungo Acquires Power and Becomes a Medicine Man.—The healer Willidjungo, one of the most active and respected white magicians among all the tribes in northeastern Arnhem Land, was a large, rather heavy-set man with a mop of straight hair. He was very amiable and inclined to joviality. He had six wives and a number of children. He belonged to the Yandjinung linguistic group, which is in the western part of the area. He had all the abilities accredited to the ordinary healer type, but unlike a few of the magicians he could not kill as well as cure.

One day when Willidjungo was a mature man having several wives and children he was out in the bush looking for wild honeybees' nests. After a time he decided to return home. On his way back to camp he felt a pain in his right leg near the hip. He knew afterwards that the familiars which he later acquired had given it to him. His leg became very stiff and stayed that way for over a week. During this time he lay in the camp and covered himself with paper bark to keep warm. One of Willidjungo's wives slept by him. The two familiars, who were a little boy and girl, started talking to him underneath the paper bark. They talked in a rhythmic chant: "Dul! dul! dul!—ter ter ter."

Said Willidjungo, "The sound was like a small frog out in the lilies."

Willidjungo woke up his wife. "You better sleep among the women tonight," he said. His wife left their hut and went over to her mother's and father's. She was very frightened of these two spirits. The two continued talking. They went back into the bush and Willidjungo followed them.

"I kept listening to that noise they were making. I listened but I did not look, and followed them. The two things came back to camp and I came with them. They sat down by my fire and talked. When it was night and dark those two spirits flew in the tops of the trees. They had the sound of a quail flying. They sat on the top of my head and on my shoulders. They had white feathers, but I did not know that at that time. I could only feel them on my head."

Morning came. Willidjungo went out to look for food and to fish. The spirits left and did not come back until the afternoon. "They did not come back for me then but I went out to look for them. I saw them out in the bush then for the first time. Their bodies looked like jabirus. Their eyes looked like your glasses. Their face and stomach looked like a man and their legs looked the same way. They had big stomachs like children. Their arms were like wings and had little feathers on them. Their wings had big feathers. They were standing on a tree. I took my spear-thrower. I put the hooked end under my arms and put sweat on it. I took it out then to reach for those two spirits. I caught them and put them under my arms. I held them in my hands like you would a small bird when you catch a wild one. They left me before I came back to camp. Before they left they said to me, 'You have a wife. It is better that you go back by yourself.' "

Willidjungo said, "Oh, no, I don't want to do that." He then said to them, "What are your names?"

"We are two na-ri [familiars]. Don't you try to cure people yet. If people are sick you let them alone and tell some other doctor to try to cure them."

"Then I came back to camp. Dorng's daughter was sick. I did nothing but look at her. She had a big hole in her chest. It had cracked open. I kept on looking. One of the old doctors tried to fix her but he couldn't do anything, but I didn't do anything. Afterwards I took the flesh and put it together and she became better right away the first time I tried. I made her well when she was half dead. Those two spirits talked to me then. They said, 'The first time you have tried you have done a good job. The next time anyone is sick you treat them. That is your work. We gave this to you and it will help you, but there are some things you cannot do. You must not go in the salt water and get covered with it. You must go along near the shore. If you go down under the salt water, we two will be dead.'

"If I should dive in the ocean these spirits would die. These two spirits come around at night, usually in the middle of the night. Yesterday I carried a kangaroo on my shoulder and pressed hard on my armpits. I hurt one of my familiars, and I am sore under my arm. Last night the little one that was not hurt left me and went into the bush to look for another spirit. The other one followed him. The sick one said, 'My master is sick now like me. You come and we will fix him.'

"The well one took something out of the sick one and they came back. They found something hard in my chest and took it out.

"When I was getting these spirits I went around very quietly and said nothing. I did not smoke very much. I only ate vegetable food and stayed in one place. I made an old doctor my friend. I fed him and gave him tobacco. One of the spirits left him and came with me."

Amburro, one of the old doctors of the western clans, watched Willidjungo's behavior very carefully. Finally he said, "He is a true doctor all right. He has some things sitting on his shoulder." Many people were skeptical about it at first, but they were convinced: Willidjungo disappeared into the bush one night, and when he came back they heard the clicking sound, a kind of beating against his shoulders. Everyone said, "He has those children there." From that time on everyone believed that he was a medicine man.

Other Powers of a White Magician.—The white magician has a number of additional powers by virtue of his familiars. The nature of these powers seems best explained by Willidjungo, the magician. All the things he claimed for himself were confirmed by his fellow tribesmen.

"When I treat people those two go right inside a man. That bone which is inside the man sticks right straight in him. I keep rubbing on the outside. Those two children of mine take hold of that bone and when I suck they jump out with it. Sometimes I can look right through a man and see that he is rotten inside. Those two go inside but they can do nothing. Sometimes when people steal a man's soul in the bush he comes here to my camp. I go look; he is empty inside. I say, 'I can't fix you up. Everything is gone. Your heart is still there, but it's empty. I can't fix you up.' Then I tell everybody he is going to die.

"Sometimes people carry a sick man to me and I see them coming a long way down the beach. I call out to those people, 'You people stand each side of him,' and I look in that man. Soon the souls of the two men who killed this sick man half dead come out. When I see this I call out the names of those two men who stole this man's soul.

"Before this, men and women have gone in the bush and have played with each other and one man's wife will be with another woman's husband. They say, 'We are going to spear kangaroo.' The man goes to spear kangaroo and then goes to find that woman. They come back. My spirit children come to me and say, 'That man and woman have played together out in the bush. You go tell that woman's husband.' I say, 'Oh, no, I won't do that. That will make trouble.' I do not tell their husbands and wives because that would make too much trouble in the camp.

"Sometimes I am sitting with a man and I look at his head and I can say to him, 'You think so and so.' The man says, 'How do you know that?' and I say, 'I can see inside your mind.'"

"Doctors like Willidjungo," I was told, "can find out about these things [soul-stealing]. They know what has happened—other people do not, they can only think, that is all." A medicine man can take the hair of a dead man, hide it in the stump of a tree and make a fire around it, after which he stands off at some distance from the fire and watches it very carefully for an hour or more: the spirits of the black magicians come out in the smoke and their faces are visible. The doctor comes back to the general camp and people say to him, "You have seen somebody, haven't you?" He replies, "Oh, no, I have seen nothing." If the magicians who have killed the man are still in the camp and hear this, they leave immediately, for they know the doctor knows who has done it and that he will tell the truth presently. The doctor then tells the relatives, who gather their spears to go kill the magicians and to avenge the death of their kinsman.

An old woman had been ill for a number of days in the camp. Willidjungo came up and looked at her and said, "That woman is going to die tonight." The other people said, "How do you know?" He replied, "My spirits told me." That night the old woman died.

Willidjungo was on Millingimbi Island in the Crocodile Group one day when he said that a certain clansman was dead on the mainland. The clansman's relatives said, "How do you know that?" He replied, "My spirit children flew over to the mainland and saw it and came back and told me." That same day some men came in a canoe from the mainland and brought the news that the man was dead.

Mun-yir-yir Acquires Power and Becomes a Medicine Man.—"I found my doctor spirits in my country, in the snake country. I was out hunting for bandicoot and I had caught one and was cooking him. I think perhaps those doctor spirits smelled that bandicoot cooking. I went down to a creek to get some water to drink. I leaned over and drank out of the water hole. When I did that a doctor soul caught my nose and made me sink down in the water. I was in a coma and fell in the water. The doctors, they were two boys and a girl, took my hand and put it in a dry place [to help him up]. They took out something from inside my body when I was sick after falling in the water and they opened my eyes and nose and mouth and made me well. They blew in my mouth. I got up and took my stone axe. I hit one of those doctor souls on the nose and I hit the others, too. They looked like opossums. When I caught them, one of the men doctor souls said, 'You make us well now.'

"I blew on the man and made him well, then I made the others well. They said to me, 'Now you go back to camp. Don't you eat dog any more, but you eat cold food and don't sleep near the fire.'

"When I got near the camp those opossums called out to me. They made a loud noise. The people said, 'Look out for Munyiryir. He has found some familiars.' These familiars hit their arms against their sides and made a popping noise. I came and sat down in my camp. I slept. I slept a little while in the night and went out in the bush. Those two took me to the bush with them. I did not try to make anybody well.

"I went to Elcho Island from the Naladaer country and then came back again to the mainland. Some of the people said to me, 'We are sick here in the chest. We don't feel well. Please, Munyiryir, help us.' I went then and took a shell and filled it with water and washed my hands. I felt over their chests and took out a bone and showed them. A man came from another country. He had a sore back. He said, 'I can't walk.' I looked from a long way and I saw that little hard thing inside him. I blew on his back and this thing came out a long way. I showed it to him. The other man went hunting for kangaroo then and his back didn't hurt him and he was very pleased.

"Those two spirits sit down on my shoulders. Sometimes they sit on my head. I call them my children. Sometimes they used to come to me in the night. They would say, 'There is a man sick over there.'

"In the early morning I would say, 'Where is that man?' and they would show me and they would say, 'He has got something inside him,' and they would show me where. Sometimes I used to take bushes and brush against the man and now blow on him and that hard thing would fall a long way from him.

"When I first started some of the people said, 'You are lying and not telling the truth.' I said to them, 'You look in my mouth.' I opened my mouth and let them see I had nothing in there."

A Case Record of Willidjungo's Treatments and Cures.—A Birkili clansman had an ache in his back. Willidjungo was called. He gave him the usual rubbing treatment, found the place that was painful, and removed a small stick. This had been placed within him, said Willidjungo, "by a mokoi. This mokoi was a swallow which swooped down over the camp. This bird is the mokoi of some very old dead person. He was angry because the victim had a yam stick in his possession that was owned by a Burera tribesman." The Burera are somewhat distant people from the Birkili and they are looked upon with extreme suspicion as great sorcerers by the tribes to the east of them. The mokoi, according to Willidjungo, had definitely tried to kill his patient. The mokois at times act in the rôle of vampire, since they can definitely attack a living man and make him ill or take away his good sense (make him insane).

Munyiryir, a former magician, had a very heavy cold in his lungs, which might have been a slight touch of pneumonia. After he had suffered a few days with it he called Willidjungo to treat him. Willidjungo brought his paraphernalia, including the spirit bag, a container of water, and, of course, his familiars. He removed a pointed stick from Munyiryir's side. He informed him that it was caused by an old mokoi. This mokoi came in the middle of the night and stood near their two camps (their huts were close together). In the middle of the night Willidjungo awakened his two wives and told them to look at the mokoi, which was standing by a tamarind tree. Both of them said that they had seen this ghost. When the ghost left, Willidjungo went back to sleep and the ghost went up to Munyiryir's and pushed the stick inside him. This was done because the victim had been given a ranga a long time back and had not returned the present to the owner of the totem.

Mahkarolla had been ill for a number of days with a very bad ache in his back which made him bend over to such an extent that he could not walk. He was in extreme pain. A number of years before he had fallen from a tree which had paralyzed his lower limbs for a short time. He sent for Willidjungo to treat him. Willidjungo arrived. He walked around him in a rather stately manner until he had covered a course of about a half circle. He then walked over to his patient, got down on his knees beside him and asked him to lie on his stomach. He washed his hands, took a mouthful of water and washed his mouth out and spat it on the ground. He felt all over the body with his fingers while examining the back carefully. He then rubbed his hand under his own armpit and again applied his hands to Mahkarolla's back. He massaged it carefully. He then removed the spirit bag from his head and rubbed it under each arm and against his head, then applied it to Mahkarolla's head and buttocks. The rubbing continued. Soon it was localized to one spot. The doctor then bent over his patient and put his mouth to the spot, in the lower part of his back. He blew against the place where the illness was supposed to be located, then sucked. He raised his mouth and spat. He spat again. He put his hand to his mouth and brought out a small stick about three inches in length and about the size of a small match in diameter. It looked like a large darning needle. Willidjungo diagnosed the case as due to a wrong that had been done his familiars, who had struck at Mahkarolla. There was probably more to it, but unfortunately this occurred when I first arrived in the field and I did not get all the details. Within two or three hours after this treatment the patient was well and walking around. He claimed that he felt all right.

Mahkarolla paid Willidjungo a stick of tobacco and some nut bread for the treatment. There must always be a payment made for a treatment by a magician.

Munyiryir, although he had been an excellent doctor and had cured a large number of people, suddenly lost his power because he unintentionally disobeyed the taboo, which, if broken, always destroys a doctor's familiars. This occurred within a few months before my arrival with the Murngin.

"I had been down," he said, "to the ocean. It was on the Goyder River side of Millingimbi Island. Those doctors of mine were sitting on my head and shoulders. I was out in a canoe standing in it when another canoe came along and hit our small one. I fell in the ocean and I was covered with the salt water. I heard those opossum children make noises. I put my hand on my head and they fell down inside the water when I came up. A little after that an old man was sick. 'I am sick inside here,' he said. [He touched his chest.] I looked to see what was inside him but I could see nothing now. My eye was too dark. I had lost my doctor children. I can't see anything now inside people. Everyone says that I have lost my very good thing that I had. It's too bad. I said to all the people then, 'I can't look out for you people any more. I fell down in the salt water and it covered me and I can't cure any more.' If I had fallen down in fresh water it would not have hurt those doctor children of mine."

Diagnosing Snake Bite.—Sometimes it is impossible for a man to determine what has stung or bitten him when he is walking barelegged through the high grass. The Murngin feel it is always necessary to know what has caused a thing. Magicians are called in to diagnose, of which there are at least two methods. In the southern and more interior clan territories, among such people as the Ritarngo, Djimba, Gunalbingu and Dai, when a man thinks he has been bitten by a snake that has crawled away without his seeing it, he finds a hollow pandanus log. He then takes some blood from the wound, places it on a handful of grass, and sticks the grass in one end of the old pandanus tree. He lights the dry grass, blows on the smoke, and watches to see it come out the other side. The snake spirit comes out of the hole. If it looks around for food the man who is bitten will die. If it hurries away he is certain to live. By the other method of diagnosing a snake bite the magician rubs the injured part with one hand while with the other he holds a long thin grass stalk. The grass stalk is moved around the ground with great delicacy and is raised and lowered a number of times. In time some little particle of earth, a grass seed or a bit of bark, will adhere to the end of the stick. If it is only a grass seed or some tiny minute particle the magician diagnoses the bite as that of a small snake. If it is large, the snake is a large one. This diagnosis is also supposed to cure the injury.

Rain Magic.—It is not necessary to be a magician in order to make rain. Anyone can do it, providing he follows the correct procedure. No one would attempt to make rain during the dry season, since this is an improper time for it and nobody wants it then. However, if the dry season continues too long a number of people, usually ceremonial leaders of the various clans, attempt to end it. To make rain, a man gathers a large bundle of green grass and fashions a human image of it, then digs a hole, puts in the image, and buries it. It is left there and starts to swell up. As soon as it does so noticeably, the rain starts.

Another method is to take a pile of dangi bark (used for poisoning fish) and beat it thoroughly with a stone. Large armfuls of green grass are then gathered, the dangi is placed inside of the grass, and all of it tied in a bundle. Stones are then placed on top of the grass, and the bundle is carried out into the sea or fresh water to the height of a man's shoulders and dropped. The man then comes up out of the water and sings the sound of rain falling and pushes the water with his hand, which causes it to splash as though rain were falling in it. He says, "In three days there will be clouds and in four days there will be rain."

The bundle can also be made into a human image, which can be and usually is given the name of the maker.

If one wants the rain to cease, the grass is taken out and thrown about so that it will dry, and the rain then stops. If it continues to such an extent that a huge flood sweeps down from the bush country a very powerful medicine man may dive into the flood water, catch the offending sacred python who is causing the flood, and send him back into his water house, which causes the waters to recede. A few years ago a tremendous flood came down the Buckingham River and went higher and higher until the people climbed the highest trees with their babies and dogs. The flood came still higher and faster, and finally it knocked some of the children, dogs, and babies, and a few of the older people into the water and drowned them. Warlumbopo, the Ritarngo medicine man, with the help of his familiars, dived in the water and caught Muit, the totemic python, pulled him back, and sent him down into the well again. The rain stopped and the flood ceased. Only medicine men understand how to do this.

Murngin believe they cannot stop rain if it comes by itself. Sometimes they think that it has been caused by people in other countries performing the magic. Nothing can be done about it unless the people themselves take the proper methods to stop the magic from working.

THE MURNGIN PHARMACOPOEIA

The Murngin do not depend entirely upon magic for curing their illnesses. They have a fairly extensive pharmacopoeia which includes both animal and plant remedies. Each illness has a special treatment applied to it. If a sick man has been treated with herbs he can also be treated by magic, which is felt to be much more potent. Some of the herb remedies have magic mixed in with them.

Vomiting and Stomachache.—A nest of green ants is gathered, placed in a water-tight container, and put over a fire to kill the ants and eggs. Water is then poured upon the contents and the ants crushed in the hands so that the acid from the insects becomes infused into the water. The water is then drunk by the person who is ill. If a baby has a stomach complaint he is forced to drink some of this liquid, and the mother's breasts are rubbed with it. The natives say that it tastes much like tamarind bean soup.

Diarrhea or Dysentery.—One of the treatments for dysentery and diarrhea is to take some of the excrement and place it near a red ant bed. The ants carry the excrement inside their mound. This is supposed to cure a man in a short time, since there is a mingling of the power of the ant bed and of the man.

Headache.—The leaves of the mu-tir (unidentified) are gathered by a woman, and an infusion of them is made and rubbed over the head, face, and upper body of the ailing person. The leaves are rough, and the Murngin say, "This is just the same as rubbing sand over the body. It feels rough. When a man has a headache it is just the same as if he had dirt on his head and this cleans it off."

Sore Throat.—Drinking an infusion of broken-up leaves of the paper-bark tree is supposed to relieve a sore throat; sometimes it is drunk only for the pleasure. The fruit from the ne-urk tree is chewed to relieve a cough.

Heavy Throat or Chest Cold (girri girri).—The inner bark of the stringy-bark eucalyptus tree is chewed and swallowed to relieve congestion.

Tooth- or Earache.—The bark of the small plum tree found in the area is removed, the trunk is put in the fire until it becomes hot, and a portion is placed over the aching tooth or against the ear.

Bungeye (bam-bai).—This ailment is frequent among the natives and goes through a group every few months. Either one or both of the eyes swell and close for three or four days. Salt water is poured on shavings of the plum tree (dangapa). The infusion is then poured into the eyes of the prone patient for half an hour or so.—Bungeye is supposed to be caused by dirt in the corner of the eye, and not by watching anything which is ritually unclean.

Granuloma, Yaws, and Wound from a Spear.—The bark is taken from the tree which produces fish poison, broken up, and placed in water. The container is put on red-hot stones to heat. When the water has boiled sufficiently to form a poultice the latter is cooled slightly and placed on the sore or wound.

Granuloma, yaws, and spear wounds can all be caused by magic. It is thought that a magician can cause them by stabbing a sting-ray prong into the track of his victim while at the same time calling out the name of the object of his magic or by singing one of the black magic songs. It is also believed that yaws in the nose and mouth can be caused by a man's throwing away his nasal septum stick, which is found by an enemy and placed between two branches of a tree that rub together. This smashes the nose piece, and the man's nose and mouth are affected by this process.

Sometimes if a man has a yaws sore on his foot a live clam is found and the foot placed over it. The clam is supposed to suck the soreness from it. When a man has been wounded, frequently one of his kinsmen places his fingers in the wound to see if the spear has gone through to a vital spot or not. If he cannot feel flesh at the end of his finger it is believed the man will die.

Sting-ray or Catfish Wound.—A variety of the bush beetle is macerated and rubbed on the wound. "It makes the sore feel quiet and easy." Cockroaches are also used in the same way.

Poisoning from Untreated Cycad Palm Nuts.—Occasionally children are made violently ill or die from eating untreated cycad nuts. The natives attempt a cure by rubbing the hair with the stickers from the leaf of the pandanus.

Ringworm (pur-o-pur-o).—This is "caused from nothing," for, according to Murngin thinking, it is due to a man's scratching himself, no magic being involved. Ringworm is treated by rubbing the offal found in a bees' nest or red ocher on the ringworm scales.

Constipation.—The yellow pollen found in a honeybees' nest is eaten dry. "It acts just like that Epsom salts you have," said my informant.

Festering Splinters.—The splinter is allowed to remain in the flesh until it festers, when it is easily taken out. Beeswax is made into a small splinter and pushed into the hole where the splinter has been. A firebrand is then touched to the end of the wax; this melts the inner part of it and allows it to penetrate farther into the sore. This is done particularly if the splinter is in the foot for it enables the man to walk more easily.

Infected Wounds.—Hot ashes or hot sand are placed on the wound to remove the soreness, or a log is heated until it is burning all over, the fire is quenched and the log covered with paper bark; the man lies on it, placing the sore part against it. This treatment is also applied to a toddling child to help him walk better; as soon as he starts walking the heated log is placed against his knees to strengthen them.

CHAPTER VIII

A SOCIOLOGICAL INTERPRETATION OF MAGIC

SECTION I. THE PROBLEM OF RITUAL AND MAGIC PRESENTED BY THE NORTHERN AND SOUTHERN AREAS

SINCE the northeastern clans share a belief in magic but lack magical techniques and magicians, the people there either are forced to travel to the south and west for treatment by white magicians, such visits being comparatively rare, or resort to other means found within their own area.

In the south and west black and white magicians are found who have definite techniques for curing and for killing.

The social organizations of the two areas are identical; the totemic situation is the same, and in general there is little variation in the culture except for magical practices. With magical treatment absent in the north, the problem arises as to what to substitute for it, since there is the obvious necessity of attempting to cure an ailing man.

Throughout the north there is a general *belief* in black magic, but it is ascribed to sorcerers operating in the south. The relevant northern thinking on illness is not different from that in the southern area where the offending magician is also an outsider of the clan and the near kinship group. The difference is that there is no sorcerer within the northern groups to whom the people can appeal for punitive magic. It is analogous to knowing the effects of heavy artillery but not possessing it. The magical folklore of the north is sufficiently gruesome to cause the most fearsome apprehension in the minds of people who believe their illnesses caused by such practices.

The two more common accounts of black magical practices believed in throughout the northern Murngin clans and among all the surrounding tribes follow.

1. Two or three magicians follow a man when he is by himself, rush upon him, and throw a spear into him. The man falls down and the others rush upon him. He is in a kind of coma. The mouth cannot move but

the heart is still beating. "He is like he is asleep." He is laid on his stomach and a log is placed across his back and another one on his neck. The magicians first make fire, next gather some grass or paper bark and warm it over the fire, then place it against the skin of the victim to make it become soft and as though it were rotting. The sorcerers next gather a branch full of green ants and shake the ants over the man. The ants start stinging and biting him. The man kicks, starts crying out. Meanwhile, one of the black magicians has climbed up a nearby tree. He places his legs over a limb and hangs with his head down and looks over his shoulder at the "dead" man. The other two magicians command the "dead" man, "Look this way," and they point at the man in the tree. The man looks. "Oh, yes, there is a mokoi [trickster spirit] there," he says. The magicians then say to him, "A snake will bite you. You are a very weak man now." They say this over to him several times to make him remember. The man then gets up and picks up his spear. He wants to hit this mokoi. The two men say, "What have you been doing?" The man is a bit groggy and says, "I have been having a very long sleep." After that the men ask him, "What is the name of this mokoi?" The man replies with his grandfather's name. The man in the tree comes down and the three magicians and their victim leave. The man who has been in the tree playing the part of the mokoi gathers handfuls of bushes while the other two magicians watch. The victim stares at him. The sorcerer with the bushes hits the ailing man with them and cries out "Phee!" The skin of the man struck breaks open, his black skin being removed and his body becoming clear and white. The other two men take hold of him then, and after a little time his skin once more turns black. The two men walk along beside their victim while the man who was in the tree runs a few hundred yards away and waits for their approach. When they get near him he yells at the victim and once more the latter's skin turns white and gradually turns black again. Again the magician who has been in the tree runs, hides and waits for the others to come near him. Once more he cries out and the white coloring comes from "the center of the body from head to feet." The magician who has waited for them now says, "This sick one is properly dead." The man who has been treated by the magicians still has a wound showing where the spear has hit him. When he gets near the camp so he can hear the murmur of the camp voices the flies come out, bite upon the wound and close it up so that when he gets into the camp there is no indication that the flesh has been disturbed. By the time he has reached the camp the magic has made him forget the operation of the medicine men although he has some kind of vague memory of it about which he tries to tell his relatives. He says to them, "I will tell you one thing." The relative says, "Yes, tell me." The victim replies, "Oh, nothing." He tries to remember but all he can say is "Oh, nothing." He lies down and goes to sleep. The next morning he walks around and feels all right. The next day he feels well, but he goes out in a canoe to fish and a shark comes up and kills him. "It might be that he goes out to hunt and a snake will bite and finish him or a crocodile catch him. He is like dead now."

2. Two or three magicians make up their minds to kill someone who has wronged one of them. The wrong may be no more than a failure to keep a promise to give one of them a bundle of spears. The magicians say to the man, "We know where there are a lot of fish and where there are a great number of kangaroo out in the bush. Come with us and we will show you." When they have gone a short distance into the bush or jungle one of the magicians winks knowingly at one of the others. They get a spear and one of them throws it into the man. The others rush upon him and hold him. When they have him down, one of them says, "I gave you a long time ago some spears and you promised me some in return and you have given me nothing." The man says, "Oh, let me go." The others say, "It is too late." They then place him on his stomach and put a log on his neck and another on his back. They sit still a little while. One man then cuts some paper bark and makes a small basket and another prepares a fire stick for future use. The victim is in a faint. They cut his side open above his heart. They open his heart and the blood runs out into the basket. "If you don't open his heart with a killing stick and let that blood out the man will not die." The fire has been made with the fire stick. Some clay is gathered and put on the sore. The clay heals the sore so that no one can see where it has been. Some green ants are gathered and thrown upon his body to force him to awaken. The victim kicks. When he does this, one of the men climbs up a tree. When the man awakens he says, "I have been in a very deep sleep." The man looks up and sees the other magician hanging down from his knees with his head looking over his shoulder at the victim. The wounded man says, "Ah, that is my grandfather looking for me. Give me a spear and I will kill him. He is my grandfather's soul." The magician comes down out of the tree then. The victim says, "I am going to tell everyone." The two magicians take hold of him and start walking with him. The other runs on in front of them and hides himself. When they get near him he cries out. This frightens the injured man and his skin turns white, then gradually black again. Once more the magician runs on ahead and hides and as they approach shouts again, and once more the body of the victim turns white and then returns to its natural color. This is repeated one or more times. The victim wants to fight but by this time he has become light-headed and talks crazily. When he says again that he is going to tell his relatives, the magicians command him to open his mouth and to stick his tongue out. He obeys and they twist his tongue upside down. The man leaves them

and goes to the camp. As he approaches it he can hear the many noises of the general camp. A swarm of flies come out from the camp, light upon the sore, and feed upon it. The sore heals rapidly so that no trace is left of the wound. When the man enters the camp he says to his relatives, "I have something I want to tell you." His relatives reply, "Yes, you must tell us." But the victim can only say, "Nothing." In a few days he dies. The magicians return to where they have opened the heart of their victim and clean up the place so that there is no trace left of their operations. They gather up the basket of blood and take it with them.

The Stealing of a Woman's Soul According to the Folklore of the Northern Clans

Two or three men sneak out into the bush and wait for the arrival of the woman they expect to kill. They pretend to hunt for food but actually they are looking for the woman. When they see her they take the stone heads out of their spears, place the spear shaft in their spear-throwers and wait. When she is close enough they throw their spears, trying to hit her in the breast. The woman drops as though she were dead. At other times one of the men pretends that he is calling her to flirt with her and she comes over. He asks her to lie down beside a clump of bushes and she thinks that he is going to lie on top of her. Instead of this he kicks her Mount of Venus with his heel. The woman faints.

The men start operating on her. They do not cut her as they would a man. The sorcerer who is to open her heart wraps his hand up very tightly with string. The doctor pushes his hand, with the killing stick in it, up through her uterus. All the men turn their heads and backs, refusing to look at the vagina. If they should look there is great danger of spoiling the effects of the magic; they are liable to be overcome with sexual desire, causing an erection which would destroy the magic because it would be bad luck.

When the sorcerer reaches the heart he thrusts the killing stick in it and allows the blood and spirit to come out. The heart's blood is buried.

The sorcerers now make a fire and put stones in it. When the stones have become red hot, they take lily leaves which have been soaked in water and throw them on the fire. They put the steaming leaves inside the woman and the steam is supposed to heal the wound and hide all trace of the effects of the black magic.

A branch which has a green ants' net on it is held by one of the men while he shakes it over the legs of the victim. She kicks and awakens. One of the men runs and climbs a tree just before she is completely awake. A sorcerer on the ground says to her, "What is the name of that woman up that tree?"

The woman replies, "That is my grandmother who has been dead a long time." The woman attempts to hit the man who is up the tree with her yam stick because she thinks him to be the soul of her dead ancestress.

The remainder of the process is exactly the same as that for a man.

Ritualistic Curing of Illness in the North

When a person is ill in the north he is placed in a specially prepared representation of the totemic well of his clan. This can be con-

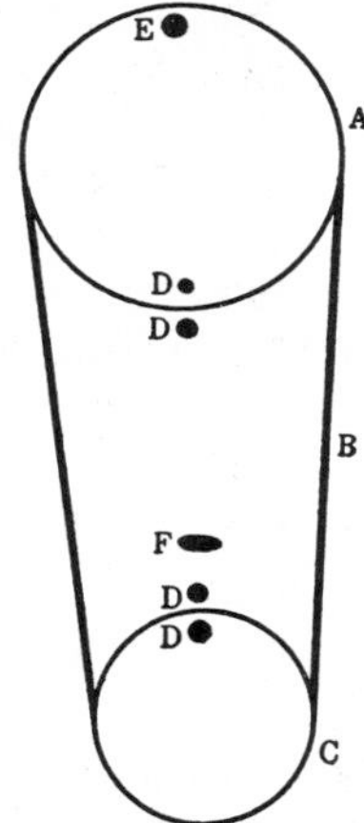

FIGURE 2.—SYMBOLIC TOTEM WELL FOR CURING RITUAL

structed at any place where the people happen to be camping, or on the ceremonial ground. The well consists of two circles connected by a channel (see Figure 2). One circle, slightly larger than the other, is about four and one-half feet in diameter (A), the other being about three feet in diameter (C). The connecting channel is about ten feet long and about two feet wide (B). The well is made by excavating earth with the hands from the center and piling it up six inches to one foot high along the outline of the channel. Leaves are placed over the heaped-up earth. The larger circle represents the actual totem well found in the clan country of the sick man. The channel is the place where the water flows out of this particular well, and the smaller circle is the "hole where the fresh water comes out." This conventional pattern is always used to symbolize a totemic well, no matter whether it be of the Yiritja or the Dua moiety. Holes are made connecting the various compartments (D), one from the large well to the channel and another from the channel to the small well. These are supposed to allow the water to come through. The holes are filled with leaves and grass. A shell full of water (E) is placed at the head end of the larger circle, and a rock (F) is placed in the channel. This represents a rock found in the actual well and the fresh water which comes out of the spring. The sick man is placed in the larger circle which is the totem well. The male members of the clan gather about it and sing the garma song, which particularly describes some activity surrounding the clan well and identifies the clan as a separate unit or part of the moiety. If a Dua man were ill, the members would sing the two old creator women, who, on coming back from hunting food, found their totemic emblems had been stolen by the men. The names of the women, references to the types of totems, and the shouts of the men who had stolen the emblems would be part of the song sequence. Red ocher is then sung by the chorus while a man is preparing some red ocher on the stone found in the smaller circle, and water is poured over the patient. The red ocher is then rubbed all over the body of the sick man. When this operation is completed the singing stops and the ceremony is over.

The Relation of a Prophylactic Ritual to Healing Magic

The relation of this ritual to the art of curing by magic is the same as the relation between preventive medicine and ordinary doctoring in our society. In modern society, preventive medicine recognizes the fundamental causes of disease and tries to prevent their being present and active in a community so that none of the members can be made ill by them; therapeutic medicine becomes active if preventive medicine fails. The disease by this time has struck certain members of the community; the cause must be removed, but by different techniques—different not in kind, but only in degree. Both are scientific methods and both combat certain types of diseases which fit into certain scientific concepts and classifications.

The prophylactic totemic ritual averts illness from anyone who participates in it and from the group generally; on the contrary, anyone who does not participate in it will be ill. Illness and general dysphoria are prevented by removing the accumulated ritualistic uncleanliness through the totemic rites of purification. During the year certain people become ritualistically unclean by breaking certain taboos and by a lax observance of the tribal laws. Magic and ritual cleanse them and the society generally.

It has been pointed out above that the source of ritual power which can kill or cure is in the totemic well and surrounding sacred rituals and objects. They belong to the general category of "inside" or sacred. The power of magic to secure these same effects comes directly from the dead, who belong to the same "inside" category as contrasted with the "outside." The two categories are both "dal" or sacred, and both ritual and magic are channels by which this power can be correctly expressed in the world of the profane.

Section II. A Sociological Interpretation of Black and White Magic—How Magic Works

Statement of the Problem

Durkheim's "church" among the Arunta is a clan organization. Each clan celebrates its spiritual unity through the unifying concept of the totem and with such objective symbols as the totemic emblem, its rituals and myths. Magic and the magician, on the other hand, fail to become part of religion and are antithetical to it because they have no church, says Durkheim. The magician as an individual manipulates techniques, and his power is the opposite of that of the priest (or ceremonial leader), who functions as ritual leader of the group. It is the thesis of this chapter that the essential nature of magic and ritual is the same, both expressing a fundamental unity and functioning alike for the individual and for the group, at least in Murngin society.

The analysis of Murngin magic to determine its nature is divided as follows: (1) a test of the magical belief of the north, which does not possess magical "techniques," with that of the south, which does; (2) an examination of the social configuration of magic in the south by (a) seeing what part ritual plays not only in the north but in the south, and (b) examining how the individual and the society behave when magic is put into effect.

The Test of the Northern and Southern Areas

The Murngin offer an excellent opportunity to study the nature of magic in relation to the social organization and society generally, particularly in relation to religion. The northern and eastern clans lack the medicine men of the southern and western clans and depend on one of the rituals for healing. The social organization of both groups is identical, the kinship system, the moiety divisions, et cetera, being the same even to minute detail. We can thus observe what elements are found in the non-personalized magic of the north and how they operate in the area of the southern shamans. From this we can possibly find out what generalized elements of the culture are organized into the social personality of the medicine man. As our analysis develops, it may be possible to determine whether ritual and magic are essentially different in their fundamentals. In the north therapeutic magic is a curative ritual; the two are one. The ritual used here is that of parts of the mourning ceremony belonging to the ordinary garma variety. This curing ritual may serve as a circumcision rite if the group needs a short ceremony to circumcise a boy before the wet season starts, for otherwise they will have to wait until the next dry season, running the chance of the boy's being too big for the operation.

The society goes through a prophylactic performance at its yearly totemic ritual;[1] at the death of a member there is a prophylactic ceremony in the mourning rite for the recently dead, which, in that aspect of its expression, is as much magical as it is religious, the purposes and social forces back of it being both. If the mourning ceremony were not held the soul would linger with the living, causing sickness and possible death. The leaf ceremony in the mourning rite chases the dead soul away. The various communions exclude the soul from the group, the entire mourning ceremony forcing it out of the society and into the totemic well. The sacred cannot remain with the profane: as Durkheim has pointed out, sacredness is contagious, hence dangerous (a lingering soul might make the living ill), and the two realms must be kept separate.

The medicine man who removes the hard object injected by a malignant mokoi, or the bone injected by an outraged totemic being or another sorcerer, is doing the same thing for the society and its individuals as the mourning rite. The magician too is performing a ritual which has no validity, since he has no position or power, unless the group sanctions it. The medicine man's social personality and the sources of his power are located within the group. The white magician is but the reverse of the coin on whose other surface appears the black sorcerer. The white magician through his personal mana helps the sick individual readjust himself to his social environment.

A prerequisite of social conditioning and adjustment is a normal organism, normal not only in biological fact but also in the values of the group. The normal human being not only among the savage Murngin but in any society, according to the evaluations of the

[1] See Chapter IX, Murngin Totemism.

group, is the "well" person. Sickness is felt by civilized man to be expectable but not normal, largely because sickness interferes with his ordinary participation in his culture. Both the savage and the civilized man consider sickness out of the ordinary, even though all organisms experience it, not only because of the lack of physical well-being but because the individual's daily social life is changed.

The effect of black magic is found only when the social personality of the victim is out of adjustment with its environment and fails to keep a satisfactory equilibrium. The victim is sick, he fails in the hunt or in fishing, he has his woman taken from him, he is wounded in a spear fight or falls from a tree, and, in general, he is not in a state of well-being. His physical energy is not sufficient to keep up the multiple activities of his social personality, he feels himself on the debit side, with his individual mana inadequate for adjustment; his social personality is dysphoric and maladjusted. Feeling the effects of black magic greatly resembles the condition of an obsessive psychotic individual in our Euro-American culture, since both the individual and his society recognize his inadequate adaptation. The extreme of this maladjustment is the person whose soul has been stolen—the ultimate in black magic. The soul, the sacred individualization of power and the epitome of the social participation of the organism, seems lost to the individual owner and is under the control of another, i. e., the human part of the man has been stolen and lost to him.

The white shaman functions as one who reestablishes the victim's social equilibrium. The society positively sanctions his actions by placing its belief in the magical and social mana under his control. The ceremonial leader in the north performs these same functions. Even here a man can be killed or made ill by magic: by black magicians, mokois, et cetera, who are outside the society, outside because magicians live to the south, and the mokois, the asocial trickster spirits, live outside the group in the jungles.

The ailing member of society in the northern area must also be cured and regain his vigor and feeling of power. There being no medicine man here, herbs are used, but the native considers them insufficient. In this area the curative technique is the well ritual—a "secret" thing caused the sickness and a sacred ritual is to remove it. The individual is placed in the well, sung over, ritually cleansed, and regarded as cured by the ceremonial leader in the clan exactly as the tribe is purified and sickness prevented by ritual, and exactly as the victim of magic is healed by the magical technique of the medicine man in the south and in the Murngin tribe country. In the north the ceremonial leader directs the healing ritual when the solidarity of the clan and the group is felt at its greatest strength. The whole of the social forces are focused on the individual through the totems, the totem well, and the attitudes and beliefs of the participants. The leader merely expresses, through his direction of the ritual, the social mana of the ritual in the group. This power is believed to go into the individual and remove his weakness. The leader functions here as in the Djungguan when he directs the ritual over the python totemic emblem to sing power into it, or at the blood-letting in this same ceremony when he places the power of the python spirit in the individual and his blood, which is to be used in the circumcision ritual. It is not the leader who has this power but the ritual of his group. The power and efficacy of the ritual come from the mana of the entire group, organized into a society of clans. The leader in the north, then cures by ritual and performs those functions carried out by the medicine man in the south. His activities are organized by his clan, he represents his church in the Durkheim sense, not only as a religious ritual leader but in the functions of a magician. In both cases, however, the clan is the "church" back of him. In the south the leader's powers are divided. The well ritual may still be used, but there is also here the white magician. His social personality is little different from that of another member of the clan; he differs only inasmuch as it is recognized that he has a special power. He is sought by the afflicted, however, exactly as a ceremonial leader in the Northern area is sought by the relatives of the dead or by the parents of a boy who is to be circumcised. The relatives of a sick man send for the shaman to cure and diagnose the illness of their ailing kinsman and either to restore him to his normal participation in the group or to pronounce his death sentence. *The medicine man then helps organize and direct the community's attitude toward the sick man.* He leads community attitude and organizes the community fundamentally as does the ceremonial leader. He examines his patient, says that he will die because his soul has been stolen, and the community at once recognizes that death is near. The society then organizes itself into a group which in effect excommunicates the patient, trying to force his soul into the realm of the dead and the sacred. If the magician diagnoses the case as curable and removes the cause, he reestablishes the individual's equilibrium, making him believe he can once more participate in his usual manner in the group. He can do this because he organizes group attitude, since the belief in the curative power of this ritual unifies the point of view of all the members. The magician, while healing, is usually watched by a number of the near and far kinsmen. They all express great satisfaction in his removal of the sickness (the foreign object) and an affirmation of the victim's cure, as do the magician and the victim.

An Examination of the Social Configuration of Magic in the South

The Part Ritual Plays as a "Magical" Instrument in the South.— Ritual can cause sickness and death as well as prevent them. When the great ceremonies such as Gunabibi, Djungguan, Ulmark and Narras are being performed, any breaking of the tribal laws is considered exceedingly dangerous and likely to cause sickness among the totemic group. If totems are hidden within the men's camp and a fight is started, or if illegal sexual relations occur, or if in some way the clan feels its totems have been profanely treated, there is general indignation and a certain amount of fear that members will become ill.

A Narra ceremony was being celebrated by some clans of the Yiritja moiety and during the preliminary part a totem was being made when a fight broke out in the camp among some of the male members because a husband believed that his wife had been having illicit relations with another man. The owners of the totem felt not only that they and their totem had been insulted but also that they were likely to become ill from the fighting and the breaking of the tribal laws.

A shark totem was hidden by a member of the Djirin clan in a hollow tree on the edge of the men's ceremonial grounds. Some women from a distant group passed near it. The owner of the totem followed their tracks and accused their husbands of not watching their women carefully. While he stood with his clansmen back of him, all of them holding their spears in readiness for fighting, he said that it was an insult not only to him and his clan but also to his totemic emblem; that it meant sickness for him or that he might be speared in the next fight he got into.

Two men were caught in illicit sexual relations with two women not their wives while several totemic emblems were on the Narra ground. The Liagaomir clan had their great fire ranga ready for the Narra ceremony. When the leader of this clan heard what had happened he expressed great indignation. He said, "Let us take them down there to our Narra ground, those men and those women, and let us show them our ranga and then kill them. Let them see first what they have done." The women were severely beaten by everybody including their brothers and sisters. The leader felt that all the clan had been endangered by this profaneness and that they might all become ill.

At other times the lack of participation in sexual intercourse will cause sickness to the man who fails and possibly to others in a group. Sometimes young and bashful men refuse to enter into the ritualistic sexual intercourse which ends the Gunabibi. It is believed that they will be sick. In his account of his first participation in the Gunabibi old Dorng said the following about his embarrassment: "My brother [distant] said to me at this time, 'You go play with my wife.' I said, 'No.' He said, 'You will be sick and maybe die if you don't play with her.'" Often the women who are to be the sexual partners of young men send word to the men that they must come and stay with them or that the young man's refusal will cause both partners to be ill.

Sometimes improper participation in a ceremony will also cause illness. Willidjungo, the medicine man, diagnosed my lame leg as caused by my not seeing all of a certain Gunabibi ceremony, which had caused the great snake to be sorry and angry with me. This diagnosis occurred in similar cases with several of the natives.

Mistreatment of ceremonial objects connected with the celebration of a great ritual can also cause illnesses. During the Gunabibi some of the feather headpieces of the leader, Ilkara, disappeared and from the indications left it appeared that a wildcat had eaten them. The young men supposed to guard these things and remain on the ceremonial ground during the night had failed in their duty. Ilkara became ill and had to have a doctor remove a large bone from his side which appeared because of this neglect of his totemic paraphernalia.

Baldness is a term of reproach among the Murngin. A man who becomes bald considers it a calamity. One man among the group was partially bald. His people believed that his condition was due to his making too many totemic emblems and giving them to other men in return for presents; in other words, he was mistreating his totem. There was no evidence that he traded his totemic emblems any more frequently than did any of the other men of the group.

Women sometimes suffer innocently from the power of the ceremonial blood smeared on the men during the Djungguan and Gunabibi ceremonies. Dundir's leg had two small infections about the size of a thumb nail. Her husband said that she could not go hunting for grubs because she was ill. "She picked cotton off me over at Rabuma when we circumcised those young men. That blood made her sick." One old man spoke up and said, "That blood made her sick. It makes women ill when they touch us after the Djungguan. It is the spirit in that blood that does this. It is the totem, not the wooden emblem, but the spirit inside with the power name. He is in that blood. A woman cannot touch it or it will make her sick."

Smaller rituals are performed by two or three individuals to cure someone who is ailing. Frequently women rub red ocher over their bodies because of an ailment, this being but an abbreviation of its use in the larger ceremonies. Red ocher string is tied around the head or body to cure a headache or abdominal pain. This act, too, is but a shortening of the ritual in which decorated string is placed around the head or body in the larger ceremonies.

Larger rituals are definitely used to remove pain. Certain parts of the Djungguan are designed to take away the pain from the boy who is being circumcised. The women relatives whip themselves in order to transfer the pain from the boy to themselves. The head of the boy's penis, they also say, is a turtle's head, so the cutting of the foreskin cannot hurt him since it is not his flesh being cut but that of the animal. These statements are also supposed to remove the pain from the boy.

Other rituals, which assure success in war, are demonstrably only elaborated magical practices. The gaingar spears represent the head of the Dua and Yiritja moieties. The souls of the dead of the moieties are supposed to be in each weapon. The ceremonial throwing of the spears to assure the killing of an enemy and to prevent the killing of their own men is definitely of a magical nature, the power of these ceremonies depending upon the souls' clustering around the spear just as the power of the magical killing stick depends upon the souls which cluster about its point.

The bone magic ceremony used in the maringo fighting (see Chapter VI, Warfare) is also an elaborate ceremony focused upon the magical idea of the soul's being associated with a bone relic. In earlier parts of this chapter the individual treats the bone in a ceremonial way to practice his magic against his enemies. Both the gaingar and the maringo ceremony from one point of view are elaborate magical practices participated in by the group and led by the ceremonial or war leader.

All the rituals, particularly the Narra, which celebrates the ascendancy of the clan totem, are commonly used to purify the group of any uncleanliness which might cause sickness and death. The group baptism in the Narra ceremonies is explicitly considered by the Murngin to be a method of preventing illness and a way of washing away the ritual uncleanliness which causes it. Participation in the Gunabibi has the exact opposite effect to non-participation, since it too prevents sickness and death of the individuals who are a part of it. The whole mourning ceremony is consciously an effort to prevent sickness from occurring to any of the members of the group by forcing the contagious soul away from the land of the living and into the land of the dead.

The Nature of Murngin Dal (Mana or Power)

Murngin mana which lies in the rituals is both helpful and harmful. Those things which are powerful and strong because of an extramundane quality are said to be *dal*, which means they have mana and possess spiritual power.

Objects Which Are Dal Because of Primary Relationship with the Totem.—A catalogue of the elements in Murngin society which are dal indicates that all the objects within their material culture can be dal provided they have been given a power name by someone who has the right to give it. Old men are the only ones who know and can use these sacred names. Most of the objects in the material culture which possess the dal quality have it only because of the power name. Dal names fit into the general classification of "inside," while ordinary words in daily use are "outside." The men's sacred camp, the place where all the sacred totemic rituals are held, is described as "inside," the common camp as "outside." The water in the clan well is considered common, ordinary, and outside, whereas the subterranean water down below, where the totems and the ancient ancestors live, is inside. All the very sacred rituals are inside, while the ordinary garma type is outside. The totem, totemic emblems, totemic ancestors and ceremonial objects are all dal. All the objects, then, which have the quality of dal may or may not be sacred in their own right, but in all cases they obtain their power because of a special connection with the inside or sacred.

Objects Which Are Dal Because Connected with the Dead.—Another category of objects is also classed as dal, but the items in this group are not necessarily associated with a totem in a primary relationship. These objects include the bones of a man killed directly by black magic or by an enemy clansman, pieces of a spear found in a wound of a dead clansman, bark or wood saturated in his death's blood, the heart's blood of a man or woman killed by magic, a hair belt from the head of a dead man, a gondjurma or killing stick used to puncture the heart of a sorcerer's victim, the body of a dead man, a burial platform where a body formerly lay but which has since been removed, the warro or soul which goes to the totemic well, and the mokoi or trickster soul. All of these items have a common element, namely, they are associated with the dead. Each one is directly and primarily related to some aspect of death. The dead, too, are looked upon as "inside," particularly because very shortly after death the sacred totemic emblem is placed upon the body of the dead. Women can no longer look at the corpse, which is immediately wrapped with paper bark and completely covered, exactly like a totemic object. The paper bark is now "outside" and something that the women can look at, while the dead, with the sacred emblem upon it, is now "inside" and dal. The dead belong to the world of the sacred (see mourning rites), and these objects, by their primary association with the dead, partake of this power.

Dal Magicians' Paraphernalia, and Relics.—A third category of dal objects—the paraphernalia of the magician and relics used by the ordinary man to give him extra-mundane aid in his hunting or fishing—are actually only a subdivision of the preceding category, since the power of magicians and the power of relics find their source in the sacredness of the dead.

The heart's blood of a man whose soul has been stolen by a magician is saved, and it often turns up in the hands of a magician or an ordinary layman in the form of a kind of resin, which is supposed to be the hardened blood. This can be used in fighting to give a little extra power, and in hunting or fishing it is used the same way as the shavings of a killing stick, to be described presently. Sometimes the heart's blood is placed inside the white magician's spirit bag to give it extra power. This blood gains extra mana by passing through the possession of a number of people and usually is traded in from more remote regions in the south.

When the body of a man killed by magic or in a spear fight is disinterred and the flesh removed from the bones, the finger bones are often distributed as relics among the clansmen and near relatives. These relics are wrapped in string and placed carefully in the possessor's dilly bag as reminders of the crime they feel has been committed. This is also true of pieces of the spear which remain in the body, and of pieces of bark or wood which the dying man may soak in his blood and present to his relatives as reminders. The power which these relics possess is due to the soul of the dead following the bones. The soul is a true or totem-well warro. It listens from the totem well and comes when it is needed for an avenging expedition or to help its possessor in time of trouble. Any account of a clan feud is always filled with the use of these relics. Usually, when a maringo expedition is starting, a magical ceremony is gone through by the avenging group in which the bone of the dead plays the central rôle and decidedly helps to a successful conclusion. The gondjurma or killing stick used by the black magician to puncture the heart of his victim has great power, first, because it is associated with the dead body, second, because it is believed that the souls of the victims cluster about the point, and third, because it gains power by passing through the hands of a great number of men as it is traded from clan to clan and from tribe to tribe. The soul which adheres to this magic is also the Wongar one. It is like a friend to its possessor and he is its master. All of these souls are in or on the stick and can be called for help in hunting or fishing. They will also come to a man when he dreams. They will help foretell the future for him. If he is to be ill, he will feel something pricking him like the end of the stick. If good things are going to happen, one of the souls will come and tell him. If a stick is supposed to have killed a large number of men, all of the souls are supposed to be with it, but actually they are looked upon as one, and it is not so much an individual soul as a kind of diffused power or mana. A killing stick can be in the possession of a magician, or he can give it to an ordinary man who is one of his friends. Such a stick is always kept wrapped in paper bark and covered just as though it were a totemic emblem or ceremonial object and must not be subjected to the profane sight of women or the uninitiated.

When a man wishes to obtain its power to help him in hunting he scrapes off pieces, chews them and swallows them the night before the hunt. Immediately afterwards he shuts his eyes, says nothing, and goes to bed. Next morning he utters not a sound and goes out with his spears looking for game or for fish. "Those souls which the stick killed before this have gone into the water or out into the bush and they have stopped the fish and game so that they can be found. When the man arrives he sees a few. He spits in the water (he is fishing) and a lot of fish come there. He spears one fish and when he spears the one all the rest go dead as if you had poison in the water."

If he were hunting kangaroo it would be impossible for him to miss, but he could kill only one, even though there were a herd of kangaroo there. The taboo of silence is placed on the man from the time he eats the gondjurma shavings until he is successful in the hunt "because it means you have the soul inside you and when you spit it goes out into the water. You can't talk or it would send him out before."

"One time," said an informant who had in his possession a killing stick he intended using, "I was down at the creek trying to catch fish. When I got there I saw Bang-gi-la. He had one of these sticks with him. He was ready to try it when I got there. He had not used fish poison. I looked at the end of the stick. It had been scraped. While I stood there the fish came to the top and were dead. I am going to try mine."

The dry heart's blood can be used in the same way and the magical process is exactly the same. "Wet blood is no good because it makes you sick. When you take wet blood you must keep it until it gets dry."

The stick insect, a creature which looks much like a praying mantis and is one of the minor totems among the western clans of the Dua moiety, is associated with the killing stick primarily because it has a stick-like shape. It is believed that dead souls are about it, and at times it is called wan-djuk by the western peoples, which means black magician. Its correct name is war-a-la war-a-la. It is believed that the warala warala sometimes helps sneak up on people and kill them. There is an ambivalent attitude taken toward this creature. The natives play with him when they see him hanging sluggishly to a limb, laugh at him, treat him rather roughly, yet in their more serious moments they speak of his association with black magic.

The power of the black magician and his technique and the power of relics used to harm one's enemies (a variety of black magic) find their source in the sacredness of the dead. It is the mana of the dead which gives this power to magic and which *is* this power. To the living, the greatest and most intense dysphoria which finds expression in the life of man is death. The more dead souls that cluster about the evil point of the killing stick, the more power the killing stick possesses; a punitive war expedition assures itself of success by the magic clustered in the power of the bone relic because the soul is with it. The ordinary living animal or fish is killed immediately by the magical power of the killing stick because the soul of the dead is associated with it. The dal of the magician is the dal of the dead. The relics express this same power because they are associated with the dead. A relic cannot kill, but it can remove many of the traits of the living and make a living man more like the dead. A man goes to sleep because a bone has been put in the fire by him and he is killed by his enemies (see the account of a clan feud in the war chapter). A man cannot run when chased by his enemies because one of them is blowing on a dead man's bone in his mouth, or an evil soul enters a man's head and makes him crazy, the power of the soul coming from that of the dead.

The two classes, that of the totem and of the dead, are but two varieties of one general type, for both of them belong to the world of the sacred. Their power is contagious and dangerous unless properly handled by ritual. The totem can cause sickness and death just as the power of the dead can produce these same effects.

The Behavior of the Individual and the Society When Magic Is Put into Effect

The isolation of the various elements in the particular social configuration surrounding the death of a victim of black magic may help illuminate the fundamental nature of Murngin magic and explain its potency and unusual effectiveness; and a general analysis of the group behavior under such a situation will be profitable.

When the supposed theft of a man's soul becomes general knowledge, the sustaining social fabric pulls away from the victim. The familiar attitudes of the kinship personalities change, the collaboration of the victim and his society, of which his social personality has always been an integral part, ceases. The group now acts with all the ramifications of its organization and with countless stimuli positively to suggest death to a suggestible individual. The ordinary daily activity of the victim's social life is removed. The society itself creates a situation which, if unchanged, makes it impossible for the individual to adjust himself to it even though he tried; and in addition he usually not only makes no effort to live and to remain part of his group but actually, through the multiple suggestions from it, cooperates in his withdrawal therefrom. He becomes what his society's attitudes make him, committing a kind of *suicide*. The social configuration in which he finds himself operating at this time is one of anomia[2] for him. His ordi-

[2] Emile Durkheim, *Le Suicide*, Librairie Felix Alcan, Paris, nouvel edition, 1930. In general, anomic suicide is a type supposed to be due to the change in the society which surrounds the individual and gives him a feeling of maladjustment and of being "lost." The change here, however, is more dynamic than one of process; that is, the society as a functioning structure regularly performs this act upon individuals whose souls have been stolen, rather than that the society changes in a structural way and becomes something different from what it was before and by so doing causes the indi-

nary social personality is removed, his part of the social structure not only having disintegrated but largely disappeared. Such a man is neither in the world of the ordinary nor in that of the sacred. He is, to use the literal Murngin expression, "half dead." Partly sacred since his soul is not in this world, he is in a position of danger, not only to himself as a spiritual entity, since his soul is neither in this world nor in its proper place in the totemic well, but also to his group, because a soul not properly ritualized and placed in the sacred well with the totemic spirits and sacred ancestors is likely to cause illnesses and death to those near him in kinship. Before death takes place the group, then, begin the mourning ritual the object of which is to transmute the social personality into a spiritual being, that is, to make the soul enter the totem well safely. Even before death the soul starts behaving like the sacred totem; the ancestors and dead relatives come for him and enter his heart; the soul "ceases" reciprocal relations with the profane living, relating itself to the sacred dead; and the living cease acting their everyday rôles and become virtually related to the sacred part of the dying person.

The personality of the victim thus has the ordinary attitudes of society removed from him, the taboo attitude of the sacred being substituted. He responds by recognizing his change of status: the wounded feudist killed by magic dances his totem dance to make himself like his totem and insure his immediate passage to the totem well; the man dying of an illness moves his hands convulsively like his crab totem or flaps his hands like his black duck totem, listening for the sounds of his ancestors' approach as he follows the suggestive sequence of the mourning song and ritual wailingly sung and danced over his body. His effort is not to live but to die.

There are two definite movements of the social group in the process by which black magic becomes effective. In the first movement the community contracts; all the victim's kin withdraw their sustaining support—everyone in his whole community, i.e., all his kin, completely change their attitudes and place him in a new category. He is seen no longer as an ordinary living being like all the other people, but as an abnormal person who is more nearly in the realm of the sacred and taboo. This movement of withdrawal by the society means that his place in the general social fabric has been taken away from him so that he now stands in an entirely different relationship to all of his

vidual to become maladjusted and suicidal. Since this is true, there are in this situation some of the elements of the type Durkheim calls the altruistic type of suicide in which the individual destroys himself because of the perfect working of the society.

kin, his clan, and the general tribal grouping. The organization of his social life has collapsed, and he is alone and isolated.

The second movement of the group is its return toward the victim under the integrating force of the mourning rite. The "half dead" man whose soul is in that dangerous position to the community of being neither sacred nor profane must be removed by ritual from any contact with his community; and its purpose now as an organized group with its ceremonial leader, a close relative of the victim's, is finally to cut him off entirely from the ordinary world and ultimately place him in his proper position in the sacred totemic world, that of the dead. The victim, on his part, reciprocates this feeling, behaving in the manner of his totem, with which he attempts to identify himself. The mourning rite is truly a *rite de passage*.

The effect of this double movement, first away from the victim and then back with all the compulsive force of one of the most powerful rituals, is obviously drastic. An analogous situation in our society is hard to imagine. If all a man's near kin, his father, mother, brothers and sisters, wife, children, business associates, friends and all the other members of the society, should suddenly withdraw themselves because of some dramatic circumstance, refusing to take any attitude but one of taboo and looking at the man as one already dead, and then after some little time perform over him a sacred ceremony believed with certainty to guide him out of the land of the living into that of the dead, the enormous suggestive power of this twofold movement of the community after it has had its attitudes crystallized can be somewhat understood by ourselves.

The magicians are the leaders who crystallize this group attitude. By the power of their rituals they organize social opinion and attitudes just as effectively and certainly as the ceremonial leader does by the sacred totemic ritual. Both depend upon the group's participation to make their power effective. It is a group situation, not an individual one, that is operative in both circumstances. It is the power of the "church" or community which integrates the total group, directed by the ceremonial leader in the totemic ceremonies, and it is the power of the church (the clan group) which destroys a man under the guidance and leadership of its magicians.

Black magic is a force expressed through the dysphoric condition of an individual member or members of a social group, and an ever present possible danger to all the members of Murngin society.

The attitude of the kinsmen of the man they believe to have been killed by black magic is most illuminating. The sorcerer belongs to a hostile group or, what is equivalent to the Murngin mind, to one so far away that it is unknown and strange. A sorcerer of one's own clan is not asked to kill any member of it or of friendly clans, but to destroy outsiders who are looked upon as enemies and who reciprocate. The source of the enemy sorcerer's power lies within the known antagonisms which connect one's group with the foreign groups. Probably it is the foreign group's mana, as thought of by the victim and his group, which attacks a member of one's own clan through the magician's ritual. It is the enemy's magician, it must be remembered, who helps organize the local community's attitudes toward the death of its own clansman, and it is likely that he also is an organizer of the outside clan's feelings. One's own sorcerer is equally feared by his clan's enemies, and the deaths in the enemies' clans are ascribed by them to the evil worked by him. The local sorcerer is not feared by his kinsmen; rather, they go to him in times of trouble and weakness, since his power can reestablish their own and their clan's sense of well-being by killing the enemy in retaliation for the slaying of their kinsman.

The power of the black magician, then, comes (1) from the very nature of the clan itself because of its antagonism and open warfare with the people of the victim, (2) from being associated with the dead, and (3) ultimately from the action of the victim's people because of their earlier withdrawal of support from him and later thrusting him from the society.

The mana of the ceremonial leader comes from his oral and ceremonial ritual, which in turn gains its power ultimately from a society or church, viz., the clan. The mana of the medicine man comes from his ritual, in which the group must participate by its belief if his technique is to be effective, which means that his source of power is in the group. He too must have and does have his church, which in Murngin society is the group of clans.

To sum up, the power of the black magician only reverses that of the white: the healer is a member of his own or a friendly group and his magic is made effective by the positive attitude of the victim's people; on the other hand, when black magic is at work, the symbolic behavior of the victim and his people is in response to what they believe to have been the magical acts of a representative of someone outside the clans of the victim and his near kin—and even though the black magician is not present, he is the symbol around which the members of the victim's group organize their sentiments in relation to the victim.

CHAPTER IX

MURNGIN TOTEMISM, I

Murngin totemism consists of a ritual relation which is established between members of the clans and certain species of plants and animals. This relationship is expressed in certain myths and rituals.

There are two general types of rituals, one of which is called the Wawilak Myth Cycle in this book, and the other, the Djunkgao Myth Cycle. The Wawilak Cycle includes four fundamental ceremonies, the Djungguan, Gunabibi, Ulmark, and Marndiella. (The Liaalaomir and certain Dua clan ceremonies and certain garma rituals will be treated separately, although they too seem to be related to the fundamental Wawilak myth.) The Djunkgao rituals in Murngin thought form a separate myth-ritual constellation with another fundamental myth—the Djunkgao Sisters myth—and comprise two major ceremonies, the Dua Narra and the Yiritja Narra. Other important but less elaborated myth and ritual groupings will also be tested by the method we propose following in this examination of Murngin ritual and myth.

The Wawilak Myth Cycle of ceremonies—very elaborate and usually extending over several months—is focused around the *rites de passage* of the individual.[1] The Narra ceremonies of the Djunkgao Myth Cycle are also long and elaborate but are pointed more directly toward totemic behavior as it centers around the totemic well.

Both the Wawilak and Djunkgao myth-ritual cycles are concerned primarily with the expression of the social logics (usually illogical thinking, if observed as the mental behavior of an individual) of the people as they are focused on the problem of adapting nature to man. The data demonstrating this thesis will be presented in this and the following two chapters.

The totemic religious behavior of the Murngin tribes is intelligible only in terms of the social organization, the relation of the technological system to society generally, and the ideas which surround the so-

[1] See Chapter IV, Age Grading.

ciety's adjustment to the natural environment. There will be no attempt to look for the origins of totemism, but rather our effort will be to determine what the totemic system is, how it works, and finally by analysis to ascertain what meanings lie implicit in the thinking and behavior of the religious activities of these people.

The task of understanding the place of the totemic myths and rituals in Murngin society and their fundamental meanings in the thought and life of the people demands that we first determine whether there is a primary or possibly an intrinsic relation between the acted ceremony or ritual, and the myth or oral rite. If there is, and it can be demonstrated that they are but two parts of one social phenomenon in Murngin culture, then we can turn our attention to the more fundamental meanings of these sacred phenomena and their place in the general religion of the people. Our order of procedure, then, will first lead us to the question of whether the Wawilak Creator Sisters myth and certain great ceremonies of the Murngin are generically connected. The same procedure will be used for the other fundamental myths and what seem to be their ritual constellations.

It should be stated explicitly that the thesis of this chapter is that, in meaning, the Wawilak myth is fundamental to, and organically related to, a certain group of rituals found in Murngin religious thought. The dramatic rituals express the oral rites.

Generally speaking, scientific method in the social sciences should include:

A. *Gathering of data:* an objective collection of the ethnographic facts from the whole of the society and from all aspects of the culture in as complete detail as possible. (*Activity in the field.*)

B. *Classifying* as like and unlike, and "near and far," *the materials* which have been collected and which in the realm of social organization form structural parts or configurations of the society being examined. (*Activity in the laboratory, checked by renewed activity in the field.*)

C. *Propounding of final generalizations* on the basis of the simpler generalizations of B. (*Activity in the laboratory.*)

SCIENTIFIC METHOD AS APPLIED TO THE ANALYSIS OF MURNGIN TOTEMISM

A. *Gathering of Data*

As many descriptions of the various ceremonies as time and opportunity in the field would allow were collected. *Before* seeing a ceremony I interviewed, as many times as possible, the leader and principal participants. *While* the ceremony was taking place I wrote careful descriptions and interviewed bystanders, or participants if possible. *After* the event I went over the two accounts and checked for discrepancies, and again interviewed. I repeated this many times. I collected a great number of accounts of the same myth and observed the variations and conformities of the several accounts. I made a detailed and accurate observation of the natural conditions to which the society is adapted—in particular, climatic changes and the adjustment of nature to them—and obtained native ideas and evaluations of the various phases of the weather and other changes in nature.[2]

B. *Classifying the Materials*

I analyzed the native accounts of myths and determined that they fell into dramatic sections or "movements," and these again into episodes. I lettered and gave descriptive titles to the dramatic sections (three in the Wawilak myth); and I numbered consecutively and summarized descriptively each of the episodes (ten in the Wawilak).

I analyzed the ceremonies and determined that these likewise fell into dramatic sections, and the sections again into groups of episodes (cohering elements of the rituals). The sections I lettered and gave descriptive names. Each subdivision (group of episodes) of a section I numbered, summarized analytically, and described fully. At the end of each *section* I wrote in the native interpretation of that section of the ceremony with respect to the myth.

In collecting these interpretations I used a free association method and did not question directly, allowing the native informants to tell what they thought about the ritual either while it was being enacted or when they were discussing it before or after its performance. These native interpretations constituted, then, a detailed study on the first level of interpretation, based on the meanings, beliefs, and attitudes the natives held explicitly and consciously about the various parts of the myths and rituals.

I ascertained that there is a connection between the myth and ritual, first by observing that the native mind *is* aware that there is a *general* connection (even though this awareness is only rationalization).[3]

[2] The Marndiella, Ulmark, and Yiritja Narra were not observed as completely and are not as completely described as the other ceremonies.

[3] In the earlier half of my field work I was unaware of the full significance of the

This established, the next step was to see *what kinds* of symbolical relations exist between myth and ritual—to determine how far and in what details the various parts of the myth-symbols are thought of by the natives as being correlated with the various dramatic symbols of the rituals. If a point-for-point connection between myth and ritual could be determined, then certain wider generalizations could be made, and certain larger associations, of the phenomena of nature and society as they are related or not related by the native mind, tested.—I summarized, referring always to native interpretations, all the symbolical meanings of the several sections of each ceremony to see which were equivalent and which were not. That is, I found, say, that ritual sections A, B, C, and D of a certain ceremony, as well as X, Y, and Z, had the same theme *according to native interpretation*, while sections N, O, and P were different and had a different theme. I could now generalize on the myth-ritual symbols in terms of major, minor, and equal religious concepts.

I next examined the various sections of the myth from the point of view of native interpretation in order to expand the meaning of the myth and to acquire a fuller and more detailed understanding than the myth alone was likely to give. It had become evident by this time *what* the *kinds* of relations were between the fundamental myths and the fundamental rituals. By the integration of the ceremonies with the myths, the larger ideological configuration became evident, which presented a more fundamental and unconscious level of native thought than could be discovered by a mere analysis of myth or of ritual by itself.

C. *Final Generalizations*

I could now safely step to the third major part of my examination, to generalize if possible on the several religious concepts which had been discovered as underlying the manifest behavior of the myths and rituals. I analyzed the relations of the concepts as social logics by the

relation of the myth to its rituals, and I failed to interview consciously for the interconnections between the two. I must confess I did not see the relation between the Wawilak myth and the seasons until well near the end of my field work. Consequently most of this material was gathered without my realizing its implications. This adds, I think, to its value, since there was little chance of the field worker biasing the result of his interview, but it also means that the native interpretation cannot be presented as systematically and in as great detail as it might have been had I known the situation as well as I did when I left the field.

use of an elaborated form of the Ogden and Richards system for the analysis of individual logic.[4]

The first myth-ritual constellation to be presented under the foregoing method of analysis is the Wawilak myth and its interlocked ceremonies. It is represented diagrammatically in the following chart:

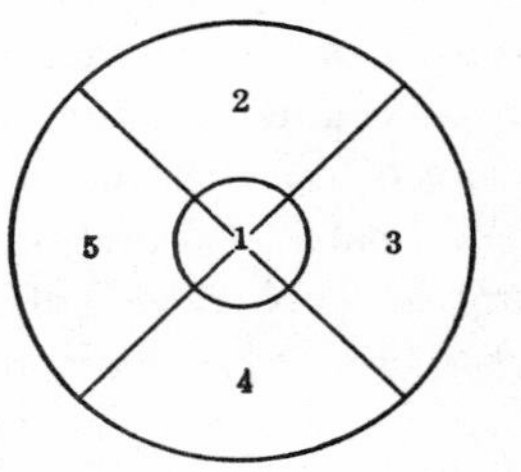

1. The Wawilak Myth
2. The Djungguan
3. The Gunabibi
4. The Ulmark
5. The Marndiella

CHART X.—CONSTELLATION OF THE WAWILAK MYTH AND ITS RITUALS

The Wawilak myth is of extreme importance to the Murngin and is always present in their thinking. I had been in the Murngin country for only three days when I heard of it. The narrator, Yanindja, leader of the eastern Djirin clan, said, "This story belongs to the Djungguan. They [myth and ritual] are all the same thing." At the first circumcision ceremony I saw, clansmen from many parts of the country were present; and in explanation of their presence I was told by the leader, "People come to a Djungguan ceremony from everywhere because when that snake swallowed those two women he stood up right to the sky and sang out and people heard him from every place." (He meant that all the clans come to attend the ceremony.)

This most important of the myths was collected a great number of times and all the fundamental features and most of the secondary ones were always present, no matter how poor the narrator. The occasion was always just before, during, or just after the ceremonies supposed to be connected with it.

The story is primarily an account of how before the time of present-day man the two Wawilak sisters and their children marched out of the southern inland after committing clan incest, and came to the Liaalaomir totemic hole. Here the older sister profaned the pool of the Great Python by accidentally allowing her menstrual blood to fall

[4] *The Meaning of Meaning*, by C. K. Ogden and I. A. Richards, with an appendix by Bronislaw Malinowski, has been a great help to me in working out the ideas expressed in this chapter.

in the water hole; because of this, the women and their children were swallowed by Yurlunggur, the python. A great flood covered the land, after which the two women were regurgitated and finally swallowed again.

The myth has three primary and ten secondary movements. The first principal movement can be called "the coming of the two sisters from the southern interior"; the second, "the python's pool is profaned and he swallows the Wawilak women"; and the last, "man learns the secrets of the Wawilak rituals."

The Murngin unquestionably associate the Wawilak myth generally with the four ceremonies. The following statement by a Liaalaomir old man summarizes what I heard probably hundreds of times: "Those two old Wawilak women made the garmas [not all of them], and Djungguan, Gunabibi, Ulmark, and Marndiella for the Liaalaomir and Mandelpui people"; or, as it was sometimes expressed, "This Gunabibi and Ulmark, Djunguan, and Marndiella are all the Wawilak story. They belong to Mirrirmina [clan well of the Liaalaomir], where those two old women found the snake. Marndiella is the same as a garma [i.e., it is a less sacred ceremony than the others] because it belongs more to the women's camp." I was told by many that all people believe that Muit (one of the sacred names of the python) caused the wet and dry season and that "the Wawilak women sang all the songs and dances [the four ceremonies mentioned above] to stop the rain and to stop the snakes who had surrounded them."

In one account I was given of the Wawilak Creation myth, "She [the older sister] sang the 'outside songs' when we cut young men. After she finished them she sang all the Djungguan songs and the Gunabibi songs. All the time she was trying to stop this rain but it wouldn't stop—she sang the 'inside' song of Djungguan—a-a-a—kak-ye!—; she sang the songs where the subsection names are called out and the men sit in a circle, and she called out the clan names for the first time."

The young sister sang like the leaders do now, with a singing stick. That young girl said, "We will take the Yiritja way now." The rain did not stop and it got harder. They tried to sing something more "inside" (i.e., more sacred). "And they sang Yurlunggur [another name for the sacred python] and menstruation blood and this is the same as when the boys bring Yurlunggur in at night to the circle." (See Djungguan ceremony, page 260.)

The story of the two Wawilak women is always told when any one of the Wawilak cycle of ceremonies is being given; continual references are made during the dancing and singing to the sisters and their antagonist, the snake; and one is always being reminded of this drama of the creation period. "What Bapa Indi [the python totem] called all these countries [the clan lands and local areas within them] and the languages he spoke [the dialects real or believed to be real which are the distinguishing marks of the clans] all we people speak today. That snake made these ceremonies then. He made this one [the Djungguan], and he made Gunabibi." "Circumcision started when those two women tried to cut their boys in the Djungguan, but the snake swallowed them before they could do it; and cutting today starts from that."

It is obvious from the above quotations that the Murngin generally connect these rituals with the Wawilak Creation myth. The difficulty with accepting the natives' verbal statement of a general connection is that it may be a mere rationalization on the part of the natives; the general relation might exist in their minds without a generic connection between the dramatically acted rituals and the oral Wawilak rite. We shall therefore examine each element of the ritual and myth to ascertain whether there is an organic connection between the two.

In general, it can be said that throughout the myth there is constant reference to the social organization and to the four rituals of the Wawilak constellation: the Djungguan, Gunabibi, Ulmark and Marndiella. When these are presented later, it will be seen that the primary locale of their drama is the Mirrirmina water hole.

MYTH OF THE WAWILAK WOMEN

A. The Coming of the Two Sisters from the Southern Interior

1. The two sisters and their children leave the Wawilak country and start toward the sea, naming the animals and plants as they go; but before they leave they have incestuous relations with their clansmen from which a child is born later in the Wawilak country.

It was the time of Bamun (the mythological period) when Wongar men walked about and modern men had not yet appeared. Everything was different. Animals were like men then! Those two Wawilak sisters had come a long distance. They were coming from the far interior to the Arafura Sea. They had come from the far interior Kardao Kardao country. This is a clan territory of the Dua moiety. They had come from the land of the Wawilak people for Kardao Kardao is their country. The wirkul (a young woman who has not had a child) was pregnant. The gungmun (a woman who has had a child; literally, "the giver") carried her own baby under her arm in a paper-bark "cradle." It was a male child.

The two women carried stone spears and hawks' down and bush cotton. On the way they killed iguana, opossum, and bandicoot for their food. They also gathered some bush yams (ippa). When they killed the animals, they gave them the names they bear today; they did the same for the yam. They gathered all the plants and animals that are in the Murngin country today. They said to each thing they killed or gathered, "You will be maraiin by and by."

When the two sisters started their journey they talked Djaun, later Rainbarngo, and still later Djinba; then they talked Wawilak, and finally Liaalaomir. They named the country as they went along. In the Wawilak country they copulated with the Wawilak Wongar men. These men were Dua, and they were Dua. This was very wrong and asocial.

The two women stopped to rest, for the younger felt the child she was carrying move inside her. She knew her baby would soon be born.

"Yeppa [sister], I feel near my heart this baby turning," she said.

The older one said, "Then let us rest."

They sat down, and the older sister put her hand on the abdomen of the younger sister and felt the child moving inside. She then massaged her younger sister, for she knew her labor pains had commenced. The baby was born there. It was Yiritja, for its mother was Dua. The country was still a part of the territory of the Wawilak clan.

After the child was born the older sister gathered more bush food, then the two moved on toward the sea. They stopped at various places and gave all of them names. They named all the clan territories and the localities within their borders. They first rested at Djirri Djirri (quail place), then at Wakngay (crow place), Dung Dunga (fish spear place), Tarbella (white oyster place), and Katatanga (falling meteor place). All these localities were Dua and were within the country of the Wawilak clan. Although the Wawilak sisters went to almost all the clans of the Dua moiety they never walked on the country of the Yiritja moiety.

"Come on, sister," said the older, "we'll go quickly now." They drank water at the last place and hurried on.

2. The flight of the food animals.

They did not stop until they sat down at the great Mirrirmina (rock python's back) water hole in the country of the Liaalaomir clan. It is in the bottom of this well in the deep subterranean waters below the upper waters that Yurlunggur, the great copper snake, or python totem of the Dua moiety, lives. They called the country for the first time Mirrirmina.

The older sister took her fire drill and made a fire. She started cooking all the yams and other bush food that she had gathered and all the animals that they had killed on their journey.

"Sister, you cook my food for me, too," said the younger one.

"Be patient," said the older. She then gathered some paper bark and fashioned a bed for her younger sister's newborn child. As she did this, she said, "By and by, sister, we must circumcise these two small sons of ours."

"Yes, sister," said the younger.

As soon as they cooked the food each animal and plant jumped out of the fire and ran to the Mirrirmina water hole and jumped into it. They all went into this Djungguan and Gunabibi well. The crab ran in first. When he did this, the two women talked Liaalaomir for the first time; before this they had talked Wawilak. The other plants and animals followed the crab. The yams ran like men, as did the iguanas, frilled-neck lizard, darpa, ovarku snake, rock python, sea gull, sea eagles, native companions and crocodiles.[5] Each ran and dived into the clans' totemic well and disappeared from sight.

B. The Python's Sacred Pool Is Profaned and He Swallows the Wawilak Women

3. The profanement of the pool.

The older woman went out to gather bark to make a bed for her sister's baby after it was born. She walked over some of the water of the Mirrirmina well. Her menstrual blood fell in the totem well and was carried down the sacred clan water hole, where Yurlunggur, the Big Father, lives.

4. Yurlunggur raises himself to swallow the women; the rain comes and the flood commences covering the earth.

When the menstrual blood dropped into the pool Yurlunggur smelled the odor of this pollution from where he was lying in the black water beneath the floor of the totem well. His head was lying quietly on the bottom of the pit. He raised his head and smelled again and again.

"Where does this blood come from?" he said. He opened the bottom of the well by throwing the stone which covers its base out of the well on to the land by the women's camp. (This stone is near the camp today and can be seen by those who go there. "It is now a snake's head.") He crawled out slowly, like a snake does, from the well. When he came out

[5] One of the Liaalaomir leaders of the Wawilak ceremonies gave me the following list of animals and plants named and collected by the Wawilak sisters: "When they came from the Roper River they named iguana, bandicoot, opossum, snake, honeybee, fish, fresh-water fish and salt-water fish, shark, jabiru, shore birds, yam, big yam and little yam, water lily, water, salt water, fresh-water turtle and salt-water turtle, fresh-water snake and salt-water snake, all the different kinds of clansmen, lizard, small rat, brush turkey, and all the animals and things they saw." It was evident that he was attempting to make a definitive list of all the plants and animals, and that he was using as a memory device the names of the things he directed the chorus to sing in the various ceremonies of the Wawilak constellation.

he sucked some of the well water into his mouth. He spat it into the sky. Soon a cloud about the size of a man's hand appeared from nowhere in the center of the sky. As Yurlunggur slowly rose from out of the bottom of the pool the totemic well water rose too and flooded the earth. He pulled himself up on the stone which he had thrown, and laid his head there. He looked around him. He saw the women and their babies. Yurlunggur was older brother to these women, and they were sisters to him. Their children were his wakus, and he was gawel to them.

Yurlunggur continued to look at them. He hissed. This was to call out for rain. There was no cloud in the sky until then, but soon the two sisters saw a small, a very small, black cloud appear in the heavens. They did not see the great python lying there watching them.

The cloud grew larger and larger, and soon the rain came down. The Wawilak sisters hurriedly built a house to be ready for the rain. They named the forked sticks they used as uprights. The women went inside the house. They did not know where this rain had come from; they did not know that the older sister's menstrual blood had defiled the Mirrirmina water hole and had made Yurlunggur angry.

The Wawilak women went to sleep, but the rain poured down harder and harder and awakened them.

5. The sisters sing the rituals to prevent the flood and the snake's swallowing them.

The gungmun said, "Sister, where does this rain come from? There's no cloud in the north or south, and there is no cloud in the east or west, but over us is this huge black cloud. I think something is wrong. I think something terrible is going to happen."

She got up and went outside. The younger one stayed within the house and sang. The gungmun beat the ground with her yam stick; she knew now that Yurlunggur was going to swallow her, and she wanted to stop the rain. She sang, "Yurlunggur, don't you come out and swallow us. We are good, and we are clean." While she sang she danced around the house. The two sisters then called out the taboo names of the Mirrirmina well.

While the older sister sang and danced around the house, and the younger sister sang inside it to stop the rain from coming down and to drive the great cloud away, they were being surrounded by all the snakes in the land. The pythons, death adders, tree snakes, black snakes, tiger snakes, iguanas, the blue-tongued lizard, snails, caterpillars, and all the Dua snakes came up around them in a circle, for they had heard the call of their father, Yurlunggur. It was night and the women did not see them.

The gungmun first sang all the songs now sung in the general camp. After this she sang all the songs sung in the general camp during the Gunabibi. These are the less powerful songs. She did this first, for she thought they would stop the rain, but it did not stop. She was afraid of this rain, for it came out of a cloud she could not understand, because this cloud had come from nowhere.

She sang then the taboo songs of the Djungguan—"Ah! Ah! Ah! Kak Ye!!!" She sang the songs when the subsection names are called out in the Djungguan. She took the Dua subsections first.

The young sister sang like the leader of the Djungguan ceremony does today. She kept time with singing sticks. She said, "We'll turn to the Yiritja subsections now. We'll call out the Yiritja peoples [subsections]."

They sang the garma songs first, for they are not "strong" and belong to the camp of the women. Then they sang the songs of the Marndiella, for it is only a little more powerful, and its songs only slightly more taboo. Then they sang Djungguan and Ulmark.

The rain continued and came down harder and harder. They decided that they must sing something even more powerful, more taboo, and deeper within the ceremonial camp of the men.

6. Yurlunggur swallows the women, and the earth is covered with a flood.

They sang Yurlunggur and menstrual blood.

When Yurlunggur heard these words, he crawled into the camp of the two women and their two children. They had suddenly fallen into a deep sleep from his magic. He licked the women and children all over preparatory to swallowing them. He bit the noses of each and made the blood come. He swallowed the old woman first, the wirkul next, and the little boys last.

He waited for daylight. When dawn came he uncoiled and went out a short distance in the bush, because he was too near the water. He wanted to leave the women in a dry place.

He raised himself and stood very straight.[6] He was like the trunk of a very tall straight tree. His head reached as high as a cloud. When he raised himself to the sky the flood waters came up as he did. They flooded and covered the entire earth. No tree or hill showed above them. When he fell later, the water receded, and at the same time there was dry ground.

[6] In some of the Wawilak stories the snake, after he has swallowed the two women and put his head in the clouds, flies over the country and names the various parts as he goes. "Wongar went on and on flying and flying and flying and naming and naming and naming with the young sister, the old sister and the children inside him." This is told in a monotone.—"Then he came down in the same country again and spit them out. They were still alive." When the snake flew over the country he also gave the people their various languages, according to some accounts. A Liaalaomir man is speaking: "I am a rock snake. I call Yurlunggur father and he calls me child. That snake flew over the country when he swallowed those women, and he talked my language. I talk that language now." In other accounts, when the snake flew about in the sky he spat on the various clan areas. The ones usually named are the Liaalaomir and Perango totemic wells. It is said that he only spat there because these snakes (Liaalomir and Perango totems) are large and the other snakes are smaller (not important).

While he was high in the sky and had the two women and children inside him he sang all the Marndiella, Djungguan, Gunabibi and Ulmark ceremonies.

7. The Dua clan snakes and Yurlunggur discuss what they have eaten and discover they have different languages but the same totemic emblems. They tell their language names, the names of their totemic water holes, and recite the list of their totems, and kinship is established.

The other Wongar Wirtits (totemic pythons) stood up too. They were all Dua, as Yurlunggur was, and none was Yiritja. Yurlunggur was higher than all the rest. He was the leader for those other snakes, and was more powerful than they.[7]

The Wessel Island python (Perango clan) raised himself. "What is your language?" he said.

"I am Liaalaomir. What is yours?"

"I am Perango Yaernungo."

"What is yours?" Yurlunggur then said to the python on the Howard Island mainland.

"I am Liagaomir."

"What is yours?" he asked the Banyan Island python.

"I am Karmalanga language. My country is Kolpaiyunala" [a tree from whose roots fiber string is made].

The Mandelpui, Wawilak, Boun, Djirin, Kalpu, Merango, Djapu, Djawark, and all Dua clans were asked by Yurlunggur what their language was, and each answered the language of his country (see pages 39 to 51).

The Mirrirmina snake said then, "I see we all talk different languages. It would be better if we talked the same tongue. We can't help this now. It is better then that we all have our ceremonies together, for we own the same maraiin[8] [totemic emblems]."

They all sang out together then, and their voices were the thunder and roared all over the land and sea.

The python Wongars still stood on their tails high in the sky. The great Yurlunggur turned to a Daii Dua snake. He said, "What have you been eating?"

"I have been eating fresh-water fish" (Dua variety).

"How did he taste?"

"Oh, he was very good. Nice and fat."

"What are you going to do, now that you have eaten him?"

[7] There is no doubt that all peoples in the area recognize the leadership of the Liaalaomir python. He is the highest in the sky and the deepest in the well. His clan leaders always lead the Djungguan ceremony when they are present, even if the other clan leaders who ordinarily lead this performance are present.

[8] See glossary of Native Terms.

"I'm going to spew him up and look at him and eat him again for the last time."

He was going to do what the live pythons do now; they eat something, swallow it, spew it up, lick it, and eat it again. It does not come up again.

Yurlunggur now asked the Djapu python what he had eaten.

"I ate a wallaby [Dua moiety]. I'm going to let him out."

He inquired of the others. The Merango snake had eaten a small plains bird; the Kalpu, a sand crab; Djirin, a green sea turtle; Naladaer, a small shellfish; Wawilak, a bird; Mandelpui, a fresh-water fish; Karmalanga, honey. All of the snakes of the Dua clan were asked. Wessel Island snake was asked last. He is second highest and only lower in rank than Mirrirmina snake.

"What have you been eating?" the Liaalaomir snake asked the Wessel Island one.

"I won't tell you."

"Come on, tell me. I've heard lightning and thunder and wind in your country. Something has happened there."

"You give me something and I'll tell you."

"Come on, you and I are brothers. Remember I call you brother."

"If I tell you, you must tell me, because I call you wawa [older brother] and you called me yukiyuko [younger brother] just as you said."

"I'll tell you. I've eaten parrot fish."

"What color?"

"Blue."

"What kind of teeth?"

"White."

"What you have eaten is no good. Why didn't you eat iguana or stone kańgaroo?"

"But what did you eat?" replied the Wessel Island snake.

"I won't tell you."

"Why not?"

The Mirrirmina snake raised itself higher and higher into the sky. He laid his neck and head on a cloud. His eyes shot lightning. He felt ashamed.

"Come on and tell me, my big brother," said the Wessel Island snake again.

The Wessel Island snake continued to insist, and his head came closer and closer as his body writhed across the clouds toward the Mirrirmina python. He was very angry.

After a long time Yurlunggur said, "I ate two sisters and a small boy and girl."

8. The fall of Yurlunggur and the decline of the flood when the southeastern wind blows.

When he said this the southeastern monsoon started blowing from off the land. As it did this the head of the Wessel Island snake hurriedly pulled back to its own well. The wind had stopped him from coming farther; he wanted to make a waterway from Wessel Island to Mirrirmina. Yurlunggur roared and fell to the ground at the same time.

When he fell, he split the ground open and made the present dance ground at the Liaalaomir ceremonial place. He lay there on the ground and thought, "Those two sisters and their children are dead inside me now."

Yurlunggur started cleansing his mouth with his cheeks and tongue. He spat several times. He said to his sons, "I'm going to spew." He regurgitated the two women and the little boys.[9] They were dropped into an ants' nest.

The Wessel Island snake, when he heard what Yurlunggur said, was disgusted. "You've eaten your own wakus and yeppas," he said. This was a terrible thing.

9. The totemic trumpet appears and Yurlunggur goes back to the Mirrirmina water hole where he gathers all the snake creatures, returns, and reswallows the women and once again falls and the flood is ended.

The Wongar Yurlunggur crawled slowly back to his water hole. He went inside but kept his head up to watch. At this time the Yurlunggur totemic trumpet came out of the well and lay beside him. No one brought it out and no one blew it, but it sang out like it does now.

The Yurlunggur trumpet blew over the two women and their two sons. They were lying there like they had fainted. Some green ants came out then and bit the women and children. They jumped.

The trumpet continued to walk around, while the Wongar Yurlunggur looked on. The women and children were alive again, and he had thought them dead. He picked up two singing sticks (bilmel) and crawled out of the water hole. Before he emerged he called all his sons, who were in the well, and put these true snakes, lizards, and snails on his head and neck.

He hit the mothers and their babies on their heads with the sticks and swallowed them again. He meant to keep them down this time.

He felt sick again, for once more he had swallowed Dua people. He decided to stand straight up.

When he raised up the Mandelpui snake shouted, "What did you eat?"

"Bandicoot," he lied.

"You do not tell the truth."

"Two Dua women and two Yiritja boys."

When he said this he fell again. This time he made the Gunabibi and

[9] In some accounts a boy and girl are swallowed, and usually also regurgitated; but in many of the stories told by the older Liaalaomir men the children are male, and not spewed up by the snake.

Ulmark dance grounds by his fall (as the first time he fell he formed a Djungguan place). After his fall, he crawled into the Liaalaomir well and went down into the subterranean waters. He put a stone over his entrance and stopped the flood of water that had been coming out. He swam in the underground waters to the Wawilak country, for he wanted to take the mothers and children back to their own country; here he spat them out for the last time. He left them there and came back to his own country. The two women turned to stone and one can still see them in the Wawilak country today. Yurlunggur kept the boys inside him, for they were Yiritja and he was Dua.

The two women did not circumcise their two sons as they intended, because Yurlunggur had interfered before they were ready. It was because they so intended, and said for other people to perform this act, that people cut their sons today.

C. Man Learns the Secrets of the Creator Sisters' Rituals

10. Man learns the secrets of the Wawilak women and at this time starts the use of these rituals by modern men through using the women's blood and the ritual paraphernalia brought with them to Mirrirmina. Man is warned by the women in a dream to continue to practice these ceremonies forever.

While all this great drama was being acted in the country of the Liaalaomir, two Wawilak Wongar men had heard the terrible noise of the snake's voice (thunder) and they had seen the skies fill with lightning and felt the downpour of the rain. They knew something was the matter, so they followed the two women's tracks. It took them many days and nights to get there. They finally saw the snake track.

"I think the sisters had trouble," said one. "I think that maybe a crocodile or python has killed them."

They arrived at Mirrirmina. They had followed the Goyder River down. They saw all the ants walking around everywhere, like they smelled something that was dead and they wanted to eat. They then found all the snake tracks. The well water shone like a rainbow. When they saw this they knew there was a snake in there.[10]

They went farther in the bush and saw the ceremonial ground where Yurlunggur's fall had made the dance places.

"Wongar python has been here," they said.

When they looked carefully at the stone, they found blood from the heads of the two women and boys.

"What will we do?"

[10] Cf. Radcliffe-Brown, A. R., "The Rainbow Serpent Myth of Australia," Royal Anthropological Institute of Great Britain and Ireland, *Journal,* London, 1926, Vol. LVI, pages 19-25.

"Run and get some paper bark and make a basket," said the older Wawilak man.

They gathered two baskets of blood, and went to the dance grounds. They made a bush house on part of the ground that represents the snake's tail.

"You take all the hawk's feathers, bush cotton, and this blood, and we'll paint ourselves. You do this, and I shall go cut a hollow log and make a Yurlunggur trumpet."

Each did his task. The hollow ridgepole from the Wawilak sisters' house was used for the trumpet totemic emblem of Yurlunggur.

The sun went down. They left the blood till morning. They slept, and while they were in a deep sleep they dreamed of what the two women sang and danced when they were trying to keep Yurlunggur from swallowing them. The Wawilak women came back as spirits and taught the two men the Djungguan songs and dances that are for the outside general camp, and the inside ones that are for the men's camp. They told the men the way to do the Marndiella, Gunabibi and Ulmark ceremonies. They sang Yurlunggur and Muit. The men slept on and dreamed that Yurlunggur brought out all the iguanas from the Mirrirmina well. (See Djungguan ritual, pages 273 to 274.)

The two sisters said to men, "This is all now. We are giving you this dream so you can remember these important things. You must never forget these things we have told you tonight. You must remember every time each year these songs and dances. You must paint with blood and feathers for Marndiella, Gunabibi and Djungguan. You must dance all the things we saw and named on our journey, and which ran away into the well."

After the men danced the new dances and ceremonies for the first time they went back to their own country. "We dance these things now, because our Wongar ancestors learned them from the two Wawilak sisters."

THE DJUNGGUAN CEREMONY

The great ceremonies all take place in the dry season, and always on the men's ceremonial grounds. Actual participation is only by initiated men, although the women, not allowed in the ceremonial grounds and not thought of by the men as in the ceremony, play an important rôle.

All the ceremonies are associated with age grading, as being participated in by men initiated into certain age grades, or serving to initiate a man into a higher status; and all are associated with moiety or clan totems.

All the rituals have ceremonial leaders. The participants paint themselves with sacred totemic designs and usually employ feather ornaments, the decorations ordinarily varying from one ceremony to another. Musical instruments are used—a drum, a wooden trumpet, singing sticks, or bull roarer.

A fundamental conceptual scheme runs through all the ceremonies; the various dramatic sections portray the myth by dance and song. For the western European, this whole totemic ceremonial behavior might be compared to a Wagnerian opera, with the myth as libretto; the motifs, like that of the snake swallowing the women, first expressed in a phrase or two, are later elaborated; and certain motifs, highly elaborate in some of the ceremonies, are only hinted at in others. For the reason that here we have ceremonies treated separately by the natives which they yet realize fit into a larger whole, the totality may, without too much stretching, be compared to the Nibelungen Ring. The fundamental difference is that the story is not a myth to them but a dogma and has the same ceremonial significance to the Murngin as the Mass to a believing Catholic.

Shortly after the rainy season is ended, the waters of the many lakes are receding, and the long dry period of plenty begins, the various clans of the Murngin and other northeastern Arnhem Land tribes perform their principal interclan circumcision, the Djungguan, which also serves as a *rite de passage* for the older boys.

A. The Preliminaries

1. Yurlunggur is made; its first blowing announces that a Djungguan has started.
2. The little boys are taken from their mothers. They are decorated and sent on a journey.
3. The camp is divided into its sacred and profane sections. The Warn-gai-tja is made and placed in the main camp.

1. When the leader of the Djungguan has conferred with his blood brothers, the other old men of the clan, and usually the older men of the surrounding friendly clans upon the advisability of having a Djungguan, the ceremony starts. A number of the older men go out into the surrounding bush and pick out a small tree the core of which has been eaten out by termites so that only a thin outer layer of the trunk remains. This is cut down, cleaned out, and formed into a large trumpet, which in a later section of the ceremony (E) is painted, and becomes a totemic emblem representative of the great python deity, Yurlunggur. It is then taken to the old men's ground and placed

either in a special house made for it or within a clearing inside the jungle thicket. All this is done without ceremony. The trumpet is usually blown to ascertain if it has good tone and carrying quality, and also to indicate to all the tribe then present that preparations are under way for a Djungguan.

Normally two boys are initiated at one time. The fathers are approached for their permission to circumcise their sons.—Frequently the fathers petition the leader to initiate their sons, saying, "I'll give you presents of spears and my totemic emblem string if you will make this little son of mine a young man [yaoer-in]."

The boy may belong to a clan of either moiety. When the father decides that his son is old enough he informs him he must cease from being a child (dje-mer-ku-li) and become a yaoerin. The fathers, if asked by the leaders, always give their permission, unless they have decided to have their boys initiated in some other locality.

2. The little boys who are to be circumcised are told by their fathers and the other older men, "The Great Father Snake smells your foreskin. He is calling for it." The boys believe this to be literally true and become extremely frightened. Usually they take refuge with their mother, mother's mother, or some other favorite female relative, for they know that the men are organized to see that they are taken to the men's ground, where the great snake is bellowing.

The men take the boys from their mothers, the other women, and uninitiated children. All the female relatives grab up spears and spear-throwers and pretend to fight the men to prevent them from removing the boys. Some of the women, as do the men, participate in this ritual act in a spirit of play, others wail ceremonially, and some of the nearer female relatives shed real tears, both for the loss of the boy and the fact that he must go through the ordeal of circumcision.—All this is to make the boy think that the women are protecting him from the great snake, and, symbolically, to keep the great snake from swallowing him.

Some of the women talk to each other while they form a ring around the boy to protect him from the men: "Our sons [brothers, et cetera] have [or they are going to have] a great multitude of relatives, and their people are to be found everywhere. Our sons have many possessions. They have killed many kangaroos, wallabies, and birds, and they have speared many fish and turtles. Our sons and brothers have gone many places and speak many languages, and they have many presents from all their people." All this is exaggerated, but it is said for its magical effect, to insure the boys' acquiring many presents on the journey on which they are sent by the older men, and to enable them always to have plenty of good things during their lives. The above quotation is not a formula and is varied according to the speaker.

The two boys, with a near relative such as an older dué (sister's husband, father's sister's son), are sent out (at times this does not occur), usually on separate paths, to visit the various relatives and clans to invite them to the coming ceremony. The relatives of the boys who are present at the time they are sent away and who belong to outside clans are always desirous that the initiates visit their clans. The father chooses a trail for the boy to follow, but the man who accompanies and protects the boy usually modifies the father's directions to fit the circumstances of the journey.

The neophytes usually stay away a month, but their journey may last two moons, or less than one. If they leave when the moon is full they return when there is a new moon. In later years a man always boasts about the many clans he visited, the great distances he traveled, the long period he was absent on his journey.

The young men are sent away, it is said by the old Murngin men, so that they will meet new people, which is felt to be a good thing, and make lifelong friends among their more distant classificatory relatives. This ritualistic making of friends is not organized among these people as highly as in West Australia, nor does the path followed by the boy occupy as important a place in his later life as it does in West Australian regions.

One Wessel Island boy of the Perango clan went down through Elcho Island, where he visited the clan of that country, through Arnhem Bay and into the country of the Gwiyamil clan.[11] A candidate for initiation from the Wangurri clan went overland to the Barlamomo of Blue Mud Bay.

Before leaving, the boys are given new armlets which are then painted with white clay; white cockatoo feather headdresses are put on them, and their faces are daubed with white paint. Usually a white clay bark band is tied around the forehead. Red ocher and kangaroo fat with a white clay outline are put on the boys' faces. A large hair belt, suspended from which is a painted opossum fur string pubic covering, is put on the initiate for the first time. Before this he has gone completely nude, as do all uncircumcised boys.

Wherever the boy goes on his journey the people are informed of the coming ceremony and invited to attend. All those who are invited give

[11] See the clan and tribal map, page 40.

presents, such as spears, hair belts, spear-throwers, and other valued articles, to the boy. Most of these things are later presented to the father, older brothers, gawel, and mari. If the boy were not treated liberally his clan would be offended, and it might lead to an open feud; but the people in the clans visited are always generous and such cause for a feud is never given. While the boy is away the women gather yams, lily bulbs, and other vegetable food to prepare for their guests. Many of the visitors come with the boy when he returns, while others precede him to participate in the preliminary ceremonies.

3. When the neophyte arrives in camp, or frequently before he comes back, the Warn-gai-tja is erected in the center of the main camp where all the people live. Two poles about six feet long are cut from trees (of any variety) in the old men's ground and tied together. A bunch of leaves is tied to the top of each pole. If three boys are to be initiated, three poles are cut and tied together; if only one boy is to be circumcised, only one pole. Grass is strewn on the ground around the foot of the pole. The sticks are Dua and the leaves are Yiritja.

The general camp of both the men and women is called Wonga. In the center of it, or sometimes at the side of this ground if better suited for dancing, is the general dance ground. The warngaitja is located in the center of the dance floor. It is here that men and women dance. This is the only part of the ceremonial ground to which women and uncircumcised boys have access. It is sometimes called Wakinu Wonga, which can be translated as "the camp of those who do not belong," and is used in a contemptuous sense (see pages 99-102).

The men bring the warngaitja into the main camp from the men's ground. They carry their spears pointing downward and beat time against the shafts with their spear-throwers. They sing meanwhile:

"War-li-mar-la din-ya
War-li-mar-la din-ya
(Dua sticks of the warngaitja)
Warn-gai-tja ngu-lai-ngu-lai
Warn-gai-tja ngu-lai-ngu-lai"
(Yiritja leaves of the warngaitja)

The following songs are also sung:

(1) Stone spear
(2) Camp made by Wawilak Sisters in the Garl-ban-uk country (Gun-al-pia)

(3) Bamboo spear with stone head (Gun-na-mar-mar)
(4) Women and boys (Mielk koon-di Djer-ku-li)
(5) Fat of the kangaroo mixed with red ocher to paint the boy's face (Ri-djil-gur-o)
(6) The taboo name for the warngaitja (Ngur-mir-go-nor-mi-a)

During the singing and dancing the warngaitja is carried in the center of the group of men.

The women meet them and, while the men stand in a compact circle, they dance around them waving branches. The pole is taken to various parts of the camp and the men form circles around it and sing the above cycle of songs while the women dance around them. Finally a permanent place in the center of the main camp is selected, and after singing once more over the warngaitja, it is placed upright on the ground and left there until the end of the Djungguan ceremony.

When a Djungguan is being celebrated a Murngin camp is divided into several geographical divisions. These territorial divisions are based on the age-grade groupings which are discussed in Chapter IV. The geographical divisions are (1) the general camp, (2) the men's ground, (3) the old men's camp and totem house, (4) the "totem well," or temporary dwelling place of the totemic emblem for one portion of the ceremony, and (5) the snake dance ground.

The territorial division clearly objectifies the grading in the men's association and the differentiation from women: the old men's camp, the holy of holies for the few; the dance ground for the circumcised, which includes the greater part of the young men; and the main camp for the uncircumcised and the women.

The men's ground is called Djungguan Wonga (camp). It is also called Ma-rai-in Wonga. Maraiin is a general word meaning, as nearly as it can be translated, powerful, sacred, taboo, or spiritual. It is used to describe anything that is taboo to the women and uninitiated boys. It is not necessarily taboo to everyone in the tribe. Totemic emblems, ceremonial grounds which certain age grades are forbidden, "sacred" names known only to the older men, and certain designs are among the things that are considered maraiin by the Murngin.

A quality possessed by a thing that is maraiin is dal. The literal translation of dal is "hard" and "strong," but dal means strength only in the magical sense of ritually "powerful." The maraiin wonga has a considerable amount of dal, but the old men's camp possesses a concentrated portion of this magical strength. The old men's part of the

Djungguan is called Wongar Dal. Wongar is the totemic spirit itself. It is one of the beings which once lived in the earth and now lives in the subterranean waters. It is also the spirit or essence which enters the totemic emblem, so that when the old men's camp is called Wongar Wonga it means totemic spirit's camp. It is here that the totemic emblem is kept when it is not in use during the ceremony. Since the essence of the totemic spirit is supposed to be within the emblem, the camp literally is the place where Wongar lives. The young men who do not belong to the upper age group are told that he actually stays in this place.

The triangular dance ground, where the various dramatic dances are presented before the initiates, represents a snake's body and is also supposed to have the Wawilak sisters and their children inside it. It is supposed to face toward the southeast.

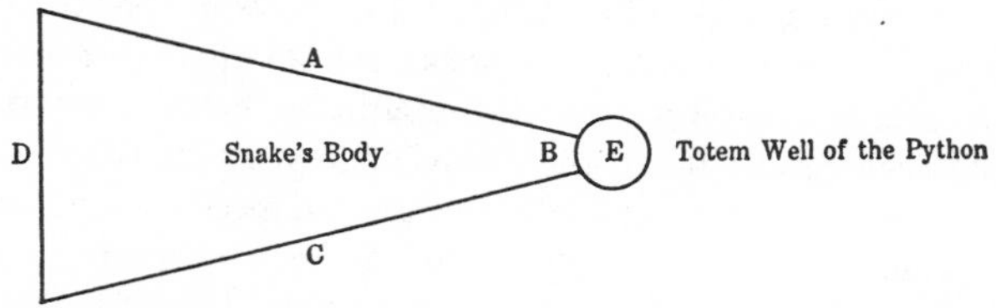

FIGURE 3.—THE TRIANGULAR DANCE GROUND OF THE SNAKE'S BODY

The old men are saturated with all the ritual power that pertains to the totem and its emblems, and the old men's camp therefore takes on a taboo quality, partly because the old men take maraiin there. To a lesser degree, this is true of the camp where the circumcised men are allowed to go. They, to a lesser extent, have assimilated some of the ritual power which allows them to be on this part of the camp ground. Even the women have a minimum of maraiin: they know a part of the ritual tradition; they dance around the warngaitja; they help in dramatizing the removal of the boy from the uncircumcised age group to the circumcised; they paint themselves with red ocher; and, of course, fundamentally they are Murngin social personalities.

The triangular dance ground is made by clearing off a smooth space and heaping a line of earth about ten inches high around its periphery. The earth is then covered with green leaves from any variety of tree. The end (D) is twenty to twenty-five feet across, and from D to B is some forty to fifty feet. A and C represent the side of the snake. "The Wawilak sisters said that (A) was Yiritja moiety and that (C) was Dua moiety." This division refers to the dance ground and not to Yurlunggur, who was Dua. B is the snake's anus; D is the head where the initiates stand, both in the circumcision part of the ceremony and also in that portion devoted to showing and explaining the totemic emblem to the older initiates.

The circle E is the special house for Yurlunggur erected on the first day of the ceremony and is a windbreak about four feet high and fifteen feet across. The dancers who paint themselves as iguanas in the totem scene ceremony hide there while the earlier part of the Djungguan is taking place.

When the Yurlunggur dance ground is made, a cycle of songs is sung over the man who gives his blood to the ceremony (see page 264) by the old men. This makes the ground maraiin because it now possesses the essence of Yurlunggur.

Native Interpretation.—The warngaitja is symbolical of the two boys who are being circumcised. "The sticks are all the same as the boys being cut. The bushes on top are all the same as the hair of those boys." I was told each time I heard the Wawilak myth that when "the little sister sang inside the house, the older sister danced around the house just the same as women do now around the warngaitja pole in the Djungguan." When new groups arrive at the Djungguan ceremony, the ritual is being started, and they dance around the warngaitja singing "A-wa!—a-wa!" it is the sound of flood water flowing or of rain falling: "They do that because those two old women did that when they tried to stop the rain." In the Djungguan ceremony older women ordinarily do the dancing and wailing. "No young women, only old women do this. Old women are better for the boys—it helps them more. Those old women when they dance are all the same as those Wongar women."

B. The Dancing Each Evening Around the Warngaitja. The Initiates Are Carried into the Men's Ground

1. The women wail over the neophytes while dancing around the warngaitja pole (or poles); the men rush in and remove the boys to their own grounds.
2. The circle of men around the fire and the sequence of songs and dances.

1. Until the last day of the ceremony dances in the Djungguan are not held during the day except occasionally in the early morning. But

when the sun sinks and dusk first appears the boys' maris (mothers' mothers), yeppas (sisters), and arndis (mothers) start wailing for him because they are going "to lose him forever." (Once the initiate is taken from the women, even before he makes his journey, he is not allowed to return to them but is kept entirely in the charge of some of the men.)

The women then dance with bent knees around the central pole, with their slow, shuffling rhythm, waving bunches of leaves in each hand. The men meanwhile pick the initiates up and gather in a group outside the general camp behind a clump of bushes.

When the boys are first taken from the women, and each evening during the opening part of the ceremony, they are carried on the men's shoulders in the same position that babies are carried by their mothers and fathers.

The men beat their spears with their spear-throwers and sing:

"Djer-ma-kun-di,[12] mielk-kun-di."
(Uncircumcised boys, women)

The men rush out and surround the pole in a solid mass. The women sing a song which, freely translated, means, "We give you men this boy child while we dance." The men then sing kangaroo fat.—This performance is repeated a number of times.

After the above ceremony has taken place on the women's ground the boys are carried upon the shoulders of the men, who go, singing, to the men's ground. The women meanwhile continue to dance around the wạrngaitja.

2. A fire is built a short distance from the triangular dance ground (see Figure 3, page 255). The little boys are put down within the group of men who sit in a circle around the fire.

A new cycle of songs is sung:

(1) Turkey (Wal-pa-run-go di-ma-run-a, Dua)
(2) Fresh-water turtle (Gai-yil-pur-o djel-gai-a-na, Yiritja)
(3) Young boy before circumcision (Mil-er-um-bur-u)
(4) Fish spear (Bar-nai-djer-yer, Yiritja)
(5) A tree with a red flower that emus eat (Warn-bar-ko ngu-nu-lai)
(6) Bamboo spear (Djir-ne-djir-ne gur-o-o)

[12] Cf. dje-mer-ku-li. Age Grading, page 114. "Djer-ma-kun-di" is from the ritual language.

At this period in the song cycle the following refrain is sung by all the men:

"Ah—ah—ah—!! ah—ah!
Sis ye!! Sis ye!!
Ay—Ay—Ay—!!
Kak ye!!"

(7) Wallaby (Nar-ku mar-rain-djur-a kam-dal main-djur-a)
Two men stand up and dance in imitation of kangaroos. They may be either Yiritja or Dua moiety, but the Wallaby dance is for the Burilung subclass.

(8) The rock kangaroo (par-de-par-de-min-ne burul-purul-min-e, Burilung subclass)

The following refrain is now sung:

"Bir—pir—!! Pir—pir—!!
Ah—oo!! Poo!!
Bir—pir—!! Pir—Pir—!!
Ah—oo!! Poo!!
Kak-ye—kak ye!!"

(9) Emu (Ur-tarn-gal-li-na), Yiritja
Emu head feathers (kurt-kurt-gal-li-na), Bur-lain subclass, Yiritja moiety

(10) A fresh-water fish (Gal-ngi mar-kunr-dur-na), Narit subclass, Yiritja moiety

(11) Ibis (Durn-di-tja gar-ran-gun-mi), Kaidjawk subclass, Yiritja moiety

(12) A small hawk (Kar-kar-ain-bir-na), Bang-ar-di subclass, Yiritja moiety

The refrain beginning "Bir—pir" is repeated.

(13) Carpet snake totem (Yur-lung-gur), Bal-lung, Ka-mer-dung and Wa-mut subclasses, Dua moiety

(The totemic emblem is brought in at this time. The chorus sings, "Djil-djil-la djil-djil-la [hiss of the snake].)

(14) Blood from the arm to paint the body in the Djungguan ceremony (Man-in-jul-or-un-gal), Yiritja or Dua moiety, since either can give his blood for the ceremony.

(15) A fresh-water, non-poisonous snake (Bog-min-bog-min)
(16) Fresh-water crayfish (Run-nar-ra-nar-ra-na), Yiritja moiety

The following dances take place:

(1) A small hawk (Kar-kar-kain-bur-na mal-le-wir-de-wir-de)
(2) Dollar bird (?) (Ko-ko-mir-ding), Dua moiety

Big gray kangaroo, wallaby, and rock kangaroo are also danced. This ends the ceremony for the evening, and the refrain "Wah! wah! wah!" (sound of running water) is sung.

Whenever wallaby is sung in the above cycle of songs two men stand up and dance at one side. Sometimes they are joined by several others. The men hold their hands in front of their chests with the fingers pointed downward to imitate the posture of the front legs and paws of the wallaby. They dance jumping sideways as one often sees the wallaby move when frightened. At intervals they fall flat on the ground, remain there a moment, then arise and start the dance over again.

While the chorus of men sing and the men at the side dance, one man stands by the side of the ring and calls out in a high shrill voice, "Kawk! Kawk!" This is supposed to be the call of the wedge-tailed eagle.

Native Interpretation.—"The warngaitja was put up the first time by the two Wawilak women. They cut off the stringy bark tree and put it up and tied it with bush string. Now men do this." "Those women said, 'We two sisters, we'll do this and make up this warngaitja dance and everybody will do this after us, but the ranga and maraiin will belong inside of the men's ground.'" (For further interpretation of the Warngaitja ceremony, see Section E, where the ceremony is performed for the last time.)

C. Yurlunggur Comes Out

1. The older men sing Yurlunggur and his totem well and several bring out the trumpet. It is blown over the uncircumcised initiates. The older boys (those about to pass into a higher age group) hide their heads under the women's mats.

1. Just before the Yurlunggur song is sung (13 of the cycle in Section B), the leader of the ceremony calls out the totems of the Liaalaomir clan and of other clans which possess the same totems as this

group beginning with the great rock python Yurlunggur.

One man of this clan (or of another clan in the Dua moiety) leaves the circle and walks to the edge of the nearby bushes in the direction of the old men's camp and cries out the totemic name of the country where Yurlunggur swallowed the two Creator Sisters and their babies. This country belongs to the Liaalaomir clan and the names are those of its sacred water hole as well as those of the country.

Finally Yurlunggur's tongue is called. All the younger men, who have not been initiated into the higher parts of the men's association by seeing the totem of the rock python, lay their heads on the ground and the older men cover them with women's pandanus mats (ainmaras). The uncircumcised boys who are to be initiated in this ceremony have usually gone to sleep long before this time. They are awakened and their heads covered in the same way.

The older men continue sitting with their heads up in an attitude of expectation. Four or five men have left the group and have quietly slipped into the bush. The men are still singing the totemic names of the python. As if from some far-off subterranean stone chamber one hears a kind of bellowing roar. It is a weird sound. To those who have been reared on stories of mediaeval knights and their dragons the sound is like that which one imagines a wounded dragon would make. The roar continues for some moments, which the initiates say appears to be a long time.

The Yurlunggur trumpet (totemic emblem) appears. It is carried by the three or four men who shortly before disappeared, while another blows it. When it is within a few feet of the circle its carriers stand still while the trumpeter continues blowing. Yurlunggur's "head" is pointed toward the circle of men and the neophytes. It is blown over them. It is then turned around, and with the man still blowing it, is carried back to the old men's camp, which is the totem house. The carriers and trumpeter sneak back to the circle and all the initiates are told to uncover their heads.

Native Interpretation.—"These two sisters sang Yurlunggur and menstrual blood. They sang blood because that is what brought the snake when Yurlunggur came. This is the same when the men bring Yurlunggur in at night to the circle. The iguanas bring him in. Yurlunggur crawled right into the camp with the women and their children. He swallowed them." (These statements are also applicable to the sacred songs sung while the subsection names are called out—see Section B.) During a Djungguan one of the older men said, pointing to the trumpet, "That is the real Great Father. He is also the real father for these boys who are going to be cut."

D. The Dances on the Triangular Dance Ground

1. The men dance a variety of animal dances, while the initiates stand on the edge of the dance ground and are instructed by the old men.

1. All the men then collect and go over to the dance ground. A fire is lighted in the center. The Yiritja men dance while the Dua men look on; then the Dua dance while the Yiritja watch. The same leader conducts the songs for the men of both moieties. Sometimes two moieties dance together instead of separately, but this is considered less proper.

After the alternation of the dances by the moieties, all the dancers join hands and, calling out in turn wedge-tailed eagle and kangaroo, they stamp out the fire. A new fire is started in the same place and all of the men go out at the anal end of the snake dance ground to the side. They divide into two groups, one representing the Yiritja gray kangaroo and the other the Dua wallaby. They squat on their haunches and hop into the dance ground at the anal end, and when they reach the fire they dance around it as one group. They fall down and lie in a heap around it. This ends the ceremony on the dance ground for the night. They return to the dance ground in the main camp calling out like hawks[13] after they have given the sound that symbolizes running water. Meanwhile in the old men's camp can be heard the low bellowing of the python trumpet "to let everyone know that the Great Father is in camp." It is late and the women have gone to bed; their fires are still burning when the men disband after the day's ceremony.

All the men participate in the above dances, except the boys to be

[13] The hawk is a Yiritja bird supposed always to be on the lookout for small snakes believed to be their chief antagonists.—Tremendous grass fires are made all over the country when the dry season has parched grass and brush to the point where they are easily burned, to clear the land so that it is easy to hunt over. They are made particularly by the women to aid them in catching bandicoot and other small game. At this time hawks gather about, intent upon catching snakes, grasshoppers and other small game which run before the fires.

circumcised and a few of the older men, who stand outside at the head of the dance ground. The old men tell the initiates the meaning of the dances. The little boys stand, each with the men's basket under his arm, with the string handle over the left shoulder, in the manner of grown men.

The entire Djungguan song cycle is repeated during all the time the boys are away to invite others to their circumcision and from two to four weeks after their return. The dances vary slightly, and occasionally a few new elements are introduced into the main camp ceremony.

Sometimes an old woman, usually the initiate's mother's mother (mari), goes through the camp snatching the men's spears from them and threatening the younger women with the weapons. She is taking a threefold rôle in this ritual act: (1) expressing the antagonism of the women's division of the sex and age structure toward the men's division; (2) disciplining the younger women and thereby increasing the solidarity of the women's division; and (3) acting the part of a very old woman, which gives her special privileges, since old women are "more like a man" (see page 91 on the relationship of older mothers-in-law to their sons-in-law).

On certain nights (there is no regular order), several fires are built outside the python dance ground in a line running from the python's anus, and several inside the triangle. After having left the warngaitja circle and starting their ceremony on the python ground, the men, instead of dancing wallaby and kangaroo, dance hawk and rock kangaroo. The fires are built, say the natives, to chase the rock kangaroos out of their hiding places, and when the hawks see the fires they appear as they do when the natives light bush fires to hunt kangaroos.

The hawks cry, "Kawk! Kawk! Kawk!" They carry under each armpit green bushes or paper bark which they shake in imitation of hawks flying, and they carry their spear-throwers to represent the birds' tails while they dance between the fires. They are plastered with white clay. A white band of clay covers the face from the eyebrows to the bridge of the nose and runs from ear to ear. Another band of clay extends laterally from jaw to jaw beneath the mouth and across the chin. The upper arms, trunk, and upper legs are daubed with parallel lines of birds' down made fast with human blood.

The rock kangaroos dance first, followed by the hawks. Both stamp out the fire on the dance ground with their feet. The hawks call out their totemic names and the rock kangaroos shout their taboo names. The kangaroos are Dua and the hawks Yiritja. Usually the men who dance the Dua animal belong to the Dua, and the men who dance the Yiritja bird, to the Yiritja moiety.

Early in the morning, before the heat of the day, ceremonies are also held. The uncircumcised initiates are again placed before the head of the dance ground with one or more old men to explain the meaning of the various dances and songs. The first set of dancers are Dua honeybees. They come in one at a time in a zigzag line from the bush and enter the dance ground at the tail of the snake. They kneel before the boys and lie down with the arms stretched above the head and the legs at full length. The last two dancers dance around the others. They all lie down on their backs in one or more lines. Each man places his head between the legs of the man above him and stretches his arms above him at an angle so that they cross the legs and form a diamond pattern, which is supposed to symbolize the honeybee and is one of the few dominant designs found in the totemic paintings of the Murngin.

They squirm forward and backward to represent bees in a hive, while they cried out, "Wah! Wah!! Wah!!" They leave the head of the dance ground and return to the bush. The faces of the little boys remain inexpressive, like masks, throughout the dance.

Yiritja kangaroos are then danced. The Dua wallabys are in a line directly back of the tail of the snake, and to the rear of them are the Yiritja kangaroos. The two lines of dancers pretend to fight with their forepaws as these marsupials box. The leader beats his singing sticks together and leads the ceremony while standing back of the dancers. He sings wallaby and kangaroo.

Farther back in the bushes a man, painted with a "string harness" worn by present-day women but representing here that of the two old Creator Sisters, stands with a spear articulated to his spear-thrower. He sneaks up toward the animals as the two lines form again after their sham fight. The two lines merge. The "hunter" throws his spear and "kills" the leader. He limps off and, followed by the wallabys and kangaroos, falls down at the head of the snake.

Native Interpretation.—The triangular dance ground in the Djungguan has the same interpretation as both the excavated and the surface dance grounds of the Ulmark ceremony. A dance ground is a snake's body and it is usually thought of as having the women and children inside it. Frequently the green leaves surrounding it are said to be the women after he has spewed them up. During one of the many times I was told the story of the Wawilak women, when the narrator got to the moment in the drama when the sisters were seeking something more powerful to stop Yurlunggur and they sang menstrual blood, he interrupted himself and said, "When the dance place for the Djungguan is square and not triangular it is a camp of these women. When it is this way [triangular] it is a snake's body. At Mirrirmina you can see the holes where all the sons of Yurlunggur crawled around the two women and you can see the dance ground where the snake fell after swallowing them."

E. The Bloodletting

1. Yurlunggur is painted.
2. Yurlunggur is blown over the men who give their blood; the names of the ancestors are called.

1. All during this section of the ceremony the totemic trumpet is kept in the old men's camp or in the specially built ceremonial hut (the python's totem well). During the preliminary stages of this section Yurlunggur is painted.

2. On the day before the circumcision a bloodletting ceremony takes place in the old men's camp. The blood is to be used as an adhesive substance to hold the birds' down and native cotton to the dancers' bodies. Before a man offers his blood for the first time Yurlunggur is blown all over his body; after the first time it is unusual. This ceremony is one of the ritual methods by which a man is admitted into the higher order of the men's association. Though it is not obligatory for him to go through this rite as it is for the young boy to go through the circumcision ceremony, all of the men feel it their privilege to contribute their blood either the first time they enter the old men's grounds or at some later period. Most men, while still in their prime, give their blood every time this ceremony is held.

Here is an account of one of the many blood sacrifice rituals witnessed by the author:

The old men sing over the man, Lika. The "mouth" of Yurlunggur is placed against him and the trumpeter blows all over his body while the trumpet's notes keep time with the slow rhythm of the singing sticks of the leader.

The cycle of songs is sung in the following sequence:

(1) Human blood (Man-in-gul-ur-un-gul)
(2) Python snake totem (Yurlunggur ar-lur-la)
(3) Snake's hiss (Djil-djil-la)

After each song the men take turns calling out the name of some of their ancestors (usually father's father or mother's mother's brother). Sometimes only the names of the ancestors are called out, but at other times men shout: "My mother's mother's brother [mari] carries a totemic emblem on his back!!"—"My mother's mother's mother's brother makes a totemic emblem!"—"My mari has a large penis!!"—"My father's father [marikmo] has a net in his hand and is catching many fish." The old men are always described by the men who use their names as making a totemic emblem or performing some other act while a totemic emblem is being made. The names of the old men are always their totemic and taboo names. The relatives referred to may be actually living, dead, or mythological ancestors. Each man continues all the relatives' names he pleases to select and then calls out, "Bilin [I'm through]." The leader then turns to the next man and he continues the same process.

(4) The fourth song sung is earthquake shaking the ground (movement of Yurlunggur)
(5) Snake's tongue
(6) Dua lightning
(7) Black rain cloud (Gor-ro-ma-la)
(8) Rain clouds covering the sky (Warn-ba-nar-ri)

The members of each subclass are taken in order by the leader to call out the names of their ancestors as well as the names of their totemic emblems. The Ballung subclass sings first, then Kamerdung and Wamut follow. All the Yiritja subclasses follow and then the fourth Dua one. Sometimes all four of the Dua subsections are called first, then the four Yiritja. Giving the ceremony a sequence of songs that follow in order of subsections grouped according to moiety definitely integrates the subsections into the ceremonial structure. At the same time the dead and the mythological ancestors are also placed in their correct subsections and moiety.

While the singing is going on, the man's arms are tied near the wrist and shoulder with some stout cord. A stone spear head is broken and a flake of it used to make a half-inch cut in the lower arm. The leader rubs the man's head with his hand while another cuts his arm. The totemic emblem is blown against the wound.

The blood runs slowly, and the rhythm of the song is conducted with equal slowness. In a second or two the blood spurts and runs in a rapid stream. The beat of the song sung by the old men increases to follow the rhythm of the blood. The blood runs into a paper-bark basin. "When Lika gets up he'll be very quick and feel very light; and he will be very happy because that blood running out of him will make him that way."

Two men hold the trumpet for a third to play. One of them keeps his hand on the blood-giver's head, occasionally rubbing it, and then massaging the forearm. He keeps one hand or part of his body against the trumpet.

The bottom of the basin fills with blood, and pieces of paper bark are taken from a supply near at hand, broken up in little pieces, and thrown into the basin. They soak up the blood and more pours in upon them. Once more small pieces of paper bark are placed in the basin to be saturated. These pieces of bark will be used later as brushes with which to put on the blood. The giver looks down at the blood coming from his arm with a smile which expresses pride, a slight embarrassment at being the center of attention, and real pleasure. Meanwhile the leader of the ceremony continues to massage his arm. The chorus now sings stringy bark tree.

The blood runs slower and the rhythm is decreased. One of the men loosens the cord on the upper arm and it is taken off. The song and the blowing of the trumpet continue. The slowly dripping blood is stopped with a bit of bush cotton or birds' down. The blood-giver massages his arm with an upward movement. He goes over to the side of the camp and lies down. Frequently the men who give their blood faint and remain in a state of coma for an hour or more because of exhaustion.

The next man opens a hole from yesterday's giving and the blood pours forth in a stream. It runs quickly, and the rhythm of the song is at a very fast tempo. There is much smiling among the men and an occasional "main-muk, main-muk (good, good)."

A third man pulls off an old scab from his arm and the blood pours forth in a larger stream than that of the others. The trumpet continues to blow (but not over the blood-giver since he is not one who is giving for the first time).

Several men proudly exhibit their arms which show five and six cuts that have been made during previous ceremonies.

The man who gives his blood for the first time is considered to be in a dangerous position. This is one of the reasons, the old men say, why he is played over. "That man who gives his blood for the first time for Yurlunggur might get killed. That is why we play over him. That blood comes straight from his heart to his arm when it runs out. That is why we tie it at the top or it might all run out. The boy might get killed because his soul is in his heart and the blood comes from there for corroborees." "It is blood [man-gu] which makes people strong all their lives; if a man's blood runs out and he is emptied of all his blood that man dies and his soul is gone. We got this body because we have that blood. If that blood goes away we are empty inside."

It is believed that this blood, when it is on a man's body as a part of his decoration for the ceremony, if touched by a woman will make her ill or produce sores on her body, because it has had a totemic name given it and the essence of the totemic spirit has gone inside this blood. The blood of a man who has been hurt in an ordinary accident will not hurt a woman. She can rub against him and be all right. "The blood that hurts a woman is the spirit of the Wongar that is inside that blood. It has a big [sacred] name that the leader sang when the men cut their arms. The spirit that is inside that blood is not just that wooden trumpet but another one more inside [more sacred] and the totemic spirit itself, Yurlunggur.—That blood that man gives in the Djungguan is Wongar Derpal. [Derpal means magically powerful and strong.] That blood the old man gives to the dance people makes them derpal and it makes their feathers and bush cotton derpal. The meaning is like this: suppose you and I have come a long way and we reach a good camp and our people have one house empty and it is a good place for us and they take us and put us in it. We get in that house and have a good sleep and no one can hurt us because we have friends. That blood is just like that. It makes us feel easy and comfortable and it makes us strong. It makes us good. That derpal is like the head man. We have that derpal from that blood. It is in our body. It goes inside when we put that blood on it. That blood makes a very big thing."

The night of the day following the bloodletting, the procedure in the main camp is changed. The old women start the evening's performance by wailing and dancing around the warngaitja. The men enter the camp, the boys on their backs now covered with bundles of bushes and leaves. The boys are placed on the ground under the pile of bushes by the warngaitja poles. The men stand with spears around them. The song ends. The men snatch the warngaitja from out of the ground, take the two boys, and run away into the men's ground. The women follow them singing flood water, stop at the edge of the men's grounds and return to the center of the camp, while the men continue on to the fire circle.

Native Interpretation.—The blood that runs from an incision and with which the dancers paint themselves and their emblems is something more than a man's blood—it is the menses of the old Wawilak women. I was told during a ceremony: "That blood we put all over those men is all the same as the blood that came from that old woman's vagina. It isn't the blood of those men any more because it has been sung over and made strong. The hole in the man's arm isn't that hole any more. It is all the same as the vagina of that old woman that had blood coming out of it. This is the blood that snake smelled when he was in the Mirrirmina well. This is true for Djungguan and Gunabibi."—"When a man has got blood on him [is ceremonially decorated with it], he is all the same as those two old women when they had blood. All the animals ran away and they couldn't cook them."

When the trumpet blows over the man giving his blood, it is Yurlunggur risen out of his well to swallow the women and their two children because he has smelled the menstrual blood of the older sister. Several well-informed men told me, "When Yurlunggur blows over them when they cut their arms it is like that snake comes up and smells that woman's blood when he is getting ready to swallow them." The songs sung refer to the profanement of the pool and the swallowing of the women by the snake, which means that the man who is giving his blood for the first time is being swallowed by the snake and is at the moment the old woman.

The first *giving* of blood was made by the Wawilak sisters themselves, since it was the blood from their heads and those of their children which was first used by man. "When the Wongar men [who came after the women had been swallowed] looked closely at the stone, they found blood from the heads of the two women and boys [where the snake had bitten them; see myth, subdivision 6]. 'What will we do?' 'Run and get some paper bark and make a panikin out of it.' "

"They tied up two panikins and put the blood in them and went to the ceremonial grounds.

"Take all the bird feathers and we will paint ourselves. You do this and I will go and cut Yurlunggur."

It is only the men's blood that is of the right quality for use in the Djungguan ceremony. Women's blood cannot be used. "Woman's and man's blood are just the same but woman's blood is no good. Wongar would not allow it to be used. He will only take men's blood." The blood is not only the menstrual blood of the women in the eyes of the old men; "That blood, that old woman's blood that ran out here [informant pointed to his pudenda], that blood is a live Wongar's blood too. He [the man who was giving the blood] does that for Wongar too. They blow that trumpet over him [the blood-giver] because the snake came out and smelled that woman's blood when she went after paper bark." These last statements were made within the totemic camp of the old men while they and I watched the young man who gave his blood for the first time.

When "Djili-djili-la" is sung after "blood" and "Yurlunggur," it, in singing form, "is just the same as when the snake comes out the first time," by which the various men who told me this meant "when Yurlunggur comes out" as described in Section C. In other words, these two parts of the ceremony are equivalent.—The next song, "Earthquake," was interpreted: "Those two women came to that place [Mirrirmina]. Yurlunggur smelled them and turned over and moved the ground." Whenever an earthquake occurs in Murngin country it is always said that Bapa Indi (Yurlunggur or Muit) is moving in the subterranean waters.—When the next song, "Snake's Tongue" was sung, a leader of one of the Djungguan said, "Those two women try to stop that snake's tongue. He wanted to swallow them. That is what this means. They gave his tongue an inside [sacred] name." Another man said, "When that trumpet blows he is singing out and asking, 'Which one has got strong blood?' It is like he is choosing the man he wants. When he gets that man he plays all over him just like he was licking him. He did those two Wongar women that way before he swallowed them. This makes the man's blood come out quick and easy."—After the next song, "Dua Lightning," the leader of one of the ceremonies said, "That is the forked tongue of the snake. Storms and thunder come from him. That is when he is after those two Wongar women." When "Rain Cloud" was sung the leader said to me, "Those two women are trying to stop that rain because it is coming like a flood and trying to cover them up, it is all the same as if they were being swallowed by a snake."—"Those women are trying to sing to stop the rain but they are only making sounds" (that is, they are having no effect on the rain or snake)—also a comment when "Cloud in the Sky" was sung. —After the completion of this cycle, the leader said to me, "No man made these songs. Those two women made them to keep the two lines [Yiritja and Dua moieties] sacred—to keep marriage straight."

The singing of the real and mythological ancestors' names is much more significant than merely recalling the names of the dead, for the souls of the dead are believed to be within the totemic trumpet itself (and within Mandelprindi and Yermerlindi in the Gunabibi ceremony and Uvar in the Ulmark ceremony). "When we have Djungguan, Gunabibi and other corroborees we men tell the women when a man is dead [recently died] that he has come back because that Djungguan has been named his big name [totemic name]. All the men believe he has come back and that all the souls of the dead on that side [moiety reference] are in the ranga [totemic emblem]. If my older brother should die, next Narra or Djungguan we have, he would come back and go in that ranga. That is why we get angry when someone does a bad thing [unsanctioned sexual relation, open fighting, and the like] when we have a Narra or Djungguan. We must stop that corroboree and throw the ritual string away because our old marikmos and maris and kutaras [et cetera] get angry with us and make us sick. The little babies when they are fish [unborn] live in the same place with marikmo and mari souls. That marikmo and mari watch us. If we are good, and we don't steal, or have other men's wives, he sends us fish to our wives." "You can't see that spirit when it comes back but you can see it in a dream. That man can be Yiritja or Dua. The man who has dreamed goes to the leader and says that so-and-so has come back, and that he says he has come to look at his children and to bring Yurlunggur. That leader asks the man which way the man in the dream said to make Yurlunggur for this next time, because he knows the man understands from this dream." This dream can come before or at the same time as the ceremony and the power name of the returning dead man can be given to the trumpet. Even though "spirits go to the islands of the dead,[14] or the whale takes them to the

[14] See Myths, Barnumbir and the Island of the Dead, pages 524-528.

Warumeri well, they come back to the ranga and go inside of it and into the well."

The souls of women likewise return: "When a woman dies she becomes a Bir-im-bir [spirit] Wongar and goes to the same well as a man. She can come back to her ranga and is like those two old Wawilak sisters."

When the men come out and take the boy away from the women, they are the snake or the flood and the women are the Wongar women who made the first camp. On the last evening when the men come out they stop at the edge of the camp and they sing rain. When the boys are left under the piles of bushes they are the children of the Wawilak women. "Those boys left there alone are all the same as those babies that were born to the Wongar women. They left their babies there the same way to dance: the women dancing around the Warngaitja mean that." When the men stand with their spears around the pole they sing rain, which means that the flood has come, and when they pull the warngaitja out of the ground and rush away and the others take the bushes off the boys and run away with them to the men's ground, the chorus sings flood. "That means that the flood came and took these two yam sticks and carried them away."—"A flood takes them away after the rain, that is why we sing Wa—wa—wa. That means that the flood water is running."

"When the boys lie there and the men pull the bushes off them that means that snake spitting them up. They are spirits now." (This refers to the first time the python swallows the two women.)

F. The Last Dances in the Men's Ground

1. The dancers are painted with human blood.
2. The boys who are to be circumcised are painted.
3. The initiates are shown the dances of the animals and the triangular ground and are instructed.
4. The older boys who have run away are caught and Yurlunggur comes out of the well and is shown to them.

1. The climax of the ceremony occurs next day. All the men paint with the blood that has been let the day before. The bloodletting occurs one day before the circumcision rite instead of the same day, because the exposure to the air gives the blood a more adhesive quality.

The blood is now sacred and powerful. It is, say the natives, as if it were a totemic emblem in itself. It has the power of Yurlunggur in it because he blew over the blood-giver. It is also powerful because the leader walks among the men, who are decorating themselves with birds' down to take the part of various birds and animals in the coming ceremonial dances, and sings a song over their heads. He sings the taboo names of the creature the man is painting himself to represent. This makes the design and the man magically powerful.

One end of a small green stick from any tree is chewed into a brush and dipped into the blood, and the blood is painted over the body of the man to form the various designs used by the dancers. The paper bark dropped into the blood the day before is also used as a brush. Two men usually paint each other at the same time. The old men paint in the old men's camp, and the younger men go off by themselves. If the old men so desire, they may paint outside where the young men do. They do not let the neophytes see them decorate themselves for the ceremony.

2. The boys who are to be circumcised are painted on the dance ground by older men. The totemic design of the clan is placed on each candidate's chest and abdomen, with the juice of an orchid bulb as the adhesive; blood is never used because it is magically too powerful for an uncircumcised boy. The man who paints the boy is always given a present by the father and mother. The neophytes are then led by the older men to the head of the snake ground. Sweat from the armpit of an old man (almost as powerful as blood) is rubbed on the eyelids of the boys to strengthen their eyes for the coming ceremony.

3. The division of dances that follows on this day of the circumcision is on a moiety basis. Dua men dance Dua animals and plants, Yiritja men dance Yiritja objects that belong to their world of culture, man and nature.

Two men run in with their spears fixed to their spear-throwers and point them straight at the boys as if they were going to throw them. The men have their baskets in their mouths as they often do when fighting. They return to the bush and rush in a second and third time. They are supposed to be fighting men and also catfish. The word for catfish is the same as that for one variety of fighters. The leader sings catfish while the men dance. Several old men stand beside the boys to instruct them and to prevent their running away.—Each group of dancers bows before the initiates just previous to leaving the dance ground.

After the "catfish" have retired, one man comes in dancing, carrying his spear-thrower and shaking it as if it were a bird's tail. He is a willy-wagtail. He pretends to pick flies off the branches of the trees and acts generally in imitation of this bird. When he reaches the boys, he bows at their feet. The leader walks along beside him beating his singing sticks and singing the taboo names of this little bird. Two men dance a grotesque step which makes them appear deformed. They are mokoi trickster spirits.

Two "wallabys" now arrive, hopping along on their hands and feet and imitating other actions of the wallaby. Following them a large gray kangaroo (kai-tjim-bal) and a black-faced kangaroo appear. The last falls down and sleeps; he is considered a very sleepy creature by the natives.

A group of dogs come out crawling on their bellies. They howl like dingoes.

The dance of the mopoke owl and the bush rat is next. The rat crawls in on his hands and knees. The owl, squatting on his haunches, follows after, carrying leaves in each hand. He pounces upon the rat, but the leader kicks him over. This is repeated a number of times, and causes much laughter among the onlookers.

Brush turkeys next appear, and fires are lit all along the dance ground and back in the bush as when the natives try to smoke out these birds in hunting them.

The Dua honeybee dance follows. Two parallel lines of men about six feet apart start at the direction of the leader about one hundred and fifty yards back in the bush. They dance in a rapid rhythm, the members of each line crossing over and taking the place of the other group. When they reach the dance ground they all lie flat on their backs in a long line with the head of one dancer lying between the legs of the one ahead of him.

The stone kangaroos dance again, as well as the big gray kangaroo and the wallabys. This finishes for the moment the initiation of the young boys. They are led away toward the women's camp and left in a convenient clump of bushes between the men's camp and the women's while the initiation of another age group into a higher grade in the men's association takes place. The young men, who are to see the totemic emblem for the first time, run away from the dance ground because they are to be put on a vegetable diet (see Section H, 3) and suffer the taboo of silence for a period of time. The older men run after them and bring them back.

4. Meanwhile, at the tail of the snake dance ground, Yurlunggur is in the "python well" of the Liaalaomir people. He can be heard roaring in a very slow rhythm. The young men stand with their heads

down. The bushes are pulled back from the "Mirrirmina well." All the men painted like iguanas lie in it on their backs with a symbol of the iguana painted on their abdomens. Yurlunggur, the trumpet, lies among them with one man blowing it. The trumpet is played over an iguana while he crawls on his belly out of the well and on to the dance ground. The trumpet then goes back for another and continues until all the iguanas are out of the well and in a line at the apex of the triangular dance ground. A trumpeter then repeats the last activity and brings the iguanas one by one before the line of initiates. The trumpeters then place the trumpet at the feet of the initiates and before the iguanas who are now kneeling in a line.

Each initiate is asked to try to blow the trumpet. Then the old men command all of them to "respect their fathers and mothers," "never to tell lies," "not to run after women who do not belong to them," "not to divulge any of the secrets of the men to the women, men who belong to a lower division of the association, or uninitiated boys," and all in all to live up to the tribal code.

Native Interpretation.—Kaitjimbal (large gray kangaroo) is repeated a number of times because, said the leaders, "We have to get in all the clan countries where he has totems." This is partly a rationalization: it is true he has rangas in a great number of places; but most of the other animals which are danced are also found in a large number of clan holes, yet they are not repeated so frequently. The use of the Yiritja kangaroo in the dance sequence shows that Yiritja as well as Dua things are ritualized in the Djungguan, despite the fact that the two old women were supposed to walk only in Dua clan territory. Kaitjimbal's ranga is his tail (see Ulmark ceremony, page 307). The mokois danced are said to be Yiritja trickster souls by some of the informants, Dua souls by others, and by another group they are declared to be of both moieties. The last category is probably correct, since the mokoi's moiety depends largely upon what clan country is being sung at that time.

Yurlunggur, the trumpet, is in the "totem well at the head of the dance ground." The iguana with him are his children. "They are initiated men who have given their blood for the Djungguan ceremony," or, as it has been concretely put by the natives, "Yurlunggur is in the Mirrirmina well. We hear him roaring out and the young men stand with their heads down." "Yurlunggur is the father of these iguana. He calls to them and brings them out one at a time, and he is calling to his yolno [black human] children for them to see him."

This section is equivalent to Yurlunggur coming out at the camp circle, Section C.

G. The Circumcision

1. The men tip their spears with human blood, pick up the two uncircumcised boys and march toward the women's camp.
2. The women paint themselves.
3. The dance of the wild geese.
4. The women apply magic to the boys.
5. The circumcision and treatment of the foreskin.
6. The removal of the feather.
7. The food taboos are imposed.

1. On this last day of the Djungguan the men, at the ceremonial ground, paint their stone spear heads with the ceremonial blood. The leader of one of the ceremonies explained this in the following way: "We take that blood on our spears to the women's camp and tell the women we have killed a very big python and we ran away after we had killed it, but that the snake did not really die. The camp women know then it's Wongar. They think that blood on the spear is Wongar's. If a woman asks, 'Why did you kill that snake?' we say, 'So he'll go down in the ground. We want to be sure he'll go down in the ground.'"

The men then form into a regular line (both those who have seen Yurlunggur for the first time and the older men) and, beating on their spears with their spear-throwers, march toward the women's camp, crying out, "Ka—ok!! ye! ye! Ka—ok!! ye! ye!" On the way they pick up the two uncircumcised boys and place them on the shoulders of two men, again in the way small babies are carried.

2. Meanwhile the women, instructed by the old men to paint themselves and get ready for the camp part of the ceremony, cover their faces with red ocher and their bodies with daubs of white paint. The painting is poorly done and not elaborate. It is only on this last day of the ceremony that the women are allowed to paint themselves, and it is explained that they are allowed to paint at this time only because it is the day of the circumcision and the men want them to look nice when uncircumcised boys see them. For some little time before the men arrive with the boys who are to be circumcised upon

their shoulders, the women carrying bunches of leaves in each hand have been dancing around the grass where the boys are to be cut.

3. When the men appear in camp with the boys there is a short period of considerable excitement and seeming confusion. The men continue crying out and march to the camp dance ground where the grass and leaves are and where the warngaitja was placed. By this time the grass has become dry, and if it has been disturbed more grass has been added. It has been placed there so that no blood from the circumcision operation can fall on the ground, for it is believed that the child operated on would become ill if this happened. After the circumcision the blood-stained grass is buried or burned. Before the circumcision and while preparing the boys, the crowd divides into two halves which call out like wild geese (this is also a part of the Narra totemic ceremony), while the leader cries out the common names of the totemic emblems:

"Gun-bor! gun-bor! (no meaning)
Main-yir-pa (goose)
Gun-bor gun-bor
Dur-a-mul (fresh water from the clan well)
Gur-um-gur-um-bo (goose)
Birn-gi (holes left in the mud where the geese
had been feeding in a swamp country)"

4. The men form a compact group with the little boys in the center. The women stand slightly at the side. Most of the latter are crying. They say they are sorry because those little boys are going to be hurt. When the cutting is actually taking place they say, "You boys are fish, you are kangaroo, you are turtle [or any other game animal], and all of you things go into this little boy's blood, and all of the blood must go down to his penis, so that it will be like cutting a turtle head or cutting a kangaroo's head off, and it won't hurt the boys." This is cried out loud, and the old men say that it helps the little boys to bear the pain. Sometimes the women carry bushes and whip themselves with them to bring all the pain from the boy to themselves. It is only the close relatives and members of the boys' own clans who cry for them or attempt to hurt themselves for the boys' sake.

5. Two men lie down on their backs. Each boy is given a shell of water and the contents are drunk so that his mouth will be wet when he is bidden to hold his basket between his teeth. It is the last drink

that he will be allowed to have for twenty-four hours. The basket is placed in the boy's mouth to prevent him from crying and to help him bear the pain.

The initiates do cry in spite of the basket. When they do, the men call out with a high trill which is supposed to be a snake's voice. The little boys beg to be turned loose. They are laid on top of the supine men and then held firmly so that they cannot move. The men's chorus surrounds the scene of the operation and it is impossible for the women to view this part of the ceremony. Some of the women dance around the men. One man cuts one boy, while at the same time a second individual circumcises the other. A neat operation is performed, and it is seldom that an infection sets in.

After each boy is cut, a man picks him up and runs with him back to the men's ground. After the man has washed his hands thoroughly with water, he warms them over a lighted fire stick. The wound is also washed and warmed by the man's hand.

The foreskin is put in a paper-bark basket filled with water. Later it is taken out and wrapped with paper bark and a pandanus string. It is hung on a basket as one of its pendants. It is supposed to be kept by the father until the boy grows up, when it is given to him. It is improbable that the boy ever receives the basket, but ideally this is the proper method of finally disposing of the foreskin.

6. Just after the circumcision is completed the leader approaches each man who has participated in the Djungguan ceremony and pulls a feather off the latter's body as a sign that the ceremony is over. This also has a magical significance: it is supposed to prevent any illness or other bad luck from coming to each participant because of his part in the "powerful" Djungguan ceremony. (The same idea exists in the leaders' rubbing the back of the dancer in the Gunabibi ceremony.)

7. Until this period in the boy's life and during the ceremony until the actual circumcision, the boy is allowed to eat any food that he may obtain, but after this he is not allowed to eat any large game until the rainy season has "made the grass come again." He is not allowed to drink water until the following day; he is told a great flood has covered the earth and made the water salty, the sea has covered the land and there is no fresh water to drink.

Native Interpretation.—When a child is circumcised the snake and the flood are supposed to have come again. Here is a typical statement from one of the older men: "When I was circumcised they told me all the water was mọnok (salty or bad) because the flood had come and covered everything. I was told I could speak to no one except gawel and bapa and only little boys, and not to women or men."

H. The Two Circumcised Youths Are Steamed

1. A fire is built in the men's ground; the boys are steamed over it while being instructed.
2. They learn the totemic language.
3. Food taboos are placed on the older boys.
4. Yurlunggur returns to the sacred pool.

1. Next day, or shortly after, the initiates are taken to the men's ground. On the part of the ceremonial ground that is nearest the women's camp two parallel logs about a foot and a half apart are laid over two other logs placed directly over a stone fire. The stones are made red hot. Lily leaves are gathered and soaked in water, or sometimes bunch grass is dampened and used for this purpose. The boy stands on the upper logs and squats over the fire.

The dampened leaves are thrown into the fire and produce a thick steam. This pours around the boy and is supposed to enter his anus, go all through his body, and come out his mouth.

This is to make him a very "strong" man. It is to prevent him from being greedy or noticing the pangs of hunger or thirst. It is to help insure his having plenty of kangaroo, fish, and other animal and vegetable food.

The old men warm their hands over the fire and put them to the boy's mouth while they are addressing him: "You must not use obscene language. You must never tell a lie. You must not commit adultery, nor go after women who do not belong to you. You must always obey your father and respect your elders. You must never betray the secrets that you have learned from us to the women or the boys who have not been circumcised."

While they are speaking they also rub the navel of the child, for this is also supposed to make him "strong" and prevent him from being greedy.

2. The leader starts the round of totemic songs he used earlier in the Djungguan ceremony and conducts the singing with his singing sticks. The boys are taken off the fire and placed on the ground. A man brings a piece of paper bark on which several small pieces of food have been placed. Every variety of food obtainable in the camp at

that time is represented on the bark tray. The boy is given a piece of kangaroo meat or some other food and an old man says, "That is not kangaroo. You tell me the name of that which you're eating. What is it?"

An old man sits beside the youth and whispers a totemic name of the animal into the ear of the boy. The boy then calls out this esoteric name as he swallows the food. As he says the totemic name all the men cry out, "Yai!!! yai!!!" The whole list of foods is gone through, the boy eating them and being told the taboo name of each. Even though the food is not represented on the bark tray, its name is told him and another pellet takes the place of the missing edible. During the ritual the little boys are informed that if they impart any of the information they have been given, "something will happen to their mothers," and that the old men will spear them if they inform any of the women or children. They are told that the old men will know by magic if they betray their secrets. All the men insist that a boy would be killed if he gave away the secrets of the men.—When the ritual is finished, the fire and logs are covered with sand and earth, and men and boys return to the main camp.

The newly circumcised boys are kept away from all women and remain with the men until the wound is healed and they can walk and urinate without pain or effort. Then the pubic coverings they have been wearing, the ones in which the women saw them before circumcision, are taken off; a short song is played over them and they are burned, others being placed on the boys to symbolize the change in biological and social status. The boys are watched over most carefully by the men during the entire ceremony, as well as during a period after the circumcision. Some older man is always with them. This attention is given both to keep them away from the women and because it is felt that during a circumcision initiation a boy should have every luxury given him and the best of everything that the group has to offer.

Older boys show greater emotion and expression of pain than the younger ones when they are operated upon. The younger ones stop crying almost immediately after the operation.

3. The older age grade of youths who have been shown the totemic emblem of the python for the first time (see Section F, 4) are put on a vegetable diet for a period determined by the leader of the ceremony, ordinarily about a week. At the end of the period the young men are taken to the men's ceremonial grounds where they are painted by

some of the older men with the totemic design of their clan, the leader and the older men meanwhile singing the totemic names of the clans, animals, and sacred clan wells over the youths. They can now eat anything they desire. The taboo of silence (see Section F, 3) is also removed at this time. The leader of this ceremony, who, as has been said before, is usually the head of the Liaalaomir clan, is always given presents by the newly initiated boys. These presents consist of all varieties of food, weapons and other elements of the material culture. The whole family of the boy, both men and women, help him. Only the old men can participate in the consumption of food that is given in payment.

4. The ceremonial trumpet (Yurlunggur) is put back in the totemic well of the clan whose leader has been giving the ceremony. It is buried at night in the mud so that the women will not see it when they are at the well. If it is in good condition at the time the next ceremony is held, it will be used for this occasion; if not, it is reburied and a new trumpet made.

Native Interpretation.—The reference in the native interpretation in Section E which says a man cannot eat anything when he has blood on him because he is unclean, indirectly explains the superficial reasons for placing the taboo on the older boys.

A general summary of the interpretation of each ritual section will be given in Chapter XI.

THE GUNABIBI CEREMONY

A. Preliminaries

1. Mandelprindi, the bull roarer, is made.
2. The young men are chosen for initiation by the leader.

1. The season chosen for the Gunabibi is always the dry period as soon as the food is plentiful, after the luxuriant spear grass has been burned and travel becomes easier. This ceremony lasts from two months to two years. At the discretion of the leaders it may be shortened or indefinitely prolonged. The information that a large group of people is coming from a long distance to participate at the Gunabibi often causes the leader to continue the preliminary stages a month or more while waiting for the visitors.

When the ceremonial leaders of the Liaalaomir clan have decided that it is time to start the Gunabibi ritual, it is usually the younger brother of the Liaalaomir leader who goes out into the men's ground and makes a bull roarer (mandelprindi). The bull roarer is attached to a human hair cord on a small stick before it is ready for whirling. It is covered with human blood or red ocher and a snake design is painted on it. The Gunabibi song sequence is usually sung over it to make it "strong," and often the painting is outlined with birds' down. The feathers are removed when it is whirled because they prevent the friction of wood and air which makes the characteristic booming sound. The mandelprindi is then wrapped in bark and hidden in a hollow tree or elsewhere within the men's ceremonial grounds.

2. The old men of the Liaalaomir clan and the leaders of the nearby local groups confer and decide which boys are to be initiated into the Gunabibi mysteries. Since all young men are in time inducted into the Gunabibi ritual, the only question to be decided is whether the boy is old enough. The leaders of the other clans must give their consent if they are present at the conference for the boy's initiation.

Native Interpretation.—There is little to comment upon in this first section of the Gunabibi except that all the natives say that the bull roarer is the snake itself and the initiates "are just the same as those in the Djungguan."

B. The First Ceremony in the Woman's Camp

1. The different clan garma songs are sung and the groups form into one.
2. Mandelprindi is whirled and the camp women and men answer its sound.
3. The initiates are taken by the two Yiritja snakes to the totemic grounds.

1. That evening, or a few evenings later, according to the whim of the leaders, the actual Gunabibi ceremony starts. The leader sends word throughout the camp where a large number of people from the nearby friendly clans are collected, and all the men, women and children gather in the main part of the camp. Each clan group sings the garma song (general camp's less sacred totemic song) that is recognized by all as belonging to that particular clan. The Djirin clan sings and dances Djirin garma songs, and the Warumeri sing and dance their garma songs.

When this is completed the members of the various clans (men, women and children) at the order of the leader all form one large group and sing the rapid Gunabibi rhythm that is used for the general "outside" camp.

2. Out in the nearby bush a Dua man whirls the mandelprindi. The sound is much like that of a bass viol: "Ah um um um um, ah um um um um."

The man whirling the bull roarer cannot be seen. The women and uninitiated are told that Muit, the great father, is calling out for the initiates (in the Djungguan they are told he is calling for the foreskin).

The bull roarer is whirled around the man's head from left to right as he slowly turns with it. He then stops and whirls it from right to left. This is continued for as long a period as the man has strength and feels inclined.

At each pause in the sound of the bull roarer caused by the change in the direction of the whirling, the leader of the camp calls out in a high, shrill, falsetto voice:

"Ah! Yai! ah! Yai! ah! Yai!"

This is in a very quick tempo. The moment he stops, the women answer in high soprano voices:

"Le le le le le le le."

This creates a pattern of musical sound: mandelprindi (bass viol tone and rhythm), male leader's voice, and female chorus.

Sometimes the leader and the bull roarer cry out at the same time. Sometimes two Yiritja water snakes answer instead of the leader. This continues for a quarter of an hour, and sometimes much longer. By this time the women may be in their camps, still chorusing, and the group of men sitting down while smoking and talking.

3. The two Yiritja moiety men who are looked upon as Yiritja water snakes and who have been designated as messengers leave the main camp and go out into the men's ceremonial grounds, where they are supposed to stay until the end of the ceremony, except when they appear for ceremonial purposes at the main camp. Both wear white forehead bands, as do most of the men in the Gunabibi. With them go the boys who are to be initiated. The Yiritja messengers act as guards for the initiates, and also serve as instructors. The boys are not supposed to return to the main camp where the women are until the Gunabibi ceremony is over. They often do come back to the camp if the ceremony lasts longer than a few months, or if there is fear of night attack; but theoretically they must remain away from the women's

camp until the ceremony is completed. The old men insist that this is the only proper way to perform the ceremony.

Native Interpretation.—Throughout the Gunabibi ceremony, the sound of the bull roarer is the voice of the snake coming from the men's ground to the women's. "When Mandelprindi sings out, it is the voice of the snake, and when the women call back, that is the old women calling out to the snake who swallowed them in their house." Throughout the Gunabibi the answer of the camp women is always the cry of the two Wawilak women trying to stop the snake. When the two Yiritja snake dancers reply to the bull roarer, they are the two children of the old women answering the snake. "Dua man always makes the bull roarer sing out and the two Yiritja snakes always answer." The bull roarer is Wirtit (Yurlunggur or Muit). Some of the men said the two Yiritja were "yellow-bellied water snakes."

C. The Morning and Evening Dance Sequence

1. The animals dance on the ceremonial ground. The men sing and the women reply. The sea gull dance.
2. Mandelprindi speaks and the women reply.
3. The song and dance sequence which is the core of the Gunabibi.
4. The opossum dance.

1. The next morning, before the morning meal has been eaten, the men leave the main camp and go to the men's ceremonial grounds. Here they stand in a line before a clear space about fifty or seventy-five yards in diameter and surrounded by heavy underbrush. They hold their spears, heads up, on the ground before them and beat time on the spear shafts with their spear-throwers. The leader often uses two boomerangs instead. They sing in a fast rhythm.

The leader stands before them as a director of the chorus. At the end of the song, which is repeated over and over, he calls out in a high, shrill voice:

"Ah! Yai! Ah! Yai! Ah! Yai!"

The women in the camp answer with the high shrill sound they make when they hear the bull roarer. After some five or ten minutes of singing a dancer appears from the bush and dances toward the leader and chorus. Neither the leaders nor the members of the chorus are decorated, but the dancer is heavily ornamented and represents a male sea gull.

On his head is a high painted headdress ("dunce cap") made of ti tree bark, topped with a bunch of native companion's feathers. The bark is covered with red ocher. The body of the dancer is completely coated with human blood, and the body from the waist up, as well as the arms and the shoulders, is covered with perpendicular parallel lines of birds' down, and bunches of leaves are attached to the upper arm. The face may have two horizontal lines running from ear to ear above and below the eye, with one additional line that crosses the face at the chin.

The dancer advances with slow deliberate rhythm in a zigzag course as though he had heavy weights attached to his feet. As he changes his course and his flight across the field, he squats and shakes his shoulders, which makes the leaves on his arms quiver like the feathers of a bird. He kneels and faces the chorus. The leader and men surround him, knock off his headgear and rub his back to rub off some of the birds' down that has been glued on it, and the leader sings, "Gunabibi! Gunabibi!" in a voice which is impressively dramatic and sounds much like a modern priest chanting a prayer. ("Gunabibi" is one of the names used for Muit and Yurlunggur.)

2. The dancing stops. A man comes out with a bull roarer and whirls it. In camp the women answer in a trilling high soprano.

3. The bull roarer is put away, and the chorus and leader sit down in a circle and sing mandelprindi. A few men stand up and move back and forth behind the others. They have their stone spears attached to their spear-throwers. They are supposed to be fighting men. The leader stands in front of all. The following song sequence, the heart of the Gunabibi ceremony and often repeated, is gone through for the first time.

Sea gull	male, female, and eggs
A small snake (bolokmi)	male, female, and eggs
Native companion	male, female, and eggs
Small rock python (wirtit)	male, female, and eggs
Muit (python totemic spirit)	male, female, and eggs
Small fresh-water snake	male, female, and eggs
Sea gulls	male, female, and eggs
A small snake (bolokmi)	male, female, and eggs
Sea eagle (dimala)	male, female, and eggs
Rock python (Wirtit)	male, female, and eggs

Muit (python totemic spirit)	male, female, and eggs
Four Muits[14]	male, female, and eggs

The song sequence may be changed and some of the animals or birds left out, but the cycle is more or less constant in order and number. When all the songs of the sequence are finished, the men go back to the main camp and eat the morning meal. The usual round of daily activities is continued until evening. Just at dusk the men again leave for the ceremonial grounds and go through the same ceremony as in the morning. Sea gull, and possibly other animals, have been danced the day before. The animal dance may be still bolokmi (small snake), or dimala (sea eagle) may now be in progress.

Each day one or two animals, sometimes more, are danced and sung in the same manner as the sea gull on the first day. The animals are taken in the order of their appearance in the song sequence, that is, following sea gull and bolokmi would come native companion, and so on, through large palm tree and Muit.

The males of the species are all danced first; when the complete list of this sex has been danced, all the females are taken in turn; and finally, both males and females. When birds are danced, as well as any egg-laying animal, the eggs appear in the last round of the song and dance cycle. After this has been completed, four pythons, two males and two females, are danced. They are coiled up, and supposed to be copulating. Following them, four native companions appear and go through the same performance, and finally four Muits are danced.

When the males or females dance by themselves, here and in later sections of the ceremony, they represent unmated animals.

The men return to the main camp and have their evening meal. It is eaten just after dark. An hour or so later they return to the ceremonial place and the Gunabibi ceremony is continued.

They all sit down in a circle around the fire and sing:

(1) Dua country
(2) Mandelprindi
(3) Human blood for the Gunabibi ceremony

[14] The division of each of the things danced, on the basis of male, female, and eggs, clearly demonstrates the Murngin way of thinking about sex and fertility, and also organizes these species in their minds on the basis of family pattern. A number of dances—such as Muit's, for example—are repeated, either because of the great importance attached to the totem itself, or because of the satisfaction the dance gives the native.—Usually certain plants, e.g., palm trees, are also danced.

(4) A small Dua bird
(5) Male opossum
(6) Female opossum
(7) Fire
(8) Male and female opossums

4. Dancers then come out grunting in imitation of the opossums. They have bark penises sticking erect from their belts. Some men without these appendages are female opossums. They may or may not simulate copulation.

After dancing for some few moments, the opossums bow before the chorus on their hands and knees, and the leader sings, "Gunabibi, Gunabibi!" The leader rubs each dancer's back with his hand.

The bark penises are removed and the dance is over. The python ritual is sung again. The opossums, a small kangaroo (Yiritja moiety), fire, and mandelprindi are also sung. This completes the day's ceremony. The two ritual periods—morning and evening—occur every day throughout the ceremony.

When the new moon (narlindi yurta) appears, this section of the ceremony is completed, and the next morning the men dance the last element of the sequence.

Native Interpretation.—The animals sung or danced are supposed to be those seen by the Wawilak women on their way north from the interior. They all belong to various clans and totem wells found specifically on the women's route and generally throughout the western and southern part of the Murngin tribe. (The totems in the east tend to center around the Djunkgao myth rather than the Wawilak.) —"Those two sisters named all those animals. As they went they said, 'By and by you will be maraiin.'" Some of the animals and plants danced, though they have totemic significance, do not have totemic emblems; but in a sense the dance itself serves to make them for the moment a totem, and the dance becomes a totemic expression, since the bodies of the dancers and maraiin express the totemic essence in the same way a totemic emblem does.

The bull roarer here, as before, is the voice of the snake, and when the women of the camp trill their answer they are the two old Wawilak sisters calling out to Yurlunggur.

When the various groups dance together, it is literally what it appears to be, making one people out of them. "The making of one mob in a dance is all the same as making one people out of all those people from [by use of] the Gunabibi."

The tall headdresses of the dancers are supposed to be the snake's neck or the neck of the animal that is being danced. They are also the house of the two women. The feather headdress on top of the dunce-cap arrangement is the snake's head looking over the house. And when the whole headdress is knocked off at the end of the dance, it means the house has been destroyed by the rain and swallowed by the snake. When the backs of the dancers are rubbed by the leader, it means the snake is licking them, preparatory to swallowing them. The cycle of songs sung and the dance, first of the male of the species, then of the female, and finally their offspring, are symbolical of reproduction. Said one of the leaders, "Black men walk about single, and by and by catch a mate who belongs to them, and by and by children come. Macassar man walks about by himself, by and by catch his woman, and more children come out. Big kangaroo walks about single and by and by he catches a woman and by and by there are children. It is all the same for opossum, fly, and bandicoot. Snake catches a mate and by and by there are children, and it is all the same for lizard, honeybee, pigeon, and bird, and turtle and everything. Black man cuts down tree and by and by little ones come up. It is all the same. Walk about single, by and by mate, and by and by children. It is all the fault of those women. If they hadn't done wrong in their own country this would not have happened. If they had not menstruated in Mirrirmina this would not have happened. Everyone, all plants and animals, would have stayed single. But after they had done these bad things, they made this new law for everyone."

Opossum is looked upon by the Murngin as a libidinous fellow.

D. The Line of Dancing Men Surround All the Women of the Camp

1. The men carry lighted torches and in a single file dance to the border of the common camp where the women are huddled in a group. Two old women beat the ground with clubs or yam sticks.

1. After this they gather some bushes, put them in their armpits and, carrying lighted torches of paper bark, leave the men's ceremonial grounds and start dancing toward the main camp.

Meanwhile the women, under the guidance of an old man, leave their camp, form themselves into a solid, circular mass, and sit down in the territory between the main camp and the men's ceremonial grounds. They hide under their ainmaras (mats). Two old women walk up and down in front of the other women, beating the ground with clubs or digging sticks, and telling the young women that they cannot eat certain taboo foods or they will become ill and probably die; they will have sores on their bodies and rot away and harm their clan's people as well.

With a line of men, two Yiritja water snakes (kak-a-war) appear before the women and uninitiated boys for the first time. The snakes call out in high tones, and the women answer in the same high trill in which they reply to the bull roarer. The men dance in a circle around the women. All the women make presents to the men, which are turned over to the two Yiritja snakes. The gift is obligatory, under penalty of illness and possible death sent by Muit, to whom the presents are supposed to be made. The two old women walk up and down, beating the ground with their clubs, and shout.

Their words can be freely translated: "Muit, do not come out any more and swallow us, for now we are clean and no longer impure":

Wal-mi Come out	Nin-ne Stop there
Nin-ni-niki Stop there	Yuk-ka norl-tur No swallow
Na-ma-tung Make us good (from)	Ir-rk-tun Sickness
Nangul Dui-yung-ur (from) Blood sickness	
Mar-yalng-nao We can live good	Mar-tjin-naerao We can be healthy (no sick trouble)

Native Interpretation.—The line of men which dances around the women huddled under the mats is the snake, and is also the two Wawilak women. The symbolic significance of the various men changes during the dance.—"When the men come out into the camp they are the two old Wawilak women at first. Then two Yiritja men at the side call out and then the line of dancers changes to proper men. When they go around the women they are snakes. The two old women who beat the ground are those two old Wawilak women who beat the ground when Yurlunggur tried to swallow them. They are beating Muit. They tell those young people they can't eat every kind of food or they will get sick and maybe die and they will have sores on their bodies and rot away. The old women walk up and down and say, 'Muit, don't you come out any more and swallow these people. We are good people, we are clean.'"

Other accounts say that when the men come out of the ceremonial grounds in a line and dance toward the group of women they are the snake who has smelled the blood of the two old women because "They are painted in that blood [meaning they have the blood from a man's arm, which is the symbolical menstrual blood of the Wawilak women]. They paint their noses and over their eyes; when the snake swallowed the women he bit them and the blood came. This makes them Wongar women too."

"The snake calls out to all the other snakes and they come up and circle around the women. [See the Djungguan for a like interpretation.] The women are in their paper-bark house. When they take their mats off, that means they have stood up before the snake swallows them. The red ocher on their faces [the women's] is blood from where that snake bit them when they were swallowed. The two Yiritja snakes who call out are the spirits of the two children of the Wawilak women. They cry out and cry out."

"The presents the women give to the two [Yiritja] snakes go inside the two snakes. Those two women are inside the snake. These presents are swallowed by the snake just the same as those two women were swallowed by the snake before." The presents given by the women are kept by the Dua leaders of the ceremony, but not before they have been put on the snake emblem (i.e., given to Muit; see E 2 below).

E. The Yiritja Messengers Leave to Invite the Other Clans to the Ceremony

1. The two Yiritja snakes leave to invite the other clans to the ceremony.
2. A symbolic well is dug, which all the dancers enter after the dance sequence of Section C is repeated.
3. The messenger snakes are sent out again to announce Gunabibi, while Section D is repeated and the presents given to the snake by the women are displayed.

[The activities of the foregoing sections, largely preparatory, have involved only the home camp. The arrival of the visiting clans marks the beginning of the most significant phases of the Gunabibi.]

1. The men then leave and go back to their ceremonial camp. The two Yiritja snakes are given a human hair string decorated with parrot feathers and tipped with white cockatoo feathers. It is a ceremonial "message stick" and represents the snake. The men leave with the message and go to the other clans, inviting them to the ceremony.

2. Meanwhile the song and dance cycle of Section C 3 is gone through, starting with the unmated male sea gull and ending with the four Muits. At the same time a large round hole is dug in the men's ceremonial grounds by the members of the Yiritja moiety. All the animals, birds and plants which dance get in the well with the two Yiritja snakes. In theory the two snakes leave with a message stick; but in practice this seldom happens, unless they go to nearby clans. They wait until the end of the ceremony, centered around the taboo hole, before departing; or if they do leave, two other men enact the rôles of the Yiritja snakes. The leader sings over them, and they all dance in the well as one people.

A month has supposedly gone by since the departure of the messengers, and the moon is once more new. Once again the men put bushes under their arms, carry lighted torches, leave their own ceremonial ground, and dance out near the women's ground, where they surround the group of women. The old women repeat their previous performance. Gifts are again made by the women.

All the men, including the two Yiritja snakes carrying the presents made by the women, return to the men's camp again. A forked stick railing is placed around the taboo well and the gifts are hung on it. The Dua leaders of the Gunabibi ceremony keep the gifts after this offering has been made to Muit.

3. The two Yiritja snakes and the initiated son or younger brother of the leader of the Gunabibi (in other words, two Yiritja moiety men and one Dua moiety man) are given a mandelprindi and told to go to all the clans and tell them they are ready for the final phases of the ceremony. The Yiritja snakes are sometimes spoken of as the waku of Yurlunggur, and the son of the leader is "all the same as the snake. He can't sing out, but the Yiritja snakes do it for him." The Yiritja men whirl the bull roarer outside the camps of the various clans as a signal that the final dance will start and also as an invitation and virtual command for all who hear to appear.

At the various camps messengers supposedly go through some of the performances that have been held at the original camp. The sounds they make are the voice of the snake. The women's reply from the other camps is that of the two old Wawilak women. The hole dug is a representation of a Mirrirmina well and is sung over to be made such by the power names of that well. The sequence of dances is the same sea-gull-to-Muit cycle; the unmated men dance first and then the females. The dancers who symbolize the unmated males and females do not go in the well. Only mated groups of males and females enter.

Native Interpretation.—The reason for keeping the unmated male and female dancers out of the well, according to the leader of several of the ceremonies, is the same as that given for separating the males and female in the cycle of songs in Section C. "That snake is all the same as a man.—[Here he was speaking of the rock python and other snakes who are the living counterparts of the totemic spirits.] He walks about single [a male dances up to the entrance to the hole]. A woman snake walks about single and lays eggs. By and by at stringy-bark flower time in the dry season they find each other. Mobs of these snakes find each other and they copulate and lay eggs for children [all the dancers go inside the hole]. When the wet season comes one man goes one way and another man goes another way looking for rat and lizard food. By and by those eggs break and the children of the snake come out. They walk about single, the female goes one way, and the male another. The dry season comes and a mob comes out and they copulate and make eggs again and go along a hole because this is a house for them." When the snakes congregate "all kinds mixed up, they all go into the one hole for copulating. In the [early] morning up in the big rocks before daylight they come out a little way and copulate. Two more come out, man and woman, man and woman, and copulate and then go into the hole."

F. The Kartdjur Is Made and the Gunabibi Well Abandoned

1. A crescent-shaped trench, the kartdjur, is dug, and the well abandoned.
2. The snakes dance in the kartdjur; the copulation of the libidinous man and woman and of the two rock pythons.

1. After the messengers leave, the round taboo hole is abandoned and a larger crescent-shaped trench is dug. The trench (kart-djur) is four or five feet deep; the earth is piled along its concave sides. It is about ten feet long, and the width is sufficient for two men to pass

by each other while dancing inside it. While the messengers are away and the new trench is being dug, the Gunabibi cycle of songs and dances from the single male sea gull to the four Muits is gone through by the leader and his chorus.

2. The snakes are allowed to dance in the kartdjur, but none of the others except the palm tree are allowed to go inside it.

After the Gunabibi cycle, a single man filled with sexual desire and looking for a mate is danced. Then a man representing a single woman, also sexually hungry and looking for a mate, is danced. And finally the two together perform a dance; meeting at the entrance to the kartdjur, they simulate copulation but do not enter the "well."

The moon is now full, and people have been coming from the other clans to participate in the ceremony. Messages are usually brought by them that the two Yiritja snakes are coming with more people. Visitors and messengers take part in the dance around the kartdjur. All the men in the ceremony dance rock pythons copulating. The last dance of the entire series is that of the blue-tongued lizard. He dances in from a long way in the bush and goes inside the kartdjur. The appearance of this symbol indicates to all that a transition is taking place in the Gunabibi.

Native Interpretation.—"The kartdjur is that head inside the woman's vagina. It is all the same as her marn-bu [clitoris]. The crescent shape [shown by curve of fingers] is the way the two women laid down in the house before the snake swallowed them."

G. Yermerlindi

1. The Yeritja make Yermerlindi—two poles symbolizing the snake and a palm tree, and covered with blood.
2. The Yiritja camp; Dua give presents to the Yiritja.
3. The neophytes are placed on the kartdjur and sweat is placed on their eyes. Various dances include a clown element, the opossums, the Wawilak sisters, and finally blue-tongued lizard.
4. The initiates see Yermerlindi and are instructed and warned by the old men.
5. The Yermerlindi are knocked down and put in the kartdjur, and the men put blood on themselves.

1. During the last period, when the kartdjur is being used, the Yiritja moiety men participating in the Gunabibi ceremony have been making the yermerlindi emblems. They are about fifteen feet long and two and a half wide. They have a pole as a solid core and are

surrounded with grass and covered with paper bark. The bark is covered with human blood, on which is pasted birds' down or bush cotton, and on one yermerlindi a representation of Muit is painted in human blood against the white-feather or cotton background. This yermerlindi is another emblem of the rock python totem. The other is called a palm tree emblem, but it is known to be a python totem too, for it has a snake design upon it. The two are stood up by the Yiritja men. They say to each other, "Oh! They are true Wongars [totemic spirits]." The leader sings a song to prevent sickness since the yermerlindi are very powerful because Muit is inside them.

2. The Yiritja camp, where the yermerlindi is made, although still on the men's ceremonial ground, is placed at one side of the actual dancing ground. No Dua man can go near it. The Dua leader asks from time to time by circumlocution if the yermerlindi is made, even when the emblem is completed.

While the Yiritja are making the yermerlindi, the Dua men send presents of food to them for making the yermerlindi. The Yiritja men send the Dua presents of kangaroo fat and red ocher with which to paint the Yiritja dancers.

The Dua leader of the Gunabibi once more asks if the Yiritja have finished their work, and they reply that yermerlindi is ready. The leader says, "One day more and then we will dance with yermerlindi." The Yiritja never say that yermerlindi is ready until the two messengers have returned with the visitors.

3. Following the blue-tongued lizard dance which marks the end of a phase of the ceremony, the Gunabibi pauses so the men may eat their evening meal.

Later in the evening the neophytes are placed on the raised ground on the concave side of the kartdjur. Two leaders now conduct the ceremony. A new phase of the Gunabibi has begun. A long shallow trench of some fifty feet is extended from one end of the kartdjur. The neophytes have bushes placed under their armpits. The Yiritja snakes and the Dua leaders put their own arm sweat on the eyes of all the initiates.

All those who are not dancing stand on the raised ground with the chorus. Two dancers sing reed warbler in a small piping tone which forms a ludicrous contrast to the heavy male chorus. The onlookers in chorus appreciate the deliberate humor of the contrast. The clown element, although not definitely and elaborately developed, is present in this part of the ceremony as well as later.

A large group of men, covered with white clay blown on them from the mouths of their fellow dancers, dance around the kartdjur and then go back to the end of the connecting trench and dance down to the kartdjur again. They are opossum dancers and grunt in time to the beating together of the two leaders' boomerangs. As they dance, the opossums and leaders start filling up the kartdjur with the loose earth around it.

The opossums are followed by two dancers who represent the Wawilak sisters. They have paper-bark bundles under their arms to represent their babies. At the end of each song of the chorus the dancers cry in a high whine in imitation of a newly born child. They squat inside the trough and cry again. The crying, in contrast with the heavy voices of the men's chorus, again has a note of absurdity in it and is a source of much laughter.

The last dance is the blue-tongued lizard. He is painted across his back with a white horizontal stripe. Keeping his legs very stiff, he wriggles along on his abdomen, with a wave-like motion, to the kartdjur. When he stops inside it the leader intones, "Gunabibi! Gunabibi!" over him. The hole is further filled until the greater part of it is covered.

4. The singing now changes to the song, yermerlindi. A fire is made. The Dua leader cries to the neophytes, "Look! See what you can see! I think Bapa Indi is coming out of the water."

The two Muit emblems are brought in; two men hold them upright with the rock pythons painted in blood on the white surfaces gleaming in the light of the many fires before the eyes of the frightened initiates.

The neophytes are told by the old men that the emblems are real pythons, that the spirit of Muit is inside them, and that they are very dangerous, even though they have been made by men, for Muit now walks around the jungle like a man. They are also warned to tell nothing of what they have seen to the women and uninitiated boys.

5. Two men bring in a pole and hold it horizontally about waist-high from the ground, on the concave side of the kartdjur. The yermerlindi are stood on the convex side. They are pushed over and allowed to hit the pole, while all the chorus cries out in shrill tones. They are picked up and again allowed to fall. This continues until the feather headpieces on the top of the emblems fall off.

The yermerlindi are put in the kartdjur. The grass around them is burned and the inner poles are charred. While this is being done, blood is let from several men's arms, and as the fire burns, all the men cover themselves with blood and kangaroo fat.

Native Interpretation.—The palm tree totemic emblem is supposed to be the palm tree "on the outside, but inside it is all the same as a snake."—"That first ranga is called the palm tree ranga because the Yiritja make it, but the inside [sacred] meaning is all the same as the snake. When we stand them up all the Yiritja say, 'they are Wongars all right,' and the leader sings to keep off sickness, for Wongar is inside them and might make us sick."

There is no question but that the Murngin believe the totemic emblems have the totemic spirit inside them, and there is considerable evidence that the totem is believed to take possession of the emblem and move around as a snake does. On one of the nights that yermerlindi totems were first shown, one of the Yiritja men came into my camp and announced to some of the natives and myself that he had gone over to the Yiritja ground where that Wongar snake was, meaning the totemic emblem. He said, "I am afraid of that one. I am small boss for him [younger brother of some of the leaders]. He is close up to the water when he is that way, and maybe he will walk about and kill me and everybody. Yermerlindi always walks about." He meant that when the totemic emblem had been made, sung over, and completed, it was in much the same condition as the totemic spirit is when it lives in the totemic water hole; and with the totemic spirit in the emblem and outside of the water hole, it was dangerous to man. This same man told me of an experience in another Gunabibi ceremony when Yermerlindi was left by himself for a night: Yermerlindi got up and walked around by himself. The discussions among the men during the ceremonies all proved that the statements of this one man are generally believed to be true of ordinary behavior for the yermerlindi emblem. There is ample direct statement from a large number of natives that when the Yiritja men make the totemic emblems for the Gunabibi they sing over them, and this puts power and the totemic spirit in the yermerlindi.

A night after a Gunabibi ceremony when the yermerlindi was shown, one of the men had the following experience: He couldn't sleep and his sleeplessness continued for some time. Presently he heard the whistle of Muit for him, he said. He raised his head and listened. Muit whistled again. The man listened very carefully to make sure it wasn't something or someone around him, but he heard it again. He laid his head back and went straight to sleep. This story indicates again how sure everyone is that the totemic spirit is about during the time of the ceremonies which celebrate his power.

H. The Ceremonial Exchange of Wives

1. Distant tribal brothers exchange wives.
2. The camp dance of the sexual pair and the exchange of gifts.
3. The night of ceremonial intercourse.

1. When the men from distant clans come in to see and participate in the Gunabibi ceremony, the older men, if they do not know their kinship to one another, work out their tribal relationships after much talk; this is mental exercise appreciated by all the more intelligent Murngin. When a local man discovers that a certain visitor from a far clan is his tribal brother, he sends his younger brother to inform this person that he may have the local man's wife for ceremonial copulation at the end of the Gunabibi ceremony. He sends presents along with the younger brother. The recipient, either through his own younger brother or through the messenger, offers his own wife in exchange, and also sends presents.

This exchange of wives for ceremonial intercourse at the close of the Gunabibi serves as the grand finale of the entire ceremony. As a consequence, it is considered very dangerous and is surrounded with a fairly intricate ritual.

The above is the formal and correct way of exchanging wives for ceremonial purposes, but there are several other methods. Sometimes men agree, without the intermediation of messengers, to exchange their wives. Sometimes a man and woman arrange matters without first gaining the consent of the women's husband; but without the final consent of the woman's spouse, this could not be recognized as legal procedure.

2. After the evening meal, and before the men return to the ceremonial grounds, they sit down in a half-circle around the fire and the women dance on the other side in front of them. The women and men wear circlets of fiber string around the head above the ears and across the forehead to indicate that the exchange arrangement has been made. While the women dance, various men arise, walk over to the women and hand them presents of food, red ocher, or some other object of value. The woman presented with such a gift is the one with whom arrangments have supposedly been made for ceremonial copulation.

The man who is the wife's partner later privately again gives her presents of spears or tobacco, red ocher, and the ordinary presents that are reciprocally exchanged. She accepts the present, keeps part of it, and gives the rest to her husband. The natives, both men and women, are much more interested in the ritual of giving and taking than in the value of the presents, which is never very great. There is usually considerable joking and amusement during this dance. Although intercourse is not to be consummated between the ceremonial partners until the last night of the ceremony, and then only for ceremonial purposes, there are a considerable number of clandestine meetings between these mates before that time. This is recognized by all, even though it is not considered regular or entirely proper.

After a man has had sexual intercourse with another man's wife, the latter male comes to him and puts his sweat on the legs and arms of his wife's partner so that the one who has been with his wife won't be "sick" from it. The position taken in the sexual act differs from the customary one (see page 67) in that the woman sits on the ground on the back of her buttocks. The trunk of the body leans back and at an angle from the legs, with the hands on the ground in back of the body to support it. The man puts his legs under hers and his hands around her so that the pudenda meet in closer contact than if he lay on her.

3. For the final occasion the men and women partners are heavily painted. On this night one woman may have sexual relations with several men because there is always a lack of women in the group attending the ceremony. If a woman shows a dislike for her ceremonial partner and refuses to join him, she is told she will be ill and make her husband and ceremonial mate ill, and she is forced to comply with her husband's demand. If a man refuses, the woman sends word that Muit will make him ill, and that she too will be sick.

Native Interpretation.—The ceremonial exchange of wives and participation in ritual intercourse is thought to be absolutely obligatory on the men and women. When a man or woman objects, the older men insist, as does the partner, that the person must do this or "Muit will make him ill" and the partner will become ill too. In speaking of the ceremonial sexual exchange I was told many times, "This makes everybody clean. It makes everyone's body good until next dry season."

The oldest leader of the Gunabibi in the area, in many ways the man best-informed on this ceremony, said to me, "Those two women [the Wawilak sisters], they walked down from the Wawilak country and they made a corroboree like this one. Two Wawilak men came up to those women and 'played' with them. 'I think, sister, we will put white feathers all over and make this one [Gunabibi] higher and more dear [valuable] than the Djungguan. We will make this one so that every man can come and play with us.' When the Wawilak men played with them, those two sisters said these words, 'We will make this corroboree more high for people to play with each other. We are Wongar women, but when people come after us they can play with their women. It is better that everybody comes with their women and all meet together at a Gunabibi and play with each other, and then nobody will start having sweethearts the rest of the time.'" This same man said, "Everybody paints himself not for nothing. We don't take this blood out of ourselves for nothing and paint ourselves with it. We don't sleep that night, and if a woman says, 'I won't go to that corroboree place with you,' the man says, 'If you don't go with me you are going to be dead.' Sometimes we kill that woman by magic, and throw spears at them if they won't do it."

I. The Forked Poles Are Erected

1. The ridgepole is placed on two forked poles.
2. The Yiritja snakes and the initiates are placed on it.
3. The women and children of the camp gather by it.
4. The line of men dances around the initiates and women.
5. The taking of bread by the initiates.
6. The initiated boys are taken to the ceremonial ground and their forehead bands removed.

1. The following morning, at the boundary line between the men's ceremonial ground and the general camp, two forked poles are placed in the ground about six feet apart from each other, and a thick connecting pole is placed in their forks. It is about four feet off the ground. The whole framework reproduces part of the framework of an ordinary house or platform. The pole is hung with branches from nearby trees so that the space from pole to ground is completely covered.

2. The two Yiritja snakes go first to the structure and sit down in the forks of each pole. They lean back against the forks and face each other. They cry out with the same shrill call heard in the earlier ceremonies of the Gunabibi. Since dawn the bull roarers have been sounding and the women answering from the general camp. The initiates are placed under the bushes that hang down from the ridgepole; they

hold on to it with their two hands. Although their feet are on the ground they are supposed to be hanging from the pole.

3. Several old men now go to the women's camp, gather all the women and children into one group, and march with them toward this ceremonial structure. The women have smeared themselves with red ocher; they advance dancing. Two old women run along beside the rest of the women and the children, beating the ground with their yam sticks and calling out to the great snake (see page 289, where they address Muit). The women sit down about twenty-five feet to one side of the structure.

4. All the men dancers remain about thirty yards from the scene, hidden in palm-tree thickets or mangrove jungles. They are decorated with bushes under their arms. The men dance into the clearing in single file. They dance around the initiates, the two Yiritja snakes, and the women and children. The two Yiritja snakes cry out and the women answer. The women then arise and return to the main camp. The men sit down in a line beside the ridgepole, and paralleling it. The initiates are taken from the pole at the same time and placed at the back of a line of men.

5. The seated men hold out their left arms (the far side from the forked pole) and the initiates crawl under them. They shake their shoulders as they advance to the head of the line. When each initiate crawls under the arm of the man who heads the line and who sits by the forked pole, the Yiritja snake sitting on this forked pole hands the neophyte a piece of vegetable (usually ground palm nut). The boy takes it, puts it in his mouth, and spits it out again. The particle of food is covered up. When the last neophyte has enacted this rite, the forked-stick phase of the ritual is finished.

6. That night mandelprindi sounds again and the women reply. The leader gathers the initiates in a circle at the edge of the men's camp and the men dance around the boys. They sing the same songs as those sung when they danced around the women and boys during the forked-stick rite. With the men leading and the boys bringing up the rear, the whole group of males then dance off in single file to the men's ceremonial place. Here the boys' forehead bands (gar-lam-ba) are removed without ceremony. They are given to the leader, who is supposed to keep them for the next Gunabibi. The older men usually elect to wear forehead pieces and also now give their bands to the leader. This ends the Gunabibi except for ceremonial purification.

Native Interpretation.—The forked sticks with the pole across are the house of the two women. The ritual of the women who answer the two snakes and beat the ground with their clubs parallels that of the two old women in Section D. The men in the bush are the snake. The boys who are hanging from the rafter are flying foxes. When the women move back and the men sit down in a line under the rafter, "This means one people, and the rafter is the snake and the people are Muit food.—They are all the same as the birimbir of Bapa himself. —They are Muit and they are one people." When the boys crawl from behind the line of men to one end of the line, they are brought to the tail of Muit and "They are the young snakes of that big one." When the boys crawl up to the head of the snake and receive the food from the head (the Yiritja snake sitting on the forked pole), "This means the children all want food [the children of the snake] and the snake spews out the two women and they [the children] eat it [the two women] and give it back to him [spit out the food again]."

All the above was told to me by the leaders of the Gunabibi, both during the actual portrayal of the ceremony itself and in conversations during the hours of rest between the morning and evening dances.

The significance of the flying fox to the Murngin is that he is a mokoi or trickster spirit of the dead who lives in the bush. He is a generally recognized symbol to all of the spirit that does not go into the water hole but goes out into the bush or the jungle or to the Morning Star Island at time of death.—"A flying fox [a large fruit bat] is all the same as the dead spirit from the bush. It is Dua."[15]

J. Ceremonial Purification

1. The men and women paint themselves with red ocher and kangaroo fat. The neophytes are brushed with smoking ironwood branches.

[15] When an uncircumcised child dies, its mother has the wings of a flying fox painted on her shoulders and the body of the fox painted on her abdomen. "This flying fox is the birimbir spirit of that dead baby. This is done for both Yiritja and Dua mothers and babies." The same painting is sometimes put on a woman when she has had her first menses. The woman is placed inside a hut and, when she wants to move, is given two yam sticks with which to turn over. The yam-stick movement is ceremonial and symbolic of the movement of the two old women who walked with the aid of a yam stick in each hand.

The condition of the boys, or women who are menstruating, of the mother of a dead child, etc., is said to be djo-ak, which means ritually unclean. "If a mother or mari or yeppa sleeps close to dead baby that sweat comes out and makes the mother unclean. Women put red ocher on after this. No one can take food from these women until the bones are dug up and she is painted by her husband with flying fox."

1. A week or ten days afterward all the men and women who have participated for the first time in the ceremony are painted with red ocher and kangaroo fat, at least twice. The last time a fire is made of ironwood, and green branches are held in it and brushed all over the initiate.

Native Interpretation.—This ritual is to keep the participants from becoming ill and to prevent them from being hurt by any of the animals seen in the Gunabibi dances. The use of red ocher for purification purposes is general. It is one of the recognized mechanisms of the Murngin ritually to prevent or stop sickness. At the end of the Gunabibi the following comment was made in a variety of forms: "After the next rain a man can come out and see a lot of emus and kangaroos and all kinds of animals. He will say, 'My word, we sang him good in that last Gunabibi.' "

THE ULMARK CEREMONY

The Ulmark ceremony is performed in the dry season. It may last a month, a season, or possibly two dry seasons. In rare cases it may be shortened to a few days. The length of time depends on the leader and the old men associated with him.

Like the Djungguan and the Gunabibi, the Ulmark too is an age-grading ceremony. The boy who undergoes its initiation is placed definitely in the men's age grade. The Ulmark is recent in this area and is still being learned by the older men. It is not yet felt to be obligatory for all men to pass through it to attain social adulthood.

Human blood is not used in the Ulmark ceremony. It is the only one of the four major ceremonies belonging to the Wawilak cycle that does not use blood. Kangaroo grease serves more or less the same symbolical function.

New feather strings are made in preparation for the Ulmark, to be used as ornaments in it. The work of collecting the feathers and making the string is supposed to take a month or more and depends on the supply of feathers available and the amount desired by the men for the dance. Four men who later play the rôle of kangaroos gather the feathers from the various camps and take them to the men's ceremonial grounds at the camp where the ceremony is to be held.

The first three sections are largely preliminary. The first two sections take place simultaneously.

A. The Four Kangaroos Run Away

1. The four kangaroos and the line of men at the boundary line between the men's and the women's camps.
2. The women appear and the kangaroos run away to the men's ground.
3. The men remove all articles of dress and ornament and cut their hair.
4. The men dance individually.

1. When it is decided to hold an Ulmark ceremony, which may or may not be every year—although theoretically it should be—the older men cut down a tall tree, take the top out of it, remove the branches, and carry the log to the ground which forms the dividing line between the men's ceremonial ground and the main camp. Next morning four men, two from the Yiritja moiety and two from the Dua, sit down on the log. The two Yiritja men represent the large gray kangaroo (kai-tjim-bal) and the two Dua men are stone kangaroos (pardi-pardi). All of the initiated men sit down in a line by them.

2. An old man goes to the general camp,[16] collects all the women, and brings them to the spot where the log has been placed. The women dance in, single file, carrying yam sticks and singing "Kait-ba! kait-ba!" The kangaroos run away from them toward the men's ceremonial ground, followed by the other men walking with high steps in slow rhythm. The women follow to the near boundaries of the men's grounds and then dance back, still singing "Kait-ba! kait-ba!"

3. When the kangaroos reach the ceremonial grounds they throw away all their body ornaments and dress, including their armlets, wristlets, and pubic coverings, until they are completely nude. They then cut their hair.

4. After the log episode, the men start dancing, morning and evening, with the day given up to any occupations they may have, as during the Gunabibi. A chorus sings and one man dances while the

[16] The grounds of the Ulmark are largely similar to those found in the Djungguan. There is the usual division of the territory into two parts: (1) the general camp where the women dance and which is sometimes referred to as the women's dance ground, and (2) the men's ceremonial ground where in the earlier part of the ceremony a bush house is made for the ceremonial totemic drum, and where two triangular dance grounds are made. In the earlier sections of the ceremony (see Section C, etc.), the triangular dance ground is on the surface of the ground and is formed by heaping up earth to demark its limits. In later sections a triangular dance ground is excavated (see Section G), referred to by the natives sometimes as the dance hole, sometimes as the snake ground, sometimes as the well. A bark house for totemic paintings is also erected on the men's ceremonial grounds.

others gather around him. His step is almost a complete reproduction of a modern "buck and wing" jig step. When he has finished he takes his spear-thrower and designates the next dancer by tapping one of the chorus on the shoulder with it. This individual also does a solo dance and then taps another. This continues until all the individuals in the group have danced at least once.

Native Interpretation.—The leader of the Ulmark ceremony told me, "The logs are the backbone of Muit." The men who sit on it are two kaitjimbal (large kangaroos who are Yiritja) and two pardi-pardi (stone kangaroos who are Dua). "They dance because those two old women named them in their dance. The two old women tried to catch these kangaroos but they ran away." The two Yiritja kangaroos are called gur-warn or messengers: "They are all the same as the kakawar [Yiritja snakes] in the Gunabibi."

The women represent the Wawilak women throughout the whole dance. "The women get up and dance around like those two [Wawilak] women did before when the rain fell down. The women carry yam sticks like those two women did. They are trying to stop the rain and to stop Muit from coming out." The words "Kait-ba! kait-ba!" were supposedly used by the two Creator Sisters in the Liaalaomir clan country.

The men take off their ornaments and "clothing" and cut their hair "so that they will go very poor and skinny and look like a man gets when there is a long wet and little food. They are all the same as waiting for the dry season to come." These acts symbolize the effect of ceremonial uncleanliness on nature and man.

Concerning the solo dance, I was told: "They dance this way because those two women did that and when one sister finished dancing, she hit the other sister with a spear-thrower and this one started dancing."

B. The Ceremonial Drum, Uvar (the Great Python) Is Made

1. A large hollow log is formed into a drum and beaten with a pandanus stump.

1. During the progress of Section A several men, including the leader or his younger brother, go into the surrounding bush and select a hollow tree, cut it down, clean it out, and remove the outer bark. The log is recut to a four- or five-foot length and carried to a small bush house that has been made for it on the men's ground. Here it is painted with snake figures, emus, and other animals, as well as plants.

A small pandanus palm stump is trimmed to a convenient size for a beating stick. As soon as the totemic drum is made, it is carried under a man's arm and struck with the pandanus palm stick. The women reply from the main camp with "Kait-ba! kait-ba!" This is symbolic of the beginning of an Ulmark, as the sounding of the bull roarer is of the Gunabibi.

Native Interpretation.—The sound of the drums is the voice of Muit, and "the women answer the same way as for Mandelprindi [in the Gunabibi] only they say 'Kait-ba! kait-ba!' [instead of making high trilling sounds]."—"The women calling out 'Kait-ba! kait-ba!' is what they said in trying to dance and keep Muit back."

C. The Kangaroo Messengers

1. They visit other groups to invite them. They have two kangaroo tail emblems with them.
2. The triangular dance ground is made; the behavior of the visitors who arrive.

1. For several weeks the men continue dancing the "buck and wing" jig step while the women gather palm nuts and put them in water to soak out the poison. Meanwhile a few of the men make two small emblems. One is supposed to be the tail of the large gray kangaroo, the other the tail of the stone kangaroo.

The kangaroos are then sent away to the surrounding clans to invite them to the ceremony. When they approach a camp they cut a large club-like stick and beat it against a hollow tree. The camp people hear it and realize that Ulmark messengers have arrived to invite them to its ritual. A man from the camp goes out to meet the messengers, who say, "We have two kangaroo tails here, one Dua, one Yiritja. We have all the food ready. You must come."

2. While the messengers are away the men in the camp make a triangular dance ground which is the same in structure, material, and form as the Djungguan dance ground. When the visitors—men, women and children—approach the camp of the clan that is giving the ceremony they paint themselves with red ocher. They sing the Kait-ba, kait-ba refrain until they arrive in the main camp. Visitors who arrive early and who have been initiated into the Ulmark are conducted by the old local men to the men's dance ground, where they start dancing the characteristic jig step of the Ulmark.

All neophytes are supposed to remain on the ceremonial grounds and not go to the main camp until the Ulmark ceremony is over. They do not dance. The women stay in the women's camp. The women form themselves into groups according to their clan, and dance and sing, "Kait-ba! kait-ba!"

The men, also grouped according to clan, sing:

(1) The honeybee (Yer-pain) of the Dua moiety
(2) Small stone kangaroo (pardi-pardi)
(3) A grub found in rotten wood floating on lakes and rivers (Ka-mer-ung)
(4) A grub found in the trunk of the pandanus tree
(5) An acacia tree grub (Bar-ler-wir-lar)
(6) A grub found in the roots of the lake grass (I-nur-i)
(7) A grub found in the lily bulbs

At the end of each song cycle a call is made that is the same as the chorus refrain of the Djungguan ceremony.

Native Interpretation.—"When they [the messengers] hit the tree it is like when those two women were walking and saw honeybees' nest and cut down the tree,"—i.e., the tree that is beaten by the messengers is hollow, as was the tree which the old women cut down. The hollow tree is also beaten as a substitute for the hollow log drum.

The triangular dance ground is "all the same as the Djungguan." It is called barn-ga-ga and means python's body. "The women dancing are the two Wawilak sisters." The songs that the men sing when they are divided into groups are "every kind of animal that the two women saw on their way down to Mirrirmina." These songs are to stop Muit and were sung by the two Wawilak women.

D. The Torres Straits Pigeon and Uvar

1. The pigeon emblem is placed twice within the drum on the triangular dance ground.

1. After the completion of the dance ground, the leader announces that the Torres Straits pigeon dance will be performed. The man who dances this dance has red ocher on his face, a white head band, dots on his body, and a red ocher surfacing from the knees to the elbows. A man brings the ceremonial drum, Uvar, and lays it down at the large end of the triangular dance ground. A small light stick is painted, and feathers are tied to one end to represent the pigeon.

The dancer lies down on the ground beside the "pigeon," crying out, "Wah! Wah!!" He picks up the pigeon, arises, and dances a short distance toward the triangular ceremonial ground and sits down again. While he does this the male chorus sings out the refrain of the Ulmark. The leader also calls out the taboo names of this variety of pigeon. The dancer rises and, when he reaches the ceremonial drum, thrusts the bird emblem into the tail end of the drum as far as his arm will reach. He then dances around to the other end of the drum and pulls the pigeon out at that end. He dances up to the head of the dance ground, returns to the drum and once more pushes the pigeon emblem into the drum, this time at the head end, and pulls it out on the opposite side. The Straits Pigeon dance is repeated for several days, and occasionally weeks, before it is abandoned for the next part of the Ulmark sequence.

Native Interpretation.—(1) This means "Wongar snake came out of his well and ate this Wongar pigeon all the same as the rock python snake today. He ate this pigeon before he ate those two women."

E. The Stone Spear-head Dance

1. Parrot-feather string is brought out of the men's baskets and is placed over the ironwood stakes.

1. When the pigeon dance is over, the four kangaroo messengers, who have kept their new parrot-feather ceremonial string ornament hidden in their personal baskets until this time, bring it out and wrap it around two small slabs of ironwood which are supposed to be stone spear heads and are inserted into spear shafts. The four men then stand in a line, one behind the other; the first and the last carry the spear emblems in the crook of their elbows. They dance up to the tail of the snake ground and then across it to the head where the chorus stands, hesitate, and then go back to the tail again. This is repeated a number of times while the chorus sings out the Ulmark refrain and the leader calls out the taboo names of stone spear heads. None of the youths being initiated is allowed to see this section of the Ulmark, which is called by the taboo name of the stone spear head (Mar-ul-pul).

Native Interpretation.—The ironwood stakes symbolize stone spear heads and are also associated with women, who use ironwood stakes as digging sticks. The two sisters were carrying the spear heads in their baskets. They "walked around their camp at the time of the rain with a stone spear looking for the snake to hit and stop him. The two women walked in a line."—"That small sister said, 'What will we do with this one [the head of the spear in her basket]?' The older sister said, 'Take it out and put it away.' The dance was after the women came to Mirrirmina. The blood has come. Those animals run away, and the rain and the thunder and the lightning have started. They dance these things to stop them."

F. The Headdress Dance

1. A dance sequence consisting chiefly of tree-grub dances is performed.

1. The next dance is the feather headdress ritual (kurt kurt). The men sit down in a line on the men's dance ground. The first man has a feathered headdress in his hand, the next has none, the third has one, and so on. The men rise and go repeatedly through the same movements as in the last dance: up to the tail of the snake, across to the head, hesitate, and back to the tail again.

The dances of Section C are repeated a number of times, always using the above movements.—When a cycle of dances is repeated, the *general* order is always the same, e.g., bees, kangaroos, grubs; but the order in which several grubs, e.g., are danced may vary.

Native Interpretation.—"The totemic name of the headdresses is darl-polng-ngo and its inside meaning is the Dar-pa snake."

Grubs are either classed as snakes or are closely associated with them. "Those women danced all these things to stop the rain. The grubs are the things they danced."

At about this time in the progress of the Ulmark all the men change baskets and fire drills, which temporarily ends the ceremony. All the participants now go to their own clan's country or remain as visitors until the ceremony starts again. Sometimes the preliminary portion of the Ulmark is extended through the whole dry season and the final part left until the following dry season, but ordinarily the complete performance is gone through at one season. If the ceremony is to last two seasons, the various participants repeat the dance sequences at their own clans throughout the rainy season, although because of the inclement weather and the difficulty of obtaining food, the dancing is not daily but only at intervals.

G. Certain Ritual Paraphernalia Are Constructed

1. Kangaroo-tail emblems are constructed.
2. The sunken triangular dance ground is dug.
3. The women's dance ground is prepared.
4. A winding path is placed around the men's ground.

5. Snail shell rattles are manufactured.
6. A bark house is constructed and is painted with ceremonial designs.

1. While the group of headdress dances of Section F dances is being performed, two emblems are under construction. They are large representations of the Dua kangaroo and Yiritja kangaroo tails. The smaller emblems previously mentioned function as message sticks for the kangaroos who announce the ceremony to the other tribes; these larger ones are used as emblems in the ceremony. They are brought out by the dancers who jump over each other. Yiritja jump over the Dua and Dua over the Yiritja in the same manner as our children play leap frog.

2. If the ceremony is to last two years the snake dance ground is not excavated, since it forms a part of what is considered the final portion of the Ulmark. If it is decided to complete the ceremony in one season, the Yiritja and Dua kangaroo messengers dig the dance place to a depth of a man's shoulder. It is in the center of the dance ground and well protected by heavy clumps of jungle growth. It has the same triangular shape as the snake ground in Section D and the one found in the Djungguan ceremony (which is not dug but is on the surface of the ground); but in addition it has a pathway dug to one side of the triangle. It is the python snake's body. It is supposed to face the southeast both in this ceremony and in the Djungguan. Bushes are piled in it at the head of the ground.

3. The women's dance ground is only a cleared space in the center of the general camp.

4. While the men are digging the triangular snake ground, the women, of both home and visiting clans, clear a small path which encircles the whole of the men's ceremonial grounds. (It winds and twists like the track left by a huge python.)

5. After the excavating has ceased, the men gather dry snail shells. These are painted with red ocher on which is dotted white clay. A half dozen of these shells are strung on one string and tied to a spear-thrower. Several of these snail-shell rattles are made.

6. A bark house is also built on the ceremonial grounds. The house is the same in structure as those used in the rainy season. The interior walls are painted with realistic and geometric figures (which illustrate the story of the two Wawilak sisters).

Native Interpretation.—The triangular and the women's dance ground are identical with the Djungguan dance places and are looked upon as the same by the natives. "Those bushes are put around a hole just the same as in the Djungguan. The two camps [dance grounds] are just the same as in the Djungguan."—"The tail [of the triangular dance ground] goes out by the women's camp. This means he has already swallowed those two women." (In the Djungguan the triangular ground also represents the snake after he has swallowed the two women. See page 263.) "The bushes are the two women who have been spewed out by the snake. They are [also] an ant bed on the ground where that snake first fell down at Mirrirmina."

When the women dance in their camp dance ground they are those two Wawilak sisters. The winding path which is made around the men's ground, and which of course surrounds the triangular dance ground as well as the bark house, is supposed to be the track of Muit when he was surrounding the two women; and the triangular dance ground always faces southeast because "that rock place at Mirrirmina looks that way."

When the snail-shell rattles appear it means that "the two women made this at Mirrirmina, and it was to show they were tired and near the finish of the dance." The snail-shell rattle is symbolical of marl-pin-pin (snail) itself. Its "inside meaning" is the garna, an ordinary wooden spear used by the women to stick in holes when looking for snails.

The bark house is that made by the two women when they tried to avoid the rain and being swallowed by the snake. There is supposedly a depression in the rocks and ground at Mirrirmina where the women had their house in which they put all their ritual properties during the rain. The two women left in it their hair belts and opossum string, and all the tools, weapons, and implements used by modern Murngin men. They were left for and found by the Wawilak men.

H. The Snail-shell Rattle Dance

1. The men dance with the snail-shell rattles on the boundary of the men's and women's grounds. The women give them gifts of "clothing."

1. The spear-throwers with the snail-shell rattles attached are brought out toward the main camp by the men. All of the male members enter the camp except the messengers, who remain in the ceremonial grounds. As they approach, the men sing and dance Flood Water. They meet the women who have marched out from their own camp and stopped on the ground intermediate to the camps. The women have gathered from

all the women of their camp, pubic coverings, head circlets, and all other articles of adornment and clothing as presents for the men.

The line of men singing and dancing Flood Water call out "Wah! Wah!" as they dance, and are answered by the women with the usual cry of "Kait-ba! kait-ba!" The men's arms are covered with leaves, the women are not painted or decorated. When the men are facing the women and only a few feet away, they stick the spear-throwers with the snail-shell rattles into the ground. The women dance up to them, the old men accept the presents of clothing from them and tell them to start gathering palm food for the guests coming to the last part of the Ulmark. The men then return to their own grounds. The old men put the women's presents in the snake house.

Native Interpretation.—"Snail is just the same as snake," and also, the snail was among the animals who ran away from the women. (See interpretation for Section K, page 313.)

I. The Messengers Leave Again

1. The messengers announce the Ulmark again. Many of the earlier sections are redanced while they are away. The initiates are treated severely. Other dances are introduced.

1. Messengers are sent out to announce the final events of the Ulmark. While they are gone, first the usual cycle, from the Torres Straits pigeon through the various grub dances, is danced in the excavated snake ground. The men also dance the jig steps of the two old women, the old men sometimes holding firebrands in their hands like penises. They shake them in the faces of the neophytes to frighten them and to amuse the initiated. The old men always appear to be extremely angry with the boys who are under initiation.

Then the clowns paint themselves to represent centipedes. They also dance the kangaroo leap-frog sequence and the line of men with spears in their arms. The little boys who are being initiated are forced to stay awake and watch this performance. The men swear at them unless they give complete attention to the ceremony. These last dances, which are not part of the cycle, are done not in the snake hole (excavated triangular dance ground) but some little distance away on the first triangular dance ground constructed earlier in the ceremony (Section D). They also dance a large flying insect (Di-kar) that comes just before the rain time, followed by a black butterfly (Burn-ba) dance, and a red butterfly dance.

Native Interpretation.—According to the natives' statements, the symbolization here is the same as in Section C when the kangaroo messengers leave the first time.

J. The Grub Dance Sequence

1. Several varieties of grubs are danced, as well as honeybees and other species.

   (1) The acacia tree grub (Bar-ler-wir-lar); a headdress made of the sulphur-crested cockatoo is worn for this dance.
   (2) A grub found in the ant beds (Gu-lung-a). Two men sit with their backs together, bend their torsos forward so that the head is as near the ground as possible, and then swing the body from left to right and back again.
   (3) The lake and river floating-wood grub.
   (4) Plain's grass grub. The bodies of the dancers are covered with small circular dots made by dipping the end of a bamboo rod into white paint and pressing it against the skin.
   (5) The lily grub.
   (6) Small kangaroo (pardi-pardi).
   (7) The Dua honeybee's honey found in a dead tree.
   (8) The Dua bee's honey found in a green tree.
   (9) The tiger snake (Dar-pa).
   (10) The sulphur-crested cockatoo headdress (Kurt Kurt).
   (11) The two Yiritja and two Dua kangaroos. The four sit down and the chorus surrounds them. The leader sings out the taboo names of the kangaroo. The chorus represents bushes and trees.

Native Interpretation.—The things sung in this all-inclusive list of songs are "the things the two women named and saw on their way."

K. The Settlement of Old Feuds

1. Old feuds are settled and a clown helps prevent open fighting and the destruction of the ritual. The ki-djin "language" is taught, and there is a repetition of earlier sections of the Ulmark.
2. The initiates are placed in a line, one behind the other.
3. Two lines of men throw the snail-shell rattles to each other.
4. A line of men and one of women on the boundary line of the male and female camps throw the snail rattles back and forth.
1. The above sequence of dances takes a month or six weeks to per-

form. When the moon is about quarter full in the west the messengers return. Everyone becomes very quiet; that peculiar type of quietness reigns in which one almost feels there is trouble brewing within a Murngin camp.—Then the people who have had trouble during the last year, or even prior to that time, begin to quarrel and fight. They are always of different clans, never members of the same group. When fights start, the leaders stop them. The people who have been keeping the Ulmark stand by, spears in hand, and talk the ki-djin "language" to them; some sing it. The "language" is a kind of native pidgin which includes words from the Mullikan, Djuan, and other native languages from the south.

A man noted for his clownish abilities takes his spear and spear-thrower from his personal basket, eats his food in an absurd manner, and generally acts the fool while he talks the kidjin language. Everyone laughs at this performance. If one of the quarreling men turns on the clown, the latter points a spear at him and pretends to spear him. The general loud laughter from everyone keeps the angry one from committing any overt act; and since the clown and his audience express no hostility, the offended man cannot cause trouble. It is clear that this clowning is a method of preventing feuds from breaking out during the ceremony.

The Torres Straits pigeon is danced again and the pigeon pulled through the drum as before. The spear is danced again, and the entire remaining sequence of Ulmark dances repeated; the snail shells are placed on the spear-throwers as before, and all the men paint their bodies and upper arms and legs with red ocher and kangaroo grease.

2. The initiates lie down in two lines. The four messengers sing near the general camp, but low enough so that the women cannot hear them. They sing in the kidjin language. Then they sing louder, and the women answer with the refrain: "Kait-ba! kait-ba!"

3. On the men's ground two lines of dancers throw the snail rattles back and forth. They, too, sing the refrain of the women. After this all go to the general camp singing the kait-ba song. They take the marl-pin-pin with them. When they get on the ground near the general camp they change the refrain to a kind of low humming noise, "m-u-mmmmmmmmm."

4. The women meanwhile have come out to the intermediate ground and stand in a line, and the men approach and form themselves into a line opposite them. The men from one clan throw a snail-shell rattle to the women belonging to the same clan. They throw the

marl-pin-pin back again. When it has gone back and forth and everyone has thrown the marlpinpin, the women finally keep it. The men now dance while singing "Kait-ba! kait-ba!" and return to the men's ground, the women following until they reach the edge of the taboo ground. The men go inside and the women return to their camp.

Native Interpretation.—"The kidjin language means talk used by the two old women when they looked up into the sky and tried to stop the rain and Muit." (It is also used in fighting and hunting; a man looks at his spear and tells it to go straight.)

"Those two women are singing to stop Muit all night and to stop the raining. The young men lie down the way the children of the two women did." When the boys lie down in two lines, "They are the two women. This is how they did it before."

"When the men come toward the general camp they dance the two Wawilak women at first." That is why the line of men sing Kait-ba! kait-ba!, for this is the cry of the two women. When they change and make the humming sound, "This is Muit coming for the two women. That is why the camp women are singing 'Kait-ba! kait-ba!' now."

The men and women throw the marlpinpin at each other "because the two women did. They did it because they knew lots of rain was coming. Snail is just the same as snake. He comes out just before the rainy season. That snail ran when the women had that blood."

L. The Fire Dance with Spears and Yams

1. A bark cylinder is made with spears at one end and yams at the other. The cylinder is fired and the men dance in the flames.

1. The men sing all night long. The old sequence of Ulmark songs and dances is followed through in one night. Songs are also sung by the chorus in which all the things the women saw and named on their march to the sea are enumerated.

Two men leave the group and paint a bush yam with red ocher. The same men roll up pieces of paper bark into a long cylinder about one foot in diameter and about twenty feet long. Several spears are tied together and also wrapped in paper bark. It is near daylight by this time. A fire is built and the bark cylinder is placed with one end near it. At the opposite end of the bark cylinder the wrapped spears are placed. Two men sit at the fire end of the paper bark where the yam has been placed. A line of men sits down on the spears and on the paper-bark cylinder. The paper bark is lit and the men get up and dance over it. Dancing the Ulmark jig step, the men break up the unburned bark and feed it to the fire. Each man dances till he feels the hair burn on his legs and it is too hot for him to continue. The bark is taken off the spears and also burned.

Native Interpretation.—The bark cylinder is the snake and the men sitting in a line on it are Muit too. The bark fire is also the snake. The burning of the paper bark is Muit disappearing. The men dance over the fires "so that they must burn their legs so that they can eat any animal." They are the two Wawilak sisters when they dance this. They are "Wawilak and unclean."

M. The Frill-neck Lizard Dance

1. Two men dance frill-neck lizard in a tree and jump into a fire.

1. This same morning the frill-neck, "big-eared" lizard is danced for the first time. It is used as a symbol to announce the end of a phase of the ceremony, just as the appearance of the blue-tongued lizard was in the Gunabibi. Two men dance it. They climb up a tree and hold on with their knees while waving their arms. A fire is lit beneath them. The two lizards jump on it and then run away.

Native Interpretation.—"When the lizards jump in the fire they are running into Mirrirmina away from the two women."

N. Flying-Fox Dance and Snake Dance

1. Two lines of flying foxes surround seated figures of kangaroos, tiger snakes, and gray kangaroos. The men enter the triangular dance ground.
2. The dance of the snakes and small kangaroos in the sunken dance ground.

1. They next dance flying foxes. The flying foxes file in to the dance ground from the bush in two long lines. On the triangular dance ground eight men sit two by two with their backs to each other. They represent black kangaroo, gray kangaroo, and darpas (tiger snakes). The two lines of flying foxes encircle each pair of sitting dancers.

2. The sitting dancers inside the circles of flying foxes shake their shoulders and fling their bodies back and forth as did the grubs in the Ulmark dance described on page 311. The kangaroos and snakes take out their feather headdresses from their baskets and place them on their heads.

The initiates are not allowed to see the rest of this part (N) of the Ulmark. All the older men get up and run to the path that has been excavated in the snake ground; they run inside the path and into the hole.

Native Interpretation.—"Two men [the pairs of sitting men] go straight inside the hole we dig for them. That means that the snake has swallowed the two women and is going down the hole."

O. The Ceremonial Camp Is Encircled by Fire

1. The men dance through the fire to the women's ground. They ceremonially wash and put on new raiment.

1. Two men paint themselves as darpa (tiger) snakes (Ma-ring-o in the Wangurri tongue, and U-var-ko in the Garl-ba-nuk dialect). One man paints himself to represent the small kangaroo (pardi-pardi). The two snakes squat down at the head end of the triangular excavated snake ground. The kangaroos sit down at the tail end, surrounded by the chorus. Lines of bushes are put on each side of the snakes. The kangaroos dance first. The chorus uses the swinging motion of the trunk described on page 311, and sings the taboo names of the kangaroo. After the snakes have danced, the men leave the ceremonial grounds and return to the women's camp. When the snake and kangaroo episode occurs, the neophytes are shown the excavation and instructed in the mythology for the first time.

The women now make a fire that follows the path made by them earlier in the Ulmark (see Section G 4), which completely surrounds the men's ceremonial camp. The fire moves in toward the men. The women return to their own camp. The men paint themselves and all their possessions with red ocher. They shave and cut their hair to give themselves a "new" appearance. The women in camp also paint themselves and all their possessions, also to make them look "new." The men come out of their ceremonial ground and through the fire to the main camp. They dance out into the water and wash themselves, as do the women. When the men and women come back, they take kangaroo grease and red ocher and paint themselves. They put on a new white headband, freshly painted arm bands, a new hair belt, and a new pubic covering.

Native Interpretation.—"That fire is all the same as the two women made to cook the animals that ran away. [It is also the snake, and the snake's tongue.] The path is Muit."

All the men and women bathe themselves and wash their belongings "to make them all the same as new people and clean people." The men wash to "clean" themselves, and put on grease and ocher and new raiment to make themselves "new and clean."

P. The Forked-Pole Dance

1. Pardi-pardi runs and climbs a tree.
2. A forked pole is erected and two women climb it and jump into the arms of the men's chorus.

1. On the intermediate ground near the women's camp the small kangaroo, pardi-pardi, climbs a tree. The chorus surrounds him, dancing and calling out the cry of the two Creator Sisters.

2. While the men were dancing tiger snake and kangaroo, a large forked pole was placed in the ground. It is much the same as that used in the Gunabibi, except that here only one forked pole is used. The women, under the guidance of an old man, are collected around this pole. Two of the older women climb up and sit in the forked branches. The men leave the ceremonial grounds and surround the stick and the women. They roar like thunder. The two women jump from the forked stick into the chorus of men, singing "Kait-ba! kait-ba!" The men roar again. Two men get up into the forked pole and jump down into the chorus and the entire group of men then returns to the men's ceremonial grounds.

Native Interpretation.—"When pardi-pardi ran up the tree and then away, he was running away from those two women. They tried to catch him."—"That forked stick is just the same as the house of the two Wawilak women. When the two men get up in the forked stick that is like Muit's head in the sky, and the [chorus of] dancing men below is Muit's body around the house."

"When the two women jump down and dance around singing Kait-ba! kait-ba! they are fighting with the snake and it means they have been swallowed and taken below the ground. The men [chorus] roar like a snake [thunder]."

Q. The Spear-Thrower Feather-Headpiece Dance

1. The spear heads are rubbed with honey and red ocher. A line of dancers is formed at the excavated grounds; they hold, one a spear, the next a feather headdress, et cetera, in their hands.

1. This element of the Ulmark is performed at the ceremonial excavated ground. The men paint their spear-throwers with red ocher.

Honey is rubbed over the central part and the two ends are dotted with white paint. The chorus sits down in the path that leads into the excavated dance ground. The first man holds a spear-thrower, the next a feather headdress, and the next a spear-thrower, etc. The spear-thrower and the feather headdress are taboo and like totemic emblems. The initiates are not allowed to see them. The men sing under the direction of the ceremonial leader the taboo names of the two objects.

Native Interpretation.—The men in the path "are the two women. They dance this to stop rain because this was right inside [very sacred and high in the totemic mysteries]. They couldn't stop because Muit wouldn't stop. The kurt-kurts [feather headdresses] are darpa snakes."

R. The Flying Fox and Kangaroo Dance

1. The kangaroos sit by the excavated triangular dance ground with lines of fire on each side of them.
2. The flying foxes enter and go into the hole.
3. The messengers appear.

1. Following the episode above, two lines of gray kangaroos (kai-tjim-bal) are formed, one on each side of the triangular dance hole. Three groups of men sit inside with their ceremonial feather headdresses on. A line of fire is placed on each side of the dance hole.

The kangaroos hop over the fire while they dance around the hole.

2. After this the group sing evening and morning star, the sun, moon, stars, and milky way. When daylight is near, everyone picks up a firebrand. Several lines of flying-fox dancers gather out in the surrounding bush. They cry out like flying foxes. They run by one another a number of times, then enter the ceremonial hole and surround each group of men there. The leader of the ceremony calls out the taboo name of the headdresses. The seated men exchange headdresses.

3. Soon after dawn messengers walk into the ceremonial camp. They are painted as Dua honeybee, darpa snake, and small kangaroo.

Native Interpretation.—When the kangaroos leap over the triangular well "they are swallowed by the snake." The men sitting in the well with kurt-kurts (feather headdresses) are darpa snakes. When the flying-fox dancers go into the triangular well the neophytes are made young men. "The messengers are Bapa Indi who swallowed the two women, and the other men are rain."

S. The Forked-pole Dance Is Repeated

1. In the camp several old men have made three or four stone fires as if they were going to cook kangaroo. The women dance out from the general camp to the forked pole where the two women climb it as earlier in the ceremony. The men come out of the ceremonial ground and surround the women on the pole. They roar like the thunder. The women jump on the ground into the chorus of men, and the two men climb up on the pole and then jump on the ground. A chorus of women dances outside the group of men.

Native Interpretation.—The natives' interpretation is the same as for the first performance of the dance (Section P, page 316).

T. The Stone Fire and Snake Dance

1. The old men build a stone fire and the men inhale the smoke and squat over the fire in order to allow the smoke to enter their anuses.

1. All the men go to the general camp and divide into groups around the various stone fires the old men have made. The women dance around them. All the men hold their heads over the fires and inhale the smoke and heat. They also squat over the fire to allow the smoke to enter the anal opening. Men, women, and young boys then paint themselves with red ocher and kangaroo grease.

Native Interpretation.—When the men inhale the smoke, "this means so we can eat any kind of food." When they put their anuses over the fire, "This is like the Wawilak women did when that baby was born." The women go through this same healing and purificatory rite today. The whole fire ceremony "means just the same as the place in the Gunabibi [Section I] when men go along the ridgepole and get food handed to them."

U. The Palm Nut Bread Is Eaten

1. The bread is divided and eaten by the men. The ironwood-leaf purification is held and the neophytes are steamed..

1. Several days later, possibly a week or more, the women bake a large palm nut loaf. The ceremonial bread is divided and eaten by all the men who participated in the ceremony. Another big stone fire is made. New body ornaments are placed on each man, and green bushes are held in the hands of each mature male to symbolize the trees that surround their ceremonial ground. The men dance around

the stone fire, and the women around them. Ironwood leaves (maipin) are put in the fire and a smoking branch is brushed over all the males and females who have been in the ceremony. To make a heavy steam, wet grass is put on the fire and the neophytes placed over it so that both mouth and anus are supposedly filled with purifying steam. This is to allow the young men to eat the large game which up to this time has been taboo to them.

Native Interpretation.—All the informants insisted that the interpretation of the steaming of the initiates is the same as in the Djungguan (Section H). The eating of the bread is a general symbol of communion which will be treated later.

General Summary of the Sections of the Ulmark

The ritual dances of the Ulmark ceremony divide themselves into two main groups of symbols: (1) the food animals' running away from the two women, and (2) the snake's swallowing the women and animals.

THE MARNDIELLA CEREMONY

A. Preparations

1. The fathers are consulted. The boys are decorated.

1. The Marndiella is used as a circumcision rite and belongs to the Wawilak group. It is usually held when it is felt that certain boys are too large to be allowed to remain uncircumcised for another year and when the time is short and the wet season is at hand. In other words, it is used when the Djungguan ceremony is considered too long for the time at their command. It is the shortest of the four general tribal ceremonies centered around the Wawilak. The Marndiella never comes first by preference and is only used as an expedient. However, at times the Marndiella is prolonged, principally because of the Murngin's keen pleasure in all ceremonies and because it is felt to be not quite fitting to rush a ceremony through in so short a time.

The ceremony starts the afternoon before the circumcision is to take place. The leader in this ritual, as in all the others, is a clan ceremonial director. He confers with the fathers of the boys to gain their permission, or to set a time for the circumcision when the fathers have requested him to make their boys young men. On the afternoon of the day chosen to start the ceremony the boys are taken to the men's ceremonial grounds where they are decorated for the coming ritual.

White string is put on their arms. The torso, the upper arms down to the elbows, and the upper part of the legs to the knees are painted solidly with charcoal. The lower arms and legs are covered with red ocher, as are the face and hair. Lines of white feathers are glued with orchid-bulb juice from each shoulder across to the opposite hip so that the lines cross at the navel. A band of white feathers is put around the body at the belt line. A bark forehead band is painted with white clay and tied across the forehead so that the white band outlines the upper part of the face. Lines of white feathers run from ear to ear on the lower part of the face. This ends the first day's preparations. The women meanwhile have been gathering food for the morrow's ceremony.

Native Interpretation.—The natives say, "Marndiella is quick because the snake came quick. The design painted on the boy's torso symbolizes a woman's 'harness' because he is all the same as a woman."

B. THE SONG SEQUENCE

1. The men cut their arms to make the blood flow, and a cycle of songs is sung.
2. The initiates have spears thrown at them.

1. In the morning the men cut their arms, as they do in the Gunabibi and Djungguan, for blood to be used in the ritual for both its magical power and its adhesive qualities. While the cutting is taking place the leader and the other men sing the following cycle of songs, time being kept by the beating of singing sticks:

(1) Flying fox (Yari-war-la)
(2) A small honeybee—Dua
(3) A large Dua honeybee
(4) The scales of the small fresh-water fish (Bi-dji-ma)
(5) Water ripples
(6) Flower of the water lily (La-barn-dja)—Yiritja
(7) Water-lily stalk (O-lo-nair-i)—Yiritja
(8) Flight of the dollar bird (Yam-yam-ming-o)—Dua
(9) Fruit tree's fruit (Djar-la-larn-a)—Yiritja
(10) Leaf of this tree (Gir-in-gir-in)—Yiritja
(11) Flower of this tree (Gar-dok-gar-dok-me-la)—Yiritja

(Children eat this food more than anyone else and it is associated with them as candy would be with European children.)

(12) Domesticated female dog (Yair-a-wa-din-ya)—Yiritja
(13) Male dog (Gorn-daort borola)—Yiritja
(14) Wild female dog (Gu-lang-na-ngang-ba)—Yiritja
(15) Wild male dog (Wart-pir-i-djin-na)—Yiritja
(16) Wild dog pup (Dir-a-ra-ko)—Yiritja
(17) Big gray kangaroo (Kai-tjim-bal)—Yiritja
(18) His face (Bo-ko-nar-wil-li)—Yiritja
(19) Hop of the kangaroo (Lor-o-to-djin-ya)—Yiritja

(When the big kangaroo song is sung two men stand up and dance in the manner described in the Djungguan ceremony. Later the entire group dances songs. They do not paint for this part of the ritual.)

(20) Buttocks of the kangaroo (Kjar-la-ba-ba)—Yiritja
(21) Path to the Kangaroo water hole (Dir-go-go)—Yiritja
(22) Depression in the ground approaching the water hole (Barng-in-dal brang-in-dal)—Yiritja
(23) Water hole for the kangaroo's drink (Lar-lar-la-war-ain-yi) —Yiritja
(24) Parasite found on the yam (Djo-go-mirn-nir-i)—Dua
(25) Salty-tasting yam's leaf (Si-ba-ma mai-al-pong-o)—Dua
(26) Teeth of the big kangaroo (Lir-a-mai-yor-o)—Yiritja
(27) Young lily (Dji-ma-rang-gal)—Yiritja
(28) The young of the gray kangaroo (Da-gan-da)—Yiritja
(29) Fire circle used to hunt kangaroos (Gan-djarl-gar-ra)—Yiritja
(30) Cycad palm nut (Bal-mar-din-gur-a)—Yiritja
(31) The shell of the cycad palm nut (Pal-mar-yir-in-i)—Yiritja
(32) Cycad palm tree (Din-gu)—Yiritja
(33) Acacia tree (nin-bal-ma)—Dua
(34) Flower of the acacia tree (Warng-gi-ir-i)—Dua
(35) Leaf of the acacia tree (Yun-bar-djun-bar)—Dua
(36) Trumpet's wood (Ma-rin-bor mar-ba)—Dua
(37) A small night bird (Tar-bo tar-bo)—Yiritja

This sequence of songs is repeated a number of times. The men sing after the evening meal until quite late at night. Sometimes the ceremony is continued until the next morning. In the morning the men paint themselves on the ceremonial grounds for the morning's dance, and then sit down in a circle within the general camp. They throw spears at the boys who are to be circumcised and then take them inside the ceremonial grounds. The chief animals represented are dog, kangaroo, and honeybee. The ceremonial leader, when the men have almost completed their painting, returns to the camp. He has a large pair of singing sticks.

Native Interpretation.—The native interpretation of this second section will be discussed in the general analysis, Chapter XI.

C. The Women's Mat Dance

1. The young initiate (or initiates) and his mother's brother's daughter are put under an ainmara.
2. Fires are lighted and clan names called out.

1. The men who do not figure in the dancing, but who take part in the ceremony as members of the men's chorus, go with the leader to the main camp.

In the cleared space in the center of the camp the initiate is put under the woman's mat with his feet sticking out from under it. A young woman, preferably his galle, is put under the ainmara with him. The boy's mother (arndi) and his mother's mother (mari) stand over him. They wave their head circlets over him because this is supposed to take away any harmful effect his eating the flesh of large animals may have had—in other words, from having eaten any of the things permitted up until this time, but which from now on he will not be allowed to include in his diet until he is married and has a child.

2. The leader and chorus sing fire (Laid-dal-ma-yao-yao) during this part of the ceremony. Fires are lighted at this point, which is a signal for the dancers to come out. The taboo names of many clan territories are called out by the leader and chorus. The women slap their thighs and keep time with the men's singing and the beating of the singing sticks. All the women are painted with red ocher except the two who stand over the boy. They are painted in a rough imitation of him. The women sit while the men stand. The men have their spear-throwers lying on the back of their necks and a hand on each end of the weapon. The scene at this part of the Marndiella corresponds to that at the end of the Djungguan at the time of the circumcision.

Native Interpretation.—"When a boy is put under an ainmara, that house is the house of the two old Wawilak women."—"Those women dancing around the ainmaras are told to do this to stop sickness and so the boy won't have trouble where he is cut."—"The couple under the ainmaras are the two Wawilak women," from the point of view of the myth and ritual.

"Marndiella was sung first by the two women before they sang the Djungguan and Gunabibi to try to stop the rain, but they couldn't stop it and the snake came and swallowed them."

D. The Dog Dancers Enter

1. Two men dance in the main camp as dogs.

1. A dog dancer comes into the dance ground of the main camp after circling about in the nearby bush and on the camp ground. He has a high peaked hat on of the same type that is used in the Gunabibi. While he comes toward the group, all the taboo names of the country belonging to the Mandelpui, Liaalaomir, and Wawilak clans are cried out by the leader and male chorus. Another dog who has on only a forehead band instead of the high hat approaches the group from another quarter. The first dog comes in and smells the feet of the boy and girl and sits down at one end of the line of men. The other dog does likewise and sits at the other end. The boy gets up then and pulls a feather from off the decorated men.

When the boy pulls the feather off it means: "Those two women had that done to them when the rain knocked the feathers off when they danced around the bark house."

Native Interpretation.—This dance "means that boy is all the same as iguana, bandicoot, opossum, and kangaroo, and that dog has come to catch him. Those two women made it that way."

E. A Line of Men Dance into the Women's Camp with Lighted Torches

1. The boy, or boys, who are to be circumcised are once more placed under the ainmara, and a line of men with torches dance around them.

1. The men then go out to the ceremonial ground and paint themselves with blood and feathers. They form a long line and dance into the women's camp carrying lighted torches of paper bark. The boy has been placed under the woman's mat and they dance around him. The leader stands by the men and sings torch fire (War-nan-bor-yo-

yor-o), honey (Bar-a-gar-la), and honeybee hive (Warl-kin-di). While the leader sings, the chorus shrilly cries, "Ai—ai!!" Two birds who frequent the salt plains (Ta-bu-ta-bu) dance in while the chorus sings the name of these birds. The leader taps them with his singing sticks and makes them go over and sit down in the line formed by the chorus. The following dancers appear and are treated in the same way by the leader: honeybee, tiger snake (darpa), leech (djal-ng-nin), and two dogs. The hat worn by one of the dogs is knocked off.

The whole chorus then dance Dua honeybee. After this they tie bunches of leaves to their ankles and, beginning with the flying fox, the entire sequence of dances is performed again.

Native Interpretation.—"That line of men come in with blood and feathers on them. They are snakes and they dance around the camp of the two Wawilak women."

F. The Circumcision and Steaming Rites

1. The same dances are used for the steaming ceremony of the Marndiella as in the Djungguan.

1. The boy is then circumcised. The same procedure and method of cutting are followed here as in the Djungguan (Section H), and the purificatory fire rite is performed in exactly the same manner.

Native Interpretation.—The same set of symbolical ideas operates here as in the Djungguan.

The next chapter turns to a consideration of the Djunkgao myth and ritual cycle, and the reader may turn immediately to the interpretative chapter if he is interested in discovering the Murngin symbolic processes.

CHAPTER X

MURNGIN TOTEMISM, II

THE DJUNKGAO CONSTELLATION

THE Djunkgao myth-ritual constellation will be treated by the same method as the Wawilak, presenting first the myths, and following them by descriptions of the ceremonies with each section named, analyzed and given its native interpretation.

Introduction to Myth

The Djunkgao sisters myth, not as well organized as the Wawilak sisters narrative, is but one part of a larger cycle of stories centering around the movements of the ocean tides and the floods of the rainy season. The totemic emblems which many native accounts insist were brought to man by the Djunkgao sisters are in all these different narratives carried by the floods or tides either directly or by some such creature as dugong or shark. The totemic wells usually are said to have been made by the two Djunkgao sisters and the rangas put in them: the common rationalization is that they made the wells and put in either all the rangas or a certain number; and porpoise, dugong or Garrawark put in the others. Sometimes the holes made by the yam sticks which the two sisters used for walking sticks are now ranga or Narra wells. In certain clans the Yurlunggur and the Djunkgao cycles overlap, and all the creatures found associated with both configurations are in the Narra wells in the overlapping areas. Generally speaking, the western clans tend to celebrate the drama of the Wawilak with the Djungguan, Gunabibi, Ulmark and Marndiella, and the eastern are more concerned with the Narra ceremonies and the Djunkgao sisters. The myths of the two sets of sisters recount the adhesion of the different totems to each, but in native thought the eastern clans emphasize the Narra and the western clans the Wawilak in the ritual expressions of the myths. Frequently the Djunkgao story jumps from one clan territory back to another, and place is not related to time as minutely as it is in the Wawilak story. The different accounts give varying locales for certain events, but essentially the stories follow one pattern.

First the women came into the Murngin country on a raft from the south and then started walking with two yam sticks to support them on their journey. They went from the east coast northward and westward and disappeared into a hole somewhere in the little-known Gunwinggu country. On the way three important events occurred: (a) they named the clan countries and the animals found there and made the totem wells with their yam sticks; (b) the younger sister was incestuously raped by an ancestor man or men in her own moiety; and (c) the men stole their totems and they became like ordinary women. The account may vary in detail and place, but these happenings appear in all.

The three stories given below present the main essentials of the general theme and demonstrate the overlapping and minor contradictions found in the separate narratives. The location of the clan of the narrator affects considerably the subordination of certain clan names and the prominence of others.

THE DJUNKGAO MYTH

A. The Wanderings of the Sisters

When things started there was only water. Those two sisters paddled into Caledon Bay (other accounts, Blue Mud Bay) on a raft. Those two Djunkgao sisters went through the Marungun country first. (They had come from out of the sea in Blue Mud Bay.) They next went to the Darlwongo, Djarwark, Kalpu, Mukka-nai-mul-mi, Karpin, Merango, Marungun, Djirin, Gwiyula, Naladaer, Liagaomir, Ding Ding, Perango, Guria Marunga Island, Mart-a-rang-a Island, Pu-djer-i-ki, Rabuma, Milpai-wa, and then went on toward the Gunwinggu country. They went to all the Dua clan countries in the tribes of the north. They walked on the outside of Elcho Island and avoided Yiritja country, and just went to the country that did not have a name and made it Dua. They always avoided Yiritja country.

Those two women had been paddling with a canoe. They left the canoe and stuck two yam sticks in the ground where they stopped. They named that country Nu-pur-a. They started there and walked and walked. They came out at another place on the mainland and called it Tak-ar-a. They crossed Arnhem Bay and came out at the mainland near Elcho Island. They landed at Maripai. These women left the canoe there. They came on land now. They found a lot of shells there, and they named all these shells, they gave them totem names. They caught a number of fish, such as mullet and flatfish and others, and they gave them all names.

"Come," said the older sister, "we must go now, for the sun has gone down. We will go quickly."

They crossed the plain the other side of Elcho Island to the bush. They went to the bush and found bush food there, and other things that black people use, such as stringy bark for houses. They named all these things.

They sat down and stopped here in the bush country. They sat down on their feet, with their knees out in front, just the way women do today. That is why the women do this now. They looked around at the people there. They looked at the people; there were very few people, and different from what they are now. The women said to themselves, "What are we going to do? We have no husbands."

They had vaginas, but they were not large the way they are now. They were not large enough for sexual intercourse, but could only be used for urination. They took a small piece of wood and hit themselves on each buttock so they could make plenty of people and their vaginas would grow larger, just as they are now. They were walking at this time by the Goyder River. They had two yam sticks with them. They sat up high on their heels like women do when they have children. Because of this there were plenty of people there.

These two women looked like women, but they also looked like Wongars and like our grandfathers a long, long time ago. Our grandfathers came out from the wombs of these women. They left the Goyder River country and the Arafura Sea country and went on over toward the Gunwinggu country. They went down in the ground there. Before they went they gave all the trees, stones, birds, animals, everything names. They named the mud and everything. That is why we have names for these things today. We did not name them ourselves. Wongars gave them their names. Our names belong to us. We can name ourselves, but everything else in the world has a name for it.

Before the two women came to us they made a wooden totem. One was a woman, and they made another one a small girl. They also made an iguana ranga, a parrot one, a stone ranga, and a fire ranga. They made a big Narra ceremony and put all these rangas in one place. When they did this they thought they would make all the water into land and have nothing but dry land, and they would have the turtles and fish live in dry places, but trochus shell talked to turtle and fish and to porpoise. He said, "Let us go back into the sea. We shells will keep ourselves halfway between on the beach and you people can go into the water. The fish can go out a little way. The turtle must stay out in the deep water. It is all right for him to come in and lay his eggs, but that's all."

Those two Djunkgao sisters paddled along in a canoe and there were no men with them. There was a very big sea. They saw the Morning Star. They caught the Morning Star and held it in their hands.

"You go first," they said, "and we'll come behind."

This was in the night time. They were covered with the white slimy substance that is found on top of the sea water. This is just the same as the semen that the young woman had upon her when the Kalpu man had incestuous relations with her, and deposited his sperm upon her body. (See the Incestuous Rape of the Young Sister, page 338.)

The sea was red at that time and not like it is now. There was no land anywhere. Next morning they saw land and they were very glad. They said, "Oh, this is very good." They said, "Oh, this is Ma-lang-o." It was the mainland. There were no islands then, either. They kept coming on in this canoe and following the Morning Star. When the star went down the sun came out. The star came out at night and the sun came out in the daytime. Those two women followed the sun. They tried to get ahead of her. They followed the sun clear around the world. (The informant illustrated by putting his hand over a box and under it and around again.)

By and by they left their canoe and walked around looking for a good place to leave a ranga. They left their god at Malango and the other places where they stopped. They left another one at Marapai. They left their canoe at Marapai, too, and it became a ranga and turned to stone. They caught a lot of fish at this place and gave all of them names. They gave them both their common names and their power names. They went inside the mangrove swamp here and they found a lot of shellfish, including crab. They called him Nu-ka. This was in the Liagaomir country. After they named the shellfish they went farther into the bush, where they found bush food. They named all this bush food.

They made all the islands along the north coast. They made Elcho Island and the English Company Islands and the Crocodile Islands.

B. The Incestuous Rape of the Young Sister

When those two women came to Caledon Bay the older went a little distance farther than the younger one. The wirkul (young girl) lay down under her ainmara (mat). One of the Wongar yolno who had been watching their arrival sneaked up and lay down under her ainmara and tried to copulate with her. He was uncircumcised. He attempted to penetrate inside her vagina. She jumped because he had frightened her while she slept. If he had asked her she would have complied willingly.

When the young girl jumped the Wongar man's penis came out of her vagina and he ejaculated all over her abdomen. His semen was on her body. She got up, ran down to the beach and washed herself. The older sister reprimanded this black man for doing it. He belonged to the ranga well called Mu-e-lung-gal. It belongs to the Kalpu Dua people. The name of the country is Kar-karng-na, after that paper-bark "canoe." This girl can still be seen standing by the shore, where she turned to stone when she took her bath. The people at this well also have the foreskin of a man for a ranga, and it can be seen in this country at the present time.

The Liagaomir and the Kalpu are all the same because they have this one for their ranga. It is found in both their wells. At the Yaor-yaor well of the Naladaer people on Napir's Peninsula, those two women squatted down there and a stone ranga fell out of the womb of the younger one. This stone can be seen a short distance from the well. Anyone can go touch it. That stone is bigger than a house. Women do not know it is a ranga. The stone is called the bir-ta (black stone).

C. The Djunkgao Sisters Lose Their Rangas

Those two Djunkgao sisters hid their dilly bags[1] with ranga string in them inside some bushes. They went out to look for shellfish in the mangrove jungles. Some of these old Wongar yolnos stole their dilly bags with the ranga string. These baskets were totemic emblems. They took the baskets away and burned the grass and bushes where the baskets had been so that the women could see the fire and think their camp fire had burned over and destroyed their totemic emblems. When the sisters returned they said, "It is no one's fault but ours. Our fire did it."

Each sister quarreled with the other for losing the red parrot feather string. They took their own baskets from their heads and put them on the ground. They thought about what they had done during the day and were sorry they hadn't put their maraiin baskets in a clear place. While they were sitting there thinking, they heard the sound of singing sticks inside the jungle. They knew that a ceremony was taking place. They knew that those old Wongar yolnos had stolen their baskets and the parrot string. They said to themselves, "We'll go and take it away from those men."

They ran out into the bush toward where they had heard the sound and where they thought their baskets were. They came close to the bush and saw the old men. The men were singing "Benbur benbur," and dancing. They had the string and baskets. The women fell down and hid their eyes because they didn't want to look at that ceremony. The men were dancing water at the time. "It is no good now for us to try to get those baskets. We must work hard now. We women must go get the food for the men from now on," said the big sister to the little one.

"Yes, sister," said the little one, "we can't do anything now. It's our own fault."

They went back to their camp and told all the women always to make plenty of food for the Narra time. Women do that now. The men who had stolen the ranga talked to each other. They said, "It is a good thing we took this ranga from those women, because now they can get food for us."

In the old times men used to get food for women and the women sat

[1] Women's carrying bags: Australian-white term.

down on the inside and looked after the rangas. Those two old women (Djunkgao), when they first came, carried the sun. They were the leaders of the sun. It was just as though he belonged to them. They left him up when they came this way. In the beginning we had the sun, the water, and those women—nothing more. The sun was first.

Out in the bush the men thought, "We must have a fire." They burned paper bark and brush. Those men said, "We stole this from the women. We can't sell this string to the Yiritja until we have a fire. We cannot put this string back into the mud because we stole it from these women. We must keep it and sell it to other men so they can make presents to us."

THE DUA NARRA CEREMONY

The Dua Narra and Yiritja Narra are not so much age-grading rituals as totemic rites. They celebrate the relationship of man to his totems and are focused on the totemic emblems.

Both Dua and Yiritja Narra are divided into two parts. The first or preliminary part is called the *Duni*; the second is looked upon as the real ceremony and is far more important then the Duni. The Duni comprises sections A, B, and C of both the Dua and Yiritja Narras.

A. Preparations

1. The leader gives his consent to his younger brothers and other members of the clan to start a Narra ritual, and totemic emblems are carved and painted.
2. The Narra dance ground is made in the men's ground and the men dance on it.

1. At the beginning of the dry season the grass is too high for travel, and the lily bulbs and cycad palm nuts are not ready for harvest. It is necessary to wait until the grass can be burned and food becomes plentiful, to start a Narra ceremony. Most of the old men watch carefully for the earliest time possible to begin. The younger men are usually the ones who start preparations. Ordinarily the younger brother of the leader goes out into the bush with some of his friends and examines the trees until he finds a straight one of the proper size. He comments upon its proper appearance and says that this is a good one: "I am going to cut it down and make a ranga."

The tree is cut down, cleaned, and the refuse burned by him and his fellows. It is brought back to the vicinity of the clan camp, to a spot on the men's ceremonial grounds in the thicker part of the jungle.

The young man then goes to see his brother or whoever is leader of the ceremony and says that he has cut ranga wood and wants to make the totemic emblem. If the time is proper the leader says, "Yes, we will go look at that log to see if it is the right size [for carving]." The old man, with other old men, goes out from the main camp to the totem grounds to see how large the ranga wood is. If it is a big log he says, "I think we'll make a woman ranga." If it is somewhat smaller he says, "I think iguana would be the thing to make." Other young men sometimes say at this time to the leader, "I would like to make a girl ranga." Another one says, "I should like to make a fish ranga," another, "I should like to make a wan-du-ma [mud fish]," and still others say, "We want to make a marn-bur [clitoris]."

The young men who are talking to the old leader are his yukiyuko, gatu, younger bapa, marelker, gurrong, mari, and kutara. The old man says to them, "When this Narra ceremony is finished you can sell the string from these rangas to your relatives, but you must come first and see me and make me a present. You can sell it to the Yiritja, you can sell it to people in the same camp. You can take out the string with parrot feathers on it and make bangles and streamers to hang down from your arms. That makes the arm strong when warding off spears. It will help break the spears." The various totemic emblems are usually made at this time.

2. Late in the afternoon the leader and the initiated men leave the main camp and go out to the men's ceremonial grounds. A small quadrangular dance place has been prepared. This ground is made and used in the same way in the Narra ceremony of the other moiety. The leader takes his singing sticks, the men form themselves into a chorus in front of him. They sing "Um-um-um-wa!" which is to symbolize the running of the fresh water from a totem well located in the interior, and they dance back and forth across the dance ground. When the dancers turn at the end of the ground, they repeat the cry again and the tempo of the rhythm increases, which means that the water is running fast. After this dance has been repeated a great number of times, the leader, followed by his chorus, dances into the main camp. They walk about the place and call out the power names of rain and flood water and the springs that appear after the floods. Finally the leader says, "We will stop." The women give them food and they return to the Narra totemic grounds for further dancing. When they get on the dance ground they cry "Um-um-sis-sis-sis-wa!" All the power names of water are now called up.

This finishes the dance for the evening. Some of the men return to their totemic grounds to eat their food, and others eat in the main camp.—Until this time the totemic emblem has not been painted with red ocher. The leader says to the young men, "Are the rangas finished?"

The young men say, "No, we have no red parrot feathers."

The leader says, "Then we will make our ceremony the du ni way [the red ocher or simple way]. We will put paint on instead of red parrot feathers. We will paint the ranga tomorrow and leave it until next year." Even the people who have enough opossum string and opossum fur of Yiritja and red parrot feathers of Dua to decorate their totemic emblems properly must make an affirmative response to this statement of the leader. He then says, "We will wait until there is more food." Many times the duni is held just before the rain in November and December. Part of the feeling for having a duni then is because of the keen interest in ceremonies and ritual; occasion is given for another ceremony before the advent of the wet season which makes any kind of large gathering almost impossible.

Most of the people who have come from other clan countries have brought carved ranga wood with them. They show these unfinished rangas to the leader and obtain his permission to complete them and use them as part of the Narra ceremony. Some of the visitors, however, cut and make their totemic emblems after they have arrived. The first procedure is the ideal, the second is the way it often happens. After the ceremony has been repeated a number of times the leader says at this point, "We will paint our rangas now." Food is brought in to the men's camp. It is cut up and eaten while the totemic emblems are painted with red ocher. There is an insistence upon these two activities being performed at the same time. While the men are painting the rangas, the leader starts a cycle of songs: first water, then mud, et cetera.

Native Interpretation.—The preparatory sections of the Dua and Yiritja Narra rites parallel very closely the preparatory ceremonies in the Wawilak constellation. The Dua rangas which are made at this time are definitely associated with the myth of the two Djunkgao women. The interpretation given by one informant, which I shall quote here, is one that is heard many times during the preparatory period. "You can't make just one ranga. You must make all the friends that belong to those two women," which means all the totemic things that were associated with the two sisters and were later made into totems. The word "can't" is not to be taken too literally, since it would be possible, although unusual, to have but one totem made.

The decorative materials used in the construction of the totemic emblems have a symbolical significance. I was frequently told: "Red parrot feathers on a ranga are all the same as fire. That log [the original totemic wood used in the Djunkgao myth] was lighted when those two women were here, and that made that fire. That fire now is red parrot feathers."

The water the men use in painting the rangas symbolizes the spring flood water coming from the totem well; and when the natives sang mud several of my informants said, "You can sing the mud song, not because we are using mud to cover our rangas with, but it is like we are painting our rangas with mud from the totem wells." The red ocher symbolizes the wet mud of the totemic wells where the totemic rangas are buried when not in use. The totemic mud has spiritual significance.

When the tempo increases during the singing of water on the dance ground, reference is not only to the water which is running faster but to the seasonal situation, since the totemic well water runs rapidly only during the heavy rain period.

After the women have given the men food and they return to the Narra dance ground to continue their dancing, the repetition of the earlier cries is supposed to be the sound of water coming after a heavy rain; it is running down a flooded creek in the wet season and is definitely associated, I was told many times, with the totemic well water.

B. The Totems Are Displayed

1. The men shave and fashion "Van Dyke" beards. The women paint. Certain dances are performed and the totems displayed.

1. All the men shave their faces and leave a small growth of beard on the point of the chin. The leader sends white clay to the camp, and the women and uninitiated boys paint themselves there. They, as well as the men who also paint at this time, use a series of lateral bands running around the body and legs and arms. They are supposed to be iguanas and kingfishers.

The totemic emblems are danced with and shown to all the men present, who include not only the men of the moiety giving the ceremony, but both Yiritja and Dua clansmen. All the men participate in the dancing except, possibly, the older men, who sit at the side and watch, and make comments and give advice. The dance is supposedly given by the Dua for the Yiritja people to see. The leader says to the younger men of the Yiritja, "See this one? He is your waku," or, "He is your gawel," or whatever term the young man calls the leader. The young man's kinship term for the totemic emblem is the same as the one he applies to the leader and possessor of the emblem.

Native Interpretation.—Shaving occurs in several parts of the ceremony, but usually as repetition of the foregoing element of the ceremony. I was told by the natives: "We shave for this Narra because Wongar people shaved when they painted their rangas and put them in the mud," which means "in the time of the Djunkgao sisters when the Wongar men took away their totemic rangas." At another performance of the Narra I was told that all men shave and leave only a little hair on their chin because, "We take this ranga out and that string and give it to the Yiritja and Dua and sometimes to kutara." It is a common rationalization that the string is traded to members of the other moieties; usually a mari gives it to his kutara. The meaning of the shaving here is syncretistically associated with the string in the sense that the hair left in the beard is thought to be like or generically the same as the totemic string.

The paint the men use is supposed to be the semen of the Wongar yolno who tried to have sexual intercourse with the younger Djunkgao sister.

C. The Ring of Women Covered by their Mats

1. The men kingfishers come into the main camp, dance around the women and children hidden under ainmaras, and thrust their spears in among them.
2. The totemic poles are placed in the mud of the clan well.

1. The men dance painted kingfisher, holding a spear in each hand. This dance leads them out to the main camp.

The women and boys are gathered in a ring and hidden under ainmaras. The men use their spears (representing yam sticks) as canes and walk along in a line, one behind the other, while the leader sings and beats his bilmal (singing sticks). They dance around and around the circle of women and uninitiated. The leader calls out, "Where was this woman born?" and someone answers the name of her totem well. "And where was this one born?" and someone answers the name of a well close to the ocean, or that this one was born in a bush well at such and such a place, until all the women's birthplaces (totem wells) have been asked for and the answer given. The leader, as each well is named, calls out the names of the old Wongar yolno men who belonged to and are part of these totemic clan wells.

The dancers continue moving around the circle of women. The leader calls out the sacred names of the yam sticks represented by the men's spears. The men then thrust them into the circle of women, while the women wiggle their buttocks back and forth under their ainmaras.

The men dance around the women in two lines, one going one way and one the other.

After the leader has "called up" the yam stick, he follows it with the power name of ainmara. The men dance this, the women still lying under the ainmaras. The leader next calls out the power name of semen. After that he calls up the ranga marikmo for the various wells. The wells and ancestors are divided according to whether they are supposed to "belong to the ocean cycle of songs or the land cycle." The women get up. The leader changes the beat of his sticks from a slow rhythm to a kind of rapid syncopation. The women still stay in the ring.

2. This section of the ceremony now ends, unless it is decided to enter the ocean for ceremonial bathing. Instead of proceeding to the water, as is done when the ceremony is not a Duni, the men usually call out water; the crowd disperses and the people return to their various clan countries. The leader says at this time, "All you men go look for red parrots and make a big supply of feather string. By and by, after the rain, we will start again. We will wait for next time until the palm food is ready." The various wooden emblems are placed in the mud of the clan wells for later use.

This part of the ceremony has taken a month, perhaps two or three months, since the dances are repeated over and over on the men's totemic ground before the men go out into the main camp to perform the final rite with the women.

Native Interpretation.—The lines of men who dance into the camp to the ring of women and boys are supposed to be the crowd of Wongar yolno who came up when the old man incestuously "raped" the younger Djunkgao sister. They are also the two Djunkgao sisters with their yam sticks. The usual interpretation of this element in the ceremony is: "Those dancers come in in two groups. They are the crowd of Wongar yolno who came up when that old man tried to play with that young girl. Those two crowds mean two 'lines' [Yeritja and Dua lineages]. Those two women said, 'We'll make two lines for marriage now.' When that woman got up the man got up too. She was frightened. Those two danced when they got up. They danced just the same as we dance now at the place in the Narra. Men and women dance now because of that."

The ring of women is supposed to be at the place where the Djunkgao sisters put their ainmaras down, and the dancing around them again symbolizes the unlawful sexual attack upon the Djunkgao sister. "That ring [the circle of women] means that smooth place those two Djunkgao women made before they put their ainmaras down. When that young girl went to sleep she did not know that old man was going to try to copulate with her. He tried and tried to enter her. By and by that white stuff came out and went all over that girl's body and not inside her. That is why they wash themselves. That is why we wash ourselves now. When the women paint themselves before they go in that ring the inside meaning is the semen of the two Wongar men who tried to have sexual intercourse with the young Djunkgao women."

The men's spears which are thrust into the group of women sometimes symbolize the yam sticks of the Djunkgao sister, as is demonstrated (1) by the men using them as canes, as the sisters did their yam sticks; and (2) by the leader's calling out the sacred names of the yam sticks for the spears. At the moment when the "yam stick" is thrust into the ring of women it is supposed to be symbolical of the penis of the incestuous Wongar yolno. "This old man who tried to play with that young sister was uncircumcised. He was not Yiritja and he was not Dua. The two sisters were Dua from the beginning." When it is explicitly thought of, these old Wongar yolno were neither Yiritja nor Dua, but there is an implicit feeling that they were Dua.

"They [the men who are painted as kingfishers] are painted that way, but 'inside' they dance those yolno. They dance those Wongar yolno and the two old women with their yam sticks at the same time." This statement signifies that the kingfisher dance has a twofold meaning. At some moments in the ceremony the dancers are the two sisters and at other moments the men. "Those kingfishers are also proper men the same as men now, and they are looking for food and for sexual intercourse." This explicitly states the relationship of their feeling toward modern man's activities and toward the activities of the old Wongar men.

D. Sea Tides and Flood Waters Are Danced

1. The tides of the ocean and the floods are danced; certain birds and animals are included.

1. The following dry season word comes in from the various clan groups that they have red parrot string ready. The leader then sends out word that a Narra ceremony can be held. The messengers are decorated with red parrot feather armlets and may carry a miniature Dua totemic emblem carefully wrapped in paper bark. The ceremony can take place in either a Yiritja or a Dua camp ground, even though the performance is Dua. This statement is true with the possible exception of the Gwiyula clan; they seem to have a strong feeling that their ceremony ought to be held at their own well. Yiritja men can dance with Dua men.

The men and women of the various clans arrive and bring the parrot feathers or parrot feather string they have accumulated during the year. Ideally, many rangas should be made, including, in addition to the others named earlier in this chapter, fire, basket, labia minora, and the other totemic emblems that belong to the clans of the Dua moiety. The rangas that were made the year before are taken out of the mud, washed, painted with red ocher, and the parrot string put on them. The men paint their bodies and faces with red ocher. White clay is put on their bangles. It takes several days to prepare the totemic emblems properly. While the men are engaged in these preparations, the women have been industriously collecting lily bulbs, palm nuts and yams to supply the men with food for the period of the ceremony. Some of the men carry food from the various camps to the Narra ground. This dance ground is the same as the small quadrangle used in the Duni, except that the borders are made with heaped-up earth.

The first dance is spring flood water. The line of men dance back and forth, following the leader or calling out, "Ai—e!! Ai—e!!" which is the water coming down; when they turn and retrace their steps they call out, "Um—um ye," which is the tide returning. They next dance the ocean. The leader calls out, "Let! Let!" and when the dancers turn, "R-R-R-irt! ! R-R-R-irt! !" the cries of the red parrot from the tree tops.

The leader again sings out, "Ai—e!! Ai—e!!" and when the dancers turn, "Um—um ye!!" and then, "Mo-mu-tun [the roar of the sea], yam-ber-wong-a [the stir of the sea water when the wave breaks], burl-ol-lum [pools of boiling sea water following the break of the wave], ma-rai-ma-ra-yun [the wash of the waves covering the sand beach]," and finally again, "Um—um ye [the tide returned from the ocean]," and "Ben-bur [conventional ending to a song and dance sequence]."

Iguana is now danced. The leader sings out, "Gun-bor gun-bor [conventional announcement in the Dua Narra that the sacred name of a totem is to be called; it means nothing, according to the natives, but the two Djunkgao women sang it in their time], Djun-dam-a-la [the iguana], Gun-bor gun-bor man-ni-mur-a, Gun-bor gun-bor kui-pi-di [iguana power names]." The chorus of dancers moves to the back of the dance ground, and a solo dancer comes out of the crowd and dances to the front, arms raised sideward, elbows bent. He is an iguana. The red parrot, represented by one of the dancers, listens while the iguanas call out. He thinks it is a man making that noise and he is afraid.

Native Interpretation.—One of the native interpretations of the various dancing of water for the Narra ceremonies is: "We dance water for the Narra because it brought those two women on those paper-bark rafts. They pulled those rafts with yam sticks for paddles. We dance the water when it is all the same as the tide going out and then coming back again. We dance the sea making a roar, and we dance the way water does when the waves stop, and the pools of boiling sea water, and the waves coming on the sand beach when those two old women came. When those two old women got ashore they heard a parrot and went farther and found iguana and danced it and a Wongar iguana danced too. That's why we dance iguana now." The parrot cries symbolize the red parrot watching the two women walking along the beach.

E. The Ceremony Around the Tree in the Women's Camp

1. The women gather around a tree in their own camp. The men march in and the women run away. The sacred names of different clan wells are called out.

1. After dancing water, the men go to the main camp; they march in single file, beating their spears with their spear-throwers. They are Wongar yolno.

Before they arrive, the women have left their separate camps and gathered around a tree. They sing out in answer to the men as the men come on. The leader calls out the big name of a catfish, "ka-pi-la." When the sacred name of the catfish is said, the women run away. This name is also supposed to represent the well of a clan which is supposed to be far in the interior, possibly near the upper waters of the Roper River (Ba-rel-ku country). The women return and gather around the tree. The leader climbs the tree and calls out the power names of the well where the women first came on shore and the names of all the old Wongar men who lived in that well. He beats his singing sticks very rapidly and then comes down. He sings out caterpillar (the edible variety). The women dance with their elbows flexed and shake their bodies in a syncopated rhythm. The leader calls out the name of another well and once more the name of the catfish, while the men put their baskets in their mouths and bite them. Two men with their hands clasped behind them then walk with long deliberate steps, much in the manner of the military goose step of the parade grounds. They dance a short distance to the right, then turn on their heels and retrace their steps. While they move back and forth they and the chorus sing out, "R-R-R-T-wa! ! ! R-R-R-T-wa! !" which is supposed to be the call of the white duck, the bird they are dancing. They are succeeded by pairs of dancers until all have gone through this performance, which finishes the ceremony for the night.

Early every morning and again in the evening this performance (Section E), from beginning to end, is repeated for possibly two or three months. The morning ceremony is performed before breakfast and the evening ceremony is held at twilight, before the evening meal. The only variations occur in the order of the sacred names of wells called out. The entire cycle of Dua totem wells is called out at one time. At times some of the well names are repeated. Only the power names of the Dua wells are said during the Dua Narra, but it is felt that it is imperative to call every one of them. It is highly possible that many of the wells which are supposed to be found in the extreme interior are not real.

On the final day the last well dance is performed in the *middle* of the day. That night the men go to the Narra ground and light bushes and paper bark and carry them to the main camp. The men sing "ben-bur." After the fire the ranga string can be given to the Yiritja in trade. Some of the men say, "Are we going to put these [strings] in the mud again?"

The leader replies, "We can't do that now. We must keep the string and sell it to another man so that he can make presents to us."

The people say, "All right, we'll do that. We'll only sell this string this time to the Yiritja people. We'll sell them to our wakus and our dués and our galles. We'll put this wood in the mud; we'll keep this string for presents."

Native Interpretation.—The fire that is carried to the main camp by the men is supposed to represent the fire which the women thought destroyed their totemic baskets but which the Wongar men had lit to fool the women when they stole their baskets from them.

"When the women dance around that tree and sing out when the men call, that means those two Wongar women put their yam sticks [rangas] in that tree. It's all the same ranga in the well."

"Those two Djunkgao mielks made those wells. They walk along, squat down, stick yam sticks in the ground and put rangas there. We people come from those wells today. We get our names from those wells. Those two mielk Wongars gave those names to our old marikmos. All our big names come from those wells from our marikmos. All the old marikmos were Wongar men and all the Narra wells are Wongar wells. All Dua wells were made with yam sticks and those two old mielks were walking."

The relation of the giving away of the ranga string to fire is given the following interpretation: "You must have fire before you can give away that ranga string to the Yiritja because those Wongar people did steal their rangas from the women. Those old men thought, 'We stole those rangas from those women. Are we going to sell them or are we going to put them in the mud, string and all?' Their leader said to them, 'We can't. We must keep them and sell them to another man so he can give presents to us.' After this the people said, 'All right, we'll do that. This will cut out the guratu [relationship] lines, and we'll sell this ranga to the Yiritja. We'll put the wood in the mud and give them the string.' We shave for this too."

"We never give that ranga wood away. It is sent back to the well. If a man gave it away his people would kill the man he gave it to." (This is the ideal, but in reality the totemic wood is given away, although there is a feeling against it.)

The information quoted above came to me when one of the better leaders of the Narra ceremonies was describing how the ceremonies were carried out. It is almost impossible for a Murngin to describe a ceremony without dropping into the mythological reasons for doing it.

"All those Dua wells are danced because those two women put their dilly bags and ranga string in their [large string] bags and they went out to look for shellfish and they went inside the mangrove. Those Wongar yolno they went and stole that dilly bag and yam sticks and ranga string and they took it away. Those yolno burned the grass around that basket so those two women could see that fire and think their camp fire had burned over and burned up that basket. When the two women came back they said, 'It's no one's fault but our own. Our fire did it.' Each sister quarreled with the other for the burning of the red parrot feather and string.

"They took their own baskets from their heads. They think about the way they had done before and were sorry they hadn't put their other baskets in a clean place. They heard the sound of singing sticks from inside the jungle. They knew then that Wongar yolno had stolen their baskets and ranga string. They thought first they would go and take it away from them. They ran with that basket. They came close and saw the men were singing the Narra song. They thought, 'It is no good now, we must work. We must get food for the men.' "[2]

"The meaning on that basket is when young people sneak up now and play with mielks they do that like old yolno did. We people do wrong the same way. We must clean him up the same way."

One man who had had missionary training said of this part of the ceremony, "It is just the same as the Heaven people do wrong when God say, 'no more touch that tucker[3] on that tree,' and they do anyway."

F. The Ring of Women Repeated (See Section C)

In the morning all the men shave and leave only the small "Van Dyke" beards. "They shave because they are taking the string off those rangas and selling it to the Yiritja." The same thing is done, however, if the string is sold to the relatives who belong to their own moiety.

After the men have shaved there may or may not be a dance, usually not. All the ceremonies, are put off until the next day, when wallaby and kingfisher are danced. At the last dance the kingfishers enter into the main camp for the first time. They behave much as

[2] This and the foregoing paragraph offer a conspicuous example of how the native, in attempting to explain the ritual, draws on the myth.

[3] Food: Australian-white term.

they did in the first ceremony. They walk with spears in their hands, which, at the moment, symbolizes the yam sticks of the two Djunkgao sisters. They continue until they come to the ring of women, as described in the duni or red-ocher part of the ceremony. The kingfishers also represent the modern Murngin man looking for food and sexual intercourse. In a way, too, they are Wongar yolno. After the kingfishers have performed a dance around the women they thrust the short spears among the group to symbolize the Wongar yolno's original breaking of taboo against sexual relations with women of one's own group; then they return to the men's ceremonial ground.

G. The Brush Turkey Totem Is Danced and Displayed

1. The totem emblem of a turkey is danced in the Narra ground.
2. The initiates are shown the totem.

1. Some distance back from the men's dance ground, groups of men have been painting themselves like turkeys. They represent the brush turkey totem. Fires are built all around the men just as fires are built on the plains when turkeys are hunted. The turkeys dance through the fires while an old man beats the singing sticks and leads them toward the men's dance ground. They carry the totem. One man dances a pantomime of a brush turkey out in the plains.

2. Small boys are put at the head of the dance ground and are shown the various lower age-grade types of totems by the old men. They cannot see the ones that belong to higher age grades. After they have looked upon the totems which have been strongly taboo to them until this time, they must eat only bush food until after they are painted and have made presents to the leader. Looking at the totem serves as an initiation rite. After the boys have seen the totems, all the men dance once more to the main camp, where again the kingfisher ceremony is gone through with the women under their ainmaras.

Native Interpretation.—"When the turkeys come in, that means by and by the Yiritja are coming up. Those fires are built all around. This is all the same as making a fire in the plain by those Wongar men. When Wongar men built the fires those Wongar turkeys came up too and looked."

H. The Men and Women Bathe Ceremonially

1. All the men, women, and children enter the sea and wash themselves.

1. When this is completed the women and children all run into

the ocean, preceded by the flatfish and catfish whose songs are being sung. A small bundle of paper bark is constructed. It represents a catfish. It is hit rhythmically against the ground while the groups of men dance the black goose dance.

On the seashore or river bank, according to where the ceremony is being held, two men come out of the chorus of geese (Dua) and dance black duck (Yiritja). The black ducks dance into the water first and stir it up. The geese (the rest of the men) follow. When the ducks enter the water they call out the names of the black duck ranga wells. All the men, women and children wash themselves. Two rings are formed out in the water.—These dances are danced only when the tide is in, for the practical reason that the dancers do not want to walk out on the long mud flats.

After they come out of the water the men dance the two fish songs again, two men at a time, chasing each other and moving back and forth across the beach.

Native Interpretation.—The men dancing catfish on their way down to the water, followed by the women, are supposed to symbolize the two Djunkgao women going down to the ocean after the illegal intercourse of one with the yolno man. A superficial interpretation or rationalization of this behavior is that "when that catfish came out and went into the water it was all the same as those two Djunkgao mielk following the fish and trying to catch them in the ocean. It's all the same too for that catfish. Those people are all the same as goose trying to catch that catfish."

"Duck goes into the water first, he makes the water dirty and goose follows. That black duck belong Yiritja well and he sings out the name of that well. This is all the same as in a billibong. We always see black duck go in and make the water dirty and goose comes behind." (This refers to the seasonal appearance of the black duck before the geese in the fresh-water lakes in the area.)

"When we wash, that means we're taking that semen off those women and making ourselves clean, and that means too the Narra is close up to finish. That white clay on the women means before this world only ocean, rain fall down and make foam, that makes this land. That white stuff goes from inside the bush, too, all the way to the Crocodile Islands."

"*Dua* people make rangas because Wongar yolnos and those two mielks did wrong a long time ago. It's all the same as two Dua play with each other now. It was a guratu [kinship] wrong. That Wongar yolno and mielk went to swim in the sea and made themselves clean and they cut out that wrong. That's why we dance the same way now to cut out that wrong."

The thinking here shows that both the Yiritja and the Dua use the same symbols, but the Dua identify the white paint with uncleanliness and the Yiritja identify it with foam.

I. THE TOTEMS ARE SHOWN TO THE YOUNG MEN

1. The lower totems are shown the youths by lines of dancing men.

1. The women give the men palm food so that the leader can feed all the men. He informs the men that they will wait to eat until they go back inside the men's ceremonial ground. They return to the dance ground and once more take their totemic emblems out of the "bush house" or from the hollow trees used as a hiding place. All the men stick red parrot feathers on their chins with honeybees' wax. Red ocher is painted on the face. The leader says, "Are you prepared now?"

"Yes," they say.

"Are all the totemic emblems here?"

"Yes; what are we going to do now?"

"Let the young men who have beards and moustaches move."

Everything is very quiet now and there is no laughter. There must not be any laughter. A bird called a djunmal (possibly a curlew) is danced by one of the men in the Narra dance ground. He represents the tide coming in. Another bird called the ka-url-dal-por-al (a variety of the kingfisher) dances with him. The djunmal climbs a tree and the kookaburra (kingfisher) another nearby. The djunmal emits the cry of this bird, which means that the tide is coming in; the natives believe the djunmal sings just before the tide comes in. A line of old men dance forward. Their backs and necks are bowed; their eyes look down to the upturned palms of their two hands, in which they carry their totemic emblems. The kookaburra now sings that the tide is going out, when the men turn and retrace their steps. Thus the old men dance back and forth, as the tide is high and then low, high and then low, while the two birds sing alternately with the dancers' change of direction.

Native Interpretation.—The Dua Narra rangas were all brought by the Djunkgao women. The Yiritja rangas have the integrating factor of the spring floods and tides. "All the Yiritja rangas were brought by the flood and tides. The big rain made that big flood."

(The beards, too, emphasize the manliness of the young men in an age-grade sense. Their beards demonstrate their belonging to the mature men's age grade. The red parrot feather decoration on the beards helps to ritualize this symbol of manliness.)

J. The Higher Totems Are Shown the Older Men

1. The old men leave the young men and show their higher totems to each other.

1. Following the ceremony of showing the totems to the older young men, who represent an age-grade stratum of the male division of the tribe higher than the recently initiated boys, iguana is repeated; then follows the sea-water dance which has been described, and finally iguana, with the usual conventional ending of "benbur benbur."

Only the older men see the higher rangas. The young men are left and the older men go inside the bush to look at the rangas which only they are allowed to see. The string is taken off all the totemic emblems at this time. This string is presented to members of the opposite moiety, or very frequently, as has been said before, kutara gives it to mari and mari to kutara (they are of the same moiety) as a demonstration of the solidarity of their relationship. If people who are somewhat distant, therefore a bit strange, ask for this ranga string, it arouses a considerable feeling of antagonism in the owner. It is usually said, "Have people lost their heads? Can't they think? We will just give them ordinary food later. We won't give them string." —"If they are very good friends we can give them food, but the food is not given a power name."

K. The Eating of the Sacred Bread, and Conclusion of the Ceremony

1. The bread is eaten by those of near kin.
2. The string is removed from the emblems and the neophytes are instructed.

1. The leader sings over the palm bread (or yams) which is put in the ashes and cooked. He calls out the totem names of the various rangas (kookaburra, banitja, etc.). This is supposed to infuse the bread with the power names of the rangas and make it "just the same as a ranga," which means that the totemic spirit resides within the bread. Only the men who understand can eat this, which means only the men who are near relations and who have been initiated.

The Murngin always eat in this way after all ceremonies. To outside tribes the people say, "This is maraiin that belongs to the Narra," but the power name is not given to the food for them. The natives agree that this food is eaten because all Wongar yolno did the same thing. If the leader gives the food with his name to it to his friends from another tribe, his own clanspeople would wait until there was an opportunity and kill him, because they do not want to have that name go to another tribe.—All my most reliable informants gave me this information.

Yiritja and Dua both eat this food, providing they are from one country, which really means, if they are closely related. My most intelligent informant said this: "Dorng and Ilkara [two men of the Liaalaomir group] can eat our food which has a big name because their sister married one of our people. It is all right for the Ritarngo to eat Warumeri and Wangurri food which has a big name because we have one ranga, because we are friends. Sometimes we give our ranga from the Warumeri side to the Ritarngo and they give us rangas from the land side. That is because that duck came from the Ritarngo to us in Wongar days."

2. The string is taken from the totemic emblems, wrapped around the hand into a neat ball, and placed in a basket. The carved-log ranga (see page 330) is hidden once more in the mud of the ceremonial leader's totem well. It is said that the leader likes to have them all remain there. The men can eat no animal food, but only bush (vegetable) food, until they have been painted. The old men say to them, "You must do what we tell you. Put your head and ears to these things. You don't want to swear at your old men or your big brothers. You want to talk a good way to them. We don't want you to steal. You don't want to go running after other men's women." The old men also tell the younger ones which rangas belong to the different totemic wells and which wells belong to the various clans. This ends the Dua Narra ceremony.

Native Interpretation.—The old men say, "This makes one people."

THE YIRITJA NARRA CEREMONY

A. Preparation

1. The same general preparations are made as those before the Dua Narra.

1. The Yiritja Narra ceremony parallels the Dua Narra rites. After a log has been cut, scraped, and carved, the leader sends out word to the various surrounding clans that a Narra is to be held. A Duni

(here Sections A, B, and C) frequently is given first, not only because of lack of materials, as was stated for the Dua Narra ceremony, but also because it is felt that it makes the log "stronger" and better. Various people arrive; they bring balls of opossum fur and string. Opossum fur is a decorative material used for Yiritja ritual and symbolizing this moiety just as red parrot feathers are the materials for decorating Dua ceremonial objects.

The same preparations are made for carving and painting the totemic emblem; "flood" from the totemic wells flowing to the sea and "ocean tides coming in" are danced on the Narra grounds which have been made on the old men's grounds. Instead of dancing red parrot and water, the Yiritja dance bandicoot and water. Flood water is danced back and forth on the small quadrangle, then the leader calls out:

> "Bir-ka bir-ka (conventional Yiritja announcement of Narra power words) djar-a (spring water)
> Bir-ka bir-ka mill-yar-ui (tree growing out of a spring)
> Bir-ka bir-ka ga-urn ga-urn (gravel boiling in spring water)
> Bir-ka bir-ka ka-ku-lor-oi (small rocks in the bottom of a spring)
> Bir-ka bir-ka kar-a-ko-ar-oi (a small valley where the water runs)."

Once more the sound of water is repeated and a new dance is started. The leader calls out the power names of bandicoot. All the chorus gets down on its knees and elbows while the leader sings out, "Gorn-djur-djur [bandicoot] yer-mer-da [bandicoot]." The bandicoot always follows water in the Yiritja ceremony, after which the men return to the general camp. As they march along in single file, the leader walking to one side, they call out "Kar-ra-ark! Ye!" This is supposed to be the name of the tree which the leader usually climbs when he calls out the power names in the main camp. It also lets the women know that they must run and be gathered at the tree when the men arrive.

When the men arrive in the main camp and approach the tree the women run away from it and return to their huts. The leader runs straight toward the tree and points at it with his singing stick while he calls out its power name. Any convenient tree is picked for this purpose and it can be of any species, providing it is large enough for the leader to climb when the occasion arrives.

Native Interpretation.—The natives make a clear distinction between the Yiritja and the Dua Narra rites, but basically they are exactly the same. The formulae at the end of the songs in the Yiritja and Dua are different, and other formalized elements have slight variations; but in the fundamentals the structures of the two ceremonies are very similar, and the interpretations given are much the same. Because the two Djunkgao sisters were supposed to be Dua, there is a feeling that the Yiritja ceremony is associated with the floods and not with the women.

The natives say they dance bandicoot right after water because he comes out of the bush first after the rain time, scratching small holes to look for food.

The women run away from the tree, say the natives, because the two old sisters ran in their time when the men approached them.

B. The Men Dance with the Carved Wood of the Totemic Emblems

1. The men shave themselves as in the Dua Narra.
2. The quail and fire dances are performed.
3. The totems are shown and the totemic bread eaten.
4. The women paint and the men go to the men's ground.

1. The men shave, leaving only the small "Van Dyke," putting heated honeybee wax on the beard and pulling it out. The leader then calls out the power name of Banitja, one of the more important Yiritja totems:

> "Bir-ka bir-ka banitja
> Bir-ka bir-ka djir-lir-war-a (barrimundi)."

2. Following this song, the leader and the chorus dance quail (djerkit). The quail is supposed to be the leader for fire and is therefore the leader for shaving with hot wax. After this dance the people become inquisitive and want to know what will be next. "What will we do?" they say. "Shall we tie our opossum string to our totemic emblems? What will we do?"

The leader says, "No, we will leave them."

3. While the totemic bread is being eaten and sung over in the men's ground, the totemic emblems are painted, the same procedure gone through, and the same attitudes taken as in the Dua Narra. The leader sings the water cycle of songs, with bandicoot taking the prominent lead. A totemic well next is sung, then mud and man-

grove fish are called out. The last is a variety of borer found in the trunks of mangrove trees and is Yiritja. The totemic emblem is then painted with yellow lines representing the totems.

4. The leader directs that red ocher and white clay be sent to the main camp. One or more old men have been left in this camp to look out for the women and children. The old men direct the women while they paint. The women paint themselves to represent barrimundi and albatross (marn-ba), creatures associated with the sea tides and not the flood.

Native Interpretation.—The association of quail with fire is interpreted by the Murngin: "Quail is the boss for fire and Narra time. We call out that one when it is time to light the fires and we carry his ranga. Quail has a ranga and he is in the Narra ceremony." The quail in Wongar days, according to myth, threw some fire about and burned his feathers. Further, the quail is usually found in the low brush when it is fired during the burning season.

C. They Dance Around the Ring of Women

1. The same general outline of dancing is followed as in the Dua Narra; different animals and birds appear.
2. The totems are placed in the clan wells.

1. The men leave the ceremonial grounds and go to the main camp, calling out the big name of white clay:

> "Bir-ka bir-ka bu-lor-mar-mar (white clay)
> Bir-ka bir-ka gar-wa-wa (yellow paint stone)
> Birka-bir-ka mar-ku-la (white bubbles caused by barrimundi biting at fish)."

When they arrive near the camp, leader and chorus sing "birka birka marnba [a sea bird]." Near the entrance to the camp two men dance marnba. One dances to the right, the other to the left. They both turn at the same time, retrace their steps, pass each other, repeat the figure a number of times, and then dance around the ring and are surrounded by the chorus.

The women by now are fully painted.

After dancing the marnba the men dance barrimundi and follow this with Yiritja honeybee. They then form a long file. An old man meanwhile has gathered the women into a ring. They are under their ainmaras. The men, with the spears in their hands, dance around the women. They are supposed to be dancing garrawark and sea foam made by barrimundi. The leader sings out the names of their totemic wells. He calls out first water and then a bangle made from the grass surrounding the well. When the bangle is called out, all the women get up at one time. All the people then go into the ocean by clans as the men call out water. The bathing ceremony can be postponed until the next year. The men and women return to their separate camps.

2. All the visitors put their totemic emblems in the mud of the totemic wells so that the women and uninitiated cannot see them; they all then leave for their homes. The leader appoints a man to see that all the rangas are properly taken care of and are not disturbed. The Duni is over. During the Duni a true Narra ceremonial ground is not constructed. This has a formal outline and is made only for the larger Narra ceremony.

Native Interpretation.—Although the same general outline is followed in this part of the Yiritja ceremony as in the Dua, the interpretations are not directly connected with the myth of the Djunkgao sisters, but are associated with Yiritja creatures, such as garrawark and other totems of this moiety, who have mythological stories attached to them. These myths have not been included with the Djunkgao myth because they fall more directly into the category of local organization stories.

The white clay on the women, according to my informants, who were the leaders of a number of Narra ceremonies that I witnessed, means, "Before this world there was only the ocean. The rain fell down and made the foam. That made some of this land. That white stuff (foam) went from the Warumeri country to the Crocodile Islands. Garrawark, the great Yiritja totem, floated in on this and made Yiritja camps by sticking his horns in the land and splitting the ground and making wells and creeks. He named these places, too; he gave them their power names. We make our rangas from that. Dua people make their rangas because that Wongar yolno and those two sisters did wrong. It was just the same as two Dua having sexual intercourse. It was a guratu [a patrilineal line of relatives] wrong. That Wongar yolno and that small Djunkgao sister went into the ocean and swam and washed themselves and made themselves 'clean' and cut out that wrong from themselves. The Dua dance that way today and do the same thing for themselves. Our Yiritja Narra is different, but all the same." (See also page 344.)

"That fish tried to stop the water with this grass, but the water came too fast and went on. The fish was a bream [mart-bu-na] and is Yiritja."

"For Yiritja that white clay on the woman and on the men too is all the same as foam. Garrawark had that foam when he dived to make Narra wells. In the Yiritja ring when the dancers come it's all the same as a fresh-water 'tide' and pushes that bream along the ocean. This tide is fresh water from a heavy rain, that takes the bream down to the ocean."

When the people divide up into groups and everyone goes into the water according to his or her clan well, they are ducks, and "They *are diving down in their ranga well water*. Those ducks are all the same as a mate for that well. It means too they are all the same as Garrawark, because that Yiritja ranga been do that. He went down in that water and came out all the same as those people do." The washing, then, is no ordinary washing but is symbolical of being cleansed by the spiritual well water, and the act is the same as the totem's. There is a general story about the "tide" (flood) carrying the rangas down to the sea and of the sea tides pushing the flood waters back.

When the leader and his men paint the rangas and sing water it means that the water is being put on the red ocher and refers also to the original flood. When mud is sung it means: "You are not painting that ranga with mud but with red ocher, but it is like you paint him with mud and that mud is all the same as mud from the ranga well and where we put the ranga when we get through with it.

"We sing water running fast and rain coming. We start from rain. We do this because of that flood water. The water comes from the rain and runs down the creeks. We sing bandicoot first because he comes with the rain time. Bandicoot comes out and makes holes looking for food. We must sing bandicoot after water."

(The water dance in all these Narra ceremonies is supposed to be the primeval floods and tides. It has been amply interpreted before under the Dua heading.)

D. The Sea Tides and Flood Waters Are Danced

1. At the beginning of the new season new dances of the floods and tides are started.

1. When the dry season arrives again, the leader sends his son or

younger brother as a messenger to all the surrounding clans to announce the beginning of the true Narra ceremony. This messenger should be decorated with bangles which have streamers of opossum fur on them, but he is not always. One or two miniature garrawark totems covered with bark are made to serve as message sticks. The leader says, "You take this small ranga to all the people [Dua and Yiritja] and tell them we are going to start now. If people make trouble for you, show them this ranga, and they won't fight you or hurt you, because you are a messenger man."

The visitors begin to arrive before the messenger returns. Some distance from the camp, they call out rain cloud; when they are near, rain; then finally, flood water. They approach the camp in groups, singing "Ka-wa!" to announce their coming ceremonially. They call out the sound of well water running in the creek as they go to the leader in the main camp. They make a ring around the tree from which the leader of the Narra calls the power names (see page 347). The leader of each group of visitors climbs it and calls out the names of the visitors' clans.

After a chorus has joined with two men in a crocodile dance, the men leave the main ground and go into the men's dance ground. They take a vegetable food with them. Each crowd of visitors goes through the same ceremony on its arrival.

After the first few visitors have appeared, the men start putting feathered string on their totemic emblems. The leader walks around among the groups and instructs them how to make the various emblems. Some people make Banitja, some Barrimundi. The Warumeri people, if they are there, will make dugong rib, garrawark, crayfish, dorsal fin of the whale, tail of the whale, as well as the other rangas named above. The Wangurri would do likewise. The Ritarngo do not have the garrawark, but in its place they make the black duck ranga.

The Narra dance ground is now constructed (or may have been constructed earlier) with heaped up earth to define its limits. The leader starts the bandicoot and water dance. If the dancers have rangas from the sea-way cycle of songs, they dance back and forth: they drag their spear-throwers on the ground, utter no sound, and run up and down the dance ground until they are almost exhausted. (This is the tide coming in and going out for a great distance.) The leader sings out: "Sis!! Sis!! Sis!!" This is the wind coming up. He waves his mangel (spear-thrower) in the air: The water is coming higher and higher. The leader calls out:

> "Bir-ka bir-ka man-bing-a (power name of water)
> Bir-ka bir-ka kir-kir (foam)"

and continues through the waters' names of the Dua Narra (see page 347).

The leader and chorus then cry "Ye! A—Ah—O! Waw! [the tide coming in hard and the waves breaking], Um-um-um [water coming back]." Following this, the leader calls out the power names for crowds (see page 359), and the chorus replies: "A—Ah—Aah—Waw-waw-um-um-um," which is the tide coming back again. They are dancing with great rapidity back and forth across the dance ground. They wave their mangels on the ground to indicate a very heavy sea. The leader then calls out the power name of the diamond fish:

> "Bir-ka bir-ka brin-ga-ye!"

All the chorus fall on their hands and knees and squat down, each individual beating the ground with his mangel, singing "Main-muk, main-muk," literally "good," but supposed to represent sheet lightning, which comes at the end of rain in the wet season.

Still sitting, the chorus hold hands and, while moving the trunks of their bodies forward and back slightly, swing arms back and forth in front of them. This is representative of the swimming of the diamond fish who is a Yiritja totem but does not have a totemic emblem made for him. He is supposed to have had one in the old days. His totem well was the sea, and his closest associate was the whale, who sometimes stands as a symbol of the sea. After this dance has been completed the men leave the Narra grounds and return to the main camp.

They call out "Kar-ra-ark Ye!" until they enter the camp of the women. The women have heard them coming and prepared themselves by gathering about the tree, as described on page 347; they run away when the men draw near. The leader of the ceremony climbs the tree and calls out the name of Wongar men who live in far-off places but who are not true yolno, then descends and calls out the power names again, and the chorus answers. Two, and possibly four, men now dance salt-water crocodile, who is Yiritja. If there are four men dancing, pairs stand abreast facing each other. They carry their knees high and move their elbows up and down while they dance back and forth, passing each other, turning, retracing their steps, repeating the figure a number of times. The pairs then dance with their heads together. It is a most intricate and difficult dance to learn, and is supposed to represent crocodiles swimming under water with only their nostrils thrust above the surface. This finishes the dancing for the evening.

The whole cycle of Yiritja wells is then called out, morning and night, until all the totem wells have been completed. Usually only one well is called out each night, although at times the names of two wells are sung by the leader and chorus. The totem well of the clan that is giving the ceremony comes last.

E. The Men Dance into the Women's Camp

1. The men go through the camp looking for food and bring the gathered food back to the leader and old men.

1. When it is almost time for a ceremony to end, the leader picks out a group of men and says, "You paint yourselves as bandicoots and water for the sea-way," and to others, "You paint whale," and to still others, "You paint jungle fowl." The men who paint themselves as jungle fowl put circular symbols all over their bodies to represent the egg. The circles are connected with straight lines which are supposed to be long string-like beans from a tree I was unable to identify. While the men are painting on the Narra grounds, five or six younger men who already have been painted as bandicoot come out into the camp. This is the way Banitja, the great totem, did in the old Wongar days. He came out looking for food because he had smelled it cooking. They have, in addition, yellow lines for the barrimundi, and white dots which represent the foam made by barrimundi biting at something. Others, supposed to be banitjas, may be painted as Yiritja honeybees, because Banitja came from the Koparpingu country, which has a honeybee totem.

When the dancers have come about halfway from the men's totem grounds the leader stops them and calls out:

"Bir-ka bir-ka bur-lum-bul (foam)
Bir-ka bir-ka ko-wa-wa (yellow paint)
Bir-ka bir-ka mar-ku-la (red and yellow paint)."

They then all dance into the camp, calling out, "Kar-ra-ark Ye!" They go from hut to hut as though looking for something. They are supposed to be Banitja looking for food. The women get up and give them some palm-food bread or yam bread which they have prepared. They also can give fish or honey. If the men received nothing from the women they would become very angry, and pick up their spears and threaten them. The women always give because, say the informants, they see this Banitja painted on the men.

After the men have made the circle of the camp they return to the dance ground. They do not eat the food they have been given, for they are young men. They take it to the older men who belong to a higher division in the men's group. If the young men should eat this food they would turn into old men immediately.

Certain totemic dances are danced and the leader then instructs all the men to shave, leaving only the small tuft of hair at the point of the chin. While everyone shaves, the leader calls out:

"Bir-ka bir-ka rao rao (power name for opossum string)."

The opossum string is put on the chin with hot honeybee wax. The strings are supposed to represent the white flowers of the lily. The above power name of the opossum string signifies to the dancers that the leader has chosen the land-way cycle of songs. If the leader had chosen the sea-way he would have called out the power name of the whale:

"Bir-ka bir-ka bul-tung-o, bir-ka bir-ka ma-rain-dji bi-lain-dji."

F. The Whale Dance

The leader and chorus dance water on the Narra ground as described in earlier sections. Bandicoot is also danced, and then the sea-way is followed through (diamond fish, waves, et cetera). No one talks then; everything is quiet. There can be no laughter. The men walk up and down the dance ground slowly and attempt to keep very still. This is supposed to be the sea water and the slow rising of the tides. The chorus splits into two groups. They stand at each side of the Narra dance grounds. They are all whales. Two men who have painted themselves like whales stand at each end of the Narra dance ground. The leader is in the middle of the ground. The leader walks up to and marches in front of one group of the chorus and stamps his foot, then turns and walks to the other group and stamps his foot. This is the way a man stamps his foot when he hits a whale with his paddle. After this, the leader covers with ainmaras the two men painted to represent whales. He then stamps his foot in front of each. As he does this the men move beneath the ainmaras. They are supposed to represent a whale diving under the sea. The men shrug their shoulders to look like the back of the whale as he goes beneath the water. The "whales" also move their hands back and forth to imitate the movement of the fins of the whale. The leader and the two whales repeat their figure of the dance a number of times. The leader then calls out the power names of the whale, wi-ma-ri and nul-lan-dji. One whale then gets up and sits on top of the other. This means that the whales are copulating. Those Wongar whales did that in the old days. (The dugong totem dance, which may be substituted for the whale, is conducted in the same way.)

Once more the leader and chorus dance slow water, keeping as silent as possible. The tide is coming in. Finally the tide is supposed to reach Truant Island. The men sing "Um-wa-um-wa." The water is coming slowly up on the beach. (A Wongar yolno is coming in on the tide. He reaches the island and startles the jungle fowl. He hears a jungle fowl sing out when he gets on shore with his paddle.)

The chorus sits down and the leader calls out:

> "Bir-ka bir-ka ka-djirk-ker-ak (the call of the jungle fowl)
> Bir-ka bir-ka bun-bung-a bun-bung-a (jungle fowl)."

The dancers move their heads slowly about, imitating the jungle fowl listening to the sound of a man or animal in the underbrush below his perch. This part of the dance is repeated a number of times.

Native Interpretation.—When the leader sings out the power name of the whale, as well as those of all the other creatures, animals, men, plants, and the general phenomena of nature, it is, say the leaders of the ceremonies, as though they were asking for something. "That Wongar whale can hear. He is all the same as the head of the clan for all those whales. If we go to the salt water and we are a long way out and a whale comes along, we can take sweat from under our arms and put our hands in the water, and we can put that water in our mouths and sing out the power names of that whale. It is just the same as if we were asking him for something. Our old Wongar mari and marikmo and gatu hear that and they go to that whale and turn him and keep us from harm. It is all the same as if we say to that Wongar whale, 'Don't hurt me.' That whale takes Warumeri dead men on his back to the Island of the Dead. Porpoise takes Dua men. We do not eat the whale because his food is not good. If one floats up on the seashore we use his ribs for rangas."

"When the dancers shrug their shoulders in the whale dance it means those whales [who are diving] are copulating. That's the way those Wongar whales did. Dugongs do the same way too."

"That jungle fowl belonged to the Wongar yolno who owned that house. He was a true jungle fowl when he was in Wongar days."—"He was not a man at this time, but a bird."

G. The Ring-of-women Dance Is Repeated (See Sections C and F)

After this the leader says, "We will all go out to the main camp now." When the women see them coming they gather in a circle and squat beneath their ainmaras. The men dancers walk, pulling their spear-throwers after them. They are calling out the power name of water and are supposed to be dancing it. Near the camp, they call out once more the name of water, and then the leader sings out power names of cloud, barrimundi, and the albatross. When they reach the women, two men who are albatross walk around the ring.

The leader calls out barrimundi. The chorus, who are standing, jump in the air in imitation of the barrimundi leaping out of the water, and then, while holding their spear-throwers, dance around the ring of women. The men form two lines, a flood group and a sea-tide group. While dancing around the women they pull their spear-throwers along the ground as before, to symbolize a low tide, then raise their spear-throwers, which means the tide is growing higher, until finally it has reached full water. The leader says now, "We'll awaken these women."

When the dancers come they are the same as fresh water and they push the bream out into the ocean. The leader then calls up rain water running in floods down the creeks, and he runs around the ring. He then calls out bangles and the grass from which they are made, found near the totem wells. (See the first account in the duni version, page 350.)

Native Interpretation.—"The albatross flies around and around a canoe when it is out at sea or when it sees anything there on the ocean."

The women are the two Djunkgao sisters but they are also bream fish, for when the bream had come a long way he lay down, using an ainmara because he was tired. When the leader says, "We'll awaken these women," the reference is to the sleep of the two Djunkgao sisters.

H. The Men, Women and Children Bathe Ceremonially

The women get up. All the men and women, both Yiritja and Dua, go down to the ocean. When they get close to the water they form into several groups. The division is made on the basis of the wells from which the men and women come (i.e., clan).

When the groups are near the water the two men who are painted as albatross leave the chorus and dance in a circle, one going to the left, the other to the right, while the leader beats his singing sticks. They approach the water, take a little from it in their hands, and throw it upon the people. In this new dance figure the chorus has changed from the bream, which has been swept into the sea by the flood water, and is now a flock of black ducks. When the men throw the water on the others it is supposed to represent the albatross shaking himself and throwing the water from his feathers on the ducks.

The chorus and the two men sit down. All the men are carrying spears. They hold their spears in front of them parallel to the ground. Once again the symbol of the dancers changes, for the spears mean that they are now water, that a heavy rain which has carried sticks and leaves has come down and left them in a line on the beach. Everyone starts moving back and forth: the fresh-water flood has taken the leaves down to the shore and the salt water is carrying them back. The dancers put the spears down: the water leaves all the logs, sticks and other refuse on the shore and the heavy fresh water has receded and left the refuse on the high banks. The leader now calls out the power name for a line of refuse on the beach or on the river bank: "Bir-ka bir-ka ka-lain-dja (a line of leaves, sticks, et cetera, left by fresh or salt water) bir-ka bir-ka rar-kal-noom (water moving this line of brush)." This song is sung while the spears are being put on the ground. The black duck call is once more given:

"Bir-ka bir-ka mu-tal-li (black duck)
Bir-ka bir-ka dirrt-dun (duck paddling with its legs)
Bir-ka bir-ka mar-ka-lai-in (duck flying away)
AA-a-ah!! A-a-ah!! (the tide coming back)
Dirk—Dirk—Wah!!!
Le—le—le (tide bringing stones [ducks' eggs])
Lir-lir-lir (tide coming up and leaving the little stones on the ground)."

The leader then again divides the people into two groups: those who belong to the totemic wells connected with the land cycle of songs, and those who are supposed to have been born into the sea cycle of totemic wells. All divide further into groups according to the wells to which they belong. All the names of the old men who belong to these wells (mythological people usually) are called out. The leader calls his own marikmo, mari, and similar relatives last. When this is done, all go into the water, one clan at a time. They swim, completely immerse themselves, and wash their faces and bodies. When the leader says "Ka-war!" they stand up. When he calls out "Ka-war!" again they once more swim and wash themselves. The leader takes each crowd and again calls out the names of its grandfathers (patrilineal line). This is continued until he has come to his own well. Everybody returns to the ground where the ring of women were. Four or more men dance the crocodile and another group dances a small fish; these two groups are fresh-water fish and crocodiles going out into the sea.

Native Interpretation.—"That fresh water is carrying sticks and leaves down from the bush and it leaves it in a line [the spears of the men dancers]. When everybody dances back and forth that means that fresh-water flood takes the leaves down to the shore and the salt water carries them back. We put the spears down because that salt water leaves all that log and sticks and leaves on the shore when the heavy flood brings it down when the creeks are high."

The cry of "kawar" is supposed to be the sound made by a duck when it is diving. The people are ducks and they are diving down into their ranga well water. These ducks, say the leaders of the ceremony, are just the same as younger brothers to the wells to which they belong. It means, too, they say, that it is just the same as garrawark or any other Yiritja ranga diving in his well.

I. The Low Totems Are Shown

The leader then says, "We will take all our food that the women have gathered and go into the Narra place. We won't cut our food here, but we will wait and go there." When they arrive at the totemic grounds the men put their opossum string on their beards. The leader then says to certain of the men, "You take the garrawark totemic emblem, and you take barrimundi, but don't bring out any of the high rangas. You must leave them there because those rangas look out for that ground. They are too far down inside the well for the young men to see." Each totemic group brings out its own rangas which belong to the lower order. The Warumeri will bring out the totems listed as crayfish, garrawark, barrimundi, whale and whale rib; but the high rangas, such as black duck's egg and large basket, will not be displayed.

The chorus of men and the leader start dancing again on the Narra dance ground. They dance spring floods and salt water. The old men hold their totemic emblems in front of them in the same way that the Dua do, except that they are supposed to be representing the movement of the fresh-water flood down to the sea and the movement of the sea back again. The young initiates stand in front of them at the head of the Narra grounds. Two men stand beside them and instruct them in the meanings of the dances and of the totems. When the garrawark totem is carried, it is thrust in the ground, and the various totemic wells it is supposed to have formed are named. The leader then calls out the power names of garrawark. He next calls out the power names of spring floods while the men dance back and forth. This is supposed to represent the original fresh-water flood which carried all the totemic emblems down to the sea. The chorus next dances crayfish. Their hands are moved jerkily to imitate its movements. They whisper "E—e—e—." The leader calls out the sacred name of the crayfish.

Native Interpretation.—See Dua Narra.

J. THE HIGHER TOTEMS ARE SHOWN (See the Dua Narra).

K. THE SACRED BREAD IS EATEN AND THE CEREMONY CONCLUDED (See the Dua Narra).

The Yiritja Narra is concluded with the eating of the totemic bread in the men's ground after the old men have displayed the higher totems to one another. The boys are admonished to conduct themselves according to the tribal standards, and food taboos are placed upon them. (See the Dua Narra.)

CHAPTER XI

AN INTERPRETATION OF MURNGIN TOTEMISM AND ITS RITUAL LOGIC

Analyses and Summaries of the Ritual Sections and the Myth-symbols of the Wawilak Ceremonies

A review of the Wawilak rituals will be presented here, but for the time being we shall postpone a summary treatment of the Narra rites. The chapter will concern itself first with a general summary of the sections of the rituals as expressions of myth-symbols, in an endeavor to determine the meaning of the rituals mythologically. These totemic phenomena will then be related to the larger society in an effort to ascertain what are their ultimate meanings in Murngin culture. Let us first consider in order the four rituals of the Wawilak myth.

Djungguan

All but the last section of the Djungguan are dramatic expressions of the myth-symbol of the snake swallowing the two women. The natives clearly recognize this, as their interpretations indicate.

In the first section—The Preliminaries—the boys who are to be circumcised are told that the Great Father Snake wants their foreskins and is calling for them. The warngaitja is erected, which is later taken away by the men who symbolize the snake. Symbols are made which are used in later sections: the snake trumpet (Yurlunggur), the decoration of the boys to be circumcised, et cetera. This section represents the entrance of the snake. There is the constantly recurring symbolic theme of the effort made by the women to stop the snake.

In the second section (B), when the dances occur around the warngaitja, it is understood that the dancers are the snake which later takes the warngaitja and the boys to the men's ground. The third section (C) explicitly states that Yurlunggur comes out and swallows the women, while in the fourth (D) the snake swallows the animals as well as the women.

The fifth section (E)—the bloodletting—is by far the most important, for here the whole of the ideology of the myth is clearly stated and interpreted in the ritual, with heavy emphasis on the profanement of the pool by the women's menstruation blood and their being swallowed by the python. The ritual power of blood is demonstrated. The last dances on the men's ground (F) symbolize the snake swallowing the women, as in the fourth section above, and some of the plants and animals collected and named by the women run away from them into the Mirrirmina well. Some of the dances also bring in the minor theme of the moiety ceremonial antagonism, Dua animals pretending to fight Yiritja. The circumcision (G) has the snake-swallowing-the-women element, and is the fulfillment of the first section above, in which the boys are told the snake is calling for their foreskins.

The last section (H) is the one in which the initiates are finally purified and, by taking the communion of food (the sacred names of the various morsels of which they have been told), are finally made a part of the male group.

In brief, all the sections of the Djungguan except the last dramatize primarily the myth symbol of the snake swallowing the women.

Gunabibi

The mythological python in the Gunabibi ceremony is known as Muit. Muit is supposed to be more powerful than Yurlunggur. The old men say he is more powerful because his ceremony is greater. Muit is sometimes looked upon as the father of Yurlunggur, as the inner spirit of Yurlunggur. Generally the two are interchangeable. Most people say they are the same, though a strict Murngin philosopher, when giving the subject careful consideration, differentiates between the two pythons by associating Yurlunggur with the Djungguan rites and Muit with the Gunabibi and Ulmark.

The first section (A) is merely the preparation of the symbols for the two elements found in opposition throughout the myth: Mandelprindi, or the snake; and the boys and dancers who are the two women. The ritual of this section is part of the general snake-swallowing-the-women symbol. In the second section (B), Mandelprindi calls, the women answer, and the initiates are taken—i.e., the snake has taken them. The third section (C) again—in the whirling of Mandelprindi, the singing of the men and the reply of the women—symbolizes the swallowing. The dance sequence here offers another major symbol—that of reproduction and fertility and the cycle of the seasons. In the fourth section (D), the line of men who surround the women symbolizes the swallowing of the two Wawilak women. The rituals while the messengers are gone (Section E), are once again symbolic of the swallowing.

The kartdjur (F) although it indirectly symbolizes the swallowing, is more concerned with the reproductive and seasonal cycle, with the animals' departure from the women and entrance into the python's pool. The rituals (G) surrounding the Yermerlindi totemic emblems symbolize the arrival of the snake and the swallowing of the women. The ceremonial exchange of wives (H) symbolizes the reproductive and seasonal cycle.

The ceremony centered around the forked sticks and ridgepole (I) is again the swallowing symbol. A minor symbol, however, is injected in this section: the flying fox, a symbol of death. He is considered a mokoi or trickster soul, personified by the young boys who hang on the rafter of the two old women and who are spiritually dead because they are yet to be completely initiated. They take food from the snake—the line of men seated on the ground by the ridgepole; they join on to the male body of the snake by seating themselves in the row of men, which symbolizes their becoming a part of the higher age grade of men.

The final section (J) is not symbolic from the myth point of view except that the two women went through a similar performance of painting with red ocher.

Sections A through E, as well as G and I, all symbolize the snake's swallowing the women. The last section (J) is merely a ritual mechanism to relate the dancers once again in a normal way to their ordinary society and to prevent any harm coming to them from having been in touch with the sacred Gunabibi. Sections F and H, as well as, secondarily, part of C and of E, depict the cycle of fertility as expressed in reproduction, seasonal fluctuation, and periods of plenty and scarcity; and these again are directly expressed in the animals and plants starting out singly, then mating, copulating, and having offspring at wet seasons of the year. Briefly stated, the snake-swallowing-the-women symbol dominates the greater part of the Gunabibi; another major theme is introduced which is concerned with the cycle of reproduction; and minor themes of naming the plants and animals and of their running away are introduced (see final summary of the four great ceremonies below).

Ulmark

In the first section the four kangaroos' running away symbolizes the animals who ran away from the women; the men who take off their clothes and shave represent men who are thin from going through a rainy season of scarcity. The snake is introduced, and the women try to stop him and the rain.

In the second section Uvar is made; its drumbeat is the voice of the snake; the women try to stop the snake from swallowing them.

The triangular dance ground in the third section has the same functions as that in the Djungguan and symbolizes the snake after he has swallowed the two women. In the fourth section (D), the swallowing of the Torres Straits pigeon corresponds to the snake swallowing the animals in the Djungguan dances.

The symbolism is less clear in the stone spear-head dance of Section E, but an analysis of Murngin thinking shows the stone spear head to be associated with the snake: it is the circumcision and the fighting and hunting instrument, and is associated generally with male pursuits.—The women dance to stop the snake.

In Section F the headdress or group dance shows considerable evidence that the groups are possibly classed as snakes (as caterpillars and snails explicitly are by the natives); but even though they do not specifically represent the snake, their dances again were danced by the Wawilak women in the myth to stop the snake from coming.

The ritual paraphernalia constructed in the seventh section (G), including the sunken triangular dance ground, the winding path around the men's ground, and the snail-shell rattle, are all symbolical of the snake; and the women's dance ground and ceremonial house represent the places where the Wawilak women danced and sang to prevent the snake from swallowing them. The kangaroo tail is associated with kangaroos who are the same as the Yiritja snakes in the Gunabibi.—The women have been swallowed by the snake in some of the elements of this section.

The snail-shell rattle dance (Section H) is Muit coming for the women. The dances performed in the ninth section (I) are repetitions of earlier dances in which the snake has swallowed or is about to swallow the women and animals.

The grub-dance sequence in Section J is a repetition in meaning of the grub-dance sequence in Section F, and also identifies explicitly the initiates with the two Wawilak women and their children. The dances performed while the feuds are being settled (Section K) are repetitions of the earlier ones which symbolized the Wawilak women fighting to keep the snake from swallowing them, and of those which symbolized the actual swallowing.

The spear, bark cylinder, yam, and fire dances (Section L) are Muit. The men are Wawilak women and when burned by the fire are being consumed by the snake (a cleansing ceremony).

The frilled-neck (big-eared) lizard of Section M is one of the animals who runs away from the women's impurity into the well of the snake. In Section N the flying-fox (associated as in the Gunabibi with the trickster soul of the dead) and snake dances are performed by the neophytes; their going into the well means the snake swallows them (and purifies them or makes them alive spiritually). The fire that encircles the camp in Section O is the Wawilak women's fire, but is also the snake and the snake's path around the camp. The communal bathing (immersion) in this section symbolizes Muit swallowing the women, and is supposed "to make the people clean and new."

In the forked-pole dance and gray-stone kangaroo dance of Section P the animals again are symbolized as running away from the women; but when the dancers get on the forked stick, they are Muit surrounding the house of the women. Q symbolizes the snake swallowing the women.

In Section R fire is again used as a snake symbol and swallows the kangaroos; and the initiation of the neophytes is symbolized by the kangaroo and flying-fox dancers entering the well. Section S is a repetition of the earlier forked-pole dance (P). In Section T, when in the stone-fire and snake dance the men inhale the smoke, "it means just the same as the Gunabibi when the men go along the ridgepole and get food handed to them" (see Section I, the Gunabibi, page 298).

In the last section, U, the palm-nut bread, spiritualized by virtue of being in the ritual, is eaten by the men as a communion, and they are purified with the burning and smoking leaves of the ironwood. (In the mortuary rites smoking leaves and branches are used to chase away unclean spirits of the newly dead or to remove generally any unclean thing.) This section parallels the Djungguan steaming rite.

To summarize, nine sections of the Ulmark are associated largely with the symbol of the snake swallowing the women: B, C, D, G, H, I, N, Q, R, and T. Five sections, E, F, J, K, and L enact part of the above symbol: they are concerned with the women trying to prevent the snake from swallowing them. Three—O, P, and S—are partly associated with the swallowing. Five—A, M, O, P, and S—either primarily or secondarily symbolize the animals running away from the unclean women into the well. One (U) is a communal eating ritual which symbolizes the unity of the group.

Marndiella

The Marndiella symbolism, like the ceremony itself, is unelaborated. The first section is concerned merely with preparing the boys by ceremonially dressing them like women for the important reason of identifying them with the women's social group. The bloodletting of Section B (found in full detail in the corresponding section of the Djungguan) ritualizes the profanation of the pool and the swallowing of the women by the snake. The flying-fox motif of the spiritually dead brought to life by the ritual is indirectly referred to.

The women's mat dance (Section C) identifies the initiate with the two Wawilak women, and covering him with the ainmara (woman's mat) symbolizes his place in the age grading. In this section we also find the snake swallowing the women.

The dog dance of Section D is one of the most difficult to interpret fully. The dog smelling the initiates means they are "all the same as animals and he is going to catch them." (Dog is best understood in the several myths in which he becomes a symbol of black men generally and therefore of the male group.) The significant fact here is that the boys are symbolical of ritually unclean food.

The blood-smeared, torch-bearing line of men of the fifth section, E, are snakes, and dance around the Wawilak women to symbolize swallowing them. In the last section, F, the initiates are circumcised and steamed exactly as in the Djungguan, and the same symbolism holds here.

The analyses of the four ceremonies show that in addition to the fundamental snake-swallowing-the-women symbol, the Gunabibi brings in also the reproductive cycle and seeing-and-naming-the-food-animals symbols. The Ulmark adds the animals-running-away-from-the-unclean-women symbol. The concluding segments of the Marndiella, Djungguan, and Ulmark bring in a communion, as does the Gunabibi in the flying-fox episode; the communion in the first three seems fairly separate from the general myth-symbols, but in the Gunabibi is part of the snake ideology.

Summary of the Ritual Logics of the Wawilak Configuration [1]

If we let

M stand for myth

[1] This same procedure could be followed for the other sections and subsections of the myth, including the women naming the animals and the coming from the south, also the animals running away from the women.

B for the section of the myth in which the python swallows the women
C for ceremony
D for Djungguan
G for Gunabibi
U for Ulmark
M for Marndiella

and allow lower-case letters corresponding with upper-case letters of the sections to stand for those sections, we can say

$$M_B = C_D(a \ldots g), C_G(a \ldots e, g \ldots i), C_U(b \ldots i, p \ldots t), C_M(c, e \ldots f).$$

The ideology of the first section of the Wawilak myth (M_A)—the coming of the two sisters from the southern interior and the flight of the food animals—although latent in a great number of the sections, appears explicitly only in G(c), G(e, f) and in U(a, c, i, m, o, p). Omission of symbolical relation of certain sections to the myth is due to lack of material.

Obviously the testimony of the natives itself has manifest in its content a great amount of interpretative material which most emphatically demonstrates that the Wawilak myth is no meaningless tale concerned with a purely mythological history of the aboriginal peoples of the area; and this evidence again proves that the dances performed have a deeper significance to the natives' own consciousness than mere aesthetic expressions or religious formulae. All four of the rituals definitely are related to the fundamental Wawilak myth and have their symbolic point of reference there. Each of the dance and song elements refers to a myth-symbol found within the Wawilak dramatic story. The Wawilak myth-rituals are, speaking generally, sacred dramas in which the mysteries of life are enacted. The same is true for the Djunkgao myths and Narra rituals; but rather than confuse our thinking by dealing with too many variables at one time, we shall postpone our interpretation of the Narra rituals until we deal further with the Wawilak story. Since the Djungguan, Gunabibi, Ulmark and Marndiella are the most important rituals, and since in them the one symbol of the snake-swallowing-the-women seems to dominate all the others, the core of our problem of meaning lies here, and we shall give it our first attention.

The Wawilak Configuration and the Seasonal Cycle

Throughout the native interpretation in which the Wawilak myth and the four rituals are connected point by point and integrated, there is a continual association of the rain and flood with the python which gives us a clue to the wider meaning of the python symbol to the Murngin. The Murngin definitely associate the Wawilak python with the weather and seasonal change. The climatic ideas which surround the python are not latent but conscious and manifest in Murngin thinking. Here we shall examine the python as a weather symbol.

The outstanding general natural phenomena are the great seasonal changes which produce heavy rainfall and floods for five months, and for seven months an extremely dry season in which there is no rain and many of the streams, lakes, water holes and inlets dry up. Correlated with this cycle of rainy and dry seasons are the attendant phenomena of changing winds and clouds, greater and less heat, growth and decay of vegetation, birth and growth of the different species of animals, and the appearance of certain birds and insects and the disappearance of others. There is constant need of drastic change in the adaptation of the Murngin economics and technology to fit the constantly changing natural environment.

The other fundamental natural phenomenon which is always dramatically before one's eyes is the relation of the land to the ocean, tidal lakes, and rivers. The great tides pour inland for scores of miles, reaching into the flat coastal plains which stretch back to the broken and difficult highlands in the interior. The flat coast land is continuous along the Sea of Arafura and the Gulf of Carpentaria.

The Murngin have a most accurate knowledge of the locational, seasonal, and daily variation of the tides. Anyone who has taken a canoe trip with them along the seacoast quickly learns that this knowledge is immense in detail, well organized, and held by all the men. To the Murngin mind the flow of the tide into the Murngin land stands in opposition to the flow of the rivers, particularly at flood time during the rainy season. The reason is obvious when we realize the great heights of the incoming tide and the tremendous flow of flood water which goes to the sea during the rainy season.

The central plain which extends from thirty-five to sixty miles inland at sea level is composed of Tertiary deposits which have produced a very poor soil. Inland the altitude increases from several hundred to a thousand feet. Arnhem Land's highest point (to the west and south of the Murngin) is said to be only 1500 feet high. Because of the combination of heavy drought and poor soil, the coastal plain of northeast Arnhem Land has hardly any jungles except patches of mangrove and palms, and is unlike New Guinea and other tropical areas of heavy rainfall in its vegetation. The vegetation has created monsoon or savannah forests which are found throughout the watered parts of the area except where soil erosion has created salt deposits which prevent tree growth. The characteristic trees are many species of eucalyptus, mangrove, acacia, ti trees, pandanus and cabbage palms. The whole country in the proper season is buried in a luxuriant growth of spear grass which grows at times to heights of ten to twelve feet.

The rainy period begins approximately in November and ends in March, although heavy thundershowers and oppressive heat start in October and are also found in March and April after the heavy-rain period has passed. The dry season of five to seven months is one of drought and there is usually no rain at all from May through September, and very little in April and October. The rains belong to one type, since they are all caused by the monsoon Low coming from the northwest. The months of maximum rain are January and February. Although the rain comes from the northwest, it moves from the west more than from the north.[2]

[2] Taylor, Griffith, *Australian Environment Memoir No. 1,* Commonwealth of Australia, page 69. To avoid all possibility of including my own or Murngin preconceptions, there is given below, in preference to my own summary, the summary of a statement by Griffith Taylor (one of the foremost authorities on Australian climate and geography) on North Australian meteorological phenomena. His description is purely from the point of view of a scientific geographer.

The yearly rainfall ranges around fifty to sixty inches, but since most of this occurs in two or three months it does not give a true picture of the amount of rain that falls daily during this short period. In January and February some fifteen inches are precipitated monthly, and in December and March ten to eleven monthly. The following chart gives some idea of the rapid rise and fall of the rain from a little over two inches in October to some ten inches in December and fifteen in January, and the almost as rapid drop when the rainy season ceases. The following account of the seasonal change in Darwin (taken from Taylor's *Australian Environment,* page 70) describes very adequately the dry and rainy cycle as it is found in the Murngin country of northeastern Arnhem Land.

"The different changes of these seasons are so uniform and regular that they may be predicted almost to a day. Signs of the approach of the wet season appear immediately after the sun has crossed the equator during the spring equinox, in September, when the strong E.S.E. monsoon—which has been blowing continually throughout the dry season—ceases, and is succeeded by calms, and light, variable winds; the weather becomes intensely hot, and small thunderclouds gather over the land, increasing in size and density day by day until they burst into terrific thunderstorms, accompanied by hurricane squalls of wind and rain. These squalls, at first, take place every four or five days, gradually increasing in numbers until the end of November, when they occur

The Wawilak myth among other things symbolizes[3] the cycle of the rainy and dry seasons. Evidence will be presented to show that the great python is the rainy season and that associated with this symbol

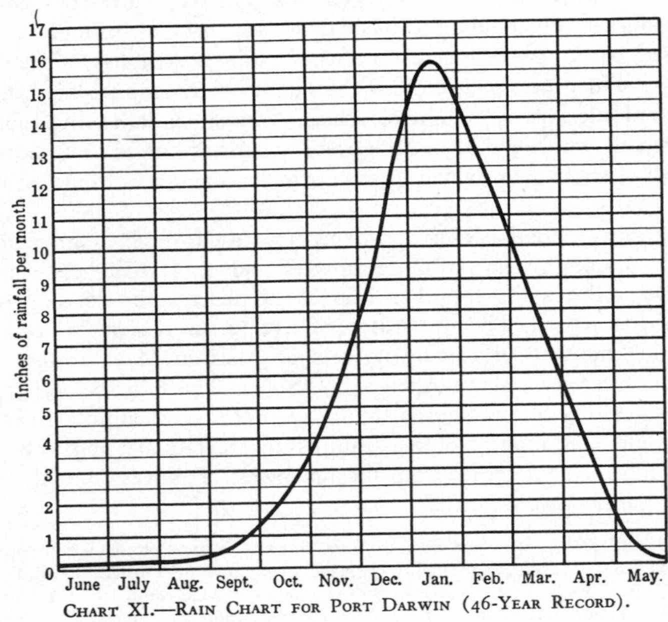

CHART XI.—RAIN CHART FOR PORT DARWIN (46-YEAR RECORD).

almost daily. They come up in a dense black bank, and travel so very rapidly that they are generally out of sight on the western horizon within 40 minutes. About an inch, or sometimes more, of heavy driving rain accompanies each storm; but in the year 1871 the writer of this article saw 2¾ inches of rain gauged within ten minutes during one of these squalls.

"During December the N.W. monsoon gradually gains the ascendancy and blows steadily, with an occasional break of calm weather. The thunderstorms disappear, the sky becomes overcast and clouded, and the atmosphere gets thoroughly saturated with moisture—so much so that leather-work becomes green with mildew; if not constantly attended to, the binding of books becomes soft; and sugar or salt, if exposed in an open vessel, will soon liquefy. This is felt to be an agreeable change after the intensely hot weather during the change of the monsoon in October and November; and, although the humid, moist atmosphere induces profuse perspiration, the effects of the weather are not nearly so unpleasant or severe as those attending the dry heat experienced in the southern portion of Australia during the same and two succeeding months.

"The N.W. monsoon is accompanied by rain almost daily, and increases in force until the latter end of January or beginning of February, when it is blowing in full heart, and penetrates with its copious and fertilizing showers into the very centre of Australia. During this period thick, damp weather prevails, the clouds being very low, and scud and banks of nimbus pass over almost constantly from the N.W. to the S.E.

is the belief in an original flood which covered the earth and, to the Murngin, was a prototype of the modern great floods that yearly inundate the countries of their clans and force them for their own safety into the high grounds, and at times even into the trees on the high grounds.

The west and northwest wind (rainy season winds) is called Barra. "Barra is Dua, it belongs to the same moiety as the snake and is sent by the snake," said the leader of one of the Dua clans to me. In other accounts it is said to be the snake. "Barra wind only brings nothing but rain and flood. After awhile that rain brings fish in the lakes and rivers and makes the grass grow up for bandicoot to eat and the tree flowers for flying-fox and opossum and plenty of fresh tucker [vegetable food] for black men. When the stringy bark comes it is Dua time."

The west wind brings grass and flood and holds until the trees flower, when the wind changes and comes from the north. "Then all the people start looking for bush tucker," and, to continue with the native comment, "Dua rain and wind bring the wet season [mai-elng-nga, no-food time]. The west-wind part is first and it is the largest part."

The dry-season monsoon comes from the southeast, and for the natives northwest of those on the Gulf of Carpentaria, it is a land wind. The dry season is called Gu-tjer-a, and the southeast wind is known as Di-mur-u. "That Dimuru brings plenty tucker and yam and other bush food. There is plenty of fish in the billibongs and plenty sea birds' eggs and yams and all kinds of plums. When the plums finish the wind goes back to Barra [northwest monsoon]. The rain

---

with great rapidity. The maximum temperature in the shade during the day in this weather is 96°, and the minimum during the night is 65°.

"On the approach of the autumn equinox the N.W. monsoon gradually dies away, and is succeeded by the calms, variable winds, thunderstorms, and oppressive weather until about the end of April, when cooler weather is felt; the S.E. monsoon sets in, and the dry season may be said to have fairly commenced. The wind is characterized by a clear sky, enjoyable weather, heavy dews, and cold mornings and nights—so much so that blankets can be used when sleeping. It blows off the coast without intermission, and with great force, almost throughout the season, being in full heart between June and July. At Port Darwin and other places adjacent to the coast, the monsoon generally drops in the afternoon, and is sometimes succeeded by a sea breeze, which is merely local, and only extends to a few miles inland. The atmosphere is clear and dry, and rather hot during the middle of the day—the maximum temperature in the day being 89° and the minimum during the night 56°."

[3] See social organization, technology and the various rituals which are connected with this myth.

clouds are Dua and those lines of clouds that come from the west are Dua.

"The north wind blows and the weather can be wet or dry. It is Yiritja. This is also the time of the wind from the south. When black clouds appear [on the horizon] and Yiritja lightning comes from them, it is when the crocodile makes his nest and lays his eggs and the sting ray appears. It is Yiritja time now."

When the inland lakes dry up and the small streams disappear and many of the clan water holes are empty, "the thunder comes then and calls out for the rain." This is Raer-un-daer, the intermediate period between the dry season and the wet. The clouds from which thunder comes are called kur-ka (penis or male) mo-la-ma (cloud); they come from the south and east. A little later gur-ding gur-ding (the "woman cloud") comes from the west. "Those two meet and copulate." When this happens the "Snakes on the ground ["tucker ones"] put their tails together and copulate. Great mobs of the snakes do this."

"The inside meaning of those clouds is all the same as the snakes. They are snakes."

"The rainbow comes then [bar-i-el-la, light; ba-pi, snake]."[4]

The rainbow is sometimes seen as the python totem itself, at other times it is the house of the snake, and at still others the totemic trumpet. Since it is believed that when the Yurlunggur trumpet is made for the circumcision initiation the snake is inside, it follows that if the rainbow is the snake's house it is also the trumpet. "That one is a snake, he is also the snake's house. Bariella shows all the people that they have to get their houses ready, and when we see this each one starts making his house."

It was because the Wawilak men, who came after the snake had swallowed the women, saw the rainbow in the Mirrirmina pool that they knew the snake was inside the water hole. To the Murngin the rainbow is an announcement not only of heavy rains but also of the heavy floods at the height of the rainy season.

The rain is believed to be Yurlunggur himself or his saliva, with which he licked his two Wawilak victims and their children before he swallowed them. "The rain," said one of the leaders of the Liaalaomir clan, "is all the same as Muit's spit, or he can send it by his voice [thunder]. He can tell it to come." The oldest leader of the Liaalaomir clan, Dorng [thunder], said, "That big fellow, Bapa Indi, he is our father. Down here we call him Wirtit [common name for

[4] Cf. Radcliffe-Brown, A. R., *The Rainbow Serpent Myth of Australia.*

the ordinary rock python]. Bapa Indi makes the rain. Rain is all the same as our brother."

Snails and caterpillars are classed as snakes by the Murngin and, although I did not attempt to get an explicit statement on certain types of grubs, I believe they are also placed in this same category; at least they are always associated with snakes. "Snail is all the same as snake. He comes out just before the rainy season. The inside meaning for that snail is the wet season." Modern Murngin women start hunting snails for food with their marl-pin-pin (snail) sticks at this time of the year.

There are two kinds of lightning. One, ordinary heat lightning, is supposed to be Yiritja; a native compared it to the light from my flashlight because it spread out and diffused evenly. Forked lightning that comes with the roar of thunder is Dua. Yurlunggur's voice is his warro (soul, shadow, or reflection). He said to those two Wawilak women, "People by and by will call my warro, bapi [snake]. When that lightning comes it is all the same as daylight, and thunder sings out in a heavy roar. Dua lightning is the forked tongue of the snake, and the thunder is the roar of the snake. That storm [see myth] and thunder were from that snake, and he was after those two Wawilak women—those two women tried to stop that snake's tongue. He wanted to swallow them. Those Dua rain clouds [see myth] bring rain. Those two women tried to stop that rain because the water came like a flood and tried to cover them all up. That is all the same as that snake swallowing them. The women tried to stop the snake because he was the flood and the wet season covering the earth."

The Great Python, Yurlunggur or Muit, is sometimes seen as the rain itself but is usually associated with or considered identical with the flood. The flood referred to in their thinking is either the great inundation that covered the earth as told in the Wawilak myth or those that come yearly.

Generally Yurlunggur is associated with the totality of the wet season. He is recognized as such by the clansmen of both moieties over the entire area. The degree of a person's philosophical and theological insight into his meanings depends largely on the individual and his social personality. An intelligent, alert Murngin will know most of the evidence recorded here in the native statements. On the other hand, a stupid one would know a few of them and understand the generalities. Muit or Yurlunggur is man and woman, but he is thought of as male. The splitting of the python into two sexual parts, a male individual and a female, is made when the totems are put into the category of natural phenomena; and since it is the nature of snakes on earth to be male and female and have young as man and all other creatures do, it is obvious to the Murngin that the totemic snakes are the same as any species. One of the clan leaders said to me, "The children are little Muits. They live here on the earth or with their father in the sky or with him in the waters down below the earth. Their children are true wirtits [actual snakes—thus the connection between the snake species and the snake totem is complete]. It is the little Muits who swallow a man or woman when they do some unclean thing such as a woman's getting into a canoe while menstruating. It is Muit who makes the rain." This account I think is less generally expressed and believed among the larger group because it is too well rationalized and bears the mark of a ritual leader and more intelligent person; yet it would be accepted by any Murngin if it were expressed to him by a leader.

The following would be generally known and was told to me numerous times during ceremonies or when the weather was being discussed: "The wet and dry seasons are caused by the snakes. During the wet the snakes curl up and have sexual intercourse; the Great Father Snake does the same. They then come out of the water and want to lay their eggs. This brings on the dry season so that they can have such a place. By and by this causes the heavy floods of the wet season."

It is believed that if, through any ritually impure act, the Wongar totem snake should be angered, he would come out and swallow the earth, and a flood would come at the same time. Several men said to me in effect what I now quote from one man: "If any Wongar snake would swallow us now the flood water would come like it did for the Wawilak sisters and cover all this land.—That snake brought the flood and the rain at the same time when he pushed the stone out of the bottom of the Mirrirmina well." Another time I was told, "When that snake took the stone from the bottom of the well the water came and the snake at the same time. He blew up to the sky for rain." Some versions say he spit water from Mirrirmina, and others say, "He spit at the same time he blew his breath."

At a moment in the Ulmark the leader said to me, "Those Wawilak women sang all night to stop Muit and stop the rain and water. They are all the same thing."

Lightning "is all the same as my brother," a Dua man said to me.

"When the lightning comes that means a light for Wongar [the totemic spirit] to see by when he makes that big noise [the thunder] and hits down at those people he fought [the Wawilak sisters in the myth]. When rainbow time comes that is the snake Wongar. He is swallowing those two women. When I see a rainbow or lightning I understand rain is coming."

The cycle of the seasons with the growth and decay of vegetation, copulation, birth and death of animals as well as man, is all the fault of those two Wawilak sisters. "If they hadn't done wrong in their own country and copulated with Dua Wongar men [an incestuous act] and then come down to the Liaalaomir country and menstruated and made that snake wild [angry]," this cycle would never have occurred. "Everyone and all the plants and animals would have walked about by themselves." There would have been no copulation between the sexes and no children and no change. "After they had done this wrong they made it the law for everyone." One of the most intelligent men said to me, "Black men walk about single and by and by catch a mate belong him and by and by yoto [children]. White man walk about by himself, by and by catch mielk and more yoto come out. Macassar man was all the same. Big kangaroo walk about single, by and by he catch a woman and by and by yoto. All the same for opossum and fly and bandicoot and everything."

"Snake catchum mate and by and by egg and yoto. All the same for lizard and native companion and bee and turtle and everything.

"Black men cut down trees and by and by little ones come up. Everything is the same everywhere. Walk about single, by and by mate and by and by pickaninny."

This was told me during a Gunabibi as well as other times. It is almost, as far as I could see, a formula in the thinking of the Murngin.

Most of the quotations that have been given were obtained while I observed the Djungguan or Gunabibi and was being told by its leaders the "inside" meaning of each part according to Murngin thought.

The statements of the natives in these last few pages clearly indicate that they are conscious of the symbolism by which they associate the rainy season with the snake or with his actions. The snake at this time comes out of the streams, the lakes, the springs, rivers and wells, which are the sacred totem wells of the Murngin, and as he raises himself the flood rises and the rain starts. He is both in the heavens (the thunder is his voice and the lightning his tongue; the clouds copulate and they are the snakes) and in the subterranean depths. When the snake rises and swallows the women the waters of the earth cover the dry land, and the snake does not fall until the southeastern monsoon blows. He falls and the earth is dry again. "He was looking for dry land to put [regurgitate] them on." The rain stops, the waters recede, and the earth dries while the southeastern monsoon blows. In the myth, then, its blowing is the coming of the dry season. The snake falls and regurgitates what he has eaten, as do the other snakes. The period of want when little food is available is over, for the wet season has "spit up" what it has swallowed in its waters. The women and the other animals swallowed are in this symbolism. The reproductive and "food-giving" parts of nature are by inference—but not, so far as I could determine, in the consciousness of the Murngin—the dry season. The great primeval flood is merely a dramatic enlargement of what takes place every year when the torrential tropical rains flood the lands, cover the earth, and bring want where there was plenty.

The Wawilak Myth and Ritual and Murngin Social Organization

The "swallowing" of the earth by the rainy season is known to be caused by the wrong actions of the two Wawilak women in copulating incestuously with their own clansmen and by the older sister's later profaning the pool of the sacred python. This is not considered an unmixed calamity, however, because the rain and water bring the plants and bulbs and flowers which are consumed directly by man or provide pasturage for kangaroo, opossum, and other animals eaten by man. In other words, the Murngin see the snake's swallowing the women and animals as necessary and part of the scheme of things, and their testimony clearly demonstrates the causal relation between the actions of the Wawilak women and the seasonal cycle. The cycle of nature is a necessary one, in which man has ordinary and extraordinary rôles to play. In the ordinary rôle he "walks about single, by and by mielk, by and by yoto," as do all the other animals; and in the extraordinary rôle he is pledged by the Wawilak women to continue producing the great rituals because of their original sins and to purify man and his society. These ceremonies are designed to aid nature, or possibly it would be better to say to restrain man from preventing by his unclean actions the coming of the dry season of plenitude. This is why the young man who refuses to copulate with the woman in the fertility rite of the Gunabibi is scolded and told that he will be sick and make his partner ill. And this is why the whole

Gunabibi or any of the other ceremonies must be completed; scarcity and sickness are likely to result if it is not.

The snake, then, in this symbolism of nature, is the wet season, and his actions become significant because he swallows the dry season and regurgitates it, which brings a period of plenty.

A number of additional elements to this symbol are suggested by the four myths. The women are swallowed because of their unclean acts. When the various ceremonial elements are listed, the snake is found to be played almost always by the men, and the Wawilak sisters by the women, uninitiated children, and those who are being initiated.

Initiated and uninitiated meet frequently on the border line of the general camp (to which the women are ceremonially restricted) and the men's grounds. At times the men invade the ground of the women. The formal grouping of the women and children and of the initiated men is emphasized by this spatial arrangement.

In all instances the male snake (Bapa Indi, Father Big) is a ritualization of the male section of society, and the Wawilak sisters who by their uncleanness have provoked the snake (men) into swallowing them are the unritualized or profane sections of the tribe, i.e., the women and uninitiated boys. The only exceptions to this generalization occur when men take the rôle of women on the men's ground from which women are barred. This brings us, I think, to a deeper level of the great Murngin rituals. The men's age grade is a snake and purifying element, and the sociological women's group is the unclean group. The male snake-group in the act of swallowing the unclean group "swallows" the initiates into the ritually pure masculine age grade, and at the same time the whole ritual purifies the whole group or tribe.

The snake is the fertilizing principle in nature according to Murngin symbolism; this explains why it is identified with the men's group rather than with the women; otherwise one would suppose that the male principle, being identified with the positive higher social values, would be associated by the Murngin with the dry season—the time of the year of high social value.

Seven institutions found in Murngin society are the elementary family, the extended kinship structure, the tribe, the clan, the moiety, the subsection, and the horde. The tribe and the horde are amorphous unities which have no formal structure. The unstable elementary family and extended kin groups are organized into larger formal unities by the clan, moiety, and subsection systems. The totemic system of the Murngin is highly elaborated and permeates all the activities of the group and all of its concepts of life in the world about it; but despite this proliferation of detail of totemic ideas, none of the informal structures have totemic elements as definite parts of their organization, whereas all the formal ones have them. The clan has multiple totems attached to it by authority of the various myths, and the moiety is given these same totems generally by the whole myth. For example, all Dua clans theoretically have the Wawilak totems or the Djunkgao totems according to the area in which the moiety is located. The subsections have definite totems given them, although they are of little importance to the Murngin.

The Murngin clan is a social category which gives spatial form to the kinship system. The ordinary kinship reciprocals can exist anywhere, since a man's father or mari could be almost anywhere in the area, and as a kinship term *mari* is not thought of spatially and in a definite locality, although one's actual father is of course identified with one's own clan. With the introduction of the clan system into the larger social order by the selection of certain lines of relatives out of the total group and the rejection of others through the use of the patrilineal unilateral principle, certain people are given a single unity with respect to the rest of the kin community and are at the same time related to a given area of land. By the inclusion of certain people and the exclusion of others from the kinship pattern, one of the chief functions of the kinship reciprocals is expressed, because the principles which exclude most of the people from one clan include these people in other clan groups and thereby create a clan system integrated into the structure of the larger kinship system. All of the people and all of the clans are related by kinship ties. The kinship system functions as an "international" social system by means of the allocation of the clans to one of two groups. This interclan organization is more simply formed than the kinship structure, and from the point of view of the moiety the segmentation into clans gives greater precision and stronger local solidarities for the people within either half of the tribe. The moiety has spatial significance only indirectly and in a derivative sense; the total territory of the clans of one moiety is its only claim to spatial character.

The Wawilak and Djunkgao myths emphasize the spatial characteristic of the clan by naming its various locations and clan wells, and by relating the wanderings of the two women through the various clan territories; further, the women's travels locate and relate the clans in the general topography of northeastern Arnhem Land. The clan structure is not a mere exogamic group which occupies a certain extended territory and whose people earn their living from this area. In the first place, all its female members are usually not attached to the land itself, for after reaching early adolescence they go as wives and potential mothers to other clans than their own; the wives and mothers of the local clan come from other areas and are therefore not thought of as belonging to this particular piece of land. Spatial unity is disrupted and the Murngin clan is seen to be an entirely different social entity from our modern state. Further, the economic unit of this people is not the clan but the horde.

The horde's membership is composed of men from a number of clans as well as of women from different groups. The clan composition of a horde becomes more hetereogeneous during the dry season when an area can support a larger number of people, than in the rainy season when food is scarce. The male membership of the clan is seldom spatially intact except during the ritual season when all of the male members are more likely to be present than in the rainy period. The clan's so-called "ownership" of the land has little of the economic about it. Friendly peoples wander over the food areas of others and, if their area happens to be poor in food production, possibly spend more of their lives on the territory of other clans than on their own. Exclusive use of the group's territory by the group is not a part of the Murngin idea of land "ownership." The ownership of the land is more in the "nature of things," as seen by the Murngin. The land is not outside the clan but is an integral part of it. As has been said, it cannot be taken from the clan, for it is of the clan and made such by the order of existence. "Wongar made it that way and that's why we have these things today."

Politically the clan is almost impotent when it comes to positive action. It is impossible to obtain group action, even for the wergild, which will function to the extent that discipline can be enforced and individual action prohibited in a blood feud. The ceremonial leader is considered head man, and if physically able and of sufficient talent, he is also war leader, but his power is at an absolute minimum except as a ritual leader; it is in the field of ritual and not of government that he exercises his leadership.

The names of the country, the names of the wells, and the list of totems as well as the names of the mythological ancestors all form fundamental parts of the clan unity. All of the names of the clan wells, both the sacred and the camp names, refer to the totemic objects either directly or indirectly and usually describe some aspect of the clan's country or rationalize its relation to the totem. The totemic mythological ancestors generally have the same names as the well. All of these elements are unified by one or more myths. These myths in turn are dramatized by the various rituals enacted by the clanspeople so that when a man is asked what totems a particular clan possesses, he ordinarily thinks of the rituals they use and the myths the rituals portray.

The names of the clan wells either elaborate the detail of the myth as it is expressed by the totem or they give distinct additions which relate other totemic myths to the well. In no case does the name of a well have no relation to the totems of the clan.

The clansmen are identified with the totemic well by the fact that they come from it and are allowed to be born by the action of the totemic spirit that resides within the well; they are identified with the well because at death they will go back to it and because all of their kin who have died and those living, with whom they have had all of their social relations, are or will be either in this well into which their own soul returns or in other like clan wells; and finally, their well-being and that of their fellow clansmen and of other clans are dependent upon the proper enactment of the seasonal rituals which demonstrate the mana or power of the totem. At death not only does the soul go into the well but it also enters into the totemic emblem itself and becomes a part of it.

The names of the living are all taken from some part of the totemic complex and refer directly or indirectly to the totem. One exception to this is the new group of Malay terms which, however, have been sacralized by the real ancestors' possessing them, and which, after a period of taboo and when the ancestors are within the totemic water hole, are passed on to the living. Another exception to the rule is the group of nicknames, which are also inheritable by the living from the dead. The spiritual life of a Murngin, then, is entirely made up from totemic elements, and his whole participation within that part of the community which makes him a social man and separates him from the adolescent children and women is within the totemic complex itself. (This of course is a fundamental aspect of age grading and is treated under that head.) As a male social personality, a man is part of the totem, and in all his social relations with the male part of his group he is identified with the totem. This is true for all other individuals in his adult age grade, so that the totality of the males' individual relations forms the whole of the totemic behavior. It is the sacred tradition of the clan groups, as held in the minds of the individuals of the adult male age grade—plus ritualistic behavior as overt demonstrations of these traditional beliefs held and possessed by the male group—which forms the totemic configuration. The group in this sense does unconsciously worship itself. The totem well and the totemic emblem, being concrete symbols of the totality of the sacred traditions, become symbols of group unity and symbolize the group; and to the extent that the ritual sanctions hold and force subordination of all behavior to their end, the sacred dominates and controls the ordinary life of the individuals within the clans, and therefore of the social life of the clans themselves. The Murngin, when asked why this is so or that exists, always reply, "Wongar did it this way," "Those two old women made it that way," or, "Such and such a totem did so and so in those Wongar times." If their associations are allowed to proceed to deeper levels of explanation, various fundamental myths make their appearance within the thinking, and it soon becomes clear that the categories to which the speakers refer their ideas and the things of the world in their ultimate meanings are these myths. The possession of all land is made absolute and final to the Murngin by the statements of the myth which describe certain behavior of the totems which took place on that land, and which identify the clan and the land as one because the clan has certain totems. The clan's totemic ancestors have certain totemic names, its children arrive by relations with certain totems, it possesses and practices certain rituals, and its dead go to certain totemically named wells. The Murngin clan itself, then, is a membership of a certain unilateral group of people whose unity is expressed by the possession of a totemic configuration and the practice of exogamy.

The mana of the Murngin well is due not to any mundane biological value its water may have for the group, but rather to the spiritual power of the water. If the water had physiologic value alone, then all the water holes would be placed in the same category by the Murngin. As it is, certain wells are considered sacred, and certain others ordinary and placed in a natural category. The spiritual elements in the sacred well include the totem and totemic ancestors as well as the souls of the dead and those who are to be born. The Narra well also acts as a repository for the totemic emblems after the Narra ceremonies.

The clan well as an organizing idea can be used in ritual and myth, but it has not the flexibility and ease of manipulation held by a small totemic object. The totemic emblem can be used in a ceremony as a concrete expression of the ideas of the sacred. It becomes a tangible expression of python, barrimundi, or some other totemic spirit. The infinite variety of ideas and feelings which are a part of the beliefs making up the totemic spirit can be symbolized and expressed in the concrete image of the totem, and this object can be manipulated in the rituals. The ritual handling of the totemic image can and does express, through a series of totemic dances, the various attitudes of awe, respect, and supplication, as well as the fundamental social ideas and myth-symbols which are a part of the totemic configuration. The neophyte holds his head down, the old men tell him of the respect and care with which he must treat the emblem, and how he must live his life under the code of Murngin morals after seeing this sacred totem. The totemic trumpet is blown over the initiates, and the myth-symbol of the great python swallowing the women is expressed; a man dances with an emblem in the Narra ground, and a certain myth of his clan is symbolically expressed; a man cuts his arm and while the blood pours from it the python trumpet is blown over him, and the profanement of the python pool with all its complex social ramifications and subtle implications of value and sanctions is expressed symbolically and simply because this concrete trumpet-emblem (imbued with totemic mana by the agency of the totemic design and totemic ritual and song) can be handled and moved and seen and heard.

The great rituals like the Gunabibi and Ulmark, which bring together, from widely separated clans and tribes, people who often have old scores unsettled and are ready to burst into open conflict, function as organizing units of these people during the period of the ritual, and also after they separate, for, with the aid of the myth, the rituals leave in the minds of the natives a feeling of oneness, of relationship to the larger group. The peoples who attend the ceremony organize themselves spatially in accordance with their location in the horde—that is, they camp in the same direction and relative distance with respect to the host clan. For example, if the Warumeri gave a Narra, the Kalpu of the English Company Islands would be north of them, the Kalpa still farther north, the Liagaomir would be west, and so on. The subsection (see Chapter III on Kinship) enters into certain ceremonies such as the Djungguan to regulate the ritual behavior.

The ritual sanction of offending the ancestors and totems by starting a fight prevents many feuds from breaking into open conflict. This sanction or a similar one is absolutely necessary to allow the ritual to remain an interclan and tribal affair. If the sanction and its attendant action were not fully established, the disintegrating effect of the clan solidarities and their associated antagonism to outside groups, organized by the blood feuds, would destroy the participation of a large number of groups and reduce the people who would participate in any one ritual to a residue composed only of clans and peoples closely connected by marriage. At times the blood-feud feeling is so intense that a ceremony is broken up, or the ceremony is not attended by the warring groups.

The rituals provide the only effective mechanisms which enlarge the social horizon of any individual or clan beyond his or its immediate neighbors. The kinship system with its asymmetrical marriage arrangements constantly pushes out into the larger culture and tends to increase the clan's participation in wider groupings; but in the face of the blood feud, organized on the basic unity of the clan and its intermarrying groups, this larger integration of the society on the basis of the kinship alone is impossible. Old rivalries for women are remembered and several generations of killings are not forgotten, which means that even though a man calls a somewhat distant tribesman "older brother" and is termed "younger brother" by him, the concepts of cooperation and solidarity that lie within these terms have no effect in restraining killings or the blood feud, since the feelings of loyalty to the local group and the near kin, as expressed in antagonism to outsiders, prevent an extension of the kinship system to others.

It is the larger rituals, then, with their most powerful religious totemic sanctions which do operate to restrain the local loyalties and seasonally allow a larger participation in the group. In certain instances they further tend to lessen the intensity of the dislikes of the conflicting groups following the dispersion of the larger groups. It must be remembered, however, that the mere bringing together of very large groups, as for example in the Gunabibi (to which people come from great distances), tends to create situations which may lead to battles after the ceremonies are over; but ordinarily a peacemaking duel follows the ceremony which is supposed to settle old fights and lead to a general friendliness.

Masculinity and Femininity as Organizing Principles of the Social Organization as Expressed in the Rituals

In addition to isolating the symbols of the snake as the rainy season and the snake as the men's age-grading group, we can separate out a further symbol which permeates all their thinking and underlies their elaborate organization and social structure. Masculinity is inextricably interwoven with ritual cleanliness, and femininity is equally entwined with the concept of uncleanliness, the former being the sacred principle and the latter the profane. This sexual dichotomy and its correlation with the Murngin beliefs of what are the sacred and profane elements of the group, are again connected with a further principle of human relations, namely, that of superordination and subordination.

The superordinate male group, made sacred through the ritual initiation of its individual members into the sacred group, and maintained as a unit by continual participation in the rituals, subordinates the female group which is unified by virtue of exclusion from the ceremonies and of ritual uncleanliness. The superordination of the male is made a mystery by the nexus of masculinity, sacredness, and the seasonal reproductive cycle. Within this mystery lies one of the strongest and most effective sanctions found in Murngin society. The male sacredness becomes more sacrosanct and "holy" as it progresses into the graded deeper mysteries through the age-graded initiations, and this sacredness controls the profane and less sacred elements of society by the invocation of the direct negative sanctions of ritual: "If you young men do not do this, such and such will happen to you." "This man married wrong or that woman has had illegal sexual relations, and our whole group is endangered ["made sick"]." Obviously it behooves everyone to live up to the code of the society; and if he does not, the whole group feels compelled to act to prevent the contagion of his harmful actions causing a general catastrophe. The ceremonial mysteries of the male group, then, help subordinate not only the women and younger boys but also the men themselves, since they too cannot profane the sacred mysteries by some impure and illegal act; if they do, the male group feels obliged to act. In other words, in the local organization of the whole social group from the pinnacle of the old men's age grade to the bottom age grade of women and children, and from the most remote northeastern clan of Wessel Island to the most southeastern one in the far interior, there is a general subordination of the several institutions of the social organization to the higher sacred realm which constitutes the Murngin system of totemism. It is in the ultimate sanctions of the totemic system that Murngin society finds its final unity. The general technology, which is the community's practical adaptation to its natural environment, is disciplined and organized through the instrumentation of social organization. For example, the rules of conduct for various kin personalities, such as gawel and waku, or father and son, regulate the distribution and consumption of the social goods produced by the technology; or, to take another example, the rules of clan membership demand certain divisions of foods, other creature necessities, and services. These and the other laws of the social organization not only discipline the economic life but also relate the individual members and the institutions of the community to each other.

The totemic system provides, first, a final set of absolute sanctions for the society which places a pressure on all the members to perform the acts dictated by the rules of the social organization; and, second, a set of concepts organized into a unified system which provides a mechanism for group integration. The totemic emblem is a concrete symbol of these two basic concepts, and an object which can be manipulated by a series of rituals (primarily the Narra), which elaborate, dramatize, and tie together the various sacred concepts of the myths in the sacred dances and songs. The latent content of these rituals is the myth, and within the myth are the fundamental symbols of the social concepts of totemism. These were the symbols which we analyzed and for which we gave the native interpretation in Chapters IX and X and summarized in the beginning of this chapter. In the present chapter we also presented some of the concepts which underlie the oral rite and dramatic ritual. We found that there is a general idea which surrounds natural phenomena, and that nature is seen as a unity, as an alternation of the dry and rainy season (that is, in the myth the seasonal alternation is symbolized by the conflict of the snake and the two women). The natural phenomena are all organized in this dichotomy. We saw that the seasonal variations are given social categories by the identification of the rainy season with the male principle and the dry period with the female principle. This classification is mechanically accomplished in Murngin thinking by giving the seasons and the age-grade dichotomy the same symbols. The relation of the social category to the natural one is implicit in the myth's account of the wronging of the two women by the ancestors of man and the profanation of the sacred pool. The general activity of nature, that is, the alternation of the seasons, is the effect of man's uncleanliness in the mythologic past and in the present, as the Djunkgao interpretations will later demonstrate. It is therefore necessary continually to cleanse the group and its individuals of all social uncleanliness. This is the function of the Narra rites and of the Garma, Marndiella, Djungguan, Gunabibi, and Ulmark.

That which organizes the two categories (the seasonal reproductive cycle of nature and the male-cleanliness female-impurity dichotomy of society) into one is the totemic symbol which can be manipulated by ritual and gives man an effective control over nature and an effective negative sanction over the members of his society. The rituals must be properly conducted yearly to keep the group and its individuals ritually clean; and in these rituals the manipulation of the sacred totem insures the proper function of the seasons, a sufficient production of food, and a continuation of the natural surroundings proper for man. Thus that which is beyond man's technology or beyond his real powers of control becomes capable of manipulation because its symbols can be controlled and manipulated by the extraordinary powers of man's rituals. At the same time the identification, in the totemic concept, of the male and female principles with the seasonal cycles gives the adult men's group the necessary power to enforce its sanctions; the providing world of nature will not function if the rules of society are flouted and man's uncleanliness contaminates nature. Hence everyone must obey. If he does not by his own volition, then he must be forced to, by restriction of his larger participation in the group (as, for example, barring him from higher age grades until he behaves himself); or by the direct sanction of clan feud; or, within the clan, by allowing the offending member to be killed by another clan. As we have said, the women's sociological group and women as physiological beings are thus subordinate to the men's group, and the Murngin age-grading system has been built on this principle. Like other Australian tribes, this peoples' "political" control might be termed a gerontocracy, but it is more than merely the rule of old men.

The analysis of the four myths shows that, besides the fundamental snake-swallowing-the-women symbol, the Gunabibi uses the reproductive cycle, and the Ulmark the animals-running-away-from-the-unclean-women as important motifs. The concluding acts of the Marndiella, Djungguan and Ulmark introduce communion rites, as does the Gunabibi, in the flying fox episode. The communion in all of the rituals except the Gunabibi seems fairly differentiated from the general symbols, but in the Gunabibi it is part of the snake idea (the initiate becomes part of the snake in the dance).

The animals-running-away-from-the-women myth-symbol given primary expression in a number of the Ulmark segments is also of secondary interest in the Djungguan and Gunabibi. The interpretation of the snake-swallowing-the-women symbol gives a sufficient understanding of the Wawilak myth to fit the animals-running-away symbol into its place. The animals leave the women and jump into the python's pool because the women are ritually impure. They arise from the pool and roar like snakes. The animals here are symbolically taken into the snake's totem well and made clean by their immersion, which is demonstrated by their roaring and acting like the snake. Further, they are being swallowed by the wet season. In the Gunabibi also the animals are running away from the women and are being made clean in the well. In the Ulmark the rainy season theme is made more explicit by having the men remove all their ornaments and clothing and shave to resemble men emaciated from lack of food. This occurs in the first section after the animals (kangaroos) have run away. It seems a possible hypothesis that the Djunkgao loss of the totems and the Wawilak loss of the animals are analogous and to the native mind, in general, the same thing. This was not told to me specifically of Murngin dogma by the native interpreters, but was often said generally about the Wawilak and Djunkgao myths and the behavior of the two sets of sisters.

The Gunabibi directly introduces the further theme of the reproductive cycle. In the Djungguan, Marndiella, and Ulmark it is subsumed under the general seasonal cycle, but in the Gunabibi it has a definite part of its own in the symbolization; and when the reproductive cycle does find expression in the song and dance symbols the seasonal cycle is understood to lie within it as a part of the process of reproduction. It can be said that part of the fundamental structure of the Gunabibi is the expression of reproductive activities in symbolical detail. First only the male animals dance, then only the females, then the two simulate copulation; and when the human species perform, they actually copulate ceremonially. The ceremonial aspect of copulation is emphasized by the exchange of tribal brothers' wives; repetition of ordinary profane sexual relations of spouses would lack the dramatic force of the copulation of strange mates.

(Incidentally, the fact that the copulation of animals is simulated by male dancers and that the human symbols of reproduction actually copulate demonstrates once more how the rituals symbolically manipulate functions of nature which cannot be directly controlled, whereas the direct form of expression is exercised when possible.)

The reproductive symbol is related point by point to the seasonal symbol by the knowledge of the seasons when the animals go about not paired, but singly, and the time of year mating and reproduction take place. The reproductive cycle of mating and birth is manifest in most of the sections of the four Wawilak ceremonies, is explicitly stated in the Gunabibi symbolism, and is latent in the concept of the season's fluctuation. The emphasis of interest in natural phenomena is shifted slightly from the seasonal variation as the organizing principle of all nature's complexities to the reproductive behavior of the animals and plants, which again generalizes on all the activities of nature. In brief, the concepts of the reproductive cycle and seasonal alternation state the same generalization and are given the same symbols in the myth.

The Gunabibi, by bringing the reproductive cycle into explicit symbolical statement in a number of segments, by retaining in others the usual seasonal symbols, and by combining seasonal and reproductive symbols in still others, gives us a better understanding of the Murngin concepts of the order of natural phenomena. The fertility of the plant and animal species is seen to be in a time relationship, and this order of time is conceived as a seasonal one. This gives us a more elaborate knowledge of the general thinking which underlies the two sister myths and Murngin totemism in general. Furthermore, the Gunabibi ritual completely demonstrates the fact that the Murngin realize the necessity of sexual intercourse as part of the reproductive cycle.

When the Liaalaomir python says, "I see we talk a different language—it is better then that we all have the same ceremonies together for we own the same maraiin," he is stating a fundamental fact of the Murngin social structure. What he is saying is that the clans ("different languages") tend to break down the larger unity with their open or suppressed antagonisms, and the ceremonies and totems tend to establish unity through the underlying agency of the rituals and myths in which Yurlunggur appears.

Comparison of the Wawilak and Djunkgao Constellations

The western Wawilak myth tells of the wanderings from the south of the two Wongar sisters who name the animals, localities, and wells of the individual clans, as well as the countries, in their progress northward. In the eastern Djunkgao myth two sisters do exactly the same things except that they travel by water and by land. The Wawilak sisters break the fundamental rule of clan exogamy by committing incest with one of their own clansmen. The Djunkgao sisters do the same thing. The only difference in this part of the two myths is that the Wawilak adds the menstruation uncleanliness to the incest impurity. In the third and final element of both myths the ritual paraphernalia and mysteries are obtained by the men from the women and the latter admit their subordination: the Wawilak women tell the men how to conduct their rituals and give them up to the men; the Djunkgao lose their totems and therefore their rituals are stolen by the men. These two myths with their essential identity of plot have superficially elaborated their rituals into quite different patterns; fundamentally they are the same. The Narra rituals focus their attention on the individual clan wells, on their clan totems, and on the process of purifying the clan of its uncleanliness. The Wawilak rituals place their emphasis on the totems of one well, although the other wells are brought in by inference (all the snakes in the myth hold a conversation in the sky). The Wawilak rituals emphasize the ceremonial uncleanliness and the final purification of the group but with a different set of symbols from those of the Djunkgao rituals. The Narra ceremony repeats and thereby emphasizes uncleanliness and purification. The Wawilak rituals accent purification by the snake's swallowing the women, but rather explicitly symbolize profanement as a separate element in the Dua Narra kingfisher and spear dances, the center of this ritual.

This identification of the two myths and the fundamental sameness of the two rituals help us to obtain a deeper insight into the concepts of the Djunkgao than we could obtain if we had only the Narra rituals to analyze. The two sisters by their incestuous act lose the totems to man. This incestuous act also causes the cycle of the seasons and of reproduction. The symbol of this uncleanliness is the semen of their incestuous partners, and their purification consists of washing this impurity off their bodies. The Murngin people reenact symbolically the mythological cleansing in the ritual of the community baptism. The water cleanses them as it does in the symbol of the snake (water) swallowing the women in the Wawilak myth. The bathers in the Djunkgao rite must cover themselves entirely just as the Wawilak women were covered by the snake (water) in the western myth. After this the males are sufficiently clean to eat their ritual bread ceremonially.

In the Narra there is less definition of the various symbols than in the Wawilak group of rituals, and in the Yiritja Narra even less than in the Dua. In the Yiritja Narra the great floods bring the totems; the dances are basically the same as in the Dua, where there is the dance with the totems on the men's ground, the calling out of the entire list of clans of the moiety, the dancing in the ring, the use of spears, the ceremonial bathing, the later showing of totems, and the eating of communion bread. In the Yiritja there is no deviation from the fundamental pattern of the Dua Narra, but the mythology is explicitly attached to the ritual by making the foam (semen in the Dua ritual) land in the Yiritja ritual; and it is only by inference that the whole of the Yiritja Narra is seen to depend on the interpretation of the Dua Djunkgao ritual for its meaning; e.g., the ascendency of men over the women is demonstrated by calling out the names of the wells each night, which symbolizes the removal of the totems from the women.

Basically the totemic Narra ceremonies are, first, purification rites by which the whole group is "baptized" (and it is this element which is most emphatically accented); second, expressions of group solidarity in communal eating of purified totemic bread by the purified group; third, rites emphasizing both clan structure and rigid dual division (by showing clan totems and calling out names of clan wells, and by the division of the Narra ceremony into two—Dua and Yeritja—rituals when in reality it is but one). Of all the rituals involved in the high totemic ceremonies, the Yiritja Narra is the simplest and least elaborated in its expression and the Gunabibi and Ulmark the most proliferated and explicit.

The individual totems found in all the wells supposedly visited by Wawilak and Djunkgao women are all pieces of the general mosaic of the myth. For example, in the Liaalaomir where the Wawilak women visited there are the following totems: carpet snake's head, carpet snake's anus, caterpillar, carpet snake, carpet snake's neck, carpet snake's tongue (this is also lightning), an iguana, green ant, singing stick, a palm tree, ridgepole of a house, house rafters, uprights, forked stick used for house construction, sea gull, wood brought in on the tide, porpoise, moon fish, a rock, young porpoise, morning star, bamboo spear, stone spear, spear-thrower, variety of the wild bee, boomerang and white feather string.

The same is true among the Djawark where the Djunkgao women visited; for example, there are the following totems: menstruating girl, woman's mat and apron, mature woman, young girl, clitoris, cane, yam stick, singing sticks, fire, tidal floatwood, red parrot, grub in lily pond, black ant's nest, sea gull, wood brought in on the tide, porpoise, moon fish, a rock, young porpoise, morning star, bamboo spear, stone spear, spear-thrower, variety of the wild bee, boomerang and white feather string.

Additional totems of a higher order as well as the lowest garma forms will be discussed below. (The garma are fully treated under Mortuary Rites.)

The totems are the concrete expression of the underlying concepts of society in its relation to nature and in the relation of the internal institutions to each other; and these concepts are embedded in the myths. This means that the concepts are a part of the myth and subject to its interpretation, as the natives testify when they interpret the rituals of the various myths as well as the myths themselves.

The usual native generalization is that "these two sisters brought all the ranga," but it can be demonstrated that some wells have additional totems which have separate myths. These latter totems and myths belong to the local organization and are secondary elaborations which symbolize either clan or moiety oppositions or solidarities. The separation of the local organization myths from the larger and more comprehensive ones gives us a clue to some of the subsidiary themes and smaller subdivisions found within the larger segments of the rituals associated with the Wawilak and Djungguan myths.

The shark myth of the Djirin, for example, is added to the general configuration of the Narra by having the shark dance symbolically his breaking through the land in Buckingham Bay. Only over a long period of years could one collect all the local organization myths and determine the exact place in which they all fit into the general pattern. I regret to say I did not accomplish this. In the time at my disposal, however, I did collect a sufficient number to discover their general patterns.

The garma totems are all lower than the rangas (high totems). The rangas are preponderantly connected with the myths of the two sisters, but the garma generally are not. The garma rituals are associated with mortuary rites or cleansing ceremonies throughout the area, but in the north and east some of them also function as curing rituals for sickness.

The Narra and garma myths all express the fundamental idea of the movement backward and forward of the tides in the spring floods either in the present period or in the mythological past; the Wawilak myth and ritual leave out the movement of the tide except in a minor way, and concentrate on the flood. The essential formula of the Narra links together the sacred names of the moiety's clan water holes: the leaders shout out during an important part of the ritual in fairly exact order in a Dua Narra first only Dua clans and in a Yiritja Narra first only Yiritja clans. The moiety clan water holes are further tied together: in the Dua Narra by relating the names of the clan wells to the wanderings of the Djunkgao sisters; in the Yiritja by the actions of the various mythological creatures. That the underlying ideas of the Djunkgao myth are ceremonial uncleanliness and purification by means of the ritual is demonstrated by its following fundamental elements: (1) the women's wanderings and planting of the totems; (2) their incest and defilement; and (3) the taking of the totems by the men.

The Yiritja Narra account shows clearly that the spring flood is made not only by the rain but also by the rise of the water in the totem water holes which overflow at this time. In this ritual it seems rather an overflow of the totem well than a flood coming directly from the rain. In any case, the well water is always a strong contributing element to the flood covering the earth. The rise of the water, then, is something more than the symbolization of the flood as male and spiritual, as in the Djungguan; it is here an actual outflow of water from the sacred centers of the land, which causes the growth of new plants and animals and the refertilizing of the earth. It is the male principle fertilizing the earth. The women are covered with semen and made fertile, as is the land. The "white stuff" on the Djunkgao women was unclean and compelled purification by washing because the clansmen of old had broken the most fundamental law of the social code. The social relations needed purification and the bathing ritual resulted. The modern social organization needs purifying for past misbehaviors, particularly those of a sexual nature (see pages 67-79 for examples of sexual code infringement). It is felt that nature, inextricably organized on the pattern of man's social organization, needs purifying as man does, since both are in the same social category, and when man "keeps from being sick" he at the same time keeps nature from being sick. The rituals keep both man and nature well and strong and allow them to reproduce and the fertility cycle of both to continue.

An Analysis of the Ritual Logic of Murngin Totemism

We have now finally reached the point where we can analyze Murngin religious thought, for we have presented in detail, first, the relations of the myths to the rituals; second, the symbolization of the phenomena of nature in myth and ritual; and third, the symbolization of the social organization and its various segments in Murngin ritual. The articulation of these very complex elements of society and nature into a conceptual configuration which is Murngin totemic logic cannot be presented coherently by description alone. It will be necessary to resort to charts.

To delineate properly the logic of Murngin totemism, it is necessary first to examine what the ritual realities are in man's relations to the physical environment of northeastern Arnhem Land. We shall be concerned not so much with the obvious realities of the natural environment as with the social attitudes which man has in relation to the various aspects of this environment; both concepts are comprised in the single statement that nature acts on man and man acts on nature.

The technological behavior of man describes his realistic and logical adjustment to his environment. Within this realm of his behavior his attitudes are entirely logical, and his techniques relate him in a scientific way to nature. It will be necessary to restate a few general facts about the natural world in which the Murngin lives. This world consists of two seasons, a rainy and a dry. Man's adaptation to the former is difficult and his adaptation to the latter is comparatively simple and without effort. The total effects on man of the dry and rainy seasons, socially and physically, are felt as comparative degrees of ill-being and well-being (in behavioristic language, the effects of positive and negative stimuli.)

The Murngin definitely recognize the real relation in nature of the wet and dry seasons, and they understand that the former is necessary to produce the latter. They are also conscious of the physical as well as the social effects on man of the two seasons (see native interpretations of the two seasons and man in them, pages 368-376). The

Murngin express these effects socially in terms of values: the dry season is considered good and desirable, the rainy season undesirable but necessary to reproduce the benefits of the dry period.

The configuration of native thinking about the rainy season, evaluated under a feeling of comparative ill-being, includes thought of a scarcity of food, unpleasant physical surroundings, a minimum of creature comforts, small horde groupings because of food scarcity, little social activity, as well as the possibility of actual hunger, sickness, and privation, and even death from floods. These last possibilities are fairly remote but nevertheless they have occurred and are in the minds of the people as things that might happen.

The natives evaluate the dry season as one of well-being; and in the configuration of items within this general attitude are included a plenitude of foods, easy and pleasant surroundings and ample creature necessities, large horde groups, intense and enlarged social activity, and pleasant exciting behavior, such as hunting and harpooning; all of these might be summarized under things which are enjoyable and pleasant, and of a positive nature.

Control of the seasons by an adaptive mechanism is necessary if man is to survive. The technology successfully adapts man only to the periods of normal and abnormal plenitude, but it does not adjust him to the abnormal period of scarcity during a long rainy season or when nature for other reasons does not provide sufficiently. Control of nature is one of the functions of totemism, and the Murngin's totemic ideology has one of its firmest and most substantial roots in the negative and positive social evaluation of nature's effects on man's physical well-being and his social groups. The aim of this control, in the light of the above statement about the Murngin's thinking on the seasons, is to endeavor to repeat the pleasant dry period and to control the wet period and minimize its effects.

In the following charts (XII and XIII) the anatomy of Murngin totemic logic as it is expressed in the Wawilak and Djunkgao constellations is analyzed, and the general relations of myth and ritual, social organization and nature as a seasonal cycle are expressed.

Chart XII: Wawilak Totemic Logic

The Wawilak myth is expressed in the rituals ordinarily by the use of four fundamental symbols: (1) the animals and countries are named; (2) the animals run away into the python pool; (3) the snake swallows the women and animals; and (4) the men obtain the rituals from the women. These underlying motifs found in the various segments of the several Wawilak rituals are expressed in the chart by the use of the arrows 1, 2, 3, and 4 which relate the myth and ritual rectangles.

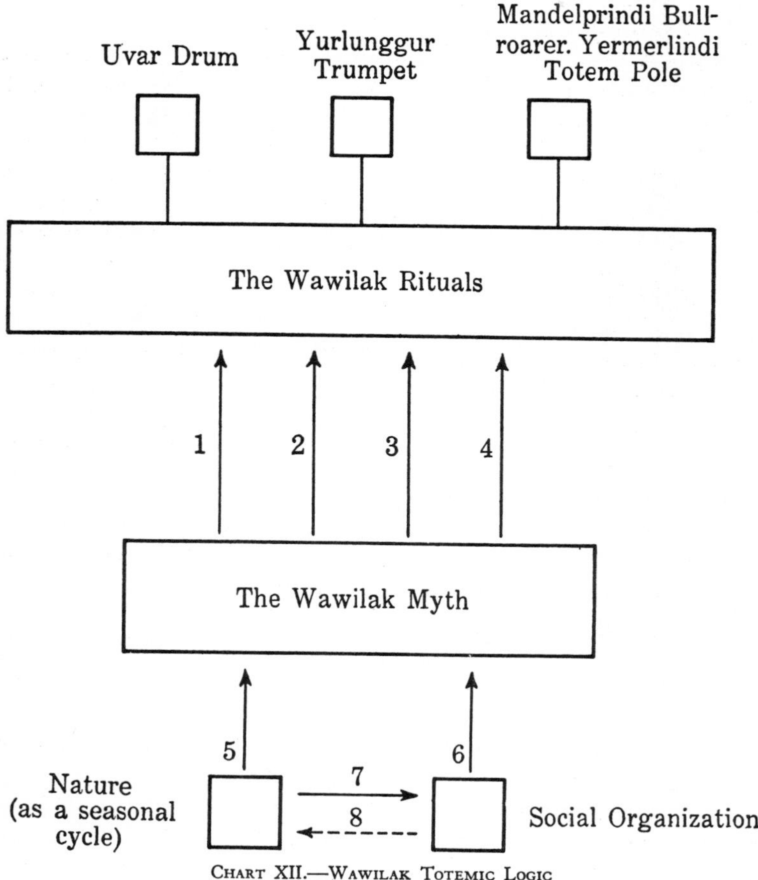

CHART XII.—WAWILAK TOTEMIC LOGIC

There is a direct relation between the myth and the seasonal cycles in the conception of the Murngin, directly symbolized in the myth. This relation is expressed by the arrow 5 leading from the square which is the seasonal cycle to the Wawilak myth. The social organization is also in direct relation with the myth, since it too is directly symbolized by it. This relation is expressed by the arrow 6 which joins the social organization to the myth.

Nature as a seasonal cycle definitely affects the activities of the social organization (see Chapter V). This is expressed by the arrow 7, relating the square of the seasonal cycles with that of the social organization. Murngin logic has it that the social organization also affects the seasonal cycle (broken arrow 8), for the rituals are believed to control the wet season. There is thus established a bilateral reciprocal arrangement in the minds of the Murngin which does not exist in reality. This bilateral reciprocal relationship between nature and the social organization is possibly due to the feeling among the Murngin for the balanced reciprocals that exist in their social relations within their social organization, and nature's relations to man are thought of accordingly.

The totemic objects at the top of the chart—the Uvar drum, the Yurlunggur trumpet, the bull roarer, and the totem pole—are manipulated by the rituals to express the symbols of the myth. The myth itself is saturated with the feelings, values and ideas which give this manipulation its meaning, and these values and meanings originate in the social organization directly as expressions of its various parts. These same meanings and values may also be direct expressions of the seasonal cycle, if it is understood that this means that the Murngin conceives the seasonal cycle to be a reality. The relations between seasonal cycle and the society are real, inasmuch as the society adjusts itself technologically to nature by means of techniques, of social values, and the meanings given to nature.

The seasonal cycle and social organization are identified as one in the myth-symbols of the Wawilak myth; and the myth-symbols are expressed and the identity of seasonal cycle and social organization is concretely stated in the manipulation of the emblems and in the rituals which surround them.

All this finally can be summarized: the totemic emblems and the ritual dances and songs express the symbols of the myth; the myth gives form to the meanings, values, and ideas of the society as one in ritual logic.

Chart XIII: Djunkgao Totemic Logic

The Narra and Djunkgao logic is a repetition of the Wawilak configuration. The totemic emblems, ritual, myth, seasonal variations, and social organization have the same set of relations and are organized into an analogous pattern which functions in the same manner in the general society. The differences which exist are: (1) the Djunkgao myth varies in detail and choice of manifest symbols (the totems are different, for example), and (2) the structure of the Djunkgao myth is not as well formalized and compact as is that of the Wawilak. The myth-symbols are: (1) the movements of the tides and floods; (2) the naming of animals and country; (3) the incestuous relations; and (4) the stealing of the totems.

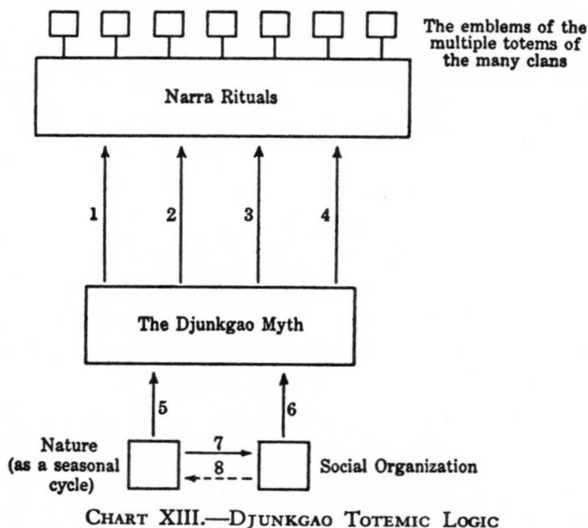

Chart XIII.—Djunkgao Totemic Logic

It is now necessary, in our examination of the logical methods of the Murngin as expressed in the fundamental pattern of their totemism, further to break down the elements found within the configuration and to look at them in the light of thought processes. To do this I have had the good fortune to be supplied with the method worked out by C. K. Ogden and I. A. Richards in their brilliant book, *The Meaning of Meaning.* Unless the reader is familiar with their technique of thought analysis it will be wise for him to read carefully the summary of their method in the accompanying footnote.[5]—Let us examine Chart XIV.

[5] See Ogden, C. K., and Richards, I. A., *The Meaning of Meaning* (Harcourt, Brace and Company, New York, 1927). The authors present their analysis of logical and illogical thinking in our society and the relation of language to it. They use a triangle to illustrate their thesis: the words used in the language are placed at the left-hand basal corner and related to the idea which is being expressed by a solid line running from the base to the apex. The idea is connected with the thing referred to (referent) by a

Chart XIV: Social Logic of Murngin Totemism

In triangle (a) the Wawilak ritual is found at the left-hand base of the triangle, the snake-swallowing-the-women symbol at the apex, and social organization at the right-hand basal corner. The line connecting the Wawilak ritual and social organization is both solid and broken. Certain ideas or meanings of the ritual, concretely expressed in song

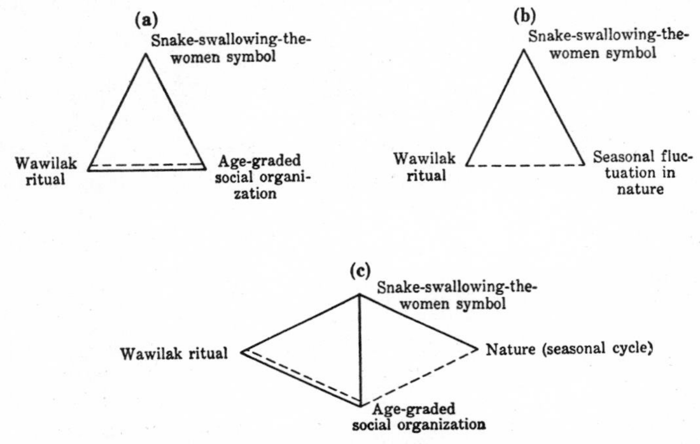

CHART XIV.—SOCIAL LOGIC OF MURNGIN TOTEMISM

and dance, relate the ritual to social organization; the meanings, however, are not to be found directly, but are expressed in the concepts of the myth. The social meanings expressed in the ritual are given symbolic form in the myth ideas.

It is felt that by manipulating the trumpet totem, one is manipulating the society (cleansing it), but the meaning of this societal cleansing can be apprehended only in the symbols and ideological relations found in the myth itself. There is also a real direct relation, inasmuch

solid line running from the apex to the right-hand base of the triangle. This, according to Ogden and Richards, illustrates the method of logical thinking; the process by which the words used and the things referred to are properly connected by thought.

The thing referred to and the words used are connected by a broken line running from the two sides to form the base of the triangle. The broken line indicates that frequently an illogical direct connection is made between the word used and its referent. The authors brilliantly demonstrate that this is a phenomenon found not only among the illiterate, but quite characteristic of the greater part of our theological philosophical thought.

Bronislaw Malinowski's article on Trobriand language further elaborates the Ogden and Richards method of analysis. (See Appendix to *Meaning of Meaning.*)

as the thing to which the ritual refers (the male group) is directly participating in the ritual. However, when the male group is thought of as the snake symbol, the rest of the triangle is necessary to explain the thought processes.

In triangle (b) the relation of the Wawilak ritual to the seasonal fluctuation of nature is expressed. The Wawilak ritual is related by a solid line to the snake-swallowing-the-women symbol, as is the symbol to the seasonal alternation. The line connecting ritual and seasonal fluctuation is broken because the Murngin's assumption that they manipulate the variations of the weather is illogical. Triangle (b) hides the basic essentials of Murngin totemic thought because it expresses only part of the symbolism and abstracts this part from its social context.

Triangle (c) expresses the whole conceptual pattern. It combines (a) and (b) and analyzes their relations. The myth-symbol of the snake and women is directly related to both social organization and the weather or nature. Although the Murngin are aware of the connections that exist between the dry season of plenitude and the high degree of social euphoria and the rainy season of want and social dysphoria, their totemic thinking is not concerned with the empirical technological realities. The line from social organization to weather is broken to indicate that the Murngin assume a direct false causal relation between the good or bad behavior of society and the state of nature. If society, it is thought, can properly care for itself in a mundane as well as in a spiritual way, the fluctuation of nature can take care of itself likewise.

Society's technological adaptation to nature with its alternation of adaptive seasonal mechanisms is expressed in the weather symbols with all the feelings and meanings which are a part of this adaptive behavior. The social organization which also undergoes considerable periodic alteration is expressed by the snake-swallowing-the-women symbols. In reality the two aspects of society are being ritualized: the social relations of man to nature and of man to man. It is man's adjustment to nature and his relations to it which are important to totemism, rather than nature as an objective reality. The totemic design symbolizes the idea of the whole group in its intra-relations, and the concept of the group and its relation to nature. The purpose of the ceremonies is to control man's relations with the changes of nature; and the effect is to subordinate, for a time at least, smaller groups to larger integrations, to prevent open conflict, and to express the relations of the various internal groups (clan, age grades, moieties and subsections) to each other.

The totemic emblem itself is not an absolute necessity for the expression of the two fundamental meanings of the Wawilak snake-women symbol, since the rituals themselves can express the meanings by dance and song, by the symbolic movements of the body and the use of certain sacred words; but in Murngin religion the totemic design and the totem serve as unifying symbols for the remainder and give concreteness and definiteness to the other symbolic actions of the ceremonies.

The other myth-symbols of the Wawilak ritual configuration could be analyzed in the same way as the snake-swallowing-the-women concept, as well as the Narra, since the several parts of Chart XV could be broken down into the same logical arrangements as Chart XIV.

Chart XV: Nature and Social Organization in Their Relation to Totemism

It is now possible to generalize on the whole of Murngin ritual logic and explain at least some of its meanings. Central oblong 1 of Chart XV is the Wawilak symbol of the snake swallowing the women, or the Djunkgao myth-symbols. Rectangle 2 represents the dramatic rituals which are organically related to the two myths. This rectangle has been redivided to represent the various ritual units which make up the two myth constellations. Rectangle 3 is nature as a seasonal fluctuation or reproductive cycle, et cetera, and is symbolized by the respective myths. Rectangle 4 is the total Murngin group with its age-graded clans and moieties.

The solid lines lettered A, B, and C express the direct connection between the myth-symbols and the two referents, nature and social organization. The thing that is important to notice is that in the general thought there is a syncretistic association of social organization and nature through the connection of the myth and the symbols. The Murngin logic to this point is verifiable and grounded in reality, provided one grants them their choice of symbols and realizes that thus far there is no attempt to connect the two referents; but at this point we must turn to the broken arrow *a*. The Murngin in their logic of controlling nature assume that there is a direct connection between social units and different aspects of nature, and that the control of nature lies in the proper control and treatment of social organization. Properly to control the social organization, the rituals must also be held which rid society of its uncleanliness. The society is disciplined by threat of what will happen to nature, the provider, if the members of the group misbehave. This brings on an identification of the social organization with nature, and they are treated as one and expressed as such in the rituals. It can be seen that if one can manip-

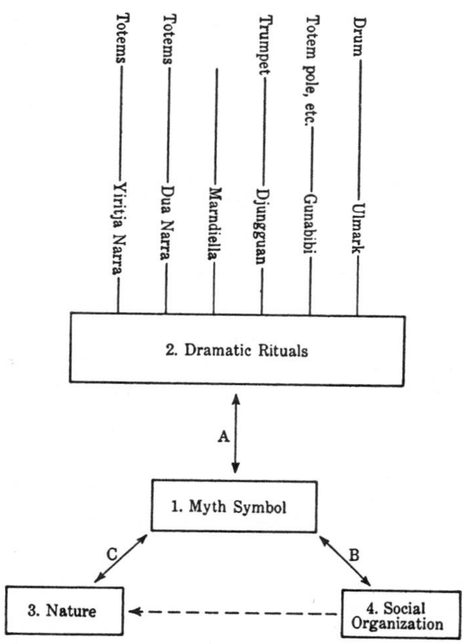

CHART XV.—NATURE AND SOCIAL ORGANIZATION IN THEIR RELATION TO TOTEMISM

ulate the various totems such as the bull roarer, trumpet, and drum through the operation of the concepts of the myths, one cleanses society and by so doing forces nature to function properly. The ritual, then, from the totemic point of view, is a series of manipulations of the totem or the totemic symbols through the use of a set of symbolic actions woven into relationship by song, dance, and word expressions. The rituals relate various parts of the group to each other by use of larger symbols which incorporate smaller ones into configurations that form a unified whole.[6]

[6] See Warner, W. L., *The Living and the Dead* (Vol. V, Yankee City Series), Yale University Press, New Haven, 1959, for further development of theory about sacred symbols; in this case, Christian.

CHAPTER XII

MORTUARY RITES

I. General Summary of the Nature of Murngin Mourning Rites

The very elaborate Murngin mortuary rite is the final rite of passage in the life cycle of the individual. The first rite of passage occurs at the individual's "birth," i.e., when the father is mystically informed of the child's arrival in his mother's womb; here the emphasis is on the male parent's changed status in the community by virtue of his consummation of a family of procreation. It is only when he is a big boy that the male child becomes the center of attention in a rite of passage; he then, through an initiatory ritual by which he becomes a part of the sacred world and partially participant in its functions, changes his status from one socially equivalent to a woman's to that of a "young man." The mark is left upon him by the removal of his foreskin at the climactic rite which is purificatory and associated with the reproductive attributes of nature (see Djungguan, et cetera). At later transitions in his age grading he goes through further initiations, *all of which increase his status within the general community by enlarging his contact with the world of the sacred and the totemic spirit.* In his increasing knowledge of the totem and in his participation in the sacred rituals, myths, and mana of the totem he has his attention fixed on the center and focal point of all totemic sacredness, the totemic well. This increase of status in life by ritual initiation is the general age-grade structure. When he is socially an old man h sees the highest grade of totem which lies deepest in the water of the totemic well. There is nothing more he can do in life to come into a deeper and more fundamental contact with the sacred; but death, the final rite of passage, transfers him from all the world of the profane and puts him (his soul) entirely into the world of the sacred with the totem in the totemic well. The age grading, then, throughout his life has been a gradual increase in his sacred participation, with a consequent lessening of his social participation within the profane (since he gives an increasing proportion of his time to ritual activities), until finally he returns to where he first originated, the totemic well.

The father's dream at a child's birth is an expression of the relation of the ordinary to the sacred, since the dream announces a soul's entering the world of the living; and the mortuary ceremony is a ritualization of the relation of the once living soul[1] and also of his mourning kin to the world of the sacred and the dead. The mourning rites symbolize the relationship of these two realms in the beliefs of the Murngin.

This chapter will first describe, without interpretation except that of the natives, the mortuary rituals and afterwards present interpretative conclusions. It might be stated that when all the field material which is given here was collected the author had no idea of where the facts led, and it was only by an analysis of the material and by relating it to the rest of the social configuration that the general ideas concerning the aboriginal mourning rites were discovered.

II. Murngin Death, Mortuary and Mourning Ceremonies and Customs

When it is believed that a man is very close to death his relatives gather about him and wail; some of them, in a plaintive voice, sing the garma water cycle of songs of his moiety and clan, the leader usually beating time on his singing sticks. The dying man is supposed to listen to these songs and to follow their suggestions; if he cannot understand what is being said, it is believed that the spirit of his marikmo (father's father) or his mari will come when he hears, and talk to the soul which is about to leave the body and instruct it on what it has to do.

"We sing these songs to make that soul a good one, so he won't hurt any of us." Sometimes when a man has been speared and is still alive a song is sung over him to tell him to die in the proper manner and not allow his soul to make any difficulties for those who are alive. A man who has been badly injured in a spear fight and thinks that he is about to die likes to have this singing because it soothes his pain and removes any worry about the disposition of his soul. "That fellow who has been speared says, 'There is no time for me to live now. I am

[1] All Murngin individuals possess two souls: one (warro) which is from the totem well and important, and the other which is a trickster (mokoi).

very close to death. I had better die,' and when that spider song comes he is dead and his soul leaves him."

The songs mean "he thinks of his totem and his totem well and he wants his spirit to go straight to his well when he dies." The man may call out the sound of water or make the cry of his totem. If, for example, a Liaalaomir were near death he would cry out like a python trumpet and "like that snake when he made rain."

As the garma song cycle reaches each totemic element in the sequence, a dying Warumeri clansman is supposed to make motions in imitation of the totemic animal; for example, when the relatives sing whale he kicks to simulate the movement of a whale's body in the sea. This is indicative of his immediate death, of which he is attempting to tell his father and mother. He is becoming like his totem. The father and mother understand the symbol and know then that death is certain. When a man dies he wants the songs of his father and his father's father's people sung into his ears and listened to by his ancestors before he passes away; i.e., he wants the songs of his own clan and his own moiety sung, so that even in death accent is on the patrilineal character of his inheritance and status in life, and the place where he is going and the change in his qualities.

The man goes into a coma. He is dead now, according to Murngin thought, even though the heart still flutters. The relatives notice that it is still moving and although they realize that the life of the body is finished they understand that the grandfather or the mari (mother's mother's brother) is looking out for him. They can tell this because the old ancestor has entered into the heart where the soul of the man has lived during his lifetime. The song cycle now repeats the words about a man going inside the jungle. The heart of the dying man is now ready for this. The soul listens for that song. "It is as though that soul had gone inside the jungle country which belongs to his clan's people. His father's father is taking the soul away." The last quick breaths come and the soul comes out of his heart and out of his windpipe and finally out of his mouth. He is dead.

The song now is to make the soul such a perfect character that he will find his ancestors and go straight to his totem well. "If we didn't sing he might go bad because evil ghosts (mokois) might catch him and take him out in the jungle country where they live. It is better that his old grandfathers and his ancestors come and get him and take him straight to his clan well where his totem came from."

Even though the garma song is being sung during a man's dying moments, there is little organization of the people to give general community expression. A kind of disorganization has occurred. The women wail, but it is not the organized wailing which one finds in some of the rituals. There is a hesitancy and uncertainty about the actions of the people. The more intense latent antagonisms rise to the surface and some of the relatives may be blamed for the death. For example, when a child dies it is often thought that the father and mother have had sexual intercourse during the later months of pregnancy, which are supposed to be a period of abstinence. The other relatives of the dead child express their antagonism by picking up their spears and attempting to throw them at the offending pair. In one sense this is an organized expression, since they well know that they will be prevented by other relatives from throwing the spears.

After the first wailing at the news of the spearing or sudden death of a member of the clan or of a near relative, a stillness comes over the camp which is very noticeable to anyone accustomed to the general noisiness of all the Murngin camps after dark when the people have eaten. It is at this quiet time that the people express their desires for revenge. A near relative throws a spear on the ground and lets everyone know that he is going to avenge the death, whether it has been caused by the spear of a known enemy or the black magic of an unknown antagonist.

The female relatives of the dead man cut their heads with stone knives or spears or sharp pointed sticks to show their great sorrow. The mothers, sisters, wives, and female maris are the relatives who show the greatest amount of grief and cut themselves the most. A few hours after the death of a man or woman the relatives belonging to his clan, led by the father if he is alive, paint the design of his clan well upon him. For example, if he were a Warumeri or Wangurri clansman he would have the duck well painted upon him. The painting and design are exactly the same as those placed on the body of a young boy when he is being circumcised, and on the body of an adolescent boy after he has seen his totemic emblem. Red ocher is painted all over the body first and then the totemic design is painted on the chest and abdomen and face. The hair is covered with white clay after most of it has been cut off or plucked out to be made into a sacred hair belt. "We pull out the hair of the dead man a few hours after he dies and put red ocher on his head after we do this. We make a hair belt from his hair and look for red parrot feathers to put on it.

Any relative can make a hair belt for the dead man but the dead man's brother gives that belt to their kutara or mari. Sometimes the brother keeps it. That belt is very good in a fight. It makes you very strong. If you wear that one in a fight you can throw a spear that will go straight and kill that man you throw it at. This belt is good for ceremonies."

The painting, according to native thought, is so done that the old ancestors can see which totem well the dead man belonged to and carry the soul immediately to its proper resting place. The old dead marikmo is supposed to announce loudly, "Oh, that is my young maraitcha." The evil mokois say, "No, this one belongs to us. We are going to take him." They argue about it, but the design upon the dead man definitely places him in the hands of his proper ancestors who prevent him from getting into the clutches of the evil mokois and take him back to his totem well.

When a man dies his relatives move their camp some little distance away from the grave. Some of them call out, usually the mother, "If you want to see us you can come back now. Don't come back by and by." She is talking to the mokoi spirit rather than the warro spirit (soul) of the man. (See footnote, page 403.) When the mokoi spirit leaves the dead all the mokois of the many men who have died before make noises in the jungle. These evil spirits are calling out to this newly released spirit of the dead man. They make sounds as if they were coughing, for this is the way that mokois talk. They are saying, "Where is our son and our grandson?" The leader of the mourning ceremony calls out when these sounds are heard and the mokoi spirit of the dead man is supposed to come away from his body. The people carry fire sticks and go out to the jungle. There are two lines of them; they join in the center of the dance area, and the spirit is supposed to be in the sac-like space between them. The leader takes a fire stick from a man. He puts the fire stick against his chest and no one can see what he is doing. He runs and shows the fire. This is supposed to drive the spirit into the jungle and to finish his life with the living. It is thought by some that this is for the good soul and by other informants that this is for the bad soul, "and by some it is not believed at all." "We did that for Narnarngo's wife when she died. Marupila and I carried fire and we did not see that spirit. We said to ourselves, 'That whole thing is a lie. You can't see a mokoi that way.' Another time when I wanted to see a mokoi with my own eyes I tried at Elcho

Island when a man died but I could see no spirit. I think that is a lie."

The father of the dead man or some other near relative has a large cake of palm-nut bread made by the women and divides this food among the members of his own moiety and those of the mother's group. This is supposed to force the dead soul to leave because he is not participating with the rest in the communion. Everyone is afraid to have the soul linger about the camp because it might go looking for fish and turtle and other animal food and frighten these animals away so that the living could not kill them.

The father or other relatives then build a small fire, gather and place on it bunches of green leaves until they are smoking, and then brush them over the bodies of all the people, both male and female, who are relatives of the dead person, with the purpose of chasing away the soul of the dead. This ceremony may be involved with a considerably longer ritual or may consist of the mere brushing of the smoking leaves on the bodies of the relatives.

After the garma fire ritual, mokul bapa, yeppa and mari (male and female) talk among themselves and then to the body and to its dead mari's and old marikmo's souls which are supposed to be by it. "Don't you cause trouble and get angry with us. We are only going to keep this dead man a little while, then we are going to give him to you and you can keep him, but don't you cause trouble." Sometimes the father or near relative dreams that the old grandfather has come to him and has said that he now should be in control of the new soul and wants that soul immediately.

The Garma or Main Camp Ceremony.—Since the various types of garma rituals are interwoven in all parts of the mourning ceremonies it seems best to digress a moment and describe all of them at once. The garma type of ceremony is found among all the clans of the tribes studied (except possibly the Liagaomir and Naladaer clans). The garmas are primarily for mortuary ceremonies but can be used for circumcisions. There is a considerable geographical variation in the kinds of garmas, particularly between those of the tribes centered around the western shores of the Gulf of Carpentaria and those among the peoples along the Glyde River. There is also a clan variation, since the various clans include in their cycle of songs objects which are of immediate significance to the clan. The clan variation is very slight, however, and usually for the purpose of including references to the totemic well and the objects surrounding it. There is a rather considerable individual variation, since some leaders will include many more items than others. The material presented here has been selected more or less on the basis of including the normal songs and of what the most informed Murngin considered the ideal way of expressing them. Selections have been made from the clans in the east and west and include garma songs of both moieties in the two regions.

The Warnt-djer (leaf), a garma type of ceremony for the removal of the spirits of the dead, is found among both the Yiritja and Dua clans, except the Liagaomir, Naladaer and Ding Ding. The mast ceremony (mar-ai-yir-ri) is found among the eastern Yiritja clans, including the Gunalbingu, the Warumeri, the Kolpa, Wangurri, Darlwongo, Birkili, Komaits, Burilung, Kiki and Maradunggimi. The Barnumbir or Morning Star ceremony is used only by the Dua clans; it has a general distribution. The western Dua groups use Yurlunggur in their garma ceremonies; the eastern people do not. The cockatoo or ni-erk type of ceremony is found only among the Yiritja clans of both the east and west. The Nierk ceremony is used for the raising of the hollow log coffin and at times for a circumcision which would come immediately after putting up the hollow log. This sequent association of mourning and circumcision rites has a rather important interpretative significance.

The garma type of songs and ceremonies as well as the Narra has a central core of ritual which is known as the land- and sea-ways. Each moiety has a land-way cycle of garma songs and a sea-way cycle. The sea-way cycle describes the movement of the tide and the sea into the land, up through the tidal rivers, and into the small lakes. The sea-way describes a canoe coming on with the tide. Various activities take place in bringing the canoe in and beaching it. The occupant of the canoe is a Wongar man. Various occurrences while the canoe is coming in show the rise of the tide and its flow into the land. The ritualistic songs and occasional dances in this sea-way cycle express the intimate relations of man to his natural environment, and transmute nature into man's social structure and social values, and man into nature's order. The land-way cycle is the exact opposite of the sea-way. It describes the clouds gathering in the high country, the rain coming from the clouds, the rivulets running into the creeks, the creeks into the larger rivers, and the great rainy-season flood going to the sea. The various creatures associated with this natural phenomenon are brought into the sequence of songs.

Eastern Yiritja Sea Tide Garma Cycle of Songs and Dances.—The members of the clan and the close relatives, including the wives and their near relatives, gather around a symbolic well, a basin about two feet in diameter scraped out of the ground. The ceremonial leader of the clan beats his singing sticks and directs the singing. The sacred totemic names of the clan well of the dead are sung over it to make it the "well" of the dead. The song, which has a wailing quality, is designed to send the soul away from the group and into the totemic well, and to force the trickster spirit out into the jungle. It also helps purify the living group.

All possessions of the people which are in intimate relation to the body, such as wearing apparel, spear-throwers, spears, tobacco, and the like, are placed in the well. This singing takes place not only in the camps where a man has died, but also in any other camp where his near relatives are living at the time. Certain members of the clan agree among themselves to go out hunting, particularly for the animals which belong to the totem, while other members of the group are selected to sing the garma songs.

The eastern cycle of songs follows:

(1) An island far out in the sea.
(2) Lightning that strikes out in the middle ocean and in the east.
(3) Black cloud (mo-dais).
(4) A wind coming in from the sea.
(5) Calm sea water (ran-gu-ra).
(6) Heavy waves on the surface of the sea (man-bui-na).
(7) A small bird, not identified, that dives into the sea for fish (ba-lin-ta-pi).
(8) Kingfish (guin-go-lo).
(9) A flat white fish (yar-war-i).
(10) Whale.

"That one who throws water like rain" (wi-ma-ri, nal-lan-gi, and mar-ping-o). (The last two names are esoteric.)

(11) Diamond fish (ring-ga).
(12) Crocodile.

"The crocodile sings lightning when it comes in the east and that's when the crocodile lays his eggs and that's when the sting ray gets fat and good to eat. When that lightning comes and the rain comes that makes the sting ray fat, that makes the crocodile lay his eggs. Before that time the sting ray has no fat and he is not worth eating."

(13) A plank floating on the tide and coming toward the shore (pa-pung, probably a Malay word).
(14) A hollow log floating on the incoming tide (u-lo-ba-ri).
(15) A small oyster found on the plank (rar-i-tji).
(16) Coconuts floating on an incoming tide (ta-on-gil).
(17) The country where the coconut, hollow log, and plank come from.
"We don't know what that country is. No people are there. We only sing it because the old old people sang it that way."
(18) The back of a turtle (near land) (go-ar-tji).
(19) The head of a tortoise-shell turtle (wil-ar-a).
(20) People where the coconuts come from—the east (ki-lur-o).
(21) Paddle (mar-ra-la).
(22) Canoe (li-pal-pa).
(23) Noise the paddle makes on the gunwale (ma-la-o-ma).
(24) A small bird crying out on the beach when it sees the people coming in from the canoe (go-lo-wit-pit).
(25) Paddle (mar-ra-la).
(26) The paddles being thrown on the beach.
(27) Canoe rolling about on the beach with the sea hitting against it.
(28) Men walking along on the beach.
(29) Men looking for turtle eggs in the sand beach.
(30) Men following the tracks of turtles going toward the nest.
(31) The turtle nest (ka-tji-ng).
(32) Turtle eggs.
The men are drinking the white of the turtle egg (i-di-ka).
(33) Basket (kan-nan-gir).
The men are putting the eggs in the basket.
(34) Putting the basket on the shoulder and carrying it down to the shade.
(35) Putting the eggs down in the shade.
(36) Walking fast down the large path to the well.
(37) Cleaning the dirt and refuse out of the well.
(38) Washing oneself with the water because of the dirt on the body from cleaning out the well.

It is at this place in the song sequence that some of the men get into the symbolic basin, the water from the melon shells is poured over them, they wash and cover themselves with red ocher. These are men to whom the dead relative has appeared in a dream. They are washing away his soul because it would make them sick. "You have a good friend of yours who is dead a little while ago; you feel very sorry. At night you go to sleep. You dream and he comes to see you. You sing this garma song the way we do this. You won't worry any more. You won't dream any more. But suppose you didn't have these songs, that spirit would come and make you sick and maybe kill you.—When we dream of our dead relative we ask our brothers to sing for us while we go hunt for turtle. We come back, get all our things, our spears and our dilly bags and our belts, put them in the well and sing over them."

(39) Taking off ornaments and drying them on the well.
(40) Going back to the turtle beach, cleaning off dirt under the big trees. (The leaves are now brought in for the fire and smoke ritual.)
(41) Gathering wood for a fire.
(42) Fire burning.
(43) Coals of a fire smoking.
(44) People are sleepy and they sleep.
(45) Waking up.
(46) Smoking a cigarette.
"The smoke goes up from the tobacco (na-rai-li)."
(47) Red cloud (ri-pa).
That smoke went up into the sky and made a red cloud. The red cloud song indicates the singing is completed.

Eastern Dua Sea Cycle of Songs.—The eastern Dua clans, namely, those found around Buckingham and Arnhem Bays along the western shores of the Gulf of Carpentaria, possess the following sequence of garma songs and dances. The first song usually sung in this area is about a Wongar yolno, who was paddling a canoe out in the ocean.

(1) Wongar yolno (mi-tja-lo).
(2) Black sea grass (dji-o-el).
(3) A sea bird (dja-rok).
(4) A very small fish (yint-gar).
(5) A salt-water snake (yar-luer).
(6) Salt-water turtle (ka-ri-wa).
(7) A floating hollow log (wir-o-ko).
(8) The tide going out (ka-pu-mon-oak).
(9) The tide is standing still far out (ka-pu u-tu nor-o-tin kan-ga).
(10) Burial log (dai-mer-i).
"He walks around on the bottom of the sea, he is a Wongar. We only see him at night and he looks like a hollow log."
(11) "The man [Wongar yolno] is coming to the shore now. The tide is rolling the canoe in and it is high tide" (tur-ri-u-na, "pumping out that canoe").
(12) Paddle (ma-tin): danced by women.
They carry the paddles on their shoulders, put them in the shade. The yolno is supposed to be walking around now look-

ing for turtle eggs. He looks down and finds the nest, puts the eggs in the basket, returns to the shade, and sits down.

(13) Ring around the fire (ko-mer-nin-na).
This is a ring of men around a fire. The Wongar yolno has brought in some fire wood and broken it up and made a fire to cook the turtle eggs.

At this place in the ceremony they take the green branches of a tree, put them in the fire, and the men ceremonially brush the smoking branches over the heads and chests of all participants and near relatives of the man who has died. "That spirit of the dead man goes away now. That means the souls of our own people, not our enemies."

(14) The man sits down and goes to sleep, wakes up and goes away.
(15) He takes fire sticks, walks around and puts fire to the grass, which makes a big bush fire. The fire smoke goes up into the heavens, into the clouds. The dancers, while this is going on, dance with fire sticks in their hands.
(16) The Wongar snake in the sky (u-var-ko).
(17) Another large snake (dar-pa).
(18) Caterpillar.
(19) The fire which has been built is in a small basin (symbolic totemic water hole). It is a snake camp.

On one side are two lines of snake dancers, one Uvarko and the other Darpa. Facing them on the other side of the fire are two lines of caterpillar dancers. (The caterpillars are classed as snakes among the Murngin.) To one side of the fire and between the two lines of dancers are the iguanas. While the snakes and caterpillars dance back and forth beside the fire the iguanas stamp on the fire and put it out. The snakes are supposed to be going to fight, but the extinction of the fire in the totem well by the iguanas means that all the people in this country are one people. Each dancer carries a basket in his mouth to symbolize a fighting man, and each carries a spear shaft or stick and moves it to represent the head of a snake.

(20) Hermit crab.
The men hold bushes up in front of themselves and hit their chests, keeping time to the rhythm.

(21) Blow fly (wor-or-lorl).
The dancers simulate the buzzing of the fly and move their hands back and forth to imitate the vibration of its wings.

(22) A shore bird (por-leur-or).
One of the dancers moves his legs rapidly up and down and

stamps on the ground and flutters his arms up and down to indicate the bird is flying away.

(23) Morning star (bar-num-bir).
Everyone carries fire sticks. The dancers move back and forth before the leader of the ceremony, moving the fire sticks up and down in the darkness. Moving them up is supposed to represent darkness, and down, daylight.

The Morning Star Ceremony. —The morning star ceremony is Dua. The song cycle starts with Barnumbir (morning star):

Gar-le-in-bui
  East
Yal-main-aoi
  Morning star
Djan-gir-ir
  Morning star
Ma-rang-in
  Morning star

Chorus: Aa-ee kai kai kai kai

Barnumbir yea-a-a

Gar-le-in-bui
  East
Yal-main-aoi
  Morning star
Djan-gir-ir
  Morning star
Ma-rang-in
  Morning star

Chorus: Kai kai kai kai

Yo yo-o-o

If the first song is at night, the men dance with firebrands, and if in the afternoon, with bunches of white cockatoo feathers tied to strings. The leader and chorus stand off at the side. The chorus are supposed to be mokois.

(2) Mokois (gurn-dju-la); the chorus is then repeated.
(3) Mokoi food, a small tuber.
(4) Butterfly (burn-ba).

The butterfly is closely associated with the morning star and lives on top of it.

(5) A small paper-bark tree, sung because the morning star and the mokois light on top of it in their flight over the jungles.

(6) Bat (gar-nat-bin).

"This one flies on top of the sky with the mokois at night time. We are afraid when we hear that noise at night that this bat makes because he has got mokois with him."

(7) Ibis, the black variety.

"When the mokois walk around they look at that ibis, and he looks at them, and we can tell when they are around because he looks at them."

(8) The name of the land on the western shores of the Gulf of Carpentaria (Cape Wilberforce) where the morning star first lights.

(9) Fire.

(10) An unidentified bird closely associated with the mokois.

(11) The darpa snake.

(12) The flower of the paper-bark tree.

(13) The bark of this tree.

"The Morning Star is going into the bush now. This tree bark wrapped around the corpse makes that spirit feel good."

(14) A small parrakeet.

This is sung because he eats the flowers in the trees.

(15) The slender long-headed type of honeybee.

(16) Crow.

(17) Pandanus basket in which the honey is placed.

(18) Grass, the kind that is dipped into the honey to eat it.

(19) Boomerang.

(20) Spear-thrower and stone spear.

(21) Kangaroo, the Dua variety.

(22) A small unidentified bird.

(23) Rock python.

(24) Rain.

(25) A rock ledge.

(26) Pandanus.

(27) The long type of yam, Dua variety.

(28) Mosquito.

(29) Rain.

"That rain makes the yam and everything grow up and good."

(30) The rope for a harpoon.

(31) The paddle used in a harpooning expedition.

(32) Porpoise.

(33) Sea grass that the turtle eats.

(34) Rain.
(35) The hollow log coffin.
(36) Small fish.
"He is that fish that goes inside the woman. It is a very small one. He floats around in the water and goes inside that hollow log."
(37) Salt-water snake with a flat tail (yarl-lur).
(38) Low tide.
(39) A stone fire.
(40) Cutting up the turtle.
(41) Lighting the fire.
(42) Smoke from the fire going into the clouds.
(43) The cloud where the snake lives.
(44) Rain.
(45) A small bird.
(46) A man standing on a rock burning off the top of the rock.
(47) Barnumbir.

The Dua Land or Flood Cycle

(1) A Wongar yolno walking around.
(2) Stone spear.
"That spear belongs to him."
(3) Spear-thrower.
(4) Wongar yolno sneaking up to kill that kangaroo.
(5) He kills that kangaroo and carries him on his back.
(6) He is sitting down now cutting him up and eating him.
(7) Red cloud.
"That is the blood that belongs to this kangaroo."

The kangaroo element in the song sequence can be removed according to the totem clan and some other animal such as turtle put in its place. Killing of the kangaroo refers to death, and cutting up the kangaroo is a reference to the exhumation of the body after death.

(8) Fire stick.
(9) Walking away.
(10) A honey basket.
(11) Carrying the honey basket.
(12) Biting the honey basket and spitting it out.
"That is to make rain."
(13) A small parrakeet.
(14) Stringy bark flower.
(15) The Dua honeybee.
(16) Wasp.

(17) Big-eared lizard.
(18) Caterpillar.
(The honeybee, wasp, lizard and caterpillar are totemic objects in the Dua moiety.)
(19) A sea gull.
(20) Barnumbir ceremonial string.
(21) Crow.
(22) Small stringy-bark tree.
(23) A small black stone found in the bush.
(24) Boomerang.
This is sung because the boomerang is associated with people in the farther interior.
(25) The tide carrying the man [Wongar yolno] down to the sea.
(26) A beach on the ocean.
(27) A bark water carrier.
(28) Making it.
(29) Pulling up water from a totem well, washing himself.
As in the other garma cycles, the various relatives ceremonially wash themselves in the symbolic totemic well.
(30) Leaving the well.
(31) Making a stick with human hair on top of it "which is just the same as the stringy-bark flower, and that flower is all the same as a man's hair."
(32) Putting the stick in the ground with other sticks like it and dancing. This offers an opportunity for the Barnumbir morning star ceremony.
(33) Putting a white feathered string on the sticks.
(34) Making a fire to cook food.
(At this part of the singing the men are brushed with smoking leaves and sometimes dance with firebrands stuck in their armpits so that the smoke pours over them.)
(35) A very low tide.
(36) A hollow tree lying on the beach.
Reference is to the hollow log in which the bones are placed.
(37) Pelican.
The pelican's bill is supposed to be a net which catches the soul (see makarata dances).
(38) Fish net.
The fish net is the same as the pelican.
(39) Salmon fish.
(40) Mullet.
(41) Dua fish.
Fish are supposed to be the souls of dead men caught in the nets.

(42) Wallaby carrying a spear and looking for fish.
The wallaby and kangaroo are always said to act like men and frequently symbolize man. "Kangaroo was a man at that time. He was just the same as we proper people that first time."
(43) The sun.
"The sun and that wallaby have gone into the bush, way inside, to make a camp."
(44) Shade in the western sky; the sun is in the east.
(45) A shade comes back this way.
(46) A kangaroo comes along with the shade.
(47) Afternoon.
"Sing Kangaroo jumping around slowly in the afternoon and going back again to the jungle."
(48) Wongar yolno.
"He goes back to his house in the bush too. He cleans the leaf away and makes him a good camp."
(49) Spear and mangel.
"He picks his spear and mangel up and dances."
(50) Red cloud.
The element used to finish the ceremony.

The red cloud is also supposed to appear in the skies just before night falls, and that is the reason, according to the Murngin, why it is used to symbolize the end of the ceremony.

Yiritja Garma Land or Flood Cycle

(1) Black rain cloud.
"That cloud is ready for rain to fall down."
(2) A very heavy rain falling down.
(3) Water running down in a small creek.
"That water is running in a larger stream."
(4) Brook in the rain season when it is swollen with floods.
(5) Fresh-water turtle.
"When the fresh water starts running up high this fresh water turtle swims along with it just like he has come up out of the ground through the spring water."
(6) Leech.
"His house is in the fresh water and he wriggles around. He is always with fresh-water turtle."
(7) Hollow log.
"This running water has thrown it across the stream and that log has stuck there"—an indirect reference to the log used for the interment of the bones.

(8) Grass used for armlets.

"The grass is growing up now because of that water."

(9) Barrimundi.

"Barrimundi is in the lily place; Barrimundi has come out from the salt water to meet the schools of fresh-water fish coming down from the bush."

(10) A small red bird with a white breast.

"That bird is looking for fish, he eats minnows and he likes lice."

(11) Slow water.

"The water is running slower now. It stops quiet and is not running the way it did."

(12) A man walking along the side of the creek.

(13) Nierk cockatoo.

"He is up in the tree and he is looking at that man and he is calling out at him"—again a reference to the mokoi soul (cockatoo) and the man walking around below who is the warro.

(14) A small bird which eats ants, butterflies and insects.

(15) The warnba's nest.

"We also sing yea for that bird when we sing that. When that small bird grows up his mother will teach him how to sing and say our language. We people talk, that bird answers back. He talks like a man."

(16) A variety of ibis.

"He is standing up looking for the fish and he sees them jumping about. He tries to catch them but he can't." The ibis is also associated with the mokois, and the fish with the true soul, and this again is an indirect reference to the attempts of the mokois to steal the true soul and prevent it from entering into the totem well.

(17) A man and woman walking around on the plain.

"They are Yiritja people."

(18) Spear fight.

"Everybody is running back and forth fighting"; a fight takes place between the ancestors and the living, a ritualistic spear fight.

(19) Crocodiles.

When a makarata is going to be fought or the time when a near fight is on, some of the fighters paint themselves with white lines to symbolize crocodiles.

(20) Fresh-water turtle.

(21) Wild dog.

The wild dog is also in this fight.

(22) A cockatoo flock.

"They see these fighting people and they fly up out of the trees, singing out."

(23) A man and woman looking for lilies.

"They are looking at the black duck in the lily places." This is a reference to the totem of the Warumeri, Wangurri, and Ritarngo Yiritja people.

(24) All the people going down to look for lilies (Yiritja people only).

(25) Mud taken up looking for lilies.

(26) Washing the lilies in the water to remove the mud.

(27) Washing themselves off after the mud has got on them.

This element in the sequence is often used for the ceremonial washing in the symbolic totemic well.

(28) Lilies in a basket.

(29) Walking from the lily place "to go look for a dry place to sit down."

(30) Taking a fire stick and burning the grass (Yiritja grass) to make a place for a camp. The burning leaves may be used to be brushed over the bodies of the mourners.

(31) Grass burning rapidly over the plains—a direct reference to burning the grass to facilitate hunting and to clear the paths, and an indirect reference to the smoke ceremony which chases away not only the mokois but the true soul of the dead.

(32) Rats.

"The rats are on the plain and they are running away from the fire. They are singing and are crying out." The rats have an inner meaning which refers to the souls of the dead leaving.

(33) Words and talk.

"The people are sitting down in the shade now and talking. They are talking about the sun going down."

(34) Spider.

"The spiders come out in the cool when the sun goes down. The spider puts up his web from tree to tree. He takes his string one place and goes to another place."

This ends the sequence of songs. At this point in the ceremony a man comes out and dances in front of the chorus holding his legs very high and moving his hands to imitate a spider spinning a large web. The spider is definitely associated with the soul of the dead. "We sing this way because our older people sang that way. All Yiritja sing that way. Dua sing different when their dead men die. I take my songs from my mari [mother's mother's brother] and my marikmo [father's father]; they [the relatives] are Yiritja."

"We sing for that warro soul and which way he has gone. He walks around the same way we sing. That food the relatives of that dead man give me when I sing this song so I can take those smoking leaves and put them in the fire and chase that spirit away and so we can go out hunting and that spirit will not bother us."

The living relatives talk to the recent dead both before burial and after, and continue until the bones have been exhumed, painted, and placed in the hollow log for their final interment.

In preparing the body for burial by painting the totemic design of the man's clan upon its chest and abdomen, one man usually stands by with his singing sticks and leads the singing while the others paint. He sings a list of garma songs, including a list of the paints being used in decorating the body. He then sings string and bark for tying up the body in a paper-bark coffin. The singing continues while the paper bark is being placed over the body and tied into position. When this operation is completed the singer sings the red cloud element in the song sequence, which is a symbol of the end of the song and of the operation.

The Mast Ceremony.—The relatives then call out for all the people to appear. They sing a new song cycle, the first element in which is a ship's mast that belonged to a Wongar Macassar.[2] Two or more men pick up the dead body and move it up and down as though they were lifting a mast. The chorus sings "Oh—a—ha—la!!" while the "mast" is laid down. When it is picked up again they sing

"O—o—o—o—a—ha—la!
A—ha—la!!
A—ha—la!!"

"The Macassar mast was like that," said my informant while viewing a burial ceremony with me. "Macassar man sang out when he raised a mast and when he did that all of us black men ran from our camps to see him go because all of us knew then that the Macassar was ready to go away. Some people would say, 'What's the matter with those Macassars, what are they doing?' and other people would say, 'Oh, they are going to another place because their mast is standing up straight.' This is all the same as that dead man because he is ready to go away. We people say the same thing about him. 'What is the matter with him?' and it is like that dead man saying back, 'I am standing up straight now, I am going away.' It is like an old Wongar

[2] For a full account of the influence of the Malay culture on the Murngin, see Social Change in North Australia, Chapter XIV.

Macassar man saying, 'I want to go over that sundown way, my grandfather is there.' "

Two men stand over the body, each with one hand over his face and one hand thrust out straight over "the mast." The first two men continue to move the "mast" up and down. Within the circle of relatives watching the ceremony and part of the center of attention are two other men who dance as though they were pulling on ropes that raise the mast. All the people are very quiet. The singing sticks continue to beat, but they accentuate the general quietness of the group. Two men in unison say what the natives believe to be a Macassar prayer (Djel-la-war, Malay term):

"Si-li-la-mo-ha-mo ha-mo-sil-li-li,"

(A native who had been with the Macassars and who understood some English because of recent mission contact said, "This is just the same as amen.")

"Si-li-nai-yu ma-u-lai,"

("They are asking something in the clouds or maybe it is in the moon.")

"Ra-bin-a-la la-ha-ma-ha-ma,"

("They ask again for something from that man god who lives in the moon.")

"Ser-ri ma-kas-si,"

(Save man,)

"Bel-la bel-la,"

(Watch,)

"Daung,"

(Me from that danger thing.)

"The Macassar man sang that when the mast broke or when a man was about to die."

After the two men have prayed in unison, the chorus cries, "Djil-li-le!" There is a repetition of the prayer, and the chorus once more cries, "Djil-li-le!" which is supposed to be the cry of the Macassar sailors when they made the mast stand up straight and it was finally attached to the deck. The last time the Djil-li-le is cried out it is continued with Li-li-li-li, which means that the anchor is up. The singing stick now speeds up its rhythm for the putting of the sail on the mast. All the people now start a very grotesque fast dance with first one leg bent at an extreme angle high in the air, and then the other, the arms going through the motion of pulling ropes on a sail. The dancing, all of which is supposed to belong to the Wongar Macassar men, continues to the open grave, the corpse being carried as though it were a mast.

Anyone can carry the body to the grave. The pallbearer can be either Yiritja or Dua. There is only one exception theoretically to that rule, and that occurs between gawel and waku; neither can carry the other's dead body. Each must keep away from the sweat of the dead man. If either should touch the body of his dead relative, he would not be able to eat food. If he should eat food, he would get a sore in his stomach.

The garma singing and dancing that now takes place may last from the early morning until the late evening, but ordinarily it would occur only in the late afternoon. The cycle of songs sung can be either the sea or land group; sometimes both of them are sung. When the body is put in the grave the leader calls out the sacred power names, and also sings the sacred names of the totem well.

If the man were Yiritja, let us say Warumeri clansman, the leader would call out the following names:

Bir-ka bir-ka djar-a
(Ceremonial expression of the Yiritja moiety, spring water)
Bir-ka bir-ka mil-yar-ui
"A tree coming from the spring"
Bir-ka bir-ka ga-urn ga-urn
"Pebbles boiling in the spring water"
Bir-ka bir-ka ka-ka-lor-ui
"Small stones in the bottom of the spring"
Bir-ka bir-ka kar-a-ki-ar-oi
"Small valley where the spring water runs."

The corpse is then put into the grave, which is symbolically the sacred well of the dead man and his clan. The grave is about four feet deep. The corpse is placed face down and the body is laid out straight. If the knee should pull up it is straightened out. Flexed burial is not practiced here. The natives do not know why they put the body face downward.

The calling out of the sacred names is supposed to be a signal to the marikmo and mari of the deceased to come and guide the soul to the totem well. After the several cycles of songs have been sung, the leader sings out earth. The earth is symbolically neither Dua nor Yiritja, and everyone including men, women, and children, throws a certain amount of earth into the open grave. The spirit is supposed to be under the dirt but the marikmo can pick him out and take him away. The earth is heaped over the body, grass is put on top and, at times, stones. Everyone leaves then and eats his evening meal.

A man is buried by his people so that he will rot and the flesh can be prepared for removal from the bones. The people who bury their dead say they do it so they won't have to see him rot.

(In platform burial the body is placed face upward so that when the abdominal wall breaks the intestines will not fall. The platform is not torn down when a body is removed. It is always avoided thereafter, although the feeling is rather slight about it. Ordinarily women feel a greater sense of taboo about it than men. They always pass by at some little distance because "they are afraid that that mokoi is still there." The men, when they are with the women, sometimes tease them by grunting and coughing like mokois, and laugh when the women jump. The women laugh too, but usually not until later.)

The men then call out the names of the dead male mari and marikmo of the dead man. The groups, singing, quarrel with the people for what they did to the deceased, and the dead ancestors are supposed to blame the living for not taking better care of the dead person when he was alive. While this singing is going on, the chorus dances with spears and knives to simulate a fight between the living and the dead. Once more the garma cycle of songs is sung. The people then clap their hands, symbolical of the Macassar drum, and finally the red cloud element in the garma sequence is sung to indicate that the ceremony is over.

The Grave Post.—The next day, or a few days after the burial, the grave post is erected and a mast of a Macassar design is also placed over the grave. Both the grave post and the mast are carried through the camp while a Murngin version of a Macassar prayer is said over it and the chorus sing a response to the prayer. Food is begged from all the members of the camp who are not participating as near relatives in the ceremony. All the male relatives of the deceased who are later ceremonially to eat the food in ritual communion, paint themselves. The designs are those of the totem of the man who died, which usually means the totem of all the men engaged in the ceremony except those on the mother's side of the kinship group. When a Warumeri dies, for example, the men paint themselves as whales just as the dead body has been painted and as his totemic emblem and poles are painted. The post also announces to the ancestors that the body is buried beneath it.

Two basins symbolic of totem wells are made over the grave by heaping up earth into two separate compartments with channels leading out from them. The wells represented are the dead man's and those of his nati, which means that they belong to both moieties, and both sides of the man's elementary family of orientation are symbolized. These wells are made for both the Yiritja and the Dua kinsmen to eat in. All the men of the nearby clans who are relatives of the dead gather there and eat the food that has been prepared in the camp. If anyone else attempted to eat there it would cause trouble among the near kin.

The putting up of the mast over the grave symbolizes the people telling the departed one a final goodbye. The grave post, in the eyes of the natives, "is just the same as the dead body. It means that you can look at the grave post and remember where the soul has gone." Grave posts are also put up in the camps which are far distant from the grave of the dead. Additional grave posts are erected if a man is felt to be important. Children and women ordinarily would not have more than one grave post erected for them. Sometimes in the case of children no posts are erected. The grave posts of the Dua people are supposed to be symbolic of the two Wawilak sisters.

The grave of a child is usually placed within the main camp. The grave of an older person is usually at the edge of the camp. Sometimes when the people have left a grave and gone to another place a chance visitor who has not heard of the death arrives in the camp and discovers the grave. This makes matters difficult for him because he is liable to be followed and have tricks played on him by the mokoi of the dead person. There is a method, however, of fooling the evil spirit. The man who has been placed in this embarrassing position goes to a nearby tree and makes a small toy spear and spear-thrower and hides his own spears and spear-thrower in the bush. He takes the play spear and spear-thrower to the newly made grave and he addresses the mokoi, "Now don't you follow me. I am going to come back." He puts the spear and spear-thrower on the grave to prove that he will return, since no man would walk around in the bush without his spear-thrower and spears. The man then returns to his own spear and spear-thrower, and the mokoi, who has been fooled, does not follow him.

While the grave post is up and before the bones have been exhumed and placed in the hollow log, outsiders are not allowed in the immediate camp of the parents or near relatives of the deceased. At this time the house of the parents is burned, the garma dance is held, and outsiders are then allowed to enter the camp itself. The mother of the dead individual paints herself with red ocher, as does the female mari of the person. This is to remove the taboo from them so that they can go out and gather fire wood and water as well as food. Before that time they must stay in the camp. The mother is not supposed to paint herself before the grave post is put up. If she does, and puts water on herself to make the red ocher spread, the body of the dead person will not decompose but stay firm so that the bones cannot be painted and properly treated. "The mother that belongs to that dead man cries every night for him. She cries a long time, maybe until one rain is over. All the people go back now to take out that dead man. They take the paper bark off his body. It has a very strong smell. Some people don't like to see that, but some people have strong hearts. We keep the young people away and the women do not look."

Exhumation of the Bones.—After a minimum of two or three months or a maximum of a season the body is exhumed under the direction of the father or some near relative of the dead man. If it is a child and has been buried beside the house, the father pulls the house down and makes a windbreak with it. The women relatives sit on one side of the windbreak and men on the other. They sit so that the wind blows between the male and female lines. At the head of the grave a small fire is built out of wet material so that it will smoke. The smoking fire, with the aid of a strong wind, prevents the stench from being too heavy. It is believed that no one should walk through the smoke that comes from the fires and grave, for the stench of the dead would make him ill. The fires are lit not only to kill the smell of decaying flesh but also so that the wind won't blow the odor a great distance, for it is believed that the stench is consumed by the smoke. The windbreak acts as a screen in front of the women so that they cannot see what is taking place. If an adult is being disinterred the screen is placed in the same way, but the material is not from the house of the parents. The mokul bapa (father's sister) can and does sit on the side of the men.

Strips of paper bark are made ready on which to place the bones. The bark is cut into sections. The inside sections of the stringy-bark tree are broken into handfuls of waste with which to clean the bones, and water is brought in large melon shells.

The men sing the garma cycle of songs while the women dance to a monotonous syncopated rapid rhythm: alternately one arm touches the head, and the hand of the other arm is lowered to the abdomen; the feet are alternately raised toward the opposite knee. The women stop dancing and sit down in a line back of the screen. All start crying, and with stone spears or any sharp instruments they may have in their hands hit their heads to the tempo of the dance. Hitting the head is purely ceremonial in the case of most of the women. The mother and female mari really cry, the mother going into a paroxysm of tears. The mokul bapa also cries and hits herself. The father or some other near relative, while all this is going on, is opening the grave while the chorus of men continues singing. As soon as the body is found in its paper-bark wrapping, an old woman is given a spear-thrower and dances from the line of women to the grave, using the spear-thrower as though it were a paddle, while another woman emerges from the line with a spear by her side, dances toward the open grave and thrusts the spear inside it. This is done twice or oftener. The body is then taken out of the grave and the covering removed. Two of the deceased's dués (father's sister's sons) clean the bones. The father pours the water over the putrid flesh to help cleanse them.

The flesh is taken off the feet first. The skin has turned white. The bones of the feet and then the leg bones are removed. When they come to the ribs the cleaners are particularly careful because they are over the heart; they are kept at times to give as relics to the relatives of the man who has been killed by spear magic. The backbone is removed next, then the lower jaw. The head is taken off and a stick is used to thrust into the occipital opening to clean out the putrid brains. Water is poured inside the skull to wash it out and clean it again. The shoulder and arm bones and hands are then cleaned and put in the paper bark. Some of the relatives prefer to take the finger bones as relics, rather than the rib bones, since they are smaller. The men say, "I want this bone to keep because I want to remember my dead relative. I am going to take this bone. I am going to take this bone because I am going to kill somebody in a little while."

If the body has not started to rot it is often believed that the father and mother are the cause: they belonged to the same moiety and were incestuous. A man on the border line between two cultures, where the culture pattern was slightly confused, married a woman whom the natives of his tribe considered to be in his own moiety. They used to point to his children and say that their bodies would never rot. Even though the man had changed his own moiety when speaking of himself, it had no effect upon tribal opinion.

The bones, after they have been washed, are placed in the paper bark and at the end of the ceremony tied up into a bundle. After the cleansing ceremony is over the father and the two dués paint themselves with red ocher so that they "won't stink" (have the soul about them).

When the grave is opened the chorus sings canoe, then paddling, which is a signal for the old woman to come out with the symbolic spear-thrower while imitating a man paddling a canoe. The chorus then sings whale hunter, harpoon, and rope. At this time the other woman sticks the "spear" in the body. The body is a whale. The whale is the totem emblem for the Warumeri. Before a man was on the earth two Wongar men went to the totem well of the Warumeri and kept hitting and hitting and cutting it up. Cutting up the whale is next sung. At this juncture in the singing the two dués start cleaning the bones. Sometimes when the grave is being opened and the bones cleaned some of the chorus of men walk around the ground imitating the actions of a dog and others call out like curlews.

The mast is removed after the exhumation and burned. Each clan at this period in the garma song cycle dances a different animal or plant. Warumeri dance the whale, the Wangurri a split mangrove wood, the Djirin the turtle, and the Liaalaomir the snake. This is also supposed to help the spirit depart to the other land and to take him out of his own society.

When the bones have been placed in the paper bark and wrapped up they are put by one of the men in the fork of a tree a short distance from the camp. It is late evening when he returns from the tree where he has placed the bones. Several men carrying fire stick brands meet him and escort him back to camp. The keeper of the bones of the dead man has bushes tied on each arm or he holds them in his hands and crosses them so that the bushes are on his chest. On the edge of the camp a brush house has been made for him. He enters and stays for the night and sometimes for a short time longer. He is not allowed out. The mother of the dead man gives him food and water and takes care of him. "He is just the same as a son of that old woman."

Men gather water in melon shells and obtain a supply of red ocher to make ready for his reappearance. They approach the hut and sit on one side of the doorway, the keeper of the bones on the other. The man puts red ocher on himself with the aid of the water. He remains one or two, sometimes three days longer, to let the newness of the red ocher wear off. Sometimes he leaves the house and moves to another house with some of his near relatives, and once more covers himself with red ocher. Meanwhile the old house is burned. He then returns and the people paint him as though he were going to be put through the circumcision ceremony. All the other relatives paint themselves with red ocher. This is particularly true of those in the patrilineal line, but the mother and wife also cover themselves. After a symbolical well is made, such as is described on page 409, the man who is in charge of the bones is supposed to give food to all of the above people.

He goes out and kills a supply of game; after it is cooked it is placed in the well, which is symbolic of the dead man's well. All the clansmen of the deceased also put in food. The man who is the keeper of the bones and who has cleaned them takes a stick and cleans out his finger nails into the hole. The finger nails are then cut off into the well. "This is to clean off that rotten flesh from his fingers and put it into the well." At this juncture of the ceremony, if the dead man is Yiritja, white maggots are sung; they are supposed to be flying away. If the man was Dua they sing the ants' larvae. Both songs symbolize change. Only the clansmen and near male relatives of the dead man can eat the food but everyone gathers about this communion.

The Hollow Log Coffin.—The keeper of the bones watches them for two or three months; then the brother of the dead man is supposed to go to him and tell him to bring the bones in. The bones are brought up to the edge of the camp, where red ocher is placed on them before they are ready to enter the main camp. The bones are placed in paper bark out in the sun and allowed to dry so that they will not smell and will have the odor of red ocher when they do arrive in camp. Frequently a small bark cylinder is made out of a stringy-bark tree and the totemic emblems of the dead man are painted upon it. The bark cylinder is really a preliminary coffin and is only smaller in size and lighter in material than the final hollow log receptacle in which the bones are placed at the end of the mortuary ceremony. The man who is carrying the bones at the time they are being painted at the edge of the camp puts red ocher on his arms and legs at the same time.

The singing at this point is split mangrove stick, which is the home for the mangrove fish, if the ceremony is Yiritja; if it is Dua, the singing is salt-water turtle. The men sing cutting up the turtle and throwing the bones away just as if the turtle were a man. They then dance mokoi, woman crying, and cockatoo, which are a part of the Nierk mokoi ceremony. The bones are then placed inside of the bark cylinder and the two ends are stuffed with grass. Sometimes red parrot feathers are stuck on it if the bones belong to a Dua man, and opossum string if to a Yiritja.

The women are off some distance from the men. The mother and female mari of the dead man dance a little to one side by themselves. The men dance up to the women and offer the bones to them. The women take them and return them to the men. This is repeated several times before the women finally stop dancing and accept the bones. The leader continues beating his singing sticks and still sings the garma songs. The men wail. The women take the bark coffin and place it in the forks of two sticks at the edge of the camp. The mother then takes the bones and carries them wrapped in paper bark for several months. (The custom of carrying the bones about is practiced only in the more central regions of the Murngin tribe and, according to my informants, is not found in the Wessel Island group among the Yaernungo.) Once more food is offered to the former keeper of the bones.

The Nierk or sulphur-crested cockatoo ceremony follows within the main camp. The principal participants in the ceremony paint themselves with white clay. The earth has been piled up into three small basins which lie side by side and represent the totem wells of the dead man and his relatives. Before the ceremony branches have been broken off the trees and placed in the well bottom to represent the leaves brought in by the tide or the spring floods. The wells are always placed under a large tree. The bones of the dead man and some of his personal property are placed within the circumferences of the three wells. During the dancing that follows members of the chorus break up the spears, shells, et cetera, owned by the deceased.

One of the painted dancers climbs a tree and hangs from a limb by his knees. The leader and chorus sit down in front of the totemic wells. They sing the sea-way cycle of songs (see pages 409-411). The cockatoo calls out in imitation of the sulphur-crested bird. He is supposed to be the mokoi spirit of a dead man.

A second dancer on the ground dances back and forth in front of the chorus of men and the leader. He is also painted white and is supposed to be the newly released ghost of the dead man who is still too timid to go out in the jungle and join the other ghosts. He tries to hide in the trees where the cockatoo is, but the bird sees him and screams out, just as the white cockatoos high in the trees do today when, as the natives suppose, they see the ghosts who hide in the jungles.

The cockatoo in the tree continues calling out, "Ni-erk! Ni-erk! Ni-erk!" while the men by the well reply with "Gar-ra! Gar-ra! Gar-ra!" They are the old ghosts of the people who are long since dead, and who are living in the bush and in the jungle.

Two dancers gather out in front of the chorus and dance, first the jungle, and then a small pigeon, lapar, which is looked upon as a ghost.

The bones of the dead man have been lying tied up in a paper-bark receptacle within the "totemic well" until the mokoi spirit gets up and dances with them. The cockatoo dancer who has been on the ground follows him about and pretends to be watching him very carefully. About a hundred and fifty feet away the women of the camp have gathered in a broken circle facing toward the totemic well. The leader at this moment leads the men to where the women's group is dancing with the monotonous rhythm which characterizes nearly all of the female dancing. The women, too, are supposed to be ghosts.

When the men reach the spot where the women are, the bones of the dead man are given to his female mari. She holds them for a moment and then gives them back to the leader but he once again returns them to her.

The taking of the bones the first time by the women is supposed to mean that they intend keeping both the bones and the spirit of the dead, they are not going to allow them to go away from their group. When the bones are given back it means that the spirit has already gone and they can't keep it. The bones are returned by the dancer to the female mari because they are only bones now and she is to keep them and the various female relatives are to carry them for the proper time.

The women wail when the bones are given to them.

When the mother is tired carrying them, she says to the leader of the clan, "I want these bones of my son to stop in that hollow log. I am not strong enough to carry them. I want them to be in that proper place for them so if I get sick and die they will be there." Sometimes the mother gives the bones to other near female relatives and they carry them and pass them on to others until finally they return to the mother, when she informs the leader they should be placed in the hollow log. From other information gathered, it seems that the leader and male relatives are largely instrumental in setting the time for taking the bones from the women and placing them in the log.

When it is decided that the bones are to be finally removed from the kin group the leader sends several men out into the bush to find a suitable tree. They go about tapping the various eucalyptus trees with their fingers until one has the right sound which indicates that the center of it has been almost completely eaten out by termites. The tree is cut down, the bark scraped off, the inside cleaned out thoroughly. It is then carried back to the edge of the camp and placed in a clump of bushes or behind a windbreak. Sometimes a house is made for it, much as if it were a totemic emblem. Forked sticks are set up in the house and the hollow log placed in them so that it will not be upon the ground. This treatment is exactly the same as that given the ranga trumpet in the Djungguan ceremony. Red ocher is now placed on the hollow log. The garma cycle of songs is sung when it is put in the forked sticks. Yiritja sing a cycle beginning with the cloud and going through to the spider element in the sequence, which takes them from back in the bush with the spring flood to the sea; the Dua sing the land-way cycle.

The log is next carved into the proper shape. The log of each moiety has a different name. The Dua call theirs dai-mer-i, and the Yiritja, char-lum-bu. Eyes are cut into the top of the hollow log which are "all the same as the time when we see in the ocean eyes that belong to that hollow log." The lower section of the hollow log is divided into three parts: the upper third is the area where the sea fish are placed, the middle portion is where salt and fresh water meet and both types of fish are found, and the lower part is the land way where fresh-water fish only are found. In the late afternoon the men dance, first salt water; then salt-water fish; the kingfish; the sea wind coming after the kingfish has jumped in the water; the hollow log that comes from another country; the coconut floating in with the tide from other countries, which means that they are getting near the land where the fresh waters meet; and the tide coming in fast. All the men have on white clay; the women, who are dancing at a little distance, red ocher.

High tide is then danced, followed by low tide. Next in the sequence is people walking along the sea rocks looking for fish. They put their hands underneath the stones to find the fish and try to break the stones off with their feet. The men sit down in a ring with the two leaders sitting at one side, and the women stop their dancing. The ring is the same as the rock pool. They then sing the tide returning and everyone calls out the high water has covered up the rock. The leader sings he has caught a fish on a line and is carrying it to shore to take home. The tempo increases and the chorus is supposed to wash itself in the rock well water. The next song in the sequence is the talk of gathering fire wood to get the fish ready for eating, followed by the eating of the fish and the sleepy feeling that comes from gorging oneself. The last dance is that a big sea takes this totem hollow log, and everyone sings that the water has carried the log away. The leader runs and is followed by the chorus. He calls out the power name of water, then the sacred names of the totem well. The sacred name of the hollow log is cried out, and the log planted in the ground in an upright position. All the women cry and wail for the dead man. Food is given by the women to the leader. It is placed near the hollow log coffin. The leader says, "This food is for the old old ancestors. Only we very old people can eat it. You middle-aged people and young men and boys cannot have any of it," which means that the fully initiated men are the only ones who can eat this totem food (marai-in, sacred, powerful; na-ta, food). The others get ordinary food which has no spiritual significance.

Before the bones are placed in the coffin they are broken up with a stone.[3] When the log rots away the bones are not burned but left to decay. If an *outsider* should burn a hollow log with bones in it he would either be killed or threatened with death.

[3] A man's or woman's bones are sent back to his clan's territory and preferably near the clan well. "We do this so that when that hollow tree and bones are burned when our people are burning grass when the dry season starts this tree and bones will be burned and they will go into the ground of their own country."

CHAPTER XIII

INTERPRETATION OF MURNGIN DEATH RITUALS—AN INTEGRATION OF MURNGIN SOCIETY

All the elements of the mortuary ritual are designed, first, to remove the profane part of the human being who has died and, second, to spiritualize his soul and make it like his totem. The first ceremony sung over the dead (see pages 403-404) demonstrates the intent of the whole ritual. The names of the totems are sung to enable the dying man to act like his totem and become like it, that is, to be completely spiritualized and to remove any of the profane part of his personality. The intent of the ceremony is further demonstrated by the direct native interpretation of the actions of the individual who is mortally wounded in a fight and who performs his totemic dance to direct his soul to his well. In addition, his grandfather or collateral dead kin are believed to come for him to aid him to his well and prevent evil spirits from getting him. The totemic emblem aids their identification of him and makes him "all the same as a totem," just as the carved wooden stick or a wad of bark becomes the totem when it has the emblem placed on it and is ritually sung over. The singing of the garma songs helps direct the soul to the water hole, for "we sing for that warro (soul)—he walks the way we sing." The grave is made symbolically into the sacred totemic well and the Macassar leaving ceremony tells the soul of the dead a last farewell. The grave post and mast are also symbols of this final goodbye. In the exhumation ceremony of some of the clans the body is symbolically speared because it is a whale (totem). The temporary bark receptacle is painted with the totemic emblems, and the coffin itself, which is the final repository of the bones, is a mythical creature associated with the totem. All this clearly shows that one of the primary motives of the ceremony is symbolically to translate the soul out of all profane and worldly contacts and place it finally in the sacred totemic water hole. Another fundamental motif in the mourning ritual is to remove all contact of the dead from the living. The dead person is powerful because he is now a soul and because he has died by magic; these two concepts enter profoundly into Murngin thinking about their dead relative. As a soul he can be properly handled by ritual and translated back to the world of the dead, but as a victim of magic—and all the dead are such victims —he is very dangerous (see the chapter on magic). There are, then, a whole series of purificatory rites which serve to sever the dead's relationship to the living. They are of two varieties: the first is symbolically to force the separation from the living, and the second to propitiate the soul and tell it to go quietly to its totem well and not hurt the living. The second variety tends to prolong the ceremony as if the living people were loath to give up the soul to the dead. The first takes concrete symbolic form in the fire ceremonies which chase the soul away, the spider web dance which catches the soul, the pelican or net dance which does the same, and the removal from the group of the scapegoat who has carried the bones. In the second the songs express the indignation of the dead ancestors toward the living because the recently dead was not given better treatment and because the bones were retained by the female relatives.

The last primary motif in the mourning rites is found in the various symbolic rituals performed to reintegrate the society, close its ranks after the removal of one of its members, and once more assert its solidarity. Ceremonial food is gathered from the whole group and eaten in the sacred wells made over the deceased's grave and at various other times during the ceremonies. The entire group paints itself and participates in the communion. This general participation is also to prevent the magic which killed the dead from harming the living. The symbolic expression of group solidarity (if the writer's theory of magic is correct) prevents the harmful effects of magic from spreading.

The relatives of the dead cannot be in too great haste to dispose of the body or remove the soul from contact with the living, but neither can they keep the soul too long, ("don't be too angry with us,"—see page 407). In either case the ancestors would not like it and would be offended. The living relatives have an ambivalent attitude toward their dead relative. They feel the strong social bond they once had for him. There is a consequent desire to keep him a part of the living and with them, and there is at the same time a feeling of abhorrence and repugnance. The long mourning ritual expresses these contradictions of attitude.

The burial of the body for several months allows the emotions of the bereaved relatives to settle; the later digging up of the bones, the women's carrying them, and the final reburial give ample time for the emotions finally to adjust themselves to this major crisis.

An examination of the kinship structure alone, without any conception of the total social personality or social participation of the former member of the living group, shows that if a man's father-in-law, for example, is taken by death from the social group, part of the social structure of the bereaved man is removed—at least the content of that part of the structure is gone. This forces a considerable readjustment by the living son-in-law, not only to his dead kin but to the dead's other relatives who are also his own. It seems highly likely that the period of mourning corresponds fairly definitely to the period of readjustment of the social structure to this social loss. The best evidence of this is that a baby, particularly a newborn child which has little or no social personality and has not become a part of the social structure, frequently has no ceremony for its burial; the women dig a shallow hole, deposit the body in it, and cover it—and it is quickly forgotten.

The social personality of a woman is less developed than that of a man (she does not participate, for example, in large parts of the ritual or directly in any of the spiritual behavior of the group, et cetera). The ceremonies for her are much less elaborate than those for a man. The ordinary man has less made of his burial than a man renowned for his feats of war, unless he has been killed by a blood feud. The death of an ordinary man by the blood feud organizes the major antagonisms and creates strong solidarities in the surviving group of kinsmen and those of the killer. The man who has participated the most in his social structure—a man, for example, who has been a great fighter, a ceremonial leader of his clan, and powerful in his kinship relations—is the person who has the strongest social bonds and who is mourned for the longest. A very old man is given less time in his mourning ritual than a man in the prime of life because his lateral and ascending kinship bonds are less strong—that is, the relatives who provide these bonds have previously died.

The Murngin Soul in Life and in Death.—Each Murngin man and woman has two souls. One is looked upon as fundamental and real, and is felt to be the true soul, the soul from the heart, while the other is considered a trickster, of little value, and only in a vague way associated with the "true man." The first is the birimbir or warro, and the second is the mokoi or shadow soul. The warro is the totemic well spirit. It can be seen reflected in the water when one looks in it. It comes to one during good dreams. The warro, when a man dies, becomes "all the same as a fish." It lives with and in the totemic emblems. "He walks about with the ranga in the water down below in the well. Our old people reckon this way: he must be all the same as a fish because if a man's canoe tips over out in the middle water of the ocean that old relative's warro comes and helps us, saves our life and takes us up to the shore. If my son went out in the deep water with his canoe he would call out for Banitja [one of the totems of his clan]. After he had taken sweat from under his arm and spit into the water, then he would call out for the warro of his marikmo and mari. Those warros of his mari and marikmo would come all the same as a fish to help him. Warros swim and look like fish. When I look in the water he looks like me. Banitja and warros will also save a man from the sharks as well as from drowning. All the people have warros."

The trickster soul is called shadow soul before death and mokoi when it leaves the body and goes into the jungle and bush country. "Our old people reckon that the shadow soul is all the same as a bad spirit. It's that thing that makes me bad. My shadow always comes with me. The shadows of other things and creatures [beside man] are not souls but only shadows." The mokoi soul is supposed to live more or less all over the body. It is a kind of vague duplicate of it. Sometimes one is told that only the head of a man is made into a mokoi at his death and that mokoi has no body. In the pictures drawn of it and the representations made in the dances, the mokoi is always possessed of a body, but it is distorted and made to appear ugly and unpleasant.[1]

The warro is constantly undergoing change of status. It originates in the totem well, comes to its human father in a dream under miraculous circumstances where it is directed to its mother's womb, lodges there, is born in a normal number of months, and then lives in the heart of the new human organism during the period of the organism's life of the flesh unless it is stolen by a black sorcerer. After death there is a period of some indecision between the land of the living and the land of the dead, but it finally returns to the totemic well whence it came. It is in the symbol of the soul and its relations to the sacred and profane elements in Murngin civilization that we find mirrored the structure and values of the society. The soul supplies the eternal element to the cultural life of an individual Murngin. It lifts man from

[1] The Murngin ideas about the mokoi spirit are varied and somewhat confused.

the simple profane animal level and allows him to participate fully in the sacred eternal values of the civilization that was, is, and will be. It finally and eternally ties the man whose heart it occupies to his totem, the symbol of all clan unity in Murngin culture, since the soul at death is one of the prominent elements in the configuration of associated items found in the clan's totemic water, the water which is the essence of life. Here live the great totemic ancestors who existed in the time of the Wawilak creator sisters when the Wongar totems walked the earth, and whose sacred names are used by the profane living only when these living have been purified by the great rituals, when they are part of the sacred and eternal elements in the culture, when man and his totems participate as one in the totemic rituals. Here, too, in the well, lie the totemic ancestors who died at the beginning of time, and the more recently dead whose emotional bonds with the living are still strong. The more recent ancestors who have gone through the long purifying mortuary ritual which removed all the profane elements of the personality (whose mokoi spirit has gone into the bush with his other evil comrades) are, in their nature, of such sacredness that they can be absorbed into the body of the totem itself. And when the totemic essence of the totem animals is induced into the emblem, they also enter and participate in the spiritual life of the Murngin during the great rituals and then return to the sacred water hole. After the ritual, the emblem is buried beneath the mud of the totem well and allowed to rot, and the ancestor spirits and the totemic spirit return to the subterranean depths. Man goes through exactly the same cycle of existence as the totemic spirit. The totemic spirit enters into the sacred water hole, goes through the ordinary water at the top of the well into the subterranean depths, and finally into the totem water beneath, where the Wongar ancestors live, becoming a part of the sacred configuration. The soul does exactly the same thing.

The soul, the totemic spirit, the Wongar or totemic ancestors, are all expressions of the fundamental sacred essence, the ultimate symbol of which is the totemic well, which is the repository of all the individual items which have been or will be incarnate in man or his religious objects.

The kinship organization classifies the social elements of ordinary behavior. The primary kinship system regulates the basic behavior such as marriage, descent of children, gift-making, economic behavior, et cetera. The moiety and clan generalize and classify this detailed kinship behavior into larger patterns; and they also articulate the ordinary daily life of the people as it is lived by the kinship group, to the totem well, and the individual to the realm of the sacred and the dead.

The unilateral clan differentiates certain lines of patrilineal kin from the kinship totality and organizes them into a spiritual group, the focal center of which is the clan totem well. The totem well as the integrating nucleus of clan solidarity organizes clan sentiments into a sacred unity. The basic factor in this spiritual organization is the relation of the living to the dead and the unborn. The dead souls are grouped into spiritual aggregates based on clan organization. They do not enter into general tribal groupings in the land of the dead, they do not divide on the dual basis of the moiety; but the various male relatives are separated in death if they do not belong to the same clan. Although in life there is an intensely close relationship between the mother's brother and his nephew, in death these relatives are separated by the division of the kinship system into clan groupings of the dead. It is, then, the clan division of the kinship system which orientates the living Murngin to the profane and sacred parts of the totem well and at death places him within the sacred part of the realm of the dead.

The two great classifying structures of Murngin culture are the kinship system and the totem well, both of which generalize the various elements in the total structure. The first basically controls the ordinary daily behavior of the Murngin, and the second organizes spiritual behavior and regulates the activities of the dead. The totem well classifies the totality of the sacred elements of the Murngin social structure. The totemic spirits, the totemic ancestors, the unborn souls and the souls of the dead are all thought to reside within the subterranean depths of the well. It is difficult to distinguish these sacred objects from one another. Even the recently dead soul can become a part of the totem and return in the totemic emblem to participate with it in the great rituals of the people.

The relation of the living to the dead and also the relation of the profane to the sacred can best be presented by Chart XVI. The line A-B separates the sacred from the profane. The seven vertical lines in the lower section which are crossed by the five lateral lines to form the checkerboard with the star at the right center, represent the primary kinship structure of the Murngin. The vertical lines are the patrilineal descent lines and the horizontal are those of generation. The cross-sections of the two form the kinship personality. The star represents Ego. His line and the line to the right of him, which is the mari-marelker, have arrows pointing up from them to a circle which is their clan; the next line at the right, kutara-gurrong line, has an arrow which points into another well. On the left side of Ego's line is found the gawel-galle line, combined with the dumungur-waku, and the dué-waku line, combined with the natchiwalker-gawel line into

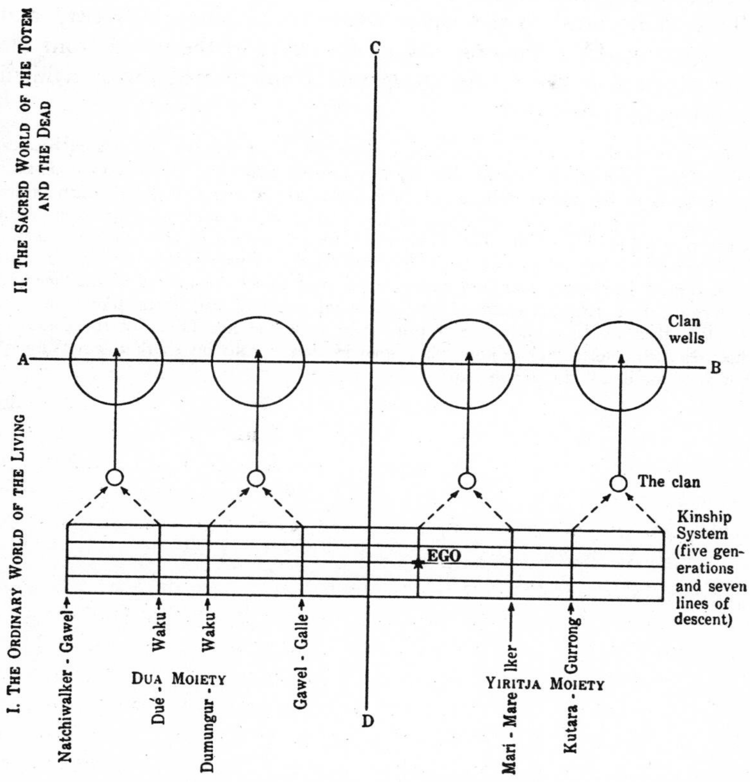

Chart XVI.—The Place of Death in the Murngin Social Structure

another clan group. Leading out of each clan circle is an arrow which enters into a circle above it which symbolizes the clan well. It will be noticed that the symbol of each clan well will be found half below the line A-B which separates the sacred and profane, and half above it. The arrow leading from the clan to the clan well symbolizes the ritual relation of the profane to the sacred and serves to illustrate how the total life of the people is organized by, and pointed into, the clan well. It also, by piercing the lower and entering the upper half of the well circle, demonstrates that part of the relationship of clan to well is profane and part sacred. By profane behavior we mean, for example, the general camp use of the well for drinking water, the women soaking palm nuts in it, et cetera.[2]

This chart sums up the whole structure of Murngin society and relates the world of the ordinary to the world of the totem from the point of view of the whole group and from that of the individual participating in it.

[2] The dead in the totem wells are related since the living relatives are related because of the organization of the kin into the primary kinship structure. This makes it possible for the souls in the totem wells on the left-hand side of the C-D line, which is the Dua moiety grouping of clans, to stand in kin relation to the souls and the totem wells on the right-hand side of the line. Because of the articulation of the kinship structure to the clans, the totems at each well are also related. This is made possible because the patrilineal lines that enter into each totemic well called the totems of that well by the terms father and grandfather. The collateral relatives call these totems by the term that they would actually use if this totem were the real father of the clansman who uses such a term. For example, if a man in clan A calls his shark totem "father," his waku would call this totem nati.

PART IV

SOCIAL CHANGE

CHAPTER XIV

SOCIAL CHANGE IN NORTH AUSTRALIA

SINCE the historian of Murngin society must depend almost entirely on indirect induction to obtain any knowledge of this people's past, any conclusions reached are likely to be tentative and usually not specific but general in their dating and statement of relationships. The Murngin do not possess organized migration myths, although there are accounts of the movements of clan ancestors, particularly during the stress of early disasters. The writer is in whole-hearted agreement with Lowie when he says: "My position, then, towards oral tradition, may be summarized as follows: It is not based, in the first instance, on a universal negative unjustifiably derived from a necessarily limited number of instances, but on the conviction that aboriginal history is only a part of that hodgepodge of aboriginal lore which embraces primitive theories of the universe generally, and that its *a priori* claims to greater respect on our part are nil. Such claims must be established empirically, if at all; but, so far as my experience extends, the empirical facts are diametrically opposed to such claims."[1] I have therefore placed no historical value on these myths or oral traditions concerning the early movements of the Murngin's ancestors but have seen them as rationalizations. I have looked upon the movements of the clan ancestors as Murngin rationalizations, in a logic of time relations, for their present spatial relationships of antagonism and friendship for certain clans and tribes in their local organization.

The following materials and methods have been used to reconstruct Murngin history:

I. Observations of present culture change, e.g., the intrusion of certain rituals such as the Gunabibi and of certain customs such as subincision.

II. Documents of earlier explorers.

III. The culture area method, by which essentially spatial facts are given an interpretation in time. This method, combined with the evidence of archaeological finds, has been used in reconstructing the possible history of Murngin modes of disposing of the dead.

IV. The archaeological method, to determine the length of time certain articles of technology have been possessed by the Murngin.

[1] Lowie, Robert H., "Oral Tradition and History"; address of the retiring president, delivered at the Annual Meeting of the American Folk-Lore Society in New York, December 27, 1916.

V. Application of the Douglass tree-ring method.[2] This was attempted unsuccessfully in an effort to date more exactly Malay intrusion into North Australia by examining the growth rings of the tamarind trees which were brought to the shores of the Arafura and the Gulf of Carpentaria by the Malay traders.

Observation of Certain Historical Processes

The Gunabibi is not found in any of the clans around Arnhem and Buckingham Bays or among the island peoples of the northeast; but large numbers of the men from these districts go south to the clans that have this ceremony and participate there. Certain features of the Gunabibi are not observed by these northern visitors, particularly the exchange of wives since they do not bring their wives with them. The Gunabibi is thought of as a southern and western ceremony. Leaders from the Rainbarngo come to the Goyder River country to assist in its direction. The Liaalaomir and surrounding clans, however, have it as an organized part of their ceremonial life. The process of diffusion, as it is observable in this case, has two elements in it: (1) the clans on the edges of its distribution tend to assimilate it, and (2) the clans farther away tend to accept it in that their men go to its celebrations, which means that a large group of men are Gunabibi initiates in areas where it is not a part of the total clan behavior. Because of its distribution among the more remote northern clans and simultaneous contacts with the general distribution of the Gunabibi, this rite is diffusing very rapidly and promises to cover the whole of the Murngin area within the next few years.

The rapidity of its diffusion is aided by the operation of a cultural selective factor: the ceremony itself is but a slight variation of the Djungguan and is dependent on the same Wawilak myth for its logic. It also emphasizes with greater clarity and satisfaction the ideas of fertility latent or explicit in all the large Murngin rituals; this would tend to make it attractive and exciting to their thinking and emotions and make them see it as "more inside" (that is, the further inside the men's ceremonial grounds one goes, the more sacred the mysteries become).

In the Roper River area the Gunabibi is associated with subincision but in the northern Murngin area it is not. Subincision is diffusing into this area as a part of the general complex, but is not a ritual element; and it is treated by the people who accept it as a separate custom, although they know that it is a part of the general Gunabibi configuration in the south. It seems probable that, in no great length of time, the two will be reassociated because the subincision songs are sung at the present time in the

[2] Douglass, Andrew E., "Dating Our Prehistoric Ruins; How Growth Rings in Timbers Aid in Establishing the Relative Ages of the Ruined Pueblos of the Southwest," *Natural History,* 1921, Vol. XVI, pages 27-30.

Gunabibi sequences and many of the men and the leaders who sing them are at present subincised.[3]

The ceremonial life of the Murngin seems to be constantly enriched by cultural waves coming from the south—that is, from Central Australia—as will be demonstrated when we examine their burial customs from an historical point of view. The technological borrowings, of recent times at least, are from the seacoast and not from the inland. We must turn to the Malay contacts to see what traits have been taken and by what cultural processes they have been chosen from the contact of the Malay traders from the north and west.

Malay Influence on the Aboriginal Cultures of Northeastern Arnhem Land

The Malays, from an early date, made yearly voyages down through the East Indian Islands and through the Arafura Sea to the northern coast of Australia. Their prows sailed into many harbors and river mouths that indent the coast, from the Victoria River, which flows into the Indian Ocean in West Australia, to the southern limits of the Gulf of Carpentaria in the east.

Sir Matthew Flinders, in the second volume of his *Voyage to Terra Australis*, reports having seen first evidences of the Malays in the Pellew Islands.[4] He next speaks of them when he was anchored at Caledon

[3] The people to the south and west of the Murngin practice subincision. It seems to have a distribution that projects up the Goyder River to the Crocodile Islands. The following people practice it; Rainbarngo, the people around Cape Stewart, the Djinba, Ritarngo, the Marunga Island people (some do, some do not—it is a matter of personal choice), and the Burera (a matter of personal choice). None of the people east of them go through this ordeal except a few who have made long visits to the people west and south of them and have gone through the Gunabibi ceremony. In the more northern parts of the subincision distribution the cutting is unritualized. Two men go out and stand in a river or pool to above their waists. One takes a sharp stone knife and splits the urethra of the other; either at the same time or later, the one who has been cut reciprocates by performing the same operation on his friend. Farther south, subincision is a definite part of the Gunabibi ceremony. Clitoridectomy also seems to be practiced in this ceremony by these southern peoples. It seems likely that if other factors do not disturb the culture, the subincision element of the Gunabibi will spread into northeastern Arnhem Land and become a part of the ritual within this area. Many of the people at the present day sing a subincision song as part of the ceremony even though they do not go through the ordeal.

[4] Page 172—"Pellew Group: December, 1802: Indications of some foreign people having visited this group were almost as numerous, and as widely extended as those left by the natives. Besides pieces of earthen jars and trees cut with axes, we found remnants of bamboo lattice work, palm leaves sewed with cotton thread into the form of such hats as are worn by the Chinese, and the remains of blue cotton trousers, of the fashion called moormans. A wooden anchor of one fluke, and three boats' rudders of violet wood were also found; but what puzzled me most was a collection of stones piled together in a line, resembling a low wall, with short lines running perpendicularly at the back, dividing the space behind into compartments. In each of these

Bay,[5] but it was not until he had reached the English Company Islands that he actually came in contact with the Malays themselves.[6]

---

were the remains of a charcoal fire, and all the wood near at hand had been cut down. Mr. Brown saw on another island a similar construction, with not less than thirty-six partitions, over which was laid a rude piece of frame work; and the neighboring mangroves, to the extent of an acre and a half, had been cut down. It was evident that these people were Asiatics, but of what particular nation, or what their business here, could not be ascertained; I suspected them, however, to be Chinese, and that the nutmegs might possibly be their object. From the traces amongst Wellesley's Island, they had been conjectured to be shipwrecked people; but that opinion did not now appear to be correct."

[5] Page 213—"Caledon Bay: February, 1803: That this bay had before received the visits of some strangers, was evinced by the knowledge which the natives had of fire arms; they imitated the act of shooting when we first landed, and when a musket was fired at their request, were not much alarmed. A quantity of posts was lying near the water, which had been evidently cut with iron instruments; and when we inquired of the inhabitants concerning them, they imitated with their hands the motion of an axe cutting down a tree, and then stopping, exclaimed Poo! Whence we understood that the people who cut the wood had fire arms. This was all that could be learned from the natives; but from the bamboos and partitions of frame work found here, similar to those of Pellew's Group, they were doubtless the same Asiatic nation, if not the same individuals, of whom so many traces had been seen all the way from the head of the Gulph."

[6] Pages 228-233—"English Company's Islands: February, 1803, Thursday 17: After clearing the narrow passage between Cape Wilberforce and Bromny's Isles, we followed the main coast to the S.W.; having on the starboard hand some high and large islands, which closed in towards the coast a-head so as to make it doubtful whether there were any passage between them. Under the nearest island was perceived a canoe full of men; and in a sort of roadsted, at the south end of the same island, there were six vessels covered over like hulks, as if laid up for the bad season. Our conjectures were various as to who those people could be, and what their business here; but we had little doubt of their being the same, whose traces had been found so abundantly in the Gulph. I had inclined to the opinion that these traces had been left by Chinese, and the report of the natives in Caledon Bay that they had fire arms, strengthened the supposition; and combining this with the appearance of the vessels, I set them down for piratical Ladrones who secreted themselves here from pursuit, and issued out as the season permitted, or prey invited them. Impressed with this idea, we tacked to work up for the road; and our pendant and ensign being hoisted, each of them hung out a small white flag.

". . . we learned that they were prows from Macassar, and the six Malay commanders shortly afterwards came on board in a canoe. It happened fortunately that my cook was a Malay, and through his means I was able to communicate with them. The chief of the six prows was a short, elderly man, named Pobassoo; he said there were upon the coast, in different divisions, sixty prows, and that Salloo was the commander in chief. These people were Mahometans, and on looking into the launch, expressed great horror to see hogs there; nevertheless they had no objection to port wine, and even requested a bottle to carry away with them at sunset.

"Friday 18, February 1803: My desire to learn every thing concerning these people, and the strict look-out which it had been necessary to keep upon them, prevented me attending to any other business during their stay. According to Pobassoo, from whom my information was principally obtained, sixty prows belonging to the Rajah of Boni,

The Malay trading in North Australia excited Flinders' curiosity, and after leaving the continent and arriving at Timor he inquired further into their trading methods and also attempted to discover when trade with Australia had first started. His statement that "but twenty years before one of their prows was driven by the Northwest monsoon to the coast of New Holland" was the beginning of the trading relations between the East

---

and carrying one thousand men, had left Macassar with the north-west monsoon, two months before, upon an expedition to this coast; and the fleet was then lying in different places to the westward, five or six together, Pobassoo's division being the foremost. These prows seemed to be about twenty-five tons, and to have twenty-five men in each; that of Pobassoo carried two small brass guns, obtained from the Dutch, but the others had only muskets; besides which, every Malay wears a cress or dagger, either secretly or openly. I inquired after bows and arrows, and the ippo poison, but they had none of them; and it was with difficulty they could understand what was meant by the ippo.

"The object of their expedition was a certain marine animal, called trepang. Of this they gave me two dried specimens; and it proved to be the *beche-de-mer*, or sea cucumber which we had first seen on the reefs of the East Coast, and had afterwards hauled on shore so plentifully with the seine, especially in Caledon Bay. They get the trepang by diving, in from 3 to 8 fathoms water; and where it is abundant, a man will bring up eight or ten at a time. The mode of preserving it is this: the animal is split down one side, boiled, and pressed with a weight of stones; then stretched open by slips of bamboo, dried in the sun, and afterwards in smoke, when it is fit to be put away in bags, but requires frequent exposure to the sun. A thousand trepang make a picol, of about 125 Dutch pounds; and one hundred picols are a cargo for a prow. It is carried to Timor, and sold to the Chinese, who meet them there; and when all the prows are assembled, the fleet returns to Macassar. By Timor, seemed to be meant Timor-laoet; for when I inquired concerning the English, Dutch, and Portugues there, Pobassoo knew nothing of them: he had heard of Coepang, a Dutch settlement, but said it was upon another island.

"Saturday 19, February 1803: Pobassoo had made six or seven voyages from Macassar to this coast. within the preceding twenty years, and he was one of the first who came; but had never seen any ship here before. This road was the first rendezvous for his division, to take in water previously to going into the Gulph. One of their prows had been lost the year before, and much inquiry was made concerning the pieces of wreck we had seen; and a canoe's rudder being produced, it was recognized as having belonged to her. They sometimes had skirmishes with the native inhabitants of the coast; Pobassoo himself had been formerly speared in the knee, and a man had been slightly wounded since their arrival in this road: they cautioned us much to beware of the natives.

"They had no knowledge of any European settlement in this country.

". . . They carry a month's water, in joints of bamboo; and their food is rice, cocoa nuts, and dried fish, with a few fowls for the chiefs. The black gummotoo rope, of which we had found pieces at Sir Edward Pellew's Group, was in use on board the prows; and they said it was made from the same palm whence the sweet sirup, called gulah, is obtained.

"My numberless questions were answered patiently, and with apparent sincerity; Pobassoo even stopped one day longer at my desire, than he had intended, for the north-west monsoon, he said, would not blow quite a month longer, and he was rather late."

Indies and Australia seems rather doubtful, and it is highly likely that trade had been going on long before this period.[7]

Norman B. Tindale, in his recent monograph, "The Natives of Groote Eylandt and the West Coast of the Gulf of Carpentaria,"[8] also speaks of evidences of the Malays in the area in which he did his field work. He mentions the tamarind trees left by the Malays, and the old anchorages, as well as the cemetery sites.

In the region from Cape Stewart and the Crocodile Islands (in the Arafura Sea and to the west and north of northeastern Arnhem Land) to Caledon Bay and the Gulf of Carpentaria there were several concentration points used by the Malays in their trade relations with the local natives. The chief centers were at Malay Bay in the east, Elcho Island, on a mound formed by an old native camp site at the eastern mouth of the Caddell Straits, and at Millingimbi Island, in the Crocodile group in the west. It was at these centers that the Malays took down the great fiber sails and mast-poles from their ships and made anchor for the rainy season.

The voyagers made their first appearance each year when the monsoons drove their cumbersome ships down from Timor Laut and Macassar through the Arafura Sea to Malay Bay and the other landing points. According to the blacks, there was considerable competition among the various ships to arrive in Arnhem Land first because of the larger harvest the first traders reaped. The competition occasionally resulted in ships remaining all through the dry season to be on location before the others arrived in October or November. The informants declare that "when the first lightning came, the Macassar man came, too."

Economic Organization of the Malay Traders.—In the whole area the Malays did not establish any permanent settlements in which a permanent

[7] Page 257—"Timor: April, 1803: I made many inquiries concerning the Malay trepang fishers, whom we had met at the entrance of the Gulph of Carpentaria, and learned the following particulars. The natives of Macassar had been long accustomed to fish for the trepang amongst the islands in the vicinity of Java, and upon a dry shoal lying to the south of Rottee; but about twenty years before, one of their prows was driven by the north-west monsoon to the coast of New Holland, and finding the trepang to be abundant, they afterwards returned; and had continued to fish there since that time. The governor was of the opinion, that the Chinese did not meet them at Timor-laoet, but at Macassar itself, where they are accustomed to trade for birds' nests, trepang, sharks' fins, &c.; and it therefore seems probable that the prows rendezvous only at Timor-laoet, on quitting Carpentaria, and then return in a fleet, with their cargoes.

"The value of the common trepang at Canton, was said to be forty dollars the picol, and for the best, or black kind, sixty; which agrees with what I had been told in Malay Road, allowing to the Chinese the usual profit of cent. per cent. (from Macassar to their own country)."

[8] Tindale, Norman B., "The Natives of Groote Eylandt and the West Coast of the Gulf of Carpentaria," *Records of the Australian Museum,* March 31, 1926, Vol. III, No. 2.

population occupied a site for the entire year. No Malay women were allowed to accompany the men on their southern voyages. With the exception of the tamarind tree and possibly the bamboo, no flora of the East Indies were deliberately transplanted to the northern coast of Australia. The Malays did not engage in any form of agriculture here. Although they brought rice for trade with the aborigines, none was ever planted by them or the natives. It may be possible that two cocoanut palm trees reported by the natives of the Kolpa clan of Cape Wessel Island were planted by the western trader, but it is also possible that the two trees sprouted from cocoanuts carried in by the tides, which bring hundreds of these nuts to the shores of northern Arnhem Land.[9]

The Malay traders made these long trips from their native islands to Australia because they wanted to acquire the native pearl shell, pearls, tortoise shell, trepang, and sandal wood, found all along the shores of North Australia. The natives received in return dugout canoes, rice, molasses, tobacco, cloth for sarongs, belts, knives, tomahawks, gin, and pipes, as well as other articles of trade. The Malay did not come to establish outposts of his civilization and promote agriculture, nor had he any desire to proselytize the aborigines to worship his gods; he came to trade for highly valued articles on which the natives placed little value, and when he had accomplished his purpose he was glad to go home to Macassar, Koepang, or Timor Laut. Consequently he had little effect on the native civilization or its racial stock.

The various head men of the coastal clans were made "kings" by Malay traders. Usually the brother of the "king" was also made a "king" to assist his older brother—apparently a Malay adaptation of native custom, since the ceremonial leader of a clan usually has his younger brother to assist him. The head men were put in charge of their clansmen in the trepang expeditions. Friendships grew up between various Malays and aborigines to the extent that the black fathers took their young sons down to the Malay boats and pointed out the men who were to be their trading friends when they were grown up. This indicates a tendency to organize the trade on the basis of the patrilineal line, which again shows that the Malays did not attempt to change native civilization, but merely adapted themselves to the native social institutions.

The gin traded to the natives caused occasional great drunken orgies, and much blood was shed in interclan fights that came to a head under this alcoholic stimulation. However, the alcohol seems to have had no effect upon the general well-being of the people.

[9] The ocean currents are exceptionally rapid in the Arafura Sea and the distances of no great length from cocoanut-growing areas, which makes it highly possible that of the tens of thousands of nuts washed ashore through the years, two of them might have taken root. Recent researches have shown that cocoanuts can remain in sea water for a considerable period of time without losing their germinating power.

Many of the black men went back to the Malay country with the returning fleets and stayed through the intervening season. There are a few cases of men who stayed permanently and married Malay women, but this was very rare.

The Malays also bought spears and spear-throwers from the blacks, but it is likely that this was done in modern times because of their interest in them as mementos rather than weapons.

The trade with the Malays seems to have been purely on a basis of exchange, with very little else in its social content. Nevertheless, it had little effect on the aboriginal ideas of trade. The Murngin trade is fairly extensive. The native sometimes exchanges things he possesses for the things he needs and cannot get from his own territory; but the larger basis of trade in northeastern Arnhem Land is one of social reciprocity which establishes a social bond between the traders and enlarges the social periphery of each. A trade between two people is considerably ritualized, and may be an exchange of the same objects, such as carved spears, spear-throwers, or baskets.

All this again shows the strong resistance of the Murngin culture to outside influence. The Malay trader came for an exchange of goods and nothing else; and it would be thought that, in the hundreds of years he is likely to have been in Arnhem Land, he would have given a new impetus to Murngin ideas of exchange. But as far as can be determined, the Murngin ideas are no different from what they were before he arrived, since the trade life fits into the general setting of their culture. Further, this system of exchange is no different from that of the interior tribes, and it is still not a matter of pure economics, but is of more significance to the social and ritualistic life of the people.

Malay Influence on the Aboriginal Material Culture.—Although the influence of the Malay was of no great importance, nevertheless it had considerable influence upon certain aspects of the material culture of the tribes who occupied the coastal plains along the Arafura Sea and the western shores of the Gulf of Carpentaria.

In brief, the Malay introduced the dugout canoe, its mast and pandanus sail, the Malay type of pipe, a fashion for cutting the beard in a kind of Van Dyke style, and an appreciation for iron and other metals. It is possible the tides had carried in wooden planks with metal on them before the Malay arrived in Australia, for at the present time the natives often find planks with nails, which they extract and use for fish hooks. The tomahawk was also brought into North Australia and became a part of the native culture, partly supplanting, along the coast, the ground stone axe. It was, of course, not made by the Australians. The technique of grinding a stone axe is still known by the men of these tribes. The metal axes did not come in sufficient number to supply all the needs of the natives. It is unlikely that many iron axes ever reached the interior peoples; and the proximity of stone and the native's tendency to lose his implements (which necessitates constant replacements) greatly contributed to the continuation of this stone-axe technique in the aboriginal culture.

The dugout canoe used by the natives possesses no outrigger; but it is a fairly well-shaped boat and is much superior to the indigenous bark canoe that the native had used as his chief means of water transport before the arrival of the Malay. The Malays who traded with the Australians used the double outrigger. Some of the present-day natives know how to make an outrigger, but this addition to the dugout was not appreciated by the more conservative aborigines, and never became part of their culture. It is likely that this was due to the influence of their own bark canoe. This latter boat lacked an outrigger, and it was easier and simpler to learn how to manage a dugout canoe without an outrigger than to learn how to operate one with it.

Judging from the direct evidence of the natives who were alive at the time when the Malays were still coming to North Australia, it is probable that the blacks did not manufacture their own dugouts until the white Australian government sent its gunboats up to the western entrance of the Arafura Sea and prevented Malay trade with the black natives. Several informants reported that when the last consignment of canoes was eventually broken up, all of the people went back to bark canoes, but that a few of the men from the English Company Islands had learned how to make the dugout, and the manufacture of this type of boat was learned from them. This story seems likely, for the termination of the Malay voyages occurred when several of the informants were old enough to observe and to remember the exact circumstances. Groote Eylandt and Caledon Bay were also concentration points of the Malays. Groote Eylandt particularly was a region where the native culture had more intensive contact with Malay traders. Possibly dugout manufacture was learned there and the English Company Island people relearned it from their southern neighbors.[10]

The conservatism of Australian material culture is more or less demonstrated by the persistence of the bark canoe. Even today men who know how to make a dugout with outrigger equipment paddle their bark canoes across the open sea from island to island and from the various points of land. The fashioning of a dugout canoe takes much longer and requires more skill than any other article in the North Australian technology; further, after it has been made, it becomes a more or less permanent part of a man's equipment. The bark canoe is easily constructed; it can be made for immediate use with very little labor, and the material for its construction is always at hand. Its value in labor is consequently little, and it can be discarded with no feeling of loss. A bark canoe is seldom used after

[10] Tindale, *op. cit.*

one voyage, for it quickly becomes unfit for use, because of the cracking and warping of the bark. Since it does not become a permanent part of a man's possessions it is not an added responsibility and care, as is the case with the dugout canoe. The material for the dugout canoe is difficult to get, the trees used are frequently a considerable distance from the inland rivers or the sea, and it involves the labor of a number of men to transport the canoe from its place of manufacture to the water. The rarity of the material adds to the value of the canoe. The labor involved and the organization of the labor contribute their share to increasing the canoe's value to the native owner; consequently an aborigine who possesses a dugout canoe feels a considerable responsibility for its safety and upkeep, and the canoe gives him a relationship with his immediate environment which is permanent and will not allow him to make his decisions with the ease that he would if he did not feel the necessity of taking care of his property.

To sum up, the bark canoe fits into the general pattern of Murngin behavior. The Murngin is not particularly interested in his material culture and would rather not be disturbed by its burdens and responsibilities. The manufacture and possession of a dugout canoe obviously do not fit into the general scheme of things as does the bark canoe. It is highly probable that the tardy and partial acceptance of the dugout in Murngin culture is due to the above set of causes. When the Malays supplied the canoes ready-made and they could be acquired each season for turtle shell that was saved during the dry season, or for pearls that the native found while eating his oysters, the burden of making the canoe and the great responsibility of ownership were not felt. The turtle shell and pearls were worthless to the native, so that if a man lost his canoe he could replace it without any effort and without loss of any property that he valued. As a result, while the Malays supplied them ready-made the natives used them, but when the Malay supply was gone the bark canoe once more returned to partial use.

The dugout finally became a trait in Murngin material culture because a man has a better chance of harpooning a turtle, dugong, or shark in the comparatively firm footing supplied by a dugout than he has from the unsubstantial bark canoe. Several informants who were excellent sea hunters declared that this was the reason they used the dugout instead of the older bark canoe.

The canoe mast and the pandanus sail are but two parts of one general invention, since the former is a mechanical device used to articulate the latter to a dugout canoe. The technical equipment to make a mast was already in the hands of the native, since he is an expert carver. The ability he shows in the manufacture of his carved totemic emblems demonstrates this fact. The mast is a very simple object to make; what is more important, it takes but a few minutes and can be discarded when it has been used only once, with no sense of real loss to the owner. It does not burden the native with "excess baggage." It is easier to make a new one than to keep an old one.

The use of the pandanus sail has become general in the north. It is easily constructed and only a few hours are needed for its manufacture. It is a labor-saving device, and any such invention is deeply appreciated by the leisure-loving blacks. It, too, fits into the general scheme; no new technique was needed for its manufacture. The simple twining method used in the construction of the native basket or mat, with only slight modification, made an excellent pandanus leaf sail, the only difference being in the size of the strands used.

The most difficult element in the learning process that would enable a man to sail a boat rather than paddle it was the actual sailing itself. As has been said, the manufacture of a mast and sail is simple; but to learn to sail a canoe with a large pandanus sail, to adjust it to the vagaries of winds and tides, and, in all, to learn the job of a sailor man, undoubtedly took a long time. From what the writer has seen of the native's lack of interest in any activity that was not pleasurable, it seems obvious to him that if the native had not had a keen interest in the sea and a strong wanderlust, both of which the dugout canoe and its mast and sail definitely satisfied, Murngin civilization would never have adopted this whole complex.

The Malay pipe is a small, straight stick with its center bored out; at about four inches from the distal end a hole is made in the side of the pipe which connects with the central chamber; this latter hole is lined with a small piece of tin and forms the bowl of the pipe. Bamboo or cane is generally used, or a small tree whose central core has been eaten out by termites. The Malays introduced both the use and the manufacture of the tobacco pipe during the period in which they traded with the aborigines. Although the aborigines know that they acquired the pipe from the Malays, they believe they practiced smoking before this time, and point to the fact that there are several native tobaccos.[11] Whether this is true or not it is impossible to say at the present time, but nearly all the evidence seems to point to the introduction of smoking into Australia from a Malay source. However, if the latter is true, the natives quickly learned how to use native substitutes after they could no longer obtain Malay tobacco.

The substitution of the iron tomahawk (brought in as an article of trade by the Malays) for the stone axe can be understood, since the iron implement is a far more capable instrument, and—a more important reason—the tomahawk was easily acquired and it was not necessary to learn

[11] The Murngin insist that they had a native tobacco before the Macassar introduced the variety they use at the present time. The leaves were macerated and wrapped in paper bark and smoked as a cigarette, or put in a cane which had a hole in one end much like the Queensland type of pipe.

how to make it. There was no arduous labor attached to collecting turtle shell to trade for an axe, for the shell came as a by-product to the pursuit of harpooning turtles. The making of the stone axe took time and a considerable amount of hard labor; but to go turtle hunting was a pleasure, since turtle harpooning expeditions are not only for the anticipated enjoyment of the flesh and to supply the family larder, but also for the pure joy of stalking the turtle, spearing it, and bringing it home to an admiring audience which could appreciate one's abilities as a hunter and a man of importance. Undoubtedly pride of workmanship is felt by a native axe-maker. His fellow tribesmen always express their appreciation of a well-turned-out axe or spear head, but the social approbation given to the two occupations is completely disproportionate.

The turtle shell had never been used, and had been discarded until the Malay came; that it should become an article of high value to the trader was an item of some amusement and a fortuitous circumstance for the aborigines. Since the women gather oysters, the trading of pearls for the Malay objects of trade was looked upon by the black as an even greater bit of luck than the trading of shell.

The trepang (*beche-de-mer*) industry demanded more effort. In this activity the Malay showed himself a practical sociologist, for he again made no vain attempt to change Murngin civilization to his liking, but merely used the institutions he found among them to satisfy his wants.

Canoes were given to certain men who, with their clansmen, gathered the sea slugs from the low-lying sand banks at low tide. All this the native understood, since it was but one added particular to a general type of behavior; and although the blacks do not eat trepang, this animal belongs to a group of seashore fauna which are gathered and eaten, and could have been added to the diet without any change in the methods of acquiring food. But there is one element in the economic structure of Murngin civilization that must have made this adaptation somewhat difficult, since the sexual division of labor allots the task of gathering mollusk and other seashore foods to the women. Men only gather these articles of diet for their own use when they have no women with them and there is nothing else to eat. It is very likely that if the natives could not have speared fish or harpooned dugong or turtle while looking for trepang beds, the Malays would have found the industry unprofitable, if not impossible.

The Malay brought the tamarind fruit with him. The seeds that were thrown away sprouted, and now the lands where he voyaged are known by their growth of the tamarind tree. Many of these trees are very large. The circles of trees which surround the spot where once a huge tamarind tree had grown show that they are secondary growths and do not represent the earliest period of the Malay contact. No one knows how long the Malay has been making his voyages to Australia. The writer attempted to find an approximate date of his first intrusion into the Arafura Sea by means of the tamarind tree. A few of the larger trees were cut down and cross-sections taken to show the number of growth rings on the tree. It was thought that by determining the amount of time shown by the tree rings and adding approximately two-thirds of the time it took the parent tree to grow, it might be possible to say at least that the Malay had been coming for the period represented by their growth, even though we could not say he had been in North Australia before this. Unfortunately, according to competent botanists, it is impossible to date a tamarind by its tree rings.

The writer excavated two large shell mounds on Millingimbi Island, in the Crocodile group, both of which had tamarind trees near, or growing on them. One of these kitchen middens surrounded a water hole that was known generally to all the aborigines as Macassar Well. Although I was able to accumulate a large collection of native artifacts in the eight feet of shell excavated, I did not find any that were Malay. This, however, does not demonstrate a late Malay invasion because negative evidence does not prove the Malay was not there. Furthermore, the bases of the trunks of the tamarind trees on the mound were well covered with refuse shell. One tree was, by measurement, well over a foot under the accumulated shell. Since the accumulated refuse was well packed and hardened by time, this seems to point to a considerable period of Malay contact with North Australia. The number of people using this mound was never large, and it would take such a group a considerable period of time to throw away a sufficient number of mollusk shells to form a foot of debris around the base of a tamarind tree.

The ripe tamarind pods are eaten and greatly appreciated by the natives. They are looked upon as a part of the general economic flora, although it is known that they were derived from the Malay. No native would ever think of planting a tamarind tree for later use.

From this brief summary of the Malay influence on the material culture of the Murngin, it is obvious that the number of Malay contributions was small, and especially when considered from the larger aspect of the total aboriginal culture, of no great numerical importance. Looked at from the point of view of Malay civilization, it can be seen that the greater part of Malay technology was not adopted. All the objects taken over by Murngin culture were but modifications of original indigenous inventions, with the possible exception of the Malay pipe. The exotic dugout canoe, with its mast and sail, partially took the place of the bark canoe, but did not entirely supplant it. The tamarind tree, although a part of the culture because it contributes, however slightly, to the Murngin larder, is not a true cultural element, since Murngin civilization is in no way responsible for its existence. It is an integral part of Malay culture, since it is planted and is part of their agricultural complex. It is probable that tides, currents, birds, and other natural causes introduced several floral species into the north that are part of the raw material used in the technological and economic life of the Murngin. Since the tamarind fruit is known to be edible, these plants, brought in by natural means, occupy the same position in Murngin life as the tamarind.

With the exception of the canoe, sail, mast, tobacco pipe, Malay beard, and tamarind tree, little else was contributed by these traders as a permanent part of Murngin material culture. Their influence on the interior people was far less than that felt by the coastal groups. The dugout, with its sail and mast, has not, even today, penetrated twenty miles inland, except by visits of the coastal people, even though there are large navigable rivers and inland lakes that would support a dugout canoe. The Malay pipe is generally used on the coast and the interior. Very few iron tomahawks ever reached the bush people. The tamarind tree is found only on the coast and the adjacent islands, for the Malay never penetrated the interior parts of Arnhem Land.

Malay Influence on the Social Life of the Murngin.—Although the contributions of Malay civilization to Murngin material culture were not large, the purely social elements added to the aboriginal civilization were still less, and probably of less importance in modifying the other social traits. The chief elements of immaterial culture that were adopted by the eastern Arafuran natives were: (1) a pidgin Malay language that was spoken by a considerable number of natives in all the coastal tribes, but not by all the male members of the society; (2) Malay personal and place names; (3) part of the mast-raising ceremony of the Malay voyagers; (4) a mourning ceremony; and (5) other fragmentary elements, such as folk tales.

A pidgin Malay dialect was spoken by most of the older men among the tribes along the Arafura coast. This language became a lingua franca among the various linguistic groups who border the coast. A man traveling from Cape Don, in the far west, could make himself understood to the people on Groote Eylandt. The language stimulated intertribal communication. The introduction of the dugout canoe, with its sail, also accelerated and intensified the interrelations of the various local groups and dialectic tribes. Anyone who has traveled a few hundred miles in a dugout, with and without sails, quickly comes to the conclusion that a canoe with a sail can average more than double the distance of a canoe depending on paddles for locomotion. The sailing canoe also made it possible for two friendly groups separated by hostile clans to communicate when the intervening peoples were on the warpath. Before this time, with the old bark canoe, it was often necessary to land on unfriendly territory because of the voyager's inability to cover the distance in one day's paddling. Although the dugout was capable of carrying more people than its predecessor, it did not develop into a war canoe.

The Malays gave all the islands, beaches, bodies of water, peninsulas, and other landmarks names from their own vocabulary, which the natives learned and used in addition to their own. All the locations in the whole territory which were touched by the Malay sailors have Malay as well as native terms. Men who do not know the Malay dialect usually know the Malay place names of a particular district.

Almost all the people of the Arafura country also have Malay personal names. These names were originally given them by the Malays, but they were passed by the natives to their own relatives through the custom of giving a sister's daughter's son, or a son's son, the name of a mother's mother's brother, or a father's father; and in the female line by giving the daughter's daughter or brother's son's daughter the name of a mother's mother or father's father's sister. The Murngin know which are Malay personal and place names and which are aboriginal in origin.

There were no Malay words adopted by the blacks to describe the various social institutions of the Murngin. No clan or local group, as far as the writer could determine, received a Malay name which was used by the black. No kinship term was adopted from the Malay terms, although it might be argued that the word for father (bapa) in Murngin nomenclature, being the same as the Malay word, was taken from the intruders. When it is realized that this same word bapa figures in the more central tribes as a kinship term, and that in some of these kinship systems it means older brother and in other places describes still different relatives, it will be seen that this likeness in the two languages was probably a coincidence. It could just as easily be argued that our word "papa" was taken over by the blacks and used for their word for father, since white civilization had been in contact with aboriginal Australian culture in the south and east for a considerable period of time. A visiting Malay, had he come to the Arafura country later than the white man, might have argued this were he as uncritical as many white theorists in their arguments for the diffusion of culture traits.

The Malays only slightly influenced Murngin mythology. Certain myths seem to have a possible Malay origin, or, if not Malay, then some other outside source, since they do not seem to fit into the general cultural background. For instance, the belief that a man acquires the soul of the man he has killed may be due to the transportation of the head-hunting idea from Indonesia to Australia by the Malay traders. On the other hand, it is also likely that this Indonesian idea came by way of New Guinea and then down to Australia at a much earlier period than this last, Malay contact.

Certain native myths have been somewhat modified to make a place for the Malay in the native cosmic ideology, just as the myths have been added to in order to account for the white man and his civilization; but all these changes are purely superficial and but additional facts seeded into native cosmologies.

At the end of their visits in Australia the Malays always lifted their masts, which had been taken down, and fastened them securely to the decks as part of their final preparation for departure. It is possible that there was a slight ceremony involved in this. The Murngin have taken the activities that surrounded the raising of the mast and transplanted them as a ritual into part of their burial ceremony. This has not been done by all of the clans, but is confined to only a few of the groups of the Yiritja moiety. The lifting of the mast by the Malays meant to the Murngin that they were leaving for that year, and, in a way, it symbolized their farewell to Australia in the minds of the Murngin. The idea of the departure of the Malay ship has been transferred to the idea of the departure of the soul of the dead.

The corpse is lifted in the same way as Malays were supposed to have raised their mast, and the natives chant a pidgin variety of Malay which seems to be a version of Malay chanting. When the body is raised from the ground to be taken to the grave, two men say a Malay prayer over it.—The prayer is supposed to mean, according to my native informants, that they are asking for a safe journey for the soul, that no trouble will come to it, just as the Malay, in his prayer, asked for a safe voyage for his ship. This prayer was said by the Malays, according to native ideas, during a storm and before they left for their homelands.—The natives then dance a ceremonial pulling-up of the anchor while taking the body to the grave. A mast is raised over the grave as a memorial.

All this is of particular interest to the student of symbolism and ritual, since it clearly demonstrates some of the methods by which abstract ideas are put into concrete form and the various elements of culture integrated into a single unity in the minds of the people and in their group actions.

Some of the coastal clans have added articles of Malay material culture to their list of multiple totems. Each clan has a large number of totems which are ranked according to their emotional mythological importance. The Malay totems usually belong to the garma class, which is the lowest and can be seen by women. This is not so much the direct influence of Malay culture as the inclusion of new facts into Murngin classifications. The whole of their world (animal, plant, mineral, cultural, et cetera), has been symbolized into a totemic system. It would be strange indeed if the culture did not find a place for the Malay and the contents of his culture. At present there is a tendency to substitute the white man and his civilization for the Malay in the totemic system.

Malay Influence on the Racial Stock.—It is surprising to the investigator to find little evidence of miscegenation among the blacks and Malays in northeast Arnhem Land. The writer measured a large number of individuals in this area and found only two individuals who might be classed as hybrid. The two skin colors were slightly lighter than the darker type of black, but no lighter than the type of pure Australoid found in the interior regions where there was no opportunity of racial mixture. These individuals also had the mongoloid broad head and straight hair. Their brachycephalism clearly marked them off from the dolichocephalic heads of the pure aborigines. The straight hair, however, was little different from that of the pure strains. There are several reasons for this lack of interbreeding. The first is the insistence of the people east of the Goyder River that their females remain monogamous and faithful. They are very different from the peoples to the west of this river, who center around the Liverpool River and Cape Don, where wife-lending and a kind of primitive prostitution are common.

The writer, although he was frequently offered the wives of many of the men from the western regions as a friendly gesture, was never embarrassed by such offers from the more eastern people, except by two men, both of whom had lived for long periods of their lives in the west, and were considered "low fellows" by their tribesmen. This insistence on the faithfulness of wives chiefly accounts for the lack of mixture. A large proportion of the white men who sailed along the Arafura coast have been killed or attacked by the natives, because, in almost every case, of a white man's attempting to have illegal sexual relations with native women. The same conditions must have prevailed during Malay times. All the native informants insist on this fact.

In addition to the above reason for lack of racial mixture, there is the fact that the Malays also displayed a considerable wisdom in preventing trouble from breaking out between the two races through attempts to interfere with native women. They organized a system of guards or "policemen" to watch their men and prevent them from having contact with native women. All the blacks in this whole area speak very highly of the Malay traders, for they always mention first their generosity and immediately after this they say, "They let our women alone." In the same breath they will tell a white man whom they consider to be their friend that the white and Japanese traders are "no good" because they are stingy in their trade and are always trying to rape their women.

A number of white pearlers have been through the islands and along the coast, but no Caucasian half-castes are found in the region east of the Goyder River and north of Groote Eylandt. When one knows the "barnyard morals" of the average white trader, this is eloquent testimony to the high standards of native morality and of the chastity of their women. The lack of white hybrids is also explained by the feeling the whites of the north have for the black men of this district. The killing of several whites and Japanese has put a heavy fear in the hearts of all intruders into these parts. The natives have a reputation for treachery, largely because of their ambushing of several white pearlers and night attacks on a few Japanese boats, where all the men were killed, in retaliation for mistreatment of their women.

These last few remarks have been added further to substantiate the possible causes which prevented race mixture when the Malays were coming into North Australia. Since the rapacious civilization of the West cannot produce half-castes in this region, it is less probable that the more gentle Malay culture would produce racial hybrids in North Australia. Tindale, in his article on the Groote Eylandt natives, says that the Malays were interested in acquiring native women to take home with them. I can find no evidence of this among the Murngin and their neighboring tribes. A number of native men, however, did go to Macassar and the other islands whence the Malays had come. The writer met one or two of these men who had served as pearlers on seasonal voyages on Malay boats.

The influence of the Malay race and culture has not been important in northeastern Arnhem Land. There are but slight traces of hybridization in race or culture. The greatest influence is found in the material culture, and the least in the social institutions of Murngin civilization. Compared with the total number of traits found in aboriginal culture, those added from the more eastern civilization are very few indeed and, with the exception of the dugout complex, have had no significant influence on the development of Murngin civilization. On the other hand, when an examination is made of the even larger number of traits found in Malay culture, and they are contrasted with the very few adopted by the Murngin from the Malays, it becomes even further demonstrable that Murngin civilization remained very near to what it was before the Malay arrived, and that the Malay gave little of his own civilization to aboriginal Australia.

History of Burial Customs

The Murngin now finally dispose of their dead by placing the bones in a symbolically carved hollow log and planting the log upright within the camp. This is true of all the tribes except those in Cape Wessel Island, where the natives, after wrapping the bones of the dead in paper bark, put them in rock shelters. I am told by island natives that the rock shelter is used also in the interior back of Blue Mud Bay. All the natives to the west, such as the Gunwingu and Maung, use the hollow-log method of disposal. Historically this situation raises an interesting problem of priority of burial customs. The distribution of the rock burial method in the far north and southeast on the periphery not only of the Murngin but also of the whole of Australia suggests that this method was first and that the hollow log is a later intrusion. Against this is the fact that the use of the hollow log as a bone repository is not an isolated item in Murngin material culture, for the log is used as a basic material for the making of a number of objects such as the trumpet and the drum and their smoking pipes.

An examination of these last three objects from an historical point of view proves fruitful when we remember that the pipe is quite recent in Murngin culture, having been brought in by the Malays. The Uvar drum seems to be fairly late because it is associated with the Ulmark ceremony wherever it is found, and the Ulmark is only partly distributed in the Murngin clans and also seems to be spreading in from the south. It is also not found in the northeastern clans where the hollow-log burial is absent. There are a number of clans farther south than Wessel Island which do not have the Ulmark drum. Of the objects made from a hollow-log form, only one seems comparatively old within Murngin culture. Their comparative recency lends color to the belief that the hollow-log burial is more recent, particularly when one remembers its distribution. This last bit of evidence is obviously insufficient by itself and is merely offered as support for the general thesis of the recency of log burial.

The conclusive proof of this historical induction comes from archaeological finds. Around Arnhem Bay, Buckingham Bay and at Caddell Straits, as well as farther inland, the bones of great numbers of skeletons can be found in the dry rock shelters at the present time. Some of them were collected by the writer. They had been laid out in burial position and some had pieces of bark lying with them. The natives said that they were the bones of very old people who once lived there but who belonged to a different race. Some of them attach the destruction myths to the disappearance of this race whose bones repose in the rock shelters, and others said they were the bones of Wongar people. The bones showed indications of having been covered with red ocher, and the skulls when measured and observed demonstrated that they were authentic remains of Australoid peoples and were undoubtedly racially the same people who occupy the region at the present time. The Murngin knew that these burials were the same as those at Wessel Island, and it was finding the rock burials which brought out the information that Wessel Island people still use this type of interment. With the evidence of a peripheral distribution of rock shelter burials at the present time associated with the findings of rock shelter burials of a former time in the central Murngin area, it seems fairly conclusive proof that the Murngin of the whole area once used the rock shelter method, and that the log coffin interment is more recent than the other.

Archaeology and the Ground Stone Axe

The ground stone axe is normally considered to be comparatively recent in Australia because it is not distributed throughout the whole of the continent; it is not found in the southwestern part of Australia. Such evidence is not conclusive since the spear-thrower, which is looked upon as an old trait by many authorities, is not found in certain sections of southeastern Australia. It is largely because European stratification shows it to be more recent than the chipping or flaking techniques found in the Old Stone Age cultures in the sites of such countries as France and Spain that this assumption has been made for Australia. The stone axe is the only ground stone implement found in Australia, for the knives, spear heads and similar tools and weapons are made by the chipping and flaking techniques. The Murngin possess this implement; the writer made a fairly large collection of them. The stone axe is little used by the people on the coast because they have acquired Malay iron axes and more recently European ones, but nevertheless they are still in use in the interior and occasionally along the coast.

Because the axe is stone and durable it gives one a good opportunity to use archaeological methods to study its approximate age in Murngin culture and possibly Australian civilization, since there were a number of large shell mounds distributed generally along the Murngin coast and in particular in the island of Millingimbi in the Crocodile group where the present Christian mission is now located. Two of these Millingimbi mounds were excavated by the writer with the help of aboriginal labor and mission picks and shovels.

The largest mound was located about one hundred yards or so from the shore and was shaped like the crater of a volcano with a rock water hole in its depths. This crater-like appearance was so real that the missionaries had called it Meteor Well because an explorer a year or two before my arrival had pronounced it the result of a meteor's fall. Actually, it was the result of human habitation spread around a clan well and the dropping of oyster and other shells around this water hole. This mound was about 425 feet long. The crater was approximately eighty-five to ninety feet across. The mound itself was eight feet wide and eight and one-half feet deep from its highest part to the earth's surface. It tapered off gradually to each side. The Murngin women were still adding shells to the heap by bringing to the water hole for opening baskets full of bivalves dug out of the mud flats along the coast or pried from the rocks of the oyster beds. The seacoast had a bountiful supply of shell food on this side of the island. A trench was sunk in the mound running from the outside to the center of the crater. It measured five feet in width and was excavated through the shell into a foot or more of earth, which gave a fair sampling of the site.

The same varieties of bivalve shells were found throughout the excavation. No stratification of any kind was found. The same tools were discovered a few inches from the bottom (as well as red ocher and white clay paints) that are being used by the modern aborigines of the area.

A ground stone axe was found within six inches from the bottom, or eight feet beneath the surface. This seemed to indicate a great antiquity for this implement in this area and therefore at least for its appearance in Australia. The finding of this axe was the most important positive contribution made by the two mounds that were excavated, since it was a positive proof of the long use of this artifact in North Australia.

The age of the shell mound must be considerable. The mound was only one of three larger ones and a number of smaller ones within a few hundred yards. All were composed of a compact mass of broken bivalve shells. The supply of bivalves in this area appears unlimited and forms a large part of the diet of the people; however, the population of the clans of this island was very small and could not have numbered more than twenty-five or thirty people, though during the shell and ritual season it might, for two or three months, rise to eighty or a hundred people; the year-round average could not have been more than approximately forty individuals. The natives said that before the mission came, no one lived there during the height of the rainy season because of its being badly infested with mosquitoes. It seems incredible that mounds the size of these could have been built by such a small group, and only a long period of occupation could account for the quantities of broken shells and the several large mounds.

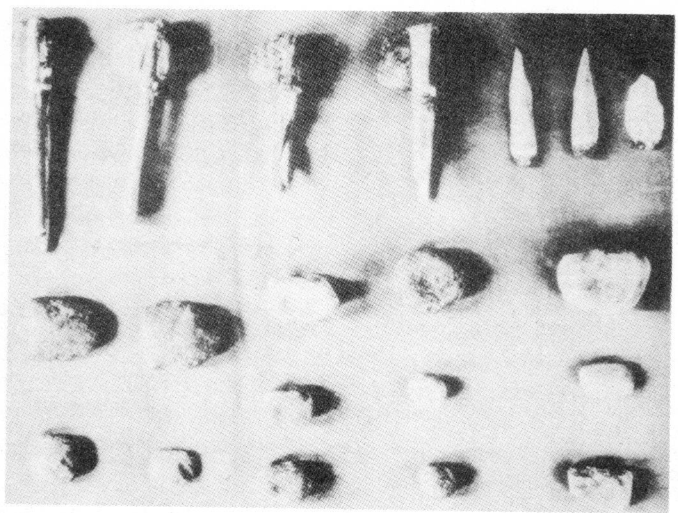

IA. *Top left:* HAFTED STONE AXES.
Top right: STONE KNIVES (or Spear Heads).
Middle and lower left: UNHAFTED AXES.
Middle and lower right: GRINDING BASINS AND MULLERS.

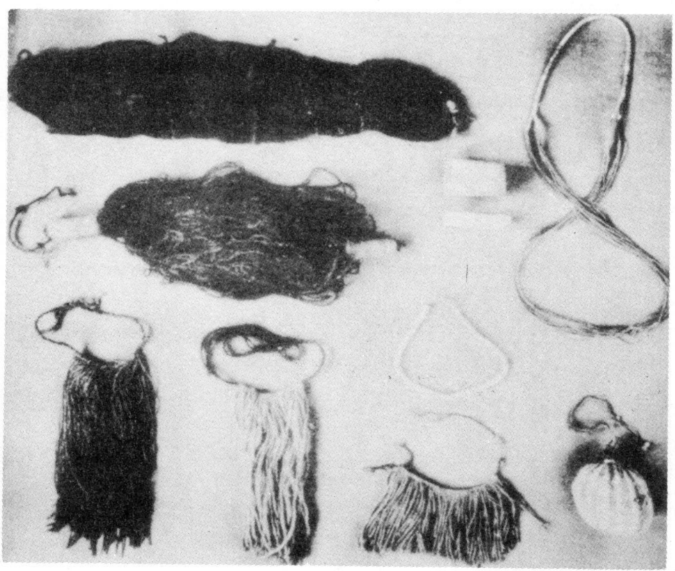

IB. *Upper left:* TWO HAIR BELTS.
Lower left: TWO MEN'S PUBIC COVERINGS.
Lower middle: ONE WOMAN'S PUBIC COVERING.
Upper right: ARMLETS AND WOMEN'S "HARNESS."
Extreme lower right: SPIRIT BAG.
Left center: NECKLACE OF FISH VERTEBRAE.

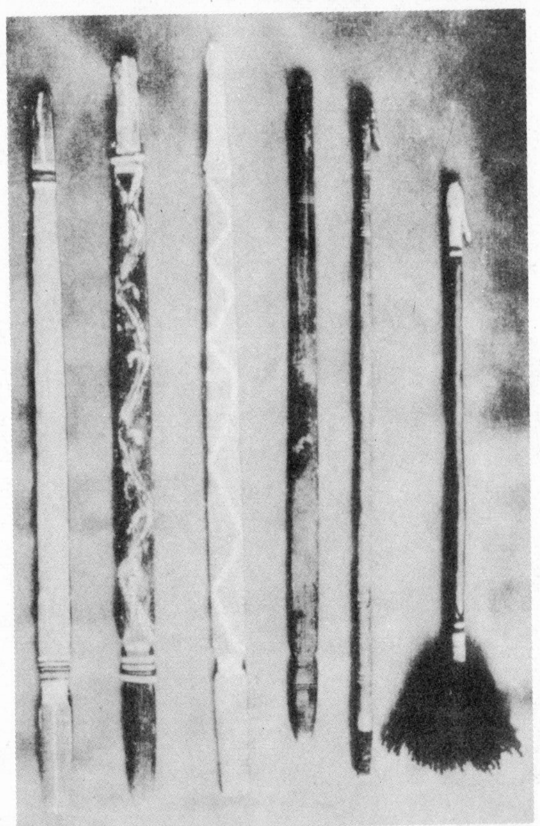

IIa. Spear-throwers. Four at Left Are Mangels.

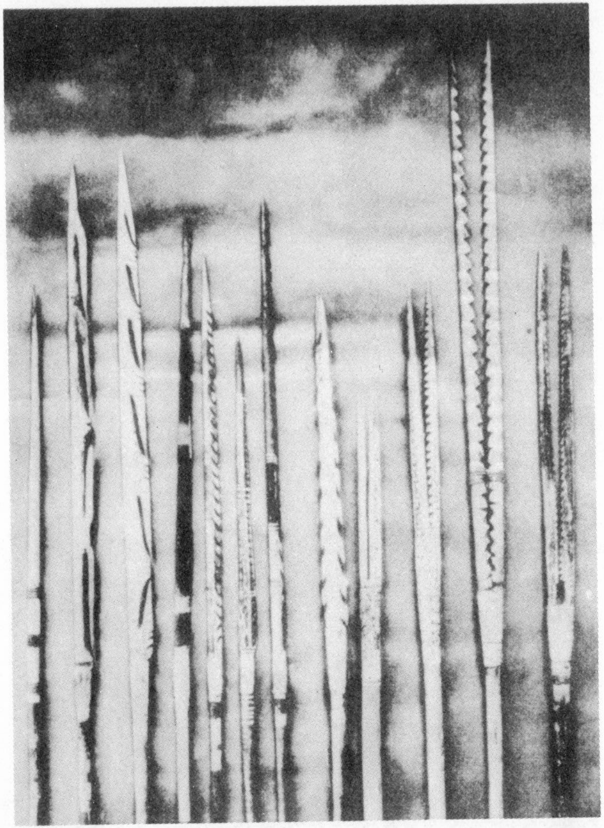

IIb. Spear Heads.

IIIA. FOUR MEN'S BASKETS;
WOMAN'S CARRYING-BASKET (*lower left*).

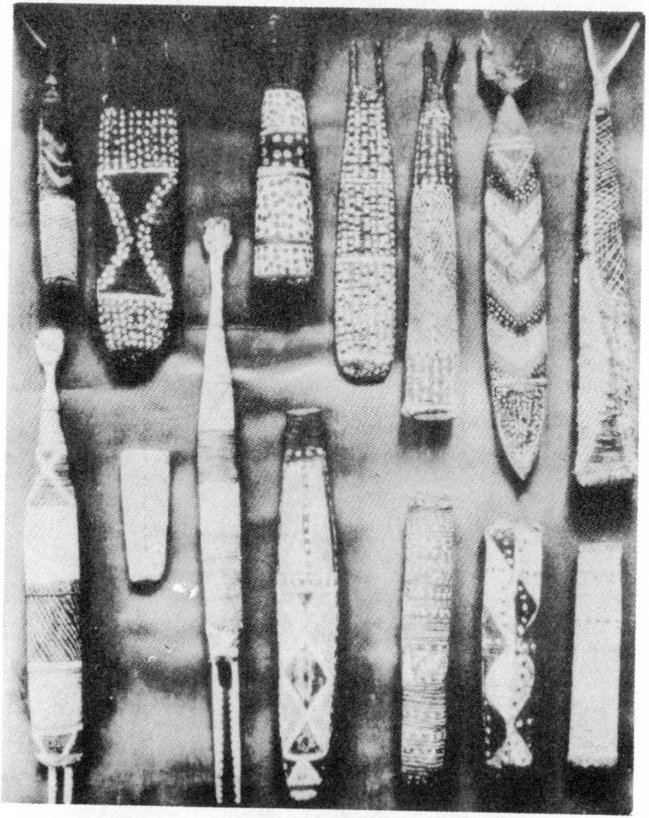

IIIB. TOTEMIC EMBLEMS USED IN NARRA CEREMONY.

IVA. WAR PARTY. (Warriors covered with white clay.)

IVB. WARRIOR PAINTED TO REPRESENT A CROCODILE.

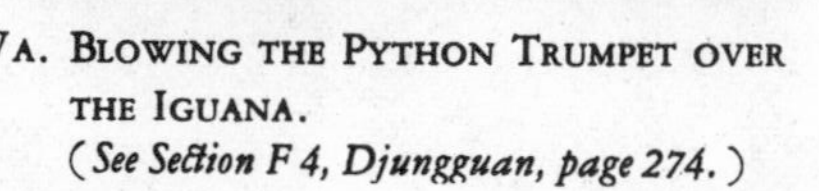

VA. BLOWING THE PYTHON TRUMPET OVER THE IGUANA.
(*See Section F 4, Djungguan, page 274.*)

VB. IGUANA DANCERS IN THE DJUNGGUAN CEREMONY.

VIa. Yermerlindi, the Python's Emblems in the Gunabibi.

VIb Preparing a Dancer for the Gunabibi Ceremony.
(*See Section C 1, page 283.*)

VIIA. CHORUS AND DANCERS IN THE ULMARK CEREMONY. (*See Section J, page 311.*)

VIIB. GRUB DANCERS IN THE ULMARK CEREMONY. (*See Section J, page 311.*)

VIIIA. DANCING FLOOD WATER IN THE NARRA CEREMONY.

VIIIB. BOYS RECEIVING INSTRUCTION IN THE NARRA CEREMONY.

PART V

PERSONAL HISTORY

CHAPTER XV

MAHKAROLLA AND MURNGIN SOCIETY

THIS section, too fragmentarily and too briefly, tells the story of Mahkarolla, a Murngin who was my friend. Although we had not seen each other for almost twenty years, we continued being intimate and close friends until his recent death. He was a member of a "stone age tribe" and I have lived most of my life in modern industrial America, yet during his life our friendship was as strong and enduring as any I have experienced with my own people. I think I knew him as well as I have ever known anyone. Most of this chapter will be in his own words; the part told by me relates incidents in our relationship which I believe reveal his mature wisdom, moral strength, and his fine qualities as a human being. Throughout the book I have striven for objective reporting and detached scientific analysis; although Mahkarolla's autobiographical sections in this chapter do conform to these criteria and the evidence was collected accordingly, I hope the last section about him will express what I felt him to be as a splendid human being, as well as express my love, respect, and admiration for him. Perhaps in any true account of a lasting friendship this is the ultimate objectivity. [Mahkarolla is the large man with his back to the viewer standing in the center of Picture IVA; white war paint covers his body and head.]

The previous chapters present the Murngin world as a social system and as a symbolic order, while "Social Change in North Australia" attempts to reconstruct something of the past Murngin life, particularly the relations of the Murngins with the Macassar people. The purpose of this chapter is different: it is designed to let the reader meet a Murngin individual and *feel* what he is like as a human being. This chapter can render no claim to being an autobiography or a personality analysis. Rather it is an incomplete account of a man's life and his feelings about himself and his world assembled from field notes which were collected to understand not Mahkarolla but his society.

Throughout the text of this chapter the social references and social significance of his remarks have been indicated by placing page references to the text of the book in parentheses. For example, when he speaks of his experiences in the circumcision ceremony the pages in parentheses refer to age grading parts of the Djungguan ceremony and other appropriate social and collective behavior. Mahkarolla tells part of what he *thinks* he remembers of how it felt and what it meant to him as an individual; the text referred to presents the norms and modes of the society.

When I arrived in the Murngin country the men who had been on board the sailing vessel with me very quickly spread the news of my arrival among all the people. A number of the older men came to see me. Among them was a man who, I discovered, could speak a fair amount of English. He and I talked. I learned his country was on the mainland farther to the east; although he spoke English his thinking was native; and he considered himself, and was looked upon, as a person of consequence and authority among his people.

Across his chest and on his upper arms were ritual scars from self-inflicted wounds which had been filled with ashes. I judged him to be a man of about 45, possibly a bit older. He told me that his name was Mahkarolla. It was not long until we began our discussions, he telling me about his people and I telling him about mine. He became my best informant. We went out hunting together. We did together many of the things common to the daily life of a Murngin. He took me on my first canoe expedition away from Millingimbi Island to some of the other islands in the Crocodile group where a great ceremony was being held in honor of Bapa Indi, the python totem. It was during this first expedition that we became aware of our mutual dependence and friendship. Thereafter we were constantly together.

The next sections are told by him. I have translated his English, much of it pidgin, and his use of Murngin into standard English and have arranged what he told me in a simple chronology.

"When I Was a Little Boy"

I don't remember myself when I was very little. When I was a little larger I wanted to go to the countries of other clans and see places like Elcho Island and the Goyder River (map, page 40) and see how people lived and what they did and learn their language, but I was too little. All this was before I was circumcised.

I had heard my older brothers and some of the old men talk about Kopang and Macassar and the black men who lived to the west and who talked a language we little children could not understand (pages 445-450). I, too, wanted to go there and see those countries and ride on Macassar prahus which came to see us when the wind was from the East, but I was too little. Some of my brothers and some of the old men had been to those countries and a few of these men, while they were there, had Macassar women for wives. Charli Charli Sit-Down, my older brother, fell to the deck from the mast of a Macassar ship. He broke his back and still lived.

We Wangurri clans-people are a bush people (pages 16-29). We are very strong and very fierce and good fighters. All the coast people are afraid of us. Our country comes to the salt water at only one place on Arnhem Bay (map, page 40). It was here that we saw the Macassar. They brought us presents of rice, syrup, calico, tomahawks, dugout canoes, knives, and gin. We gave them pearl shell, pearls, tortoise shell, sandalwood, and other woods they use for medicine. We helped them gather trepang (pages 448-450).

At these times, when the Macassar prahus took down their sails and masts and their men disembarked, our old men drank plenty, for it was then they got all the gin they wanted for the presents they gave the Macassar men. There would always be big fights. In the morning you could see blood everywhere and many people were killed. While the old men fought with the knives from around their belts and with tomahawks, clubs, and spears, we children used to sneak in and eat the food that they had left. We always waited our chance and rushed in and ran away again.

I can remember one day my father's giving me some tortoise shell and saying, "Mahkarolla, you go and give this to that Macassar man and make friends with him so that when he comes again he will know you, and you will know him, and you will have a feeling of friendship for each other." I did. The Macassar man talked to me but I didn't understand him. I forget the rest.

Another thing I remember when I was very small: I went with my father through the Gwiyamil clan country to the Wulkara people for a corroboree. This is the path our ranga took in the stories we know about him, and those people are also Sand Fly people (pages 33-35), just as we Wangurri are.

Before we were circumcised we little boys played spear-fighting games, talked about sneaking up and killing a man, and we threw clay mud balls at each other. When it was hot in the rainy season we swam in the sea (pages 114-117).

Later we played being grown men and women with the little girls. We made little fires in the sand beaches. We went out just like our fathers and pretended to spear fish, and the little girls went into the bush and brought home bush food (vegetable food). We made little bark huts just like our fathers' and mothers'. The girls would come in and lie beside us as our wives and we were their husbands.

When we were little boys, others boys who were a little bit bigger joked us about the wives we were going to marry. This made me feel very ashamed. Little girls joked the same way. They also became ashamed. When we got bigger we weren't ashamed any more. We were glad.

I think I always knew it was wrong to "play with" a girl of the Yiritcha moiety because I always knew I was Yiritcha (pages 29-33). I just knew it. No one told me. I cannot remember anyone telling me. I just knew it. Yiritcha people belong to my half of the people, and I knew it was wrong to play husband and wife with my sister, even though I was a small child and knew nothing. I talked to my sister then. Now I never talk to my sister (pages 54-55). I never do any of those things with my sister. I am just the same with her as I am with my Mokul Rumeru and my Momelker (pages 92-93).

Long before I was circumcised I was told to stay away from my Mokul [Mother-in-law] and her mother. They were taboo. I was told by my father and my mother and the other old people that I could not speak to them and that I must not look at them. I must never touch them, and I could not use their names. If I wanted to give them anything I must give it to another man or woman to give to them, but never could I give anything to them from my hand to theirs. If I went near them or did any of these things, the old people told me, I would get a sore in my groin and a very large swelling in that place and I would become very sick. When I was very little I walked around anywhere, and I touched anybody, and I did as I pleased, and I went near these taboo people because I didn't know any better.

I didn't know anything at that time. I thought women were just the same as men. I did not think at all. By and by, when I had grown a little, I saw that the little girls were different when I looked down at them. I thought then that they were just like my mother. About this time I noticed that some of the little boys looked different when I looked at them there. They had no foreskin on their penises, but I had foreskin just as I had when I had come out from my mother. At first I did not say anything—I was ashamed. By and by I asked one boy why he was like that and he said he was circumcised. I asked him how it was done. He said he did it. He was lying to me because the old men had told him they would kill him by magic if he told the truth to us small boys. We could not know this until we had been circumcised ourselves. I did not know he was lying, but I felt maybe he was not telling me the truth.

When we little boys and girls played together we did it by ourselves so that no one could see. We were ashamed if we thought older people were watching and listening to what we were doing. We said things to each other about sexual intercourse and other sexual things which we did not understand. The other day I heard a little girl say to the little boy she was playing with, "You are my husband. I am your wife. Come have sexual intercourse with me." That was the kind of things we said to each other. I laughed because I remembered when we said those things and we did not know what they meant. She said it because it was part of their game. But when we grew larger we did find out and some of us became sweethearts. Even today these old sweethearts still get food from us and we get food and presents from them (pages 63-81).

When I was a little bit bigger, after I was circumcised, we little boys always made fish spears and we always carried them with us. We hunted birds and fish with them. Sometimes we hit a bird, and often we caught small fish. We learned then to carry our baskets over our shoulders, under our arms, just like grown men do, just as our sisters learned to carry their baskets over their foreheads.

When a boy gets a little bit large and he has been circumcised, he sleeps with other boys and the unmarried men and he stays away from his father's and mother's camp most of the time. It is no good for young people around where married people are. They learn too much. They see women too much. Sometimes you see these boys sitting down in a camp with the women. They are not learning the way to live properly. It is all right when they play around in their own camp and they eat there and sleep there (page 116).

Mahkarolla's Circumcision

One day I went with an older brother down through the Barlamomo country to Blue Mud Bay to invite them all to come up to my country for my circumcision (pages 249-280).

When I came back from the Blue Mud Bay country many of our relatives came with me. They brought many presents. My father took me and gave me to a man who painted me very pretty with many colors. I was afraid but I tried not to show it. I looked like I did not care what happened. I was a little bit pleased, too. I was afraid because I did not understand what was going to happen to me. I did not know it then, but my father had given that man a present to paint the picture of my totem well on my breast and belly, and also to put some of my totems (symbols) on me to get me ready (page 252).

When the old men painted me for my circumcision ceremony they put kangaroo teeth stuck in beeswax on a string and tied it around my forehead. The teeth hung on my forehead over my nose.

When some of the old men were away I asked some of the little boys what they were going to do, and one of them said he thought they were going to cut me. I was very frightened. My father had taken me a little way away from the main camp where the women stay and had brought me part way to the sacred camp of the Python, where only men can go. This also frightened me.

When I heard the little boys say the old men were going to cut me I sneaked away from the little boys' camp and ran to my mother. It was nighttime when I heard this and I thought if I went to my mother she would hide me and I could sleep. I asked her to hide me under her sleeping mat. She put me there but said I would have to be cut. She said all men had to have that done to them for it was like that (page 251).

Next day, when it was time for me to be circumcised, my galles, who were big men, caught me and took me from my mother. All the women got spears and they pretended to fight the men. They threw spears without spear-throwers. They did not hurt anybody. It was a little bit like fun. I thought, "Those women are fighting for me." It made me feel good. The men made a ring around me and took me. They chased the women away. I was taken to the sacred ground of the great Bapa Indi, where the men held their ceremonies to celebrate the fact that they were Dua (pages 29-33).

I thought I was going to see a real python. When I stood and looked at the leaves and piled up earth that surrounded the dance ground I thought that big snake would come out there. I stood at the head of the ground with another little boy who was also going to be circumcised and two old men stood beside us (pages 255-256). Two dancers came. They were all painted, but I was too little and I did not know what their paint meant. One old man said they were Wongar kangaroos (pages 261-264). He also said, "When you get through with this ceremony you can't talk any more to any of your people except your father and your mari and to the little boys." He said if I did talk a little bird which was all the same as a spirit would listen to me and come and tell all the old men and the old men would kill my mari and my mother and kill me. They would have a bad medicine and do it.

All the dancers who come out in the circumcision ceremony appeared. While they came the two old men told me the story of the two Wawilak sisters who made the world and our life the way they are today (pages 236-245). In one of the dances several old men ran at us little boys, holding spears in their spear-throwers and pretending they were going to kill us with them. We were very afraid but we did not show it. We stood still. Then they told us that this was the way Wangurri people were and this was the way our fathers and our grandfathers had always acted and that they had never been afraid and they always had been great fighters. After this they took us away, back to the bush which separated the men's ceremonial ground from the main camp of the women. Some old men stayed with us. When we had been there a few moments we could hear the roar of Yurlunggur, the great Father Python of the Dua moiety (pages 255-256). He seemed very near. I tried not to tremble, but I was very afraid. The old men told me he was more than a real snake. He was a spirit. The old men told me he was the great Father Python who had come in the spirit and was made true for us black men at this ceremony for him. They said when I grew older I could see him, but that now I was too little and that my eyes were not strong enough and that it took much "power" to look at him like old men must have when they see him.

After a little while I heard all the men calling out with some strange sounds. I knew later that they were using the cry of a wedge-tailed eagle. They were beating their spears with their spear-throwers. They came nearer and nearer and finally two of them picked us up and put our legs around their necks and over their shoulders. We rode on their backs as we marched to the main camp where the women were. When they carried me on their shoulders I thought they were sure to kill me. I was more afraid. I held my head down and shut my eyes. I thought first, "Maybe they will kill me," then I would think, "No, maybe they are going to burn me." I would think back and forth like that. When we got in the women's camp they took me down from off the man's shoulders and one man lay down on the ground and I was placed on top of him and some other men held me with my legs spread apart so that I could not move. I cried and cried. Just before they did this one old man gave me a drink of water. When I started crying one of the men put a small basket in my mouth for me to bite on and so the women couldn't hear my crying. All the men had surrounded me and I was in the middle of a circle. I could hear the women crying while they danced around our circle (pages 276-278).

One man took a stone spear and broke it and took a small piece of it and cut the skin from off the head of my penis. Then I was picked up and a man ran with me back to the men's ground. I was crying and crying, for I was very afraid and the cutting had hurt me. When we got near the men's ground he put me down by a small fire and took some water and washed where I had been cut and took his hands and put them over the fire and heated them and placed them over my penis. This made me feel much better. I was thirsty. I asked for water. The old men said that while we had been out in that ground the whole world had been covered with salt water again because the tide had come in and covered everything. There was no drinking water now, he said. They told me this for one day and would not let me drink. All that day I went without water; next day they gave me some (pages 277-278).

A day or two after I had been cut some old men took me, with my father, to the men's ground. When we got there I found they had two logs laid down and two more laid across them. They were placed over some stones that were as hot as fire. A big fire had been built over these stones to make them hot, before the logs were placed on top of them. All the old men were sitting around singing. I was afraid again because I did not know what they were going to do. I did not cry. I just looked down and said nothing. They told me to stand up on the logs and squat down over the hot stones. An old man stood by. He had some lily leaves that had been soaked in water. He threw the lily leaves on the hot stones. Steam came up all around me. This went inside my anus and into my body and all through it and came out my mouth. That is what those old men told me.

They told me it would make me very strong and clean me all out and make me all the same as the power song. I know now they did this for this reason and so that I wouldn't be greedy and could go a long time without food and without drink.

Two or three old men warmed their hands over the fire and put them to my mouth and talked to me. They said, "You are no longer a baby. You are growing up and going to be a big man. You must not swear at anybody. You must not lie. You must not chase after other men's wives."

Another old man rubbed my navel. He said, "This will make you very strong and you won't get hungry quickly and you won't try to eat too much food." One old man sat beside me. He picked up a piece of kangaroo. He said, "This one is not kangaroo. What do you call this one?" Another old man sat on the other side of me and whispered the power name of kangaroo in my ear. I called out the secret name of this food when I swallowed it. When I said this, all the old men who were sitting around in the men's chorus sang out, "Yai! Yai!"

That first old man then named all the kinds of foods that grow in the bush and that are game and that are fish, and he said this same thing to me and that other old man told me their power names. All the time the leader beat his singing sticks and sang the sacred names of these foods. This was the first time I had ever heard the secret language which only we men understand. No women hear these things. Women are profane and they would spoil them. These are things only for men to know. Children and women are not strong enough (pages 278-280).

He Grows Up—A Foreign Woman Seduces Him

My father and I went to visit my nati's people at Elcho Island (map, page 40). I was larger then, and my circumcision had been a few dry seasons in the past. Some Macassar men were there, and they said that the white men were getting very mean and cheeky and that they were going to stop the Macassar men from coming. They said that this was their last voyage and they would never come again. They said that white men were all the same as animals and that they were big men and had hair on them and were very fierce and they just killed people because they liked to kill.

They said that white men always stole all the women of a people they visited, and when the people complained they killed them. Our old men believed them. We were all very afraid. We were sorry that the Macassar men were not coming again, for they brought us tomahawks and calico and other things we liked (pages 443-462).

One day after they had gone we saw out in the middle ocean the sail of a big boat. My older brother said he would go out and look. He was always very curious and wanted to see things for himself. He was sent out by the old men, who stayed back, for old men are like that. The old men thought he would be killed, but all the time I thought, "No, white men have fathers and mothers and wives just the same as black men." I thought a minute. I got in the canoe with my brother. We rode out to the lugger. A man threw down a rope for us to come up on. Everybody in our canoe jumped, for we thought something was going to kill us. When we saw it was a rope we were a little bit ashamed and we laughed. We crawled up the rope and went on deck.

There was a black man on board. He belonged to the tribe of Cape Don. He was called Cape Don Tommy by the white men on board. We did not know him then, but because he was a black man and he looked happy we felt better. He talked Macassar. We could talk Macassar, too. We did not talk his language, and he could not talk ours. Macassar was always the language black men talked when they could not understand each other's language. There were a white man and some Malays on board. This white man wanted some tortoise shell and pearls. We all talked in our own language and they could not understand us. My brother said that when it came night we would all sneak on board and steal all the things that this white man had. The white man, when he saw me, liked me. The Malays also liked me. They told Cape Don Tommy to ask me if I would come with them and be their cabin boy. I was a little bit afraid, but always when I was a little boy I wanted to go places and see other people. I said I would go. My brother was very afraid and wanted me to come with them, but I stayed on the ship and they went away. My brothers came after me and tried to catch me. They thought that white man was going to shoot me.

Our sailboat went on as far as the Crocodile Islands. When we got there I was very sorry I had gone with them, for I did not know what they were going to do with me. We put down our anchor. We got in the dinghy and were going ashore. I cried and cried. There was a Chinaman on board who was their cook. He liked me and he gave me food. We left the islands and went out to Junction Bay. I found some pelican and sea gull eggs and ate a lot of them. I asked if black fellows lived there. I did not know then that black men lived all around this seacoast. I looked around and tried to find some. I thought to myself, "I'll talk a little Macassar to them, and I'll run away from these white men and go back home." I felt very sorry I had left it. I was afraid maybe that these white men would take me some place and kill me. Then I thought, "No, they won't." I was afraid. I don't know why now.

I hunted for some people, but I didn't find any. I came back from the bush singing a mourning song (pages 403-405). It said how sorry I was and how unhappy, and it is the song we sing when people are dead or when they have gone away and we want them to come back. I got on the boat and went on with these people, for I could not stay by myself. We went on past Cape Don, but there was no lighthouse there then. We went to Port Darwin, where I found many tribes. They had not all died. They were most of them alive then.

We stayed there a little while and came back to the country of Cape Don Tommy. I was still very young and I had no beard and no pubic hair when we arrived there. I stayed there two rains. When I left I had both pubic hair and a beard. When I came there I did not know their language. When I went away I spoke it. One night one of their women made a large bark hut and fixed a fire in front of it and put paper bark on the ground to lie on. She told me I could go inside. I went inside, thinking there would be another boy with me.

When I went into that hut that woman crawled on top of me and put her legs around mine so I couldn't move. I was still young. I did not know what she wanted. I thought she was holding my legs that way and someone would come up and spear me. I could not talk her language and she did not understand Macassar. The girl was young and had young breasts on her like this [he cupped his hands over his nipples]. I wriggled loose from her and ran outside. I found Cape Don Tommy. I said to him, "What does that woman want?"

That girl was his half-daughter. He said, "I think she wants you for a sweetheart."

I said, "I don't like that. In my country we don't make sweethearts that way. We don't make sweethearts before everyone in the middle of the camp. Boys and girls sneak away from the camp and do it there so that the old people can't see us and we won't be ashamed."

He said, "Don't be afraid of her husband. He won't fight you. That is a custom here. He is away now. When he comes back you give him presents, and he will know that you belong to another country, and that our people took you from there, and we must see that you have a sweetheart just as we must see that you have plenty of food."

I slept, though, with the other boys that night. Next morning I was sitting by the fire when three young women came by. One of them was the girl. She said, "Come on with us. We are going to look for honeybee nests."

I did not know what to do. They were going to look for honeybee nests all right, but they wanted me to come along for other reasons. People were about when they asked me. I was ashamed not to go, and I was ashamed to go. I went. When we walked away, one of them saw some honeybees flying and we followed them to their hive in a hollow tree trunk. One of them cut a long forked stick and put it on the side of the tree as a ladder. They got up and cut away at the side of the tree. By and by they found the honey and brought it to the ground. When they did this they called for me to come and help eat it.

I like honey very much, but I was ashamed to be with those three women, and I was afraid of what they might do. While all of them were down on their hands and knees eating the honey I sneaked away and hid behind a big tree that had fallen down. They looked up and called for me, and they tried to find me, but they couldn't. I lay there very quiet.

That noon I came into camp. There was an old man there. He called me over and said he wanted to talk to me. He was very quiet, and he seemed kind, and I believed he wanted to help me.

"Why did you run away from that girl this morning?" he said. "She likes you. Don't be afraid. No one will hurt you. Tonight when she comes to her hut she will want you to go with her. You go in with her." he talked Macassar.

I thought then, "These people are all right. They won't hurt me. I'll sleep with her tonight." But I was still ashamed and a little afraid. Everything was all different from the way it was in my country. I had never been with a woman before, and this also made me ashamed.

That night I watched people. I could not understand what they said so I watched. If a man picked up a spear I held my spear. If men picked up spears and walked around I followed them with my eyes. Under my half-closed eyelids, as I sat by the fire, I watched the girl to see what she would do. I saw by the way she acted she wanted me, but I was still afraid and ashamed, and we do not make sweethearts like that in my country.

I sneaked away from the camp and went out to the beach and sat down in the canoe. There was a boy there. I pointed to the canoe and then to my tongue and said by sign language, "What do you call this?"

He told me. I pointed to a stone. He told me. We did this for a while. At last I hit the thigh of my right leg and pointed to my pudenda to ask him what he called wife. He told me. I was very surprised to find that they had the same word for wife as they did for husband. That seemed to me very silly, for we have a word for each in my country.

I was doing all this to learn the language and find out if it was all right for me to live with that girl. We went back to camp that night, but I slept with all the other unmarried men. In the morning all the young men laughed at me. I couldn't tell what they said, but I knew by the signs they made they were making a fool out of me for not sleeping with that girl.

Cape Don Tommy talked to me again. "She is my daughter. Don't be afraid of her." That night I went into her hut. She came in and lay beside me. I was very ashamed. I tried to lie quiet, but I shook all over.

She was a young girl. Maybe I was no older than she, but she had had sweethearts, I think, before this, from the way she acted. I had never had a woman before this. It was my first time.

She tickled me and made me laugh. She rubbed her fingers all over my body, being careful to keep away from my penis. This made me feel better and did not frighten me. I laughed. She pushed her stiff index finger into my stomach. After this I lost my fear and I had intercourse with her.

In the morning she took me with her. She told me by sign language she was going to teach me her language. I wanted to learn it very much. That day she taught me how to say mangrove tree and barrimundi and palm fruit and all other things women gather for food. She did this as we walked along. I lived with her all the time I was in her country, and she taught me the language, and I can speak it now. When I went with the same white man, who had come back with his lugger, to Elcho Island I left her and told her I would be back in a little while. That white man and his Malays had brought some gin, and I was drunk. It all seemed like a dream. I remember she cried and cried and wanted me to take her, but I said no. When we were away at sea I was sober and I said, "Where is my girl?"

They said, "You left her behind."

I said, "I must go back and get her." I was going to get up and go back, but I was told to wait and get her when we once more came back to her country. They said they were older men and understood those things better than I did. I was a fool to have left her. I was very angry with the Malay for giving me that gin. It may be that he wanted her for himself.

We went on and got to Cape Stewart, where we shot same geese with the white man's gun. Soon we reached Elcho Island. It had been so long I had forgotten it. I did not know it when I saw it, and Cape Don Tommy told me it was Elcho Island. All the people ran away when they saw us for they were afraid of the white men, and they had thought that I had been killed when I left with them before. Finally some of them back back out of the bush. They had no canoes then because the Macassar men had stopped coming and they had not yet learned how to make them from the Kalpu on the English Company Island, people who still remembered how to do it (pages 451-452). Some of the people came out to our boat by lying on a large log and paddling with their hands and feet. I got in the dinghy and went ashore with some of the people on the boat. When my mari saw me he cried and cried. Some people are like that among us black men. We cry when we meet people just as we cry sometimes when we tell them goodbye. I tried to talk to him, but I couldn't say anything. It was just the same as if I had lost my language. I had to talk to him in the sign language. I felt very foolish. I brought flour with me, but they did not know what it was. They cooked flour in paper bark just like they did palm tree flour.

All the people were very angry with the white man for keeping me away so long, and some of them sneaked out in the bush and got their spears and clubs and were going to kill the white man. I said no, that it was no good. I said, "The white men talk very hard and sometimes they swear at you, but inside they are all right. Sometimes when they swear, they mean good." While we were there I got my people to make gifts of turtle shell and pearl to the white man, and he gave them hatchets and knives and calico. I got in the boat and started to go back to Port Darwin with the white man. Cape Don Tommy and the white man quarreled when we got to Croker Island because Cape Don Tommy wanted to sleep on shore. We got out at Croker Island and went by canoe to Cape Don. There I met that girl again, but her husband was there then. We went on to Port Darwin for a moon and came back to Elcho Island. Once more I went into the bush and stayed.

His Wives and Their Parents

Black men walk about single and by themselves. At first they have no mates. By and by they find one that belongs to them. By and by children come. White men walk about by themselves. By and by they find a woman, and more children come out. The Macassar man was all the same.

Big old man kangaroo walks about single and by himself. By and by he catches his woman, and then there are little kangaroos. Opossum and fly and bandicoot—they are all the same.

Python catches his mate and by and by there are eggs, then there are children. Frilled-neck lizard, native companion, honeybees, pigeon, hawk-billed turtle, and all those animals—they are just the same.

Black men cut down trees and by and by little ones come up. Everywhere and all the time it is always the same. Walk around single, by and by a mate, and by and by children. There is an inside meaning to this. Some of us old men who are not fools understand. If those two Wawilak creator sisters had not done wrong in their own country and fornicated with those

Wongar men, things would have been different. Both the men and the women were Dua. They were incestuous. It was like a brother and sister being together. Those two sisters left that country, one pregnant and the other menstruating. If they had not done this, this cycle would never have happened. Everyone and all plants and animals would have stayed single. But after the Wawilak sisters had done this they made it the law for everyone (pages 240-241).

When I was a small boy I walked about single. One day my gawel came to me and said, "Look at me. I am your gawel. You must give me kangaroo and turtle and spears. By and by I will give you my gatu mielk" (pages 82-87).

I gave him spears and spear-throwers, hair belts, and all kinds of food because he would give me his daughters. When I first started making presents to him for my wife, my younger brothers all helped me. By and by, when they get ready to have a wife, I shall help them make presents to their gawels. My gawel gave my father presents of spears and food, and he also gave my arndi presents because I was her son and because she is my gawel's sister.

We like our wives' fathers very much. Suppose my gawel and my father quarrel and suppose they fight. I can do nothing. I cannot help my father. I cannot help my father-in-law. I must do nothing. They are all the same to me. I must try to stop any fight.

All men try to get plenty of wakus in other countries. This is because they send presents to their gawels. They send things that aren't in this country. This country, where we are now, has no stone. Relatives here send presents to the Ritarngo country for stone spear heads. They send bamboo to the Goyder River people for it. Some others have no white clay and they send to other countries for it. Fathers-in-law and sons-in-law are the people who do this (pages 84-85).

Sometimes a no-good gawel promises his daughter to three wakus. All these "half" sons-in-law give presents to him. They all think they are going to get that girl. By and by one gets her. This means a big row. The other two want to fight this lucky one, and they always fight the father of the girl because he has been two-faced. They think this gawel maybe is a little bit crazy. Sometimes two or three boys, when they are all trying to get a girl, see that her father is no good and they all quit.

When a man marries a woman his father-in-law tells him to take good care of her. When a man has two daughters from his father-in-law, sometimes the old man comes and says to him, "It is better that I give your younger brother this next girl." The older brother says, "Yes, you tell him to feed her [give her to him]"; but if he is a greedy fellow he says, "No, I want to keep her myself."

The black man's custom is different from the way white men are. A black man takes a wife when she is very young, sometimes before her breasts have come. He sleeps with her, loves her, and does everything but have intercourse with her. This makes his girl want him and makes her breasts come large and start sticking out. That is before her blood comes. When blood first comes to a woman it is after she has copulated with a man for the first time. That is what causes it. She has blood a few more times, and then she has a baby, and then the blood stops.

If my wife gave me no children, I would go to my gawel and tell him. He would say, "Wait a little while and I will give you another daughter of mine so that you can have children." If my wife died, my father-in-law would give me another one right away. If he hasn't a grown daughter, he would wait until his little one got larger and then he would give that girl to me.

When my second wife got large enough her father and mother brought her to me and said for her to stay with me and that I was her husband (pages 84-85). My first wife [the new wife's older sister] did not growl at me but kept very quiet when I was around. When I was away she growled at her little sister and told her to go on away. "Mahkarolla belongs to me and not to you." By and by my new wife told me about this. She also told her mother and father.

They said to my first wife, "You must stop this quarreling with your sister. She is just the same as you. You are our daughter and she is our daughter. You have Mahkarolla for a husband, and we have given her to him and she has him for a husband. She is your young sister. You will now have someone to look out for the wood for you, and she can help you get food for your husband."

My wife kept quiet then. Those two sisters live together just like good friends. They never fight like the wives of some husbands do. They look out for each other's children.

When another gawel liked me he went to my proper father-in-law and said, "I like that son-in-law that belongs to you. I would like to give him my daughter. He can be a son-in-law of mine, too." My gawel, because he is a good man, said, "You haven't promised that girl of yours to somebody else, have you?" If that man had said, "Yes," mine would have said, "No, you can't because that will make trouble for my son-in-law." That man said, "No," so my father-in-law said, "Yes."

My mother-in-law—I don't talk to her. I can't go close to her camp, can't go pick up something close to her camp, can't take food from her. I can't give food to her straight; I must give it through my wife. When I am around her I can't talk high; I must talk low. It is just the same for her. I can't look at her when we are close. If I go along a path and meet my mokul I must leave that path. I must leave that path and go another way. If I walked along a path and did not see her and accidentally touched her, her sweat would make me swell up in the groin. My sweat would do the same thing for her.

My mother-in-law is a very good woman. I like her very much. She is very good to me. She always saves all the tobacco she gets and keeps it for me when I have no more. I always send her the best of the kangaroos I kill and the turtles I spear. She always says nice things about me to other people. I hear them and it makes me feel good. When my mokul gets a little bit old and she can't have any more children and she looks a little like a man and has hair on her face, then I can talk to her and she can talk to me. We must be very serious when we do this (pages 90-92).

I like my mother's mother [mari] very much. I like her best of all. She is more my mother than my own mother. When I was little, she looked out for me more than my own mother. She gave me plenty of food. She carried me when I was a baby. I like my mother's sister next best, then my mother. My mother's sister was very good to me, too (pages 85-87).

My true father died when I was small. My mother and we children went to my father's yukiyuko [younger brother], as is the law of our people.

Having an old woman for a wife is no good. She can't have a baby. She is too old. If a man doesn't have children he won't have any sons and daughters-in-law, and he, when he is old, won't have any food and plenty of spears and plenty of tobacco. It is no good having an old woman. She is all the same as rubbish.

My wife is not like that—she is young. She is a very good woman. She always looks straight ahead and keeps her mouth very still when she is around other men. She never talks loud. Sometimes, when I am away too long, she won't give me food when I come back. She thinks I have been away too long. When she does this I sit down and wait a while and say nothing. It is better to keep quiet. Then I say, "Well, what are you mad about?" She says nothing, and her face looks different. I can see by how her heart is beating that she is wild inside. I keep asking and asking. Then she tells me she thinks maybe I have stayed away a long time and have been with some other woman. She thinks maybe I haven't been hunting and I have been fooling her. Clear inside she knows this is not true, and by and by she gets quiet and gives me something to eat. Sometimes she thinks when I have been away that I have an old sweetheart and that I go out all the time to see her. After she has growled for a long time I say nothing and then I say, "No, I have no sweetheart. If I did have I would come and tell you. You're not a man." This makes her quiet. I think sometimes if I did have a sweetheart I wouldn't tell her, because none of the other men do when they have them.

When I was a young man, women were more careful and better than they are now. My brother, Badunga, is just starting to grow a mustache. This no-good woman we call the Mokoi [evil ghost] has already tried to seduce him. My brother was out hunting the other day with some other boys, and when he was a little bit away from them that Mokoi woman saw him. She was getting shells, away from the rest of the women. She is no longer a young woman. She has no children because she has copulated with too many men who were not her husbands. She sneaked up on him and talked very nice to him, but my brother Badunga did nothing and came away. He was afraid, and besides he did not like the woman.

Badunga told me. I went down to her husband's camp and told him. I called that Mokoi out and gave her a very hard beating. Her husband, who is my "half-father," did nothing. When I had finished he took a spear-thrower and started beating her too. All the people in the camp said that was very good and was what she needed.

Women before were different. They sat down more quiet than they do now. This one, who is now Dimala's wife, who used to be my sweetheart when I was a young boy, seduced one of the Ritarngo boys. He is too young. I said, "I don't know what is the matter with you women now. You are going after younger and younger boys all the time for sweethearts. I shall have to watch Marl-ma-leen and Pulli [his 18-months-old son and three-year-old boy], or you will have them out too. You are ruining our young men because you are teaching them to have too many women who don't belong to them. They won't sit quiet with their own wives when they have them because you women teach them another way. When we old men were young, a man had one sweetheart and no more until he was married and had proper wives of his own."

If the sweetheart I had a long time ago would come to me now and ask for food I must give it to her. I would not have sexual relations with her now because I am a married man and that would be wrong. When I go to her camp she gives me food. Her husband is a good man; he says to that woman, "Give Mahkarolla some food. He used to be your sweetheart." If he were no good and jealous, he would growl at the woman and tell her not to give me anything to eat. I haven't any sweethearts now. Dimala's wife used to be my sweetheart a long time ago. She likes me very much now. Sometimes she comes around and wants me to go out to the bush with her but I say, "No, I've got a wife. I have children." I will not "play" with another woman. I would get a baby (pages 63-81).

Sometimes a man and a woman run away because they like each other too much. This is a bad thing. Marriages should be arranged properly and people should do things that we do here when things are right. No one here likes runaway marriages. When people like each other too much it always makes trouble for all their relatives and for them (pages 75-77).

Some women stay no good. A man can give them a good hiding and what do they do? They go straight away and look for a new sweetheart. They are all the same as someone with an evil spirit in their heads.

His Children

When my son was born, I was very happy. Many moons before I had come back from a Djungguan python dance. I went to sleep by my campfire and had a dream. In the dream the spirit child came to me and said, "I am bringing something from Wongar to you. I am looking for my mother." I said to him, "Where do you come from?"

He said, "I came from your totem well. I am bringing a barrimundi fish for you" (pages 56-58).

I got up and walked around in the morning time. I went down close to the water along the beach. I saw a large barrimundi floating on the water. When he came close up, the tide threw this fish right up on the sand bank. I looked at him. His tail was moving. I thought quickly, "Oh, this one is from that dream." That fish was all the same as dead when I came up close. I took my spear-thrower, hooked it inside his mouth, and pulled him all the way along through the water and carried him back to camp. I left him there. I called out to a man. "You come help me," I said. "Come help carry this fish and get a fire ready."

The man said, "You lift him up yourself."

I said, "No, he is too big for me."

We two carried the barrimundi back to camp. We cooked him. One man cooked the liver and tasted it. He said, "It is very sweet and very fat but tastes very different."

I said, "Yes, it is different. I dreamed this one."

We started next day for a ceremony. We danced all night. We danced for over a moon.

Before my daughter came I did not dream at first. One day I was out hunting turtles. I saw a little bird. It was like a little fish in the sea. The little bird flew on one side of me and then the other. I heard him say, "Whee!! Whee!!" It was all the same as the wind in the trees. I thought then, "This is a spirit after me." I went ashore. I slept and I dreamed. This little bird came to me in the dream and said, "Father, I have come to you. Where is my mother?"

I said, "Your mother is here alongside of me." Her mother had not had children yet. We had no family. She was only a young girl. I awakened my wife and told her my dream, for I thought straightaway, "I am going to have a daughter." I said to her, "I dreamed a girl for you." My wife knew then she was going to have a daughter.

After my daughter was born we knew we were going to have a son because I dreamed a son. One moon went by. My wife felt a little bit heavy. She told me. I said, "Yes, that is what I told you before in the dream." A few months later a son was born.

I like my children. If a father and mother do not take care of their sons and daughters all the women everywhere start gossiping about them. They say that they are crazy, that maybe they have an evil spirit in their heads, and they say they are no good. We men talk the same way, too. We do not like to see little children mistreated. My little son is just the same as my spear-thrower. He is just the same as my right arm (page 60). I think it is a good thing for a man to have a lot of children. It makes a lot of people in his tribe. It always gives him, when he gets old, all the things he wants to eat and use for himself. If he has trouble, and all men have trouble, he does not have to go to his mother's people or his wife's people for help. He has it himself. He can take his own sons and fight any people because he is strong. When a man has no sons and no daughters, then when he gets old he can do nothing. We black men like daughters too because when they marry that gives us many wakus and makes us very strong. Good sons-in-law always make many gifts. Good wakus make men proud. We like sons too because nobody can hurt us.

Sometimes people talk out loud in the camp at night, and they say, "Which one did you promise this daughter of yours to?"

I say, "I don't know." I say, "No one." I say, "If I have a sister and she has a son I can't wait any longer then. I must point at that waku [sister's son and son-in-law]. He must get her. But now I must keep quiet. I can't say anything. My sister has no son and I must wait. My little boy's mother has a brother; by and by when he has a daughter, I must go to him and get that girl for my son. That will make everything right and keep our family straight" (pages 54-56).

Mahkarolla as a Friend and a Murngin

Those who believe that the savage has a prerational mentality have not known natives intimately, either because of not being in contact with them or because of the mental barrier of scientific or religious dogma. The larger ideas and more general concepts of primitive people are much the same as our own. They have their philosophers and thinkers, their fools and their ordinary men, in about the same proportion as we do. However, no matter how much we like natives and their culture, there is always a tendency to assume an ethnic superiority and to look upon a "primitive" man as "just like a child." This assumed mental superiority is part of our thinking and difficult to dislodge.

A "council" of the important old men had gathered under a large tamarind tree on the border of the totem grounds (page 31). Mahkarolla, as one of the older and more important men of the Murngin, had a place in the circle. [I was also present.] The members of this council were discussing the perplexities of the great war in which their various clans were involved. A few months before there had been complete quiet. In the whole of northern Arnhem Land there had been peace. All the old blood feuds were quiet and inactive. The great ceremony to celebrate the recognition of Yurlunggur, the python god, had started. Leaders from the upper reaches of the Roper River had come down to the coastal plains of the Arafura Sea for this great fertility rite.

One night two young men, against the wishes of their elders, killed a boy and wounded another who belonged to clans that had been their traditional enemies. In the early morning the bush people gathered their belongings and hurried back to their own country. The younger men of all the clans of the Murngin and the other tribes made new spears and tested their spear-throwers in preparation for trouble. War started. The ceremonies ceased. Many battles were fought and many people were killed (pages 161-163).

The ceremony which had been interrupted was a fertility rite. Without this celebration to help nature perform her many functions, the animals would not multiply, the grass would not grow, and the seasons of the year would lose their symmetry. The absolute necessity for the celebration of this ritual was felt by all the men who had accepted the responsibilities of Murngin society.

The council had met, therefore, to find ways of stopping the war and of bringing peace to all the clans of the black world as they knew it. The war must be stopped if life were to continue.

The causes of the war were considered in the effort to find a solution which would bring peace to the people. The reasons for the failure of the peace-making ceremonies were considered. Blame was attached to various individuals. The old men criticized especially the hot-headedness of their youths, with slightly more emotion expressed when they spoke of the misdeeds of their enemies' young men.

After several hours of talk consensus was reached. It was felt that the warlike peoples of the bush were really responsible for the trouble. It was clearly seen that those not represented at the conference were the real instigators of the war and that their actions were without tribal sanction.

One old man then suggested sending a messenger with a message stick to the bushmen, who were not represented, to tell them that there would be a great makarata or peace-making ceremony (pages 163-165). Someone replied that this was foolishness for makaratas had been tried and they had failed because the enemies violated the rules. Instead of bringing peace the makaratas had only brought more trouble and greater conflict. Discussion of this point finally brought victory to the one who opposed the makaratas because the antagonism of the coastal people against the inland clans was still very strong and they wanted vengeance as well as peace.

What, then, could be done to stop the fighting? The situation was desperate; drastic efforts must be made. One of the older men said, "Let us stop all war. This killing of our young men is no good. It is better that we have ceremonies all the time and never have war. Let us have a gaingar."

Everyone agreed he was right. The speaker continued, "We will have a spear fight to end all spear fights."

A gaingar is the most deadly form of Murngin warfare. Later I learned that 17 men had been killed in one gaingar. In proportion to the population this meant a higher mortality rate than in all of the battles of World War I. This old man was proposing that today's young men be sacrificed so that the young men of tomorrow could be saved.

I was asked what I thought of the idea. I did not respond for it was too much. I sat there, among a council of the wisest men of a Stone Age culture. In one sense several millenniums separated their civilization from mine. Yet I had been a soldier in a war in which our leaders and those of our allies had said, "This is a war to end all wars," and had sent millions of young men to die with this rallying cry.

The discussion continued. Most of the group were enthusiastically in favor of the gaingar. The minority, Mahkarolla among them, grudgingly agreed.

When the meeting disbanded Mahkarolla and I walked back to my camp. "When I was a boy I saw a spear fight to end all spear fights," he said. "Many men were killed. It was no good. We must not have it. My people did not stop fighting. As you see, we are fighting today just as we did before. Spear fights do not end spear fights."

One day Mahkarolla and I started on an expedition with two canoeloads of Murngin men, I to map clan territories, he to visit the sacred pools where his totems lived. As we sailed in the dugout around the rocky cliffs of Point Napier, across the channel from the English Company Islands, we entered almost open sea where the wind sweeps down from the northeast and Cape Wessel with terrific force. The western side of Napier's Peninsula was quiet and calm, but the moment we rounded the point we entered a heavy, stormy sea. To go back would have risked being dashed to pieces against the rocky cliffs of the point; we had to go on—across many miles of open sea.

Mahkarolla was in my canoe. Each canoe was equipped with a small sail and a paddle used as a rudder. Along the sides the men used paddles to steady the canoe and keep it from tipping over. The dugout canoes with no outriggers that are constructed by the natives of North Australia are unwieldy and easily upset even in calm water.

As the storm increased Mahkarolla became anxious and asked his older brother, Charli Charli Sit-Down, to act as steersman. In spite of his broken back he was probably the best canoeman in North Australia. He was entirely dependent upon the water for long distance traveling and had become an excellent sailor. Mahkarolla distributed the other men about the boat and took charge of the sail. He placed me in the center in front of Charli Charli.

I thought the waves would submerge us or dash up against the rocks, but the little canoe rose slowly over them and plunged into the troughs beyond. Sometimes the waves were so high that we could not see the sail of the other canoe. Finally, I suggested to Charli Charli that we go back. He shook his head and pointed to the rocks, indicating with a gesture that we would be swamped and killed.

The wind and waves were increasing. One man bailed furiously with a bivalve shell, for although the waves did not strike us the heavy spray filled our canoe. The natives mumbled to themselves. They were calling on their totem ancestors and their totems to help them. I said nothing and looked straight ahead. Then I started to swear in native at the storm. Charli Charli tapped me on the shoulder and asked me to stop because I would offend the Great Serpent and he might swallow us.

In gripping the gunwales I had one hand underwater. Charli Charli again tapped my shoulder and shook his head. He pointed to my hand and said, "Bult-main-dji" (gray shark). I pulled my hand out of the water and turned it so that the fingers were inside the boat. The day before our canoe had been struck several times by large sharks which had come to prey on a crocodile we had harpooned.

We sailed on. We had lost sight of the other canoe and wondered whether it had sunk or gone back. The wind increased and the waves rose higher and higher. We took down the sail because it was no longer possible to control it. It seemed only a matter of minutes before one of the waves would strike us and sink us all.

I called to Mahkarolla, "What shall we do?" He said nothing. He did not so much as glance back. I called his name. He paid no attention. I wondered if he were sulking. This seemed unlike him, but most Murngin occasionally sulk and I wondered if he might feel that I had brought him into this very dangerous situation and blame me for it. With the foolish hope that it might be possible for us to get back to safety, I yelled again and asked if it were necessary for us to go on. He ignored me. After several more futile attempts to get his attention and some profane comment I subsided. There was complete silence in the boat.

Hours went by. Everyone remained quiet. I felt isolated and alone. The sun had gone down behind a bank of red clouds. In many of the Murngin ceremonies red clouds are a symbol of the end of things. The sea had turned blood red, ugly and morbid.

Darkness came, and with the night the waves quieted and the wind lessened. About midnight we came to a desert island lying a few hundred yards off the shore. The island was formed like a semicircular hill with one small beach at the bend. We saw a campfire on the beach and were afraid to land because the coastal and bush peoples had been fighting. Marauding bands from the interior had been coming down to the coastal country. We drew closer and discovered the party to be Murngin—the other canoe had landed safely.

Everything I had with me was soaked through except my camera and photographic material which, fortunately, were in waterproof bags. Mahkarolla and I with the others sat by the fire to dry and warm ourselves. We dried out enough tobacco to have a smoke. Mahkarolla turned to me and then said, "I am very sorry I did not answer you when you called to me, Bungawa. I could not because I was crying too much. I was afraid you were going to lose your life. I thought those waves were going to tip our canoe over and you would die. I am very sorry."

I tried to answer him. All my words seemed inadequate. However, even in my shame I knew he understood my feelings because he had once said that when white men swore they did not mean what they said. After we had had some food and what little water was left in my canteen we hovered around the fire and went to sleep.

When I left the Murngin country I took the mission lugger from the Crocodile Islands to Port Darwin to get the boat to Sydney. Mahkarolla came with me. I had to wait ten days for the boat and during this time he and I were together a good part of each day. When the boat came in Mahkarolla helped me aboard with my luggage and scientific equipment. Then my white friends in Darwin came aboard for a farewell whiskey and soda. Natives were not allowed to stay on board. When I realized we were about to sail I rushed out to find Mahkarolla. The pier was filled with Darwin whites who were there to feel in touch with the homeland. Out at the far corner of the crowd I saw Mahkarolla. He was standing still, his head bent down. I waved but he did not reply. I called to him but received no answer. There came to my mind the memory of the storm at sea when he thought I was going to lose my life. Our parting now had death in it, too, because it was certain that we would never see each other again. I hurried down to the other end of the boat to be nearer him to try to attract his attention. The whisle blew and we started to leave the pier. I called again. Mahkarolla looked up, waved, then lowered his head again. He was crying. That was the last time I saw him.

GLOSSARY OF KIN, NATIVE, AND TECHNICAL TERMS

Kin Terms

arndi—mother.
bapa—father.
dué—father's sister's son (husband); father's sister's daughter.
dumungur—father's sister's daughter's daughter's son; father's sister's daughter's daughter's daughter.
galle—mother's brother's son; mother's brother's daughter (wife).
gatu—son; daughter.
gawel—mother's brother.
gurrong—father's sister's daughter's son; father's sister's daughter's daughter.
kaminyer—daughter's son; daughter's daughter.
kutara—sister's daughter's son; sister's daughter's daughter.
maraitcha—son's son; son's daughter.
marelker—mother's mother's brother's son.
mari—mother's mother's brother; mother's mother.
marikmo—father's father; father's father's sister.
mokul bapa—father's sister.
mokul rumeru—mother's mother's brother's daughter (mother-in-law).
momelker—mother's mother's mother's brother's daughter.
momo—father's mother.
nati—mother's father.
natjiwalker—mother's mother's mother's brother's son.
waku—sister's son; sister's daughter; father's father's sister's son; father's father's sister's daughter.
wawa—older brother.
yeppa—sister.
yukiyuko—younger brother.

Native Terms

Bamun—the mythological period when "things were different" and the totemic spirits and the ancestors of man inhabited the land.
Bapa Indi—*see* Muit.
baperu—native name for moiety, meaning four subsections that belong to each moiety.
billibong—a general term used by the Australian whites for a small lake or pool.
bilmel, bilmal—singing sticks.
birimbir—the totemic soul of man (*see* mokoi).
corroboree—a general term used by the Australian whites for native ceremonies.

dal—ritually powerful, a quality possessed by things that are *maraiin.* Literally, "hardy," "strong."

diramo—man, male.

Djungguan—an elaborate totemic ceremony associated with the rock python cult. The myth of the two Wawilak sisters is connected with this ritual. There are three other major ceremonies also related to the myth of the Wawilak sisters: the Gunabibi, Marndiella, and Ulmark. The Djungguan is "owned" by the Dua moiety.

Djunkgao—the two creator sisters of the East (*see* Narra).

Dua—one of the two moieties in the dual organization.

garma—the Murngin totems are classed chiefly into higher and lower orders, the higher being more sacred, the lower more profane and used in the general camp. The higher totems are called ranga, and the lower totems garma. Emblems, myths, rituals, songs, and dances belong to this lower totemic configuration and are so graded. Garma usually refers to the emblem or to the ceremony. Garma totems may be seen by women, whereas ranga may not.

Gunabibi—*see* Djungguan.

gungmun—a woman who has had a child, literally "the giver."

Makarata—ceremonial peace-making duel.

mangel—spear-thrower.

maraiin—sacred, spiritual, powerful, taboo, connected with the totem. It sometimes is used as a synonym for totem.

Marndiella—*see* Djungguan.

mielk—woman, female.

mokoi—all men have two souls, according to the Murngin: the totemic (birimbir or warro) and the trickster or mokoi one. The former goes to the totemic well at death, and the mokoi to the jungle.

Muit—the python totem. *Also called* Yurlunggur, Bapa Indi, and Great Father.

Narra—this term refers to the totemic well or hole, or a variety of totemic ceremonies associated with the totemic emblem. A Narra totem belongs to the higher order and is connected with the myth of the Djunkgao sisters.

ranga—a totem of a higher order. The word usually refers to the emblem. *See* garma.

Ulmark—*see* Djungguan.

warntdjer (leaf)—a garma type of ceremony for the removal of the spirits of the dead.

warro—same as birimbir, the true soul, "the soul from the heart."

Wawilak—the two creator sisters of the West. The term Wawilak refers to a clan of the interior as well as to the two mythological sisters whose careers are traced in the Wawilak creation myth. The term as an adjective is used to refer to the myth, several rituals (*see* Djungguan), and so on.

wirkul—a young woman who has not had a child.
wirtit—native term for the rock python. *See* Muit.
womera—spear-thrower.
Wongar—a general name applied to the totemic spirits. "In the time of Wongar" refers to the mythological period (Bamun) when the totems inhabited the earth and were frequently like man. Wongar men or Wongar animals are, respectively, totemic ancestors and totemic animals.
Yermerlindi—a totemic python emblem used in the Gunabibi ceremony.
Yiritja—one of the two moieties in the dual organization.
Yurlunggur—*see* Muit.

Technical Terms

age grade—a social division based primarily on sex and the position of the male in the family and ritual structures.
All Father—a vague, otiose, spiritual being who is of little importance in Murngin thought.
black magic—the magic which is harmful to man
clan—the Murngin clan is a unilateral kinship group which traces the descent of its members through the father. Marriage must take place outside the group. It is totemic and owns a more or less definite territory.
classificatory kinship—in the anthropological literature this term usually refers to the system of classifying certain collateral relatives with the lineal kin and of placing people who are of no blood relationship in the categories of other kin who are. For example, a man's or woman's father's brothers are classed as fathers, and the father's father's brothers are classed as paternal grandfathers (marikmo). The mother's sisters are called mother, and their mother and her sisters are all called maternal grandmother (mari). This particular form of the classificatory system, by which the father's kin and the mother's kin are separated, has been called the Dakota System (*see* Robert H. Lowie, *Primitive Society*).
cross-cousin marriage—marriage of the children of unlike siblings; i.e., marriage of ego to mother's brother's daughter or to father's sister's daughter.
symmetrical cross-cousin marriage—system whereby ego may marry *either* mother's brother's daughter *or* father's sister's daughter.
asymmetrical cross-cousin marriage—system whereby ego may marry *only* mother's brother's daughter or *only* father's sister's daughter.
equivalence of brothers—the social rule by which brothers are seen as occupying the same sociological position and are treated as such by the society; as, for example, in the Murngin kinship system.
exogamic—marriage outside the group.
family, limited—father, mother, and their children.
family of orientation—immediate family into which ego (male or female)

is born, including upper generation: mother and father; lower generation: sisters and brothers.

family of procreation—family created by ego by marriage, including upper generation: father (ego) and mother (also ego); lower: their sons and daughters.

function—what a technical object, social unit, or social element does in the group economy.

Great Father—*see* Muit in glossary of native terms.

horde—the Murngin horde is an economic group of people temporarily occupying a certain area of land. The membership of this social unit consists of from a small number of individuals to possible hundreds. It includes the members of several clans and the two moieties.

"inside"—a word used to describe the sacred part of the dichotomy made by the Murngin between the ceremonial world of the totem and the profane world of the general camp. "Inside" also means deeper and more profound, since it refers to the totem.

killing stick—a sharp, hard, short stick supposedly used by the black magician in his killings.

levirate—the inheritance of a dead man's wives by his brothers; in the junior levirate, by his younger brothers.

mana—the impersonal spiritual power or essence found everywhere according to Murngin thought and which can take tangible form in a man, totem, animal, totemic object, and so on.

moiety—a moiety among the Murngin is a unilateral kinship group which traces descent of its members through the father. Marriage must be with a member of the opposite moiety. The several clans are divided between the two moieties. These two divisions of the tribe are sometimes referred to as a dual organization.

"outside"—this term applies to the profane and ordinary meaning of a word, and when used as a geographical expression it means the camp inhabited by all the people, including women and children. (*See* "inside.")

patrilineal line—a lineage of fathers, sons, brothers, fathers' fathers, sons' sons, and the sisters of these men.

phratry—a phratry in Murngin society is a loose grouping of several clans within a moiety, usually on the mythological or ritual basis. It is not exogamic.

power—*see* mana.

reciprocal (in kinship)—summation of all the relations between two people who constitute a kinship bond, as mother's brother (gawel) and sister's son (waku).

rite de passage—a formal ceremony by which the status of an individual changes from that of one age group to another.

sororate—the right of a husband of a woman to the remainder of her sisters after he has acquired the first of these female siblings.

subincision—incision of the urethra. In the southern part of the Murngin area, as in Central Australia, it is part of one of the important ceremonies.

subsection system—a reclassification into eight groups or subsections.

totemism—a form of religion found in primitive society by which a group establishes ritual relations with spiritual beings who are generally species of plants or animals. The totems of the Murngin include not only the plants and animals but certain physical and social items taken from the world of man. In the Murngin totemic complex are included the totems (spiritual beings), totemic ancestors (the mythological ancestors of modern man who consorted with the totems in the creation period [Baumun]), and religious totemic emblems (objects made by the Murngin which symbolize the spiritual reality of the totemic spirits). Other elements in the complex are totemic myths, totemic rituals, dances, songs, etc. (*see* garma and ranga).

tribe—the Murngin tribe is a loose grouping of clans based largely upon a general linguistic unity. It has no chiefs, head men, or formal political structure.

white magic—the magic which is helpful to man.

INDEX[1]

Abortion, 85.
Absolute logics, 10-11, 183-440. (*See also* Avoidance; Magic; *Rites de passage,* Mortuary; Sanctions; Taboo; Totemism.)
  in relation to natural environment, 400-401.
  of death rituals, 433-440.
  of totemism, 393-400.
Adaptation, 393-401.
  primary, secondary, and tertiary, 10-11, 11 Chart I.
  primary, and technology, 127-143.
Adaptive mechanisms, 4, 10, 135, 394.
Adultery, *see* Intercourse, illicit.
Age grades, bases of position in, 6.
Age grading, 5-7, 11, 11 Chart I, 114-126, 380-381, 402. (*See also* Gerontocratic principles; Initiates; Puberty; *Rites de passage.*)
  Narra rites totemic rather than age grading. 330.
  status of men, 5, 6, 115, 125-126.
  status of women, 5-7, 96, 122. (*See also* Women.)
All-Father, 469.
Archaeology, Murngin, 443, 455, 461-463.
  and cave burials, 460-461.
  and the ground stone axe, 462-463.
  and shell mounds, 455.
Arndi (mother), 22-23, 29, 31, 44-46, 54, 57, 60-61, 66, 85-88, 90, 101, 118-119, 322, 404-405, 425, 428, 430. (*See also* Kinship reciprocals; Mother.)
Arndi, little, 61, 71, 87.
Arnhem Land, 35-36, 111, 145, 171, 368-369, 449-450.
  location of the Murngin, 3.
  northeastern, battle ground at frequent intervals, 145.
  northeastern, ritual realities in, 393-401.
Arnhem Land—(*Continued*)
  problem of ritual and magic presented by the northern and southern areas in, 213-233.
Arunta, 23, 36, 36 fn 15, 105, 107, 108, 110.
Asia, southeastern, and Australia, 12.
Australia, 12, 41, 107, 137, 462.
Australia, Central, 23.
  cultural influence on Murngin, 445.
Australia, Northern, 23, 29.
  social change in, 443-463.
"Australian Blacks," 4 fn 2.
Australo-Dravidian linguistic group, 4.
Australoid race, 4.
Avoidance, 51, 87, 89, 92, 93. (*See also* Taboo.)
  brother-sister, 42, 54, 100, 116, (*See also* Kinship reciprocals, Yeppa, Wawa.)
  mother-in-law, 69, 90-91, 121.
  mother-in-law's mother, 105.
  of "keeper of the bones" of the dead, 427-428.
  of platform burial, 423.

Bamapama (Uré, trickster hero), 55. (*See also* Wakinu.)
Bamun (Wongar, mythological times), 10, 34-35, 69. (*See also* Myths; Narra ceremony; *Rites de passage.*)
Bands, *see* Hordes.
Banitja (Barrimunid, totem), 34. (*See also* Narra ceremony; *Rites de passage.*)
Bapa (father), 16, 29-31, 46, 55, 62-64, 66, 76, 89-90, 98-102, 118, 121, 137, 150, 187-188, 251, 319, 331, 378, 404, 425-427. (*See also* Kinship reciprocals.)
  "thrown away," 94.
Bapa Indi, *see* Muit.

[1] The index does not include *all* the numerous and detailed aspects of the culture referred to in the totemic rituals, e.g., technology, hunting, food animals, social organization. Murngin culture is permeated by totemism, and references to the culture permeate the rituals.

Baperu, *see* Moiety; Subsection system.
Island of the Dead, 270, 300, 356.
Mortuary ceremony, 136, 413-415.
Biological configuration, man a species in, 138-143.
Birimbir (soul, Warro), 25, 62, 122, 186 fn 4, 270-271, 300, 373, 403, 403 fn 1, 433, 435-437, 438. (*See also* Mokoi.)
behavior of, at death, 403-404.
close association of, with clan members, 25.
enters killer, 152-155, 457.
enters totemic emblems, 270, 380, 433.
goes to Morning Star Island, 270, 300, 356.
in life and in death, 435-440.
leads killer to game, 154.
living speed departure of, 403-407. (But see all of *Rites de passage,* Mortuary.)
returns to sacred water hole, 16, 22-25, 57, 62, 380, 404, 433.
spider associated with, 419, 434.
Birth, 5, 23, 57-58, 66, 86, 119. (*See also* Procreation.)
control, 23.
from sacred water hole, 16, 21.
rebirth, 22.
"Black Civilization," "Blackfellows," 4 fn 2.
Blood, *see* Ritual, blood.
as relic reminder of vengeance, *see* Dead, bones of.
feud, *see* Feud.
heart's, different from body's, 185.
heart's, extracted by black magician, 184-196. (*See also* Magic, black, case histories.)
kin, *see* Kin, consanguine.
sacred qualities of, *see* Dal; Maraiin.
Boys, 59-60, 115-121, 131, 150, 334-335. (*See also* Camp, boys'; Children; Gifts; Initiates; *Rites de passage.*)
Brother, 26-27, 42, 56, 63, 99-102, 250, 296-298, 406, 428. (*See also* Equivalence of sibs; Kinship reciprocals; Wawa; Yukiyuko.)
Burial, 33, 420-438, 434-435, 460-461. (*See also* Ceremonial masts; Exhumation; Grave posts; Technology, coffin.)
cave, 461-462.
Burial—(*Continued*)
history of customs, 456-461.
platform, 170, 423, 427.
"Buying back" the killed, 166-179, 193-194.

Camp, boys', 114-116, 124-126.
brawls, *see* Fights.
geographical division of, for Djungguan, 250, 254-255; for Ulmark, 302 fn 19.
location, 18.
married people's (main, general), 114, 116-119, 124-126, 253. (*See also* Narra ceremony, *Rites de passage.*)
names, *see* Names, "camp."
of horde, 128.
spatially organized during ceremonies according to location in horde, 382.
Cannibalism, 134 fn 3.
Capture, *see* Warfare.
Census, 17.
Ceremonial, cleansing, *see* Ceremonial purification.
leader, 26, 32, 52, 59-60, 117, 146, 208-209, 249, 379; of Djungguan, 250-251, 279-280; of Gunabibi, 280-284, 289-291, 293-295; of Marndiella, 319-320, 322-324; of Mortuary ceremonies, 413, 420, 422, 429-431; of Narra ceremonies, 330-340, 342, 345-346, 347-360; of Ulmark, 305-316. (*See also* Clans, leaders of.)
as healer, 221-223.
as war leader, 17.
life, influenced by Central Australia, 445.
masts, 33, 423-425. (*See also* Burial.)
names, *see* Names, sacred.
paraphernalia, luxuriance of, 137.
purification, 53, 65, 67, 86, 220-226, 277, 288, 297-298, 300-301, 315-316, 318-319, 322-324, 335-336, 342-344, 349-351, 358-359,380, 386, 389-390, 392-393, 398-399, 402, 434, 437. (*See also Rites de passage,* Mortuary; Ritual curing.)
sickness, *see* Sickness due to ritual.
uncleanliness, 53, 86, 123, 183, 279, 300 fn 18, 303, 376, 384, 389. (*See also* Ritual injury.)

Ceremonies, 15, 19, 21, 32, 42, 59, 77, 111, 115, 128, 135. (*See also* Narra ceremony; *Rites de passage.*)
and dreams, 270.
and myths, close association of, 239-240.
basis of age-graded status, 6, 249.
express dual organization, 33. (*See also* Moiety.)
minor, 65, 67, 119.
only effective mechanism for enlarging social horizon, 383.
owned by clans, 16.
owned by moieties, 32.
reproduction, *see* Bamapama ceremony; Gunabibi; Narra ceremony. Dua and Yiritja.
totemic, as curing rituals, 220, 222.
Ceremony, myth, and warfare, 145-146.
Chiefs, *see* Ceremonial leader; Clans, leaders of.
tribal, non-existence of, 9.
Childlessness, fear of, 76, 83, 120-121.
Children, 6, 32, 43-44, 54, 59, 64, 66, 76, 80, 85-86, 89-92, 100, 106, 109, 114, 118, 120, 212, 300 fn 18, 321, 377, 402, 424, 435. (*See also* Age grading; Birth; Boys; Death; Girls; Kinship reciprocals; Procreation; Puberty; *Rites de passage.*)
taken by war, *see* Warfare.
Circumcision, 5, 59, 64, 81, 86, 114, 116, 120, 124-126, 225, 275-280, 324. (*See also* Puberty; *Rites de passage.*)
origin of, 240.
Clans, 11 Chart I, 15 fn 4, 21, 36-37, 41, 59, 102, 106, 111, 135, 136, 238, 281, 377-383, 437-440.
and moiety garma songs sung to dying man, 403-405.
boundary of lands, 18. (map, 40).
ceremonial leaders of, *see* Ceremonial leader.
ceremonies owned by, 16.
creation of, 16, 18-19. (*See also* Myths, Wawilak, Djunkgao.)
defined and described, 16-29.
distribution of mortuary ceremonies among, 408.
eastern, tend to celebrate Djunkgao cycle, 325.
exogamic, 4, 16, 378, 381.

Clans—(*Continued*)
feuds of, *see* Clans, inter-clan antagonism; Feud.
formed by creator totems, 16.
give spatial expression to kinship system, 378.
given spatial expression, 8, 9.
grouping of, 8, 9, 35-37. (*See also* Moiety; Phratry; Subsection.)
history of a clan feud, 166-179
identification of one's totems through, 5, 10, 25.
ideology of, 19.
insult to, 148. (*See also* Ritual injury.)
inter-clan antagonism, 16, 27, 28, 35, 99-102, 128, 145, 405. (*See also* Feud; Social antagonism; Warfare.)
inter-clan efforts at solidarity, 25, 99-102, 128, 145, 281, 286-287, 300, 311-313, 345-346, 382-383. (*See also* Makarata; Ritual eating of food communally.)
inter-clan rivalry for women, 27, 29, 32-33, 35, 57, 75-77, 84, 144.
intra-clan antagonism, 405.
intra-clan solidarity, 16-17, 19, 27-28, 35, 99-102, 145, 166-167, 379-383. (*See also* Social solidarity.)
intra-clan solidarity strongest during healing ritual, 222.
kin found in, *see* Kin.
land and localities named, 240. (*See also* Myths, Djunkgao, Wawilak.)
land inalienable, 18-19, 379.
land owned by, 16 ff., 135, 379, 381.
largest units of solidarity, 5, 19.
leaders of, 28, 32, 59, 174, 281, 379.
(*See also* Ceremonial leaders.)
location of, 17-18.
map, 40.
members of, closely associated with dead, 25.
membership regulates distribution of economic goods, 385.
mothers', called on for aid, 34.
names of, 15 fn 4, 16. (*See also* Language.)
naming of, in ceremonies, 239-240, 274, 326. (*See also* Narra ceremony; *Rites de passage.*)
northern, folklore on stealing of women's souls, 216-217; ritual curing

Clans—(*Continued*)
northern—(*Continued*)
in, 217-218. (*See also* Magic, sociological interpretation of.)
overlapping areas celebrate both Wawilak and Djunkgao cycle, 325.
own right to ritual variations, 136; to totemic designs and emblems, 136.
own totems, 16, 18, 28, 33, 136, 286, 378; in common, 28-29, 33.
patrilineal, *see* Lineage, patrilineal.
politically impotent, 379.
problem of ritual and magic presented by the northern and southern areas, 213-219.
sacred water holes of, 4, 16, 19-22, 24-25, 42-43, 122, 271, 286, 381-382, 438-440. (*See also* Clans, water holes of; Death, return to totemic water hole at; Mirrirmina well; Narra; Ranga; Wongar.)
and kinship system, two great classifying structures of Murngin culture, 438.
as organizing idea of myth and ritual, 382.
birth from, see *Birth;* Procreation.
focal point of sacredness, 402, 439-440; of clan solidarity, 438; of patrilineal kin, 438.
origin of, 325.
representation of, used in northern ritualistic curing, 217-218.
symbol of, 119; painted on dead, 25, 62, 405-406, 420; on initiates, 26.
size of, 16 ff.
southern, *see* Magic, sociological interpretation of.
spiritual strength of, *see* Ritual injury.
spiritual symbol of, 20.
sub-clans, 27 fn 13.
territorial extension of, 8, 16, 26, 378-379.
totemic references of land to, 4, 16, 26.
war-making groups, 17, 17 fn 7, 144.
water holes of, 20, 381; sacred and natural categories of, 381-382; sacred names unknown to women, 26.
water holes owned by, 17, 18. (*See also* Clans, sacred water holes of; Narra.)
western, tend to celebrate Wawilak cycle, 325.
Classificatory, *see* Kinship.
Climate, 3. (*See also* Environment; Seasonal cycle.)
Clowns, 292-294, 311-312.
Conception, prevention of, 23.
Conquest, *see* Warfare.
Corroboree, *see* Ceremonies; Ritual.
Creation stories, *see* Myths, Djunkgao, Wawilak.
Creator totems of clans, 16, 18-19; of wells, *see* Narra; Ranga.
Creator women, 10, 21, 30, 32-33, 64, 218. (*See also* Djunkgao sisters; Wawilak sisters.)
social meaning and value in journey of, 10.
Crime, 151. (*See also* Avoidance; Intercourse, illicit; Law, tribal; Ritual injury; Sanctions; Taboo.)
Crises of life, *see* Birth; Death; Marriage; Puberty; *Rites de passage*.
Cross-cousin marriage, *see* Marriage.
Cultural groups of Arnhem Land, 36.
Culture, 4, 15, 36, 36 fn 15, 138. (*See also* Technology.)
conservatism in, 447-458.
kinship system and totem well two great classifying structures of, 438.
permeated by totemism, 377-378.
Curing, *see* Magic, white; Medicine.
ritual, *see* Ritual curing.

Dal (mana, maraiin, ritually powerful), 78, 219, 254, 468. (*See also* Mana; Maraiin.)
magician's paraphernalia, relics, 227-230.
nature of, 226.
objects dal because connected with dead, 226-227.
Daughter, *see* Gatu.
Dead, the (ancestral), 22, 25, 33, 111, 120, 122, 265, 270, 356, 359, 404, 432, 437-438, 441. (*See also* Kin, totemic reference to; Kinship terminology applied to totems; Gatu (old); Mari; Marikmo (old); Wongar.)
Dead, the (recent), 26, 33, 122, 150, 437. (*See also* Birimbir; Mokoi.)
bones, blood, and hair of, as relics for good luck, 405-406; as relics to remind of vengeance, 150-151.

Dead—(*Continued*)
bones of, carried by female relatives, 430-431.
burial of, *see* Burial.
ceremonial mast for, 33, 423-425.
ceremonies for, see *Rites de passage,* Mortuary.
dal (mana) quality of objects connected with, 226-227.
exhumation of, *see* Exhumation.
go to Morning Star Island, 270, 300, 356.
grave posts for, 33, 423-425, 433.
hollow log coffin for, 428-432. (*See also* Technology, coffin.)
"keeper of the bones" of, 426-427.
mourning for, 405, 425-426, 429-430, 432.
painted with symbol of clan well for identification by ancestor escorts to well, 25, 62, 405-406, 420
power of, and magic, 188, 433-434.
related because of primary kinship structure, 440 fn 2.
relation of, to living, 438-440 (chart, 439).
soul of, *see* Birimbir; Mokoi.
source of power and danger, 219, 404-405, 433-434.
Death, 5, 6, 25, 42, 55, 62, 88, 89-90, 102, 123, 380, 402-432.
caused by magic, 183-200. (*See also* Magic, black.)
the culmination of progressive participation in sacred, 402-404, 433.
dance, 24-25, 168, 404, 434.
flying fox as a symbol of, 300, 314, 363, 365-366.
Mortuary, and mourning ceremonies and customs, 403-432.
natural, 183.
of brother, 51.
of child, 22-23, 67, 81, 85, 404, 424.
of father, 60.
of son, 52, 60.
of unfaithful wives, 68-70.
return to totemic water hole at, 16, 22, 24-25, 57, 62, 380, 404, 433.
rites, see *Rites de passage,* Mortuary; interpretation of, 433-440. (*See also* Integration.)
social disorganization at time of a, 404-405.
Demography, 17 f. (*See also* Population.)
Descent, *see* Lineage.
Dialect, *see* Language.
Disease, *see* Sickness.
Division of labor, *see* Men, Women, economic functions of.
Djambarpingu people, *see* Clans; Language.
Djungguan ceremony, 25, 32-33, 89-90, 111, 114, 118, 121, 123, 126, 146, 223, 234, 238-240, 249-280, 281-282, 298, 304-305, 308-309, 319-321, 323-325, 385, 431, 442.
summary of, 361-362.
Djunkgao constellation, 234-235, 325-360, 367.
analysis of totemic logic of, 396-397 (chart, 397).
myth, *see* Myths.
sisters, 325-360. (*See also* Myths.)
Doctors, *see* Magicians, white.
Domestic animals, dogs, 169.
Douglass, Andrew E., 442.
Dreams, 21-23, 57-58, 407, 410-411.
and magic, 199.
birth announced in, *see* Procreation.
birth announcement in, expresses relation of ordinary to sacred world, 403.
dead appear to killers in, 152-155.
relating to totemic ceremonies, 270.
Dua moiety, 5, 29-32, 58, 73-74, 135-136, 154, 166, 196, 218, 272, 336, 343-344, 350, 356, 378, 408, 419, 424. (*See also* Myths; Narra ceremony; *Rites de passage.*)
Dual organization, 5, 35, 106, 135-136, 385. (*See also* Environment; Moiety; Social bifurcation.)
Dué (father's sister's son [husband], father's sister's daughter), 27, 27 fn 13, 31, 56, 58, 62, 83-84, 98, 101, 118, 147, 252, 340, 426-427. (*See also* Kinship reciprocals.)
Dumungur (father's sister's daughter's daughter's son), 31, 44, 98, 105. (*See also* Kinship reciprocals.)
Durili people, 159.
Durkeim, Émile, 9, 184, 219-220, 230 fn 2.

Economic, activities, *see* Men, Women, economic functions of; Technology.

Economic—(*Continued*)
goods, distribution of, regulated by clan membership and kinship rules, 385.
group, 15, 127-129, 378.
organization of the Malay traders, 448-450.
reciprocity, 96.
structure, 12.
value, 52.
Environment, adaptation to, *see* Adaptation.
dual organization of, 5, 30-31, 135-136. (*See also* Dual organization.)
organized by myths, 10.
Environment, natural, 3-4, 11, 20, 135-137, 376-377. (*See also* Geography; Seasonal cycle.)
classification of objects in, 140.
control of, one of functions of totemism, 394.
earthquake, 269.
Integration of, with myth, ritual, and social organization, 393-401 (chart, 401).
materials selected from, 140-143.
Murngin related to his, 138-140.
need of purification for, 392-393.
Equivalence of sibs, 42-46, 110, 112.
Exchange, *see* Feud, "buying back" in; Gifts; Malay traders; Ritual exchange; Ritual gifts; Trade.
Exhumation and carrying of bones, 60, 62-63, 176, 425-432, 435.
Exogamy, 4, 16, 378, 381.

Familiars, *see* Magicians, black, white.
Family, 11 Chart I, 52, 58, 60, 66-67, 285 fn 16. (*See also* Kin; Kinship.)
and age grading, 124-125.
and kinship structure, 41-113.
elementary, immediate, 15, 41-45, 96, 98, 100-101, 114, 124-126, 377.
of orientation, 7, 41-45, 114, 116, 424.
of procreation, 7, 41-45, 114, 121-122.
structure, position in, related to rituals, 6.
Father, *see* Bapa; Kinship reciprocals; Procreation.
birth presaged by dream and mystical experience of, *see* Procreation.
descent through, *see* Lineage, patrilineal.
group of, 31, 43.
Snake, *see* Muit.
Fertility rites, 444. (*See also* Gunabibi; Narra ceremony, Dua and Yiritja.)
Fertilization, spiritual, *see* Procreation.
Feud, blood, 5, 17, 29, 35, 59, 87, 118, 122, 128, 144, 148, 151, 157-165, 228 253, 383, 435. (*See also* Fighting; Makarata; Warfare.)
"buying back" in, 166-179, 193-194.
history of a clan feud, 166-179.
settlement of, 311-312. (*See also* Makarata.)
Fighting, by ambush, 17, 51, 66.
language for good luck in, 311-313.
Fights, 54, 60, 83-84, 89, 120, 150. (*See also* Killings; Warfare, *especially* types of armed conflict.)
camp brawls, 70, 73-75, 77, 79, 89, 99-102, 117, 155-157, 174, 190, 223.
with mokoi for spirit of dead, 62.
women's, 70, 79, 165.
Fire, in mortuary rites, 411-416, 425, 427, 434.
ritual to drive away soul of dead, 220, 406-408, 411-413, 416, 434.
totemic use of symbolism of, 135, 261-263, 278-279, 286-287, 290, 294, 296, 301, 307, 313-316, 318-319, 321-323, 333, 337, 339-342, 348-349.
Flinders, Matthew, 445-448.
Flood, primeval, *see* Myths, Djunkgao, Wawilak.
Folk tales, 65, 68, 69, 92, 213, 216. (*See also* Myths.)
Food, *see* Gifts; Ritual eating of food; Ritual exchange; Taboo; Technology.
French school of sociology, 9, 184.
Function, *see* Integration; Interpretation.
of ceremonies, 386.
of family, 41 fn 1.
of Mirriri custom, 100.
of totemism, control of nature, 394.
Functional view of technology, 139.

Galle (mother's brother's son, mother's brother's daughter [wife]), 27, 27 fn 13, 31, 49-52, 57-58, 61-62, 75, 98-99, 102, 147, 340, 405, 428. (*See also* Kinship reciprocals.)
Garma, 20, 32, 124-126, 164, 391-392. (*See also* Clans, water holes of.)

Garma—(*Continued*)
ceremony, 25, 32, 220, 239, 386. (*See* also *Rites de passage,* Mortuary.)
cycle sung to dying man, 403-405, 433.
song used in curing ritual, 218.
songs of Gunabibi, 281.
Garrawark, creator totemic fish, 18, 325.
Gatu (son, daughter), 16, 27-28, 31, 43, 56 fn 7, 62, 74-75, 81, 98-102, 331, 351-352. (*See also* Kinship reciprocals.)
old, as totemic ancestor, 25.
Gawel (mother's brother [father-in-law]), 27, 27 fn 13, 29, 31, 43-44, 49-51, 60, 66, 72, 74-75, 88-90, 97-98, 102-105, 117, 137, 150, 187-188, 422. (*See also* Kinship reciprocals.)
Genealogies, 17, 147.
Generation, *see* Kinship, generation in.
Geographical, divisions, dual organization of, 135-136.
features, totemic reference to, 8.
location of ceremonies, 325.
space and social system, 8.
Geography, climate, 3. (*See also* Australia; Environment; Seasonal cycle.)
Gerontocratic principles, 6, 57, 59, 77, 120, 151-155, 158, 250, 280, 283, 302, 330, 333-334, 345-346, 355, 386, 432.
Gifts, 33, 50, 69, 75, 77, 82-84, 86, 89-92, 119, 166, 174, 251-253, 331.
exchange of, 97-98, 134-135, 224. (*See also* Ritual exchange.)
ritual, *see* Ritual gifts.
to neophytes, 59, 86.
Girls, 115, 118. (*See also* Children; Puberty.)
Government, *see* Ceremonial leaders; Clans, leaders of; Gerontocratic principles; Law; Political control; Sanctions.
Grave post, 33, 423-425, 433.
Great Father, *see* Muit.
Gunabibi (age-grading ceremony), 21, 32-33, 121, 123, 145-146, 223-224, 238-240, 270, 277, 280-301, 314, 316, 318, 320, 323, 325, 385.
associated with subincision, 444.
diffusion of, 443-445.
summary of, 362-363.
Gunwingu people, 37, 326, 460.
Gurrong (father's sister's daughter's son, father's sister's daughter's daughter), 26, 31, 66, 98, 331. (*See also* Kinship reciprocals.)
Gurrong-Kutara lineage, *see* Lineage.

Historical connections, 138.
History, archaeological method, 443, 455, 461-463.
archaeology and the ground stone axe, 462-463.
cave burials, 460–461.
culture area method combined with evidence of archaeological finds, 443.
diffusion of Gunabibi ceremony, 442-443.
documentary, 441, 443-446.
Douglass tree-ring method, 442, 452-453.
Malay culture influences, 138, 420-423, 444-460. (*See also* Malay.)
Malay influences on material culture, 450-456; on racial stock, 458-460; on social organization, 456-458.
materials and methods used for reconstruction of, 443-444.
observation of present culture change, 443-445.
of burial customs, 460-461.
of clan feud, 166-179.
of dugout canoe, 450-454.
of ground stone axe, 450-451.
Horde, the, 9, 15-16, 30, 134, 377, 379.
the economic group, 127-129.
Hospitality, 73.
wife, 459.
Hubert and Mauss, 184 fn 2.
Hunting, *see* Technology.
Husband, *see* Galle; Kinship reciprocals.

Ilpara tribe, 23.
Incest, 31-32, 41-42, 55, 71-72, 85, 426. (*See also* Myths, *especially* Bamapama, Djunkgao, Wawilak, and related ceremonies.)
Infanticide, 85.
Inheritance, of ceremonial leadership, 59.
of clan totems, 57-58, 95.
of magical power, 137, 187-188.
of names, *see* Names.
of right to perform dances, 59.
of wives and children, *see* Arndi, little Levirate; Sororate.

Initiates, 20, 281.
  instruction of, 261-262, 272-273, 279, 282, 315, 346, 360, 382.
Initiation, 26, 59, 119-120, 249. (*See also* *Rites de passage*.)
Integration (*see also* Function; Interpretation).
  family fundamental factor of, 41.
  kinship system basis of social integration, 7.
  of family position and age grading, 124-126 (chart, 124).
  of group, provided by totemic system, 385-388.
  of Malay and Murngin culture, 443-463.
  of material culture into symbolism and ritual, 456.
  of Murngin society, 11, 11 Chart I, 12, 15, 433-440.
  of myth and ritual, 236-238, 332-333, 340-341, 341 fn 2, 361-401.
  of myth, ritual, environment and social organization, 393-401 (chart 401).
  of nature and society, 237.
  of religious concepts and social organization, 237-238.
  of sacred and ordinary realms, in mourning rites, 402-403.
  of subsections with ceremonial structure, 265.
  of Wawilak constellation, and seasonal cycle, 368-376; and social organization, 376-393.
  of Yiritja ranga with flood and tides, 344.
Intercourse, 23, 31-32, 41, 54, 63-65, 67-69, 116, 147, 192. (*See also* Procreation.)
  during black magic, 185, 194.
  illicit, 50, 53, 61, 67-79, 85, 100, 118, 120, 146, 150, 156, 195, 204, 223, 240, 297, 341, 384. (*See also* Myths.)
  licensed, 53, 224, 291-292, 296-298.
  promiscuous, 74, 78, 78 fn 12.
Interpretation (of) (*see also* Function; Integration).
  death rituals, and the integration of Murngin society, 433-440.
  function of warfare, 144-155.
  lateral relationships (Gawel-Waku gift and daughter exchange), 96-98.
Interpretation (of)—(*Continued*)
  Makarata peace-making duel, 163-165. (*See also* Makarata.)
  mari-kutara kinship solidarity, 102-105.
  Murngin history, 443-463.
  Murngin magic, 213-233.
  Murngin totemism and its ritual logics, 361-401.
  perpendicular relationships, 95.
  the subsection system, 106-112.
  wakinu and mirriri custom, 98-102.
Intoxicating drink, supplied by Malay trader, 449.
Intrusion, *see* Sickness, due to intrusive object.

Joking, 64, 297.

Kaminyer (daughter's son, daughter's daughter), 31, 54, 71, 98. (*See also* Kinship reciprocals.)
Kariera, 36, 36 fn 15, 105, 107-108, 110, 112.
Killings, 60-61, 72, 74, 77, 78, 79, 99, 118, 144, 346, 432.
  bones of the killed as relic reminders of vengeance, 150-151.
  "buying back" the killed, 166-179, 193-194.
  by black magic, 183-199, 298.
  for illicit viewing of totems, 148-150.
  social effect of, 145.
  for unfaithfulness, *see* Women, discipline of.
Kin, 11 Chart I.
  behavior toward dying man, 403-405.
  classed according to moiety, 31.
  classificatory, *see* Kinship, classificatory.
  collateral, 46, 56, 433.
  consanguine, 17, 26, 46-48, 51-52, 56; comprise horde in rainy season, 127.
  groups, extended, 377.
  number of, 45-46.
  sexual division of, 46.
  totemic reference to, 265, 270. (*See also* Dead, ancestral; Kinship terminology applied to totems.)
  tribal, 26, 296.
  who are found in clan, 16, 26, 27 fn 13.

Kinship (*see also* Clans; Family; Integration; Marriage; Moiety; Phratry; Subsection.)
charts, 48, 93, 97, 103, 108, 109, 124.
classificatory, 8, 15, 17, 26, 44-48, 106.
customs, 12, 66, 98-105. (But see entire chapter on Kinship, 41-112.)
with regard to gifts, 134-135.
Dakota system, 45.
elaboration, *see* Kinship recognition.
generation in, 41 fn 1, 42-43, 66, 90, 96-97, 102-112, 439-440.
generation recognition, 7, 46-47.
lateral relationships, 7, 96-98, 102, 105, 112.
organization, 4, 34, 41-113.
perpendicular relationships, 7, 95-98, 102-105, 112. (*See also* Lineage.)
personality, 106, 122, 135; of Ego, 93-95.
personality, rules of, regulate distribution of economic goods, 385.
reciprocals, 47, 49-91, 93-98, 112, 113, 134, 145, 152, 378. (*See also* Social antagonism; Social solidarity.)
Arndi (mother)—Waku (child), 41-42, 85-87, 117.
Bapa (father)—Gatu (child), 41-46, 56-61, 67, 121-122, 137, 385.
Dué (father's sister *son* [husband])—Galle (mother's brother's *daughter* [wife]), 21-22, 27, 43, 56, 63-81, 97-99, 112, 145, 322-323.
Dué (father's sister's *son*)—Galle (mother's brother's *son*), 58, 63, 81-82.
Dué (father's sister's *daughter*)—Galle (mother's brother's *son*), 63, 82.
Dué (father's sister's *daughter*)—Galle (mother's brother's *daughter*), 63.
Marelker (mother's mother's brother's son)—Gurrong (father's sister's daughter's children), 58, 92, 145.
Mari (mother's mother, mother's mother's brother)—Kutara (woman's daughter's child, sister's daughter's child, 44-45, 88-90, 102-105, 134, 145, 334, 345. (*See also* Lineage.)

Kinship—(*Continued*)
reciprocals—(*Continued*)
Marikmo (father's father, father's father's sister)—Maraitcha (son's son, brother's son's son), 61-62.
Mokul Bapa (father's sister)—Gatu (brother's child), 62-63.
Mokul rumeru (mother's mother's brother's daughter [mother-in-law]—Gurrong (father's sister's daughter's children), 58, 66, 90-92.
Momelker (mother's mother's mother's brother's daughter)—Dumungur (father's sister's daughter's daughter's child), 92-93.
Momo (father's mother)—Kaminyer (daughter's child), 88.
Natjiwalker (mother's mother's mother's brother's son)—Dumungur (father's sister's daughter's daughter's child), 92.
Nati (mother's father)—Kaminyer (daughter's childr), 87-88.
Waku (sister's child, father's father's sister's child)—Gawel (mother's brother [father-in-law], mother's brother's son's son), 58-60, 64, 82-85, 102, 134, 137, 145, 385, 422, 435, 438.
Wawa (older brother)—Yukiyuko (younger brother), 46, 49-53, 72.
Yeppa (sister)—Yeppa, 56.
Yeppa—Wawa, Yukiyuko, 43, 45, 54-56, 63, 66. (*See also* Mirriri custom.)
recognition, principles of, 7, 8, 45-46, 64.
social organization built wholly on, 7.
solidarity, *see* Mari-Kutara solidarity; Social solidarity.
structure, and family, 41-113.
and social position, 7.
elaboration of immediate families, 7, 98.
equilibrium of, 102-104. (*See also* Kinship reciprocals; Mari-Kutara solidarity; Social solidarity.)
principles of, 95-113.
projected among dead, 440 fn 2.
readjustment of, required after a death, 425.
system, 15, 16 fn 6, 26-28, 27 fn 13, 41-113, 437-438.

Kinship—(*Continued*)
system—(*Continued*)
and totem well, two great classifying structures of Murngin culture, 438.
articulated with subsection system, 109-111.
based on Ego, man speaking, 47, 112.
extends scope of feud, 145.
given spatial form by clans, 378.
terminology, 16 fn 6, 42, 44, 46–47, 94, 112-113. (*See also* in index under kin terms as listed on page 467.)
applied to totems, 29, 95, 177, 334, 440 fn 2. (*See also* Dead, ancestral; Kin, totemic reference to.)
subsectional, 106-111.
wrong (guratu), *see* Incest; Myths, Djunkgao, Wawilak, and attendant rituals.
Koparpingu people, *see* Language, Koparpingu.
Kutara (sister's daughter's son; sister's daughter's daughter), 26, 31, 97-98, 102-105, 331, 406. (*See also* Kinship reciprocals.)
Kutara-Gurrong lineage, *see* Lineage.

Land, inalienable, 18-19.
ownership, 16 ff., 135, 379, 381.
Language, 4, 9, 30, 33-34, 36-39.
abusive, obscene, 55, 61, 68, 74-75, 87, 99-102, 150, 165.
Djambarpingu, 30, 37-38; Koparpingu, 30, 37-38; Mandjikai, 34. (*See also* Clans; Murngin tribes; Phratry.)
"kidjin," used in Ulmark, 311-313.
of clans as preferred clan name, 16, 30.
pidgin, contributed by Malays, 456.
sacred, 39, 39 fn 18, 122, 257 fn 12. (*See also* Ceremonies.)
sign, 69.
Law, tribal, 61, 66, 68, 71-72, 146, 151, 222. (*See also* Avoidance; Crime; Intercourse, illicit; Ritual injury; Sanction; Taboo; and chapters on local organization and kinship, 15-113.)
Levirate, 43-44, 49-52, 64, 70, 76, 78, 80, 83, 86, 99, 118, 147. (*See also* Polygyny; Sororate.)
Life, crises of, *see* Birth; Death; Marriage; Procreation; *Rites de passage.*
Life—(*Continued*)
cycle, 402, 437.
Lineage, 27 fn 13, 43-46, 63, 95-96, 102-105, 106-112, 437, 439-440, 449
applied to totems, *see* Kinship terminology applied to totems.
dumungur-waku, 44.
Ego's brother's, 16-17.
gawel-galle, 105.
gurrong-kutara, 17, 27 fn 13, 102, 105.
mari-marelker, 17, 27 fn 13, 29, 102, 105.
matrilineal, 26-27, 27 fn 13, 31, 109-113.
natjiwalker-gawel, 44, 105.
patrilineal, 4, 15-16, 26-27, 27 fn 13, 31, 42, 49, 57-58, 62, 95, 110-111, 359, 378, 381, 404, 428, 438.
(vertical) recognition, 7.
recognition, related to cross-cousin marriage, 7.
Local organization, 15. (*See also* Clan; Moiety, Phratry; Social organization; Tribe.)
Logics, *see* Absolute logics.
Lowie, Robert H., Introduction, xiii-xvi, 443.
Luck, bad, *see* Magic, black.
good, *see* Dal; Mana; Maraiin.
Luritcha tribe, 23.

Macassar, 287, 375, 420-423, 433. (*See also* Malay.)
Magic, 60. (*See also* Ceremonial purification; Ritual curing.)
and dreaming, 199.
and excretion, 199-200.
and medicine, 183-212.
and ritual, the problem of, presented by northern and southern areas, 213-219.
and war, 152-155, 158, 162.
comparison of, in northern and southern areas, 184.
curing, *see* Magic, White.
description of, with detailed data, 183-212.
effect of relics, 151.
extent of belief in, 188-189.
how it works, 219-233.
image, 196-197.
image-whipping, 199.
in northern area, 184-200, 213-219.

Magic—(*Continued*)
in southern area, 184, 213.
not property of individuals, 136-137.
power inheritable, 137, 187-188.
rain, 208-209.
singing, 197-198.
sociological interpretation of, 12, 213-233; statement of the problem, 219; test of the northern and southern areas, 219-226.
vs. religion, theories concerning, and test situation for, 9, 184.
women's, to aid boys, 276.
Magic, Black, 74, 78 fn 12, 89, 183-200 213-216.
bad luck due to, 183.
case histories, 188-196, 216-217.
cause of war, 148.
in northern area, 213-217.
instruction and power from relatives, 187-188.
sociological effect of 9, 220-223, 230-233.
sociological mechanisms of, 9.
Magic, White, 183-184, 213.
and the healer, 200-208.
case records, 206-207.
payment for, 207.
relation of prophylactic ritual to, 218-219.
Magicians (doctors, medicine men, shamans, sorcerers), 123.
crystallize group attitude, 232.
none in northern area, 183-184.
paraphernalia of, contains mana, 227 230.
social personality of, 187, 200-208, 220 222.
Magicians, Black, absent in north, present in south, 213-221.
familiar spirits of, 186-187.
methods of killing of, 184-196.
Magicians, White, diagnose snake bite, 208.
familiar spirits of, 200-209.
loss of power of, 207-208.
name black-magician killer, 186, 204-205.
other powers of, 204-205, 209.
power acquired by, 202-206.
Makarata, 118, 119, 128, 144-145, 155, 163-165, 168, 175-176, 178-179, 383, 416, 418.
Malay, culture influence of, 138, 420-423, 444-450. (*See also* History; Macassar.)
terms furnish personal names, 380.
traders, 38, 132, 444-450; economic organization of, 448-450. (*See also* Trade.)
Malinowski, Bronislaw, 96 fn 14, 397 fn 5.
Man, a species in a biological configuration, 138-143.
life cycle of, duplicates that of totem, 437.
Mana (good luck, power), 57, 60, 86, 267, 380-382, 402. (*See also* Dal; Maraiin.)
and magic, 188.
individual, 221.
of ceremonial leader, 233.
of magician, 230, 233.
of relics, 405-406.
of ritual totemic string, 331.
social, 121.
Mandelprindi (bull roarer), 269, 279-285, 289, 297-299.
Mandjikai people, *see* Language, Mandjikai.
Mara-Anula social organization, 36, 36 fn 15.
Maraiin (powerful, sacred, taboo, totem), 166, 254, 256, 345. (*See also* Dal; Mana.)
Maraitcha (son's son, son's daughter), 16, 22, 31, 44, 111. (*See also* Kinship reciprocals.)
Marelker (mother's mother's brother's son), 26, 27 fn 13, 29, 31, 44, 58, 89, 92, 98, 109, 331. (*See also* Kinship reciprocals.)
Marelker-Mari lineage, *see* Lineage.
Mari (mother's mother's brother, mother's mother, 26, 27 fn 13, 29, 31, 44-45, 58, 60, 67, 97-98, 102-106, 192, 270, 323, 331, 378, 403-407, 419, 423, 425, 430, 433. (*See also* Kinship reciprocals.)
Mari-Kutara solidarity, 113-116.
Marikmo (father's father, father's father's sister), 16, 22, 26, 29, 31, 44, 88, 89, 106, 111, 403-404, 419. (*See also* Kinship reciprocals.)
Marikmo (old), as totemic ancestor, 24-25, 270, 406-407, 423.

Marndiella ceremony, 32, 126, 234, 238-240, 319-325, 386.
 summary of, 366.
Marriage, 41, 43, 46-47, 49-51, 54, 57, 61, 63-85, 90-91, 94, 96-97, 106-109, 112, 117-119, 147, 270, 437. (*See also* Kinship reciprocals; Levirate; Polygyny; Sororate; Warfare, women taken in.)
 affection in, 78-80, 99.
 betrothal, 64.
 cross-cousin, asymmetrical, 7, 46-47, 105, 383.
 exogamous for clan and moiety, 4, 16, 378, 381. (*See also* Incest.)
 inter-clan, 28-29. (List of intermarrying clans, 28-29.)
 inter-moiety, 5, 16.
 lovers' unions, 73, 76-77.
 preferred, 64.
 runaway, 61, 66, 71, 75-77, 84, 99.
 stealing women for, 58, 65-66, 71, 74-77.
 wrong, 26-27, 27 fn 13, 65-66, 72, 94-95, 108-109.
Material culture, *see* Technology.
Matrilineal descent, *see* Lineage, matrilineal.
Matrilocal, *see* Residence.
Maung people, 37, 460.
Mauss, Marcel, 184 fn 2.
Medicine, 65.
 natural remedies, 60, 184, 221.
 pharmacopoeia, 209-212.
 treatment of wounds, 179.
Medicine men, *see* Magicians.
Men, attitude toward sex, 72.
 control of, by older, *see* Gerontocratic principles.
 economic functions of, 67, 79, 119, 122-123, 128-135, 449-455. (*See also* under various articles of the technology.)
 few who wish no wives, 78.
 —masculinity and femininity as organizing principles of social organization as expressed in rituals, 384-388.
 segmentation of, 5, 6, 121-123. (*See also* Age grading.)
 spiritual statuses of, 5, 6, 115, 124-126. (*See also* Age grading.)
 technological behavior of, *see* Men, economic functions of.
Men—(*Continued*)
 —unmarried men's camp, 114-116, 124-126.
Men's group, always represent Snake, symbol of rainy season and of fertilizing principle in rituals, 377.
 represent sacred purifying section of society, 377, 384.
 women's group antagonistic toward, 262.
Menopause, references to, 121, 256, 262, 267, 288.
Menstruation, 26, 64, 87, 239, 268, 300 fn 18. (*See also* Myths, Wawilak, Djunkgao; *Rites de passage;* Ritual blood giving.) (*See also* Totemism.)
Messengers, 175, 282, 289-292, 296, 303-305, 308, 317, 352.
Mirriri, custom of, 8, 55-56, 98-102.
Mirrirmina (great sacred well of Liaalaomir clan), 20-21, 239-240, 264, 269, 272-274, 287, 291, 305, 307, 309, 343. (*See also* Clans, Liaalaomir.)
Moiety (baperu), 5, 8-9, 11 Chart I, 15, 17, 29-33, 34-35, 37-38, 41, 57-58, 62, 106-107, 109, 111, 113, 136, 162, 270, 272, 274, 326, 334, 336, 345-346, 362, 377-378, 408, 424, 437, 439-440. (*See also* Dua; Dual orgnization; Environment, dual organization of; Incest; Myths; Yiritja.)
 ceremonies owned by, 32.
 exogamic, 16.
 fighting within, *see* Clans, inter-clan antagonism, rivalry for women; Warfare, intra-moiety.
 garma songs sung to dying man, 403-405.
 given spatial definition and location, 135-137.
 myths, 16.
 non-war-making, 144.
 totemic emblems and designs owned by, 136.
 totems owned by, 26, 29, 33, 111, 378.
 wells, 26.
Mokoi (evil, trickster soul), 62, 89, 206-207, 214, 216, 220-221, 300, 406, 424, 434-437. (*See also* Birimbir; *Rites de passage,* Mortuary; Soul stealing.)

Mokoi—(*Continued*)
ceremony (Nierk ceremony), 428-432.
possession by, 183-184, 198-199.
Mokul bapa (father's sister), 16, 31, 54, 67, 76, 87, 90, 407, 425-426. (*See also* Kinship reciprocals.)
Mokul rumeru (mother's mother's brother's daughter [mother-in-law]), 26, 27 fn 13, 31, 43-45, 50, 58, 66, 76, 89-90, 92, 102, 105. (*See also* Kinship reciprocals.)
Momelker (mother's mother's mother's brother's daughter), 31, 43-45, 72, 92, 105. (*See also* Kinship reciprocals.)
Momo (father's mother), 27 fn 13, 31, 67, 71-72. (*See also* Kinship reciprocals).
Morning Star, *see* Barnumbir.
Mortuary rites, see *Rites de passage,* Mortuary.
Mother, *see* Arndi.
descent through, *see* Matrilineal.
spiritually fertilized, *see* Procreation.
Mother's brother, *see* Gawel; Kinship reciprocals.
Mother's group, 31, 43.
Mother-in-law, *see* Avoidance; Mokul rumeru.
Mourning, *see* Dead; *Rites de passage,* Mortuary.
Muit (Bapa Indi, Father Snake, Great Father, Rock Python, Wirtit, Wongar, Yurlunggur), 25, 65, 118, 121, 123, 126, 209, 238-240, 269, 238-401, 362. (*See also* Myths, Djunkgao and Wawilak; Snake.)
Murngin, *see* Culture.
demographic aspects of, 17 f.
language, 4. (*See also* Language.)
location of, 3.
racial affiliations, 4.
reason for choice of name, 15 fn 2.
society, *see* Integration; Kinship; Local organization; Society.
tribes, 15, 15 fn 1, 16, 29, 30, 34, 35-39 (map, 40), 53. (*See also* Clans; Language.)
Barlamomo, 36-38, 168.
Burera, 28-29, 34, 36-37, 149, 190, 192, 194, 206, 445 fn 3.
Dai (Barrimundi), 36-37.
Djinba, 36-37, 84, 445 fn 3.
Murngin—(*Continued*)
tribes—(*Continued*)
Murngin, 15 fn 2, 36-39.
Ritarngo, 35-37, 62, 95, 166 ff., 346, 352, 445 fn 3.
Yaernungo, 17, 34, 36-37.
Yandjinung, 29, 36-37, 176, 191.
Musical instruments, *see* Technology.
Myth, 11 Chart I, 19, 31-32, 34-35, 166, 326.
and ceremony, close association of, *see* Integration.
and ritual, integration with environment and social organization, 393-401. (*See also* Integration; Social organization.)
as dogma, 250.
as unifying principle, 380.
ceremony, and warfare, 145-146.
creation, *see* Myths, Djunkgao, Wawilak.
cycles, *see* Djunkgao cycle; Wawilak cycle.
Mythological ancestors, *see* Wongar.
times, *see* Bamun.
Mythology, influence on, of Malays, 457-458.
Myths, 15-16, 18-19. (*See also* Bamapama ceremony; Creator women; Folk tales; Muit; Wongar.)
express local organization, 16.
local organization myths clue to subsidiary ritualistic themes, 391.
Murngin have no organized migration myth, 443.
Nara and Garma, fundamental ideas expressed in, 392-393.
organize environment, 10.
Wawilak, 136, 189, 238-240, 240-249, 378-379, 444. (*See also* Wawilak constellation, sisters.)

Names, from sacred language, 39, 39 fn 18, 279.
geographical, totemic significance of, 26.
nicknames, 380.
of clans, 15 fn 4, 16. (*See also* Clans.)
of phratries, *see* Phratry.
of tribes, *see* Murngin tribes.
personal, 4, 26, 43, 62, 88-89, 102, 136, 380; contributed by Malays, 456-457. (*See also* Natives.)
place, contributed by Malays, 456-457.

Names—(*Continued*)
sacred (personal), 55, 61-62, 111, 122, 265, 270.
taboo, 92.
Narra, rituals totemic rather than age-grading, 330.
totems, *see* Ranga; Wongar.
wells, *see* Clans, sacred water holes of.
Narra ceremonies, 24-26, 32-33, 126, 146, 223, 276, 367, 385-386, 400.
preliminary Duni, 330-337, 342, 346-351.
summary of, 390-393.
Narra ceremony, Dua, 330-346, 347-348, 350.
Yiritja, 330-331, 346-360.
Nati (mother's father), 27 fn 13, 31, 88, 98, 424. (*See also* Kinship reciprocals.)
Natives, Amburro, white magician, 201-213. Badunga, 55-56; Balli, 55-56, 100; Balliman, 70, 171 ff.; Balliman's sister, 198; Banggila, 229; Benaitjimaloi, 74-75, 79; Bengaliwe, 57, 171 ff.; Berundais, 170 ff.; Binindaio, 70; Birindjaoi, 174 ff.; Blumberi, 175; Bomlitjirili's sister, killing of, 192-193; Bomlitjirili's wife, killing of, 189-190; Bruk Bruk, 70; Danginbir, 167 ff.; Dangra, 55; Danitcha, 68; Daoper, 54, 76; Daurlung, 51, 170; Dimala, 56, 71; Djingaran, 170; Djoli, 70; Djowa, 74-75, 170 ff.; Dorng, 79, 192-193, 203, 224, 346, 372; Drona, 170 ff.; Dulperro, magician, 187; Dundir, 224-225; Garawerpa, 70; Ginda, 170; Goonga, magician, 187-188; Gunnumbilli, aid in magic killing, 194-196; Gurain-gurain, 74-75; Gurlbailli, 173; Gurnboko, 172 ff.; Ilkara, 189-191, 223, 345; Indjoka, 192; Inyinyerri, 76; Kamata, 157, 167 ff.; Kamata (2nd), 172; Kaperara, killing of, 192-193; Kutjerino, 74-75; Laindjura, magician, 187, case histories of, 188-196; Lianunga, killing of, 195; Lika, 70, 264-266; Mahkarolla, 80, 155-156, treated by white magician, 207; Maiangula, 157, 170 ff.; Malambunu, 55-56; Marawa, killing of, 190-192;

Natives—(*Continued*)
Maritcha, 87, 149, 170 ff.; Marupila, 406; Milanginunga, 195; Minyipiriwi, 176; Monali, 76; Mumulaiki, 70; Munyiryir, 78, 139, white magician, 205-206, loss of power of, 207-208; Murindit, killing of, 195-196; Narnarngo, 22, 74-75, 81, 172 ff., 406; Natjimbui, 157-158; Natjurili, 56-100; Nayilliwilli, killing of, 193-195; Opossum, 79; Parpar, 170 ff.; Raiola, 76, 173 ff.; Tjari, 175; Waltjimi, 85, 158, 171 ff.; Warlumbopo, 51, 157, 166-179; Waryi Waryi, 192-193; Willidjungo, white magician, 202-208, 224; Yanindja, 149, 238.
Natjiwalker (mother's mother's mother's brother's son), 31, 45, 98, 105. (*See also* Kinship reciprocals.)
Natural environment, nature, *see* Environment.
New Guinea culture, 138, 457.
Nomadism, 136-138, 143. (*See also* Transportation; Travel.)
Nullikan tribe, 69.

Ogden, C. K., and I. A. Richards, 238, 397 fn 5.
Organization, *see* Age grading; Clan; Family; Kinship; Local organization; Moiety; Phratry; Social organization; Tribe.
Orientation, *see* Family of.
Ownership, *see also* Property.
of ceremonies, 16, 32.
houses, *see* Technology, shelters.
land, 16 ff., 135, 379, 381.
natural objects, 135.
totems, *see* Clans, Moiety, Subsections, totems owned by.
water holes, *see* Clans, water holes owned by.
Ownership, communal, of incorporeal property, 136-137.
of land, 136.
of personal property, 136.
of totems, *see* Clans, Moiety, Subsection, totems owned by.

Patrilineal descent, *see* Clans, patrilineal; Lineage, patrilineal.
Patrilocal, *see* Residence.

Payment and buying, 89. (*See also* Exchange; Trade.)
"buying back" killed, 166-179, 193-194.
for white magic, 207.
Phratry, 9, 15-16, 29, 33-35, 37, 39.
reason for, 144.
Physiological conception, *see* Procreation.
"Political," control, 386.
impotence of clan, 380.
Polygny, 5, 42, 61, 63, 66-67, 147. (*See also* Levirate; Marriage; Sororate.)
warfare basis of, 144-145, 147-148.
Population, 146-147. (*See also* Clans, size of; Demography; Warfare.)
effects of war on, 146-147, 155-156.
Possession by mokoi (evil ghost), 183-184, 198-199.
Pregnancy, 23, 67, 85, 115, 121, 404. (*See also* Procreation.)
Presents, *see* Gifts.
Procreation, 5, 21-25, 42, 55, 57, 121, 269, 321. (*See also* Family of; Fertility Rites; Pregnancy.)
Murngin knowledge of, 5, 23-25, 24 fn 11.
Property, *see also* Ownership.
incorporeal, 136.
material, 52, 84, 135-138. (*See also* Technology, canoe, shelters.)
ritual, value enhanced by use in ceremonies, 135.
undeveloped sense of, 136-138.
value of, 137-138.
Psycho-physiological effects of black magic, 9. (*See also* Magic, Black.)
Puberty, 20, 64-65, 135-138. (*See also* Age grading; Circumcision; Gifts; Initiates; *Rites de passage*.)
Punishment, reciprocity in, 148, 151-152. (*See also* Intercourse, illicit; Ritual injury; Women, discipline of.)
Purification, *see* Ceremonial purification.
"Pusher," *see* Social personality; Warfare.
Python well, *see* Mirrirmina.

Race, little affected by Malay traders, 449.
of Murngin, 4.
Radcliffe-Brown, A. R., 94 fn 13; 105, 248 fn 10, 372 fn 4.
Raids, *see* War.
Rainbarngo tribe, 69, 176, 444, 445 fn 3.
Rainbow, 372, 374.
Ranga, 20-21, 25, 34, 124-126. (*See also* Clans, sacred water holes of; Narra; Totemism; Wongar.)
Reciprocity, economic, 96. (*See also* Exchange; Kinship reciprocals; Trade.)
in punishment, 148, 151-152.
Relatives, *see* Kin.
Religion, *see also* Magic; Totemism.
church not antithetical to magic, 184, 219-233.
white magic as a "church," 219-233.
Residence, 19, 66.
Ridicule, *see* Sanctions.
Rites, fertility, 444. (*See also* Gunabibi; Narra ceremony, Dua and Yiritja.)
magical, 183-233.
totemic, 234-401.
Rites de passage, 5, 6, 12.
Age grading, 120-121, 405. (*See also* Djungguan; Gunabibi; Initiates; Marndiella, Ulmark.)
Blood-letting ceremony of Djungguan, 264-272.
in Djungguan, 262-274, 279-280.
in Dua Narra, 342-345.
in Yiritja Narra, 359-360.
"birth," 121-122, 124-126.
Circumcision, 26, 59, 428. (*See also* Djungguan; Gunabibi; Marndiella.)
curing ritual used as, 220.
Nierk ceremony used as, 408.
Mortuary ceremonies, clan distribution of, 408-411.
interpretation of, 434-440. (*See also* Integration.)
part of, used as curing ritual, 220.
primary motifs of, 433-434.
purpose of, 433-435.
summary of, 402, 433-435.
Mortuary ceremony, 5, 12, 25, 52-53, 60, 122, 230-233, 402-432.
Eastern Dua garma flood cycle, 415-417; sea cycle, 411-413.
Eastern Yiritja garma flood cycle, 417-420; sea cycle, 409-411.
Exhumation of bones, 425-428, 433.
Mast ceremony, 420-425; contributed by Malays, 454, 456.
Morning Star (Barnumbir) ceremony, 413-415.
Nierk (hollow log coffin) ceremony, 428-432.

Rites de passage—(*Continued*)
Mortuary ceremony—(*Continued*)
Warntdjer (leaf) ceremony, 408. *See also* Fire ritual to drive away soul of dead.
Ritual, and magic, the problem of, presented by northern and southern areas, 213-219.
and myth, integration of, with environment and social organization, 393-401 (chart, 401). (*See also* Integration.)
blood, 224-225, 271-272, 275, 281, 289, 293-295, 298, 301.
blood giving, 123, 126, 264-269, 274, 294-295, 320, 382.
cleansing, *see* Ceremonial purification.
curing, 220-226; as circumcision rite, 220; in the north, 217-223; relation of, to white magic, 218-219.
danger, *see* Sickness due to ritual.
eating of food, 33, 279, 299; communally, 318-319, 332, 344-346, 348, 360, 390; to speed departure of dead, 407, 423-424, 428, 432, 434.
exchange, 450; of gifts, 33, 224, 296-297; of wives, 296-298.
for success in war, 225.
gifts, 134, 280, 288, 295, 309-310, 341, 345, 420.
injury, 60, 78, 115, 146, 148-151, 177, 222-226, 270, 279. (*See also* ceremonial uncleanliness.)
intercourse, 53, 224, 291-292, 296-298.
language, *see* Language, sacred.
logic of totemism, analysis of, 393-398.
logics, *see* Absolute logics.
making of friends, 252.
myth, and social organization, interconnection of, *see* Integration; Social organization.
pain removing, 225.
power for curing derives from totems, 218-219.
sickness, *see* Sickness due to ritual.
steaming, 278, 318-319, 324.
use of fire, *see* Fire.
Ritually powerful, *see* Dal; Mana; Maraiin.
Rituals, *see also* Ceremonies.
as tertiary adaptation, 12.
media for individual expression, 10.
social meaning of symbols of, 10.
Rock Python, *see* Muit.

Sacred, "inside," *see* Dal; Mana; Maraiin; Narra; Ranga.
change in personality, 5, 6, 402-403, 432-440.
names, *see* Names, sacred.
participation, progress in, 5, 6, 120, 402-403.
phenomena, place of, in Murngin culture, 235.
relation of, to profane (ordinary), 438-440 (chart, 439).
water holes, *see* Clans, sacred water holes of; Mirrirmina.
world, death the culmination of progress in participation in, 402-403.
world, identification with, through father's mystical experience, 5, 121, 403. (*See also* Procreation.)
world, totemically conceived, 9.
Sanctions, *see also* Absolute logics; Avoidance; Law; Sickness; Taboo.
absolute, provided by totemic system, 385.
of totemic system, final unity of Murngin society found in, 384-388.
ritual, 11, 120, 128, 383.
Seasonal cycle, 4, 20, 143, 368-376, 385-386, 389, 393-401. (*See also* Environment.)
caused by Muit, 239.
cycle regulates size of hord, 127.
Seasons, dry, great ceremonies take place in, 249, 280.
period of high social value, 377.
Seasons, rainy, symbolized by the Snake, 377.
myth cycles center around, 325.
Section system, *see* Subsection system.
Sexual bifurcation, *see* Social bifurcation.
ratio, 146-147.
relations, *see* Incest; Intercourse; Kinship reciprocals, Dué-Galle; Marriage; Polygyny.
Shaman, *see* Magicians.
Shell mounds, *see* History.
Sickness, 60, 133, 213. (*See also* Magic; Medicine; Wounds.)
and social adjustment, 220-223.
baldness, 224.
cured by white magic, 200-208.

Sickness—(*Continued*)
due to bad dreams, 199; breaking food taboos, 288-289, 422; breaking mother-in-law taboo, 91; intrusive object, 200-201, 204, 206-207, 220, 223 (*see also* Magic, White, and the healer); lingering soul, 220; magic, 183, 196-200; magic applied to excreta, 199-200; ritual, 124-150, 223-226, 267, 276, 295-298, 300-301; spirit possession, 199.
ritualistic curing of, in north, 217-219.
snake bite, 208.
Sign language, 69.
Sister, *see* Yeppa; Equivalence of sibs; Kinship reciprocals.
Sisters, Two, *see* Creator women.
Snake(s), totemic reference to, 26, 33, 159-161. (*See also* Muit.)
Social, antagonism, organized, 107-116. (*See also* Clans, inter-clan antagonism, intra-clan solidarity; Social solidarity.)
asocial behavior, 71-72, 98.
attitudes toward environment, 393-401.
bifurcation, 5, 6, 59, 115, 120-126, 262, 385. (*See also* Age grading.)
is within totemic complex, 380.
—masculinity and femininity as organizing principles of social organization as expressed in rituals, 284-288.
symbolized in spatial arrangement of rituals, 377.
change, 107; in North Australia, 12, 443-463.
customs, *see also* Kinship customs; Mari-Kutara solidarity; Mirriri.
bones of killed as relics, 150-151.
death, Mortuary, and mourning, 403-432.
sweethearting, 73-77.
effects of seasonal cycle, 368-376, 393-395.
life, Malay influence on, 454-458.
logics, clues to, 10; expressed in myth cycles, 234; of totemism, 398-401 (chart, 398).
maladjustment due to black magic, 183.
meanings of symbols, 10. (*See also* Social value.)
Social organization, 15-179. (*See also* Integration.)
Social organization—(*Continued*)
Arunta, Kariera, Mara-Anula, Murngin, 36, 36 fn 15.
as secondary adaptation, 10.
briefly characterized, 4.
disorganization of, at time of a death, 404-405.
expressed in rituals by organizing principles of masculinity and femininity, 384-388.
integration of, with myth and ritual, 240, 393-401.
integration of, with Wawilak constellation, 376-393.
local, 15-40.
organizes and disciplines technology, 385.
Social participation, lessening of, with increase in sacred participation, 402-403.
Social personality, position, participation, 6, 11 Chart I, 7, 41-113, 115, 119, 122-126, 373, 380-381, 402-403, 435. (*See also* Kinship personality.)
effect on, of Mortuary rites, 230-233.
of black magician, 187, 220.
of "pusher" in warfare, 157-158, 164, 174, 178.
of white magician, 200-208, 220, 222.
of Women, *see* Women.
Social reciprocity in trade, 450.
Social solidarity, 96-105, 165, 262, 345, 434. (*See also* Clans, intra-clan solidarity, inter-clan antagonism; Kinship reciprocals; Mari-Kutara solidarity; Social antagonism.)
and warfare, 145-148.
Social structure, 11, 15-39, 52-190.
mirrored in symbol of soul, 446-450.
organized by myths, 10.
ritual taboos basic to, 150.
warfare fundamental to, 144, 157-158.
Social system, 15-39, 52-190.
geographical space injected into, 8.
Social value, comparative, of men and women, 7, 120, 122-123, 435.
expressed in journey of Creator women, 10.
of seasons, 393-394.
of women, 100.
Society, integration of, 433-440. (*See also* Integration.)

Sociological effects of black magic, *see* Magic, Black.
Sociological interpretation of black and white magic (*see also* Interpretation).
ritual as a "magical" instrument in the south, 223-226.
social configuration of magic in the south, 223-226.
statement of the problem, 219.
test of the northern and southern areas, 219-223.
Sociology, American, English, French, and German schools of, 9.
Son, *see* Gatu.
Son-in-law, *see* Waku.
Songs, *see* Garma; *Rites de passage*.
Sorcerer, *see* Magicians, Black.
Sororate, 43-44, 147. (*See also* Levirate; Polygyny.)
Soul, *see* Birimbir; Mokoi.
children, 186-187, 200-209.
lingering, cause of sickness, 220.
of newborn, *see* Procreation.
stealing, 9, 183-184, 198-199, 201, 204-208, 221-222, 230, 230 fn 2, 406. (*See also* Magic, Black.)
stealing of women's, according to northern clans, 216-217.
unborn, 21. (*See also* Procreation.) 42, 62, 270, 438.
Spencer and Gillen, 23-24.
Spirit, *see* Birimbir; Mokoi; Soul.
Spirits, familiars, 186-187, 200-209.
warning by, 172.
Spiritual, change in personality, 5, 6.
fertilization, *see* Procreation.
Steaming, 278, 318-319, 324.
Subincision, 23, 443-445, 445 fn 3.
Subsection, names called out in ceremonies, 239, 261, 265.
system, 8, 11 Chart I, 15, 30, 33, 45, 105-112, 377.
totems owned by, 111, 378.
Sucking, *see* Sickness due to intrusive object.
Symbol, of avoidance, 42.
of clan well, *see* Clans, sacred water holes of, symbol of.
of masculinity and of femininity as organizing principles of the social organization as expressed in the rituals, 384-388.
Symbol—(*Continued*)
of social bifurcation, 126.
of totems, *see* Totemic emblems.
water most important, 19, 20.
Symbolic, processes, 324, 361, 401, 333-340.
relation between myth and ritual, 237.
Symbolism, *see also* Clans, sacred water holes of; Fire.
of death dance, 24-25, 404.
of Murngin totemism, 361-401.
of ritual decorations, 333.

Taboo, 43, 56, 62. (*See also* Avoidance; Maraiin.)
camp of near-relatives of recent dead, 425.
food, 57-58, 117, 119, 121, 154, 200, 205, 273, 277-280, 288-289, 322, 346, 355, 360.
incest, *see* Incest.
menstruation, 65. (*See also* Menstruation.)
names, *see* Names, sacred.
of silence, 229, 273, 277-278, 280.
ritual, basic to social structure, 150. (*See also* Ritual injury.)
sexual, during pregnancy, 67, 404.
symbolic, well hole of Gunabibi, 290-291.
to uninitiate, 135. (*See also* Maraiin.)
to women, 20, 26, 78, 120-121, 280, 425.
Taylor, Griffith, 369 fn 2.
Technological, behavior, 393, 437.
borrowings from seacoast, 445.
Technological processes, used in making artifacts, 141-143.
bark technique, 142.
cooking, 116, 129-131, 133.
fire-making, 257, 261.
food gathering and preparation, 73, 129-134. (*See also* Women, economic functions of.)
hafting, 143.
hunting, 68, 116, 128-133, 428, 452, 454. (*See also* Men, economic functions of.)
aid of dead enemy in, 153-155.
first kill, 55, 85, 90, 117, 119, 150.
language for good luck in, 311-312.
luck in, *see* Dal.
stone technique, 42.

Technological processes—(*Continued*)
trepang industry, 449, 454.
Technology, 52. (*See also* Narra ceremonies; *Rites de passage;* Totemic emblems.)
functional view of, 139.
Malay contributions to, 449-456.
organization and discipline of, 385.
primary adaptations and, 10, 11, 127-143.
canoes, 38, 52, 59, 62, 65, 81, 132.
cements, 135, 142.
ceremonial mourning mast, 33, 423-425.
clothing, 252.
coffin, 119, 150, 459. (*See also* Burial.)
"dunce cap" ceremonial headdress, 284, 287, 323.
fish, hooks, 159.
poison, 132-133.
food, 60, 63, 72, 77, 90, 128-133, 314-318, 321, 454-455, 463.
supply, shifting, *see* Nomadism.
grave posts, 33, 423-425, 433.
head bands, 74-76.
iron, and other metals, 137, 159, 453, 462.
marlpinpin, 309.
musical instruments, 250, 282.
pipes, 461; introduced by Malays, 450, 453.
raft, 38, 326, 338.
sails, 453.
shelters, 79, 88, 90, 118.
spear-throwers (mangel), 139.
spirit bags, 201-202.
tobacco, introduced by Malay, 449, 453; believed indigenous by natives, 453.
Uvar (ceremonial drum), 393.
Tindale, Norman B., 448, 451 fn 10.
Totemic, ceremonies, *see* Ceremonies.
conception of sacred world, 9, 10.
emblems (artifacts), 78, 134-135, 146, 382. (*See also* Narra ceremonies; *Rites de passage;* Banitja; Barnumbir; Garma; Garrawark; Mandelprindi; Ranga; Snake; Totems; Warngaitja; Yermerlindi.)
origin of, 325.
essence, enters totems through singing, 25. (*See also* Totemic spirits; Totems; Wongar.)
knowledge, possession of older men, 6.
names, *see* Names, sacred.
Totemic—(*Continued*)
rituals, as prophylaxis, 220; as tertiary adaptation, 11.
spirits, *see* Totems; Wongar.
believed actually to reside in emblems, 295-296.
of ancestors and unborn, 4, 16. (*See also* Dead, ancestral; Wongar.)
symbols, *see* Totemic emblems.
system, permeates all activities, 377-378.
provides absolute sanctions, 385-388.
provides mechanism for group integration, 385-388.
well, *see* Clans, sacred water holes of.
Totemism, 11 Chart I, 222, 234-360. (*See also* Integration; Narra ceremonies; *Rites de passage.*)
analysis of ritual logic of, 393-397.
interpretation of, and its ritual logics, 12, 361-401.
scientific method applied to analysis of, 235-240, 325.
social logic of, 398-401.
Totems, 26, 33-35, 42-43, 111, 166-179.
change of status with seeing, *see* Age grading.
hierarchically grouped, 10.
identification of, through one's clan, 5, 10, 25.
in clan wells related, 440 fn 2. (*See also* Kin, totemic reference to; Kinship terminology applied to totems.)
influence on, of Malays, 458.
insult to, *see* Ritual injury.
multiple, 4.
owned by clans, *see* Clans own totems.
owned by moieties, 26, 29, 33, 111, 378.
owned by subsections, 111, 378.
reside in wells, 21.
vengeance of, 146.
Trade, 52, 84, 134-135, 137, 450. (*See also* Exchange; Malay trader.)
ritual, 134. (*See also* Ritual exchange.)
selling ranga strings in Narra ceremony, 331, 334, 340-341, 345.
social reciprocity in, 450.
Trading friends, Malay, 449
Transportation, 137-138. (*See also* Nomadism; Technology, canoe.)
Travel, 38, 84, 86-87, 146, 445, 450-452, 456. (*See also* Messengers.)

Tribe, 11 Chart I, 15, 35-38, 41, 59, 146. (*See also* Language; Law; Murngin tribes.)
dialectic unity of, 9.
non-war-making or law-enforcing, 9, 35, 144.
vagueness of, 9, 15 fn 2, 35, 377.
Twins, 85.

Ulmark ceremony, 32, 223, 234, 238-240, 263, 270, 301-319, 385, 461.
summary of, 363-365.
Universe, dual organization of, *see* Dual organization; Environment; Moiety.
Uvar (totemic symbol, painted wooden drum), 270, 303-306, 461.

Value, 11 Chart I. (*See also* Social value.)
Values, mirrored in symbol of soul, 436-440.

Wakinu, 8, 55-56, 99-102, 168, 253. (*See also* Bamapama; Mirriri.)
Waku (sister's son, sister's daughter, father's father's sister's son, father's father's sister's daughter), 27, 27 fn 13, 31, 43, 49-50, 66-67, 72, 74-76, 81, 97-98, 102-105, 192, 290, 340, 420. (*See also* Kinship reciprocals.)
War leaders, 17, 158-159, 163, 171
Warfare, 5, 17, 17 fn 7, 29, 51, 53, 66, 72, 75, 102, 144-179. (*See also* Fights; Killings.)
and magic, 152-155.
between white and black magicians, 183.
cause of, 144, 148-152.
ceremony, and myth, 155-156.
due to black magic, 148.
effects of, on population, 146-147, 155-156.
fundamental to maintenance of social structure, 144, 147-148.
intra-moiety, 32-33, 35, 144.
land inalienable by, 18-19.
types of, 155-156.
gaingar (pitched battle), 155, 161-163.
makarata (ceremonial peace-making duel), *see* Makarata.
maringo (night attack), 150, 155, 157–161.

Warfare—(*Continued*)
types of—(*Continued*)
milwerangel (two-group open fight), 155, 161.
narrup (secret killing), 150, 155, 157-158. (*See also* Fighting by ambush.)
nirimaoi yolno, *see* Fights, camp brawls.
weapons used in, 156. (*See also* Technology.)
women and children taken in, 19, 28, 66, 71.
Warner, W. Lloyd, 108 fn 21.
Warngaitja, 121, 250, 253-254, 256-257, 259, 268, 271.
Warramunga tribe, 23.
Warro (totemic soul of the dead), *see* Birimbir.
Water, symbol of spiritual life, 19-20.
Water holes, *see* Clans, water holes of.
Wawa (older brother), 16, 28-29, 31. (*See also* Brother; Kinship reciprocals; Yukiyuko.)
Wawilak constellation, 234-235, 238-324.
analysis of totemic logic of, 395-397 (chart, 395).
and seasonal cycle, 368-376.
integration of, with social organization, 376-393. (*See also* Integration.)
summary of ritual logics of, 366-367.
Wawilak myth, *see* Myths, Wawilak.
Wawilak sisters, 424, 437. (*See also* Myths, Wawilak.)
Wells, *see* Clans, water holes of; Technology, clan wells.
Wergild, 166. (*See also* Feud, "buying back" in; Makarata.)
Wife, *see also* Galle; Kinship reciprocals; Levirate; Marriage; Polygyny; Sororate.
exchange, 53, 224, 291-292, 296-298.
hospitality, 459.
runaway, 61, 66, 71, 75-77, 84, 99.
stealing, 58, 65, 66, 71, 74-77, 148.
Wirtit, *see* Muit.
Women, *see also* Levirate; Marriage; Menopause, Menstruation; Polygyny; Pregnancy; Sororate; Wife.
and uninitiated children's group always symbolize Wawilak women in rituals, 377.

Women—(*Continued*)
as group, represent unclean, profane section of society, 377, 384; restricted to general camp in ceremonies, 377.
attitude toward sex, 72.
discipline of, 99, 146, 298. (*See also* Intercourse, illicit; Mirriri; Ritual injury; Wakinu.)
economic function of, 6, 67, 73, 79, 118-119, 122-123, 128-135, 253, 320, 331, 333, 337, 344, 355, 373, 454.
fights between, 70, 79, 165.
magic of, 225, 276.
—masculinity and femininity as organizing principles of the social organization as expressed in the rituals, 384-388.
participation of, in ceremonies, 121, 249; in Djungguan, 251, 253-254, 256-258, 275-277; in Marndiella, 323; in Ulmark, 302-303, 308-310, 315-316, 318-319; in Gunabibi, 281-284, 287-291, 296-299; 301; in Dua Narra, 334-339, 342-344; in Yiritja Narra, 342-353, 355-359; in mourning rites, 405, 425-432.
rivalry for, *see* Clans, inter-clan rivalry for women.
social personality of, 6, 7, 96. (*See also* Age grading.)
solidarity of, and antagonism to men's group, 262.
spiritual statuses of, 5, 6, 122.
stealing of, 58, 65-66, 71, 74-77, 148. (*See also* Warfare, causes of.)
taken in war, 19, 28, 66, 71.
technological behavior of, *see* Women, economic functions of.

Women—(*Continued*)
things taboo to, 20, 26, 78, 120-121, 280, 425. (*See also* Women, participation in ceremonies.)
undifferentiated, 6, 121-123. (*But see* Menopause.)
Wongar, 255, 267, 269, 295, 378, 381, 408, 437-438, 461. (*See also* Bamapama; Dead, ancestral; Gatu (old); Mari; Marikmo (old); Myths and Folk tales.)
as creators, 19.
days of, *see* Bamun.
dwell in totemic wells, 16, 21, 25. (*See also* Clans, sacred water holes of.)
spirit of the totem, mythological ancestors, 21-22, 25, 120.
Wounds, ants used to close, 185 fn 3, 189 ff. (*See also* Magic, Black, case histories.)
made by black magician, 183-196.
treatment of, 211-212.
Wulaki tribe, 176.

Yeppa (sister), 16, 31, 61, 81, 83, 99-102, 405, 407. (*See also* Kinship reciprocals; Mirriri; Wakinu.)
Yermerlindi, 33, 270, 292-294.
Yiritja moiety, 5, 29, 30-32, 58, 84-85, 146-147, 165, 177, 249, 351, 354, 418, 429 (*See also* Moiety; Narra ceremonies; *Rites de passage*.)
Yukiyuko (younger brother), 16, 28, 31, 61, 280, 295-296, 330-332, 351-352. (*See also* Brother; Kinship reciprocals; Mirriri; Wakinu; Wawa.)
Yurlunggur, 32, 250, 255-256, 259-261, 264-271, 273-275, 280, 408, 431. (*See also* Muit.)

Revised August, 1964

harper torchbooks

HUMANITIES AND SOCIAL SCIENCES

American Studies

JOHN R. ALDEN: The American Revolution, 1775-1783.† *Illus.* TB/3011

RAY STANNARD BAKER: Following the Color Line: *American Negro Citizenship in the Progressive Era.‡ Illus. Edited by Dewey W. Grantham, Jr.* TB/3053

RAY A. BILLINGTON: The Far Western Frontier, 1830-1860.† *Illus.* TB/3012

JOSEPH L. BLAU, Ed.: Cornerstones of Religious Freedom in America. *Selected Basic Documents, Court Decisions and Public Statements. Enlarged and revised edition with new Intro. by Editor* TB/118

RANDOLPH S. BOURNE: War and the Intellectuals: *Collected Essays, 1915-1919.‡ Edited by Carl Resek* TB/3043

A. RUSSELL BUCHANAN: The United States and World War II. † *Illus.* Volume I TB/3044, Volume II TB/3045

ABRAHAM CAHAN: The Rise of David Levinsky: *a novel. Introduction by John Higham* TB/1028

JOSEPH CHARLES: The Origins of the American Party System TB/1049

THOMAS C. COCHRAN: The Inner Revolution: *Essays on the Social Sciences in History* TB/1140

T. C. COCHRAN & WILLIAM MILLER: The Age of Enterprise: *A Social History of Industrial America* TB/1054

EDWARD S. CORWIN: American Constitutional History: *Essays edited by Alpheus T. Mason and Gerald Garvey* TB/1136

FOSTER RHEA DULLES: America's Rise to World Power, 1898-1954.† *Illus.* TB/3021

W. A. DUNNING: Reconstruction, Political and Economic, 1865-1877 TB/1073

A. HUNTER DUPREE: Science in the Federal Government: *A History of Policies and Activities to 1940* TB/573

CLEMENT EATON: The Growth of Southern Civilization, 1790-1860.† *Illus.* TB/3040

HAROLD U. FAULKNER: Politics, Reform and Expansion, 1890-1900.† *Illus.* TB/3020

LOUIS FILLER: The Crusade against Slavery, 1830-1860.† *Illus.* TB/3029

EDITORS OF FORTUNE: America in the Sixties: *the Economy and the Society. Two-color charts* TB/1015

LAWRENCE HENRY GIPSON: The Coming of the Revolution, 1763-1775.† *Illus.* TB/3007

FRANCIS J. GRUND: Aristocracy in America: *Jacksonian Democracy* TB/1001

ALEXANDER HAMILTON: The Reports of Alexander Hamilton.‡ *Edited by Jacob E. Cooke* TB/3060

OSCAR HANDLIN, Editor: This Was America: *As Recorded by European Travelers to the Western Shore in the Eighteenth, Nineteenth, and Twentieth Centuries. Illus.* TB/1119

MARCUS LEE HANSEN: The Atlantic Migration: 1607-1860. *Edited by Arthur M. Schlesinger; Introduction by Oscar Handlin* TB/1052

MARCUS LEE HANSEN: The Immigrant in American History. *Edited with a Foreword by Arthur Schlesinger, Sr.* TB/1120

JOHN D. HICKS: Republican Ascendancy, 1921-1933.† *Illus.* TB/3041

JOHN HIGHAM, Ed.: The Reconstruction of American History TB/1068

DANIEL R. HUNDLEY: Social Relations in our Southern States.‡ *Edited by William R. Taylor* TB/3058

ROBERT H. JACKSON: The Supreme Court in the American System of Government TB/1106

THOMAS JEFFERSON: Notes on the State of Virginia.‡ *Edited by Thomas Perkins Abernethy* TB/3052

WILLIAM L. LANGER & S. EVERETT GLEASON: The Challenge to Isolation: *The World Crisis of 1937-1940 and American Foreign Policy* Volume I TB/3054, Volume II TB/3055

WILLIAM E. LEUCHTENBURG: Franklin D. Roosevelt and the New Deal, 1932-1940.† *Illus.* TB/3025

LEONARD W. LEVY: Freedom of Speech and Press in Early American History: *Legacy of Suppression* TB/1109

ARTHUR S. LINK: Woodrow Wilson and the Progressive Era, 1910-1917.† *Illus.* TB/3023

ROBERT GREEN McCLOSKEY: American Conservatism in the Age of Enterprise, 1865-1910 TB/1137

BERNARD MAYO: Myths and Men: *Patrick Henry, George Washington, Thomas Jefferson* TB/1108

JOHN C. MILLER: Alexander Hamilton and the Growth of the New Nation TB/3057

JOHN C. MILLER: The Federalist Era, 1789-1801.† *Illus.* TB/3027

† The New American Nation Series, edited by Henry Steele Commager and Richard B. Morris.

‡ American Perspectives series, edited by Bernard Wishy and William E. Leuchtenburg.

* The Rise of Modern Europe series, edited by William L. Langer.

‖ Researches in the Social, Cultural, and Behavioral Sciences, edited by Benjamin Nelson.

§ The Library of Religion and Culture, edited by Benjamin Nelson.

Σ Harper Modern Science Series, edited by James R. Newman.

° Not for sale in Canada.

PERRY MILLER: Errand into the Wilderness TB/1139

PERRY MILLER & T. H. JOHNSON, Editors: The Puritans: *A Sourcebook of Their Writings* Volume I TB/1093 Volume II TB/1094

GEORGE E. MOWRY: The Era of Theodore Roosevelt and the Birth of Modern America, 1900-1912.† *Illus.* TB/3022

WALLACE NOTESTEIN: The English People on the Eve of Colonization, 1603-1630.† *Illus.* TB/3006

RUSSEL BLAINE NYE: The Cultural Life of the New Nation, 1776-1801.† *Illus.* TB/3026

RALPH BARTON PERRY: Puritanism and Democracy TB/1138

GEORGE E. PROBST, Ed.: The Happy Republic: *A Reader in Tocqueville's America* TB/1060

WALTER RAUSCHENBUSCH: Christianity and the Social Crisis.‡ *Edited by Robert D. Cross* TB/3059

FRANK THISTLETHWAITE: America and the Atlantic Community: *Anglo-American Aspects, 1790-1850* TB/1107

TWELVE SOUTHERNERS: I'll Take My Stand: *The South and the Agrarian Tradition. Introduction by Louis D. Rubin, Jr.; Biographical Essays by Virginia Rock* TB/1072

A. F. TYLER: Freedom's Ferment: *Phases of American Social History from the Revolution to the Outbreak of the Civil War. Illus.* TB/1074

GLYNDON G. VAN DEUSEN: The Jacksonian Era, 1828-1848.† *Illus.* TB/3028

WALTER E. WEYL: The New Democracy: *An Essay on Certain Political and Economic Tendencies in the United States.‡ Edited by Charles Forcey* TB/3042

LOUIS B. WRIGHT: The Cultural Life of the American Colonies, 1607-1763.† *Illus.* TB/3005

LOUIS B. WRIGHT: Culture on the Moving Frontier TB/1053

Anthropology & Sociology

BERNARD BERELSON, Ed.: The Behavioral Sciences Today TB/1127

JOSEPH B. CASAGRANDE, Ed.: In the Company of Man: *20 Portraits of Anthropological Informants. Illus.* TB/3047

W. E. LE GROS CLARK: The Antecedents of Man: *An Introduction to the Evolution of the Primates.° Illus.* TB/559

THOMAS C. COCHRAN: The Inner Revolution: *Essays on the Social Sciences in History* TB/1140

ALLISON DAVIS & JOHN DOLLARD: Children of Bondage: *The Personality Development of Negro Youth in the Urban South*‖ TB/3049

ST. CLAIR DRAKE & HORACE R. CAYTON: Black Metropolis: *A Study of Negro Life in a Northern City. Introduction by Everett C. Hughes. Tables, maps, charts and graphs* Volume I TB/1086 Volume II TB/1087

CORA DU BOIS: The People of Alor. *New Preface by the author. Illus.* Volume I TB/1042 Volume II TB/1043

LEON FESTINGER, HENRY W. RIECKEN & STANLEY SCHACHTER: When Prophecy Fails: *A Social and Psychological Account of a Modern Group that Predicted the Destruction of the World*‖ TB/1132

RAYMOND FIRTH, Ed.: Man and Culture: *An Evaluation of the Work of Bronislaw Malinowski*‖° TB/1133

L. S. B. LEAKEY: Adam's Ancestors: *The Evolution of Man and his Culture. Illus.* TB/1019

KURT LEWIN: Field Theory in Social Science: *Selected Theoretical Papers.*‖ *Edited with a Foreword by Dorwin Cartwright* TB/1135

ROBERT H. LOWIE: Primitive Society. *Introduction by Fred Eggan* TB/1056

BENJAMIN NELSON: Religious Traditions and the Spirit of Capitalism: *From the Church Fathers to Jeremy Bentham* TB/1130

TALCOTT PARSONS & EDWARD A. SHILS, Editors: Toward a General Theory of Action: *Theoretical Foundations for the Social Sciences* TB/1083

JOHN H. ROHRER & MUNRO S. EDMONSON, Eds.: The Eighth Generation Grows Up: *Cultures and Personalities of New Orleans Negroes*‖ TB/3050

ARNOLD ROSE: The Negro in America: *The Condensed Version of Gunnar Myrdal's* An American Dilemma. *New Introduction by the Author; Foreword by Gunnar Myrdal* TB/3048

KURT SAMUELSSON: Religion and Economic Action: *A Critique of Max Weber's* The Protestant Ethic and the Spirit of Capitalism.‖° *Trans. by E. G. French; Ed. with Intro. by D. C. Coleman* TB/1131

PITIRIM SOROKIN: Contemporary Sociological Theories: *Through the First Quarter of the Twentieth Century* TB/3046

MAURICE R. STEIN: The Eclipse of Community: *An Interpretation of American Studies. New Introduction by the Author* TB/1128

SIR EDWARD TYLOR: The Origins of Culture. *Part I of "Primitive Culture."§ Introduction by Paul Radin* TB/33

SIR EDWARD TYLOR: Religion in Primitive Culture. *Part II of "Primitive Culture."§ Introduction by Paul Radin* TB/34

W. LLOYD WARNER & Associates: Democracy in Jonesville: *A Study in Quality and Inequality*** TB/1129

W. LLOYD WARNER: A Black Civilization: *A Study of an Australian Tribe.*‖ *Illus.* TB/3056

W. LLOYD WARNER: Social Class in America: *The Evaluation of Status* TB/1013

Art and Art History

EMILE MÂLE: The Gothic Image: *Religious Art in France of the Thirteenth Century.§ 190 illus.* TB/44

MILLARD MEISS: Painting in Florence and Siena after the Black Death. *169 illus.* TB/1148

ERWIN PANOFSKY: Studies in Iconology: *Humanistic Themes in the Art of the Renaissance. 180 illustrations* TB/1077

ALEXANDRE PIANKOFF: The Shrines of Tut-Ankh-Amon. *Edited by N. Rambova. 117 illus.* TB/2011

JEAN SEZNEC: The Survival of the Pagan Gods: *The Mythological Tradition and Its Place in Renaissance Humanism and Art. 108 illustrations* TB/2004

OTTO VON SIMSON: The Gothic Cathedral: *Origins of Gothic Architecture and the Medieval Concept of Order. 58 illus.* TB/2018

HEINRICH ZIMMER: Myths and Symbols in Indian Art and Civilization. *70 illustrations* TB/2005

Business, Economics & Economic History

REINHARD BENDIX: Work and Authority in Industry: *Ideologies of Management in the Course of Industrialization* TB/3035

THOMAS C. COCHRAN: The American Business System: *A Historical Perspective, 1900-1955* TB/1080

ROBERT DAHL & CHARLES E. LINDBLOM: Politics, Economics, and Welfare: *Planning and Politico-Economic Systems Resolved into Basic Social Processes* TB/3037

PETER F. DRUCKER: The New Society: *The Anatomy of Industrial Order* TB/1082

ROBERT L. HEILBRONER: The Great Ascent: *The Struggle for Economic Development in Our Time* TB/3030

ABBA P. LERNER: Everybody's Business: *A Re-examination of Current Assumptions in Economics and Public Policy* TB/3051

ROBERT GREEN McCLOSKEY: American Conservatism in the Age of Enterprise, 1865-1910 TB/1137

PAUL MANTOUX: The Industrial Revolution in the Eighteenth Century: *The Beginnings of the Modern Factory System in England*° TB/1079

WILLIAM MILLER, Ed.: Men in Business: *Essays on the Historical Role of the Entrepreneur* TB/1081

PERRIN STRYKER: The Character of the Executive: *Eleven Studies in Managerial Qualities* TB/1041

PIERRE URI: Partnership for Progress: *A Program for Transatlantic Action* TB/3036

Contemporary Culture

JACQUES BARZUN: The House of Intellect TB/1051

JOHN U. NEF: Cultural Foundations of Industrial Civilization TB/1024

PAUL VALÉRY: The Outlook for Intelligence TB/2016

History: General

L. CARRINGTON GOODRICH: A Short History of the Chinese People. *Illus.* TB/3015

BERNARD LEWIS: The Arabs in History TB/1029

SIR PERCY SYKES: A History of Exploration.° *Introduction by John K. Wright* TB/1046

History: Ancient and Medieval

A. ANDREWES: The Greek Tyrants TB/1103

P. BOISSONNADE: Life and Work in Medieval Europe.° *Preface by Lynn White, Jr.* TB/1141

HELEN CAM: England before Elizabeth TB/1026

NORMAN COHN: The Pursuit of the Millennium: *Revolutionary Messianism in medieval and Reformation Europe and its bearing on modern Leftist and Rightist totalitarian movements* TB/1037

G. G. COULTON: Medieval Village, Manor, and Monastery TB/1022

HEINRICH FICHTENAU: The Carolingian Empire: *The Age of Charlemagne* TB/1142

F. L. GANSHOF: Feudalism TB/1058

J. M. HUSSEY: The Byzantine World TB/1057

SAMUEL NOAH KRAMER: Sumerian Mythology TB/1055

FERDINAND LOT: The End of the Ancient World and the Beginnings of the Middle Ages. *Introduction by Glanville Downey* TB/1044

STEVEN RUNCIMAN: A History of the Crusades. Volume I: *The First Crusade and the Foundation of the Kingdom of Jerusalem. Illus.* TB/1143

HENRY OSBORN TAYLOR: The Classical Heritage of the Middle Ages. *Foreword and Biblio. by Kenneth M. Setton* [Formerly listed as TB/48 under the title *The Emergence of Christian Culture in the West*] TB/1117

J. M. WALLACE-HADRILL: The Barbarian West: *The Early Middle Ages, A.D. 400-1000* TB/1061

History: Renaissance & Reformation

R. R. BOLGAR: The Classical Heritage and Its Beneficiaries: *From the Carolingian Age to the End of the Renaissance* TB/1125

JACOB BURCKHARDT: The Civilization of the Renaissance in Italy. *Introduction by Benjamin Nelson and Charles Trinkaus. Illus.* Volume I TB/40; Volume II TB/41

ERNST CASSIRER: The Individual and the Cosmos in Renaissance Philosophy. *Translated with an Introduction by Mario Domandi* TB/1097

EDWARD P. CHEYNEY: The Dawn of a New Era, 1250-1453.* *Illus.* TB/3002

WALLACE K. FERGUSON, et al.: Facets of the Renaissance TB/1098

WALLACE K. FERGUSON, et al.: The Renaissance: *Six Essays. Illus.* TB/1084

MYRON P. GILMORE: The World of Humanism, 1453-1517.* *Illus.* TB/3003

JOHAN HUIZINGA: Erasmus and the Age of Reformation. *Illus.* TB/19

ULRICH VON HUTTEN, et al.: On the Eve of the Reformation: *"Letters of Obscure Men." Introduction by Hajo Holborn* TB/1124

PAUL O. KRISTELLER: Renaissance Thought: *The Classic, Scholastic, and Humanist Strains* TB/1048

NICCOLÒ MACHIAVELLI: History of Florence and of the Affairs of Italy: *from the earliest times to the death of Lorenzo the Magnificent. Introduction by Felix Gilbert* TB/1027

ALFRED VON MARTIN: Sociology of the Renaissance. *Introduction by Wallace K. Ferguson* TB/1099

MILLARD MEISS: Painting in Florence and Siena after the Black Death. *169 illus.* TB/1148

J. E. NEALE: The Age of Catherine de Medici° TB/1085

ERWIN PANOFSKY: Studies in Iconology: *Humanistic Themes in the Art of the Renaissance. 180 illustrations* TB/1077

J. H. PARRY: The Establishment of the European Hegemony: 1415-1715: *Trade and Exploration in the Age of the Renaissance* TB/1045

HENRI PIRENNE: Early Democracies in the Low Countries: *Urban Society and Political Conflict in the Middle Ages and the Renaissance. Introduction by John Mundy* TB/1110

FERDINAND SCHEVILL: The Medici. *Illus.* TB/1010

FERDINAND SCHEVILL: Medieval and Renaissance Florence. *Illus.* Volume I: *Medieval Florence* TB/1090 Volume II: *The Coming of Humanism and the Age of the Medici* TB/1091

G. M. TREVELYAN: England in the Age of Wycliffe, 1368-1520° TB/1112

VESPASIANO: Renaissance Princes, Popes, and Prelates: *The Vespasiano Memoirs: Lives of Illustrious Men of the XVth Century. Introduction by Myron P. Gilmore* TB/1111

History: Modern European

FREDERICK B. ARTZ: Reaction and Revolution, 1815-1832.* *Illus.* TB/3034

MAX BELOFF: The Age of Absolutism, 1660-1815 TB/1062

ROBERT C. BINKLEY: Realism and Nationalism, 1852-1871.* *Illus.* TB/3038

CRANE BRINTON: A Decade of Revolution, 1789-1799.* *Illus.* TB/3018

J. BRONOWSKI & BRUCE MAZLISH: The Western Intellectual Tradition: *From Leonardo to Hegel* TB/3001

GEOFFREY BRUUN: Europe and the French Imperium, 1799-1814.* *Illus.* TB/3033

ALAN BULLOCK: Hitler, A Study in Tyranny.° *Illus.* TB/1123

E. H. CARR: The Twenty Years' Crisis, 1919-1939: *An Introduction to the Study of International Relations*° TB/1122

WALTER L. DORN: Competition for Empire, 1740-1763.* *Illus.* TB/3032

CARL J. FRIEDRICH: The Age of the Baroque, 1610-1660.* *Illus.* TB/3004

LEO GERSHOY: From Despotism to Revolution, 1763-1789.* *Illus.* TB/3017

ALBERT GOODWIN: The French Revolution TB/1064

CARLTON J. H. HAYES: A Generation of Materialism, 1871-1900.* *Illus.* TB/3039

J. H. HEXTER: Reappraisals in History: *New Views on History and Society in Early Modern Europe* TB/1100

A. R. HUMPHREYS: The Augustan World: *Society, Thought, and Letters in Eighteenth Century England* TB/1105

HANS KOHN, Ed.: The Mind of Modern Russia: *Historical and Political Thought of Russia's Great Age* TB/1065

SIR LEWIS NAMIER: Vanished Supremacies: *Essays on European History, 1812-1918*° TB/1088

JOHN U. NEF: Western Civilization Since the Renaissance: *Peace, War, Industry, and the Arts* TB/1113

FREDERICK L. NUSSBAUM: The Triumph of Science and Reason, 1660-1685.* *Illus.* TB/3009

RAYMOND W. POSTGATE, Ed.: Revolution from 1789 to 1906: *Selected Documents* TB/1063

PENFIELD ROBERTS: The Quest for Security, 1715-1740.* *Illus.* TB/3016

PRISCILLA ROBERTSON: Revolutions of 1848: *A Social History* TB/1025

ALBERT SOREL: Europe Under the Old Regime. *Translated by Francis H. Herrick* TB/1121

N. N. SUKHANOV: The Russian Revolution, 1917: *Eyewitness Account. Edited by Joel Carmichael*
Volume I TB/1066
Volume II TB/1067

JOHN B. WOLF: The Emergence of the Great Powers, 1685-1715.* *Illus.* TB/3010

JOHN B. WOLF: France: 1814-1919: *The Rise of a Liberal-Democratic Society* TB/3019

Intellectual History

HERSCHEL BAKER: The Image of Man: *A Study of the Idea of Human Dignity in Classical Antiquity, the Middle Ages, and the Renaissance* TB/1047

J. BRONOWSKI & BRUCE MAZLISH: The Western Intellectual Tradition: *From Leonardo to Hegel* TB/3001

ERNST CASSIRER: The Individual and the Cosmos in Renaissance Philosophy. *Translated with an Introduction by Mario Domandi* TB/1097

NORMAN COHN: The Pursuit of the Millennium: *Revolutionary Messianism in medieval and Reformation Europe and its bearing on modern Leftist and Rightist totalitarian movements* TB/1037

ARTHUR O. LOVEJOY: The Great Chain of Being: *A Study of the History of an Idea* TB/1009

ROBERT PAYNE: Hubris: *A Study of Pride. Foreword by Sir Herbert Read* TB/1031

BRUNO SNELL: The Discovery of the Mind: *The Greek Origins of European Thought* TB/1018

ERNEST LEE TUVESON: Millennium and Utopia: *A Study in the Background of the Idea of Progress.*‖ *New Preface by Author* TB/1134

Literature, Poetry, The Novel & Criticism

JAMES BAIRD: Ishmael: *The Art of Melville in the Contexts of International Primitivism* TB/1023

JACQUES BARZUN: The House of Intellect TB/1051

W. J. BATE: From Classic to Romantic: *Premises of Taste in Eighteenth Century England* TB/1036

RACHEL BESPALOFF: On the Iliad TB/2006

R. P. BLACKMUR, et al.: Lectures in Criticism. *Introduction by Huntington Cairns* TB/2003

ABRAHAM CAHAN: The Rise of David Levinsky: *a novel. Introduction by John Higham* TB/1028

ERNST R. CURTIUS: European Literature and the Latin Middle Ages TB/2015

GEORGE ELIOT: Daniel Deronda: *a novel. Introduction by F. R. Leavis* TB/1039

ETIENNE GILSON: Dante and Philosophy TB/1089

ALFRED HARBAGE: As They Liked It: *A Study of Shakespeare's Moral Artistry* TB/1035

STANLEY R. HOPPER, Ed.: Spiritual Problems in Contemporary Literature§ TB/21

A. R. HUMPHREYS: The Augustan World: *Society, Thought, and Letters in Eighteenth Century England*° TB/1105

ALDOUS HUXLEY: Antic Hay & The Gioconda Smile.° *Introduction by Martin Green* TB/3503

ALDOUS HUXLEY: Brave New World & Brave New World Revisited.° *Introduction by C. P. Snow* TB/3501

ALDOUS HUXLEY: Point Counter Point.° *Introduction by C. P. Snow* TB/3502

HENRY JAMES: The Princess Casamassima: *a novel. Introduction by Clinton F. Oliver* TB/1005

HENRY JAMES: Roderick Hudson: *a novel. Introduction by Leon Edel* TB/1016

HENRY JAMES: The Tragic Muse: *a novel. Introduction by Leon Edel* TB/1017

ARNOLD KETTLE: An Introduction to the English Novel. Volume I: *Defoe to George Eliot* TB/1011
Volume II: *Henry James to the Present* TB/1012

JOHN STUART MILL: On Bentham and Coleridge. *Introduction by F. R. Leavis* TB/1070

PERRY MILLER & T. H. JOHNSON, Editors: The Puritans: *A Sourcebook of Their Writings*
Volume I TB/1093
Volume II TB/1094

KENNETH B. MURDOCK: Literature and Theology in Colonial New England TB/99

SAMUEL PEPYS: The Diary of Samuel Pepys.° *Edited by O. F. Morshead. Illustrations by Ernest Shepard* TB/1007

ST.-JOHN PERSE: Seamarks TB/2002

O. E. RÖLVAAG: Giants in the Earth. *Introduction by Einar Haugen* TB/3504

GEORGE SANTAYANA: Interpretations of Poetry and Religion§ TB/9

C. P. SNOW: Time of Hope: *a novel* TB/1040

DOROTHY VAN GHENT: The English Novel: *Form and Function* TB/1050

E. B. WHITE: One Man's Meat. *Introduction by Walter Blair* TB/3505

MORTON DAUWEN ZABEL, Editor: Literary Opinion in America Volume I TB/3013 Volume II TB/3014

Myth, Symbol & Folklore

JOSEPH CAMPBELL, Editor: Pagan and Christian Mysteries. *Illus.* TB/2013

MIRCEA ELIADE: Cosmos and History: *The Myth of the Eternal Return*§ TB/2050

C. G. JUNG & C. KERÉNYI: Essays on a Science of Mythology: *The Myths of the Divine Child and the Divine Maiden* TB/2014

ERWIN PANOFSKY: Studies in Iconology: *Humanistic Themes in the Art of the Renaissance. 180 illustrations* TB/1077

JEAN SEZNEC: The Survival of the Pagan Gods: *The Mythological Tradition and its Place in Renaissance Humanism and Art. 108 illustrations* TB/2004

HELLMUT WILHELM: Change: *Eight Lectures on the* I Ching TB/2019

HEINRICH ZIMMER: Myths and Symbols in Indian Art and Civilization. *70 illustrations* TB/2005

Philosophy

HENRI BERGSON: Time and Free Will: *An Essay on the Immediate Data of Consciousness*° TB/1021

H. J. BLACKHAM: Six Existentialist Thinkers: *Kierkegaard, Nietzsche, Jaspers, Marcel, Heidegger, Sartre*° TB/1002

ERNST CASSIRER: Rousseau, Kant and Goethe. *Introduction by Peter Gay* TB/1092

FREDERICK COPLESTON: Medieval Philosophy° TB/76

F. M. CORNFORD: From Religion to Philosophy: *A Study in the Origins of Western Speculation*§ TB/20

WILFRID DESAN: The Tragic Finale: *An Essay on the Philosophy of Jean-Paul Sartre* TB/1030

PAUL FRIEDLÄNDER: Plato: *An Introduction* TB/2017

ETIENNE GILSON: Dante and Philosophy TB/1089

WILLIAM CHASE GREENE: Moira: *Fate, Good, and Evil in Greek Thought* TB/1104

W. K. C. GUTHRIE: The Greek Philosophers: *From Thales to Aristotle*° TB/1008

F. H. HEINEMANN: Existentialism and the Modern Predicament TB/28

IMMANUEL KANT: The Doctrine of Virtue, *being Part II of The Metaphysic of Morals. Translated with Notes and Introduction by Mary J. Gregor. Foreword by H. J. Paton* TB/110

IMMANUEL KANT: Lectures on Ethics.§ *Introduction by Lewis W. Beck* TB/105

WILLARD VAN ORMAN QUINE: From a Logical Point of View: *Logico-Philosophical Essays* TB/566

BERTRAND RUSSELL et al.: The Philosophy of Bertrand Russell. *Edited by Paul Arthur Schilpp* Volume I TB/1095 Volume II TB/1096

L. S. STEBBING: A Modern Introduction to Logic TB/538

ALFRED NORTH WHITEHEAD: Process and Reality: *An Essay in Cosmology* TB/1033

WILHELM WINDELBAND: A History of Philosophy I: *Greek, Roman, Medieval* TB/38

WILHELM WINDELBAND: A History of Philosophy II: *Renaissance, Enlightenment, Modern* TB/39

Philosophy of History

NICOLAS BERDYAEV: The Beginning and the End§ TB/14

NICOLAS BERDYAEV: The Destiny of Man TB/61

WILHELM DILTHEY: Pattern and Meaning in History: *Thoughts on History and Society.*° *Edited with an Introduction by H. P. Rickman* TB/1075

RAYMOND KLIBANSKY & H. J. PATON, Eds.: Philosophy and History: *The Ernst Cassirer Festschrift. Illus.* TB/1115

JOSE ORTEGA Y GASSET: The Modern Theme. *Introduction by Jose Ferrater Mora* TB/1038

KARL R. POPPER: The Poverty of Historicism° TB/1126

W. H. WALSH: Philosophy of History: *An Introduction* TB/1020

Political Science & Government

JEREMY BENTHAM: The Handbook of Political Fallacies: *Introduction by Crane Brinton* TB/1069

KENNETH E. BOULDING: Conflict and Defense: *A General Theory* TB/3024

CRANE BRINTON: English Political Thought in the Nineteenth Century TB/1071

EDWARD S. CORWIN: American Constitutional History: *Essays edited by Alpheus T. Mason and Gerald Garvey* TB/1136

ROBERT DAHL & CHARLES E. LINDBLOM: Politics, Economics, and Welfare: *Planning and Politico-Economic Systems Resolved into Basic Social Processes* TB/3037

JOHN NEVILLE FIGGIS: Political Thought from Gerson to Grotius: 1414-1625: *Seven Studies. Introduction by Garrett Mattingly* TB/1032

F. L. GANSHOF: Feudalism TB/1058

G. P. GOOCH: English Democratic Ideas in the Seventeenth Century TB/1006

ROBERT H. JACKSON: The Supreme Court in the American System of Government TB/1106

DAN N. JACOBS, Ed.: The New Communist Manifesto *and Related Documents* TB/1078

DAN N. JACOBS & HANS BAERWALD, Eds.: Chinese Communism: *Selected Documents* TB/3031

ROBERT GREEN McCLOSKEY: American Conservatism in the Age of Enterprise, 1865-1910 TB/1137

KINGSLEY MARTIN: French Liberal Thought in the Eighteenth Century: *A Study of Political Ideas from Bayle to Condorcet* TB/1114

JOHN STUART MILL: On Bentham and Coleridge. *Introduction by F. R. Leavis* TB/1070

JOHN B. MORRALL: Political Thought in Medieval Times TB/1076

KARL R. POPPER: The Open Society and Its Enemies
Volume I: *The Spell of Plato* TB/1101
Volume II: *The High Tide of Prophecy: Hegel, Marx, and the Aftermath* TB/1102

JOSEPH A. SCHUMPETER: Capitalism, Socialism and Democracy TB/3008

Psychology

ALFRED ADLER: Problems of Neurosis. *Introduction by Heinz L. Ansbacher* TB/1145

ANTON T. BOISEN: The Exploration of the Inner World: *A Study of Mental Disorder and Religious Experience* TB/87

LEON FESTINGER, HENRY W. RIECKEN, STANLEY SCHACHTER: When Prophecy Fails: *A Social and Psychological Study of a Modern Group that Predicted the Destruction of the World* ‖ TB/1132

SIGMUND FREUD: On Creativity and the Unconscious: *Papers on the Psychology of Art, Literature, Love, Religion.*§ *Intro. by Benjamin Nelson* TB/45

C. JUDSON HERRICK: The Evolution of Human Nature TB/545

ALDOUS HUXLEY: The Devils of Loudun: *A Study in the Psychology of Power Politics and Mystical Religion in the France of Cardinal Richelieu*§° TB/60

WILLIAM JAMES: Psychology: *The Briefer Course. Edited with an Intro. by Gordon Allport* TB/1034

C. G. JUNG: Psychological Reflections. *Edited by Jolande Jacobi* TB/2001

C. G. JUNG: Symbols of Transformation: *An Analysis of the Prelude to a Case of Schizophrenia. Illus.*
Volume I TB/2009
Volume II TB/2010

C. G. JUNG & C. KERÉNYI: Essays on a Science of Mythology: *The Myths of the Divine Child and the Divine Maiden* TB/2014

SOREN KIERKEGAARD: Repetition: *An Essay in Experimental Psychology. Translated with Introduction & Notes by Walter Lowrie* TB/117

KARL MENNINGER: Theory of Psychoanalytic Technique TB/1144

ERICH NEUMANN: Amor and Psyche: *The Psychic Development of the Feminine* TB/2012

ERICH NEUMANN: The Origins and History of Consciousness
Volume I *Illus.* TB/2007
Volume II TB/2008

C. P. OBERNDORF: A History of Psychoanalysis in America TB/1147

JEAN PIAGET, BÄRBEL INHELDER, & ALINA SZEMINSKA: The Child's Conception of Geometry TB/1146

RELIGION

Ancient & Classical

J. H. BREASTED: Development of Religion and Thought in Ancient Egypt. *Introduction by John A. Wilson* TB/57

HENRI FRANKFORT: Ancient Egyptian Religion: *An Interpretation* TB/77

WILLIAM CHASE GREENE: Moira: *Fate, Good and Evil in Greek Thought* TB/1104

G. RACHEL LEVY: Religious Conceptions of the Stone Age *and their Influence upon European Thought. Illus. Introduction by Henri Frankfort* TB/106

MARTIN P. NILSSON: Greek Folk Religion. *Foreword by Arthur Darby Nock* TB/78

ALEXANDRE PIANKOFF: The Shrines of Tut-Ankh-Amon. *Edited by N. Rambova. 117 illus.* TB/2011

H. J. ROSE: Religion in Greece and Rome TB/55

Biblical Thought & Literature

W. F. ALBRIGHT: The Biblical Period from Abraham to Ezra TB/102

C. K. BARRETT, Ed.: The New Testament Background: *Selected Documents* TB/86

C. H. DODD: The Authority of the Bible TB/43

M. S. ENSLIN: Christian Beginnings TB/5

M. S. ENSLIN: The Literature of the Christian Movement TB/6

H. E. FOSDICK: A Guide to Understanding the Bible TB/2

H. H. ROWLEY: The Growth of the Old Testament TB/107

D. WINTON THOMAS, Ed.: Documents from Old Testament Times TB/85

Christianity: Origins & Early Development

ADOLF DEISSMANN: Paul: *A Study in Social and Religious History* TB/15

EDWARD GIBBON: The Triumph of Christendom in the Roman Empire *(Chaps. XV-XX of "Decline and Fall," J. B. Bury edition).*§ *Illus.* TB/46

MAURICE GOGUEL: Jesus and the Origins of Christianity.° *Introduction by C. Leslie Mitton*
Volume I: *Prolegomena to the Life of Jesus* TB/65
Volume II: *The Life of Jesus* TB/66

EDGAR J. GOODSPEED: A Life of Jesus TB/1

ADOLF HARNACK: The Mission and Expansion of Christianity *in the First Three Centuries. Introduction by Jaroslav Pelikan* TB/92

R. K. HARRISON: The Dead Sea Scrolls: *An Introduction*° TB/84

EDWIN HATCH: The Influence of Greek Ideas on Christianity.§ *Introduction and Bibliography by Frederick C. Grant* TB /18

ARTHUR DARBY NOCK: Early Gentile Christianity and Its Hellenistic Background TB/111

ARTHUR DARBY NOCK: St. Paul° TB/104

JOHANNES WEISS: Earliest Christianity: *A History of the Period A.D. 30-150. Introduction and Bibilography by Frederick C. Grant* Volume I TB/53
Volume II TB/54

Christianity: The Middle Ages, The Reformation, and After

G. P. FEDOTOV: The Russian Religious Mind: *Kievan Christianity, the tenth to the thirteenth centuries* TB/70

ÉTIENNE GILSON: Dante and Philosophy TB/1089

WILLIAM HALLER: The Rise of Puritanism TB/22

JOHAN HUIZINGA: Erasmus and the Age of Reformation. *Illus.* TB/19

JOHN T. McNEILL: Makers of Christianity: *From Alfred the Great to Schleiermacher* TB/121

A. C. McGIFFERT: Protestant Thought Before Kant. *Preface by Jaroslav Pelikan* TB/93

KENNETH B. MURDOCK: Literature and Theology in Colonial New England TB/99

GORDON RUPP: Luther's Progress to the Diet of Worms° TB/120

Judaic Thought & Literature

MARTIN BUBER: Eclipse of God: *Studies in the Relation Between Religion and Philosophy* TB/12

MARTIN BUBER: Moses: *The Revelation and the Covenant* TB/27

MARTIN BUBER: Pointing the Way. *Introduction by Maurice S. Friedman* TB/103

MARTIN BUBER: The Prophetic Faith TB/73

MARTIN BUBER: Two Types of Faith: *the interpenetration of Judaism and Christianity*° TB/75

MAURICE S. FRIEDMAN: Martin Buber: *The Life of Dialogue* TB/64

FLAVIUS JOSEPHUS: The Great Roman-Jewish War, *with* The Life of Josephus. *Introduction by William R. Farmer* TB/74

T. J. MEEK: Hebrew Origins TB/69

Oriental Religions: Far Eastern, Near Eastern

TOR ANDRAE: Mohammed: *The Man and His Faith* TB/62

EDWARD CONZE: Buddhism: *Its Essence and Development.*° *Foreword by Arthur Waley* TB/58

EDWARD CONZE, et al., Editors: Buddhist Texts Through the Ages TB/113

ANANDA COOMARASWAMY: Buddha and the Gospel of Buddhism TB/119

H. G. CREEL: Confucius and the Chinese Way TB/63

FRANKLIN EDGERTON, Trans. & Ed.: The Bhagavad Gita TB/115

SWAMI NIKHILANANDA, Trans. & Ed.: The Upanishads: *A One-Volume Abridgment* TB/114

HELLMUT WILHELM: Change: *Eight Lectures on the I Ching* TB/2019

Philosophy of Religion

RUDOLF BULTMANN: History and Eschatology: *The Presence of Eternity* TB/91

RUDOLF BULTMANN AND FIVE CRITICS: Kerygma and Myth: *A Theological Debate* TB/80

RUDOLF BULTMANN and KARL KUNDSIN: Form Criticism: *Two Essays on New Testament Research. Translated by Frederick C. Grant* TB/96

MIRCEA ELIADE: The Sacred and the Profane TB/81

LUDWIG FEUERBACH: The Essence of Christianity.§ *Introduction by Karl Barth. Foreword by H. Richard Niebuhr* TB/11

ADOLF HARNACK: What is Christianity?§ *Introduction by Rudolf Bultmann* TB/17

FRIEDRICH HEGEL: On Christianity: *Early Theological Writings. Edited by Richard Kroner and T. M. Knox* TB/79

KARL HEIM: Christian Faith and Natural Science TB/16

IMMANUEL KANT: Religion Within the Limits of Reason Alone.§ *Introduction by Theodore M. Greene and John Silber* TB/67

PIERRE TEILHARD DE CHARDIN: The Phenomenon of Man° TB/83

Religion, Culture & Society

JOSEPH L. BLAU, Ed.: Cornerstones of Religious Freedom in America: *Selected Basic Documents, Court Decisions and Public Statements. Enlarged and revised edition, with new Introduction by the Editor* TB/118

C. C. GILLISPIE: Genesis and Geology: *The Decades before Darwin*§ TB/51

BENJAMIN NELSON: Religious Traditions and the Spirit of Capitalism: *From the Church Fathers to Jeremy Bentham* TB/1130

H. RICHARD NIEBUHR: Christ and Culture TB/3

H. RICHARD NIEBUHR: The Kingdom of God in America TB/49

RALPH BARTON PERRY: Puritanism and Democracy TB/1138

WALTER RAUSCHENBUSCH: Christianity and the Social Crisis.‡ *Edited by Robert D. Cross* TB/3059

KURT SAMUELSSON: Religion and Economic Action: *A Critique of Max Weber's* The Protestant Ethic and the Spirit of Capitalism.¶° *Trans. by E. G. French; Ed. with Intro. by D. C. Coleman* TB/1131

ERNST TROELTSCH: The Social Teaching of the Christian Churches.° *Introduction by H. Richard Niebuhr* Volume I TB/71, Volume II TB/72

Religious Thinkers & Traditions

AUGUSTINE: An Augustine Synthesis. *Edited by Erich Przywara* TB/35

KARL BARTH: Church Dogmatics: *A Selection. Introduction by H. Gollwitzer; Edited by G. W. Bromiley* TB/95

KARL BARTH: Dogmatics in Outline TB/56

KARL BARTH: The Word of God and the Word of Man TB/13

THOMAS CORBISHLEY, S. J.: Roman Catholicism TB/112

ADOLF DEISSMANN: Paul: *A Study in Social and Religious History* TB/15

JOHANNES ECKHART: Meister Eckhart: *A Modern Translation by R. B. Blakney* TB/8

WINTHROP HUDSON: The Great Tradition of the American Churches TB/98

SOREN KIERKEGAARD: Edifying Discourses. *Edited with an Introduction by Paul Holmer* TB/32

SOREN KIERKEGAARD: The Journals of Kierkegaard.° *Edited with an Introduction by Alexander Dru* TB/52

SOREN KIERKEGAARD: The Point of View for My Work as an Author: *A Report to History.*§ *Preface by Benjamin Nelson* TB/88

SOREN KIERKEGAARD: The Present Age.§ *Translated and edited by Alexander Dru. Introduction by Walter Kaufmann* TB/94

SOREN KIERKEGAARD: Purity of Heart. *Translated by Douglas Steere* TB/4

SOREN KIERKEGAARD: Repetition: *An Essay in Experimental Psychology. Translated with Introduction & Notes by Walter Lowrie* TB/117

SOREN KIERKEGAARD: Works of Love: *Some Christian Reflections in the Form of Discourses* TB/122

WALTER LOWRIE: Kierkegaard: *A Life*
Volume I TB/89
Volume II TB/90

GABRIEL MARCEL: Homo Viator: *Introduction to a Metaphysic of Hope* TB/97

PERRY MILLER: Errand into the Wilderness TB/1139

PERRY MILLER & T. H. JOHNSON, Editors: The Puritans: *A Sourcebook of Their Writings*
Volume I TB/1093
Volume II TB/1094

PAUL PFUETZE: Self, Society, Existence: *Human Nature and Dialogue in the Thought of George Herbert Mead and Martin Buber* TB/1059

F. SCHLEIERMACHER: The Christian Faith. *Introduction by Richard R. Niebuhr* Volume I TB/108
Volume II TB/109

F. SCHLEIERMACHER: On Religion: *Speeches to Its Cultured Despisers. Intro. by Rudolf Otto* TB/36

PAUL TILLICH: Dynamics of Faith TB/42

EVELYN UNDERHILL: Worship TB/10

G. VAN DER LEEUW: Religion in Essence and Manifestation: *A Study in Phenomenology. Appendices by Hans H. Penner* Volume I TB/100
Volume II TB/101

NATURAL SCIENCES AND MATHEMATICS

Biological Sciences

CHARLOTTE AUERBACH: The Science of Genetics Σ TB/568

A. BELLAIRS: Reptiles: *Life History, Evolution, and Structure. Illus.* TB/520

LUDWIG VON BERTALANFFY: Modern Theories of Development: *An Introduction to Theoretical Biology* TB/554

LUDWIG VON BERTALANFFY: Problems of Life: *An Evaluation of Modern Biological and Scientific Thought* TB/521

JOHN TYLER BONNER: The Ideas of Biology. Σ *Illus.* TB/570

HAROLD F. BLUM: Time's Arrow and Evolution TB/555

A. J. CAIN: Animal Species and their Evolution. *Illus.* TB/519

WALTER B. CANNON: Bodily Changes in Pain, Hunger, Fear and Rage. *Illus.* TB/562

W. E. LE GROS CLARK: The Antecedents of Man: *An Introduction to the Evolution of the Primates.*° *Illus.* TB/559

W. H. DOWDESWELL: Animal Ecology. *Illus.* TB/543

W. H. DOWDESWELL: The Mechanism of Evolution. *Illus.* TB/527

R. W. GERARD: Unresting Cells. *Illus.* TB/541

DAVID LACK: Darwin's Finches. *Illus.* TB/544

J. E. MORTON: Molluscs: *An Introduction to their Form and Functions. Illus.* TB/529

ADOLF PORTMANN: Animals as Social Beings.° *Illus.* TB/572

O. W. RICHARDS: The Social Insects. *Illus.* TB/542

P. M. SHEPPARD: Natural Selection and Heredity. *Illus.* TB/528

EDMUND W. SINNOTT: Cell and Psyche: *The Biology of Purpose* TB/546

C. H. WADDINGTON: How Animals Develop. *Illus.* TB/553

Chemistry

J. R. PARTINGTON: A Short History of Chemistry. *Illus.* TB/522

J. READ: A Direct Entry to Organic Chemistry. *Illus.* TB/523

J. READ: Through Alchemy to Chemistry. *Illus.* TB/561

Geography

R. E. COKER: This Great and Wide Sea: *An Introduction to Oceanography and Marine Biology. Illus.* TB/551

F. K. HARE: The Restless Atmosphere TB/560

History of Science

W. DAMPIER, Ed.: Readings in the Literature of Science. *Illus.* TB/512

A. HUNTER DUPREE: Science in the Federal Government: *A History of Policies and Activities to 1940* TB/573

ALEXANDRE KOYRÉ: From the Closed World to the Infinite Universe: *Copernicus, Kepler, Galileo, Newton, etc.* TB/31

A. G. VAN MELSEN: From Atomos to Atom: *A History of the Concept* Atom TB/517

O. NEUGEBAUER: The Exact Sciences in Antiquity TB/552

H. T. PLEDGE: Science Since 1500: *A Short History of Mathematics, Physics, Chemistry and Biology. Illus.* TB/506

GEORGE SARTON: Ancient Science and Modern Civilization TB/501

HANS THIRRING: Energy for Man: *From Windmills to Nuclear Power* TB/556

WILLIAM LAW WHYTE: Essay on Atomism: *From Democritus to 1960* TB/565

A. WOLF: A History of Science, Technology and Philosophy in the 16th and 17th Centuries.° *Illus.*
Volume I TB/508
Volume II TB/509

A. WOLF: A History of Science, Technology, and Philosophy in the Eighteenth Century.° *Illus.*
Volume I TB/539
Volume II TB/540

Mathematics

H. DAVENPORT: The Higher Arithmetic: *An Introduction to the Theory of Numbers* TB/526

H. G. FORDER: Geometry: *An Introduction* TB/548

GOTTLOB FREGE: The Foundations of Arithmetic: *A Logico-Mathematical Enquiry into the Concept of Number* TB/534

S. KÖRNER: The Philosophy of Mathematics: *An Introduction* TB/547

D. E. LITTLEWOOD: Skeleton Key of Mathematics: *A Simple Account of Complex Algebraic Problems* TB/525

GEORGE E. OWEN: Fundamentals of Scientific Mathematics TB/569

WILLARD VAN ORMAN QUINE: Mathematical Logic TB/558

O. G. SUTTON: Mathematics in Action.° *Foreword by James R. Newman. Illus.* TB/518

FREDERICK WAISMANN: Introduction to Mathematical Thinking. *Foreword by Karl Menger* TB/511

Philosophy of Science

R. B. BRAITHWAITE: Scientific Explanation TB/515

J. BRONOWSKI: Science and Human Values. *Illus.* TB/505

ALBERT EINSTEIN: Philosopher-Scientist. *Edited by Paul A. Schilpp* Volume I TB/502
Volume II TB/503

WERNER HEISENBERG: Physics and Philosophy: *The Revolution in Modern Science. Introduction by F. S. C. Northrop* TB/549

JOHN MAYNARD KEYNES: A Treatise on Probability.° *Introduction by N. R. Hanson* TB/557

STEPHEN TOULMIN: Foresight and Understanding: *An Enquiry into the Aims of Science. Foreword by Jacques Barzun* TB/564

STEPHEN TOULMIN: The Philosophy of Science: *An Introduction* TB/513

G. J. WHITROW: The Natural Philosophy of Time° TB/563

Physics and Cosmology

DAVID BOHM: Causality and Chance in Modern Physics. *Foreword by Louis de Broglie* TB/536

P. W. BRIDGMAN: The Nature of Thermodynamics TB/537

A. C. CROMBIE, Ed.: Turning Point in Physics TB/535

C. V. DURELL: Readable Relativity. *Foreword by Freeman J. Dyson* TB/530

ARTHUR EDDINGTON: Space, Time and Gravitation: *An outline of the General Relativity Theory* TB/510

GEORGE GAMOW: Biography of Physics∑ TB/567

MAX JAMMER: Concepts of Force: *A Study in the Foundation of Dynamics* TB/550

MAX JAMMER: Concepts of Mass *in Classical and Modern Physics* TB/571

MAX JAMMER: Concepts of Space: *The History of Theories of Space in Physics. Foreword by Albert Einstein* TB/533

EDMUND WHITTAKER: History of the Theories of Aether and Electricity
Volume I: *The Classical Theories* TB/531
Volume II: *The Modern Theories* TB/532

G. J. WHITROW: The Structure and Evolution of the Universe: *An Introduction to Cosmology. Illus.* TB/504

A LETTER TO THE READER

Overseas, there is considerable belief that we are a country of extreme conservatism and that we cannot accommodate to social change.

Books about America in the hands of readers abroad can help change those ideas.

The U. S. Information Agency cannot, by itself, meet the vast need for books about the United States.

You can help.

Harper Torchbooks provides three packets of books on American history, economics, sociology, literature and politics to help meet the need.

To send a packet of Torchbooks [*] overseas, all you need do is send your check for $7 (which includes cost of shipping) to Harper & Row. The U. S. Information Agency will distribute the books to libraries, schools, and other centers all over the world.

I ask every American to support this program, part of a worldwide BOOKS USA campaign.

I ask you to share in the opportunity to help tell others about America.

EDWARD R. MURROW
Director,
U. S. Information Agency

[*retailing at $10.85 to $12.00]

PACKET I: Twentieth Century America

Dulles/America's Rise to World Power, 1898-1954
Cochran/The American Business System, 1900-1955
Zabel, Editor/Literary Opinion in America (two volumes)
Drucker/The New Society: *The Anatomy of Industrial Order*
Fortune Editors/America in the Sixties: *The Economy and the Society*

PACKET II: American History

Billington/The Far Western Frontier, 1830-1860
Mowry/The Era of Theodore Roosevelt and the Birth of Modern America, 1900-1912
Faulkner/Politics, Reform, and Expansion, 1890-1900
Cochran & Miller/The Age of Enterprise: *A Social History of Industrial America*
Tyler/Freedom's Ferment: *American Social History from the Revolution to the Civil War*

PACKET III: American History

Hansen/The Atlantic Migration, 1607-1860
Degler/Out of Our Past: *The Forces that Shaped Modern America*
Probst, Editor/The Happy Republic: *A Reader in Tocqueville's America*
Alden/The American Revolution, 1775-1783
Wright/The Cultural Life of the American Colonies, 1607-1763

Your gift will be acknowledged directly to you by the overseas recipient. Simply fill out the coupon, detach and mail with your check or money order.

HARPER & ROW, PUBLISHERS • BOOKS USA DEPT.
49 East 33rd Street, New York 16, N. Y.

Packet I ☐ Packet II ☐ Packet III ☐

Please send the BOOKS USA library packet(s) indicated above, in my name, to the area checked below. Enclosed is my remittance in the amount of ____________ for ____________ packet(s) at $7.00 each.

_____ Africa _____ Latin America

_____ Far East _____ Near East

Name____

Address____

____

NOTE: This offer expires December 31, 1966.